Native Women's History in Eastern North America before 1900

D0913853

Native Women's History in Eastern North America before 1900

A Guide to Research and Writing

EDITED BY REBECCA KUGEL

and

LUCY ELDERSVELD MURPHY

UNIVERSITY OF NEBRASKA PRESS | LINCOLN AND LONDON

Acknowledgment for the use of previously published material appears on
pp. 461–62, which constitutes an extension of the copyright page.

Library of Congress Cataloging-in-Publication Data
Native women's history in eastern North America before 1900: a guide to
research and writing / edited by Rebecca Kugel and Lucy Eldersveld Murphy.
p.   cm.
Includes bibliographical references.
ISBN-13: 978-0-8032-2779-8 (cloth: alk. paper)
ISBN-10: 0-8032-2779-5 (cloth: alk. paper)
ISBN-13: 978-0-8032-7831-8 (pbk.: alk. paper)
ISBN-10: 0-8032-7831-4 (pbk.: alk. paper)
1. Indian women—East (U.S.)—History—Sources.   2. Indian women
activists—East (U.S.)—History—Sources.   3. Indian women civic
leaders—East (U.S.)—History—Sources.   4. Indian women in literature.
I. Kugel, Rebecca, 1952–   II. Murphy, Lucy Eldersveld, 1953–
E78.E2N38   2007
305.48'897074—dc22
2007016247

Set in Minion by Bob Reitz.
Designed by R. W. Boeche.

For our students past, present, and future

Contents

Illustrations

Acknowledgments

This volume has been a long time in the making, more than seven years since we began discussing the possibility of collecting some of our favorite articles in a volume for students and other scholars interested in Native women's history. As our ideas began to evolve, we asked other scholars for their advice, and many people were generous with their nominations of favorite articles or with ideas about ways to organize and focus the collection. In particular, we would like to thank Regna Darnell, Allan Greer, Carol Higham, Craig Howe, Clara Sue Kidwell, Neal Salisbury, Nancy Shoemaker, Susan Sleeper-Smith, Helen Tanner, and Laurier Turgeon, who took the time to send us their thoughts and helped us greatly. Although we could not incorporate all of their suggestions, it was with their help that we settled on the idea of demonstrating the genealogy of scholarship and providing sample documents to demonstrate historical research methods. In addition, we are grateful for all the encouraging comments from friends and colleagues at conferences and programs. There are doubtless friends and colleagues we have neglected to mention; our thanks go out to you all.

Tricia Bradley of Ohio State University did the difficult work of tracking down books, articles, and other sources, organizing texts, and producing electronic versions of our chapters. Always cheerful and meticulous, she made an enormous contribution to this project. She was assisted with the proofreading by Elaine Denman and Jaime Conard. We would like to recognize The Ohio State University, Newark, which provided funding for editorial assistance for this project through the History Department under the kind direction of Dr. Richard Shiels, and the Professional Standards Committee. Rebecca Kugel also acknowledges the support provided by several small University of California, Riverside, Academic Senate Research Grants. The librarians at osu Newark and University of California, Riverside have also been terrific in their support, as have the History Department staff at ucr and the osu Newark Services Center staff.

During the spring quarter of 2004, the thirty-four students in Rebecca Kugel's "History of Native American Women" course "test-drove" this essay collection. As part of their course work they read the essays and offered their views, criticism, and suggestions. We are particularly grateful for the extensive and thoughtful written comments they provided on each article. Most will have graduated and gone on to careers or graduate school by the time this book is published, but their contributions have been invaluable. Our thanks to you all.

Gary Dunham of the University of Nebraska Press has been extremely helpful and supportive, not to mention patient, as we plodded along, frequently distracted by teaching, service, family, and other research projects. Thank you, Gary!

We very much appreciate the authors of these essays, who took time from their busy schedules to write thoughtful introductions for this collection, and in some cases to locate primary sources for inclusion here. Special thanks here to Christine Gailey, former Chair of Women's Studies at the University of California, Riverside, for her introduction to the late Eleanor Leacock's article.

Finally, we could not do our work without the support, encouragement, and cheerful distractions of our families. Larry, Sky, Dylan, Tom, Colin, Beth, and Danni provide the spice of life that helps us keep our efforts in perspective. Our larger extended families of parents, siblings, aunts, and cousins have also long provided encouragement for our work. Our love and thanks to you all!

Introduction

Searching for Cornfields — and Sugar Groves

REBECCA KUGEL AND LUCY ELDERSVELD MURPHY

During La-a-ni, the First Summer Moon, on the date Anglo-Americans called June 7, 1831, the Sauk community of Saukenuk, located on the Rock River in present-day northwest Illinois, met once more with representatives of the American military to discuss the long-sought American objective of removing the village to the western side of the Mississippi River.[1] Saukenuk's people had long resisted Anglo-American demands to remove, and its war leader, Black Hawk, remained "determined to hold on to my village" in spite of mounting pressure. In the negotiations that followed, corn and cornfields figured prominently. Black Hawk and other Sauk spokespersons drew on the culturally significant image of cornfields in their efforts to persuade the Americans to let them remain at their long-established village. Americans, in particular Major General Edmund P. Gaines, who led the negotiations, badly misunderstood the Sauks' imagery and references to corn.[2]

In their efforts to get the Americans to grasp the significance of the cornfields, the Sauks undertook extraordinary political measures, according to Black Hawk's autobiography. In Sauk society, political negotiations with foreigners were usually undertaken by men. In this instance, a delegation of Sauk women, led by a woman of a leadership family, "the daughter of Mat-ta-tas, the old chief of the village," came to the negotiations. Mat-ta-tas's daughter carried "a stick in her hand," probably a digging stick or hoe, a tool emblematic of women's work and power, when she met with Gaines and voiced the women's firm opposition to the village's removal. Black Hawk, whose own opposition to removal had garnered him considerable support among the women, explained the women's position to an uncomprehending Gaines: "the women having worked their fields till they had become easy of cultivation, were now unwilling to leave them." The Sauk women further attempted to explain why, as women, they had the ultimate authority over the cornfields. "[S]he was a woman," Mat-ta-tas's daughter explained, "and had worked hard to raise something to support her children!" In Sauk thought, the earth's cycles of reproductive growth mirrored the remarkable reproductive abilities of human females. Corn, as a cultivated product of the earth, was uniquely connected to women, its cultivators. Not only did women grow corn, but the land on which corn grew was a uniquely female space. When the women of Saukenuk, as the owners of the fields, asserted that "they had decided not to move," that should have been the end of the discussion.[3]

Gaines for his part could not grasp the argument about use rights and female control of food products of their own making that Mat-ta-tas's daughter advanced. The idea that women controlled property apart from men was completely foreign to his thinking, as was the idea that women might be entitled to a voice in political decision making. He did not understand the symbol of the digging stick or the significance of cornfields or why being a woman gave Mat-ta-tas's daughter the right to speak about the cornfields. He could not imagine how any of these actions were relevant to a land sale. The Sauks were trying to underscore the seriousness of their opposition to removal by involving women as direct political participants. They were also trying to get Gaines to understand that the particular lands under discussion, a village and its cornfields, were properly the female domain, and that if men had negotiated a land sale at some distant time and place without consulting the women, it could have no bearing on these female-controlled spaces. Unable to understand any of this, Gaines fell back on what he imagined to be culturally accurate Native male contempt for women. "[T]he president did not send him here to make treaties with the women," he blustered, "nor to hold council with them!" Implying that the women's presence was an affront, he abruptly called off the negotiations, leaving the stunned Sauks believing they had been left no option but armed resistance.[4]

Unfortunately, later scholars have proven themselves almost as unable to recognize the importance of Native women as Edmund Gaines was. The source material of historical study — the letters, diaries, memoirs, autobiographies, newspaper accounts, ethnographies, census data, and legal proceedings — contains copious information on Native women's lives. Yet both scholars of the New Indian History and its methodological cousin, ethno-history, have not generally made Native women's lives and experiences central to their analyses. Black Hawk's autobiography makes clear that Sauk women were central to Sauk society, that they exercised both political and economic power, and that Sauk conceptions of land ownership were gendered in complex ways. Sauk women were anything but invisible.

The insights to be gained from analyzing gender in the study of Native history are numerous. Native women will emerge as dynamic members of their communities and families; their lives and actions will assume importance in their own right. At the same time, analysis of Native women's experiences sheds further light on Native history overall, as the Sauks' understanding of cornfields as female property reveals. Native women's experiences and their relationships to men, children, and each other will provide deeper insights into the reconstructions of Native history, into Native thoughts and actions, than reliance on just male voices and perspectives can do.

The field of women's history can also benefit greatly from more culturally accurate interpretations of Native women's experiences. As the field seeks to decenter women's experiences away from those of European-descended middle-class women, Native American women's history offers compelling alternative stories. Women's historians have generally treated Native women as a homogeneous group, a situation that has given rise to all Native women being characterized by the experiences of a select few, usually nations such as the Iroquois or the Cherokees, where women's political status was visibly different from that of European women. There has been a parallel tendency to view all Native societies as according women "equality" with men, although the term "equality" is rarely explained in such formulations. As is revealed in the Sauk women's ownership of the cornfields and their political participation when that ownership was threatened, Native women's "equality" could be (and was) very differently constructed from the Anglo-American ideal of "equality," with its emphasis on possessing the same individual political or social rights.

Women's history has tended to view Native societies as an alternative to patriarchy, but this, too, is problematic. Male dominance is neither monolithic nor unchanging nor universal. Studies of Native American women have much to offer in refining this important theoretical debate. Locating Native women within the specific cultural traditions of their nations offers opportunities to explore whether or not male dominance, or "patriarchy," existed, and whether or not male dominance was the same at all times and in all places.

For many Native nations, the Sauks among them, gender relations between women and men can best be understood as complementary, as is suggested by the imagery of the female world of the cornfields and the male world of game hunting. The fact that many Native cultures conceptualized three or four genders represents another opportunity for women's historians to probe a series of questions relating to European-derived constructions of gender, as well as to consider how male-female relations might be constructed in a world where there were multiple points of gendered reference rather than an either/or opposition of male and female. Finally, the study of Native women's history represents an opportunity to explore the lives of women of color who were shaped by very different understandings of themselves and their place in their societies than Anglo-American and other European-descended women.

Objectives

The objectives of this book are several. The editors seek to bring together a number of classic articles in the field of Native women's history, works that first articulated important ideas about Native women and theories about writing histories of Native women. The ideas in these works have been echoed in the work of other scholars, among them several included in this book, influencing their thinking, building the foundation for the historical study of Native women. It is often daunting to consider researching Native women's history, since so few sources were written by Native women and because reconstituting their stories becomes a matter of reading a work — such as Black Hawk's autobiography — against the narrative, searching for the selected moments when women's thoughts and actions are described. This guidebook will pay particular attention to research methods and sources, showing how it is possible to utilize a range of materials in our efforts to reveal elements of Native women's past. The book is conceived of as a guide for scholars and students with a number of interests, whether they seek to incorporate gender into their studies of Native history or to explore Native women's experiences in the framework of women's history or gender history.

In scope, this book examines Native women's experiences in the Eastern Woodlands of North America in the centuries between initial encounters with Europeans and 1900. We have opted to focus on one region of North America, where important overarching similarities of culture, ecosystem, and history existed, precisely because we recognize that not all Native wom-

1. Tribal locations in the late eighteenth century

en's lives and histories were the same and that they cannot be treated as if they were. The Eastern Woodlands share a temperate climate, receive adequate rainfall for farming, and are laced with rivers and lakes that provided good transportation for people, their products, and their ideas. Nearly all Woodlands peoples practiced agriculture, with corn the most important staple, and in nearly all Woodlands societies, women were the farmers. Although numerous languages were spoken and cultural traditions, political organization, and family structures were varied, a Cherokee woman from Georgia and a Menomini woman from Wisconsin would have recognized in each other's communities basic patterns of village life, of female work centered on crop production and the village itself, while males, frequently absent from the village in pursuit of game, were both literally and symbolically linked to the forest.

At the same time that we recognize similarities existed, we balance that recognition with attention to differences. Eastern Woodlands Native women lived in societies with different political structures and economies; their access to formal political power and their control of economic resources might vary widely. Similarly, they might trace descent matrilineally in some instances and patrilineally in others, a situation that could shape the lives of women and their children in very different ways. The manner in which children might be incorporated into the kinship structure mattered very much to the woman whose children's father was a Frenchman or an Englishman instead of a tribal member.

Within the same community, defining features of the female life cycle, such as age and motherhood, also defined women's status, responsibilities, and authority differentially. Age nearly always accorded respect regardless of the elder's gender. Young women might not have been encouraged to participate in community political deliberations, but the reasons for excluding them might have had more to do with their perceived immaturity and lack of wisdom than with their gender. In many Eastern Woodlands societies, young men were considered equally unsuited for mature reasoned political debate. In a work that emphasizes historical change over time, it is also crucial to remember that Native women's lives were affected greatly by when and where they lived. A grandmother and granddaughter might share a cultural orientation but inhabit very different worlds of work and personal autonomy because the younger woman's community had become enveloped by Euro-American settler-colonists, a situation Jean O'Brien's work on New England Native women clearly demonstrates.

Our decision to limit this study to the years between first encounters and the start of the twentieth century—roughly from 1600 to 1900—was also guided by our aims. The most problematic sources are those that date from before the twentieth century, and it is these sources that we particularly want to address. Native oral historical sources are of tremendous value in recounting the Native past, and are most common in the twentieth century. The further back a researcher goes into the nineteenth, eighteenth, and earlier centuries, the more difficult it is to salvage Native oral narratives and the more one must rely on the several kinds of written documents that have survived. Frequently ethnocentric, if not outright racist, generally androcentric, if not misogynistic, these are highly problematic sources. Nevertheless, much valuable information is buried within them. An astonishing amount of Native speech was recorded, numerous Native actions were described, and Native cultural practices were frequently, if uncomprehendingly, detailed.

Indeed, the painting we have chosen for the cover of this volume, Seth Eastman's *Indian Sugar Camp*, represents one variant on this last category. The grandfather of the famous Dakota physician and author Charles Eastman (Ohiyesa), Seth Eastman, a U.S. Army officer and prolific artist, was married to Wakaninajinwin (Stands Sacred), a Mdewakantonwan Dakota woman, from 1830 to 1832.[5] While Eastman was neither Native nor female, he had Dakota kin and painted this and other scenes based on careful observation. While a painting rather than a document, *Indian Sugar Camp* can be "read." A group of Dakota women are engaged in making maple sugar, each absorbed in different elements of the task: boiling the sap, cutting wood to stoke the fires, sorting and storing the processed sugar. Although men are present (two men are seated by the wigwam), this is nonetheless a female workspace; this is female-controlled production. It is also group labor, as a number of women, probably kinfolk, cooperate in the process of sugar making. And finally, the picture conveys the many skills possessed by Dakota women, belying the Euro-American notion that Native life was "simple" and "primitive." Sugar making involved both heavy physical labor and detailed knowledge of the several procedures involved in rendering raw maple sap into granulated sugar.

Although written documents and visual images are filtered through the biases of non-Native observers and writers, they can and should be utilized for the insights they provide into the lives of Native women. This book focuses on the ways in which scholars have sought to theorize and implement

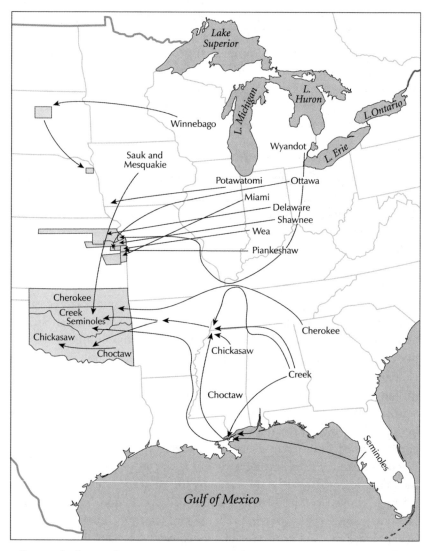

Lake Superior

L. Michigan

L. Huron

L. Ontario

L. Erie

Winnebago

Wyandot

Sauk and Mesquakie

Potawatomi — Ottawa

Miami

Delaware

Shawnee

Wea

Piankeshaw

Cherokee

Creek
Seminoles

Chickasaw

Choctaw

Cherokee

Chickasaw

Creek

Choctaw

Seminoles

Gulf of Mexico

2. Removed tribes ca. 1830s

the use of such sources, extracting information while recognizing and discounting their biases. We can never completely recover the past, but, as the articles in this collection demonstrate, we can recover much and go a long ways toward returning Native women to their historical presence. We can recognize the significance of spaces such as cornfields and sugar camps.

We have chosen to focus on the period between 1600 and 1900 not only because the historical research is so challenging but also because the period is extremely important to American — and Native American — history. Although it was during these centuries that Native peoples were gradually dispossessed of the continent, such a statement belies how uncertain that process was and how tenaciously Native peoples remained (and still remain) on the North American land. With the advantage of hindsight, Euro-Americans and Euro-Canadians have tended to view these three hundred years as an "inevitable" process of Native decline, though closer examination of actual historical events reveals a history that was anything but a foregone conclusion. Indigenous people continued to be a majority of the population of the Americas overall until around the 1770s, and Euro-Americans would not emerge as the majority population — that is, 51 percent of the people — until the mid-nineteenth century.[6] These demographic facts should remind us that Native people did not disappear or "vanish," although they certainly experienced dramatic population losses due to disease, violence, and forced dispossession. The centuries before the twentieth are better understood as a period when Native peoples, often under the harshest of conditions, forged new strategies of survivance, as Gerald Vizenor has termed them, efforts at physical survival but also struggles for cultural and spiritual continuity.[7] At the same time we recognize Native survivance, we must be aware that, increasingly over these centuries, the histories of Native peoples and European and African newcomers became intertwined. Native peoples were also affected by the significant events of North American history, conflicts such as the American Revolution, the controversy over slavery, the Civil War, and settler-colonist expansion across the continent. More importantly, Native peoples often sought to utilize the opportunities presented by something like a war or a hotly contested political debate to assert their own interests.

To further emphasize the importance of this early period, before 1900 many of the Native peoples in eastern North America faced similar challenges aside from the obvious experiences of conquest and colonization. In the nineteenth century, as the nation-states of the United States and Canada emerged from former European empires, Native peoples confronted similar policies of removal, confinement to reservations, and assaults on their cultural integrity in the name of "civilizing" them. Closely related are issues of identity, both as they were negotiated by people in their own times and in the telling of history from the past to the present day. During the period before 1900, concepts of "race" were evolving in ways that powerfully affected gender relations. The essay in this volume by Rebecca Kugel illustrates this shift, and other articles, including those by Jennifer S. H. Brown and Lucy Eldersveld Murphy, also consider how "race" was invented and transformed.

Previous Studies

The field of Native women's history has grown substantially in the last twenty-five years. In several excellent essay collections, both historians and anthropologists have contributed key works and suggested a number of thematic approaches. A pioneering volume edited by anthropologists Patricia Albers and Beatrice Medicine is *The Hidden Half: Studies of Plains Indian Women* (1983).[8] Like this guide, it takes a regional focus, examining the lives of Native women from a number of Plains societies, mainly in the pre-reservation period, but also with some consideration of the contemporary reservation period. Laura Klein and Lillian Ackerman's *Women and Power in Native North America* (1995), another anthropological collection, employs a topical approach, exploring Native women's access to and control of power, a concept they define broadly to include such forms as political participation, control of economic resources, and communication with spiritual beings.[9] Mona Etienne and Eleanor Leacock's *Women and Colonization* (1980) was pathbreaking for its effort to theorize the impact of colonization on indigenous women in a worldwide context.[10] Historian Nancy Shoemaker's *Negotiators of Change* locates Native women in specific historical contexts, ranging from Virginia Algonquians confronting the Jamestown colony in the early 1600s to Salt River Pima and Maricopa women's involvement with community action programs in the 1960s and 1970s.[11] Theda Perdue's anthology *Sifters* employs a biographical approach, providing insight into different historical periods from the early seventeenth century through the early twenty-first through portrayals of a number of Native women.[12]

   While books such as these have provided fine studies of Native women at different times and in numerous cultures, none has as its central concern untangling the processes by which scholars read and interpret their source material. The "how to" of analyzing the raw materials of history—letters, diaries, newspaper accounts, government reports, court records, estate inventories, baptismal registers — is a central component of this guide. We envision this book as a complement to other collections. While it considers theories for conceptualizing Native women's history, it focuses on the methods by which scholars piece together Native women's experiences from admittedly difficult sources.

We have selected the essays for this collection to illustrate the ways scholars have influenced each other, and to show a range of approaches and sources, rather than attempting broad topical coverage. Many of the essays reprinted here intersect in terms of the issues they consider, providing opportunities for readers to compare and contrast different research strategies and the utility of various types of documents.

Methods

Improving research on Native women's history will require adapting new research methods, looking for new sources, and mining those sources carefully. But to a great extent, it will also require rethinking old assumptions and paradigms. Gerda Lerner invigorated women's history by reminding us that, in most times and places, women have been a majority of their society's populations, and by urging scholars to write history from that point of view rather than treating women as "minorities."[13] In the same way, we should recognize that indigenous people were 100 percent of the population of the Americas for thousands of years and that they did not become a minority in North America overall until the mid-eighteenth century, a demographic pattern with thousands of regional and local variations. One consequence of this fact is that the part of "American" history in which *non*-Native people lived and acted is but a small percentage of the history of North America — a realization difficult to appreciate if one looks at the typical U.S. history survey textbook. If one group was a majority, ought that not to have consequences for the ways we assign the concepts of "norm" and "other"?[14] Scholars, then, might work to center the experiences and perspectives of Native people in more general studies, and to center — or at least draw back from the margins — the experiences of women and questions about gender in any study.

Scholars with experience in studying non-Native women will face the conceptual challenges common to all who study Native people. These include a need to problematize the concept of "progress" in history, and to fight the urge to think of American history, as Frederick Jackson Turner did, as a narrative and process of social evolution that moved overland from the Atlantic coast westward across the continent.[15]

Women's historians will also find that many concepts they have used in the past will not be particularly useful. One example of this would be the public/private dichotomy as a tool for sorting social roles and actions. In Native societies there was often no clear distinction, as some of the following articles make clear, and a "private" or personal decision such as whether to marry could have consequences of diplomatic, religious, and political importance for an entire community or group. Another conceptual tool that women's historians have employed to great effect in studying Anglo-American women, but which is extremely problematic when used to examine Native women's lives, is the idea of "separate spheres." In nineteenth-century Anglo-America, the idea that men and women lived and worked in "separate spheres" was part of an ideology that justified female disenfranchisement and supported a patriarchal society. Native peoples often agreed that the roles of men and women ought to be different, but they viewed work roles and gender relations as mutually supportive and complementary. Unlike Anglo-Americans, they did not assign more importance, prestige, or social worth to the work of one gender, nor did they view gender separateness as proving female inferiority. The articles by Nancy Shoemaker and Michelene Pesantubbee explore how Native women in two societies accepted, appropriated, and resisted the Anglo-American gender ideals held out to them as superior to those of their own societies.

It is equally important to jettison the idea that the patriarchal family was the norm among Native peoples. Generally speaking, it was not, as the essays in this volume make clear. Researchers looking at a Native family will want to ask: Was there a single head of household? Was the household head a woman or a lineage of elderly women? What are the implications of such household structures for that society?

On a related note, another important paradigm shift requires us to abandon the old historical method that looks at individual men as disconnected actors, and to recognize that with very few exceptions, Native people were members of families, lineages, kinship groups, clans, and other social organizations. If we think of indigenous societies as being made up of networks of people, we can often understand Native women's actions and influence more clearly. Sometimes finding the connections requires painstaking genealogical research. The essays by Susan Sleeper-Smith and by Carl Ekberg demonstrate this methodology and reveal the important historical insights to be gained from this admittedly tedious reconstructive work.

As these examples suggest, the scholar who hopes to study Native women must possess considerable knowledge of Native cultures. Without such knowledge, the women's historian can easily make the mistake of many of her or his sources and assume that western European cultural norms apply to Native peoples. The interdisciplinary methodology of ethnohistory, combining the anthropologist's focus on knowledge of human cultures with the historian's interest in reconstructing and interpreting change over time, has undergirded much of the dynamic work of the New Indian History since the 1970s, and it should be utilized to explore the lives and history of Native women within culturally accurate frameworks. Neither Native historians nor women's historians can ignore the specificity of individual Native cultures in their considerations of women's lives.

Indigenous perspectives are likewise paramount. While Native women left few records, we can learn much about their lives from knowledge of the languages they spoke. For example, what does it say about the structuring of Native thought if pronouns are ungendered and one always refers to "he/she" or "her/his"? Native cultural knowledge should not be confined to examinations of basic anthropological categories such as linguistics, politics, and economics. Spirituality is another avenue suggestive of Native women's status. Is it significant if the spiritual being who created a given Native people is female? Finally, it is important to remember that Native women lived their lives (and often still do) within nations that considered themselves independent, distinct, and sovereign, not as a part of European nations, even if encapsulated within one. The political status of Native communities was thus always different from that of other so-called racial minorities.

Native American history has been of particular interest to women's studies scholars because it demonstrates that patriarchy is neither universal nor inevitable. Yet traditional Native societies were organized with distinctive gender roles, the rigidity of which varied from time to time and place to place. And importantly, as Kathryn Shanley's article in this volume demonstrates, Native women's experiences, especially in the twentieth and twenty-first centuries, have been shaped by colonialism's legacy of racial, sexual, and class oppression. Shanley urges scholars, historians in particular, to consider how past events converged to create the often harrowing reality of twentieth-century Native life. The several scholars in this guidebook have, each in his or her own way, considered aspects of that larger problem.

Applying the methodology of women's history requires us to do several things. First, we must assume that what women did was important, a task made possible when we move away from the old emphasis on wars and leaders to issues of society and economy, and to new ways of looking at such old topics as military and political history. We then shift our gaze from violence, speeches, and gallantry, for example, to beliefs, production, mediation, and family, among other topics. Evident here is the importance of social history, with its emphasis on the thoughts and deeds of ordinary people, and its array of methodologies for reconstructing their experiences.

Second, we can train ourselves to "cherchez les femmes," that is, "look for the women." We know that, whether or not they are evident at first glance, women were present in most societies, groups, and communities. Maintaining an awareness of this fact when working with documents created by non-Native men for other non-Native men takes some doing, but if we are aware that women are present, if invisible, we can look for clues to their existence — in their economic production, perhaps, or in the children they bore, in their marriages and baptisms, in their names on scattered records, or in the material goods such as moccasins and baskets, left in attics or mentioned in ledgers and estate inventories. Whenever possible, find out and mention women's names.

Third, we can use gender as a tool of analysis, in Joan Scott's memorable phrase.[16] This requires us to ask three sets of questions:

1. What were women's experiences? What did women do? Was this different from what men did?
2. What were the expected gender roles? Did women and men do different kinds of work? Were their social and political activities different? How rigid were these roles? Did they change over time?
3. What were gender relations like? How did women and men get along?

Topics

Most historical studies begin either with a set of questions for which the researcher seeks answers or with one or more sources the scholar has found — sources that offer up information if one only knows how to recognize it. Sometimes a project evolves as a combination of the two. The creative historian, as the essays in this volume attest, is both lucky and observant, and keeps an open mind about how to structure an inquiry.

The articles collected here focus on stereotypes, politics and leadership, religion, kinship, culture change, economics, and the concept of race. There are plenty of other topical roads into Native women's history, some already charted — such as the boarding school experience, the impact of government policies, and third and fourth genders — and many more yet to be explored. Furthermore, we suggest that there is a general need to rewrite early American history to center Native experiences and perspectives, and a similar need for the revision of Native history to include women.[17] In addition, we urge students and scholars looking for topics to reexamine intergroup relations (such as frontier studies) with an eye to gender relations, to study the lives of urban Native women, and to look for previously invisible Indians, such as those living on the margins in eastern North America. It may also be useful to take a labor history approach or to examine Native participation in sports and the arts.

Key Questions and Issues

Research into Native women's history builds upon basic knowledge of Native history and culture, of course, recognizing the specific characteristics and experiences of people in the chosen group or region. Kinship is central to this type of inquiry, and there are many key points to be kept in mind. First, what were the typical family patterns for this community? Ethnographies will often mention whether inheritance of relationships — such as clan membership — was matrilineal or patrilineal, whether couples usually lived with the wife's family (matrilocal residence) or the husband's (patrilocal residence). One will want to ask how rigid these patterns were and how much they shifted during times of change for the community. Other questions about kinship involve the role of clans and moieties in the society. Did clan mothers have particular roles and authority? How did clan mothers, beloved women, or other important women who played key roles in families exercise authority? Did they have an effect on politics and the justice system? Essays in this volume by Jennifer Brown, Carl Ekberg, Clara Sue Kidwell, and Susan Sleeper-Smith illustrate such research.

Other kinds of networks may have linked Native women, their families, and communities. Susan Sleeper-Smith and Rebecca Kugel consider the ways that religious organizations extended kin affiliation and built political alliances. Given European and Anglo-American anxiety to convert Native peoples to Christianity, religious explorations and encounters are often valuable avenues to explore.

Names are important; historians have too often ignored the wives and mothers. How often have we heard that a Native person was the son, daughter, or other relative of a given male chief? Who was that Native person's mother, wife, or sister? Naming people gives them identity—but keep in mind that Native people often had more than one name and that, in some Native cultures, etiquette required that one's formal name not be used. Thus, for instance, the name Pocahontas was a nickname for a woman who had at least three other names. She revealed her secret name, Matoaka, only after she converted to Christianity and was baptized as Rebecca. Pocahontas, meaning "little wanton," or "the mischievous one," was a pet name, but she also carried the formal name of Amonute.[18] When Black Hawk referred in his autobiography to "the daughter of Mat-ta-tas" without giving her name, this suggests that, from his Sauk male cultural perspective, her political role was less as an individual than as a female member of a leadership family. Certainly, since the autobiography was the composite work of Black Hawk, the bilingual Métis man Antoine LeClaire (to whom he narrated his story), and John B. Patterson (a white editor), the possibility exists that the name of Mat-ta-tas's daughter was dropped by one of these men as unimportant, but this need not be the only explanation. It would have been more important to Black Hawk to emphasize the woman's kin connections to a leadership family than to provide a personal name.

Recovering names of Native and Métis women can be a necessary corrective to the tendency of Euro-American writers to erase the identities of all Native people. As Euro-Americans wrote the initial histories of those regions they colonized, they ignored the significance of Native women and downplayed their own interactions with them. A typical example can be found in an article written in 1914 about James Allen Reed by Eben D. Price. Describing Reed as the "First Permanent Settler in Trempealeau County and Founder of Trempealeau [Wisconsin]," Price further stated: "During his army life Reed married a Potawatomi woman, by whom he had five children, Elizabeth, Joseph, Mary, Madeline, and James. Upon her death in 1830 he was married a second time to a Menominee mixed blood, widow of the trader, Russell Farnham. Two children, Margaret and John, resulted from this union. He later married the widow of Amable Grignon, whose son Antoine was the chief source of this biography."[19] While the article does state, several pages later, that "the widow Grignon . . . was a relative of the Sioux chief Wabashaw" and that her "relationship with the noted chief gave Reed great prestige among this band of Sioux,"[20] Reed's Native wives remain otherwise anonymous. Here the resourceful researcher should be aware that other sources are available that reveal their names. Crawford County Clerk and Catholic Church records record the wives as Marguerite Oskache, Agathe Wood, and Archange Barret.[21] It is equally typical of early histories that Reed's Native predecessors in the Trempealeau region were not considered actual "settlers" and that Reed by himself was considered the "first permanent settler" rather than, with one of his Native wives, being viewed as the first couple or the first family.

In thinking about families, it is important to keep in mind that for much of eastern North America, exogamy or outmarriage was often seen as a virtue, because it enriched communities culturally, intellectually, and physically, creating links to other peoples and bringing in new ideas, skills, and options. Here, Clara Sue Kidwell's concept of Native women as cultural mediators can be helpful. Similarly, captives and newcomers were often adopted, and refugees were welcomed. Thus, many people had multiple ethnicities, and many villages — as Helen Hornbeck Tanner's essay illustrates — were multiethnic and/or multitribal. Families thus served to assimilate outsiders into the community, exerted social control over them, and taught them local mores and culture. Fur traders, for example, found that they were not trusted if they did not marry into a community with which they hoped to do business. Yet we should be careful when approaching sources that claim Native families "sold" their daughters or arranged marriages with total strangers. Very likely these marriages were proposed after families had carefully vetted the outsiders and the daughter's willingness had been ascertained, as the example of Old Buck's family and Horatio Newhall in Lucy Eldersveld Murphy's essay illustrates.

Native peoples of the Eastern Woodlands also recognized a number of different types of marriage, including temporary, trial, and permanent relationships, depending on the people and the time period. In addition, many nations considered it proper for a husband to have more than one wife at a time, although the wives' consent was usually required and co-wives were often sisters or otherwise closely affiliated. Divorce was generally possible and could be initiated by either wife or husband. Although fidelity within marriage was usually expected, many communities accepted that young women as well as young men might experiment sexually before marriage, and any children of these liaisons belonged to the mother, whose family helped to raise them. In all these ways they differed from Euro-Americans and Euro-Canadians, who were not shy about reading these differences as moral failings and evidence of Native "savagery."

Probably the aspect of Eastern Woodlands Native societies that Europeans had the greatest difficulty understanding was that marriage did not form the core social and economic unit of society. Because of this, Native women's most important affiliations were not with their husbands but with their natal kin groups of parents, siblings, and children. Native marriages did not invest the husband with the same types of economic and social control over his wife and children as did European marriages, nor was Native marriage the vehicle for the inheritance of property. This was especially the case with regard to land. Where Europeans viewed land as a commodity that could be divided and inherited, Eastern Woodlands Native peoples saw land as a community resource available to those kin groups that worked it but which ultimately belonged to the tribal community as a whole.

Of course, European Christians did not simply acknowledge cultural differences between themselves and Native peoples: they struggled mightily to compel or persuade Native people to change. Articles in this volume by Rayna Green and David Smits address the ways that Europeans and Euro-Americans misunderstood and misrepresented Native women and Native gender roles, sometimes intentionally. Researchers need to keep in mind the cultural differences between Native and European societies relative to gender, both when they think about historical encounters and as they evaluate and work with different types of sources. Scholars should also remember that not only did Native gender patterns vary depending on time, place, and circumstance, but so too did those of Euro-American and Euro-Canadian societies.

For projects that focus on moments of contact or the processes of colonization, historians do well to investigate the roles that women played in these arenas. Often, issues of gender are important because most indigenous societies that encountered invaders and migrants had balanced sex ratios or greater numbers of women than men. However, the "cycles of conquest" (to use Edward Spicer's term) brought in waves of explorers, armies, missionaries, government officials, fur traders, miners, and land speculators, the vast majority of whom were male.[22] The very low incidence of non-Native women in these groups meant that these male strangers often sought Native women to fulfill traditionally female roles as cooks, guides, and nurses as well as traders, interpreters, converts, sexual partners, wives, and rape victims. A key goal of any study of contact should be to ask what roles women played in the processes of colonization, what the gender relations were between Native women and non-Native men, and how this affected the gender relations between Native women and men in their own communities, and between Native and non-Native men.

A question many historians raise concerns the power and status of women in Native societies and whether it changed during a particular time period or due to a particular event or policy. Examples will be found in this guide in articles by Eleanor Leacock, Theda Perdue, Michelene Pesantubbee, Nancy Shoemaker, and Helen Hornbeck Tanner. These scholars make clear that there are a number of ways to measure these abstractions, and the issues are a good deal more complex than one might imagine. The issue of women's power is complicated because the tribal societies in question were themselves losing power in relation to the U.S. government or other Euro-American institutions, as Shoemaker, Perdue, and Pesantubbee discuss.

As if all these considerations were not complex enough, one must keep in mind several other variables. One is place: even within eastern North America there was a wide range of ecosystems and local realities to think about, including everything from water and food resources to nearness of sacred sites or immigrant settler colonies. Although most of the Native cultures discussed in this guide are considered part of the Eastern Woodlands cultural complex, there was great variability both locally and over the course of time. Certain realities changed from one time period to another. During certain eras, tribes were able to maintain a balance of power with incoming Europeans by playing one off against another or if Native people held a demographic advantage, to cite two examples. During times of disease epidemics, heightened warfare, or forced migration, social patterns and choices might change. Linda Kerber has observed that wars are times when gender can be renegotiated: it seems clear that race relations are also open to review at such moments of unrest and chaos.[23] Finally, the people's relation to land is an important factor, as Jean O'Brien's and Theda Perdue's articles illustrate. This is true for all Native people, whose landholdings were gradually eroded, and particularly relevant for women, whose roles as cultivators of the soil gave them a special cultural and spiritual connection to the earth.

Sources

Using problematic sources is always a matter of reading critically. One must realize that a written source contains both information and interpretation. The scholar's job is to differentiate between the two, to be alert to contradictions in the text. An excerpt from the journal of English fur trader Alexander Henry provides a good example while at the same time highlighting the invisibility of Native women. In 1775, Henry visited an Ojibwe village near Rainy Lake, Ontario, where he described the people as "poor, dirty and almost naked." Such remarks give a reader the impression of poverty and economic distress, yet Henry's next words belie his first description. He adds that from this community he "bought fish and wildrice, which latter they had in great abundance."[24] The fact that Henry could buy food — and in "great abundance" — from "poor" Ojibwes suggests that he is using the word "poor" to refer to something other than a state of generalized socio-economic want. When one recalls that Henry was a fur trader, it seems likely that he was assigning a specific meaning to the word "poor," one that reflected his interest in obtaining furs. To Henry, the word "poor" indicated that the Rainy Lake Ojibwes had few furs to trade, not that they were economically destitute. Equally important, wild rice was a female-harvested food source. If Henry bought wild rice from Ojibwe villagers, he almost certainly bought it from Ojibwe women. Yet his journal is silent on this point, effectively erasing the village's women as historical figures, creating a situation where later scholars have assumed that women had no part in transactions with fur traders.[25]

If Henry's use of language is specialized, sometimes a source uses language that obviously signals bias and alerts the researcher to separate carefully interpretation from information. When an Anglo-American male refers to Native women as "squaws" or characterizes Native men as oppressing "their women," a phrase that suggests notions of male ownership of women that are incompatible with Native gender relations but are very much in keeping with how Anglos thought about Native gender relations, a researcher is warned to be on her or his guard.

At other times, sources may contain unexpected information about Native people. The New York State census excerpted with Nancy Shoemaker's article asked for the clan affiliation of Iroquois people being enumerated, providing clear proof of the continuing vitality of the clan system. Careful reading of the clan affiliations listed by individual Iroquois also shows that clan membership was matrilineal, with children inheriting their mother's clan.

Different types of sources are likely to reveal different types of information and contain different sorts of biases. Narrative sources, such as letters, memoirs, and travel accounts, in which an author describes events and people and places, are perhaps easiest to work with, because it is obvious that, as products of individual minds, they will contain distinct points of view. An author's gender and class will powerfully refract his or her assumptions; so, too, will her or his race. Church records, account books, and census records, sources that were generated to record societal information, contain other sorts of biases. As Susan Sleeper-Smith points out in her essay, church baptismal records often disguised Native women's ethnicity by referring to them only by European baptismal names. Not every census could be counted on to ask questions aimed at describing Native social structures such as clans. Too often census takers distorted Native family structure by forcing it into the Anglo-American male-headed household model. Even sources that are considered to contain objective, strictly factual information, such as ethnographies, official government reports, and legal testimony, contain biases.

Whenever possible, scholars should try to present the voices of Native people. The significant amount of writing by Native peoples themselves in the years between 1600 and 1900 is often overlooked. Native peoples were quick to grasp the potential of the written word. They utilized European documentary forms, such as wills and other legal procedures. They became literate in European languages, and, significantly, in their own languages as well. The written records they produced were sometimes meant for their own communities, but sometimes also for non-Native outsiders they wished to educate or influence. Black Hawk's autobiography would be a representative work in this genre, and, while written with certain objectives in mind, it is also a good example of how a work ostensibly not about women can reveal much about their lives. Of course, this source, like many others, including Mountain Wolf Woman's autobiography, was a collaborative project between the author, an interpreter, and an editor, and one must be aware of the difficulties involved in works authored by multiple persons.

Conclusion

At times, many of the Native peoples in eastern North America faced similar circumstances in their experiences of conquest and colonization. As Canada and the United States grew in power and ability to exert control over territory, Native peoples had to consider the policies of these nation-states toward themselves very seriously. In the aftermath of the American Revolution, the U.S.-Canada border was created and a number of Native peoples found themselves living in newly different countries. In the first half of the nineteenth century, U.S. Indian policy mandated Native removal from lands the United States sought to occupy. Many Woodlands peoples confronted removal threats, and many were physically relocated from their traditional homelands. Some avoided removal but faced threats of other kinds, as they were declared to be extinct or their members were reclassified in other "racial" groups. As U.S. Indian policy shifted from removal to creating reserved land bases for Native peoples, many Native peoples of the Eastern Woodlands also faced the realities of reservation living.

Given these massive changes, Native women's roles and relationships were extremely important. As women, they not only reproduced their own populations, but they might intermarry, bringing children to their spouses' communities and creating connections between communities. They continued to work to provide for their families, often under changing, challenging, and even frightening circumstances, adapting to new ecosystems and to different economic systems and shifting opportunities. As men's roles changed, women's might compensate. New political realities and religious campaigns, military violence, land loss, and boarding schools affected women, men, and children, who struggled to maintain their spiritual, cultural, and physical vitality. That so many succeeded is a bittersweet triumph, and it is time to think of Native history as a struggle for survivance that succeeded on some important levels rather than as a story of dispossession and defeat. Native women's history goes a long way toward showing that struggle and that success.

We hope this collection will help scholars recover both Native women's history and the history of writing that history. When we began working on this project several years ago, we referred to it jokingly as a "greatest hits" collection. Some of the articles printed here are classics, while others show the evolution of approach and method that took place as later writers were influenced by earlier scholars. We have selected these essays as much to demonstrate a variety of methodological approaches and research materials as for their subject matter.[26] If this collection of essays and sources stimulates creative thinking, discussion, and research, it will have achieved our goals.

Notes

1. Sauk Language Series no. 2. Thanks to Christy Lyons of the Sac and Fox Nation Library, Stroud, Oklahoma, for this information,
2. Donald Jackson, ed., *Black Hawk: An Autobiography* (Urbana: University of Illinois Press, 1964), 107.

3. Quotations "the daughter of Mat-ta-tas," "a stick in her hand," "[S]he was a woman," and "had worked hard," from Jackson, *Black Hawk*, 112. Quotations "the women having worked" and "they had decided" from "Memorandum of Talks between Edmund P. Gaines and the Sauk," in *The Black Hawk War, 1831–1832*, ed. and comp. Ellen M. Whitney (Springfield: Illinois State Historical Library, 1973), 2:30.

4. Jackson, *Black Hawk*, 112.

5. Marybeth Lorbiecki, *Painting the Dakota: Seth Eastman at Fort Snelling* (Afton MN: Afton Historical Society Press, 2000).

6. Colin McEvedy and Richard Jones, *Atlas of World Population History* (New York: Facts on File, 1978), 280.

7. Gerald Vizenor, *Manifest Manners: Postindian Warriors of Survivance* (Lincoln: University of Nebraska Press, 1999).

8. Patricia Albers and Beatrice Medicine, *The Hidden Half: Studies of Plains Indian Women* (Lanham MD: University Press of America, 1983).

9. Laura F. Klein and Lillian Ackerman, *Women and Power in Native North America* (Norman: University of Oklahoma Press, 1995).

10. Mona Etienne and Eleanor Leacock, eds., *Women and Colonization: Anthropological Perspectives* (New York: Praeger, 1980).

11. Nancy Shoemaker, ed., *Negotiators of Change: Historical Perspectives on Native American Women* (New York: Routledge, 1995).

12. Theda Perdue, ed., *Sifters: Native American Women's Lives* (New York: Oxford University Press, 2001).

13. Gerda Lerner, *The Majority Finds Its Past: Placing Women in History* (New York: Oxford University Press, 1979).

14. McEvedy and Jones, *Atlas of World Population History*.

15. Frederick Jackson Turner, *History, Frontier, and Section* (Albuquerque: University of New Mexico Press, 1993); Patricia Nelson Limerick, Clyde A. Milner II, and Charles E. Rankin, eds., *Trails: Toward a New Western History* (Lawrence: University Press of Kansas, 1991).

16. Joan W. Scott, *Gender and the Politics of History* (New York: Columbia University Press, 1988).

17. For an admirable effort to center Native historical experiences, see Daniel K. Richter, *Facing East from Indian Country: A Native History of Early America* (Cambridge: Harvard University Press, 2001).

18. Helen C. Rountree, *The Powhatan Indians of Virginia: Their Traditional Culture* (Norman: University of Oklahoma Press, 1989), 80.

19. Wisconsin Historical Society, *Proceedings* (1914), 108.

20. Wisconsin Historical Society, *Proceedings* (1914), 112.

21. James L. Hansen, "Crawford County, Wisconsin Marriages, 1816–1848," *Minnesota Genealogical Journal* 1 (May 1984): 48, 54, 55; Hansen, "Prairie du Chien and Galena Church Records, 1827–29," *Minnesota Genealogical Journal* 5 (May 1986): 18. Oskache may have been Ojibwe — according to the Crawford County marriage record (54).

22. Edward H. Spicer, *Cycles of Conquest: The Impact of Spain, Mexico, and the United States on the Indians of the Southwest, 1533–1960* (Tucson: University of Arizona Press, 1962).

23. Linda Kerber, "'I Have Don . . . Much to Carrey on the Warr': Women and the Shaping of Republican Ideology after the American Revolution," in *Toward an Intellectual History of Women, Essays by Linda K. Kerber* (Chapel Hill: University of North Carolina Press, 1997), 104.

24. Quoted in Harold Hickerson, *Land Tenure of the Rainy Lake Chippewa at the Beginning of the Nineteenth Century, Smithsonian Contributions to Anthropology* 2, no. 4 (1967): 46.

25. For an insightful discussion of fur traders' specialized word usage see Mary Black-Rogers, "Varieties of 'Starving': Semantics and Survival in the Subarctic Fur Trade, 1750–1850," *Ethnohistory* 44, no. 4 (1986): 353–83. For women as traders of wild rice and other foods of their own production, see Bruce M. White, "The Woman Who Married the Beaver: Trade Patterns and Gender Roles in the Ojibwa Fur Trade," *Ethnohistory* 46, 1 (1999): 109–47. See also Tanis C. Thorne, "For the Good of Her People: Continuity and Change for Native Women of the Midwest, 1650–1850," in Lucy Eldersveld Murphy and Wendy Hamand Venet, eds., *Midwestern Women: Work, Community, and Leadership at the Crossroads* (Bloomington: Indiana University Press, 1997), 95–120.

26. We chose to retain the original capitalization style of these essays with regard to the words "white" and "Native" to demonstrate that conventions vary over time and from one publication to another.

I. Theory

The essays reprinted in this section are almost all older pieces. This selection was deliberate, for these older works remind us of several important things. They reveal the genealogy of scholarship, allowing us to note which scholars developed what theories and to assess the intellectual impact of those theories. These influential pieces have mapped some of the most important contours of the field of Native women's history. They are also a historiography in and of themselves. They remind us of the social moment when scholars first began to theorize about Native women, and they reveal the historical and anthropological paradigms Native Americanists confronted. If we have arrived at a time when scholars can critique and transcend these theories, it is because they created the foundation upon which we built; they gave shape and meaning to our thinking in the first place. They remind us, too, that scholarship is an ongoing dialogue, that on a very real level it is always a collaborative process.

Scholars initially paid serious attention to Native women during the 1970s, when multiple new fields of historical study were emerging. Among them were the New Indian History, as it was called, and women's history, both of which were interested in Native women's historical experiences, and both of which challenged older histories that emphasized the experiences of white males to the exclusion of nearly everyone else. If Native people had been stereotyped in earlier historical treatments, Native women had been doubly so. It is not surprising that early studies of Native women such as Rayna Green's classic, "The Pocahontas Perplex," focused on identifying and debunking the stereotypic Princess/Squaw dichotomy. Writing in 1975, Green combined analysis of what she terms "vernacular artifacts" with literary sources to show how pervasive and influential in Anglo-American society this inaccurate binary image of Native women was. Seven years later, David Smits produced a sweeping review of primary texts revealing how western European gender ideals and roles, particularly regarding the gendered division of labor, deeply influenced the views of Native women held by European colonists and their Anglo-American and Anglo-Canadian descendants. And indeed, those perceptions of Native gender roles played into the "perplex" that Green identified as distorting the realities of Native women's lives ever since.

If early treatments emphasized what Native women were not, scholars also began to probe what Native women's lives actually were. Clara Sue Kidwell's article reflects on Native women's social importance as mediators, paying particular attention to how this role gave women in a wide range of Native societies an important place in political relationships with outsiders. Jennifer Brown looks to another, equally important arena of indigenous life, the family. Where Kidwell considers what it was about Native female life that made women such likely political mediators, Brown revisits the masculinist bias in the fur-trade literature. She argues that mixed-race, or Métis, people were matricentric and that Métis and Native women, far from being simply appendages of males, whether European traders or Native hunters, were critical to creating and sustaining the communities that made the centuries-long fur trade possible. In the process, she reminds us that five centuries of colonization and contact created, in her words, "new peoples," Native-descended and offering by their mere existence a counternarrative to the story of heroic western expansion. Their history further reminds us that all human beings exist in families, that a history emphasizing individuals divorced from families and communities represents an inaccurate reading of the past.

The final two essays in this section critically engage feminist theory. The late Eleanor Leacock was one of the first anthropologists to consider seriously what women's lives were like in what she termed "egalitarian societies." Writing in the late 1970s, when most anthropologists still confidently asserted that male dominance was universal in human societies, Leacock presented an important early challenge to that view. Her Marxist theoretical orientation has been dismissed as too evolutionist, but such a critique minimizes her contribution to both Native and women's histories. Leacock took it as a given that all aspects of Native cultures and societies, including gender relations, had been powerfully influenced by five hundred years of colonization. This fact is widely recognized today, testimony to the enduring significance of her thought.

The final essay, by Kathryn Shanley, presents a contemporary Native scholar's reflections on Native women's history. Like earlier scholars, Shanley emphasizes the importance of kinship to Native identity and underscores the enduring problem of stereotypes, but she adds a sober reminder that Native women have often faced racialized and feminized poverty, a grim reality with roots in the histories of colonialism that the authors in this volume seek to uncover. Her essay invites us to consider how distinctive Native women's realities were and are. Tribal and Euro-American worldviews differ dramatically; so, too, do understandings of "race" and "ethnicity." The unique relationship between the federal government and Native people looms large in the lives of many (but by no means all) Native women. Shanley also urges feminist scholars to consider how well they have understood the ways these differences have shaped Native women's lives. At the same time, she demonstrates that Native women may care deeply about many of the same issues that feminists care about, such as the feminization of poverty, domestic abuse, or inadequate child care. She reminds us of the intersection of past and present and challenges historians to write histories that do not simply valorize a more egalitarian past but instead chart the connections between the two, all in the service of building better futures.

Further Reading

Students and scholars who would like to read further in theory might explore the following works. Although they and the authors represented in the present collection have addressed a number of important issues, there is plenty of room for further theoretical writing on Native women.

Allen, Paula Gunn. *The Sacred Hoop: Recovering the Feminine in American Indian Traditions*. Boston: Beacon Press, 1986.

Ford, Ramona. "Native American Women: Changing Statuses, Changing Interpretations." In *Writing the Range: Race, Class, and Culture in the Women's West*, ed. Elizabeth Jameson and Susan Armitage, 42–68. Norman: University of Oklahoma Press, 1997.

Fur, Gunlög. "'Some Women Are Wiser Than Some Men': Gender and Native American History." In *Clearing a Path: Theorizing the Past in Native American Studies*, ed. Nancy Shoemaker, 75–103. New York: Routledge, 2002.

James, M. Annette, and Theresa Halsey. "American Indian Women: At the Center of Indigenous Resistance in North America." In *The State of Native America*, ed. M. Annette Jaimes, 330–31. Boston: South End Press, 1992.

Medicine, Beatrice. "North American Indigenous Women and Cultural Domination." *American Indian Culture and Research Journal* 17, no. 3 (1993): 121–30.

Mihesuah, Devon Abbott. *Indigenous American Women: Decolonization, Empowerment, Activism*. Lincoln: University of Nebraska Press, 2003.

Ross, Luana. *Inventing the Savage: The Social Construction of Native American Criminality*. Austin: University of Texas Press, 1998.

Smith, Andrea. "Native American Feminism, Sovereignty, and Social Change." *Feminist Studies* 31, no. 1 (2005): 116–32.

———. "Sexual Violence and American Indian Genocide." In *Remembering Conquest: Feminist/Womanist Perspectives on Religion, Colonization, and Sexual Violence*, ed. Nantawan Lewis and Marie Fortune, 31–52. Binghamton NY: Haworth Press, 1999.

Strong, Pauline Turner. "Feminist Theory and the 'Invasion of the Heart' in North America." *Ethnohistory* 43, no. 4 (1996): 683–712.

Van Kirk, Sylvia. "Toward a Feminist Perspective in Native History." In *Papers of the Eighteenth Algonquian Conference*, ed. William Cowan, 377–89. Ottawa: Carleton University, 1987.

Young, Mary. "Women, Civilization, and the Indian Question." In *Clio Was a Woman: Studies in the History of American Women*, ed. Mabel E. Deutrick and Virginia C. Purdy, 98–109. Washington DC: Howard University Press, 1980.

What Native Women Were Not

1. The Pocahontas Perplex

The Image of Indian Women in American Culture

RAYNA GREEN

New Introduction by Rayna Green

"The Pocahontas Perplex" is not about the cultures and lives of Native women. The essay is about the imaginative construction and representation of Native women's lives and histories by non-Indians, about cultural constructions and cultural practices that affect and dislocate Native lives and histories. The essay names and defines the barriers between "Americans" and Native women. It suggests an American obsession, played out through time and space, that stands between Pocahontas and her sisters and their history, a Native history, a women's history, my history, our history, an American history.

I wrote "The Pocahontas Perplex" in 1975 in response to a request from two colleagues, then editors for the *Massachusetts Review*. For the American Bicentennial they wanted material from an American Indian perspective, work on and by women, and writing that might reach and influence an audience beyond the academy. We were all engaged in what we thought was canonical, pedagogical, and social reform in the midst of the academic and political movements that produced new, interdisciplinary, often applied, advocacy, and activist studies—scholarship with an agenda for change. "Pocahontas," then, was driven more by the promises of the New Feminism, Red Power, and Radical Pedagogy than by the opportunity afforded an untenured assistant professor to get another publication posted to the record. I do not mean to suggest that this little essay alone bore the burden of that big political agenda, but rather that the big agenda—pretentious, even futile as it may sound now—was very much on our minds in post-1960s America.

"Pocahontas" did come out of my dissertation, a study of American Indian images in American culture, for a degree in Folklore and American Studies (Indiana, 1973). The material on Native women was from that larger study, where I had begun to note particularly pervasive and significant gendered patterns to the American cultural behaviors I'd described. Examining the image of Native women became a central part of a more comprehensive description of the major form of American identity I'd identified. Moreover, "The Pocahontas Perplex" had as its "inspiration" an all-pervasive scholarly silence on gender, sexuality, and identity. It was also motivated by the conventional and skimpy body of anthropological and historical work on Native women, the singular inspirational exception to which was Nancy Lurie's *Mountain Wolf Woman*.[1] I suppose I thought of "Pocahontas" as a stand-in for activist and community-centered scholarship, and (with the wonderful work of others that had begun to appear in that time period) potentially as a Native/woman's voice emergent. That emergence was directed to a new audience—not altogether an academic one, but a general, complex audience that actually might include both Indians and women. I was writing to, for, and about women and Indians, some of whom were the new academics. And, as it happens, I realized that I was writing for me, an Indian woman, making the personal political, as my friend Gloria Steinem had urged, an act of indulgence long forbidden us by the customary distanced, third-person standards of academic publishing.

Thus the audience, the historical context in which it appeared, the "inspirations" negative and positive, and the political intent (mine and my editors) of the piece were and are as important to consider—in retrospect—as the theoretical or analytical framework of the essay. Actually, I was and remain a resistant-to-theory kind of gal. In a way, the title of the piece tells the reader that; while it offers hints to a hypothesis about the very nature of American culture, it also makes a joke about theorizing it. The title offered homage to a monograph very popular with countercultural scholars, Frederick Crews's spoof of current literary theory and literary criticism entitled *The Pooh Perplex*. In short, the title proposes a theory, the essay supports, then mocks its truth. I suppose, had I written the piece in the 1980s and 1990s, with the (de)volution of Critical Studies, I would have had to parody my own essay as a poststructuralist, Marxist, feminist, new historicist, postcolonialist, deconstructionist, and counterhegemonic theory. And the piece would have been called "(De)Constructing the Post-Colonial Pocahontas."

I do recognize that everything I was doing then, both in "Pocahontas" and much of my later work, were precursors to the thoroughly interdisciplinary and theoretical study of "identity" and "whiteness," particularly through "representations." They were then and remain today studies of cultural expression and cultural practice in order to examine race, class, gender, sexuality, identity both national and racial, belief, and ideology.

But there was more. I was using "evidence" that was not (then as now) generally accepted or used by historians or even most anthropologists. "The Pocahontas Perplex" used as its "data" songs, stories, items of common linguistic usage, oral histories, jokes, sayings and proverbs, popular novels and plays, poems, paintings, commercial advertising materials, prints, drawings, nineteenth-century photographs, sculptures, carvings (cigar-store Indians, figureheads), craft items (quilts, weathervanes). What I called vernacular culture was evidence, not merely supplemental "illustrations." These were arti-facts, not unreliably interpretive art, of what Americans, through and over several centuries, were thinking about Pocahontas, about Native women, about themselves.

In spite of the virtual flood of stellar, corrective, and visionary scholarship on Native women in the last twenty years, some of it by writers in this volume, the Perplex still has us in its deadly embrace. I had come to think in the 1980s that the Perplex was losing its hold on Americans, that we'd lost our collective need for her and her sisters (and Indian team mascots). But, no! She's back! Every time (often) I meet an upper-class Virginian who tells me she is a "Daughter of Pocahontas"; every time (regularly) I meet someone who tells me that their grandmother was a Cherokee Princess; whenever (frequently) I pick up a Land O'Lakes butter carton with that Indian maiden on it; and whenever (still too often) I am confronted with the ever-reified and -renewable Pocahontas mythologies that appear in the movies (e.g., *Pocahontas*, 1995, and *The New World*, 2005), I know it's not just a theory. It's a reoccurring pandemic. I just gave it a name. So, six reprintings and thirty years of appearances on college course lists haven't done the job I intended "Pocahontas" to do, in the pretentious optimism about social change I described for this article. In fact, the very durability of the Perplex guarantees the perpetual popularity of the essay. That's scary! But I have to believe that somehow, all those college course lists and reprints will eventually vaccinate enough Americans against the Perplex and they'll just laugh the next resurgence right out of the box office. That's why I keep writing.

The Pocahontas Perplex
The Image of Indian Women in American Culture (1975)

In one of the best known old Scottish ballads, "Young Beichan" or "Lord Bateman and the Turkish King's Daughter" as it is often known in America, a young English adventurer travels to a strange, foreign land. The natives are of a darker color than he, and they practice a pagan religion. The man is captured by the King (Pasha, Moor, Sultan) and thrown in a dungeon to await death. Before he is executed, however, the pasha's beautiful daughter—smitten with the elegant and wealthy visitor—rescues him and sends him homeward. But she pines away for love of the now remote stranger who has gone home, apparently forgotten her, and contracted a marriage with a "noble" "lady" of his own kind. In all the versions, she follows him to his own land, and in most, she arrives on his wedding day whereupon he throws over his bride-to-be for the darker but more beautiful Princess. In most versions, she becomes a Christian, and she and Lord Beichan live happily ever after.

In an article called "The Mother of Us All," Philip Young suggests the parallel between the ballad story and the Pocahontas–John Smith rescue tale.[2] With the exception of Pocahontas's marriage to John Rolfe (still, after all, a Christian stranger), the tale should indeed sound familiar to most Americans nurtured on Smith's salvation by the Indian Princess. Actually, Europeans were familiar with the motif before John Smith offered his particular variant in the *Generall Historie of Virginie* (1624).

Francis James Child, the famous ballad collector, tells us in his *English and Scottish Popular Ballads* that "Young Beichan" (Child #40) matches the tale of Gilbert Beket, St. Thomas Aquinas' father, as well as a legend recounted in the *Gesta Romanorum*, one of the oldest collections of popular tales. So the frame story was printed before 1300 and was, no doubt, well distributed in oral tradition before then. Whether or not our rakish adventurer-hero, John Smith, had heard the stories or the ballad, we cannot say, but we must admire how life mirrors art since his story follows the outlines of the traditional tale most admirably. What we do know is that the elements of the tale appealed to Europeans long before Americans had the opportunity to attach their affection for it onto Pocahontas. Whether or not we believe Smith's tale—and there are many reasons not to—we cannot ignore the impact the story has had on the American imagination.

"The Mother of Us All" became our first aristocrat, and perhaps our

Ætatis suæ 21. Aº.1616.

Matoaks als Rebecka daughter to the mighty Prince
Powhatan Emperour of Attanoughkomouck als Virginia
converted and baptized in the Christian faith, and
Wife to the Wor.ᵗ Mʳ Tho: Rolff.

1. *Pocahontas*, oil on canvas, ca. 1595–1616, by an unidentified artist, probably after Simon Van de Passe, after 1617. National Portrait Gallery, Smithsonian Institution, gift of the A. W. Mellon Educational Charitable Trust, no. 65.61.

2. *Smith Rescued by Pocahontas* by Edward Corbould, ca. 1880, engraving by George Virtue after T. Knight. Courtesy Rayna Green.

3. Pocahontas tobacco label, ca. 1880. Library of Congress Prints and Photographs Division, 11365.

4. *America*, ca. 1775, copy of engraving by Adrian Collaert II, after Martin de Vos, ca. 1595. Courtesy Winterthur Museum, 57.83.8.

5. *Holland Recognizes American Independence*, engraving by G. Brouwer after A. Borghers and P. Wagenaar, ca. 1782. Courtesy National Park Service, Franklin D. Roosevelt Presidential Library and Museum, NPX62-148.

6. Cherokee Liniment medicine label from Louden and Co., ca. 1856. Library of Congress Prints and Photographs Division, LC-USZ62-55633.

7. Advertising poster of Wildroot Dandruff Remedy. Courtesy Warshaw Collection of Business Americana, National Museum of American History, Smithsonian Institution Archives Center.

8. Indian Girl Chewing Tobacco label from James Moran and Co., ca. 1874. Courtesy Library of Congress Prints and Photographs Division, LC-USZ62-57904.

9. Watercolor of Princess figure carved for cigar store or shop in Samuel Robb's workshop, ca. 1850. Courtesy National Gallery of Art, Index of American Design.

first saint, as Young implies. Certainly, the image of her body flung over the endangered head of our hero constitutes a major scene in national myth (fig. 2). Many paintings and drawings of this scene exist, and it appears in popular art on everything from wooden fire engine side panels to calendars. Some renderings betray such ignorance about the Powhatan Indians of Virginia—often portraying them in Plains dress—that one quickly comes to understand that it is the mythical scene, not the accuracy of detail that moved artists. The most famous portrait of Pocahontas, the only one said to be done from life (at John Rolfe's request), shows the Princess in Elizabethan dress, complete with ruff and velvet hat—the Christian, English lady the ballad expects her to become and the lady she indeed became for her English husband and her faithful audience for all time (fig. 1). The earliest literary efforts in America, intended to give us American rather than European topics, featured Pocahontas in plenty. Poems and plays—like James Nelson Barber's *The Indian Princess; or, La Belle Sauvage* (1808) and George Washington Custis' *The Settlers of Virginia* (1827), as well as contemporary American novels, discussed by Leslie Fiedler in *The Return of the Vanishing American*—dealt with her presence, or sang her praises from the pages of literary magazines and from the stages of popular playhouses throughout the east.[3] Traditional American ballads like "Jonathan Smith" retold the thrilling story; schoolbook histories included it in the first pages of every text; nineteenth-century commercial products like cigars, perfume and even flour used Pocahontas' name as come-on (figs. 6, 7, 8); and she appeared as the figurehead for American warships and clippers. Whether or not she saved John Smith, her actions as recounted by Smith set up one kind of model for Indian-White relations that persists—long after most Indians and Anglos ceased to have face-to-face relationships. Moreover, as a model for the national understanding of Indian women, her significance is undeniable. With her darker, negatively viewed sister, the Squaw—or, the anti-Pocahontas, as Fiedler calls her—the Princess intrudes on the national consciousness, and a potential cult waits to be resurrected when our anxieties about who we are make us recall her from her woodland retreat.[4]

Americans had a Pocahontas Perplex even before the teenage Princess offered us a real figure to hang the iconography on. The powerfully symbolic Indian woman, as Queen and Princess, has been with us since 1575 when she appeared to stand for the New World. Artists, explorers, writers and political leaders found the Indian as they cast about for some symbol with which to identify this earthly, frightening, and beautiful paradise; E. McClung

Fleming has given one of the most complete explications of these images.[5] The misnamed Indian was the native dweller, who fit conveniently into the various traditional folkloric, philosophical and literary patterns characteristic of European thought at the time.[6] Europeans easily adopted the Indian as the iconographic representative of the Americas. At first, Caribbean and Brazilian (Tupinamba) Indians, portrayed amidst exotic flora and fauna, stood for the New World's promises and dangers. The famous and much-reproduced "Four Continents" illustrations (circa early sixteenth century) executed by artists who had seen Indians and ones who had not, ordinarily pictured a male and female pair in America's place.[7] But the paired symbol apparently did not satisfy the need for a personified figure, and the Indian Queen began to appear as the sole representation for the Americas in 1575. And until 1765 or thereabouts, the bare-breasted, Amazonian Native American Queen reigned (fig. 4). Draped in leaves, feathers, and animal skins as well as in heavy Caribbean jewelry, she appeared aggressive, militant, and armed with spears and arrows. Often, she rode on an armadillo, and stood with her foot on the slain body of an animal or human enemy. She was the familiar Mother-Goddess figure—full-bodied, powerful, nurturing but dangerous—embodying the opulence and peril of the New World. Her environment was rich and colorful, and that, with the allusions to Classical Europe through the Renaissance portrayal of her large, naked body, attached her to Old World History as well as to New World virtue.

Her daughter, the Princess, enters the scene when the colonies begin to move toward independence, and she becomes more "American" and less Latin than her mother. She seems less barbarous than the Queen; the rattlesnake (Jones' "Dont Tread On Me" sign) defends her, and her enemies are defeated by male warriors rather than by her own armed hand. She is Britannia's daughter as well as that of the Carib Queen, and she wears the triangular Phrygian cap and holds the liberty pole of her later, metamorphosed sister, Miss Liberty (the figure on the Statue of Liberty and the Liberty dime). She is young, leaner in the Romanesque rather than Greek mode, and distinctly Caucasian, though her skin remains slightly tinted in some renderings. She wears the loose, flowing gowns of classical statuary rather than animal skins, and Roman sandals grace her feet. She is armed, usually with a spear, but she also carries a peace pipe, a flag, or the starred and striped shield of Colonial America. She often stands with The Sons of Liberty, or later, with George Washington (fig. 5).

Thus, the Indian woman began her symbolic, many-faceted life as a

Mother figure—exotic, powerful, dangerous, and beautiful—and as a representative of American liberty and European classical virtue translated into New World terms. She represented, even defended America. But when real Indian women—Pocahontas and her sisters—intruded into the needs bound up in symbols and the desires inherent in daily life, the responses to the symbol became more complex, and the Pocahontas perplex emerged as a controlling metaphor in the American experience. The Indian woman, along with her male counterparts, continued to stand for the New World and for rude native nobility, but the image of the savage remained as well. The dark side of the Mother-Queen figure is the savage Squaw, and even Pocahontas, as John Barth suggests in *The Sotweed Factor*, is motivated by lust.

Both her nobility as a Princess and her savagery as a Squaw are defined in terms of her relationships with male figures. If she wishes to be called a Princess, she must save or give aid to white men. The only good Indian—male or female, Squanto, Pocahontas, Sacagawea, Cochise, the Little Mohee or the Indian Doctor—rescues and helps white men. But the Indian woman is even more burdened by this narrow definition of a "good Indian," for it is she, not the males, whom white men desire sexually. Because her image is so tied up with abstract virtue—indeed, with America—she must remain the Mother Goddess–Queen. But acting as a real female, she must be a partner and lover of Indian men, a mother to Indian children, and an object of lust for white men. To be Mother, Queen and lover is, as Oedipus' mother, Jocasta, discovered, difficult and perhaps impossible. The paradox so often noted in Latin/Catholic countries where men revere their mothers and sisters, but use prostitutes so that their "good" women can stay pure is to the point here. Both race conflict and national identity, however, make this particular Virgin-Whore paradox more complicated than others. The Indian woman finds herself burdened with an image that can only be understood as dysfunctional, even though the Pocahontas perplex affects us all. Some examination of the complicated dimensions of that image might help us move toward change.

In songs like "Jonathan Smith," "Chipeta's Ride" and others sung in oral tradition, the Indian woman saves white men.[8] In "Chipeta's Ride," she even saves a white woman from lust-enraged Indian males. Ordinarily, however, she rescues her white lover or an anonymous male captive. Always called a Princess (or Chieftain's Daughter), she, like Pocahontas, has to violate the wishes and customs of her own "barbarous" people to make good the

rescue, saving the man out of love and often out of "Christian sympathy."
Nearly all the "good" Princess figures are converts, and they cannot bear to
see their fellow Christians slain by "savages." The Princess is "civilized"; to
illustrate her native nobility, most pictures portray her as white, darker than
the Europeans, but more Caucasian than her fellow natives (see fig. 2).

If unable to make the grand gesture of saving her captive lover or if
thwarted from marrying him by her cruel father, the Chieftain, the Princess
is allowed the even grander gesture of committing suicide when her lover is
slain or fails to return to her after she rescues him. In the hundreds of "Lover's Leap" legends which abound throughout the country, and in traditional
songs like "The Indian Bride's Lament," our heroine leaps over a precipice,
unable to live without her loved one. In this movement from political symbolism (where the Indian woman defends America) to psychosexual symbolism (where she defends or dies for white lovers), we can see part of the
Indian woman's dilemma. To be "good," she must defy her own people, exile
herself from them, become white, and perhaps suffer death.

Those who did not leap for love continued to fall in love with white men
by the scores, and here the sacrifices are several. The women in songs like
"The Little Mohee," "Little Red Wing," and "Juanita, the Sachem's Daughter" fall in love with white travellers, often inviting them to share their bliss-
ful, idyllic, woodland paradise. If their lovers leave them, they often pine
away, die of grief, or leap off a cliff, but in a number of songs, the white
man remains with the maiden, preferring her life to his own, "civilized" way.
"The Little Mohee" is a prime example of such a song.

> As I went out walking for pleasure one day,
> In the sweet recollection, to dwell time away.
> As I sat amusing myself on the grass,
> Oh, who should I spy but a fair Indian lass.
>
> She walked up behind me, taking hold of my hand,
> She said, "You are a stranger and in a strange land,
> But if you will follow, you're welcome to come
> And dwell in my cottage that I call my home."
>
> My Mohea was gentle, my Mohea was kind.
> She took me when a stranger and clothed me when cold.
> She learned me the language of the lass of Mohea.
>
> "I'm going to leave you, so farewell my dear.

The ship's sails are spreading and home I must steer."
The last time I saw her she was standing on the strand,
And as my boat passed her she waved me her hand.

Saying "when you have landed and with the one you love,
Think of pretty Mohea in the coconut grove."
I am home but no one comes near me nor none do I see,
That would equal compare with the lass of Mohea.

Oh, the girl that I loved proved untrue to me.
I'll turn my course backward far over the sea.
I'll turn my course backward, from this land I'll go free,
And go spend my days with the little Mohea.

Such songs add to the exotic and sexual, yet maternal and contradictorily virginal image of the Indian Princess, and are reminiscent of the contemporary white soldier's attachments to "submissive," "sacrificial," "exotic" Asian women.

As long as Indian women keep their exotic distance or die (even occasionally for love of Indian men), they are permitted to remain on the positive side of the image. They can help, stand by, sacrifice for, and aid white men. They can, like their native brothers, heal white men, and the Indian reputation as healer dominated the nineteenth-century patent medicine business. In the ads for such medicines, the Indian woman appears either as a helpmate to her "doctor" husband or partner or as a healer herself (fig. 6). In several ads (and the little dime novels often accompanying the patent medicine products), she is the mysterious witch-healer. Thus, she shares in the Caucasian or European female's reputation for potential evil. The references here to power, knowledge, and sexuality remain on the good side of the image. In this incarnation, the Princess offers help in the form of medicine rather than love (fig. 7).

The tobacco industry also capitalized on the Princess' image, and the cigar-store figures and ads associated with the tobacco business replicate the Princess figures to sell its products (figs. 8, 9). Cigar-store Princesses smile and beckon men into tobacco shops. They hold a rose, a bundle of cigars, or some tobacco leaves (a sign of welcome in the colonial days), and they smile invitingly with their Caucasian lips. They also sell the product from tobacco packages, and here, like some of the figures in front of the shops, Diana-like or more militant Minerva (Wonder-Woman)-like heroines offer the comforts of the "Indian weed." They have either the rounded, infantile, semi-naked (indicating innocence) bodies of Renaissance angels or the bodies and clothes of classical heroines (fig. 9). The Mother Goddess and Miss Liberty peddle their more abstract wares, as Indian Princesses, along with those of the manufacturer. Once again, the Princess comforts white men, and while she promises much, she remains aloof.

But who becomes the white man's sexual partner? Who forms liaisons with him? It cannot be the Princess, for she is sacrosanct. Her sexuality can be hinted at but never realized. The Princess' darker twin, the Squaw, must serve this side of the image, and again, relationships with males determine what the image will be. In the case of the Squaw, the presence of overt and realized sexuality converts the image from positive to negative. White men cannot share sex with the Princess, but once they do so with a real Indian woman, she cannot follow the required love-and-rescue pattern. She does what white men want for money or lust. In the traditional songs, stories, obscene jokes, contemporary literary works and popular pictorializations of the Squaw, no heroines are allowed. Squaws share in the same vices attributed to Indian men—drunkenness, stupidity, thievery, venality of every kind—and they live in shacks on the edge of town rather than in a woodland paradise.

Here, Squaws are shamed for their relationships with white men, and the males who share their beds—the "squaw men" or "bucks," if they are Indian—share their shame. When they live with Indian males, Squaws work for their lazy bucks and bear large numbers of fat "papooses." In one joke, a white visitor to a reservation sees an overburdened squaw with ten children hanging on her skirts. "Where's your husband?" the visitor demands. "He ought to be hung!" "Ugh," says the squaw, "pretty well-hung!" They too are fat, and unlike their Princess sisters, dark and possessed of cruder, more "Indian" features. When stories and songs describe relationships with white men, Squaws are understood as mere economic and sexual conveniences for the men who—unlike John Smith or a "brave"—are tainted by association with her. Tale after tale describes the Indian whores, their alcoholic and sexual excesses with white trappers and hunters. A parody of the beautiful-maiden song, "Little Red Wing," speaks of her lewd sister who "lays on her back in a cowboy shack, and lets cowboys poke her in the crack." The result of this cowboy-squaw liaison is a "brat in a cowboy hat with his asshole between his eyes." This Squaw is dark, and squat, and even the cigar-store Indians show the changes in conception. No Roman sandals grace their feet, and their features are more "Indian" and "primitive" than even their male counterparts. The cigar-store squaws often had papooses on their backs, and some had corrugated places on their hips to light the store patrons' matches. When realities intrude on mythos, even Princesses can become Squaws, as the text of the ragtime song "On an Indian Reservation" illustrates.

> On an Indian reservation, far from home and civilization,
> Where the foot of Whiteman seldom trod.
> Whiteman went to fish one summer,
> Met an Indian maid—a hummer,
> Daughter of Big-Chief-Spare-the-rod.
> Whiteman threw some loving glances, took this maid to Indian
>   dances,
> Smoked his pipe of peace, took chances living in a teepee made of
>   fur.
> Rode with her on Indian ponies, bought her diamond rings, all
>   phonies,
> And he sang these loving words to her:
>
> Chorus:
> You're my pretty little Indian Napanee.
> Won't you take a chance and marry me.
> Your Daddy Chief, 'tis my belief,
> To a very merry wedding will agree.
> True, you're a dark little Indian maid,
> But I'll sunburn to a darker shade,
> I'll wear feathers on my head,
> Paint my skin an Indian red,
> If you will be my Napanee.
>
> With his contact soon he caught her,
> Soon he married this big chief's daughter,
> Happiest couple that you ever saw.
> But his dreams of love soon faded,
> Napanee looked old and jaded,
> Just about like any other squaw.
> Soon there came papoose in numbers, redskin yells disturbed his
>   slumbers,

Whiteman wonders at his blunders—now the feathers drop upon his
   head.
Sorry to say it, but he's a-wishing, that he'd never gone a-fishing,
Or had met this Indian maid and said:

Chorus:

The Indian woman is between a rock and a hard place. Like that of her male
counterpart, her image is freighted with such ambivalence that she has little
room to move. He, however, has many more modes in which to participate though he is still severely handicapped by the prevailing stereotypes.
They are both tied to definition by relationships with white men, but she
is especially burdened by the narrowness of that definition. Obviously, her
image is one that is troublesome to all women, but, tied as it is to a national
mythos, its complexity has a special piquance. As Vine Deloria points out in
Custer Died for Your Sins, many whites claim kinship with some distant Indian Princess grandmother, and thus try to resolve their "Indian problem"
with such sincere affirmations of relationship.[9]

Such claims make it impossible for the Indian woman to be seen as real.
She does not have the power to evoke feeling as a real mother figure, like
the black woman, even though *that* image has a burdensome negative side.
American children play with no red mammy dolls. She cannot even evoke
the terror the "castrating (white) bitch" inspires. Only the male, with up-
raised tomahawk, does that. The many expressions which treat of her image
remove her from consideration as more than an image. As some abstract,
noble Princess tied to "America" and to sacrificial zeal, she has power as a
symbol. As the Squaw, a depersonalized object of scornful convenience, she
is powerless. Like her male relatives she may be easily destroyed without
reference to her humanity. (When asked why he killed women and children
at Sand Creek, the commanding general of the U.S. Cavalry was said to have
replied, "nits make lice.") As the Squaw, her physical removal or destruction
can be understood as necessary to the progress of civilization even though
her abstracted sister, the Princess, stands for that very civilization. Perhaps
the Princess had to be removed from her powerful symbolic place, and replaced with the male Uncle Sam because she confronted America with too
many contradictions. As symbol and reality, the Indian woman suffers from
our needs, and by both race and sex stands damned.

Since the Indian so much represents America's attachment to a romantic past and to a far distant nobility, it is predictable but horrible that the

Indian woman should symbolize the paradoxical entity once embodied for the European in the Princess in the tower and the old crone in the cave. It is time that the Princess herself is rescued and the Squaw relieved of her obligatory service. The Native American woman, like all women, needs a definition that stands apart from that of males, red or white. Certainly, the Native woman needs to be defined as Indian, in Indian terms. Delightful and interesting as Pocahontas' story may be, she offers an intolerable metaphor for the Indian-White experience. She and the Squaw offer unendurable metaphors for the lives of Indian women. Perhaps if we give up the need for John Smith's fantasy and the trappers' harsher realities, we will find, for each of us, an image that does not haunt and perplex us. Perhaps if we explore the meaning of Native American lives outside the boundaries of the stories, songs, and pictures given us in tradition, we will find a more humane truth.

Notes

1. I would later formalize my critique into an extensive review of that literature (*Signs*, 1980; *Native American Women: A Contextual Bibliography*, 1984). In that piece I would also ask how scholarly treatment of Native women had affected Native women's lives and histories, as well as how scholarly embrace of the specific cultural behaviors I outlined in "Pocahontas" had affected the very nature and intent of scholarship on Native women. "Pocahontas" was the beginning of an interrogatory that lasted over twenty years.
2. Philip Young, "The Mother of Us All," *Kenyon Review* 24 (summer 1962): 391–441.
3. See Jay B. Hubbell, "The Smith-Pocahontas Story in Literature," *Virginia Magazine of History and Biography* 65 (July 1957): 275–300.
4. The many models, stereotypes, and images operative for the Indian in Anglo-American vernacular culture are discussed in my dissertation, "The Only Good Indian: The Image of the Indian in Vernacular American Culture" (Indiana University, 1973).
5. E. McClung Fleming, "Symbols of the United States: From Indian Queen to Uncle Sam," in *The Frontiers of American Culture*, ed. Ray B. Browne et al. (Lafayette IN: Purdue University Press, 1967), 1–24; Fleming, "The American Image as Indian Princess, 1765–1783," *Winterthur Portfolio* 2 (1968): 65–81.
6. For a summary of the philosophical backgrounds of the "Noble Savage" complex of beliefs and ideas, see Roy Harvey Pearce, *Savagism and Civilization: A Study of the Indian and the American Mind* (1953; reprint, Baltimore: Johns Hopkins University Press, 1967). For references to folk motifs in Indo-European tradition, see Stith Thompson, *The Motif Index of Folk Literature*, 6 vols. (1932–36; reprint, Bloomington: Indiana University Press, 1955–58).
7. See Clare de Corbellier, "Miss America and Her Sisters: Personification of the Four Parts of the World," *Bulletin of the Metropolitan Museum of Art* 19 (1961): 209–23;

James Hazen Hyde, *L'iconographie des quatre parties du monde dans les tapisseries de Gazette des Beaux Arts* (Paris: Beaux Arts, 1924).

8. Austin Fife and Francesca Redden, "The Pseudo-Indian Folksongs of the Anglo-Americans and French-Canadians," *Journal of American Folklore* 67, no. 266 (1954): 381; Olive Wooley Burt, *American Murder Ballads and Their Stories* (1958; reprint, New York: Citadel Press, 1964), 146–69.

9. Vine Deloria, *Custer Died for Your Sins* (New York: Avon Books, 1968), 11.

2. The "Squaw Drudge"

A Prime Index of Savagism

DAVID D. SMITS
Excerpts

New Introduction by David D. Smits

After much reading in Anglo-American primary sources about Native Americans, it became clear to me that the preponderance of commentators, from the time of first contact through the nineteenth century, depicted Indian women as little more than "drudges," overworked and otherwise exploited by their indolent Indian husbands. It was also apparent that the least-biased commentators, admittedly many fewer, directly contradicted the majority viewpoint. Having been indoctrinated in the virtues of hard work since my boyhood on a dairy farm in Wisconsin, and being intrigued by peoples' attitudes toward the same, I set out to determine the true nature of Native American gender roles. My research ultimately persuaded me that the stereotypical "squaw drudge" and her work-shirking Indian husband were based on Euro-American misconceptions, ethnocentrism, and particularly on whites' deeply felt need to rationalize their budding hegemony in America.

To prove the "savagism" of the Native Americans, thereby negating their rights to their homelands, English colonists and later Euro-Americans routinely alleged that "abominably slothful" and oppressive aboriginal husbands forced their "poor squaws" to perform the most laborious and fatiguing essential chores. Such mistreatment of women was thought to be a defining characteristic of "savagism." Incidentally, these accusations also helped to refute the Old World charge that colonial women were oppressed by their backward and "Indianized" white husbands. Euro-Americans' condemnation of the mistreatment of Indian women deflected the charge and helped to reassure the colonists that their "civilized" condition was not being threatened by the forbidding American wilderness and the pernicious influence of its Native inhabitants.

I approached my research with a recognition that Anglo-Americans had long regarded labor as a Christian virtue, a crucial instrument of human advancement, and, in its sweaty physical form, an index of lower-class affiliation, among other moral and sociocultural judgments. To accuse another human being of deliberately evading labor was a serious indictment. Work-shirking males were given no sympathy. Anglo-Americans were apt to contend that indolent aboriginal men ought to make way for a higher civilization, one which embraced the "work ethic."

It is no surprise that the stereotypical images of Indian men and women persisted well into the nineteenth century. By then distinct historical developments had actually reinforced Euro-Americans' self-serving misrepresentations. Large numbers of lower-class white women had gone into low-skill, low-pay, low-status industrial work. Middle- and upper-class women, freed from such traditional domestic tasks as carding, spinning, and weaving, had gained time for leisure pursuits. Historian Gerder Lerner had made me aware that such women commonly aspired to become "ladies," the cultural ideal of femininity. Idleness had become a status symbol for American women.

The genteel "lady of leisure," who came to personify Euro-American civilization's highest attainments, was smugly contrasted with the lowly "squaw drudge," the symbol of unregenerate savagism. Privileged whites made the vaunted idleness of the "Victorian lady" a key index not only to class affiliation but also to sociocultural progress.

In contrast, nineteenth-century Euro-America's ideal male was an assiduous worker, especially one who, like Horatio Alger's fictional heroes, advanced from rags to riches. Historian Irvin G. Wyllie's writings helped me to see that America's nineteenth-century cult of success viewed hard work as a positive religious duty, a proof of exemplary personal character, and the key to a nation's socioeconomic advancement. For the fortunate, notoriously lazy Indian men served as a negative reference group, both to demonstrate white moral and cultural superiority and to account for Euro-America's impressive socioeconomic progress. Civilization's instruments and most-esteemed males were the hardworking yeomen farmers of an agrarian America and the indefatigable "self-made men" of the industrial age. Predictably, white America's male and female role models were diametrically opposed to their stereotypical Indian counterparts.

Euro-Americans' ethnocentrism and efforts to justify imperialism by systematically denigrating its victims blinded both the perpetrators themselves and subsequent generations to a fundamental reality. The sexually defined roles of Indian societies were much more complementary, equitable, and harmoniously integrated than the historical record, written by the victors, generally asserts.

The "Squaw Drudge"
A Prime Index of Savagism (1982)

From the earliest contacts between Europeans and Indians in North America, White commentators censured Indian men for subjugating and overworking native women. Through three centuries of relations, Whites persisted in citing the drudgery of Indian women and the indolence of Indian men as major proofs of savagism. By the nineteenth century, Indian women and men had been transformed into negative reference groups representing exact counter-images of Euro-Americans' ideal sexual statuses and roles. Contrasting their male and female ideals with their stereotyped views of native men and women, Euro-Americans generally concluded that Indians personified savagism. The Euro-American concept of savagism, associated with a degraded and fierce condition of human life, served as the grand rationale for imperialism. Ethnocentrism, misunderstanding, and the need to justify continued expropriation of Indian land and relieve personal anxieties about the destruction of Indian society distorted White views. As a rule, Indians' sexually defined rights and duties were much more in equilibrium than Whites acknowledged.

English males in seventeenth-century Virginia were largely responsible for initiating the distorted images of "squaw drudges" and indolent braves. Captain John Smith (1612a, 356–57), the English explorer and colonizer, described the sexual division of labor among the Powhatan Indians of Virginia and condemned the men whose complacent idleness was supported by the hard work of the women: "The men bestowe their times in fishing, hunting, wars and such manlike exercises, scorning to be seen in any woman like exercise, which is the cause that the women be verie painefull [industrious] and the men often idle." George Percy, an English aristocrat who made the 1607 voyage to Virginia, shared Smith's judgment. Percy ([1608], 141) recounted evidence of the Powhatans' savagism: "I saw Bread made by their women which doe all their drugerie. The men takes their pleasure in hunting and their warres." Determined to rise in the world by availing himself of

America's abundant opportunities, Smith sought to justify colonization by calling attention to the superiority of English culture. Percy, a political enemy of King James, and a man with no immediate future in England, shared this outlook. Both Smith and Percy attempted to demonstrate Indian savagism by citing the oppression of native women by slothful males.

Seeking to establish their right to colonize by virtue of superior civilization, Englishmen saw or ignored what they wanted to in native societies. "The Indian became important for the English mind, not for what he was in and of himself, but rather for what he showed civilized men they were not and must not be" (Pearce 1965, 5). One thing civilized men must not be, to Smith and countless other Euro-Americans since, was lazy. Too many Englishmen had come to America expecting to prosper without labor. These "idle contemplatours," fumed Smith, were "no lesse plague to us in Virginia, then the Locusts to the Egyptians. For the labour of twentie or thirtie of the best onely preserved in Christianite by their industry, the idle livers of neare two hundred of the rest" (1612a, 374). In what may have been a remark designed to shame English gentlemen for their unproductivity, Smith (1624, 49) contradicted his contention that Indian men eschewed "women like exercise." Even Chief Powhatan performed such labors, as well as many others: "For the King himselfe will make his own robes, shooes, bowes, arrowes, pots; plant, hunt, or doe anything so well as the rest."

What particularly galled Smith and other White Virginians was the Indian man's supposed carefree idleness, an enviable condition that lured many colonists into the wilderness. Smith (1612b, 448) reviled those Englishmen who deserted Jamestown "to live Idle among the Salvages." Englishmen's resentment toward lazy braves reflected their envy, their self-deflating recognition that Indians were better equipped than themselves to thrive off Virginia's fecundity, and their frustrated intentions to employ the natives as a labor force in agriculture or other enterprises. Ralph Hamor (1615, 2), the Henrico recorder, still believed in 1615 that the Indians could be converted into laborers: "They are easily taught, and may by lenitie and faire usage . . . be brought, being naturally though ingenious, yet idly given, to be no lesse industrious, nay to exceed our English." Hamor's remarks reveal how white characterizations of Indians were shaped by the commentators' interests.

Europeans had long argued that the Indian man's idleness demonstrated the savagism of his society. Savages, as characterized by Montaigne (in Frame 1957, 153), had "no occupations but leisure ones." Bounteous nature presumably lavished sustenance without labor on the savage. Englishmen who visited America often described a munificent land of natural abundance. Arthur Barlowe (1584, 108), who reconnoitered the North Carolina coast for Walter Raleigh in the 1580s, reported that "the earth bringeth foorth all things in aboundance, as in the first creation, without toile or labour." Montaigne and Barlowe idealized savagism; Englishmen more often denounced the toil-free life of America's savages because it promoted vices. Raleigh (in Sheehan 1980, 13), obsessed with finding the earthly paradise, doubted its existence in the West Indies despite their salubrious climate. Such lands were "vicious" because "nature being liberal to all without labour, necessity imposing no industry or travel, idleness bringeth forth no other fruits than vain thoughts and licentious pleasure." To Smith (1624, 22), Virginia was a luxuriant land whose indolent natives had not begun to realize its full potential: "Heaven & earth agreed better to frame a place for mans habitation; were it fully manured and inhabited by industrious people." The image of slothful American savages living dissolutely off nature's liberality was long held by European writers. William Robertson (1788, 2:51), the widely read eighteenth-century Scottish historian, wrote of native America: "The greater part of its inhabitants were strangers to industry and labour, ignorant of arts, imperfectly acquainted with the nature of property, and enjoying almost without restriction or countroul the blessings which flowed spontaneously from the bounty of nature."

Early censorious judgments of lazy Powhatan men were sometimes qualified or negated by other contemporary Englishmen whose observations, while reflecting their own predispositions and interests, were more balanced and reliable. William Strachey, a gentleman who sailed for the New World in 1609 to recoup his fortune, gathered impressions of the Powhatans during a sixteen-month stay in Virginia. As the colony's secretary, Strachey was associated with a group of investors seeking to promote trade overseas. His writings attempted to justify the English claim to American territory. Colonization would be in the best interest of the Indians—savage "Infidells" who should be brought Christianity and the benefits of trade. Though hoping for profitable trade with the Powhatans, Strachey feared their potential for "vyolence or treason against us" (1612, 22, 25). Having a mind preoccupied with hope and fear, Strachey wrote with mixed feelings about Powhatan culture. He appears to have borrowed many of Smith's derogatory phrases, while sometimes altering their import. Powhatan men were industrious—excellent potential suppliers of trade goods—and eager to please their women. Native men took "extreme paynes" in their hunting and fishing because by such prowess "they wyn the loves of their women who wilbe the sooner contented to live with such a man." Powhatan women did many tasks, including farming, but they, "as the weaker sort be put to the easier works" (1612, 83, 84, 114). Strachey thus provides impressions of a more equitable and harmonious sexual division of labor among the Powhatans. Physically fit and strong men, accustomed "to endure hardness" in the hunt, earnestly provided for the indulged women, who performed lighter labors (1612, 74).

Alexander Whitaker (1613, 44, 25), a Jamestown minister engaged in promoting colonization for religious and economic purposes, furnished in 1613 a characterization of robust, intelligent and diligent Powhatans, presumably of both sexes. Englishmen who adventured to Virginia could "be assured" of finding "riches and honour in this world, and blessed immortality in the world to come." Conversion of the Powhatans could be accomplished, for they were not "so simple as some have supposed." They were, rather "of bodie lustie, strong, and very nimble . . . a very understanding generation, quicke of apprehension, suddaine in their dispatches, subtile in their dealings, exquisite in their inventions, and industrious in their labour." Although Whitaker's characterization may reflect personal interests, his otherwise generally censorious attitude toward the Powhatans lends credence to his disavowal of the notion that they were lazy and sluggish (Kupperman 1980, 27).

Powhatan culture was not significantly different from that of the natives of Roanoke Island painted by John White during his visit in 1585. White, a gifted artist, returned to England with meticulous watercolor drawings of the southeastern Algonquians, sometimes called "Pamlicos" or "Secotans." The frequent use of White's drawings by modern archaeologists, ethnologists, and historians attests to scholarly confidence in their accuracy. The drawings portray the orderly existence of villagers whose dwellings are neat and whose cultivated fields are extensive and carefully tended. Men are shown busily engaged in various forms of fishing, a native subsistence activity seldom stressed by Europeans (Hulton and Quinn 1964, vol. 2). Theodore de Bry, a German publisher, made slightly altered engravings of White's drawings for a widely read promotional book by Thomas Hariot, a scientist who had accompanied White to Roanoke. The accuracy of the engravings was confirmed by Robert Beverley (1705, 149) in his brilliant description of colonial Virginia's history and its aboriginal inhabitants. De Bry depicted men busily engaged in hunting, fishing, constructing canoes, and broiling fish; one print even shows a man tending a fire at which a woman cooks. No images of idle native men emerge from De Bry's illustrations. Hariot, who had acquired a working knowledge of the Carolina Algonquian dialect, described how Indian men and women worked together to prepare the earth for planting. Seeding, cultivating and harvesting, mostly native women's work, involved "small labour and paines." Indeed, Hariot estimated that "one man may prepare and husbane so much grounde (having once borne corn before) with lesse the foure and twentie houres labour, as shall yeelde him victuall in a large proportion for a twelve month." The notes that Hariot prepared for De Bry's engravings disclose that Indian women, far from being overworked, found leisure time to enjoy strolls through fields and beside rivers to watch the men hunt and fish (Hariot 1588, 14, 15, illustrations, n.p.). Despite the popularity of Hariot's book, however, it did not radically alter the prevailing White images of native male "drones" and "squaw drudges."

The first English colonists in Virginia, dependent upon hunting and fishing for survival, recognized that these endeavors required the expenditure of much energy. Still, Englishmen viewed neither hunting, which was reserved to the English gentry, nor fishing, as true labor. Strachey (1612, 83–84) conceded that Powhatan men took "extreme paynes" when hunting and fishing, but, imposing an English viewpoint on the natives, he concluded that "they place them [hunting and fishing] among their sports and pleasures." To an Englishman, subsistence activities should not be pleasurable. Labor was a Christian virtue, an instrument for human advancement, an index of lower-class affiliation, and an English remedy to prevent social unruliness (E. S. Morgan 1975, 61–66). It could not be taken lightly.

After the Virginia colony became established, and hunting and fishing diminished in economic importance, they were even more consistently classified as sports, in the traditional English manner. In 1705 the Virginia planter Robert Beverley (1705, 156) wrote that wild animals, birds and fish were "the natural Production of that Country, which the Native Indians enjoy'd without the Curse of Industry, their Diversion alone, and not their Labour, supplying their Necessities." William Byrd II, a Virginia plantation aristocrat, employed this view to chastise idle native men for overworking women. In the 1720s and 1730s, while surveying the boundary between Virginia and North Carolina, Byrd (1968, 1:382–83) discussed the few remaining Indians: "The little Work that is done among the Indians is done by the poor Women, while the men are quite idle, or at most employed only in the

Gentlemanly Diversions of Hunting and Fishing." Despite viewing the hunt as sport, however, Byrd recognized that when Indians engaged in either it or war, they endured exhausting efforts. He told how "one of the Indians shot a Bear, which he lugg'd about half a Mile for the good of the Company. These Gentiles have no distinction of Days, but make every day a Sabbath, except when they go to war or hunting, and then they will undergo incredible Fatigues."

Nowhere do English views of native culture correspond less to reality than in their unwillingness to characterize Indians as farmers. Savages were thought of as hunters and gatherers. Preconceptions about the nature of savagism allowed the colonists to dismiss the importance of native farming, even while surviving on native agricultural products. Edmund S. Morgan (1971, 172) has documented that as late as 1620–21 the Jamestown colony's improvement depended upon supplies of the Indians' corn which provided "plentie of victuall everie daie." Englishmen were not oblivious to the magnitude or productivity of native agriculture. In 1607, Percy ([1608], 137) described the Indians' cultivated lands along the James River as "the goodliest Corn fields that ever was scene in any Countery." Strachey (1612, 67) estimated that the Kecoughtans had cleared fields of up to three thousand acres. Hariot (1588, 15) contended that southeastern Algonquian farmers produced more per unit of land than English farmers. An acre of land, declared Hariot, "doeth there yeeld in croppe or ofcome of corne, beanes, and peaze, at least two hundred London bushelles. . . . When as in England fourtie bushelles of our wheate yeelded out of such an acre is thought to be much." The problem was that Indian farming did not conform to the intensive agriculture practiced in the south and east of England. Virginia's natives did not plow with the aid of draft animals; rather, the women, working with hoes and digging sticks, scraped up the soil between stumps to make small mounds in which were planted, all together, corn, beans, squash, and melons. Fields were not manured. Indian agriculture was designed to provide subsistence and reserves for lean times; surpluses were not accumulated for commercial exchange (though starving colonists often initiated purchases of stored corn) or foreign export.

Not only did native farming seem slipshod, technologically backward, and unprofitable, but equally important in shaping English judgments was the arresting distinction that Indian women did most of the farming tasks. The colonists observed native women and children planting, weeding, and gathering crops. Ironically, John Smith (1624, 52, 29), who procured

much Indian corn for hungry Jamestown colonists, and who on one occasion traded a pound or two of blue beads to Chief Powhatan for two or
three hundred bushels of corn, dismissed the importance of native farming:
"When all their fruits be gathered," wrote Smith, "little els they plant, and
this is done by their women and children, neither doth this long suffice
them, for neare three parts of the yeare, they onely observe times and seasons, and live of what the Country naturally affordeth from hand to mouth,
&c." That Smith underestimated native stores of corn is evident from his
own account of Chief Powhatan's payment of five hundred bushels of corn
to ransom Pocahontas from the English (1624, 112). Smith and his countrymen simply would not classify a society as agricultural if its men, who
ought to be the main providers as husbandmen, were not the farmers.

The seventeenth-century English applied a rigid sexual division of labor
to farming tasks. Historian Carl Bridenbaugh (1968, 83) has written that
"all matters pertaining to the land, shelter, and field husbandry became the
responsibility of the man, whatever his degree." The woman managed "all
indoor affairs and those of the dairy, barn yard and kitchen garden, and the
orchard where such existed." Englishmen carried to America their dogmatic
notions about the proper spheres of farm work for the sexes, as is clear from
the writings of the seventeenth-, eighteenth-, and nineteenth-century commentators. John Hammond (1656, 290–91), who spent twenty-one years in
the infant Virginia and Maryland plantations, observed that contrary to
Old World reports, no typical colonial woman labored in the fields:

> The Women are not (as is reported) put into the ground to
> worke, but occupie such domestique imployments and house-
> wifery as in England, that is dressing victuals, righting up the
> house, milking, imployed about dayries, washing, sowing, [sew-
> ing], etc. . . . yet som wenches that are *nasty, beastly and not fit
> to be so imployed* [emphasis added] are put into the ground, for
> reason tells us, they must not at charge be transported and then
> maintained for nothing, but those that prove so awkward are
> rather burthensome then servants desirable or usefull.

Eighteenth-century Virginians continued to exempt White women from
field work. Tax laws even discouraged planters from employing White female servants in the fields, though slave women, unrelieved by such stat-
utes, commonly worked in the ground (Beverley 1705, 271–72). Nineteenth-
century Anglo-Americans also discountenanced work in the fields for

White women. Scottish-born freethinker Frances Wright (1821, 219), while touring the United States (1818–20), observed that "no field labour is ever imposed upon a woman, and I believe that it would outrage the feelings of an American, whatever be his station, should he see her engaged in any toil seemingly unsuited to her strength." Like most of her Anglicized American contemporaries, Wright surmised that "the condition of women affords, in all countries, the best criterion by which to judge of the character of men. Where we find the weaker sex burdened with hard labour, we may ascribe to the stronger something of the savage." Thus, the performance of husbandry by native women long served to demonstrate Indian savagery. Furthermore, male-dominated British colonial and Anglo-American societies, from John Smith's time through the nineteenth century, belittled native agriculture because, in the Eastern Woodlands, it was primarily women's work.

The eighteenth-century Scottish theorists of staged human progression furnished a new rationalization for disparaging America's aboriginals by stressing the importance of modes of subsistence in ranking societies. Adam Smith, prominent in this school, conjectured that mankind had progressed through the successive stages of hunting, pasturage, agriculture, and commerce. In assigning the North American Indians to the lowest stage of social development, Smith (in Meek 1976, 118) was forced to minimize the productivity of native women's agriculture: "They [the Indians], tho they have no conception of flocks and herds, have nevertheless some notion of agriculture. Their women plant a few stalks of Indian corn at the back of their huts. But this can hardly be called agriculture. This corn does not make any considerable part of their food; it serves only as a seasoning or something to give a relish to their common food; the flesh of those animals they have caught in the chase." It would have surprised New England's Captain John Mason to know that the fifty canoes "laden with corn" which he bought for hungry Connecticut settlers in 1638 from the Nipmucks came from a few stalks behind their huts (Mason 1736, 22). The Indians of southeastern New England were seldom without corn, for the women raised bountiful crops. In the 1630s Roger Williams (1643, 124) reported: "The woman of the family will commonly raise two or three heaps of twelve, fifteen, or twentie bushells a heap . . . and if she have helpe of her children or friends, much more." Harold E. Driver (1967, 14) estimates that the shelled corn to which Williams almost certainly referred "would amount to nearly 1700 pounds per family, or almost a pound per day per person."

Lewis Henry Morgan, the "father" of American anthropology and the foremost nineteenth-century proponent of the idea that all societies evolved through the stages of savagery, barbarism, and civilization, likewise discounted the importance of women as farmers. In his *League of the Iroquois* (1851), called the first scientific account of an Indian tribe, Morgan (1851, 143) classified the Iroquois as a "hunter state," which was the "zero of human society." Moreover, hunting societies were "enchained" to their "primitive state" (1851, 57). As long as the Indian was bound by the "spell" of hunting, "there was no hope of his elevation" (1851, 143). Though Morgan defined the Iroquois as a "hunter state," he pointed out that it was Iroquois women "who, by the cultivation of the maize, and their other plants, and the gathering of wild fruits, provided the principal part of their subsistence" (1851, 329). He also recounted that Iroquois village fields consisted "often times, of several hundred acres of cultivated land," that warriors subsisted on "charred corn" when on the warpath, and that the Iroquois' enemies acknowledged the importance of their agriculture by destroying their crops in wartime (1851, 314, 340). Morgan's model of Iroquois society was clearly androcentric.

By disregarding Indian agriculture, Euro-Americans could defend their territorial dispossession of the native Americans. Agricultural societies were thought to have superior rights to the soil. Whites propounded this rationale from the first.[1] Strachey (1612, 22, 25–26) averred that Virginia colonists could in justice occupy and defend uninhabited regions "in a world of which not one foot of a thowsand, do they either use or know how to turne to any benefitt." Beyond proferring trade and Christianity to the Indians, the English would "open unto them likewise a new way of Thrift or husbandry." John Winthrop (1629, 2:no. 50, 7) defended the appropriation of native lands for the Massachusetts Bay colony because, among other reasons, the Indians "inclue noe land neither have any setled habitation nor any tame cattle to improve the land by." To Winthrop (in Pearce 1965, 21), the Puritans' right to aboriginal lands was established by divine law: "The whole earth is the Lord's garden, and he hath given it to the sons of Adam to be tilled and improved by them." In the late eighteenth century the Pittsburgh literary figure Hugh H. Brackenridge (1782, 115) spoke for Westerners in proclaiming their rights to settle Indian country: "What use do these ringed, streaked, spotted, and speckled cattle [the Indians] make of the soil? Do they till it? Revelation said to man, 'Thou shall till the ground.' This alone is human life. It is favorable to population, to science, to the information of a human mind to the worship of God. . . . To live by tilling is *more humano* [the way of humans], by hunting is *more bestiarum* [the way of beasts]."

A century later, Theodore Roosevelt, defending his nation's westward movement, assumed that the native inhabitants were nothing more than nomadic hunters. Roosevelt (1926, 8:65, 56) reviled the northwestern Algonquians, "the tigers of the human race"; their men were hunters and warriors, "while the squaws were the drudges who did all the work." Contrary to "foolish sentimentalists," the frontiersman could not be accused of trespassing, for "the man who puts the soil to use must of right dispossess the man who does not, or the world will come to a standstill" (1926, 8:82, 73). A "restless, idle, bloodthirsty people of hunters and fishers" had no valid claim to American lands. "To recognize the Indian ownership of the limitless prairies and forests of this continent—that is, to consider the dozen squalid savages who hunted at long intervals over a territory of a thousand square miles as owning it outright—necessarily implies a similar recognition of the claims of every white hunter, squatter, horse thief, or wandering cattleman" (1926, 8:77, 79). Roosevelt's remarks evince the tenacity of White myths about Indians. In blatant disregard of native cultural realities and differences, Euro-Americans, after three centuries of contact, still defended their conduct by advancing a generic image of native Americans as hunting nomads whose male drones overworked their squaws. . . .

The most convincing evidence that tribal women were not drudges comes from White women who lived with Indians. Mary Jemison (Seaver 1824, 46–47), a White woman captured in 1758 by a French and Indian war party, and later adopted by the Senecas, recounted that Seneca women's work was less inclusive and their cares fewer than White women's:

> Our labor was not severe; and that of one year was exactly similar, in almost every respect, to that of the others, without that endless variety that is to be observed in the common labor of the white people. Notwithstanding the Indian women have all the fuel and bread to procure, and the cooking to perform, their task is probably not harder than that of white women, who have those articles provided for them; and their cares certainly are not half as numerous, nor as great.

In sum, when allowances are made for the predispositions, ethnocentrism, and interests of Euro-Americans, it appears that they encountered in Virginia and elsewhere in the Eastern Woodland culture area tribes whose women and men were much less overtaxed and slothful, respectively, than was claimed. Among the Powhatans, sexual division of labor was not along

European lines, but, in the words of anthropologist Nancy O. Lurie (1959, 57), it "was approximately equal, the men hunting, the women gardening."

Englishmen who settled New England also helped to establish the convention of the "squaw drudge" and her indolent spouse as a prime indicator of savagism. To the Puritan oligarchy, the New England Algonquians represented a satanic challenge to a wilderness Zion. Captain Edward Johnson, a champion of militant Puritanism, published an early history of the Massachusetts colony. Johnson saw the Puritan settlement as a holy experiment in which the Lord had continually manifested His approval by assisting His chosen people. To Johnson (1654, 41), the epidemic of 1616–17, which devastated the native inhabitants of Massachusetts, represented a divine intervention. By desolating the region of the Massachusetts Bay colony, "Christ (whose great and glorious workes the Earth throughout are altogether for the benefit of his churches and chosen) not only made roome for his people to plant; but also tamed the hard and cruell hearts of these barbarous Indians." To confirm the "barbarous and uncivilized" nature of the Indians, Johnson (1654, 262) cited the oppression of the women and the idleness of the men: "The Women . . . are generally very laborious at their planting time, and the men are extraordinary idle, making their squaws to carry their children and the luggage beside; so that many times they travell eight or ten mile with a burden on their backs, more fitter for a horse to carry then a woman. The men follow no kind of labour but hunting, fishing and fowling." Cotton Mather (1702, 1:559), who viewed the Indians as instruments of the Devil, likewise established their savagism with the conventional indictment: "Their way of living is infinitely barbarous: the men are most abominably slothful; making their poor squaws, or wives, to plant and dress, and barn and beat their corn and build their wigwams for them: . . . their chief employment, when they'll *condescend* unto any, is that of hunting." . . .

A reliable indication that the labors of some tribeswomen were not unduly demanding is provided by John Heckewelder (1876, 155, 157, 154), an eighteenth-century Moravian missionary who spent over thirty years living among or near the Delawares: "The work of the women is not hard or difficult. They are both able and willing to do it, and always perform it with cheerfulness." Delaware women did not consider their tasks more laborious than men's, "for they themselves say, that while their field labour employs them at most six weeks in the year, that of the men continues the whole year round." Women's work was "periodical and of short duration"; men's "constant and severe in the extreme." Easy divorce precluded mistreatment:

"As women are not obliged to live with their husbands any longer than suits their pleasure or convenience, it cannot be supposed that they would submit to be loaded with unjust or unequal burdens."

To a much greater degree than was acknowledged by Whites, the sexually defined roles of Indian societies were complementary, equitable, and harmoniously integrated. Euro-Americans believed that farming ought to be men's work. Given the nature of European agriculture, with its plows pulled by domesticated animals, men, with their extra quantum of muscle power, were physically better equipped to farm. Women played the dominant role in most native farming, as they generally do in cultures where the plow is not used. Indian women combined farming, as well as other subsistence work, with their maternal duties in conformance to a widespread cultural pattern. Judith K. Brown (1970, 1073–74) suggests that women participate in subsistence activities to the extent that these labors are compatible with simultaneous child-care responsibilities. Women play an important role in subsistence when: they can remain close to the home; the tasks are relatively monotonous and do not require intense concentration; and the work is not dangerous, can be done despite interruptions, and is easily resumed once interrupted....

Whites who alleged the subjugation of the Indian woman usually cited the character and extent of her labors, failing to recognize that, as Karen Ordahl Kupperman (1980, 60) states, "politically, economic responsibility meant power." Perceiving this reality among the Columbia River tribes, Meriwether Lewis (in M'Vickar 1847, 2:44) concluded: "Where the women can aid in procuring food for the tribe, they are treated with more equality, and their importance is proportioned to the share which they take in that labour." Citing the Clatsops and Chinooks, who subsisted on roots and fish procured by both men and women, Lewis noted: "The females are permitted to speak freely before the men, whom, indeed, they sometimes address in a tone of authority. On many subjects their judgment and opinions are respected, and in matters of trade their advice is generally asked and followed. The labours of the family are shared almost equally."

To be sure, the Indian woman's work was an important determinant of her social status. By dwelling overmuch on it as evidence of her degradation, however, White observers neglected such other status determinants as the native woman's control over her body, right to initiate divorce, old-age security, participation in public activities, treatment by men, and influence in tribal decision-making. When these determinants are considered, the position of eastern Algonquian and many other tribeswomen, in terms of power, prestige, and privilege, compares favorably to that of contemporary White women.[2] Early historical records scarcely ever afford an Indian woman's view of her condition by comparison to that of White women. An exception is a judgment ascribed to Mrs. Henry Rowe Schoolcraft, a half-breed Ojibwa familiar with sex roles and statuses in both her own and White society. The Indian woman's position, she said, "compared with that of the man, is higher and freer than that of the white woman" (in Wade 1941:75).

Frequently White women held captive by Eastern Woodland tribes resisted or refused the opportunity for release. Such White acculturation was exemplified in 1764 when Colonel Henry Bouquet invaded the Muskingum River Country and forced the Shawnees to release their White captives. The Reverend William Smith (1868, 80), the historian of Bouquet's expedition, described how the disconsolate Indians "were obliged to bind several of their prisoners and force them along" to Bouquet's camp. Moreover, "some white women, who had been delivered up, afterwards found means to escape and run back to the Indian towns. Some who could not make their escape, clung to their savage acquaintance at parting, and continued many days in bitter lamentations, even refusing sustenance." Albeit the captives' behavior may indicate fear of ostracism by Whites, it probably also demonstrates genuine attachment to their Indian husbands and families, and perhaps, since the captives were evidently frontier women, a preference for a less socially isolated and less demanding life. Although the Indian woman's place in the social order varied greatly from culture to culture, Nancy O. Lurie (1972, 32) is probably justified in concluding that "given the general and pervasive freedom of tribal life, however sorry her condition in the eyes of white observers, the Indian woman generally enjoyed a good deal more independence and security than her white sister."

Beyond the repeated references to the squaw's drudgery, Whites cited polygyny and the alleged buying and selling of wives like chattel as further proofs of Indian women's degradation. Overlooked were the socioeconomic implications of plural marriage and "bride-price," and the realization that these customs reflected the crucial importance of women's productive and reproductive capacities. Where patterns of Indian male dominance were found, they were frequently balanced, limited, or negated by such cultural factors as equality of opportunity for divorce, matrilineal descent, and matrilocal residence. Whereas some Indian women were surely misused, this demonstrates the misconduct of aberrant individual males, not cultural patterns of behavior. Some tribal men viewed native women with a respectfulness akin to reverence. The advice of a Winnebago father (in Radin 1970, 122) to his son reveals this: "My son, never abuse your wife. The women are sacred. If you abuse your wife and make her life miserable, you will die early. Our grandmother, the earth, is a woman, and in mistreating your wife you will be mistreating her. Most assuredly will you be abusing our grandmother if you act thus. And as it is she that is taking care of us you will really be killing yourself by such behavior."

Despite their tenuous nature, the denigrating Euro-American stereotypes of Indian men and women became more widespread and intense during the nineteenth century. White American commentators of that period generally assumed that women's condition in a society was a standard by which to define savagism and civilization. The artist George Catlin (1973, 1:118) wrote: "Women in a savage state, I believe, are always held in a rank inferior to that of the men, in relation to whom in many respects they stand rather in the light of menials and slaves rather than otherwise." The pioneer ethnologist Henry Rowe Schoolcraft (1821, 231) concluded that "the savage state is universally found to display itself in the most striking degree in the situation, dress, personal accomplishments, and employments of females, and these evidences may be looked upon as unerring indexes to the degree of civilization, to the mental powers, and to the moral refinements of the other sex." Colonel Richard Irving Dodge (1890, 345–46), whose books on Indians were "excellent," according to Theodore Roosevelt (1936, 8:81), articulated his contemporaries' commonplace assumption that the position of women in a society was the principal index of sociocultural progress: "No high order of civilization is possible without the advancement and independence of women; and in fact, the present progress of each nation and people from the utmost degradation to the highest enlightenment, can be fairly and accurately measured by the condition of its women." In his essay entitled "Civilization," Ralph Waldo Emerson (1870, 7:23–24) argued that a trustworthy "index" of social progress was the "right position of woman in the State," and that "a sufficient measure of civilization is the influence of good women." At the close of the nineteenth century, what had become an article of faith was succinctly stated by Thorstein Veblen (1899, 353): "It has been well and repeatedly said by popular writers and speakers who reflect the common sense of intelligent people on questions of social structure and function that the position of women in any community is the most striking index of the level of culture attained by the community, and it might be added, by any given class in the community."

To many nineteenth-century White observers, then, women's condition was the single most important criterion for contrasting savagism with civility. Mark Twain (in Geismar 1973, 196) grasped the inherent weakness in this assumption: "We easily perceive that the peoples furtherest from civilization are the ones where equality between man and woman are furthest apart—and we consider this one of the signs of savagery. But we are so stupid that we can't see that we thus plainly admit that no civilization can be perfect until exact equality between man and woman is included."

Several explanations help to account for the persistence of the conventional images of native men and women held by nineteenth-century Euro-Americans. First, Victorian morality was a severe standard against which Indians could be found even more wanting. Second, Whites encountered on the prairies and plains tribes whose principal subsistence was derived from hunting and who seemed more primitive and warlike than their eastern cousins. Equally important, however, were several historical developments which transformed the Indian woman and man into exact counterimages of their idealized White counterparts.

Historian Gerda Lerner has called attention to the status changes of American women from 1800 to 1840. Industrialization increased the variations in status and life-style of white women from different classes. Large numbers of lower-class women went into low-skill, low-pay, and low-status industrial work. Middle- and upper-class women, freed from hard work once done in the home such as carding, spinning, and weaving, had time for leisure pursuits. They could become ladies. "The image of 'the lady' was elevated to the accepted ideal of femininity toward which all women would strive" (Lerner 1973, 89–90). Idleness became a status symbol for American women. Arbiters of taste and values simply ignored the lower-class women who toiled in factories or on the frontier. The genteel lady of leisure, who personified civilization's highest attainments, was smugly contrasted with the "squaw drudge," the symbol of savagism. Prestige-seeking Whites made the presumed idle lifestyle of the esteemed lady a key index to class affiliation and to sociocultural progress.

Female devotees of the cult of the lady were often disposed to view Indian women with disdain. This haughty attitude was described by Margaret Fuller (in Wade 1941, 80), who mixed with Ojibwa and Ottawa women on Mackinac Island in 1843, to the chagrin of her lady-companions:

> I have spoken of the hatred felt by the white man for the Indian:
> with white women it seems to amount to disgust, to loathing.
> How I could endure the dirt, the peculiar smell of the Indians
> and their dwellings was a great marvel in the eyes of my lady ac-
> quaintance; indeed I wonder why they did not quite give me up,
> as they certainly looked on me with great distaste for it. "Get you
> gone, you Indian dog," was the felt, if not the breathed, expres-
> sion towards the hapless owners of the soil—all their claims, all
> their sorrows quite forgot in abhorence of their dirt, their tawny
> skins, and the vices the whites have taught them.

Those White women spared the luxury of idleness could depart from conventional judgments and censure "squaws" for their laziness. Margaret I.
Carrington (1911, 220–21), who saw hard frontier life as an army officer's
wife, and experienced the frenzied preparations for an Indian attack at Fort
Phil Kearney in 1866, disparaged Crow women as "lazy squaws" after seeing
the "filth" of their lodges.

If the lady of leisure was both the role model for aspiring White women
and a standard of advanced civilization, the diligent worker was the ideal
male. Idleness in American men was condemned on religious, personal, and
social grounds. Historian Irvin G. Wyllie (1954, 34–45) has shown that proponents of the nineteenth-century cult of success made hard work a positive religious duty, a proof of exemplary personal character, and the key to
socioeconomic progress. Of the qualities that helped men to succeed, none
was more prescribed or elaborated by self-help theorists than assiduous labor. Orison Marden (in Wyllie 1954, 37), a leading publicist for the gospel of
success, affirmed: "The genius which has accomplished great things in the
world, as a rule, is the genius for downright hard work, persistent drudgery.
This is the genius that had transformed the world, and led civilization from
the rude devices of the Hottentots to the glorious achievements of our own
century." Nineteenth-century American men, imbued with the work ethic,
again found in the Indians, in this case native men, a negative reference
group to demonstrate White superiority and to account for Euro-America's
progress. To explain the Indian's lack of progress toward a civilized state,
Whites constantly cited his slothfulness. The widely read historian George
Bancroft (1890, 2:127) wrote: "No tribe could be trained to habits of regular
industry. Their hatred of habitual labor spoiled all."

Nineteenth-century developments in the science of anthropology, particularly the work of Lewis Henry Morgan, helped to further denigrate Indian culture. Following his early studies of Iroquois kinship systems, Morgan went on to investigate kinship throughout the world. His studies convinced him that the human family had progressed from an abhorrent stage of promiscuous sexual intercourse to the highest stage of civilized monogamy. Morgan learned from his studies of the Iroquois that they did not own property individually and that they reckoned descent through the female line. He hypothesized that descent through the mother originally arose because of the inability to identify fathers in the stage of promiscuous intercourse. He concluded that a universal matrilineal kinship system preceded modern "patriarchal" monogamy. Morgan then correlated marriage practices and kinship systems with "savagery," "barbarism" and "civilization," the consecutive stages through which, he theorized, all societies passed. He concluded (1877, 67) that matrilineal descent "remained among the American aborigines through the Upper Status of savagery, and into and through the Lower Status of barbarism, with occasional exceptions." In middle barbarism, the Indians "began to change descent from the female line to the male, as the syndyasmian [impermanent] family of the period began to assume monogamian characteristics." Morgan held that no Indian tribe had advanced beyond the stage of middle barbarism. The monogamous, patrilineal family had developed later, so as to assure paternity and regularize the inheritance of property. "Between the two extremes, represented by the two rules of descent, three entire ethnical periods intervene, covering many thousands of years."

Morgan, who attained eminence among American social scientists, thus offered the authority of science to those who would denigrate Indians. John Fiske (1892, 1:68) described the momentous results of the patrilineal and monogamous family's development: "Even in its rudest form it was an immense improvement upon what had gone before, and to the stronger and higher social organization thus acquired we must largely ascribe the rise of the Aryan and Semitic peoples to the foremost rank of civilization." Morgan's culture-bound and moralistic scheme of staged social progress ranked native forms of marriage well below his own Presbyterian monogamy. English anthropologist Edward B. Tylor (1903, 1:26) saw the basic flaw in Morgan's evolutionary scheme: "The educated world of Europe and America practically settles a standard simply placing its own nations at one end of the social series and savage tribes at the other, arranging the rest of mankind between these limits according as they correspond more closely to savage or to cultured life."

By the nineteenth century, then, Euro-Americans generally regarded the condition of women as the principal index of sociocultural progress. America's prime symbol of civility had become the refined lady of leisure. Civilization's instruments and most esteemed symbolic males were the yeoman farmers of an agrarian America and the hardworking "self-made men" of the industrial age. These idealized self-images were placed in stark contrast to "squaw drudges" and lazy braves—counterimages and negative reference groups by which to demonstrate superiority and rationalize dispossession. By projecting onto Indians those values and behavior patterns most scorned in themselves, Whites may have viewed warfare with Indians as both a purge of their own society's defects and the destruction of an obstacle to civilization. Nineteenth-century social science, with its proclivity for rigid schemes of universal social development, assisted Euro-American cultural imperialism. The arbitrary application of ethnocentric criteria in the ranking of cultures instead insured that Indian societies would be assigned to lowly developmental stages.

Notes

1. Nicholas P. Canny (1976, 13) observes that in justifying the conquest of the Irish, the English government seized virtually any evidence to advance the idea that the native Irish were a "semi-nomadic people opposed to all civility."

2. Robert Beverley (1705, 171) reported that among Virginia's natives "the Maidens are entirely at their own disposal, and may manage their persons as they think fit." John Lawson (1709, 193, 184) drew attention to the ease of divorce among the southeastern Algonquians, noting that either spouse had "Liberty to leave the other, upon any frivolous Excuse they can make." An Indian widow's old age was economically secure for, according to Lawson, "such a Person they always help, and make their young men plant, reap, and do everything she is not capable of doing herself." Artist John White (in Hulton and Quinn 1964, vol. 2) depicted southeastern Algonquian women participating with men in such public activities as ceremonial dancing and a ritual around a fire. Mary Jemison (in Seaver 1824, 44, 104) told how during her captivity among the Iroquois she married a Delaware man whose "good nature, generosity, tenderness, and friendship" won her love. After this "agreeable husband" and "comfortable companion" died, Mary became the wife of a Seneca warrior with whom she lived happily for nearly fifty years. She reported that her Seneca husband "uniformly treated me with tenderness, and never offered an insult." John Heckewelder (1876, 56) described the influence of Iroquois and Delaware women as peacemakers: "It must be understood that among these nations wars are never brought to an end but by the interference of the weaker sex." Heckewelder (1876, 58) also noted that in calling the Delawares "women," the Iroquois referred to the Delawares' role as peacemakers; no disgrace was attached to the term "women."

References

Bancroft, G. 1890. *History of the United States of America*. 6 vols. Author's last revision. New York: D. Appleton.

Barlowe, A. 1584. "Discourse on the First Voyage." In *Roanoke Voyages*, ed. D. B. Quinn, 1:91–116. London: Hakluyt Society (1955).

Beverley, R. 1705. *The History and Present State of Virginia*. Ed. L. B. Wright. Chapel Hill: University of North Carolina Press (1947).

Brackenridge, H. H. 1782. "Indian Atrocities." Cincinnati, 1867. In *The Indian and the White Man*, ed. W. E. Washburn, 111–17. Garden City NY: Doubleday (1964).

Bridenbaugh, C. 1968. *Vexed and Troubled Englishmen*. New York: Oxford University Press.

Brown, J. K. 1970. "A Note on the Division of Labor by Sex." *American Anthropologist* 72:1073–78.

Byrd, William. 1968. "William Byrd's Histories of the Dividing Line Betwixt Virginia and North Carolina, William K. Boyd, ed., Raleigh, 1929." In Mortimer J. Adler, ed., *The Annals of America*, vol. 1. 18 vols. Chicago: Encyclopedia Britannica, 1968.

Canny, N. P. 1976. *The Elizabethan Conquest of Ireland: A Pattern Established, 1565–76*. New York: Barnes and Noble.

Carrington, Mrs. M. I. 1911. *Absaraka: Home of the Crows*. Ed. M. M. Quaife. Chicago: Lakeside Press (1950).

Catlin, G. 1973. *Letters and Notes on the Manners, Customs, and Conditions of the North American Indians*. 2 vols. New York: Dover.

Dodge, R. I. 1890. *Our Wild Indians*. Hartford: A. D. Worthington.

Driver, H. E. 1969. *Indians of North America*. 2nd ed., rev. Chicago: University of Chicago Press.

Emerson, R. W. 1870. "Civilization." In *Society and Solitude*, vol. 7 of *The Complete Works of Ralph Waldo Emerson*. Boston: Houghton Mifflin.

Fiske, J. 1892. *The Discovery of America*. 2 vols. Boston: Houghton Mifflin.

Frame, D. M., trans. 1957. *The Complete Works of Montaigne*. Stanford: Stanford University Press.

Geismar, M., ed. 1973. *Mark Twain and the Three R's*. Indianapolis: Bobbs-Merrill.

Hammond, J. 1656. "Leah and Rachel; or, The Two Fruitful Sisters Virginia and Maryland." In *Narratives of Early Maryland, 1633–1684*, ed. Clayton Coleman Hall. New York: Barnes and Noble (1910).

Hamor, R. 1615. *A True Discourse of the Present State of Virginia*. Richmond: Virginia State Library (1957).

Hariot, T. 1588. *A Brief and True Report of the New Found Land of Virginia*. Ann Arbor: University Microfilms (1966).

Heckewelder, J. 1876. *History, Manners, and Customs of the Indian Nations Who Once Inhabited Pennsylvania and the Neighboring States*. Reprint. New York: Arno Press and the New York Times (1971).

Hulton, P., and D. B. Quinn. 1964. *The American Drawings of John White, 1557–1590.* 2 vols. Chapel Hill: University of North Carolina Press.

Johnson, E. 1654. *Johnson's Wonder-Making Providence, 1628–1651.* Ed. J. F. Jameson. New York: Barnes and Noble (1910).

Kupperman, K. O. 1980. *Settling with the Indians: The Meeting of English and Indian Cultures in America, 1580-1640.* Totowa NJ: Rowman and Littlefield.

Lawson, J. 1709. *A New Voyage to Carolina.* Ed. H. T. Lefler. Chapel Hill: University of North Carolina Press.

Lerner, G. 1973. "The Lady and the Mill Girl: Changes in the Status of Women in the Age of Jackson." In *Our American Sisters: Women in American Life and Thought*, ed. J. E. Friedman and W. G. Shade. Boston: Allyn and Bacon.

Lurie, N. O. 1959. "Indian Cultural Adjustment to European Civilization." In *Seventeenth-Century America: Essays in Colonial History*, ed. J. M. Smith, 33–60. Chapel Hill: University of North Carolina Press.

——. 1972. "Indian Women: A Legacy of Freedom." In *Look to the Mountain Top*, ed. R. L. Iacopi. San Jose CA: Gousha Publications.

Mason, J. 1736. *A Brief History of the Pequot War.* Ann Arbor: University Microfilm (1966).

Mather, C. 1702. *Magnalia Christi Americana.* 2 vols. Hartford: Silus Andrus and Son (1853).

Meek, R. L. 1976. *Social Science and the Ignoble Savage.* Cambridge: Cambridge University Press.

Morgan, E. S. 1971. "The First American Boom: Virginia 1618 to 1630." *William and Mary Quarterly* 28:169–98.

——. 1975. *American Slavery American Freedom.* New York: Norton.

Morgan, L. H. 1851. *League of the Ho-de-no-sau-nee, Iroquois.* Rochester: Sage and Brother.

——. 1877. *Ancient Society.* Ed. E. B. Leacock. Cleveland: World Publishing Company (1963).

M'Vickar, A. 1847. *History of the Expedition under the Command of Captains Lewis and Clarke.* 2 vols. Revised and abridged by A. M'Vickar. New York: Harper and Brothers.

Pearce, R. H. 1956. *The Savages of America.* Rev. ed. Baltimore: Johns Hopkins Press.

Percy, G. [1608]. "Discourse." In *Jamestown Voyages*, ed. P. L. Barbour, 1:129–46. Cambridge: Hakluyt Society (1969).

Radin, P. 1970. *The Winnebago Tribe.* Lincoln: University of Nebraska Press.

Robertson, W. 1788. *History of America.* 3 vols. 5th ed. London: A. Strahan; T. Cadell, in the Strand; and J. Balfour.

Roosevelt, T. 1926. *The Winning of the West. Vols. VIII–IX of the Works of Theodore Roosevelt.* 20 vols. New York: Scribner.

Schoolcraft, H. R. 1821. *Narrative Journal of Travels.* Albany: E. and E. Hosford.

Seaver, J. E. 1824. *A Narrative of the Life of Mary Jemison.* New York: American Scenic and Historic Preservation Society (1942).

Sheehan, B. W. 1980. *Savagism and Civility*. Cambridge: Cambridge University Press.

Smith, J. 1612a. "A Map of Virginia." In *Jamestown Voyages*, ed. P. L. Barbour, 2:327–74. Cambridge: Hakluyt Society (1969).

——. 1612b. "A Map of Virginia: Part II." In *Jamestown Voyages*, ed. P. L. Barbour, 2:375–464. Cambridge: Hakluyt Society (1969).

——. 1624. *The Generall Historie of Virginia, New-England, and The Summer Isles*. Ann Arbor University Microfilms (1966).

Smith, W. 1860. *Historical Account of Bouquet's Expedition against the Ohio Indians*. Cincinnati: Robert Clarke and Company.

Strachey, W. 1612. *The Historie of Travell into Virginia Britania*. Ed. L. B. Wright and V. Freund. London: Hakluyt Society (1953).

Tylor, E. B. 1903. *Primitive Culture*. 4th ed., rev. 2 vols. London: John Murray.

Veblen, T. 1890. *The Theory of the Leisure Class*. New York: Viking.

Wade, M., ed. 1941. *The Writings of Margaret Fuller*. New York: Viking.

Washburn, W. E., ed. 1964. *The Indian and the White Man*. Garden City NY: Doubleday.

Whitaker, A. 1613. *Good Newes from Virginia*. London: Imprinted by Felix Kyngston for William Welby.

Williams, R. 1643. *A Key into the Language of America*. Ed. J. H. Trumbull. 4th ed. Providence: Narragansett Club (1866). Reissued by Russell and Russell (1963).

Winthrop, J. 1629. "Conclusions for the Plantation in New England." In *Old South Leaflets*. 9 vols. Boston: Directors of the Old South Work (1895).

Wright, F. 1821. *Views of Society and Manners in America*. Ed. Paul R. Baker. Cambridge: Harvard University Press (1963).

Wyllie, Irvin G. 1954. *The Self-Made Man in America: The Myth of Rags to Riches*. New Brunswick NJ: Rutgers University Press.

What Native Women Were

3. Indian Women as Cultural Mediators

CLARA SUE KIDWELL

New Introduction by Clara Sue Kidwell

The inspiration for "Indian Women as Cultural Mediators" was necessity. I had to come up with a talk for the presidential luncheon at the American Society for Ethnohistory meeting in Tulsa. Although scholars still debate the exact nature of ethnohistory, it seemed to me that studying cultural factors that motivate human behaviors should necessarily be part of history. Since I was teaching in a Native American Studies program where we examined the history of encounters between Indians and Europeans, it was impossible not to be conscious of culturally based motivations. Finally, I had come increasingly to question the myths of American history, particularly those centered around Indian women—Pocahontas, Sacagawea, and Doña Marina. Why had they formed liaisons with European men?

It occurred to me at last that at one fell swoop I could deal with issues of race, class, and gender (the holy trinity of the Ethnic Studies Department at Berkeley in the early 1990s). By deconstructing the myths, I could try to reach some understanding of these women and their cultural motivations. The exercise was fascinating. It was certainly not deep scholarly research per se, but it led me to a much broader knowledge of the world of the seventeenth-century Powhatan Confederacy, the saga of Lewis and Clark, and the horrors of the Spanish conquest of the Aztec Empire.

The talk was well received, and my parents, who attended the luncheon, didn't flinch when I described Pocahontas cartwheeling naked down the streets of Jamestown with the English ship's boys. The fact that the article that resulted from the talk seems to be fairly widely used in college courses on topics like gender and intercultural communication is rewarding. If I have succeeded in demonstrating how history can be told from different viewpoints and how cultural factors are essential in understanding historical actions, I shall have some feeling of accomplishment (although I am sure I will never be able to counter the influence of movies such as Walt Disney's *Pocahontas*).

Indian Women as Cultural Mediators (1992)

Wherever Europeans and native people encountered each other in the New World, cultural ideas and perceptions were at work, and processes of cultural change began to take place. Hernando de Soto and his men encountered the "Lady of Cofitachequi" near the present site of Augusta, Georgia. She arrived for their meeting in a litter draped in white cloth and "borne on the shoulders of men," and she gave de Soto her own string of pearls as a sign of goodwill.[1] Did she intend to welcome him? To appease him with gifts? To encourage him to move on? We have no words from the lady herself about her motives and intentions.

There is an important Indian woman in virtually every major encounter between Europeans and Indians in the New World. As mistresses or wives, they counseled, translated, and guided white men who were entering new territory. While men made treaties and carried on negotiations and waged war, Indian women lived with white men, translated their words, and bore their children. Theirs was the more sustained and enduring contact with new cultural ways, and they gave their men an entrée into the cultures and communities of their own people. In this way, Indian women were the first important mediators of meaning between the cultures of two worlds.

Some of these women have entered the mythology of American history, and the myths have obscured the reality of their situations. Pocahontas continues to lay down her body if not her life to save John Smith and assure the survival of the Jamestown colony. Sacagawea stands pointing west, the leader of the Lewis and Clark expedition.[2] Explicitly, their actions led finally to the loss of Indian land and to destructive changes in Indian culture. But implicitly, they acted from motives that were determined by their own cultures.

The mythology of Indian women has overwhelmed the complexity of their roles in the history of Indian and white contact. Indian women stand in history as stereotypes such as the hot-blooded Indian princess, à la Pocahontas, or the stolid drudge, the Indian squaw plodding behind her man. They are not real people. The myths of colonialism and manifest destiny raise questions about their associations with European men. Their roles must be interpreted in two cultures. If American history portrays them as saviors and guides of white men and agents of European colonial expansion, were they explicitly or implicitly betraying their own people? Were they driven by passion, or were they victims of fate, forced to submit to men of a dominant society?[3]

The voices of Indian women are not heard in the written documents or in the history books. They did not write their own accounts to analyze their own actions. They were, nevertheless, actors in history, and their actions affected its course. But how, if at all, can we ever understand their actions and intentions in what they did?

The notion of authorial intention is currently fashionable in literary theory, and it has spilled over into history. At its heart, it questions how or whether we can understand the intentions of the author of any historical document when cultural context changes over time. Intentionality is particularly problematic when the sources are not written. Native people have written little in their own words, and what there is has been written primarily by men. Women's words are not the stuff of history.[4]

If we are to discover women's intentions in their actions, then the methods of ethnohistorians are particularly appropriate to the study of their history. If women did not explain their actions in documents, we must attempt to re-create the cultural context of their actions and to move beyond the myths that have been woven around their lives. We can discover some clues to intention by examining the cultural context of women's lives. Women, perceived as powerless by European men and voiceless in the historical records, are nevertheless powerful in the roles that they play in their own cultures, and even more powerful in the impact that they have on their husbands or consorts and on the children of those liaisons. We can examine some of the myths surrounding the roles of Indian women to see how complex their roles in intercultural contacts were.

The Indian woman Doña Marina, La Malinche, was crucial in Hernando Cortez's conquest of the Aztec empire. She was presented to Cortez as a captive, one of twenty women the Tabascan people gave him along with other tribute as he was on his march toward the Aztec capital of Tenochtitlan. The Tabascan people had obtained her originally as a slave from merchants in Xicalango. She had been given away or sold by her own people in Oluta. She was evidently of high rank in Aztec society, but not high enough to escape a condition akin to slavery. Her value to Cortez was that she spoke

Nahuatl and a dialect of Mayan, and she could communicate with Jeronimo de Aguilar, a Spaniard who had been abandoned in the Yucatan by a previous expedition. He spoke Mayan and Spanish. In a triadic relationship, Marina communicated to Aguilar in Mayan, and he in turn spoke Spanish to Cortez.

Marina also advised Cortez in his overtures to the subject peoples of the Aztec empire, whose alliances ultimately led to his conquest of Tenochtitlan and the fall of the Aztec empire. She learned that the Cholulans intended not to assist but to kill Cortez and his men. This timely warning saved his expedition. Through Marina's linguistic skills, Cortez was able to exploit the fractures among tribes held together only by the military might of the Aztecs.

Did Marina indeed deliberately betray her people and contribute finally to the European conquest of the Indians of the New World? As a woman who had spent her life as a slave, she probably had no sense of place or loyalty to her captors. If she perceived Moctozuma as a cruel emperor, as the subject tribes largely did, then she had reason to aid Cortez in his overthrow of the empire.

If La Malinche acted out of passion (she was also Cortez's mistress), she was never his wife. Cortez gave her in marriage successively to two of his subordinates, although she bore him a son during one of these marriages. If we accept that she was virtually a slave in a state under military subjection to the Aztecs at Tenochtitlan, her actions become clearer. Whatever personal passions drove her we can never know. She was, however, an essential intermediary between Spaniards and native communities. To contemporary Mexican people, her role is particularly problematic, since she is both betrayer of their ancestors and mother, by Cortez, of a new mixed-blood people. From the historical accounts she emerges as an intelligent and articulate woman whose actions, whatever their motivation, had a significant impact on the history of the Americas.[5]

The story of Pocahontas, daughter of Powhatan, is taught to every schoolchild. The perplexing question is, did it really happen? The account of her dramatic rescue of John Smith, leader of the Jamestown colony, comes from his *General History*, published in 1624 and embroidered with many details not present in his earlier writings. Smith, who had been taken captive after killing two members of Powhatan's confederacy, was brought before the chief and feasted; then his head was laid on a large rock, where the Indians prepared to smash it with their clubs. Smith was rescued from this predicament when Pocahontas got his "head in her armes, and laid her owne upon his to save him from death."[6]

Why? Was she overcome by passion? Smith described her as a girlchild about twelve or thirteen years old; given the nature of hormones, passion was a possible motive. (Might we say that she had a crush on him?) Was she moved by compassion? That option is unlikely, since she came from a culture where torture of captives was accepted and carried out by men and women.[7] Or was she exercising a prerogative of women in her tribe to choose captives to be adopted into the tribe? The later history of the Southeast is replete with accounts of women who were recognized as leaders.[8] If "queens" or "squaw sachems" were recognized as rulers, could not Pocahontas as a woman (albeit a very young one) decide the life of a captive, particularly if it was to test her own newly emerging power?

Pocahontas certainly does not disappear from history after this dramatic episode with Smith. She continued to visit the Jamestown colony. In one particularly vivid English account of such a visit, she is described cartwheeling naked through the town square with the ship's boys. In another, she and a group of young women, dressed only in paint and feathers, entertained Smith with a dance.[9]

Pocahontas also became an intermediary between her own people and the English. Powhatan sent her with one of his senior advisors to intercede for the return of some of his men, whom Smith had captured. The episode was evidence of the increasingly tense relations between Powhatan's people and the Jamestown colonists. Meanwhile, Pocahontas continued to visit the colony and to bring it food and supplies. Smith did not understand her motivation. "Were it the policies of her father thus to employ her, or the ordinance of God thus to make her his instrument, or her extraordinarie affection for our nation, I know not."[10]

Taken in the cultural context of women's power in coastal Algonquian societies, Pocahontas's actions make sense. Having saved Smith's life, she simply continued to take responsibility for it. She was not acting out her father's will, since she would not take presents from Smith for fear that her father would discover her. She was acting out her own power as a woman in her society.[11]

Pocahontas could not escape the consequences of the cultural contact that was happening around her. The English made her their instrument in 1613 when Samuel Argall, an English captain, lured her aboard his ship and held her hostage pending her father's return of stolen goods, weapons, and runaway servants. Powhatan finally sent back seven men with broken muskets, at which Pocahontas complained that he valued weapons more than her.

Pocahontas did not return to her father. The English sent her to school to be educated as a Christian. They gave her a new name, Rebecca. Soon after, she was married to John Rolfe, an English tobacco planter. Rolfe described the union as one of love, not lust, as a properly restrained Englishman should do. But beyond the personal feelings of the participants, the marriage was part of a deliberate English strategy to promote the intermixing of the Indian and white populations and to establish peaceful relations. Although Pocahontas and Rolfe consummated the most famous interracial marriage in American history, there were probably forty or fifty others in this period.[12]

The final encounter between Pocahontas and John Smith was in England, where she had gone with Rolfe after their marriage. It is revealing of her thoughts and values, even after some time spent in her husband's world. She declared that she would consider herself Smith's daughter now that she was in his land, as he had declared himself the son of Powhatan when he had entered her father's land. This declaration of kinship is telling. Among her own people, Pocahontas could exercise certain prerogatives toward Smith because he was a stranger. She could take responsibility for his life. In England, where she was the stranger, she offered her life to Smith's care, as she had taken care of him. However much she might have moved in white society, she still saw her relationships in very Indian terms.

The life that Pocahontas offered Smith was a short one. She died at the start of a voyage back to Virginia, leaving behind her a son by John Rolfe and an enduring myth in American history.[13]

Sacagawea is another mythic heroine in American history. She was one of two (or perhaps three) Indian wives of Toussaint Charbonneau, who joined the Lewis and Clark expedition in Montana in 1805.[14] Shoshone by birth, she was captured by Minatarees in her youth, and Charbonneau bought or traded for her and another woman. She gave birth to a son and carried him with her on the expedition. She did not lead it. She recognized certain landmarks in the Bitterroot Mountains and was able to indicate what might lie ahead. When Lewis and Clark encountered a band of Shoshones, she was brought forward to interpret and recognized her brother Cameahwait, their leader. Cameahwait and his people gave the expedition horses and led it part of the way over the mountains to the west.[15]

Although Sacagawea returned to her own people, she did not stay with them. She learned at the meeting with the Shoshones that most of her relatives were dead. She went on with the expedition. As a captive and the wife of a white man, she no longer had a place within the social structure of her own tribe, and indeed that structure was largely destroyed. Charbonneau was evidently an abusive husband, but he and the expedition were now Sacagawea's main reference points. Having been removed from her tribe, she could not go back; indeed, she may have chosen freely not to go back.

Sacagawea's role in American history may be symbolic of westward expansion, but her presence in the expedition was important for what it told Indian people. Since Indian tribes did not take women on war parties, she was a sign that Lewis and Clark came in peace. Indeed, Clark wrote that her presence assured the Indians that the expedition's intentions were peaceful. Her importance in history is to show us how she was valued by two cultures: Lewis and Clark needed her as a translator, but the Indian people whom the expedition encountered saw her as a sign of peace.[16]

Sacagawea has entered not only the mythology of American history but also the history of one contemporary American Indian reservation. She left the expedition with Charbonneau, and the later historical record notes the death of "Charbonneau's squaw" from "putrid fever" in 1811. John Luttig praised her in death as the most honorable woman at Fort Mandan. Most historians have accepted that statement as a record of Sacagawea's death, but the record also shows that Charbonneau had more than one wife, and it is not clear which one died.

There are stories told on the Wind River Shoshone reservation today that Sacagawea left Charbonneau, went her own way through the West, and finally returned to her people. According to this tradition, she died on the reservation in 1884.[17] If her symbolic role as guide and translator is problematic in its consequences for American Indian people today, her myth lives on in American history and has become an important source of identity for contemporary Shoshones.

Nancy Ward, "beloved woman" of the Cherokees, played most dramatically the role of mediator during the period of turbulent relations between Cherokees and colonists in the latter part of the eighteenth century. She was with her husband when he was killed in a battle against the Creeks at Taliwa in 1755. Picking up his rifle, she fought in his place, and the Cherokees prevailed. Not only was she valiant; she was also the grandniece of Old Hop, a leading man of the Cherokee nation, and niece of Attakullakulla, a skillful

Cherokee diplomat and leader. By personal valor and lineage she was an extraordinary woman.

After her demonstration of bravery, Ward was appointed to the office of Ghighau, the head beloved woman, in which role she exercised ceremonial and ritual powers and served as a leader of the "white" (peace) town of Chota, also a "mother" town, a designation of the oldest Cherokee towns. In the traditional dichotomy between war (red) and peace (white), Nancy, in her role as a beloved of Chota—the oldest "white" town—stood as a symbol of peace. In that role she also mediated relations among the Overhill Cherokees, white settlers in the Watauga Valley, and the British and American governments during the Revolutionary War.

After her first husband's death, Nancy married Bryant Ward, an Irishman and a trader. Her daughter, Betsy Ward, married Joseph Martin, Indian agent for the Virginia colony. Martin, one of the first whites in Cherokee territory, became important in upholding Cherokee land claims.[18] Ward's daughter Kate married Ellis Harlin, another trader. Joseph Martin maintained a trading post at the Long Island of Holston; it became the major depot for goods moving into the Cherokee country, as well as the site of several treaty negotiations. Martin, Harlin, Isaac Thomas, and other "countrymen" who married Cherokee women were integrated into the tribe. They moved between two worlds, and they gathered military intelligence on the actions of British troops and Cherokee war parties.

Recruited as intelligence agents by the British, Harlin and Thomas gave misleading information about Cherokee war intentions. Sent by Nancy Ward, Harlin warned the white people of the Watauga region about an impending Cherokee attack against them by the dissident Chickamaugas. Nancy intervened to save the life of one white captive, Mrs. Lydia Bean, taken during the Cherokee raid on the Watauga settlement. She also informed the British commander Joseph Campbell about the activities of the Chickamaugas.[19]

Nancy Ward was a powerful woman in her own right in Cherokee society, but the Cherokees were faced with the push of white colonists passing through the Cumberland Gap to settle a new land. The Cherokees had been decimated by disease and warfare with whites and among themselves.

Was Nancy Ward a traitor to her people when she informed British military officers of the plans of Cherokee warriors? As a beloved woman and councillor at a traditional Cherokee peace town, she was committed to preserving peace. She spoke eloquently to her male kinsmen and to the Americans, who after 1785 pressed the Cherokees for cessions of land. She played her role as it was defined in her own culture—advocate for peace. To that end she protected American settlers and informed British military agents of the hostile intentions of Cherokee men.

As a Cherokee woman, Nancy brought new resources into the Cherokee nation through her marriage and the marriages of her daughters. Betsy Ward's husband, Joseph Martin, acted as an advocate for Cherokee interests, but ultimately Nancy's efforts to maintain peace failed, and the white men who entered the Cherokee nation were agents of change rather than protectors of culture.

There are no dramatic women like Nancy Ward among the Choctaws, but they too were participants in cultural change. Levi Perry and Charles Durant married Choctaw women and introduced domesticated cattle into the nation. Nancy and Rebecca Cravat, daughters of a Frenchman and a Choctaw woman, together married Louis LeFlore, a French trader. They were reputedly the nieces of Mushulatubbee, one of the principal chiefs of the Choctaw nation. Greenwood LeFlore, son of one of these marriages, was the chief of the Choctaws who signed the removal treaty of 1830.[20]

There were many such marriages between Choctaw women and white traders and settlers. Nathaniel Folsom sired twenty-four children by two Choctaw wives. His son David became a leading man and ultimately a chief of the Choctaws in 1826. The mixed-blood leaders of the Choctaws struggled during the 1820s under pressure from the U.S. government for cessions of land in Mississippi. They encouraged missionaries to educate their children and represented forces of change in Choctaw culture, but they also wrote a constitution that they hoped would allow them to live peacefully with their white neighbors. They worked to preserve the Choctaw nation as they had come to know it, and they still considered themselves Choctaws.[21]

In this brief survey of history we can mention only some of the more problematic figures. Mary Musgrove Matthews Bosomsworth was crucial to James Oglethorpe's establishment of the Georgia colony in 1733. She was the niece of Old Brim, chief of the Creeks, and, like Nancy Ward, was important because of her family connections, but since her father was white, she was sent away from the Creek nation to go to school. Mary persuaded her people to give Oglethorpe land for his colony, and she and her respective husbands, all white, became traders—colonial entrepreneurs of a peculiar sort.[22]

We cannot give full attention to Molly Brant, who became the mistress of William Johnson's household in 1759 and bore him eight children during a relationship that probably began in the early 1750s. Her presence in his household must have given him a special insight into Iroquois culture.[23]

There is a growing body of literature on the roles that Indian women played in relations between cultures. The studies of fur trade families by Jennifer S. H. Brown and Sylvia Van Kirk document the importance of Indian women both as laborers and as intermediaries between their own people and white men in the fur trade.[24] The offspring of mixed marriages are the next important mediators of cultural change. As products of two cultures, they must find their own places in history.[25]

If historians do not have the voices of Indian women to listen to, anthropologists have a sense of women's lives and positions in their own societies. If historians despair of intentionality, anthropologists may be able to re-create from historical sources and personal observation the continuity of women's roles and motivations in their own cultures. Out of this joint inquiry we may be able to understand how cultures meet, how they change, and the important role that women play in that process.

Notes

1. Garcilaso de la Vega, *The Florida of the Inca*, trans. and ed. John Grief Varner and Jeannette Johnson Varner (Austin, 1988), 298–99; John R. Swanton, *Final Report of the United States De Soto Expedition Commission*, 76th Cong., 1st sess., 1939, H. Doc. 76 (reissued, Washington DC, 1985), 169–70, 182–83.

2. The supposed place of her birth is marked by a monument near Salmon in eastern Idaho. See Ella E. Clark and Margot Edmonds, *Sacagawea of the Lewis and Clark Expedition* (Berkeley and Los Angeles, 1979), 7.

3. A concise and perceptive overview of stereotypes of Indian women in American history is Rayna Green, "The Pocahontas Perplex: The Image of Indian Women in American Culture," *Massachusetts Review* 16 (1975): 698–714.

4. See David Harlan, "Intellectual History and the Return of Literature," *American Historical Review* 94, no. 2 (1989): 588, 608. James Axtell, in a session at a National Endowment for the Humanities Summer Institute entitled "Myth, Memory, and History," held at the Newberry Library, Chicago, in 1990, maintained that contemporary historians are as distant culturally from their eighteenth-century relatives as they might be from American Indian cultures. See also Kathleen Barry, "The New Historical Synthesis: Women's Biography," *Journal of Women's History* 1, no. 3 (1990): 76.

5. Rachel Phillips provides a perceptive reading of Doña Marina's personal history and her role in the larger history of Spanish-Aztec contacts. See Phillips, "Marina/Malinche: Masks and Shadows," in *Women in Hispanic Literature: Icons and Fallen Idols*, ed. Beth Miller (Berkeley and Los Angeles, 1983), 97–114. Nigel Davies is one

historian who questions Marina's actions, saying, for instance, that the warning about a Cholulan plot against Cortez was an "old wives' tale" and that she did nothing to prevent the death of certain Native leaders who were condemned on false allegations. See Davies, *The Aztecs: A History* (New York, 1975), 238, 252, 288. The most sympathetic account of Marina is found in the accounts of Bernal Diaz del Castillo, *The Bernal Diaz Chronicles*, trans. and ed. Albert Idell (New York, 1956). Pictorial representations of Marina as a large figure positioned close to Cortez are found in Bernardino de Sahagún, *Florentine Codex: Manuscript in Nahuatl of Fray Bernardino de Sahagún*, trans. James O. Anderson and Charles E. Dibble, 12 vols. (Salt Lake City UT, 1950), pt. 12, plates 22, 44, 51.

6. John Smith, *The Complete Works of Captain John Smith* (1580–1631), ed. Philip L. Barbour, 3 vols. (Chapel Hill NC, 1986), 2:258–60.

7. Samuel Purchas, *Purchas His Pilgrimage; or, Relations of the World*, 2nd ed. (London, 1614), 767. The account is of the Chickahominys' torturing and killing George Cassen, an Englishman. Given Smith's experience, such ritual killing was culturally accepted.

8. For examples of female leadership, see Robert Steven Grumet, "Sunksquaws, Shamans, and Tradeswomen: Middle Atlantic Coastal Algonkian Women during the Seventeenth and Eighteenth Centuries," in *Women and Colonization: Anthropological Perspectives*, ed. Mona Etienne and Eleanor Leacock (South Hadley MA, 1980), 43–62; and Martha W. McCartney, "Cockacoeske, Queen of Pamunkey: Diplomat and Suzeraine," in *Powhatan's Mantle: Indians in the Colonial Southeast*, ed. Peter H. Wood, Gregory A. Waselkov, and M. Thomas Hatley (Lincoln NE, 1989), 173–95. The written accounts of women leaders are, of course, postcontact, which might suggest that disruption of traditional male leadership patterns put women into leadership roles because there were no male claimants. The strength of matrilineal kinship patterns, mythological traditions, and women's roles in subsistence activities militate against the idea that women assumed powerful roles simply because men had died off.

9. William Strachey, *The Historie of Travell into Virginia Britania*, ed. Louis B. Wright and Virginia Freund (London, 1953), 72. Strachey did not arrive at Jamestown until 1610, and it is unclear whether the cartwheel episode occurred before or after the famous rescue. John Smith includes the account of the entertainment. See Smith, *Complete Works*, 1:182–83.

10. Smith, *Complete Works*, 2:198–99.

11. Smith, *Complete Works*, 2:198–99.

12. Ralph Hamor, *A True Discourse of the Present State of Virginia* (1615; rpt., Richmond, Virginia State Library Publications, no. 3, 1957), 53–54.

13. Smith, *Complete Works*, 2:260–61; Samuel Purchas, *Hakluytus Posthumus; or, Purchas His Pilgrimes, Contayning a History of the World in Sea Voyages and Land Travels*, 20 vols. (Glasgow, 1905–7), 19:104–6, 117–18; Philip L. Barbour, ed., *The Jamestown Voyages under the First Charter, 1600–1609*, Hakluyt Society Publications, 2nd

ser., vol. 137 (Cambridge, 1969), 459–62. Stuart E. Brown Jr. summarizes the primary literature in *Pocahontas* (Pocahontas Foundation, 1989).

14. Clark and Edmonds, *Sacagawea*, 13.

15. Elliott Coues, ed., *History of the Expedition under the Command of Lewis and Clark,* 3 vols. (New York, 1965), 2:546–49.

16. Harold P. Howard, *Sacagawea* (Norman OK, 1973), 34. See James P. Ronda, *Lewis and Clark among the Indians* (Lincoln NE, 1984), for a succinct summary of the scholarship on Sacagawea.

17. Clark and Edmonds, *Sacagawea*, 106–7; John Luttig, *Journal of a Fur Trading Expedition on the Upper Missouri, 1812–1813*, ed. Stella M. Drum (New York, 1964). I would like to thank Sally McBeth for her ideas expressed in "Metaphorical Transformations of the Myth, Memory, and History of Sacajawea," the manuscript of a presentation given at a National Endowment for the Humanities Summer Institute entitled "Myth, Memory, and History," held at the Newberry Library, Chicago, 1990.

18. Norma Tucker, "Nancy Ward, Ghighau of the Cherokees," *Georgia Historical Quarterly* 53 (June 1969): 192, 199. See also Ben Harris McClary, "Nancy Ward, Beloved Woman," *Tennessee Historical Quarterly* 21 (December 1962): 352–64.

19. Sara Parker, "The Transformation of Cherokee Apalachia" (PhD diss., Department of Ethnic Studies, University of California, Berkeley, 1991). I would like to acknowledge Ms. Parker's insight that white men married to Indian women brought new resources into tribes rather than taking them away from them. The primary sources on Nancy Ward and Joseph Martin are found in the Draper Papers, Wisconsin Historical Society, Madison.

20. Horatio B. Cushman, *History of the Choctaw, Chickasaw, and Natchez Indians* (New York, 1972), 331–32; Samuel J. Wells, "Choctaw Indians and Jeffersonian Policy" (PhD diss., Department of History, Southern Mississippi University, 1987), 66–67.

21. Cushman, *History of the Choctaw*, 331–32; American Board of Commissioners for Foreign Missions, *Report of the American Board of Commissioners for Foreign Missions, Compiled from Documents Laid before the Board, at the Seventeenth Annual Meeting, Which Was Held in Middletown (Con.) Sept. 14, and 15, 1826* (Boston, 1826); Henry S. Halbert, "The Last Indian Council on Noxubee River," *Publications of the Mississippi Historical Society* 4 (1901): 271–81.

22. E. Merton Coulter, "Mary Musgrove, 'Queen of the Creeks': A Chapter of Early Georgia Troubles," *Georgia Historical Quarterly* 2, no. 1 (1917): 1–30.

23. Isabel Thompson Kelsay, *Joseph Brant, 1743–1807* (Syracuse NY, 1984), 68–69; Milton W. Hamilton, *Sir William Johnson: Colonial American, 1715–1763* (Port Washington NY, 1976), 35, 304–5; James Thomas Flexner, *Lord of the Mohawks: A Biography of Sir William Johnson* (Boston, 1959), 319–22.

24. Jennifer S. H. Brown, *Strangers in Blood: Fur Trade Company Families in Indian Country* (Vancouver, 1980); Sylvia Van Kirk, *Many Tender Ties: Women in Fur-Trade Society, 1670–1870* (Norman OK, 1980).

25. See Jacqueline Peterson and Jennifer S. H. Brown, eds., *The New Peoples: Being and Becoming Métis in North America* (Lincoln NE, 1985).

4. Woman as Centre and Symbol in the Emergence of Métis Communities

JENNIFER S. H. BROWN

New Introduction by Jennifer S. H. Brown

The following article began life as a paper presented at a small conference on the Métis in Winnipeg, Manitoba, in 1982. "Métis" is a term well established in Canada, though less well known in the United States. In Canadian popular usage, it is a shorthand way of describing people of mixed Native-European descent who in most cases trace their roots back to unions of Native women with English or French fur traders of the mid-1700s to late 1800s. Thousands of people share that dual heritage. Many descendants, however, have followed paths to other ethnic identities; some retained their maternal First Nations or Indian affiliations if involved with communities that were signing Native treaties, while others moved into mainstream Canadian or U.S. society if opportunities arose. Western Métis commonly descend from people who had opportunities to claim land or equivalent compensation in the form of "Halfbreed" scrip grants in western Canada from the 1880s to the early 1900s (when "Indians" were signing treaties); but many other people across Canada also (and increasingly) identify as Métis based on their dual familial roots and connections. Identity depends on many factors besides "blood" (always a problematic criterion) and genealogy.[1]

The years from 1980 to 1982, when this piece was written, were seminal for the Métis in Canada, as well as for Métis studies. In 1982, after extended negotiations both internally and with Great Britain, Canada received its own constitution. The Constitution Act, section 35, recognized three Aboriginal peoples in Canada: Indians, Inuit, and Métis—a major development, although the text did not define "Métis"—understandably, given the many issues that definitions of this term present. Métis studies themselves took a leap forward in 1981 with the holding, at the Newberry Library in Chicago, of a first international conference on the Métis, and in 1985, with the publication of most of its papers. Work in the field has proliferated ever since.[2]

My particular interest in 1981 and 1982 lay in the parental involvements, connections, and interventions, maternal and paternal, that influenced the destinies of the offspring of these mixed families. My studies showed some evidence of a bilineal descent pattern along gender lines, whereby lines of cultural and social transmission traveled from mothers to daughters and from fathers to sons. Men of relatively high status in the fur trade often drew their sons into their own circles and sometimes into their line of work; class standing could trump race despite the racial prejudices of the nineteenth century. Daughters remained closer to their mothers, or so it often seemed, and their adult identities were formed by whom they married. Some married outward and upward, but many retained attachments to the communities from which their mothers and grandmothers had sprung and stayed in the "Indian country," or as it was more formally known, Rupert's Land, the Hudson Bay watershed that was royally chartered to the Hudson's Bay Company from 1670 until its annexation to Canada in 1870.

"Woman as Centre" was published in 1983, the same year I joined the Department of History at the University of Winnipeg, Manitoba. Over the years, my Native history classes have included various descendants of the fur-trade families I had been studying and writing about for the previous decade; they themselves (most often women) and their relatives have increasingly been doing oral history and genealogy to recover family stories that I had approached mainly through documents. Their research has set Métis history on a new course. Escaping a legacy of racism that led many to deny or forget their Native connections, the newer generations are making their history their own, with a mixture of pride, fascination, and a new sense of what their families experienced, good and bad, over the last two centuries. And through the internet they are finding one another, linking up with long-lost relatives, rebuilding networks that help them with research. These links also contribute to renewals and reconstructions of identity; the number of people identifying as "Métis" in Canada has increased exponentially since "Métis" appeared as a category in the 1981 census, and is now (2006) well over two hundred thousand.

Research methods are shaped by the contexts and communities in which one works. I have seen immense changes in three decades of work in this field. I began in relative isolation, in the silence of archives, before computers, e-mail, and the internet. Now, when I return to this subject matter, I work in a forest of family trees, amid people who often know far more about their roots and branches than I do. I can help them with archival sources, but they have been checking and cross-checking those sources with family records, memories, photographs, and stories that may prove the archives wrong, or at least problematic.[3] I still watch for the patterns, for the larger questions about descent, marriage, inheritance, socializing of children, identity formation. But the old isolation is ended; these are other people's stories too, and they have powerful claims as well as much to offer in a collaborative way. My best advice, for those researching Native women and families of the past, is first to keep your eye on the larger picture—the theories and patterns you want to explore. But also take as a working assumption that other people exist who may relate to and care about the families you are looking at. They and you will have a tremendous amount to offer one another, if you make connections and establish reciprocities, and are open to their interests and questions as well as your own. The lights will go on, illuminating corners and angles into which you otherwise never would have looked.

Woman as Centre and Symbol in the Emergence of Métis Communities (1983)

Biologically, *métissage* in North America can be described in a unitary way, as the meeting and mingling of Indian and white racial groups. Socially and culturally, it has had a complex history over many generations—one that continues into the present, as people of this dual descent decide which of their many ancestral roots they wish to tap in defining a contemporary identity. This history-in-process has always been multifaceted and has become more complicated with the passage of time, as much recent research is demonstrating (for samplings of work in this field, see, besides these proceedings, the papers in Peterson and Brown 1985).

By the early nineteenth century, biracial families in the fur-trade context of northern North America numbered in the thousands. Their progeny were moving in varied cultural and ethnic directions—Indian, white, Métis. We still have much to learn about the dynamics of the diverse courses they followed in their lives as individuals and as familial and community members. This paper suggests that women's studies provide one important perspective, among several, that is especially useful in tracing these processes. The study of women's roles, social, economic, and symbolic, in the critical years before the mid-nineteenth-century ascendancy of white settlers, missions, and rampant officialdom, requires further attention and will repay us in broadened insights and understanding of the human backgrounds, contexts, and consequences of *métissage*.

One initiative for this discussion comes from a recent paper by Charles A. Bishop and Shepard Krech III, entitled "Matriorganization: the Basis of Aboriginal Subarctic Social Organization." Bishop and Krech argue that early postcontact subarctic Indian groups were typically matrilocal, i.e., a new husband took up residence, at least temporarily, with his wife's relations. They also call attention to evidence for early matrilineality among the Montagnais and Cree as well as among some western Athapaskan groups (1980, 35–36). During the nineteenth to twentieth centuries, disruptions of resource availabilities and subsistence patterns led to replacement of matriorganizational emphases by the modern "flexible and fluid bilocal-bilateral organization" documented by ethnographers of this century (1980, 36). But if subarctic Indian societies were indeed characterized by matriorganization through their earlier histories and until ca. 1800 to 1900 (depending on location), it seems that we should inquire whether native women in emergent Métis groups looked for and found ways to maintain this organizational bias in their own families and social lives. To what extent did women form the consistent nuclei of such groups? To what extent did biracial families later trace ancestry through women, or at least back to a female apical ancestor who represented in herself the meeting of races that founded a new lineage? Jacqueline Peterson (1981, 1982) has been concerned with such questions in the Great Lakes–Red River area, and we might usefully ask them of data from many other localities. Some continuities with aboriginal matriorganization (on which we also need more data) may emerge from such questioning.

Another starting point for this discussion is the work of Sylvia Van Kirk (1980) on the socioeconomic role of women in the fur trade. It is clear that Indian women's traditional productive capacities, in preparing furs, netting snowshoes, foraging, securing small game, etc., often came to be fully utilized and much valued in both the Hudson's Bay Company and Montreal fur trades. In the post setting, Indian wives of traders often transmitted these skills to daughters of mixed descent. The maintaining, in this way, of women's traditional productivity was little respected or understood by the white women and other newcomers who began to penetrate the Northwest from the 1820s on. But again it raises questions for Métis history: did the persistence of such economic roles afford women a special place among the new peoples or help to maintain a sense of their continuity with the aboriginal past? The sources may fail us on this point, but any Métis statements contrasting the productivity of these women and the practical value of their heritage with the relative frailty and oft-idolized economic uselessness of their "fairer sisterhood" would be very interesting evidence on this question.

A third incentive for writing this paper comes from pursuing the implications of what I have called the patrifocality that characterized some upper-level fur-trade families in the late eighteenth to early nineteenth centuries (Brown 1980, 218). Numbers of company officers made more or less large and lasting commitments of resources and affection to their native families, although not required by law or church to honour their marriages "according to the custom of the country." By this period, however, these families tended to be large, ranging from six to a dozen or more surviving children (Brown 1976). Officer fathers who maintained these bonds often did so selectively, choosing or being obliged financially to favour certain children to education and a "civilized" upbringing. A sampling of these fathers, consisting of Nor'Westers who had native children baptized in Montreal's St. Gabriel Street Presbyterian Church between 1796 and 1821 (Brown 1982), indicates that sons were selected over daughters for such attentions by a margin of about two to one. The other side of this picture is that daughters of these families were more likely by a two-to-one margin to remain in the Indian country, marrying there and contributing to the very rapid growth of biracial population in the Northwest at that time. As daughters of officers, they were unlikely to revert to the Indian communities of their maternal heritage. They often continued to bear European surnames that were well remembered and respected. They might marry relatively well in fur-trade terms, as did the daughters of Patrick Small and William Connolly, or they might marry lower-ranked employees of French descent. Perhaps it seemed that their high-ranked fathers ultimately abandoned them, and perhaps they did. Yet if a father had been on the scene long enough to begin investing in certain of his sons, he probably conveyed to the daughters, too, a sense of their distinctiveness and non-Indianness.

Some such daughters eventually lived out their lives among the white fur-trade elite, although perhaps leaving children who joined Métis groups.

Others may be more immediately identified with *métissage* (sociocultural) in the Northwest. Louise Frobisher, daughter of Joseph Frobisher, was by the time of the late-nineteenth-century halfbreed scrip commissions the founder and perhaps matriarch of a numerous, three-generation descent group. As I suggested in discussing matriorganization, it would be interesting to investigate systematically how many Métis families by the late nineteenth century looked back to an apical woman ancestor who, like Louise Frobisher, combined femaleness and a European father's surname. The obverse of patrifocality—white fathers pulling sons more than daughters into the orbits of their own lives and "civilization"—might in the Northwest be matrifocality, daughters remaining, more often than not, with their mothers in the Indian country, and having that familial tie as a continuing core of their lives. Nineteenth-century HBC records can shed some light on comparative figures regarding daughters and sons, since district officers became required early in that century to enumerate their fur-trade post populations. In the Ile à la Crosse district in 1823, besides numerous intact fur trade families, there were listed fifteen daughters and ten sons who had been left behind by retired, transferred, or deceased traders and were evidently with their mothers or with other families.[4] This sample by itself is too small to generalize from. But in combination with the St. Gabriel church records and numerous other indications about the ratios of female to male offspring remaining in the orbit of the fur trade in the Northwest, it is suggestive of a broader pattern.

One might carry this discussion a step farther, with respect particularly to residence patterns. Michael Asch has called attention to a pattern that he calls unilocality among the Slavey Indians: that is, a tendency for the siblings of one sex only (sisters *or* brothers) to remain with their parental groups upon marriage (1980, 48). There may be use in looking for unilocal residence patterns in at least a proportion of fur-trade and early Métis families. We might watch for tendencies of two or more sisters to maintain "matrilocal" residence with their descendants in the Indian country, while their brothers gravitated to the father, and into the male-linked kin groups that characterized in particular the fur-trade-oriented society of Montreal. Some such brothers, of course, eventually themselves returned to the fur-trade country, as did Cuthbert Grant whom William McGillivray described in 1818 as "principal chief of the half-breed tribe" (Anonymous 1819, 142). In his case, a sister's residency and relations in the Northwest no doubt provided a base for him to renew his contacts there after an extended absence, and the same may have been true for other native sons returning in this way.

The development and roles of semiautonomous female-headed family units need further attention in looking at Métis emergence. There are a few signs that by the early 1800s native women with a background of ties to fur traders could be found living with their offspring, relatively independently, in the orbit of one or another of the posts. The journals of Nor'Wester George Nelson in the Lake Winnipeg area around 1810, for example, refer to at least two such instances. In this northern region where Métis groups were just becoming visible as such, the offspring of such female-headed units would have contributed to Métis emergence, being themselves neither Indian nor trading post residents.

A further line of inquiry relates to women's symbolic roles in the formulation of concepts of Métis descent and identity, in contradistinction to the patrilineal European identities that were not readily available to this new people. Parliamentary and court testimonies bearing on the Hudson's Bay/ North West Company conflicts over Red River Settlement between 1812 and 1819 show that the issues of just who these people were and of their problematic legitimacy were discussed in public at that time. These officially published texts probably reflected broader currents of discussion among both whites and Métis, as problems of Métis identity and legal status began to draw general attention. Three such texts are of particular interest in their content and in their contrasts and similarities.

First, we have the pronouncements of the Hon. William B. Coltman, a commissioner hearing witnesses on the Red River troubles and testifying in court at York (Toronto) in October 1818. Being an outsider to the fur-trade country, he took a simpler view of its natives than some. The halfbreeds, he said, were all "the progeny of Indian women, living with their mothers," although they varied "in character, information, and manners," some having been educated in Montreal or England. Overall, they ranged along a continuum: "they may be considered as filling every link, from the character of pure Indians to that of cultivated men" (Anonymous 1819, 177). As for those halfbreeds involved in the Seven Oaks massacre, they should be punished in accord with their place on this continuum. An example should be made of those Canadians and halfbreeds who had had a civilized education and religious instruction, whereas the crimes of those who had never been out of the Indian country were palliated by "their half savage state," and by their being accustomed to "the general system of revenge recognized among the Indians" (1819, 193).

Fur trader–witness Pierre Pambrun, in contrast, gave emphasis to Métis distinctiveness and to the Métis consciousness thereof, although raising the spectre of their illegitimacy. "The Bois-brules," he said, "are the bastard children either of French or English fathers, by Indian women; . . . some of them I know have been sent to Lower Canada, and received their education at Montreal and Quebec. I do not think they consider themselves as white man, or that they are so considered by white men, nor do they consider themselves as only on a footing with the Indians" (Anonymous 1819, 112).

Significantly, William McGillivray, North West Company partner and leader, and himself the father of a half-Cree family, went the farthest of the three in his analysis both of Métis identity and of the legitimacy question. Writing to Coltman on 14 March 1818, he observed that many of these half-breeds were more or less linked to the North West Company "from the ties of consanguinity and interest . . . yet they one and all look upon themselves as members of an independent tribe of natives, entitled to a property in the soil, to a flag of their own, and to protection from the British Government." He went on to enlarge upon the "independent tribe" concept, after spelling out his view of the legitimacy question:

> It is absurd to consider them legally in any other light than as Indians; the British law admits of no filiation of illegitimate children but that of the mother; and as these persons cannot in law claim any advantage by paternal right, it follows, that they ought not to be subjected to any disadvantages which might be supposed to arise from the fortuitous circumstances of their parentage. . . .
>
> That the half-breeds under the denominations of *bois brules* and metifs have formed a separate and distinct tribe of Indians for a considerable time back, has been proved to you by various depositions. (Anonymous 1819, 140)

McGillivray, then, was unequivocal about Métis identity and separateness. But his legitimacy argument is also very interesting. The denial of paternal filiation meant, under British law, the affirmation of maternal right. McGillivray did not specify what this might entail. But in British legal practice, the maternal filiation of illegitimates would have comprised the right to use the mother's surname and to inherit from her as a blood relative. We might surmise that, by extension, McGillivray had in mind upholding Métis rights to Indian tribal status and to land and other inheritances, through such maternal filiation. Although he did not spell it out, he urged the point indirectly: "the fortuitous circumstances of their parentage" should not subject them "to any disadvantages."

Of course, as a Nor'Wester, McGillivray spoke with an element of self-interest; the new nation was politically useful to his company. Yet he also spoke truth: Métis identity and solidarity were indeed taking form. And his argument on legitimacy was expressed in accord with commonly held Canadian and North West Company views regarding marriages "according to the custom of the country" as unions without legal standing (for amplification of this point, see Brown 1980, 90–96); he simply extended that argument logically in the direction of explicitly asserting mother right or maternal filiation as a positive claim.

Although McGillivray's statement is the most detailed, he, Coltman, and Pambrun were all in accord in calling attention to the maternal element as formative in Métis emergence. One could respond that they were simply saying the obvious: we all have mothers. But the reiteration of this theme in these writings suggests its centrality in early thinking about the Métis.

It is also of interest that Louis Riel, who would not have known the texts cited above, returned to this theme in his own thought, focusing on the symbolism of motherhood in at least two different ways. There was first his well-known recommendation that the Métis attend to their maternal as well as their paternal descent: "It is true that our Indian origin is humble, but it is indeed just that we honour our mothers as well as our fathers" (Tremaudan 1982, 200). In a second and different vein was his statement to the court during his 1885 trial, on his homeland as mother: "The North-West is also my mother, it is my mother country . . . and I am sure that my mother country will not kill me . . . because a mother is always a mother, and even if I have my faults if she can see I am true she will be full of love for me" (Morton 1974, 312).

The data and examples gathered here are of varied origins and substance. But it seemed useful in this forum to present some preliminary ideas and evidence about possible avenues for thought and research on the numerous topics relating to women in Métis history. A full range of subjects concerning the social, economic, cultural, and symbolic roles of women are available for investigation, and can be pursued in the context of a variety of social science and humanistic disciplines.

I would like to conclude by suggesting one specific research strategy that could serve to make our knowledge of women in Métis communities more precise. It would help to refine available data on this topic in generational terms. We often tend to collapse fairly broad time spans and to telescope generations in looking at developments over a century or more, when it would be useful to distinguish these phases of familial and domestic cycles more clearly as the microcosms from which Métis communities grew. The alliances of white traders and Indian women in fur-trade-post contexts were qualitatively different from second-generation alliances involving the first women of biracial descent, and second-generation from third-generation ones. More detailed family histories with time depths of three, four, and five generations could bring out important and subtle comparisons and paths of change, as the experiences of these native families accumulated, and as persons outside them in turn responded and reacted to them, helping to confer on them a new ethnicity. More broadly, such studies would also contribute to better knowledge of Métis demographic profiles. The rapid expansion of Métis families between the late eighteenth and mid-nineteenth centuries is a major phenomenon whose implications, social, economic, and political, remain to be fully worked out. Its analysis, along with that of many other issues in Métis history, must begin with the family—the dynamics of relationships between women and men, parents and children, and their close kin and contemporaries. It is all too easy to learn more about the men than the women; but new kinds of systematic study can redress the balance, contributing richer perspectives not only on individuals and families, but on Métis social history in its broadest sense.

Notes

1. Preferred terminologies for Native people vary between the United States and Canada. Whereas "Indian" appears current and accepted in the United States, Canadian formal usage avoids it as a negative term, despite its persistence in the 1982 constitution and in the federal Department of Indian Affairs and the Indian Act that governs those affairs. "First Nations" is the term of choice for those people formerly recognized as "Indian" by treaty or by other means. "Aboriginal" is used in the 1982 constitution to subsume all the three peoples recognized as such by that document. For a comparative discussion of "Métis" as a category in a broader North American perspective, see "Métis, Mestizo, and Mixed-Blood," which I coauthored with Theresa Schenck, in *Blackwell Companion to Native American History*, ed. Neal Salisbury and Philip Deloria (Malden MA: Blackwell, 2002), 321–38.

2. *The New Peoples: Being and Becoming Métis in North America*, edited by Jacqueline Peterson and J. S. H. Brown, was published in 1985 in Winnipeg by the University of Manitoba Press and is still in print. A recent bibliography, *Resources for Métis Re-*

searchers, compiled by Lawrence J. Barkwell, Leah Dorion, and Darren R. Prefon-
taine (Winnipeg and Saskatoon: Louis Riel Institute of the Manitoba Métis Federa-
tion and Gabriel Dumont Institute of Native Studies and Applied Research, 1999),
lists more than two thousand sources on the Métis.

3. A model for the best of this work is Heather Devine, *The People Who Own Them-*
selves: Canadien Freemen and the Emergence of the Métis in Western Canada (Calgary: University of Calgary Press, 2004). Building on her dissertation research,
Devine traces the branches of her ancestral Desjarlais family from New France into
the fur trade and across western and northern North America, from the Athabasca
River country of the western subarctic to the northern plains and into the St. Louis
fur trade as well; she also offers valuable advice on French and Aboriginal naming
patterns that researchers of such families need to understand.

4. Hudson's Bay Company Archives, 1823, District Report on Ile à la Crosse, by George
Keith. B.89/e/l. Winnipeg: Provincial Archives of Manitoba.

References

Anonymous. 1819. *Papers Relating to the Red River Settlement*. Includes "Report of the
proceedings connected with the Disputes between the Earl of Selkirk and the
North-West Company at the Assizes held at York, in Upper Canada, October
1818." London: House of Commons.

Asch, Michael I. 1980. "Steps toward the Analysis of Athapaskan Social Organization."
Arctic Anthropology 17 (2): 46–51.

Bishop, Charles A., and Shepard Krech, III. 1980. "Matriorganization: The Basis of Aboriginal Subarctic Social Organization." *Arctic Anthropology* 17 (2): 34–45.

Brown, Jennifer S. H. 1976. "A Demographic Transition in the Fur Trade Country: Family Sizes and Fertility of Company Officers and Country Wives, ca. 1750–1850."
Western Canadian Journal of Anthropology 6 (3): 61–71.

———. 1980. *Strangers in Blood: Fur Trade Company Families in Indian Country*. Vancouver: University of British Columbia Press.

———. 1982. "Children of the Early Fur Trades." In *Childhood and Family in Canadian*
History, ed. Joy Parr, 44–68. Toronto: McClelland and Stewart.

Morton, Desmond, ed. 1974. *The Queen v. Louis Riel*. Toronto: University of Toronto
Press.

Nelson, George. 1808. 11 unpublished journals. George Nelson Papers. Metropolitan Library of Toronto.

Peterson, Jacqueline. 1981. "The Matrons of Michilimackinac: A Female Métis Lineage." Paper presented at the American Society for Ethnohistory, Colorado
Springs.

———. 1982. "Honoring Our Mothers: Intergenerational Female Métis Networks and
the Transmission of Métis Culture in the Great Lakes Region." Conference on
the History of Women, College of St. Catherine, St. Paul, Minnesota.

Peterson, Jacqueline, and Jennifer S. H. Brown, eds. 1985. *The New Peoples: Being and*

    Becoming Métis in North America. Winnipeg: University of Manitoba Press.
    Reprint, University of Minnesota Press, 2001.
Tremaudan, Auguste Henri. 1982. *Hold High Your Head: History of the Métis Nation in
    Western Canada.* Trans. Elizabeth Maguet. Winnipeg: Pemmican Publica-
    tions.
Van Kirk, Sylvia. 1980. *"Many Tender Ties": Women in Fur-Trade Society, 1670–1870.* Win-
    nipeg: Watson and Dwyer.

Equality and Feminism

5. Women's Status in Egalitarian Society

Implications for Social Evolution

ELEANOR BURKE LEACOCK
Excerpts

Introduction by Christine Ward Gailey

Eleanor Burke Leacock (1922–87) blazed the ethnohistorical trail for feminist anthropologists, conducting highly influential research on the impact of colonialism and capitalist development on indigenous peoples. In 1949, while a graduate student at Columbia University, she undertook archival research in Paris on the Montagnais-Naskapi (as the Innu of Labrador were then known). The *Jesuit Relations* provided information on women's work, gender relations, and changes in production and community dynamics following introduction of the European fur trade. This research provided a basis for her contention that Christian conversion and commodity production had restricted women's authority.

Upon her return to Columbia, Leacock commenced field research among Innu groups. In the summer of 1951 she left her daughter with her father and stepmother (her husband, filmmaker Richard Leacock, was filming in Latin America) and took her infant son to Labrador. With contemporary evidence to complement her archival research, Leacock disputed Frank Speck's prevailing contention that foraging societies were based on private property, a characterization well in keeping with the anti-Marxist and anti-Communist atmosphere of postwar America. Leacock found that even hundreds of years after the introduction of commodity trade, basic resources among the Innu remained communal: only rights to trapping lines and pelts had become privatized.

Leacock's thesis also challenged Julian Steward's evolutionist view that

hunting and trapping as men's activities predisposed such societies to pat-
rilocality and patrilineality. Indeed, most contemporary anthropologists
simply assumed that all societies were patriarchal. Leacock showed how
Innu postmarital residence remained flexible, even as she found evidence
that in the past there had been a greater degree of matrilocality. Moreover,
she described arenas in Innu life that showed the distinctly comparable status of women and men.

Leacock gave birth to her third child shortly before defending her dissertation in 1952. Although her doctoral committee pronounced her dissertation "unpublishable," with encouragement from Elman Service, Leacock
sent it to the American Anthropological Association. It was published in
their prestigious Memoirs series (1954).

Despite such recognition, Leacock could not secure a regular academic
position. In retrospect she considered that she had two hefty strikes against
her: she was a mother and a committed leftist in the McCarthy era. For fully
eleven years she continued to write, present papers, teach on an adjunct
basis, and work at jobs she considered anthropologically relevant outside
the profession.

Finally, in 1963 Brooklyn Polytechnic Institute hired her for a full-time anthropology position and she obtained the stability and professional anchor to
publish extensively. Her reevaluation of Lewis Henry Morgan's *Ancient Society* (1963) was acclaimed; her introduction to Engels's *The Origin of the Family, Private Property, and the State* (1972) influenced an entire generation of
emerging Marxist feminist scholars. In 1972 she became chair of the anthropology department at the City College of the City University of New York.

A high-profile Marxist feminist scholar, Leacock was attacked as an evolutionist, but careful reading reveals that she always emphasized historical
transformation rather than inevitable or progressive stages. Her ethnohistorical work with Nancy Lurie (1971) brought issues of colonialism, capitalist development, and transformations of gender relations to the attention of ethnohistorians. She deployed her research on Innu and Iroquoian
women to challenge theories that patriarchy is somehow rooted in cogni-
tive structures and is therefore timeless (Leacock and Nash 1977). Long before contemporary scholars undertook postcolonial research, *Women and
Colonization* (Etienne and Leacock, 1980) traced transformations of gender
relations during missionary forays and other colonial processes, stressing
local resistance to colonial impositions in a range of societies as a major
reason for the uneven quality of gender hierarchies.

The article reprinted here (1978) is her first comprehensive treatment of the thesis that, in a number of less-stratified Native American peoples, egalitarian gender relations not only existed but have been defended in the face of state expansion and cultural imperialism. Leacock's thesis sparked controversy at the time and flies in the face of ahistorical postmodern and poststructuralist approaches, but her rejoinders to critics always grounded theoretical points in the lived experiences of real women and men.

References

This sketch draws on interviews I conducted with Leacock on January 26, 1986.

Etienne, Mona, and Eleanor Leacock, eds. 1980. *Women and Colonization*. New York: Bergin and Garvey/Praeger.

Leacock, Eleanor Burke. 1954. *The Montagnais-Naskapi "Hunting Territory" and the Fur Trade*. American Anthropological Association Memoir 78.

———. 1963. "Introduction." Lewis Henry Morgan, *Ancient Society*, ed. Eleanor B. Leacock, i–xx. New York: Meridian Books.

———. 1972. "Introduction." Frederick Engels, *The Origin of the Family, Private Property, and the State*, 7–67. New York: International Publishers.

———. 1978. "Women's Status in Egalitarian Society: Implications for Social Evolution." *Current Anthropology* 19 (2): 247–55, 273–75.

Leacock, Eleanor Burke, and Nancy Oestreich Lurie. 1971. *North American Indians in Historical Perspective*. New York: Random House.

Leacock, Eleanor, and June Nash. 1977. *Ideologies of Sex: Archetypes and Stereotypes*. New York Academy of Sciences Annals 285.

Women's Status in Egalitarian Society
Implications for Social Evolution (1978)

The analysis of women's status in egalitarian society is inseparable from the analysis of egalitarian social-economic structure as a whole, and concepts based on the hierarchical structure of our society distort both. I shall argue that the tendency to attribute to band societies the relations of power and property characteristic of our own obscures the qualitatively different relations that obtained when ties of economic dependency linked the individual directly with the group as a whole, when public and private spheres were not dichotomized, and when decisions were made by and large by those who would be carrying them out. I shall attempt to show that a historical approach and an avoidance of ethnocentric phraseology in the study of such societies reveals that their egalitarianism applied as fully to women as to men. Further, I shall point out that this is a fact of great importance to the understanding of social evolution.

Demonstrating that women's status in egalitarian society was qualitatively different from that in our own presents problems at several levels. First, the societies studied by anthropologists are virtually all in some measure incorporated into world economic and political systems that oppress women, and most have been involved in these larger systems for centuries. Anthropologists know this historical reality well, but commonly ignore it when making generalizations about pre-class social-economic systems.

A second problem follows from the selectivity of research. Too many questions about women have not been asked, or not of the right people, and gaps in ethnographic reports are too readily filled with clichés. To handle women's participation in a given society with brief remarks about food preparation and child care has until very recently met the requirements for adequate ethnography. Hence a once-over-lightly of cross-cultural data can readily affirm the virtual universality of the Western ideal for women's status. Ethnocentric interpretation contributes to this affirmation. Women are commonly stated or implied to hold low status in one or another society without benefit of empirical documentation. Casual statements about menstrual blood as polluting and as contributing to women's inferior status may be made without linguistic or other supporting data to demonstrate that this familiarly Western attitude of repugnance actually obtains in the culture under discussion.

A further problem for the analysis of women's status in egalitarian society is theoretical. That women were autonomous in egalitarian society—that is, that they held decision-making power over their own lives and activities to the same extent that men did over theirs—cannot be understood unless the nature of individual autonomy in general in such society is clear. (I prefer the term "autonomy" to "equality," for equality connotes rights and opportunity specific to class society and confuses similarity with equity. Strictly speaking, who can be, or wants to be, "equal" to anyone else?) Non-class-based societies are usually not seen as qualitatively different from those that are class-organized when it comes to processes of leadership and decision making. Differences are seen as purely quantitative, and the possibility that altogether different sets of relationships from those involving economic power might be operating in non-class society is not followed through. Instead, as a result of intellectual habits that stem from Platonic metaphysical traditions, universalistic categories are set up on the basis of individual behavior and are named, counted, described, or otherwise reified by the failure to move on to a discovery of the social-economic processes that lie behind them.

It is difficult to apply the principle that all reality involves interacting processes, and not interacting "essences" or things. Respects may be paid to the concepts of process and conflict, which may then be reified as well. Since these reified concepts are derived from our own culture, it is no accident that hierarchical patterns similar to our own are found to be "incipient" wherever they are not well established. From band to tribe, tribe to chiefdom, chiefdom to state, the development of decision-making processes is seen quantitatively as progressive change toward Western forms of power and control. Fundamental qualitative distinctions between egalitarian and class societies are lost. A hierarchical view of sex roles fits easily into the scheme. That sex roles exist is, after all, a human universal, and to assume that any difference between the sexes necessarily involves hierarchy is seen, not as ethnocentrism, but as common sense.

The reification of the concept "tribe," pointed out by Fried (1968, 1975), affords a good example of what I mean. Fried argues that insofar as tribes exist as culturally and territorially bounded and politically integrated groupings of bands or villages, they are the creatures of colonial relations. However, for want of a clear conception as to what might replace it, the term "tribe" continues in use and fosters the misconception that egalitarian peoples were organized in closed territorially defined units, uniformly obeying the mandates of custom and controlled by the authority, weak though it might be, of a chief and/or council. The structure is not merely "cold"; it is positively frozen. In reality, people were far more cosmopolitan than the term "tribesmen" suggests. They moved about, traded and negotiated, and constantly chose among the various alternatives for action.

In relation to the study of sex roles, the core of tribal structure is commonly seen in terms of unilineal agnatic systems that represent formal, jural authority, as counterposed to the "familial" sphere of influence accorded to women. The polarization of public male authority and private female influence is taken as a given of the human condition. Thereby areas in which women exercised socially recognized authority are obscured or downgraded. The reality of the distinction between unilineal and segmenting kinship systems has recently been questioned on the basis of comparison of Melanesian and African data (Barnes 1971; Keesing 1971). It is my contention that the public-private dichotomy is similarly inadequate for understanding societies that are (or were) not structured along class lines. Instead, insofar as social processes of the precolonial world can be reconstructed, the delineation and opposition of public and private spheres can be seen as emergent in many culture areas, where individual families were becoming more or less competitive units in conflict with the communality of family-bands or kin groups. Furthermore, the complex of processes involved, concerning specialization, exchange, and the expenditure of labor on land, together constituted initial steps toward class differentiation. Although the accidents of history caused these processes to become thoroughly entangled with colonial relations throughout the world, some of their essential outlines can still be defined through ethnohistorical research and comparative analysis.

In the case of foraging societies, the control women exercised over their own lives and activities is widely, if not fully, accepted as ethnographic fact. However, assumptions of a somehow lower status and deferential stance toward "dominant" men are made by most writers on the subject. The very existence of different roles for females and males is seen as sufficient explanation, given women's responsibility for childbearing and suckling. The possibility that women and men could be "separate but equal" is seldom considered, albeit not surprisingly, since it seems to tally with the adjuration to women in our society to appreciate the advantages of the liabilities maternity here incurs. That an equal status for women could be interwoven with childbearing is a notion that has only begun to be empirically examined (Draper 1975).

My point is that concepts of band organization must be reexamined if the nature of women's autonomy in foraging societies is to be understood. To describe the band as "familistic" (Service 1966, 8) or "only a simple association of families" (Sahlins 1961, 324) may serve in a rough-and-ready way to convey something of the nonhierarchical and informal character of social-economic life among foragers, but it implies a universal "family" to be at the core of all society. Such a view of the band, whether implicit or explicit, leaves no alternative than for sex roles in band society to present a glimmer of what was to develop in class society. It implies historical evolution to be a continuum in which social forms become quantitatively more and more like those we experience, rather than to be constituted by a series of qualitative transformations, in the course of which relations between the sexes could have become altogether different.

To argue the point of sexual egalitarianism, then, involves a combination of theoretical and empirical reexamination. In the following pages, I shall give several examples of what I think is called for. The materials are everywhere at hand; they form the corpus of the ethnographic record.

The Band

As a student of the Montagnais-Naskapi people of the Labrador Peninsula, some twenty-five years ago, I looked at changing relations to the land and its resources among hunters turned fur trappers and traders. At that time I confronted the fact that the band as then conceived (Speck 1926, 277–78)—a rather neat entity, with a leader, a name, and a more or less bounded territory—had simply not existed in the past. Missionaries, traders, and government representatives alike bemoaned its absence and did what they could to bring it into existence, while the fur trade itself exerted its inevitable influence. "It would be wrong to infer . . . that increasing dependence on trade has acted to destroy formerly stable social groups," I wrote at that time. Instead, "changes brought about by the fur trade have led to more stable bands with greater formal organization" (Leacock 1954, 20). The *Jesuit Relations*, when analyzed in detail, reveal the seventeenth-century Montagnais-Naskapi band to have been, not a loose collection of families, but a seasonal coalition of smaller groups that hunted cooperatively through most of the winter. These groups, in turn, were made up of several lodge groups that stayed together when they could, but separated when it was necessary to cover wider ranges for hunting. The lodge groups of several families, not individual families, were the basic social-economic units (Leacock 1969; Rogers 1972, 133).

Among foraging peoples, seasonal patterns of aggregation and dispersal vary according to the ecological features of different areas and the specific technologies employed to exploit them (Cox 1973; Damas 1969). However, that aggregates of several families operate as basic social-economic units which coalesce with and separate from other such units remains constant. These aggregates are highly flexible. Congeniality as well as viable age and sex ratios are fundamental to their makeup; kin ties are important but do not rule out friendships; and when formal kinship is important, as in Australia, the focus is on categorical relationships that define expectations for reciprocity, rather than on genealogical linkages that define status prerogatives.

Distinctions between bands of this sort and bands as they have come to exist may seem slight, but in fact they are profound. The modern band consists of loosely grouped nuclear families that are economically dependent to one extent or another on trade or work outside of the group or on some governmental allowance or missionary provisioning. Therefore the modern band has a chief or leader of some sort to represent its corporate interests in negotiations with governmental, business, or missionary personnel, or individual men, who are accepted by outsiders as heads of nuclear families, take on this role. As an inevitable concomitant of dependence on political and economic relations outside the group, a public domain becomes defined, if but hazily, as counterposed to a private "familial" sphere. Furthermore, the public domain, associated with men, is either the economically and politically more significant one or is rapidly becoming so.

What is hard to grasp about the structure of the egalitarian band is that leadership as we conceive it is not merely "weak" or "incipient," as is commonly stated, but irrelevant. The very phrases "informal" and "unstable" that are typically applied to band society imply a groping for the "formality" and "stability" of the band as we comfortably construe it and hinder the interpretation of the qualitatively different organizational form, of enormous resiliency, effectiveness, and stability, that preceded the modern band. The fact that consensus, freely arrived at, within and among multifamily units was both essential to everyday living and possible has implications that we do not usually confront. Individual autonomy was a necessity, and autonomy as a valued principle persists to a striking degree among the descendants of hunter/gatherers. It was linked with a way of life that called for great individual initiative and decisiveness along with the ability to be extremely sensitive to the feelings of lodge-mates. I suggest that personal autonomy was concomitant with the direct dependence of each individual on the group as a whole. Decision making in this context calls for concepts other than ours of leader and led, dominant and deferent, no matter how loosely these are seen to apply.

In egalitarian band society, food and other necessities were procured or manufactured by all able-bodied adults and were directly distributed by their producers (or occasionally, perhaps, by a parallel band member, ritualizing the sharing principle). It is common knowledge that there was no differential access to resources through private land ownership and no specialization of labor beyond that by sex, hence no market system to intervene in the direct relationship between production and distribution. It is not generally recognized, however, that *the direct relation between production and consumption was intimately connected with the dispersal of authority.* Unless some form of control over resources enables persons with authority to withhold them from others, authority is not authority as we know it. Individual prestige and influence must continually validate themselves in daily life, through the wisdom and ability to contribute to group well-being. The tragically bizarre forms personal violence can take among foraging peoples whose economy has been thoroughly and abruptly disrupted, as described recently for the Ik by Turnbull (1972) and for the central and western Australians of an earlier period by Bates (1938), do not vitiate this principle; the bitter quality of collective suicide they portray only underlines it.

The basic principle of egalitarian band society was that people made decisions about the activities for which they were responsible. Consensus was reached within whatever group would be carrying out a collective activity. Infringements upon the rights of others were negotiated by the parties concerned. Men and women, when defined as interest groups according to the sexual division of labor, arbitrated or acted upon differences in "public" ways, such as when women would hold council among the seventeenth-century Montagnais-Naskapi to consider the problem of a lazy man, or would bring a male ceremony to an early conclusion among the Pitjandjara of west-central Australia because they were having to walk too far for food and were ready to move (Tindale 1972, 244–45). The negotiation of marriages for young people would seem to be an exception to the principle of autonomy in those societies in which it occurred. However, not only did young people generally have a say in the matter (Lee 1972, 358), but divorce was easy and at the desire of either partner.

The dispersal of authority in band societies means that the public-private or jural-familial dichotomy, so important in hierarchically organized society, is not relevant. In keeping with common analytic practice of setting up quantitatively conceived categories for comparative purposes, it could be argued that decisions made by one or several individuals are more private, while decisions that affect larger numbers are more public, and decision-making processes could be tallied and weighted accordingly. My point here is that analysis along any such lines continues to mystify actual decision-making processes in egalitarian societies by conceptualizing them in terms of authority and dependence patterns characteristic of our own society.

The Status of Women

With regard to the autonomy of women, nothing in the structure of egalitarian band societies necessitated special deference to men. There were no economic and social liabilities that bound women to be more sensitive to men's needs and feelings than vice versa. This was even true in hunting societies, where women did not furnish a major share of the food. The record of seventeenth-century Montagnais-Naskapi life in the *Jesuit Relations* makes this clear. Disputes and quarrels among spouses were virtually nonexistent, Le Jeune reported, since each sex carried out its own activities without "meddling" in those of the other. Le Jeune deplored the fact that the Montagnais "imagine that they ought by right of birth, to enjoy the liberty of wild ass colts, rendering no homage to any one whomsoever." Noting that women had "great power," he expressed his disapproval of the fact that men had no apparent inclination to make their wives "obey" them or to enjoin sexual fidelity upon them. He lectured the Indians on this failing, reporting in one instance, "I told him then that he was the master, and that in France women do not rule their husbands." Le Jeune was also distressed by the sharp and ribald joking and teasing into which women entered along with the men. "Their language has the foul odor of the sewers," he wrote. The *Relations* reflect the program of the Jesuits to "civilize" the Indians, and during the course of the seventeenth century they attempted to introduce principles of formal authority, lectured the people about obeying newly elected chiefs, and introduced disciplinary measures in the effort to enforce male authority upon women. No data are more illustrative of the distance between hierarchical and egalitarian forms of organization than the Jesuit account of these efforts (Leacock 1975, 1977; Leacock and Goodman 1977).

Nonetheless, runs the argument for universal female subservience to men, the hunt and war, male domains, are associated with power and prestige to the disadvantage of women. What about this assumption?

Answers are at several levels. First, it is necessary to modify the exaggerations of male as hunter and warrior. Women did some individual hunting, as will be discussed below for the Ojibwa, and they participated in hunting drives that were often of great importance. Men did a lot of non-hunting. Warfare was minimal or nonexistent. The association of hunting, war, and masculine assertiveness is not found among hunter/gatherers except, in a limited way, in Australia. Instead, it characterizes horticultural societies in certain areas, notably Melanesia and the Amazon lowlands.

It is also necessary to reexamine the idea that these male activities were in the past more prestigious than the creation of new human beings. I am sympathetic to the skepticism with which women may view the argument that their gift of fertility was as highly valued as or more highly valued than anything men did. Women are too commonly told today to be content with the wondrous ability to give birth and with the presumed propensity for "motherhood" as defined in saccharine terms. They correctly read such exhortations as saying, "Do not fight for a change in status." However, the fact that childbearing is associated with women's present oppression does not mean this was the case in earlier social forms. To the extent that hunting and warring (or, more accurately, sporadic raiding, where it existed) were areas of male ritualization, they were just that: areas of male ritualization. To a greater or lesser extent women participated in the rituals, while to a greater or lesser extent they were also involved in ritual elaborations of generative power, either along with men or separately. To presume the greater importance of male than female participants, or to casually accept the statements to this effect of latter-day male informants, is to miss the basic function of dichotomized sex-symbolism in egalitarian society. Dichotomization made it possible to ritualize the reciprocal roles of females and males that sustained the group. As ranking began to develop, it became a means of asserting male dominance, and with the full-scale development of classes sex ideologies reinforced inequalities that were basic to exploitative structures. . . .

The record on women's autonomy and lack of special deference among the seventeenth-century Montagnais-Naskapi is unambiguous. Yet this was a society in which the hunt was overwhelmingly important. Women manufactured clothing and other necessities, but furnished much less food than was the usual case with hunter/gatherers. In the seventeenth century, women as well as men were shamans, although this is apparently no longer remembered. As powerful shamans, they might exhort men to battle. Men held certain special feasts to do with hunting from which women were excluded. Similarly, men were excluded from women's feasts about which we know nothing but that they were held. When a man needed more than public teasing to ensure his good conduct, or in times of crisis, women held their own councils. In relation to warfare, anything but dominance deference behavior is indicated. In historic times, raids were carried on against the Iroquois, who were expanding their territories in search of furs. The fury with which women would enjoin men to do battle and the hideous and protracted intricacies of the torture of captives in which they took the initiative boggle the mind. Getting back at the Iroquois for killing their menfolk was central, however, not "hailing the conquering hero."

Errors Crude and Subtle

Despite this evidence, relative male dominance and female deference is a constant theme in the ethnographic record. The extent to which data can be skewed by a nonhistorical approach that overlooks centuries-old directions of change and by ethnocentric interpretation based on assumptions about public-prestigious males versus private-deferent females becomes apparent when we consider the following two descriptions of hunting society.

In one, women are extremely self-sufficient and independent and "much more versatile than men." They take much pride and interest in their work, especially in the skills of leatherwork and porcupine or quill embroidery. "Girls are urged to do work of such quality that it will excite envy and admiration." The prestige of a good worker spreads far, and others seek her out to learn from or obtain some of her work. Men listen in on women's discussions in order to hear about "gifted women" they might wish to seek in marriage. Women also gain "public recognition" as midwives and as herbal doctors (also a male occupation). Some women become so interested that "they trade with individuals in distant groups . . . to secure herbs that are not indigenous." They achieve renown as runners or participants in other sports, where they at times compete with, and may win over, men, and occasionally in warfare, where "a girl who qualifies as a warrior is considered as a warrior, and not as a queer girl" by her male colleagues. Women compose songs and dances that may become popular and pass down through the generations, and they make fine masks used in important bear ceremonials.

Young girls often accompany their fathers on hunting trips, so they commonly learn men's as well as women's skills. There are more variations in women's lives than in men's, and many women at some time in their lives support themselves by hunting, in mother-daughter, sister-sister, or grandmother-granddaughter pairs. Some support disabled husbands for a while in this way. If need be, women who are resourceful can make their own canoes. On the whole, "women who adopt men's work are characteristically resourceful and untroubled." Women actively pursue, choose, or desert husbands or lovers, or choose to remain unmarried for long periods of time. Too open, casual, or disruptive promiscuity is frowned upon, and there is some feeling against an unmarried girl's having a baby. However, should she or the child's father not wish to marry, a woman with a child has little trouble finding a husband if she wants one.

Women have visions that bring them supernatural powers more easily than do men; visions have to be induced in boys through isolation and re-peated fasting. Elder women spend long hours in winter evenings telling sto-ries about women, some factual, some semihistorical, and some legendary.

By contrast, the second description deals with a hunting society in which women are "inferior" and lack "distinct training," in which the general-ization is made "that any man is intrinsically and vastly superior to any woman," and in which women are taught to be "recipients of male favors, economic and sexual, and are supposed to be ignored by men." Men's ac-tivities are widely spoken of and publicized, while women's tasks are "un-published"; the "mythology occupies itself with the pursuits and rewards of men." "Artistic women—in marked contrast to gifted men—are given no title nor are they regarded with the awe that indicates general respect." In-stead, women "fall into the role of onlookers who watch and admire [men] with bated breath." "No individual woman is distinctive" in the world of men, and although women "discuss the merits of their work just as men do the merits of theirs, . . . these discussions and boasts are not formal, as the men's are; they belong to the level of gossip." A double standard with regard to sex is enjoined on women. Attention is paid to the adolescent activities of boys, while girls, at their first menses, are isolated as full of "maleficent power."

The latter society sounds quite familiar, but one may wonder about the first. The trick is that the two accounts not only describe the same people, but are taken, selectively, from the same monograph, *The Ojibwa Woman*, by Ruth Landes (1938, viii, 5, 11, 18–19, 23–25, 42, 128–32, 136, 140, 180). I regret being critical of a study that offers full and rich documentation of women's activities and interests, but Landes has undermined her own con-tribution to the understanding of sex roles in a hunting society through the downgrading of women that is built into unexamined and ethnocentric phraseology.

Unacknowledged contradictions abound in her account. Landes is clear and unequivocal about the resourcefulness of women and the fact that they are allowed greater latitude in their activities than men, but then ascribes this to "the general atmosphere of cultural indifference which surrounds them" and "the sketchy and negatively phrased ideals with which tradition makes a pretense of providing them" (181). In another context, however, she speaks of women who "become self-conscious in terms of their work" and "develop a self-respect which finds satisfaction in the recognition ac-corded it." She calls this bringing "men's motivations into women's work" and pursuing "feminine occupations as a masculine careerist would" (154–55). Women are "not trained to these attitudes" of competitive striving and shame in defeat while learning female skills, Landes writes, but learn them in games where the emphases "are the same for boys and girls, for men and women," and both "feel that their self-respect hangs upon the outcome of the game" (23, 27, 155). Yet in another context, she states, "girls are urged to do work of such quality that it will excite admiration and envy" (19). Furthermore, in the context of case examples of renowned women, Landes makes a non-sex-linked statement about abilities, writing that "individual differences in ability are clearly recognized by the people, and include such careful distinctions as that of small ability hitched to great ambition, or that of potentially great ability confined by small ambition" (27).

Girls, Landes writes, are given "protective" names like "Shining of the Thunderbird," while boys are given names with more "vocational promise" like "Crashing Thunder" (13). Then she writes, without comment, of the shaman "Thunder Woman" (29, 37), of the woman warrior "Chief Earth Woman" (141), and of "Iron Woman," a shaman who was taught by her "medicine" father and her grandfather and who defeated "even the best men players" at games of chance and skill (26–27, 62–63, 137).

The basic division of labor, Landes writes, "is in the assignment to the men of hunting and of securing raw materials, and the assignment to the women of manufacturing the raw materials" (130–31). Men's work is less varied than women's, "but it is appraised culturally as infinitely more interesting and honorable," Landes writes. It has "an indescribably glittering atmosphere" (131). "Women's work is conventionally ignored" by men (18). How, then, does Landes handle the interest shown in women's work by both women and men? She writes that the "excellence of handiwork excites the *informal* attention of women as widely as the boy's talent in hunting excites the attention of men" (18–19, italics added); that a man may brag of his wife's handiwork, which "had led him to walk many miles" to claim her, "in an *unguarded moment*" (11, italics added); and that men learn about gifted workers that they might want to seek in marriage "from *eavesdropping* upon the *chatter* of their own women folk" (19, italics added). The "private" and less prestigious world of women thus having been established, Landes later implies another common stereotype—that of women as "passive" vis-à-vis men in relation to sex: "Men seem to be more articulate than women about love. It is men who are said to be proud of their wives, not women of their husbands" (120).

I am not suggesting that Landes did not record statements from both men and women about the greater importance of men's work, as well as statements to the contrary. In fact, when she was in the field, men's work *was* more important. The reciprocity of the sexual division of labor had long since given way to considerable dependence upon trade goods. "Since the advent of the traders," Landes writes, "Ojibwa men have learned how to barter. They trade furs and meat which they have secured in hunting, and since the men, rather than the women, possessed the materials desired by the Whites, they became the traders" (134). She describes the men returning from the post and showing "the results of their trade; ammunition, weapons, traps and tobacco for themselves; yard print, ribbons and beads for the women and children; candy, fruit, whiskey for all" (17). The fact that women remained as autonomous as they did among the Ojibwa was apparently related to the fact that hunting continued to be the main source of food and women could and did often support themselves and their families by hunting. Furthermore, "Today [1932–33], when rice and berries and maple sugar are commanding some White attention, the women also are learning to function as dealers" (134).

Landes's downgrading of women's status among the Ojibwa, in the face of her own evidence to the contrary, flows in part from contradictions due to the changes taking place in women's social-economic position[1] and in part from her lack of a critical and historical orientation toward her material. Nonetheless, Landes deserves credit for making available such full material on women that explicit criticism of her work is possible.

Iroquois materials offer similar contradictions. Horticultural but still egalitarian, Iroquois society of the seventeenth and eighteenth centuries is well known for the high status of its women. Lands were handed down in matrilineages, and the matrons managed the economic affairs of the communal "long houses," arranged marriages, nominated and deposed the sachems of the intertribal council, and participated in equal numbers with men as influential "Keepers of the Faith." Postmarital residence was uxorilocal, and a woman could divorce a man who did not please her with little ceremony, sending him back to his own family. Women's value was expressed in the fact that a murdered woman called for twice the compensation of a murdered man.

Yet one can have one's choice among contradictory statements about the status of Iroquois women. In the early eighteenth century, Lafitau wrote of Iroquois women (or perhaps of the similar Huron), "all real authority is vested in them. . . . They are the soul of the Councils, the arbiters of peace and of war" (Brown 1970, 153). On the other hand, there is the more commonly quoted sentence of none other than Morgan himself: "The Indian regarded woman as the inferior, the dependent, and the servant of man, and from nurture and habit, she actually considered herself to be so" (1954, 315; cited, for example, in Goldberg 1973, 40, 58, 241; Divale 1976, 202).

The contrast between the two generalizations is partly a matter of the period. Morgan was working with Iroquois informants in the nineteenth century, when the long house was but a memory and the Iroquois lived in nuclear families largely supported by wage-earning men. Morgan, however, later quoted Rev. A. Wright on the high position of women among the Seneca: "The women were the great power among the clans, as everywhere else. They did not hesitate, when occasion required, to 'knock off the horns,' as it was technically called, from the head of a chief and send him back to the ranks of the warriors" (1974, 464).

During the period between the *League of the Iroquois* and *Ancient Society*, Morgan was developing his thinking on human social evolution and on the decline in women's relative status with the advent of "civilization." "The mother-right and gyneocracy among the Iroquois . . . is not overdrawn," he wrote later. "We may see in this an ancient phase of human life which has had a wide presence in the tribes of mankind. . . . Not until after civilization had begun among the Greeks, and gentile society was superseded by political society, was the influence of the old order of society overthrown" (1965, 66). With monogamy, the woman "was now isolated from her gentile kindred, living in the separate and exclusive house of her husband. Her new condition tended to subvert and destroy the power and influence which descent in the female line and the joint-tenement houses had created" (128).

Yet this is not the end of the matter, for Morgan continued (128): "But this influence of the woman did not reach outward to the affairs of the gens, phratry, or tribe, but seems to have commenced and ended with the household. This view is quite consistent with the life of patient drudgery and of general subordination to the husband which the Iroquois wife cheerfully accepted as the portion of her sex." The question is how such a characterization squares with the description of Wright, who lived many years with the Seneca (Morgan 1965, 65–66):

> Usually, the female portion ruled the house, and were doubtless
> clannish enough about it. The stores were in common; but woe

to the luckless husband or lover who was too shiftless to do his share of the providing. No matter how many children, or whatever goods he might have in the house, he might at any time be ordered to pick up his blanket and budge; and after such orders it would not be healthful for him to disobey; the house would be too hot for him; and unless saved by the intercession of some aunt or grandmother, he must retreat to his own clan.

An explanation comes readily to mind in terms of the familiar discrepancy between ideal and real wifely roles in our society. Ideally, the wife is the patient and cheerful "helpmeet" in an entrepreneurial nuclear family. A common reality, behind an acceptable public facade, may be a frustrated wife bolstering up, manipulating, and dominating an emotionally dependent husband. Hence an assumption of male dominance as a cultural ideal and the "henpecked husband" as an alternate reality in societies where women's private "power" is constrained by exclusion from public authority is projected into much ethnography. Furthermore, variations on the theme can be observed in erstwhile egalitarian societies in which trade, various forms of sharecropping, wage work, or outright slavery have been important in recent times. These economic relations transform household collectives that were largely controlled by women and that took communal responsibility for raising children; women and children become dependent upon individual men. However, when the previous structures of such societies are reconstructed and the range of decisions made by women is considered, women's autonomous and public role emerges. Their status was not as literal "equals" of men (a point that has caused much confusion), but as what they were—female persons, with their own rights, duties, and responsibilities, which were complementary to and in no way secondary to those of men.

Women's status in Iroquois society was not based on their economic contribution per se. Women make an essential economic contribution in all societies, but their status depends on how this contribution is structured. The issue is whether they control the conditions of their work and the dispensation of the goods they produce. In egalitarian societies, women are limited by the same technological and ecological considerations as men are, but there is no socially defined group that directs their activities. Brown (1970) documents this point for the Iroquois, and its ramifications have been explored by other researchers (Caulfield 1977; Sanday 1974; Sacks 1975; Schlegel 1977).

Iroquois matrons preserved, stored, and dispensed the corn, meat, fish, berries, squashes, and fats that were buried in special pits or kept in the long house. Brown notes (1970, 162) that women's control over the dispensation of the foods they produced, and meat as well, gave them the de facto power to veto declarations of war and to intervene in order to bring about peace: "By supplying the essential provisions for male activities—the hunt, the warpath, and the Council—they were able to control these to some degree." Women also guarded the "tribal public treasure" kept in the long house, the wampum, quill and feather work, and furs—the latter, I would add, new forms of wealth that would be their undoing. The point to be stressed is that this was "household management" of an altogether different order from management of the nuclear or extended family in patriarchal societies. In the latter, women may cajole, manipulate, or browbeat men, but always behind the public facade; in the former case, *"household management" was itself the management of the "public" economy.*

The point that household management had a public character in egalitarian society was made by Engels (1972, 137); it was not understood by Morgan. Like most anthropologists today, Morgan saw the status of women in Iroquois society as quantitatively higher, but not as qualitatively different from what it later became.

Indeed, to pursue Morgan's views on Iroquois women is interesting. Despite his contribution to the understanding of historical factors underlying women's changing status, his *League of the Iroquois* is hardly free of derogatory innuendos with regard to them. From reading the *League* alone, one would not know that the matrons nominated the sachems, and their role as providers is dispensed with in the statement that "the warrior despised the toil of husbandry and held all labor beneath him" (1954, 320), although Morgan elsewhere refers to how hard the men worked at hunting. Ignoring women's agriculture, he writes as if the Iroquois were primarily hunters. Without the influence of cities, he states, Iroquois institutions "would have lasted until the people had abandoned the hunter state; until they had given up the chase for agriculture, the arts of war for those of industry" (132). When he describes women's formal participation in tribal affairs, he writes, "Such was the spirit of the Iroquois system of government, that the influence of the inferior chiefs, the warriors, and *even* of the women would make itself felt" (66, italics added); and "If a band of warriors became interested in the passing question, they held a council apart, and having given it full consideration, appointed an orator to communicate their views to the sachems. . . . In like manner would the chiefs, and *even* the women proceed" (101, italics added).

Richards (1957) argues that "the aboriginal matriarchy pictured by Lafitau, Morgan, and Hewitt was . . . a mistake" and that the status of Iroquois women had increased by 1784, the beginning of reservation life. Her documentation reveals, however, not an increase in status, but a change from the informality of a fully egalitarian society to the formalization of powers necessary for handling a new and complicated set of political and economic conditions.

Richards takes up two of women's formal powers, the right to dispose of war captives and the right to decide about marriage. On the basis of incidents in the *Jesuit Relations* and other early sources, she concludes (40) that there was "a gradual increase in the decision making power of the women and a corresponding loss by the men" as a "product of a long continued contact situation." Richards presents eleven incidents pertaining to the disposition of war captives, eight between 1637 and 1655, one in 1724, and two in 1781. She states (38) that "women in the early period had little if any decision making power," that later they shared power with the men in their families, subject to acceptance by the captors of the prisoner and by the council, and that later still "they were able to intervene and even actually instigate the capture of an individual though it was still necessary to complete the formality of obtaining council approval." However, among the eight cases in the first period, several indicate the active and successful intervention by a woman on behalf of a captive, concluded with the formal presentation of wampum to the council, and there is an instance in which a woman insists on the death of a captive given her to replace her dead brother, in spite of the council's wish to the contrary.

True, in no case do women exercise power equivalent to that held by bodies of men in patriarchal class-based societies. Instead, the cases illustrate the flexibility of decision-making processes characteristic of egalitarian societies. The captors, the council, and interested individuals all had a say in the disposition of captives, and individual women or men apparently won or lost according to the depth of their conviction and the persuasiveness with which they presented their case. What is of significance to the present line of argument is that in all instances, scattered as they are over time and among different Iroquois peoples, women operated formally and publicly in their own interest, with ceremonial gift giving, use of the arts of rhetoric, and other public display. Richards (41) quotes Radisson's report of his return from a war foray; his adoptive mother, he says, "comes to meet me, leaping and singing. . . . Shee takes the woman slave that I had and would not that any should medle with her. But my brother's prisoner was burned ye same day." Radisson's mother had first claimed him in the following fashion: "The old woman followed me, speaking aloud, whom they answered with a loud ho, then shee tooke her girdle and about me she tyed it, so brought me to her cottage."

In relation to marriage decisions in the earlier period, Richards cites several examples in which matrons did not have the clear-cut power to decide on spouses for their sons and daughters. However, the early records instead indicate that young women lived in dormitories, took lovers, experimented with trial marriages, and made the decisions about whom they were going to marry, albeit with the advice and formal recognition of their parents. Cartier wrote of this "very bad" custom for the girls, who "after they are of an age to marry . . . are all put into a common house, abandoned to everybody who desires them until they have found their match" (Richards 1957, 42). Other early accounts report both parents as involved in selecting spouses for their children, but girls as having the right to reject a suitor after trying him out (40, 43). Marriage arrangements were apparently flexible and included both polygyny and polyandry.

The fact that matrons' powers over disposition of war captives and over marriage became more clear-cut with the formalization of the Iroquois constitution betokens not an increase in power, but a formal recognition of prestige and influence that had long operated. With relation to marriage, in a society where consensus was essential, the young were *influenced* rather than *ordered* by their elders with regard to the conduct of their personal lives. However, the formal codification of women's social position took place in a situation in which their autonomy was already undermined. The subsequent history of the Iroquois polity involved a temporary strengthening of the "public sphere" represented by the confederacy at the point at which it was being supplanted by colonial rule. The long-house communities were replaced by settlements of nuclear family units; what remained were some of the interpersonal styles and traditions of cooperation and personal autonomy.

Transition

Like the Iroquois, societies around the world have been transformed by the economic system that emerged in Europe in what Wallerstein terms "the 'long' sixteenth century" of 1450–1640 (1974, 406–7). Unfortunately, this fact has been obscured in anthropology by the practice of separating the "internal" functioning of societies from their total economic and political contexts, in order to reconstruct supposedly "traditional" cultures through deletion of "modern" involvements. Wallerstein's article is not specifically directed at anthropologists, but his criticism of ahistorical methods (389) is apt: "The crucial issue when comparing 'stages' is to determine the units of which the 'stages' are synchronic portraits (or 'ideal types'). . . . And the fundamental error of ahistorical social science (including ahistorical versions of Marxism) is to reify parts of the totality into such units and then to compare these reified structures." To be effective in the interpretation of history, stages must be of total social systems.

Wallerstein distinguishes social systems as "mini-systems" or "world-systems." A mini-system is "an entity that has within it a complete division of labor, and a single cultural framework," such as "are found only in very simple agricultural or hunting and gathering societies" (390). He continues: "Such mini-systems no longer exist in the world. Furthermore, there were fewer in the past than is often asserted, since any such system that became tied to an empire by the payment of tribute as 'protection costs' ceased by that fact to be a 'system,' no longer having a self-contained division of labor." Other factors that have been undermining the self-contained division of labor of mini-systems for centuries are trade, involvement in raiding or being raided for slaves (in the New World as well as in Africa), taxation of various kinds (often as an incentive to wage work), and wage labor, often entailing men's absence from home villages for long periods. In all cases, missionizing played an important role in urging people toward an individualized work ethic and a nuclear family form. Since mini-systems no longer exist, says Wallerstein, social analysis must take into account that "the only kind of social system is a world-system, . . . a unit with a single division of labor and multiple cultural systems." This world-system is "the capitalist world economy."

Recognition of this fact has serious implications for the cross-cultural study of women, since involvements with a developing capitalist world economy have had profound effects on their relation to the production and distribution of basic group needs, hence to sources of decision-making power. The practice of stacking contemporary peoples in "historical" layers—as hunter/gatherers, simple agriculturalists, and advanced agriculturalists with domestication—does, it is true, yield some insight into the nature of women's decline in status, since a people's involvement in the world-system starts within each "layer" from a different basis. Furthermore, cultural traditions can be remarkably strong, and people can wage stiff battles for those they value. Hence the method of comparing near-contemporary cultures can be used with care to suggest historical trends (see, e.g., Sacks 1975). However, socioeconomic systems separated from the economic and political constraints that in part define them cannot be treated as direct representations of sex-role definitions in contrasting societies.

Two recent books, *Woman, Culture, and Society* (Rosaldo and Lamphere 1974) and *Women and Men* (Friedl 1975), share an ahistorical orientation and assume from recent and contemporary evidence the universality of male dominance and the cultural devaluation of women. The assumption is neither documented nor argued on the basis of ethnohistorical materials. Instead, nineteenth-century concepts of matriarchal power—incorrectly ascribed to Marx and Engels (Friedl 1975, 4) or Morgan (Rosaldo and Lamphere 1974, 2)—are cited briefly as inadequate, and the alternative of women's equal prestige and autonomy in egalitarian societies is given but passing reference and subsequently ignored (Friedl 1975, 4–7; Rosaldo and Lamphere 1974, 3). Yet the authors eschew simplistic psychobiological explanations for an assumed universal male dominance and see the structure of women's position as critical to relative subordination or autonomy in different facets of cultural life, making for an open-ended future according to structural changes.

Friedl offers thoughtful discussions of women's participation in the production and control of food and goods in a variety of cultures, but with no reference to the fact that both ethnohistorical and recent materials indicate a general decline in women's control with the advent of trade (certain notable exceptions do not pertain to the peoples she describes). Rosaldo and Lamphere (1974, 9) write of the papers in their book that they "establish that women's role in social processes is far greater than has previously been recognized" and that they show that "women, like men, are social actors who work in structured ways to achieve desired ends" and who "have a good deal more power than conventional theorists have assumed." However, they reveal their entrapment in the anthropological ethos that sees contemporary Third World peoples as virtually unchanged representatives of the past in stating (14) that "the papers . . . do not, on the whole, address questions concerning female roles today." With the exception of a paper on the nineteenth-century Mende of Sierra Leone, the empirical papers do treat "female roles today"—among the Igbo and Ijaw of Nigeria, the Mbum Kpau of Tchad, the Javanese and other Indonesian groups, Lake Atitlán villagers in Guatemala, and people of rural Montenegro, pre- and postrevolutionary China, and urban black communities in the United States. By what fiat are such peoples removed from the world of today?

The upshot of an ahistorical perspective is to see giving birth and suckling as in and of themselves furnishing the basis for a presumed past subordination, though subject to change in the future. Since the division of labor by sex was central in the evolution of cultural life, it is easy to fall into the trap: women bear children; the early division of labor is related to this fact, as is women's present subordination; hence there has been a quantitative but not a qualitative shift in women's status relative to men, which took place as egalitarian social forms were transmuted into hierarchical ones. The structural implications of the fact that, when labor is not specialized beyond the division by sex, goods are completely shared within a band or village collective are ignored, as is the concomitant control by every member of the group over the distribution of the resources and products that each acquires or manufactures. Thereby the source of transformation in women's status is bypassed: the development of trade and specialization to the point that relations of dependence emerge outside of the band, village, or kin collective, undermine individual control and personal autonomy, and lay the basis for hierarchy.

Brown (1970) contrasts the public control exercised by Iroquois women, based on their responsibility for the collective household and its stores, with women's loss of such control, and concomitant loss of status, among the centralized and hierarchical Bemba. In comparative studies, Sacks (1975) and Sanday (1974) affirm the relationship between control of production and distribution by women and their "public" participation and status. Goldhamer (1973) shows the variability in women's control over the products of their labor in the New Guinea highlands and the significance of these variations to their status.

For example, among the Mae Enga women are responsible for the daily allocation of their produce, but "men retain the 'right and duty' involved in the 'important' distribution of pigs, pork, and produce—for prestation, trade and debt-payments" (Goldhamer 1973, 6). By contrast, among the Tor of West Irian, "men say that it is women's total control over the food supply that affords them the 'exceptionally high position' that prevails throughout the district" (10). Food presentation may be a "public" or political act or a private service, according to the structural setting. Among the Tor, as among the Iroquois of the past, women's dispensation of food to strangers is a public act; it sets the stage for the reception of newcomers. "The women's expressed attitude toward strangers coming into the villages determines how they will be received by the men" (10). By contrast, Bemba women dispense food as a family service that redounds to the husband's stature and enjoins obligations to him on the part of the recipients in the same way as does chiefly extending of hospitality. Among the Mae Enga, women's labor furnishes produce that is consumed by the pigs which are distributed in political negotiations by men.

The relatively higher status of women among the Iroquois and Tor, where they control their work and its distribution, than among the Mae Enga and especially the Bemba, where they do not, suggests that preliminary phases in the process of class development did in fact accompany women's decline in status, as Engels originally proposed. The link between women's reduced status, on the one hand, and the growth of private property and economic classes, on the other, was in Engels's view the emergence of the individual family as an independent economic unit. Taking shape within and subverting the former collective economy, the family as an economic unit transformed women's work from public production to private household service. The critical development that triggered the change was the specialization of labor that increasingly replaced the production of goods for use by the production of commodities for exchange and set up economic relationships that lay beyond the control of the producers.

Commodity production, Engels (1972, 233) wrote, "undermines the collectivity of production and appropriation" and "elevates appropriation by individuals into the general rule," thereby setting in motion "incorporeal alien powers" that rise up against the producers. The seeds of private property and class exploitation are planted, and the single family as an economic property-owning and inheriting unit develops within and destroys the collective. "The division of labor within the family . . . remained the same; and yet it now turned the previous domestic relation upside down simply because the division of labor outside the family had changed" (221). Instead of carrying out public responsibilities in the band or village collective within which goods were distributed, women became dependent on men as the producers of commercially relevant goods. In the context of the individual family, "the woman was degraded and reduced to servitude, . . . a mere instrument for the production of children" (121).

Engels described the process as unfolding through the domestication of animals in the ancient East and the exchange of cattle, which were cared for, and hence came to be owned, by men. Since unequal control over resources and subjugation by class and by sex developed in very different ecological settings in many parts of the world prior to, as well as within, the period of European colonialism, it is important to separate Engels's statement on women's subjugation from the specific context of his discussion. The processes associated with the transformation of goods produced for use to "commodities," produced for future exchange, then become apparent in all world areas. These are: specialization of labor in connection with trade, and warfare to ensure or control trade; intensive work on agricultural land and unequal access to or privatization of prime lands; differences in economic status expressed in categories of "slaves," "rubbish men," perpetual youth, and the like; competition among lineage groups, within which the individual family as an economic unit begins to take shape; the institutionalization of "political" functions connected with warfare and property as separate from "social" functions and the dichotomization of "public" and "private" spheres; and the institutionalization and ideological rationalization of male superiority.

Summary

I have argued that the structure of egalitarian society has been misunderstood as a result of the failure to recognize women's participation in such society as public and autonomous. To conceptualize hunting/gathering bands as loose collections of nuclear families, in which women are bound by dyadic relations of dependency to individual men, projects onto hunter/gatherers the dimensions of our own social structure. Such a concept implies a teleological and unilineal view of social evolution, whereby our society is seen as the full expression of relations that have been present in all society. Ethnohistorical and conceptual reinterpretation of women's roles in hunting/gathering societies reveals that qualitatively different relationships obtained. The band as a whole was the basic economic unit; individuals distributed their own produce; property did not exist as a foundation for individual authority; and decisions were on the whole made by those who would be carrying them out.

Failure to appreciate the structure of egalitarian relations renders more difficult the problem of unraveling the complex processes that initiated class and state formation. Ethnohistorical research indicates that in precolonial horticultural societies where egalitarianism still prevailed, women continued to function publicly in making economic and social decisions, often through councils that mediated their reciprocal relations with men. The comparison of such societies with those characterized by differences in rank and wealth indicates that the main concomitant of women's oppression originally outlined by Engels is indeed found cross-culturally. The transmutation of production for consumption to production of commodities for exchange (usually along with intensive work on land as a commodity for future use) begins to take direct control of their produce out of the hands of the producers and to create new economic ties that undermine the collectivity of the joint households. Women begin to lose control of their production, and the sexual division of labor related to their childbearing ability becomes the basis for their oppression as private dispensers of services in individual households. The process is by no means simple, automatic, or rapid, and where women retain some economic autonomy as traders they retain as well a relatively high status. In West Africa, women were organized to maintain and protect their rights well into the development of economic classes and political states.

The documentation and analysis of women's social roles, then, show that family relations in pre-class societies were not merely incipient forms of our own. Social evolution has not been unilineal and quantitative. It has entailed profound qualitative changes in the relations between women and men.

Note

1. For studies of comparable changes in women's status, cf. Hamamsy 1957 and Leacock 1955.

References

Barnes, John A. 1971. "African Models in the New Guinea Highlands." In *Melanesia: Readings on a Culture Area,* ed. L. L. Langness and John C. Weschler. Scranton: Chandler.

Bates, Daisy. 1938. *The Passing of the Aborigines: A Lifetime Spent among the Natives of Australia.* London; Murray.

Brown, Judith K. 1970. "Economic Organization and the Position of Women among the Iroquois." *Ethnohistory* 17:151–67.

Caulfield, Mina Davis. 1977. "Universal Sex Oppression? A Critique from Marxist Anthropology." *Catalyst,* nos. 10–11:60–77.

Cox, Bruce, ed. 1973. *Cultural Ecology: Readings on the Canadian Indians and Eskimos.* Toronto: McClelland and Stewart.

Damas, David, ed. 1969. *Contributions to Anthropology: Band Societies*. National Museums of Canada Bulletin 228.

Divale, William Tulio. 1976. "Female Status and Cultural Evolution: A Study in Ethnographer Bias." *Behavior Science Research* 11:169–211.

Draper, Patricia. 1975. "iKung Women: Contrasts in Sexual Egalitarianism in Foraging and Sedentary Contexts." In *Toward an Anthropology of Women*, ed. Rayna R. Reiter. New York: Monthly Review Press.

Engels, Frederick. 1972. *The Origin of the Family, Private Property and the State*. New York: International.

Fried, Morton H. 1968. "On the Concepts of 'Tribe' and 'Tribal Society.'" *Proceedings of the 1967 Annual Spring Meeting, American Ethnological Society*, pp. 3–20.

———. 1975. *The Notion of Tribe*. Menlo Park CA: Cummings.

Friedl, Ernestine. 1975. *Women and Men: An Anthropologist's View*. New York: Holt, Rinehart and Winston.

Goldberg, Steven. 1973. *The Inevitability of Patriarchy*. New York: Morrow.

Goldhamer, Florence Kalm. 1973. "The 'Misfit' of Role and Status for the New Guinea Highlands Woman." Paper read at the 72nd annual meeting of the American Anthropological Association.

Hamamsy, Laila Shukry. 1957. "The Role of Women in a Changing Navajo Society." *American Anthropologist* 59:101–11.

Keesing, Roger M. 1971. "Shrines, Ancestors, and Cognatic Descent: The Kwaio and Tallensi." In *Melanesia: Readings on a Culture Area*, ed. L. L. Langness and John C. Weschler. Scranton: Chandler.

Landes, Ruth. 1938. *The Ojibwa Woman*. New York: Columbia University Press.

Leacock, Eleanor. 1954. *The Montagnais "Hunting Territory" and the Fur Trade*. American Anthropological Association Memoir 78.

———. 1955. "Matrilocality in a Simple Hunting Economy (Montagnais-Naskapi)." *Southwestern Journal of Anthropology* 11:31–47.

———. 1969. "The Naskapi Band." In *Contributions to Anthropology: Band Societies*, ed. David Damas. National Museums of Canada Bulletin 228.

———. 1975. "Class, Commodity, and the Status of Women." In *Women Cross-Culturally: Change and Challenge*, ed. Ruby Rohrlich-Leavitt. The Hague: Mouton.

———. 1977. "Women in Egalitarian Society." In *Becoming Visible: Women in European History*, ed. Renate Bridenthal and Claudia Koonz. Boston: Houghton Mifflin.

Leacock, Eleanor, and Jacqueline Goodman. 1977. "Montagnais Marriage and the Jesuits in the Seventeenth Century." *Western Canadian Journal of Anthropology*. In press.

Lee, Richard B. 1972. "The iKung Bushmen of Botswana." In *Hunters and Gatherers Today*, ed. M. G. Bicchieri. New York: Holt, Rinehart and Winston.

Morgan, Lewis Henry. 1954. *League of the Ho-De-No-Sau-Nee or Iroquois*. Vol. 1. New Haven: Human Relations Area Files.

————. 1965. *Houses and House-Life of the American Aborigines.* Chicago: University of
    Chicago Press.

————. 1974. *Ancient Society.* Gloucester MA: Peter Smith.

Richards, Cara B. 1957. "Matriarchy or Mistake: The Role of Iroquois Women through
    Time." *Proceedings of the 1957 Annual Spring Meeting, American Ethnological
    Society,* pp. 36–45.

Rogers, Edward S. 1972. "The Mistassini Cree." In *Hunters and Gatherers Today,* ed. M. G.
    Bicchieri. New York: Holt, Rinehart and Winston.

Rosaldo, Michelle Zimbalist, and Louise Lamphere, eds. 1974. *Woman, Culture, and So-
    ciety.* Stanford: Stanford University Press.

Sacks, Karen. 1975. "Engels Revisited: Women, the Organization of Production, and Pri-
    vate Property." In *Toward an Anthropology of Women,* ed. Rayna R. Reiter. New
    York: Monthly Review.

Sahlins, Marshall D. 1961. "The Segmentary Lineage: An Organization of Predatory Ex-
    pansion." *American Anthropologist* 63:322–45.

Sanday, Peggy R. 1974. "Female Status in the Public Domain." In *Woman, Culture, and
    Society,* ed. Michelle Zimbalist Rosaldo and Louise Lamphere. Stanford: Stan-
    ford University Press.

Schlegel, Alice, ed. 1977. *Sexual Stratification: A Cross-Cultural View.* New York: Colum-
    bia University Press.

Service, Elman. 1966. *The Hunters.* Englewood Cliffs NJ: Prentice-Hall.

Speck, Frank G. 1926. "Culture Problems in Northeastern North America." *Proceedings of
    the American Philosophical Society* 65:272–311.

Thwaites, R. G., ed. 1906. *The Jesuit Relations and Allied Documents.* 71 vols. Cleveland:
    Burrows.

Tindale, Norman B. 1972. "The Pitjandjara." In *Hunters and Gatherers Today,* ed. M. G.
    Bicchieri. New York: Holt, Rinehart and Winston.

Turnbull, Colin M. 1972. *The Mountain People.* New York: Simon and Schuster.

Wallerstein, Immanuel. 1974. "The Rise and Future Demise of the World Capitalist Sys-
    tem: Concepts for Comparative Analysis." *Comparative Studies in Society and
    History* 16:387–415.

6. Blood Ties and Blasphemy

American Indian Women and the Problem of History

KATHRYN W. SHANLEY
Excerpts

New Introduction by Kathryn W. Shanley

I wrote this essay for *Is Academic Feminism Dead? Theory in Practice* as part of a Rockefeller-funded effort to encourage "respectful engagement" among a diverse group of feminist scholars. To be candid, I found this piece difficult to write. Being interested first in individual stories of women's lives, I find the category "Native American woman" impossible, given the diversity among Native American groups and tribes. Yet, at the time, so many stereotypes overwhelmed academic thinking about who Native American women might be that I felt I had to address some basic issues. The question of difference carries with it assumptions that are difficult to avoid—worldview questions such as what is a person? what power is available to persons in the universe?

Within indigenous thought, "gender" relates more to complementarity and cosmic kinship than it does to biology, and therefore, may require other terms altogether. Moreover, the gap between the way contemporary Indian women live their lives and Native life in post-contact times cannot be easily described. Those issues continue to pose unique challenges for feminist understandings and "respectful engagements."

As I look back, I am grateful so much good work has been done and is being done to define indigeneity and women's experiences within and outside that worldview, as well as in relation to twenty-first-century life. Somewhere between "essential" differences and universalisms lies a real turf where people live and breathe. We need first to listen to one another, without judgments, categories, or theories.

Blood Ties and Blasphemy
American Indian Women and the Problem of History (2000)

> Writing is an act of courage for most. For us, it is an act that
> requires opening up our wounded communities, our families,
> to eyes and ears that do not love us. Is this madness? In a way
> it is—the madness of a Louis Riel, a Maria Campbell, a Pauline
> Johnson, a Crazy Horse—a revolutionary madness. A love that
> is greater than fear. A love that is as tender as it is fierce.
>
> Beth Brant, *Writing as Witness*

Writing and speaking about American Indian literatures, histories, and cultures, as I so frequently do, does not trouble me nearly as much as writing
about American Indian *women* does. Yet it seems I have been writing this
essay all my life. I am Indian because of blood ties, my ancestral links to a
people who have lived—indeed thrived—on the Plains long before they
were gathered up on the Ft. Peck Reservation to live a different kind of
life.[1] (My grandmother was the first person in my family to be born on the
reservation, a little over a century ago.) But my "Indianness" is more than
blood heritage—it is a particular culture, Nakota, and a history of the place
where I grew up and much more. I am also a mixed-blood, though I prefer
Gerald Vizenor's term "crossblood" (Vizenor 13). What owning the term
"crossblood" implies, in part, is that I am also Indian (or tribal) because of
blasphemy, my position on one side of a binary opposition, which connotes
resistance—a "not that" on the other side of a dubious Christian "blessing." Oppositional pairs such as native/white, pagan/Christian, primitive/
civilized, or savage/citizen bespeak the historical relations that have shaped
me—all of that Indianness is, largely, easy to talk about, since it is fueled by
the madness of which Beth Brant speaks. Woman, however, is the first skin
around me, and I do not know entirely what it is or even how to talk about
it. I do know it is not my story alone; my story belongs also to my mother,
grandmothers, sisters, friends, relatives, and so many others, including non-
Indians, and all their perspectives must be respected in whatever I say. So
my approach to the subject of American Indian women and history requires a shifting discourse, one that circles its subject and even circles my
own subjectivity.

In their introduction to *Feminisms: An Anthology of Literary Theory and
Criticism*, Robyn R. Warhol and Diane Price Herndl remark that "beginning

with a personal anecdote is practically obligatory" (ix); they say there are good reasons for this: feminism holds that "the personal is political," and that feminists believe that the traditional academic boundaries between professional and personal experience ought to be undermined. While I agree with Warhol and Price Herndl about the imperative to undermine boundaries between personal and professional experiences, an imperative the theoretical term "subject position" is meant to capture, I also believe that both epistemological and ontological realms differ considerably for American Indian women, in comparison to non-Indian women, so much so that audience becomes a problematic in the positioning of oneself to speak. Moreover, an Indian woman speaking out risks being seen as a representative of Indian women; I must disavow that role, yet I hope to share thoughts from an Indian woman's perspective that will be helpful in feminist discussions.

Simply put, Americans need to embark on a general reeducation in order to know how to situate new perspectives and voices wisely, because misinformation and mythologies about native women's lives and experiences prevail in such abundance (particularly in popular culture media). We need a common knowledge base, something more than television perspectives or single-issue alliances (i.e., antihomophobic or activism against sexual abuse), that at the very least illuminates governmental policies toward American Natives and proceeds with a recognition of basic differences between tribal and Christian worldviews. Clara Sue Kidwell, a Choctaw/Anishinaabe historian, offers a useful set of questions to begin:

> The mythology of Indian women has overwhelmed the complexity of roles in the history of Indian and white contact. Indian women stand in history as stereotypes such as the hotblooded Indian princess, a la Pocahontas, or the stolid drudge, the Indian squaw plodding behind her man. They are not real people. The myths of colonialism and manifest destiny raise questions about their associations with European men. Their roles must be interpreted in two cultures. If American history portrays them as saviors and guides of white men and agents of European colonial expansion, were they explicitly or implicitly betraying their own people? Were they driven by passion, or were they victims of fate, forced to submit to men of a dominant society? (98)

One thing is certain: their voices "are not heard in the written documents or in the history books," a fact that leads Kidwell to conclude, "we must attempt to recreate the cultural context of their actions and to move beyond the myths that have been woven around their lives" (98). Inquiries into the cultural contexts of the lives of historical figures such as Pocahontas, Doña Marina (La Malinche), or Sacajawea, begun or continued by scholars such as Kidwell, still leave a gap between those Indian women's lives and the lives of women living today. A similar gap exists between the notable Indian woman non-Indians tout and those women who serve Indian communities first and foremost.[2] With the aim of reopening the destructive and stereotypical narrative closures surrounding contemporary Indian women, I will begin with a story, a sort of truncated Indian version of *Fried Green Tomatoes at the Whistle Stop Café*. It is a story about women working to survive, to find ways to raise their families, to make meaning of their places in the world.

When I was nineteen, a year out of high school, I worked as a waitress at Skelly's truck stop in a town thirty-some miles off the reservation—it was truly one of the only jobs open to me. There I met a woman I will call Dorothy.[3] She was one of several cooks who rotated onto the day shift. Dorothy was on the chubby side, nervous, even driven, and she was, for the most part, toothless. Although she could not have been much more than fifteen years older than I was at the time, the egocentrism of my youth prevented me from seeing any relationship between who she was and who I was, other than our both being Indian—let alone who she was becoming in relation to my goals and directions.

She was married to an abusive man, an alcoholic, a fact I only knew by the way or perhaps I intuited it, since my mother was also married to an alcoholic. Dorothy and I did share, however, in our commiseration over our working conditions. Later, I would remember my time at Skelly's when I read Richard Wright's story in *American Hunger* of how he moved north and took a job at a restaurant, read of his flight toward freedom and his subsequent disillusionment. The rules seemed to work against the employees, and the employees, in turn, worked against the rules and the boss—an old story of class struggle. Dorothy and I were the exceptions, both too sincere (also read: naive) and too driven to become something else to recognize that things were set up to prevent us from doing that. For example, the boss—the brother of the man who had before managed the restaurant part of the business, but who ran away to Alaska, leaving a stack of bills behind—was understandably worried about his profit margin. He had limited Dorothy in her preparation of the "daily special": she could use either fruit or whipped cream in the dessert, but not both, so Dorothy made Jell-O on cookie sheets, then cut the Jell-O into little cubes. A neat trick, I thought, and she looked so proud when she gazed on those thick parfait glasses filled with ruby red cubes, topped (of course) with whipped cream—with the powdered substitute the boss passed off as whipped cream.

Dorothy was honest, unlike one cook, Sandy, who sometimes had her husband drive up in back at the end of the afternoon shift to load up packages of frozen chicken and steak; or another cook, Ralph, who drank on the job and, I imagine, spit in the stew, like the immigrant woman character in Richard Wright's book. . . .

Few employees could be trusted to handle the till. Sherry, one of the senior waitresses, wasn't safe within a mile of the cash drawer, any vacated table with a tip lying on it, or our purses, which we kept unlocked in the back room. I knew she stole, but couldn't, didn't dare try to, prove it. She was "one tough lady," as they say, and I didn't mess with her. She also made extra money at night in the bunk area where truckers slept while their rigs were being serviced, or so I was told. She too was Indian, and a single parent with four children.

Ten years later, I moved back home to take care of my mother, who had to have eye surgery and needed help during the recovery time. By that time, I had grown up, had made my own mistakes, had worked at many different jobs—I had sold Avon, been a legal secretary, an outreach worker in a high school for what we now call "at-risk" kids, a secretary for the Dominican Sisters of the Sick Poor, and, finally, had gone back to school to become a registered nurse. A marriage, a divorce, and two nursing jobs later, I returned home with child in tow, the memories still vivid of the folks I had worked with at Skelly's. Now as I recount those memories, the phrase, popular nowadays in the academy, "intersections of 'race,' class, and gender," echoes in my head. Inasmuch as any single phrase can describe a psychosocial reality, I suppose that one does; but for me it will always be a matter of the heart, of "survivance," as Vizenor terms it: the mornings Sandy (the cook I told you about who stole food from the boss) would show up for work with her eyes blackened and her temper sharpened (she was non-Indian and married to an unemployed Indian man with whom she shared five kids); . . . the days when Sherry stole the tip I earned from waiting on the entire staff of the local telephone company.

I found out that Dorothy had moved away, and that Sandy had become a licensed practical nurse. I never found out what happened to the others. . . . But I ran into my buddy, Violet, the waitress I most liked to work with, at the local Woolworth lunch counter. She had gotten her two girls through high school, and like the plodding, devoted Mole in the Coyote tales of the Okanagan, she had to struggle against her trickster husband to do so. She too is Indian, a Chippewa displaced to Trenton, North Dakota, one of many Chippewas who were shut out of allotment on Turtle Mountain Reservation largely because it was situated on a tract of land desirable for Euro-American settlement.

I tell this story, just one of many I could tell, and not one of the worst, as a way of describing the gulf we all know that exists between feminism as we theorize and practice it in the academy, American Indian women's history as we conceive of it—if we do in fact conceive of it at all—and the way women live their lives in (post)colonial times and places. In communities where these women work, jobs for Indians in the banks or white-owned stores and businesses are few or none. Indian women living on reservations have many different stories to tell; some of them like the stories of these women, and some focused on links to past generations and continuing religious and cultural practices (though religion and cultural worldview are one and the same in my estimation). The "old ways" stories, tales of exotic Indian life ways, always seem to interest wider audiences the most. Urban Indian women no doubt offer another set of stories entirely, however, not without common ties to their sisters' stories from rural America, for working-class experience and continuing traditions may provide common denominators. In regard to urban Indian experience and all the stories associated with that experience, more literature is available.[4] Whether living off-reservation in rural America, on-reservation in America's internal colonies that would be sovereign, or in America's cities, Indian women and their histories cannot be adequately represented or understood if we do not also understand their centuries-old oppressions. Answers to questions of why some families stay on the reservation, why some leave never to return, and why some go back and forth lie in understanding the allotment decades before the 1920s, tribal government under the Indian Reorganization Act of the 1930s and 1940s, and the Termination Policy years of the 1950s, and all against the backdrop of specific cultural histories. Canadian Native history also must be explored; many Canadian Native families like Brant's migrated to U.S. cities to find work in factories.

American Indian and Canadian Native women's stories remind us that social oppression based on class, gender, and "race" is by no means a thing of the past, despite the laudable gains the women's movement has made. But I do not need to tell you that changes have occurred or that oppressions continue: we now have new words, phrases, and metaphors in our vocabularies to connote those changes and the continuing need for change: "sexual harassment," "glass ceilings," "battered women and children's shelters," "sexual predators," "homophobia," and so on. What I do hope to make clear is how the means for and terms of realizing gains against gender/"race"/class oppression differ for American Indian women—a point I hope to make implicitly if not explicitly. Nevertheless, I fully recognize that "From the outside 'feminism' may appear monolithic, unified, or singularly definable," and I agree with Warhol and Price Herndl that "the more one sees the multiplicity of approaches and assumptions inside the movement," the clearer it becomes that feminist projects can provide "a model for cultural heterogeneity" (x). Dialogues and coalitions must be encouraged to grow. In order to discuss what American Indian women's history might look like, what kind of history they have written themselves or carried within their hearts, we need to come to something approximating common terms: what cultural differences between Indians and non-Indians persist in (post)colonial situations; who are American Indians and American Indian women to themselves; what would social justice be in regard to American Indian women's history; what are "subjectivity" and "agency" in the context of American Indian women's lives; and what constitutes activism? Through an exploration of what I mean by "race"/class/gender, I hope that the issues outlined above will take on a more particularized meaning, although more suggestively than prescriptively so.

Who is the/an American Indian? By now we know "race" to be more of an ideological construct than a fact of essential biological difference. While the terms "class" and "gender" are in some senses as ideologically constructed as is the term "race," I would argue that "race" as a term stands apart, not as the greatest in a hierarchy of oppressions, but as an overarching global designation tied to a particular colonial history of economic power and privilege. In other words, the legacy of racism among postcolonial people along with continued oppression have created a reality for "race," far beyond any genuine biological differences. Gender and class oppressions, in my opinion, can be equally destructive to groups and individuals, but how those oppressions are "racially" configured shapes them in primary, paradigmatic ways.

Books such as Michael Banton's *Racial Theories*, Stephen Jay Gould's *Mismeasure of Man*, and other, more recent works, such as Henry Louis Gates Jr.'s edited anthology, *"Race," Writing, and Difference*, and Dominick LaCapra's edited anthology, *The Bounds of Race*, amply establish how scientific studies of "racial" difference are most often used to create a superior/inferior distinction between groups. Such theoretical clarity remains theoretical, however. There remains a gap between such academic discussions and the people most affected by constructs of "race," between theory and the practice of justice. . . .

For a fuller picture of American Indian life, feminist scholarship that incorporates "race" as a term connoting an aspect of oppression must take kinship into account as well, in its most tribally specific, qualitative dimensions. Discussion of blood ties must be set against the idea of blasphemy or sin that has been associated with tribal social practices in missionary and anthropological renderings of tribal life and women's roles in those societies. The sexualities of individuals informed by identities that are other-than-heterosexual have likewise suffered distortion under the missionary's and scholar's gaze.

What do we mean by "race" then? Werner Sollors, the author of *Beyond Ethnicity* and editor of *The Invention of Ethnicity*, provides a conflicted jumping-off place. He argues that "it is most helpful not to be confused by the heavily charged term 'race' and to keep looking at race as one aspect of ethnicity" (*Beyond Ethnicity* 39). Eventually, he argues, we must also abandon the term "ethnicity," for "we may be better served by the vocabulary of kinship and culture codes than by the cultural baggage that the word 'ethnicity' contains" (39). While I agree both with the general principle of moving beyond "race" as a construct (an effort that may ultimately render "racism" less ideologically powerful) and with his impetus for also replacing "ethnicity" with terms that capture a greater complexity of being, I would argue that racism maintains material/real boundaries between "racially" designated groups and other Americans and that those boundaries figure essentially in the groups' culture codes (Shanley). While strong in his undoing of "race" as a biological denotation, Sollors is weak in accounting for the ideological power that "race" categories have carried and continue to carry with them; he perhaps believes (certainly more than I do) in a trickle-down of academic theorizing and philosophizing to the level of institutional and cultural spheres of influence.

I see another problem in Sollors's leap to a different terminology—the leveling effect of ethnicity or its less loaded equivalents designating all matters of cultural difference. Euro-Americans have, in many respects, invented an ethnic identity around the Indian presence in their history, often based on, as Sollors notes, "a presumptuous reconstruction of American kinship" (*Beyond Ethnicity* 125). In order for such appropriations of American Indian cultural identities to be effective, however, a simultaneous silencing needs to occur. Vizenor remarks on the phenomenon of Euro-American silencing, appropriation, and absorption of tribal realities, using the adjective "scriptural" in a deconstructionist mode to describe the stature such constructions have had and continue to have in American national consciousness: "The various translations, interpretations, and representations of the absence of tribal realities have been posed as the verities of certain cultural traditions. Moreover, the closure of heard stories in favor of scriptural simulations as authentic representations denied a common brush with the shimmer of humor, the sources of tribal visions, and tragic wisdom; tribal imagination and creation stories were obscured without remorse in national histories and the literature of dominance" (16). For Vizenor, visions and wisdom arise from humor; humor, in turn, keeps representations shimmering with life and unpredictability, while science is based on predictability.[5] Appropriations of Indian culture, whether under the guise of anthropological objectivity or New Age religiosity, invariably take themselves very seriously. Vine Deloria, Jr., in his book *Custer Died for Your Sins*, humorously comments on how many proud and serious-minded non-Indians announce that they, too, have Indian heritage, and always through a Cherokee grandmother (10–11). (There are, by the way, living Cherokee people who suffer from such generalizations.) A female ancestor must be infinitely more palatable in the blood ties equation than would be the "brutish and savage" (albeit noble) Indian male. Deloria employs a scathingly ironic humor in speaking of such appropriations. Sollors comments on the hegemonic nature of such gestures, noting that "the popular image of the Indian exists in a web of subdued love relationships" (*Beyond Ethnicity* 121).

Historical figures such as Pocahontas ("the first mythical Indian," as Betty Louise Bell refers to her) have become Euro-Americans, common ancestor with Natives, a usurpation tied with love in the American representational economy—"the white ventriloquism of her motives and desires . . . have made her a metaphor for the colonizing of native identity by settler imagination" (Bell 67). . . .

While such appropriations and romantic constructions continue in Disney's recent feature-length cartoon *Pocahontas*, actual Indians have difficulty obtaining the health care they need or the education promised them by their treaties, because the government has constructed a mound of red tape requiring proof of Indian identity, and legal jargon as to whether their identity is to be determined by ancestry and to what degree, or by affiliation.[6] Tribes themselves struggle for clarity in approaching the government. Sharon O'Brien writes of the complex and convoluted nature of Indian law, "Scholars have written several major works and over 1300 articles on American Indian law in their attempts to explain and define" the relationship between the United States and tribal governments (1462).

On the one hand, the Supreme Court has emphasized that the government's relationship with tribes "is not defined by race, but is of a political nature" (O'Brien 1462). On the other hand, as of 1978 "federal legislation contained thirty three definitions of Indians" (O'Brien 1485), based on various racial and cultural formulas. The government's fiduciary responsibility toward Indians (its trust relationship based on treaties and other agreements, as well as on legal precedents) falls subject to the conflicts between the branches of government, when Congress by its fiscal principles and politics (determining who actually gets served with monetary appropriations) decides to support the interests and concerns of non-Indian constituents over and above those of Indians. Such conflicting positions on Indians illustrate why it is important not to subsume "race" into the larger category of ethnicity. Regardless of whether or not the Supreme Court decides over and over again that Indians are political entities, the legislative and executive branches of the government deal with Indians according to Indians' degree of Indian blood and Indians' ability to document that blood, rather than as individuals and nations with whom the government has a special relationship and toward whom it has a special charge. (The Bureau of Indian Affairs, for example, continues to manage millions of dollars' worth of American Indian resources, and it has a poor record of doing so honestly and ethically.)[7] "Race" determines the particulars of many Indian lives, through government regulations, as O'Brien notes: "The most outstanding (although largely historical) use of race is in regard to competency. Whether or not the Bureau was willing to declare an Indian competent, thereby capable of alienating his or her land, depended upon the person's possession of one-half or more blood quantum. Individuals possessing less than one-half Indian blood were considered 'more competent' than those with one-half or more" (1483–84). Competence has always meant different things to the Washington-appointed bureaucrats than it has to tribal people themselves. Being Indian, culturally setting oneself apart as such in Indian communities within quasi-sovereign nations, depends to a large extent on tribes' being able to make gains in economic development; their ability to educate Indian citizens to acquire the skills necessary to live productive, satisfying lives and, in turn, to enable those citizens to serve their communities; and a nation's hope to provide for the health and social needs so pathetically underserved.[8]

Urban Indians present similar needs, and have largely ended up in cities because their home communities are lacking in economic opportunities. Unrelenting efforts on the part of the U.S. government over the past century to assimilate Indians into the mainstream, or simply to make them disappear from America's bureaucratic landscape and ledgers, involve perceptions of who Indians were and who they are today—contemporary "poor relatives" who represent a continuing burden, one President Bush declared he could "terminate" at will. Back in 1969, Vine Deloria described a situation that continues to this day: "With so much happening on reservations and the possibility of a brighter future in store, Indians have started to become livid when they realize the contagion trap the mythology of white America has caught them in. The descendant of Pocahontas is a remote and incomprehensible mystery to us. We are no longer a wild species of animal loping freely across the prairie. We have little in common with the Mohicans" (33). Meanwhile, as of the latest census, more and more Euro-Americans choose to identify as Indian, while "livid" Indians struggle to set the terms of membership in their own spheres of life and influence. Tribes often employ self-destructive blood quantum measures to determine who is Indian in an effort to prevent shrinking tribal resources from going to wannabes. It is often a lose-lose situation.[9]

American Indian women figure centrally in vague, blood-tie identities, as I have noted above, but Indian women constructed in popular culture media have difficulty surviving to the end of the movie. . . . Indian women fulfill their mythological purpose only in liaisons with white men. As Rayna Green notes of Pocahontas legends:

> Whether or not she saved John Smith, her actions as recounted
> by Smith set up one kind of model for Indian-White relations
> that persists—long after most Indians and Anglos ceased to have

face-to-face relationships. Moreover, as a model for the national understanding of Indian women, her significance is undeniable. With her darker, negatively viewed sister, the Squaw—or, the anti-Pocahontas, as Fiedler called her—the Princess intrudes on the national consciousness, and a potential cult awaits to be resurrected when our anxieties about who we are make us recall her from her woodland retreat. (700–701)[10]

The virgin/whore dichotomy is nothing new and is so essentially a part of the American Christian worldview that it dies hard, but its implications for Indian women and Indian people in general are chilling in their genocidal potential. The American Indian woman, Green concludes, "[a]s some abstract, noble Princess tied to 'America' and to *sacrificial* zeal, . . . has power as a symbol" (713, emphasis added), but her binary sister, the Squaw, represents a repugnance for Indian sexuality. . . .

Making use of the Indian Princess image is not limited to masculinist movies or Anglo male writers, however. In "Who Is Your Mother? Red Roots of White Feminism," Paula Gunn Allen recounts how Eva Emery Dye co-opted the image of Sacajawea to be used as a feminist heroine in the late-nineteenth-century women's movement (Allen). Sacajawea functioned as a cultural mediator, no doubt, but much controversy surrounds the particulars of her life and her role on the expedition. The questions raised by historian Clara Sue Kidwell, quoted earlier, resurface, when one reads accounts of Sacajawea's abuse by her husband, Charboneau, guide to the Lewis and Clark expedition. Sally Roesch Wagner reconstructs another of the early American feminist movement's connections to Native women's lives in her article "The Iroquois Influence on Women's Rights." According to Wagner, the antebellum suffragettes around Seneca Falls, New York, were influenced and inspired by their neighbor clanmothers among the Haudenosaunee. Such alliances were not always exploitative or appropriative, but rather were based on mutual benefit and respect. Wagner's research provides a model for feminist scholarship on Indian women.

More recently, however, Mary Dearborne, who draws on Werner Sollors's work for her book *Pocahontas' Daughters*, gropes toward a definition of "female ethnicity," beginning with American Indian women, and along the way poses the question, "Did Pocahontas know that she was an ethnic woman?" Because Pocahontas did not leave a written record of her thoughts and experience, Dearborne concludes, we cannot know. Aside from the privileging of textual records implied in Dearborne's conclusion, how could Pocahontas *not* know that she was viewed by colonists differently than European women were viewed?[11] For one thing, as the favorite daughter of Powhatan, she was kidnapped by the English and held for over a year as ransom for demands that Powhatan met; the English continued to wage war nonetheless, and Pocahontas was not returned to her father (Vaughan 114). Moreover, if there are parallels to Phillis Wheatley, an eighteenth-century black woman slave who did leave a written record in her poetry, one would have to say, yes, Pocahontas knew she was "other," "heathen," in the eyes of many. In her earlier historical moment, Pocahontas was set apart by her "race," no doubt, despite her marriage to a European man, just as Wheatley was considered black, and therefore subject to slavery on the earthly plane, despite her Christian salvation—racism dictates no less. In other words, even in well-intentioned works by capable scholars, such as Dearborne, a sort of theoretical blindness to America's racist history occurs.[12]

One of the more chilling recent representations of Indian women appears in a recent publication aimed at youth. The author of a new comic book, *Ghostdancing*, presents an Indian princess/whore, dancing nearly naked in a prison cell in a "furious fit of dementia. A death rattle."[13] "She wants to scream . . . but that is not her way. . . . Instead she grinds her teeth hard through her lip. There is no pain and, after a while, everything is still and dead again" (Delano and Case 13).

The erotic images accompanying the prose revive the tragic view of Indian women's existence, at the same time as they make her "yours for the taking," depicting her as scantily rag-clad and voluptuous. The author takes refuge in what he sees as his right as a writer to appropriate Indian sacred traditions toward his own ends. After explaining that he has "read *Bury My Heart at Wounded Knee*, and all the other 'Indian books' I could lay my hands on," he states:

> Doubtless with countless other pseudo-hippie romantics, I fantasized a Utopian, dignified nomadic coexistence with the land, and heaped opprobrium on the callously indifferent heads of our colonial ancestors—almost ignoring, in my arcadian reverie, the contemporary extermination of Native Brazilians. History repeats itself endlessly. The Christian cultures rob and pillage instinctively. It's depressing.
>
> So what do I do? I write a mad, symbolic, apocalyptic dra-

ma—a millennial western epic, in which I animate representations of beings sacred to various Native mythologies. I put
words in their mouths, and feelings in their hearts. I distort
their context and use them to express my own prejudices, preconceptions, and guilts.

But that's what writers do. We rob and pillage instinctively.
We're cultural and emotional pirates. . . .

But hey, we don't mean any harm. We're just passing through.
(Delano and Case 25)

I am not sure whether Delano's recognition of his own egregious appropriation makes him better than a Lynn Andrews or Jamake Highwater
(the former claiming her "right" to appropriate Indian spirituality through
a vision and the latter claiming his "right" to represent Indians through a
vague blood heritage, seriously in dispute), but I tend to think not.[14] More
to the point, what most would-be-Indian frauds and writing "pirates" often
have in common is their desire to reach into Indian cultures and histories
for gender and spiritual constructions more appealing than those they apparently see before them in their own cultures or histories. . . .

By these examples, we can see the dangers inherent in subsuming "race"
into ethnicity, maneuvers that hasten to link us all together in multicultural America without a proper understanding of our historical differences.
While the definition of Indians as peoples historically set apart in a "racial"
category by themselves is a generalization that by no means fully incorporates the urban Indian communities that have grown considerably over
the past several decades, nor the individuals deracinated through adoption,
sovereignty movements of necessity define "Indianness" as a personal and
tribal identity—in other words, an identity that cannot be claimed without corroboration by the tribe, band, or nation. Within those definitive
boundaries, terms such as "fiduciary" and "fiscal" take on special meanings
or simply retain the meanings Indians invested in them when they made
those treaties with the Great White Father in Washington—treaty making
as quasi-kinship bonding, which also apparently meant different things to
the parties involved.

A well-documented aspect of the fiduciary or trust institution *within
tribal societies* encompasses an intricate network of kinship relations.
Among the Lakota, such ties are referred to as the *tiyospaye* (literally, a circle
of tipis), which is a reference to extended families who camped together.

Kinship ties are established through blood ties, marriage, and ceremonies of adoption, such as those of the *kola* and *hunka*. While generalizing from one tribal tradition to something one might designate as a pan-Indian perspective can be dangerous, I believe it is not a stretch to generalize that all indigenous tribes organize themselves around kinship. On the other side of the continent, Mary Jemison, a white woman captured at the age of fifteen, went through Haudenosaune (Iroquois, specifically Seneca) adoption rituals, so that she could be made into a relative to replace a brother who had died. Of that experience she writes:

> I afterwards learned that the ceremony I at that time passed through, was that of adoption. The two . . . [sisters) who had lost a brother in Washington's war sometime in the year before, and in consequence of his death went up to Port Pitt, on the day on which I arrived there, in order to receive a prisoner or an enemy's scalp, to supply their loss. . . . It was my happy lot to be accepted for adoption. . . . I was ever considered and treated as a real sister, the same as though I had been born of their mother. (Seaver 17)

Neither "race" nor biological sex factors into the Haudenosaune need to create this bond. Moreover, Jemison's descriptive phrase "happy lot" suggests much about the belonging that kinship ties can bring. She died at age ninety-nine, a Seneca grandmother. I do not mean to diminish the trauma she experienced seeing relatives killed and then being captured and taken from her own family and home; nevertheless, I would add that Jemison was one of many "white Indians" who preferred Indian life to their repressive and oppressive positions in non-Indian colonial societies—a topic beyond the scope of this essay.[15] Nonetheless, the trust implied in such ties exceeds not only "race," but class loyalties of a capitalist, profit economy. In *The Gift: Imagination and the Erotic Life of Property*, Lewis Hyde argues that such "erotic bonding" involving people as "commodities" of exchange functions as the center of gift-giving cultures. "Erotic," in the context of Hyde's argument, stands for bonding that is consummately dynamic and vital, the stuff that holds communities together.

In her novel *Waterlily*, Ella Cara Deloria, a Lakota anthropologist, offers a unique perspective on the practice of kinship bonding among the Lakota, the "buying" of wives—a practice considered the most honorable way to be married. As the aunt of the protagonist, Waterlily, attempts to put an end to speculations about whether Waterlily will accept the offer of marriage, made through the presentation of horses and other gifts placed at Water- lily's tipi by the young man's female relatives, the cultural values become clear: "Dream Woman spoke up, 'We do not yet know how our niece will decide, of course. But if she says no, we must accept it. That is as it should be. Some families, who set greater store by things than by kinship, might force their girls to marry. In our family, Father says, no girl need marry un- less she wishes. And he is right'" (151).

Although the people in the novel and their way of life are idealized, Delo- ria succeeds in her intention to make some of her people's ways sensible to the non-Indian readership of the 1940s. Not only does Waterlily "sacrifice" for the kinship bond, she also enables her uncle to replace the horses he lost that were intended as give-away items at her grandmother's ghost-releasing ceremony; it was nonetheless a difficult decision for her to make. Generos- ity is one of the four essential Lakota virtues (the others being fortitude, bravery, and gratitude), and as a beloved child, a *hunka*, it was Waterlily's role to be generous in all ways. Men had equally demanding social roles.

While these examples of gift-giving may seem dated, out of some distant idyllic past, it is not so. Valuing generosity and personal sacrifice was a vital aspect of the training I received as a child, as was respect for elders. In the late nineteenth century, laws were passed to prohibit Indians from com- munal practices such as give-aways and their attendant rituals. Even before the passage of the American Indian Freedom of Religion Act in 1978, tribes across the country began reviving their ancient traditions. A couple of sum- mers ago, I attended an annual celebration in my home community, and was pleased to see that the *heyoka* (sacred clowns) had come back to taunt the people and to beg money for the poor....

As "contraries" who did things backwards and even mocked the sacred during ceremonies, *heyokas* fulfilled a unique role in tribal communities; humor functions centrally in many indigenous religious practice as a force to check pomposity and to highlight both human frailty and absurdities in the human condition. Sacred themselves, they were not to be contradicted or in any way harmed, no matter how outrageous their antics. They also represented a unique gender category, since they seldom married—indeed, they were greatly feared because of their Thunder Being dream power—and they "played" at traditional male and female roles. *Winktas* (men who chose to take on women's roles in society) and manlyhearted women (women who chose to take on men's roles in society) also died away with religious and government censorship, or at least were shamed from public view.[16] I suspect that, given the homophobia in American society in general, it will take a while for *heyokas* (or whatever the equivalent would be among other indigenous peoples) to return to the full power they once had and for alternative gender roles to be fully accepted. Many Indians today are Christian themselves and slow to see the oppressive legacy of the Christian worldviews forcibly imposed on them and their ancestors.

I hope that my discussion of "race," class, and gender gives a sense of the complexity of how those terms have come to bear on American Indian women. Appropriations of American Indian women's experience and stereotypes of our identities, historical and contemporary, pose serious obstacles to realistic and humane renderings of our lives. In order for class differences and struggles, such as in my story of Skelly's truck stop, to be understood adequately, we must make sure that "racial" history and cultural kinship values enter our thinking. Regional histories must also be given their due.

However clarifying, my own writing risks seeming both like a "tour of the exotic country" and like the voice of "the imperial tongue." I do recognize my own privilege as one who lives and works among the writing elite; nevertheless, my deepest loyalties lie elsewhere. . . .

Indian cultures are growing and changing today as they always have been; hence, we would do well to avoid the sightseer's mistake in trying to "capture" (as with a photograph) their essence. Rather, our inquiries need to involve us as dynamically as possible in listening, without succumbing to the temptation of hasty closures of mind or lapses into national mythologies. . . .

What I call "subjectivity" and "agency" approximates what Walter Percy calls "personal sovereignty," a willing abandonment of preconceived packaging of ideas, coupled with a delightful and liberating empowerment in discovering truth. My sense of "personal sovereignty" also includes tribal sovereignty, a strong link to the concerns of a people much greater and more important than myself. I must confess, to tell a public story of my own personal sufferings would make me ashamed of myself, both because my sufferings seem like nothing in relation to the sufferings of others I have known and because to focus on myself that way would seem inappropriate. A full story of my mother's and my grandmother's lives deserves to be told, and mine folded into theirs, but I would rather postpone that telling until I can sufficiently cloak it in fiction and humor so as to celebrate their strengths as well as to probe their failures. Yet I honor those Indian women who do and can tell stories about the oppressions they have suffered as women and as Indians, their stories and the ones they carry for others; all those stories need to be told. Certain stories can eat a hole in the center of our being, trying to get out. As Beth Brant tells us, "The secrets I am told grow in my stomach. They make me want to vomit. They stay in me and my stomach twists—like [Betty Osborne's] lovely face—and my hands reach for a pen, a typewriter to calm the rage and violence that make a home in me" (*Writing as Witness* 13).[17]

Such a writing response goes beyond compassion or empathy to commitment. In the Lakota language, the term *cante ista* means "the heart's eye," a way of seeing that comes from both the deepest of emotional and spiritual experiences and the awe, humility, and compassion engendered by suffering. "Heartfelt" would, I suppose, be the English equivalent, but "cordial" also means "heartfelt." *Cante ista* connotes something more than the individualistic way in English we customarily use "heartfelt" to designate a knowledge based on experiences that have moved us. *Cante ista* implies responsibility toward others, a trajectory of feeling into action for the greater good, the good of others. Humiliation and shame (in the Lakota sense of *unsiga*, frequently translated as "pitifulness"), which are at the core of ceremonies of deprivation and flesh offerings, liberate the religious seeker into generosity and sacrifice as a means of both giving back and belonging once again to a world of relatives—"relatives" includes all other living beings.

Of all the people I knew at Skelly's truck stop, knowing Dorothy has moved me to the depths of my being. When I returned ten years later, Dorothy had moved away to go to school, but her daughter Bobbie had become a good friend and helper to my mother. She was also taking care of her grandparents. Bobbie became my best friend—we were bound to one another through gift-giving and sacrifice. She was bright, had been valedictorian of her high school class. Her three-hundred-pound body was exceeded in abundance only by her sense of humor and generosity. That spring, as the tadpoles grew into baby frogs, she went to the river and gathered up a handful, then headed for her grandparents' trailer home. She knocked on the door, and when Grampa opened it Bobbie smiled, liberating a mouthful of baby frogs in one green streak. I tell of that afternoon to honor her, her memory and her life. But despite her being wise beyond her years, she despaired, feeling there was no place for her in the world. That summer, drunk, she drove her car into a cement wall—it was probably on a dare, since she took three other young people with her.

Several years ago Doreen, my sister Indian-way, drank herself to death, leaving five children for her no-good husband to raise. We were the same age. Throughout our childhoods growing up on the reservation, we vowed that we would make something of ourselves. I would like to be able to tell you more of her story, to honor her in that way, but the time is not right to do that. As Brant says, to do so takes courage, a courage to open up "our wounded communities, our families, to eyes and ears that do not love us" (*Writing as Witness* 53). To tell Doreen's story would require "the shimmer of humor . . . tribal visions . . . and tragic wisdom" Vizenor calls for to thwart "scriptural simulations" in the "literature of dominance." Doreen was known for her sense of humor, and deserves that sort of story. I name her here to mark a place in the world, in writing, for her story—not as a sensational, sentimental, or tragic example of pain, but as my heart's punctuation mark for the importance of remembering to remember. I know I live too much with a survivor's grief and guilt. But survivors carry more than grief and guilt—they must live their dreams doubled, perhaps multiplied many times over. I would rather close with a happier story, a story of empowerment: Dorothy now has a Ph.D. She is happily remarried and working actively in Indian education. Skelly's burned down sometime in the 1970s, but I am sure Dorothy remembers as I do what it meant to work there.

Activism for me means first hearing and telling stories "seen" with the *cante ista*. When stories of a people's heroism and suffering are presented as a transparent history—an old, safe story, another legend of "the Indian's" fall from dignity in history—no new insights into our common humanity are possible. The most important conclusions to be made about the lives of the women whom I worked alongside at Skelly's are first their own, and unlike Pocahontas or Sacajawea or Bobbie or Doreen, they may still be able to make their stories known, in their own words.

Notes

1. I use the terms "American Indian," "Native American," "Native," "indigenous," and "tribal" fairly interchangeably in speech, as a sign to my listeners that they need not struggle for the politically correct term. But I do make a distinction in my thinking and in my writing. "American Indian" or simply "Indian" is my preferred term for indigenous peoples in the lower forty-eight states; Alaskan and Canadian Natives often prefer those name designations. Differences in the historical and legal backgrounds of Alaska Natives and Native Hawaiians require that they be seen in their

own distinct political and cultural contexts and referred to by their terms for themselves. This essay is primarily about indigenous peoples in the lower forty-eight
states. "First Nations" is also used by groups and individuals in Canada and the
United States. "Native American" came into usage with the political movements of
the 1960s and 1970s and began more or less in the academy among Indian edu-
cators and activists. Most of the American Indian peoples I know refer to themselves
by their tribally (band-, community-, or clan-) specific names first, then to themselves as "Indian." See Matthew Snipp, *American Indians: The First of This Land*, for a
fuller discussion of the issue of naming and Indian identity, as well as for demographics on American Indians and tribes. I am an enrolled member of the Assiniboine (Nakota) tribe of the Ft. Peck Reservation, a reservation that is also home to
Dakota people.

2. M. Annette Jaimes and Theresa Halsey, in their article "American Indian Women: At
the Center of Indigenous Resistance in North America," present a compelling story
of the Indian women who are heroines among Indian people today.

3. All the names of the women in this story are fictitious, but the events are true from
my point of view. Special thanks to David L. Moore for his comments on this manuscript and his unwavering support, and to Beth Brant for our many discussions
about the issues contained here and for inspiring me to believe that it is not oxymoronic to see writing as a "brilliant and loving weapon of change."

4. In particular, Beth Brant's stories in *Mohawk Trail* and *Food and Spirits* offer portrayals of urban life.

5. "Pure" science in Western traditions strives for results that can be predicted and du-
plicated. Indigenous people similarly conduct such experimentation and study in
their realms, though they may be guided by decidedly different interpretations of
outcomes and predictions of possible outcomes.

6. The difficulty in interpreting the Native American count through the U.S. census
illustrates the trouble one can get into in accounting for the various ways of identifying as Indian. While in the 1980 and 1990 census figures many researchers associated inflated numbers of Native Americans with positive media portrayals of Indians, those planning for the 2000 census fear the opposite, that 10 to 20 percent of the
actual Native American population will be missed.

7. Secretary of Interior Babbitt, in his testimony during the recent suit against the Bureau of Indian Affairs, admits that the fiduciary responsibility of the federal government toward tribes and Native American individuals who own trust lands has been
woefully neglected if not criminally violated.

8. Casinos and other forms of gambling are relatively new to Indian tribes and have
barely begun to provide the capital necessary for building a sustaining infrastructure
for a few Indian nations. Largely through the efforts of Donald Trump, Congress is
attempting to tax casino profits—a move that flies in the face of the sovereign nation
status tribes assert for themselves. Moreover, tribal gaming comprises 8 percent of
the total gaming in the United States, and 85 percent of tribal casino employees are

non-Indian, according to Richard Hill, head of the Indian Gaming Commission in a speech before Congress.

9. For a fuller account of the blood-quantum dilemma, see M. Annette Jaimes, "Federal Indian Identification Policy: A Usurpation of Indigenous Sovereignty in Contemporary North America."

10. It is interesting to note that the stereotypical Indian male is of Plains origins—never from a Pueblo tribe, for example—while stereotypical Indian females most often belong to Woodlands tribes. Plains Indian women apparently do not conform to non-Indian ideals of beauty and femininity; while, in the economy of American image-making, Plains Indian men represent the rugged individualism non-Indians hope to achieve.

11. Two recent pieces on Pocahontas provide enlightening readings on her life: Jennifer Gray Reddish's "Pocahontas" and Beth Brant's "Grandmothers of a New World," in *Writing as Witness*.

12. According to Alden T. Vaughan, in *Roots of American Racism*, Pocahontas's people were not easily subdued by the British. Vaughan argues that in an effort to end Indian resistance to English colonization in the time immediately preceding Pocahontas's kidnapping, the English military commanders "rapidly abandoned all regard for customary rules of war and gained much of their success by guile and merciless treatment of captives" (114). "[Thomas] Gates lured some Indians into the open with a music-and-dance act by his drummer, then slaughtered them. Percy routed the Paspahegh tribe, destroyed its village and fields, and allowed his men to throw the Indian queen's children into the river and shoot their brains out for sport. Lord De La Warr wanted to burn the queen; Percy convinced him to let her die by the sword instead" (114).

13. Special thanks to Juan Mah y Busch, a doctoral student at Cornell University, for bringing the comic book to my attention. Other recent studies of indigenous American gender relations and constructions include Sue-Ellen Jacobs, Wesley Thomas, and Sabine Lang, eds., *Two-Spirited People*; Sabine Lang, *Men as Women, Women as Men*; and Laura Klein and Lillian A. Ackerman, eds., *Women and Power in Native North America*.

14. Ward Churchill discusses the work of Lynn Andrews and Jamake Highwater in his book *Fantasies of a Master Race*, and mentions the two in his more recent work, *Indians Are Us?*: "Think about the significance of charlatans like Carlos Castaneda and Jamake Highwater and Mary Summer Rain and Lynn Andrews churning out 'Indian' bestsellers, one after the other, while Indians typically can't get into print" (82). Of Lynn Andrews, Churchill writes in *Fantasies*:

> And, as if all this were not enough, we are currently treated to the spectacle
> of Lynn Andrews, an airhead "feminist" yuppie who once wrangled herself
> a weekend in the company of a pair of elderly Indian women of indistinct
> tribal origin. In her version of events, they had apparently been waiting
> their entire lives for just such an opportunity to unburden themselves of

every innermost secret of their people's spiritual knowledge. They immediately acquainted her with such previously unknown "facts" as the presence of kachinas in the Arctic Circle and the power of "Jaguar Women,"
charged her with serving as their "messenger," and sent her forth to write
a series of books so outlandish in their pretensions as to make Castaneda
seem a model of propriety by comparison. Predictably, the Andrews books
have begun to penetrate the "popular literature" curriculum of academe.
(189)

Also see Kathryn W. Shanley, "The Indians America Loves to Love and Read."
A version of my discussion of the term "race" as it appears in the present essay first
appeared in the above-cited article.

15. For a fuller accounting of "White Indians," people captured by various tribal groups
    who did not want to return to non-Indian life, see James Axtell, "The White Indians
    of Colonial America."

16. Walter L. Williams, in *The Spirit and the Flesh*, explores the topic of gay sexual ori-
    entation in traditional North American Indian, Alaskan Native, and Mexican Indian
    cultures, and also touches on Indian lesbian sexuality and gender construction. Also
    see Evelyn Blackwood, "Sexuality and Gender in Certain Native American Tribes:
    The Case of Cross-Gender Females"; and Claude E. Schaeffer, "The Kutenai Female
    Berdache: Courier, Guide, Prophetess, and Warrior."

17. Beth Brant began her career as a writer after editing an anthology of North Ameri-
    can Indian women's writing, *A Gathering of Spirit*. In commencing that project, she
    decided she had to draw together the voices of all Native women, not just those
    recognized for their literary achievements, so she contacted tribal communities,
    prisons, and every other place where Indian women are likely to be. Her efforts
    resulted in an extraordinary collection of writings, but also in her becoming the re-
    pository for many Indian women's stories and secrets, as a friend and sometimes a
    lone confidant.

Works Cited

Allen, Paula Gunn. "Who Is Your Mother? Red Roots of White Feminism." In *The Sacred
    Hoop: Recovering the Feminine in American Indian Traditions*, 209–21. Boston:
    Beacon Press, 1986.

Axtell, James. "The White Indians of Colonial America." In *The European and the Indian:
    Essays in the Ethnohistory of Colonial North America*, 168–206. New York: Ox-
    ford University Press, 1981.

Banton, Michael J. *Racial Theories*. New York: Cambridge University Press, 1998.

Bell, Betty Louise. "Pocahontas: 'Little Mischief' and 'the Dirty Men.'" *SAIL* 6, no. 1
    (1994): 63–70.

Blackwood, Evelyn. "Sexuality and Gender in Certain Native American Tribes: The Case
    of Cross-Gender Females." *Signs* 10, no. 11 (1984): 27–42.

Brant, Beth. *Mohawk Trail*. Ithaca NY: Firebrand Books, 1985.

————. "Preface: Telling." In *Food and Spirits*, 11–17. Ithaca NY: Firebrand Books, 1991.

————. *Writing as Witness: Essay and Talk*. Toronto: Women's Press, 1994.

————, ed. *A Gathering of Spirit*. Toronto: Women's Press, 1984; 1989.

Churchill, Ward. *Fantasies of a Master Race: Literature, Cinema, and the Colonization of American Indians*. Ed. M. Annette Jaimes. Monroe ME: Common Courage Press, 1992.

————. *Indians Are Us? Culture and Genocide in Native North America*. Monroe ME: Common Courage Press, 1994.

Dearborne, Mary. *Pocahontas' Daughters: Gender and Ethnicity in American Culture*. New York: Oxford University Press, 1986.

Delano, Jamie, and Richard Case. *Ghostdancing* 1 (March 1995) (DC Comics).

Deloria, Ella C. *Waterlily*. Lincoln: University of Nebraska Press, 1988.

Deloria, Vine, Jr. *Custer Died for Your Sins: An Indian Manifesto*. 1969. Norman: University of Oklahoma Press, 1988.

Flagg, Fannie. *Fried Green Tomatoes at the Whistle Stop Café*. New York: Random House, 1987.

Gates, Henry Louis, Jr. *"Race," Writing, and Difference*. Chicago: University of Chicago Press, 1985, 1986.

Gould, Stephen Jay. *Mismeasure of Man*. New York: Norton, 1981.

Green, Rayna. "The Pocahontas Perplex: The Image of Indian Women in American Culture." *Massachusetts Review* 16 (autumn 1975): 698–714.

Hyde, Lewis. *The Gift: Imagination and the Erotic Life of Property*. New York: Vintage Books, 1983.

Jacobs, Sue-Ellen, Wesley Thomas, and Sabine Lang, eds. *Two-Spirited People: Native American Gender Identity, Sexuality, and Spirituality*. Urbana: University of Illinois Press, 1997.

Jaimes, M. Annette. "Federal Indian Identification Policy: A Usurpation of Indigenous Sovereignty in Contemporary North America." In *The State of Native America: Genocide, Colonization, and Resistance*, ed. M. Annette Jaimes, 123–38. Boston: South End Press, 1992.

Jaimes, M. Annette, and Theresa Halsey. "American Indian Women: At the Center of Indigenous Resistance in North America." In *The State of Native America: Genocide, Colonization, and Resistance*, ed. M. Annette Jaimes, 311–44. Boston: South End Press, 1992

Kidwell. Clara Sue. "Indian Women as Cultural Mediators." *Ethnohistory* 39, no. 2 (1992): 97–107.

Klein, Laura, and Lillian A. Ackerman, eds. *Women and Power in Native North America*. Norman: University of Oklahoma Press, 1995.

LaCapra, Dominick, ed. *The Bounds of Race: Perspectives on Hegemony and Resistance*. Ithaca NY: Cornell University Press, 1991.

Lang, Sabine. *Men as Women, Women as Men: Changing Gender in Native American Cultures*. Austin: University of Texas Press, 1998.

O'Brien. Sharon. "Tribes and Indians: With Whom Does the United States Maintain a Relationship?" *Notre Dame Law Review* 66, no. 5 (1991): 1461–1502.

Percy, Walker. "The Loss of the Creature." In *Message in the Bottle: How Queer Man Is, How Queer Language Is, and What One Has to Do with the Other*, 46–63. New York: Farrar, Straus, and Giroux, 1975.

Reddish, Jennifer Gray. "Pocahontas." *Tribal College* 6, no. 4 (1995): 22–33.

Schaeffer, Claude E. "The Kutenai Female Berdache: Courier, Guide, Prophetess, and Warrior." *Ethnohistory* 12, no. 3 (1965): 193–236.

Seaver, James E. *A Narrative of the Life of Mrs. Mary Jemison*. Ed. June Namias. Norman: University of Oklahoma Press, 1992.

Shanley, Kathryn W. "The Indians America Loves to Love and Read." *American Indian Quarterly* 21, no. 4 (1991): 675–702.

Snipp, Matthew. *American Indians: The First of This Land*. New York: Russell Sage Foundation, 1989.

Sollors, Werner. *Beyond Ethnicity: Consent and Descent in American Culture*. New York: Oxford University Press, 1986.

———, ed. *The Invention of Ethnicity*. New York: Oxford University Press, 1989.

Vaughan, Alden T. *Roots of American Racism: Essays on the Colonial Experience*. New York: Oxford University Press, 1995.

Vizenor, Gerald. *Manifest Manners: Postindian Warriors of Survivance*. Hanover: Wesleyan University Press, 1994.

Wagner, Sally Roesch. "The Iroquois Influence on Women's Rights." *Akwe:kon Journal* 19, no. 1 (1992): 4–15.

Warhol, Robyn R., and Diane Price Herndl, eds. *Feminisms: An Anthology of Literary Theory and Criticism*. 1977. New Brunswick NJ: Rutgers University Press, 1991.

Williams, Walter L. *The Spirit and the Flesh*. Boston: Beacon Press, 1986.

Wright, Richard. *American Hunger*. 1977. New York: Perennial Library, 1983.

II. Method

The following ten chapters illustrate a variety of methodological approaches to Native women's history. They are paired according to key similarities to encourage reflective comparison. We hope readers will note how scholarship has evolved over time, the ways that scholars have influenced one another, and the wide range of sources and approaches these essayists have employed. Chapters 7 through 15 include one or more samples of sources that informed this research.

The first pair of essays models the use of a biographical approach to Native women's history, considering the experiences of Coocoochee, a Mohawk woman of northeastern Ohio, and Susie Bonga Wright of the Leech Lake Ojibwes. While researching other or more general topics, Helen Hornbeck Tanner and Rebecca Kugel were fortunate to come across sources providing information about women who were not well known. In the case of Kugel's study of Susie Bonga Wright, luck included locating letters written by Bonga Wright herself, allowing us to hear her "voice." Most of the sources informing these two essays, however, were written by men, both Native and Euro-American. Thus, part of each story concerns the attitudes of those writers toward the Native women in question. In the case of Coocoochee, an important source is a captivity narrative written by O. M. Spencer, who was a boy when he met and lived with Coocoochee, but who wrote about her years later.

Another approach scholars have taken is to identify a theme or pattern they have recognized in their research and then craft a monograph exploring that theme. The second pair of essays provides examples—one following upon the other—of articles created with a central theme, in this case the ways that kinship intersected with Catholic conversions and ceremonies. In Carl Ekberg's exploration of Marie Rouensa's life, we see a biographical case study of a single convert, while Susan Sleeper-Smith builds upon

Ekberg's research but adds other case studies as well. Readers will note how two scholars coming from different historical subfields, and writing nine years apart, differ in their interpretations.

All four of the above articles consider the experiences of religious women, as does Michelene Pesantubbee's article in the Oral History section. Questions about religion, an important aspect of culture, have intrigued many scholars. As these essays demonstrate, the topic can intersect with a wide range of others, including concepts of race, politics, families, gender roles, and acculturation. Of course, there are many other themes that scholars may explore with an eye on issues of gender.[1]

While some scholars design their studies after examining and being inspired by primary sources, others begin with research questions and proceed to imagine—and then locate—the types of evidence that might be used to answer those questions. Here, Theda Perdue and Nancy Shoemaker asked similar questions about women's power and status in separate tribes in different eras, and then had to consider how these vague concepts might be measured and what variables might indicate greater or lesser authority or autonomy.

Another way to practice Native women's history is to incorporate gender analysis into studies that are about many things *in addition* to gender. In any study, scholars have a list of questions they consider about the who, what, and why of the events and people of the inquiry; any study may be enriched by adding the following questions: What were the women's experiences? What were the gender ideals of these people—that is, what did they expect women and men should do, and did they all agree? What were gender relations like—that is, how did women and men get along? Answering these questions can add greater understanding to projects that might not have necessarily begun as women's history projects per se. The articles by Jean O'Brien and Lucy Eldersveld Murphy demonstrate studies of this type that used gender as one of many factors considered in examining two colonizing, transitional, multiethnic societies.

The ethnohistory umbrella has always covered anthropologists as well as historians, but most historians have been trained to base their research on documents alone. Native American history, however, is becoming increasingly interdisciplinary, and scholars benefit from using a variety of research methods, including oral histories and interviews. In the final pair of chapters for this volume we include two selections that were informed by interviews with Native people. Nancy Lurie's classic fieldwork with Mountain Wolf Woman of the Wisconsin Ho-Chunk nation illustrates the type of ethnography from which historians may draw significant information. We provide excerpts from three sections of that book, covering the period before 1900. In addition, Michelene Pesantubbee's look at Choctaw women ranging from the eighteenth century to the present is based not only upon written sources but also upon interviews with Choctaw religious leaders. Unlike the other authors—historians all—whose articles appear in the Methods section of this volume, Lurie is an anthropologist and Pesantubbee a religious studies scholar.

We urge readers to examine the ways that these studies were designed, including the authors' choices of the who, where, and when of their projects, and the types of central questions they posed. Some of them examine gender relations and gender roles, and inquire into the impact of particular changes and events on women.

Historians have always had to grapple with questions about the purpose, goal, and intended audience of each document, and often with problems of its translation, transcription, and recovery. In Native women's history these difficulties are often acute. The writers of these articles drew information from a broad range of evidence; all of them worked with sources that were problematic in some way. We include here a sample of sources, selected to represent a wide variety of types.

As noted in the general introduction to this volume, researchers should become familiar with the tribal cultures as well as the history of the people being studied. Furthermore, many primary sources were written by non-Native people, whose points of view the researcher should recognize. We must consider the biases and goals of these long-ago observers and wonder how well they understood what they were seeing; we must separate opinion from basic information. Knowing a great deal about the people who created the sources helps scholars to recognize biases and assumptions. It takes practice to train oneself to recognize but "read through" attitudes that labeled Native people as "primitive" or spiritually deluded or which saw Native women as "drudges" or "princesses." Similarly, one must train oneself to note Euro-American writers' commitment to patriarchy and yet recognize evidence they provide of women's economic production, leadership, family patterns, or protest activities, to cite several examples. In addition, we need to ask what observers were *not* seeing, and what was seen but *not* reported.

Many of these articles were also informed by non-narrative sources such as estate inventories, census rolls, petitions, church records, and laws. Often it is necessary to deduce something about women's actions from evidence of material objects or to notice the absence of certain information, such as a butter churn missing in an estate inventory.

Collectively, these works seek to recover Native women's experiences, and they demonstrate many of the tools we may use in this effort. As the first six essays in this volume demonstrated, there are numerous ways we might organize, theorize, and analyze the historical experiences of Native women, as well as several we ought to avoid. At the same time, there are certainly other theories and methods we do not touch upon. We hope readers will be inspired to continue developing additional techniques for recovering more of Native women's history.

Note

1. Readers may find the following of interest in this regard: *Ethnohistory* 43, no. 4 (1996): "Special Issue: Native American Women's Responses to Christianity," edited by Michael Harkin and Sergei Kan.

Biography

Both of the following essays illustrate the use of a biographical approach to Native women's history, and both treat the lives of women who were leaders in their own communities but who were not well known to outsiders. In fact, the existence of Coocoochee and Susie Bonga Wright might have escaped the notice of historians had not these two scholars—Helen Hornbeck Tanner and Rebecca Kugel—come across revealing sources as they researched the larger histories of these regions, the Ohio valley in the eighteenth century and the Minnesota Ojibwe country in the late nineteenth century. Both studies situate their subjects in the context of changes that were taking place in their worlds, and demonstrate the ways that these women and their neighbors responded to specific challenges.

Tanner's essay on Coocoochee provides a much-needed alternate perspective of the Ohio valley region in conflict, to balance the typical narratives focused on male military and diplomatic leaders. This insider's view, made possible in large part by a captivity narrative remembering the experiences of a boy who lived in her household, portrays a woman who had substantial influence in her multitribal community. Unlike most portrayals of Native women who lived before 1900, Coocoochee's was not of a "cultural mediator" (described by Clara Sue Kidwell in the third chapter of this volume) between her people and Euro-Americans. By contrast, Kugel characterized Susie Bonga Wright as this type of mediator.

Published eighteen years apart, these essays illustrate the efforts of ethnohistorians of two generations. Clearly influenced by the work of Tanner, Rayna Green, Kidwell, David Smits, Jennifer S. H. Brown, and Eleanor Leacock, among others, Kugel's work also follows some of the trends in women's history since the mid-1970s. She examined here issues of leadership, women's work groups and their political roles, and the negotiation of gender ideals between Ojibwes and Episcopalian missionaries. She also addressed issues of race and racism, and to a lesser extent, considered the import of expectations about class on Susie Bonga Wright's marriage controversy.

Although Coocoochee and Susie Bonga Wright lived a century apart in different places and circumstances, it is tempting to compare and contrast the religious leadership roles available to them, the former in a non-Christian multitribal community where a woman could have substantial religious influence in her own right, and the latter in a Christian congregation where women's leadership was subordinated to male ministers and deacons. The collective nature of women's religious activities is more evident in the latter study, yet both essays demonstrate the participation of religious women in local politics—whether Ojibwe policy making or Shawnee-Delaware military planning.

7. Coocoochee

Mohawk Medicine Woman

HELEN HORNBECK TANNER

New Introduction by Helen Hornbeck Tanner

Coocoochee impressed me as an exceptional figure in the frontier scene when I first read the story of Oliver Spencer's 1791–92 captivity and his experiences as a member of her household in present-day Defiance, Ohio. Throughout all Ohio, the 1780s and 1790s seemed dominated by repeated incidents of violence in which fighting men played the leading roles. Yet the account by this eleven-year-old youth revealed the spiritual power and influence of a Mohawk woman in guiding military leaders of the Indian alliance in the northwest Ohio battles against American militia and troops. In the 1970s, when I was working to reconstruct Coocoochee's life story, I questioned a number of Iroquois scholars to find out about the role of women spiritual leaders among the Mohawk people or any other Iroquoian group. Anthropologists appeared to know nothing of a figure like Coocoochee, or any society of "medicine" women who were skilled as healers and also possessed special intuitive abilities.

In 2003, however, I learned of a contemporary Mohawk woman who is a practicing midwife and healer, active in promoting Canadian government recognition of the skills of women with her own traditional training. I sent her a copy of the "Coocoochee" story, asking if this eighteenth-century Mohawk filled a social role that was familiar to her. In response I received a long and enthusiastic phone call, explaining that she herself identified immediately with Coocoochee, a readily understandable figure to any woman reared with appreciation of the many skills and responsibilities of Mohawk women. Clearly, the key knowledge of the functioning of Indian communities still belongs to the people themselves.

History comes alive as soon as one visits the terrain where the action took place. The opportunity to see Coocoochee's home site finally occurred in September 2003 in conjunction with a speaking engagement near Defiance. From the row of houses on the bluff overlooking the conjunction of the Auglaize and the Maumee rivers on the edge of town, it was possible to pick out the one or two homes that must be situated on the former site of Coocoochee's residence, 1790–94. Opposite the bluff, on the west bank of the Auglaize River, stone remnants of Fort Defiance that replaced the "trader's town" where her daughter lived are still visible in a historic preservation area. A village street close to the west side of the river must follow the same course as the late-eighteenth-century trail upriver. At the first bend, the site of Captain Johnny's town is easy to identify using eighteenth-century information. Local residents remark that they still find artifacts in the course of gardening along the banks of the river. Historical markers identify the sites of Snake's town and Blue Jacket's town to the east of modern Defiance, along the north bank of the Maumee River.

The details in Oliver Spencer's story have proved to be of interest to a variety of ethnohistorians and other scholars to whom I have recommended this narrative. Caribbean specialists are fascinated to learn that news of the uprising on the island of Santo Domingo was brought to the attention of midwestern American Indians. European historians are likewise amazed that the events of the French Revolution were a matter of interest to the American "savages." In addition, Coocoochee's "story" has been translated into Spanish and included in a volume published in Mexico City to give Latin American students a picture of the North American frontier.[1] Historians who have read the "running the gauntlet" and "burning at the stake" literature of Indian warfare are struck by the way captives were incorporated into the daily life of the Indian society that existed at "The Glaize" when Coocoochee lived there. After I sent a copy of "Coocoochee" to William N. Fenton, the recognized dean of Iroquois studies, he commented that the story included the earliest mention he had seen of the use of the blowgun by northern Indians. This weapon, common among Creeks and other southern Indians, had been noted only in 1806 in the New York area. These examples point to the fact that each reader brings different background knowledge and objectives to the examination of a personal account, and can add different observations. He also pointed out that the proper orthography for her name would be "Ku ku ci."

Erminie Wheeler-Voegelin, founder of the American Society for Ethnohistory, was almost unbelieving when I pointed out that Coocoochee obviously was speaking an Algonquian language, probably Shawnee, when she exclaimed "Michi! Michi!," clearly meaning "great." Dr. Voegelin felt that an Indian woman would not give up her native language; yet here was a clear case of a non-Mohawk expression, and indeed perusal of the literature revealed increasing evidence of the multilingual capacity of Indian people. In reading the Spencer narrative, I myself fastened attention on the fact that she lived in Blue Jacket's village. Since I had been following the different locations of this Shawnee leader's town, I felt that I had a key to the general pattern her life must have followed after she and her husband left the Richelieu River for the Ohio country. Sometime after the first publication of the Coocoochee story, a helpful scholar reported that he had found the record of her baptism in archives of the St. Lawrence valley missions. Wish I had a copy of that document!

Coocoochee
Mohawk Medicine Woman (1979)

On the borderland of Canadian settlement southeast of Montreal, the Mohawk woman Coocoochee was born about 1740, grew to maturity, and acquired skill in herbal medicine and the special ability to contact the powerful world of the spirits. Although her childhood was sheltered in territory remote from the North American fighting frontier, her adult years were destined to be spent in a traumatic environment threatened almost perpetually by warfare.[2] Five times over a period of a quarter-century her household was uprooted, forced to move either by a sense of insecurity, by Indian defense strategy, or by direct attack. Following the initial transfer of Coocoochee's family from the hinterland of Montreal to the Ohio country about 1769, subsequent dislocations were brought about by major developments in Indian-White warfare west of the Appalachian Mountains.

Coocoochee lived during an era that was critical for all Indian people in eastern North America. In the annals of western history, her life spanned the French and Indian War between France and England (1754–63), Lord Dunmore's War against the Shawnee in Ohio (1774), the American Revolution (1775–83), and the Indian-White warfare continuing in territory northwest of the Ohio River until 1794. For Indian people, this was a time when the kings of France and England unfairly extended their imperial rivalry into the Indians' country, and when American land speculators and fron-

Indian Confederacy Headquarters at The Glaize, 1792

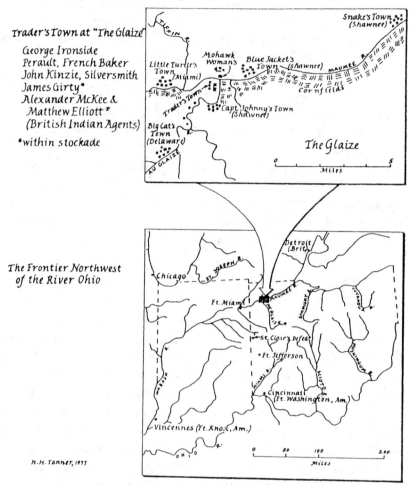

Trader's Town at "The Glaize"

George Ironside
Perault, French Baker
John Kinzie, Silversmith
James Girty*
Alexander McKee &
Matthew Elliott*
(British Indian Agents)

*within stockade

Snake's Town (Shawnee)

Mohawk Woman's

Little Turtle's Town (Miami)

Blue Jacket's Town (Shawnee)

MAUMEE

Trader's Town

Cornfields

Capt. Johnny's Town (Shawnee)

Big Cat's Town (Delaware)

AU GLAIZE

The Glaize

0   Miles   5

The Frontier Northwest of the River Ohio

Detroit (Brit.)

Chicago

ST. JOSEPH R.

Ft. Miami

MAUMEE

AU GLAIZE

SANDUSKY

WABASH

St. Clair's Defeat

Ft. Jefferson

MIAMI R.

SCIOTO

Cincinnati (Ft. Washington, Am.)

Ft. Washington, Am.

Vincennes (Ft. Knox, Am.)

OHIO

0   50   100   200   Miles

H.H. Tanner, 1977

3. Indian Confederacy headquarters at The Glaize in 1792, originally appearing in "The Glaize in 1792: A Composite Indian Community," *Ethnohistory* 25, no. 1 (1978): 17. © 1978 by the American Society for Ethnohistory. All rights reserved. Used by permission of the publisher.

tiersmen turned Indian land into individual personal property.[3] No matter how these generalized developments on the historic scene may be analyzed today, in the eighteenth century they constituted a series of direct threats to the way of life and very survival of Coocoochee and her family.

Intercolonial warfare broke out during Coocoochee's teenage years. In the summer of 1755, rumbles of distant battles on the upper Ohio River reached Indian settlements around Montreal including the Mohawk village where Coocoochee lived.[4] Her original homeland was the upper Richelieu River, the outlet to Lake Champlain emptying into the St. Lawrence River among the ribbon farms of the French *habitantes*.[5] By the fall of 1755, aggressive British troops had won a victory close at hand at Lake George, south of Lake Champlain. Two years later, Mohawk life on the upper Richelieu was disrupted as the river valley, along with Lake Champlain and the Hudson River, became a great war road between the British at Albany and the French forces at Montreal. Finally, British troops converged at Montreal to win a decisive victory over the French in September 1760.[6]

The war years were personally eventful for Coocoochee, born into the important Wolf clan. About 1757, the year when intercolonial strife invaded the St. Lawrence region, she married Cokundiawsaw, a member of the Bear clan. They had a baby daughter by the time the military campaigns were over in Montreal. During the next eight years, while three sons were added to the family, Coocoochee and Cokundiawsaw became increasingly apprehensive about their future near British-dominated Montreal.[7] The new government promoted colonization of the upper St. Lawrence valley and appeared in many ways far less friendly to Indian people than the previous French regime. The Mohawk couple finally made the decision to emigrate to the Ohio country following the land cession treaty in 1768 establishing the Ohio River as the boundary between regions of White and Indian settlement on the trans-Appalachian frontier.[8] They looked forward to life in a region from which white settlers would forever be excluded by the terms of the treaty. Coocoochee still carried her youngest son on a cradle-board, and had an active toddler in tow, when the family of six embarked on the seven-hundred-mile journey to central Ohio. Their move was not unusual; a number of families of Mohawk and other divisions of the Six Nations had preceded them to the Ohio country and others followed in the wake of the American Revolution. These Indian emigrants from Six Nations country, known as "Mingoes" in Ohio, joined Delaware, Shawnee and Wyandot villages, or established separate communities of their own.

This particular Mohawk family settled among the Shawnee villages on the edge of a broad prairieland on the west side of the Scioto River between the present towns of Circleville and Chillicothe, Ohio. By 1770 they were living in a small village of about a dozen log houses whose inhabitants included the rising young Shawnee chief Blue Jacket.[9] Nearby, six or seven other Shawnee villages were dispersed over a distance of twenty-five miles.[10] In these new surroundings, Coocoochee and her husband hoped for a more serene future. From the economic point of view, it was a convenient location. Fur traders from Pennsylvania lived in every village, bringing the kettles, guns, needles, blankets, and other European-made supplies that had become indispensable commodities for Indian people by the eighteenth century. Furthermore, a blacksmith and gunsmith who could keep these new implements and weapons in working order resided in the principal Shawnee village, Chillicothe, only fifteen miles away. Land for corn fields and vegetable gardens was neatly marked out beyond the town houses.[11]

Unfortunately, Coocoochee's move to the Shawnee town coincided with the time that Virginia frontiersmen were beginning to infiltrate the Shawnee hunting grounds in Kentucky. In 1769, Shawnee leaders first captured Daniel Boone in the Kentucky hunting grounds, seized the proceeds of his winter's hunt, and sent him home with two pairs of moccasins and a gun. But he and his companions returned within two years, the vanguard of the first few hundred Kentucky pioneers.[12] Thereafter, tension built up rapidly along both the Indian and the Kentucky shores of the Ohio River.

The first hostilities to alarm Coocoochee in her new situation erupted in 1774 when Lord Dunmore, Governor of Virginia, led an assortment of militia against the Shawnee. The main target for this expedition was the group of five Shawnee towns located near Delaware communities in the Muskingum valley of eastern Ohio, a hundred miles from Coocoochee's home. With apprehension, the Shawnee on the Scioto received news of the destruction of the Muskingum valley towns, but fortunately the advancing army halted before reaching the Scioto. Fearing imminent attack, the Scioto Shawnee sent a message of peace to Lord Dunmore, and arranged for a treaty council that prevented further violence that year.[13]

The outbreak of the American Revolution soon precipitated a general flight of the Shawnee to safer territory in northwestern Ohio. When the Indians first learned of the Revolution, which they interpreted as a family quarrel between father and children, they felt that they need not become involved. But by 1777, the Indian people in Ohio were all caught between the American base at Fort Pitt (Pittsburgh) and the British base at Detroit.[14] Realizing that they lived in a potential war zone, Coocoochee's family joined other members of Blue Jacket's town in the Shawnee migration to the Mad River at the headwaters of the Great Miami River. Here they relocated in a tight formation where they were further from the Ohio River and closer to the British supply base at Detroit.[15]

Beginning in 1777, Coocoochee took on the demands and underwent the sacrifices of a warrior's wife. Her husband, Cokundiawsaw, and their eldest son, Wapanoo, joined in expeditions directed against the Kentuckians and the increasing American traffic on the Ohio River. On more than one occasion, Cokundiawsaw returned with a fresh scalp which he prepared carefully and fastened into a circular wooden hoop for drying and preserving.

During the nine-year interval 1778–86, that Blue Jacket's town remained in the Mad River valley, Coocoochee's only daughter was married and in turn became the mother of a baby girl, born in 1779. The first tragedy to strike the family came only a short time afterward, when Coocoochee's son-in-law died, probably in defense of the Shawnee towns or in an attack on a station in the interior of Kentucky.[16] Three years later, the widowed daughter bore a son, whose father was said to be Simon Girty, the man most feared and hated by the American frontier settlers.[17] In his capacity as liaison for the British Indian department, Simon Girty was a frequent visitor at the Shawnee towns, where his brother James, a paid interpreter, continued to ply the Indian trade.[18] The young widow and her two children were all part of the household over which Coocoochee was presiding when the Revolution ended.

The end of British-American hostilities in the American colonies in 1781, and the acknowledged independence of the United States, in no way brought peace to the Ohio-Kentucky frontier. Kentuckians were responsible for the destruction of Delaware towns on the Muskingum in 1781 and the massacre of Christian Indians who returned to their fields on the Tuscarawas River the next year.[19] In 1782, Kentuckians also directed an unsuccessful attack on the Wyandot towns at Sandusky, Ohio, and destroyed Shawnee villages on the lower Miami River near modern Piqua.[20] Retaliatory raids of the Indians took a toll in Kentucky. Many scores remained unsettled from this separate frontier vendetta.

As a result of the local developments during the latter years of the American Revolution, the Indian society of which Coocoochee was a part increasingly became multitribal. In addition to the Shawnee villages, Delaware,

Wyandot, and Mingo gathered on the Mad River, along with contingents of Cherokee warriors and visiting Creek delegations. In 1786 the entire inter-tribal region on the headwaters of the Great Miami became the major objective of resolute Kentuckians. The white militia had become formidable during the course of the American Revolution. Kentucky's population rose from a few hundred in 1775 to more than thirty thousand by 1786.[21]

The post-Revolutionary phase of hostilities in the Ohio country drew into active combat Coocoochee's two youngest sons, White Loon and Black Loon, along with others of a new generation of young warriors. But the combined Indian manpower of northwest Ohio was unable to prevent Benjamin Logan's Kentucky expedition in 1786 from destroying crops, gardens, and homes in Blue Jacket's town and nine others on the Mad River.[22] Coocoochee's family and neighbors fled to dispersed hunting grounds, the only safe refuge under these circumstances.

Emerging from a winter in an isolated hunting camp, Coocoochee and her husband built their next home among Blue Jacket's warrior families at a new base of operations, the Miami Towns, at present Fort Wayne, Indiana. During 1787, Delaware and Shawnee groups moved from Ohio to the Miami country, establishing new towns in the locale where the St. Joseph and St. Mary's rivers unite to form the Maumee, a stream flowing northeastward into Lake Erie at Toledo, Ohio.[23] For Coocoochee, her third home in the west may well have brought feelings of nostalgia. A small French population lived at Fort Miami, a fur trading center long in existence at the Miami Towns; and Canadian volunteers manned the small British post. Other residents included a few British traders and a silversmith connected with mercantile firms at Detroit.[24]

The Shawnee community adjacent to the Miami Towns was located on the Maumee River a few miles east of Fort Miami. Indian people often visited the trading town, and traders circulated among the Indian villages and hunting camps to collect furs. Through some of these connections, Coocoochee's daughter became acquainted with George Ironside, a highly respected trader at Fort Miami, and soon lived with him as his wife. An unusual figure in the rough and competitive trading world, Ironside had received a university education at Aberdeen before entering the fur trade in America.[25] The marriage alliance received Coocoochee's enthusiastic approval.

The three years that Coocoochee spent near Fort Miami from 1787 to 1790 were critical in her personal life history. At first it seemed as though the omnipresent threat of attack by Kentuckians might come to an end. In the spring and summer of 1787, the leading Shawnee war chiefs, Blue Jacket and Captain Johnny, rounded up white prisoners in the Indian country and arranged a peace conference and prisoner exchange at Limestone (now Maysville), Kentucky. Daniel Boone hired wagons to bring Shawnee prisoners from Danville and paid for food and drink as well as musical entertainment at the great peace convocation in July.[26] The speech by Captain Johnny, who said that the villages at the Miami Towns were now peaceably inclined, as well as the speech by Benjamin Logan, who said that Kentuckians were interested in trade but not territory north of the Ohio, were printed in the *Kentucky Gazette*.[27] Momentarily, peace rather than war appeared imminent.

The actions of the newly consolidated American federal government during 1787 were more ominous. In New York plans were developed to organize the Northwest Territory, including Ohio's Indian country, and to sell large blocks of land there for immediate settlement. The laying out of new town sites on the north bank of the Ohio River, and the establishment of Fort Washington in 1790 at fledgling Cincinnati forecast a problematic future for the Indian allies gathered at the Miami Towns.[28]

In the fall of 1790, the first large military expedition under General Josiah Harmar set out for the allied towns at the head of the Maumee River. Warned in advance, the Indian people fled to the woods, but again their homes, fields, and food stores were put to flames, except for supplies that could be consumed by the under-provisioned soldiers. The Indians nevertheless administered a severe defeat to Harmar's retiring army.[29] In this engagement, with fierce hand-to-hand fighting using tomahawks and bayonets, Coocoochee's husband, Cokundiawsaw, was mortally wounded. He lived only a few hours after the battle, and was buried near the banks of the Maumee River.[30]

Although some of the Indians immediately rebuilt their homes at the Miami Towns, and one faction of Shawnee and Delaware took refuge in Spanish Louisiana, Coocoochee and her remaining family joined the staunchly militant Indian contingent that moved sixty miles down the Maumee River to establish the next allied headquarters at a place called "The Glaize."[31] The distinctive name of French origin referred to the steep clay banks, earlier a noted buffalo wallow, at the juncture of the Maumee and north-flowing Auglaize rivers (now present Defiance, Ohio). Coocoochee's solitary dwelling at The Glaize was centrally situated among the Indian towns that moved soon after Harmar's defeat.[32] She lived a mile west of Blue Jacket's town and three miles east of Little Turtle's town. Within a few miles were two more Shawnee and two Delaware villages, as well as a traders town of refugees from Fort Miami.[33]

Overlooking the north bank of the Maumee River, Coocoochee's house commanded a view of the entrance of the Auglaize River and along several miles of wooded scenery in the Maumee bottom lands. Directly across the river, her daughter and George Ironside occupied a three-room log cabin with a loft that served as a combined dwelling, store, and warehouse. This was the largest establishment in the small trading community.[34] Wapanoo and his wife built their cabin in a Shawnee and Delaware settlement that straggled along the east bank of the Auglaize River, south of the trading town.[35] White Loon and Black Loon were also married and lived in Blue Jacket's town a mile downstream from Coocoochee's home.[36] The two grandchildren Coocoochee had raised continued in her care.

A more detailed description of Coocoochee's life as a widow, once more in unfamiliar surroundings, indicates the resources she had developed and the status she had achieved by the time she survived more than fifty winters of frequently hazardous existence. In physical appearance, Coocoochee was of medium height but somewhat stout, and consequently awkward in her movements. She was customarily attired in a long calico shirt fastened in front with a silver brooch, a skirt of blue cloth with white edging belted at the waist with a striped sash, matching blue cloth leggings, and deerskin moccasins.

When withdrawn in her private world of contemplation, Coocoochee's features appeared stern and forbidding, but she was also capable of sociable conversation, exchanging anecdotes, and showing a great interest in all the events going on around her. Throughout the nearby villages, Coocoochee was esteemed for her skill in preparing and administering medicines, and for the power of her incantations which gave her insight into the future. War leaders generally consulted her before starting out on any important expedition, and she shared the spoils of their victories.[37]

A woman of great physical vigor, Coocoochee at times was sensitive and compassionate, but always was capable of soul-stirring emotional energy. At middle age, she viewed her own past and future in the context of the long stream of existence of all her people, a panorama of experience that evoked a kaleidoscope of visions, ranging from depressing to inspiring. Often her thoughts dwelled on the larger world of events that had produced the present circumstances of her life. In this darker mood, she recalled the traditional accounts handed down by her ancestors on the St. Lawrence River, who had seen the first landing of the pale-faced people from their gigantic canoes with the spreading white wings. Motivated by insatiable avarice, these pale-faced people had rapidly grown in strength and power, and remorselessly continued to encroach on the land of the red men, who were weakened by disease, civil strife and extended warfare against the British and the "Long Knives" (Americans).

Coocoochee believed that these aggressive newcomers would not be satisfied until they had crowded the Indians northward to perish in the Great Ice Lake, or pushed them westward until those who escaped their rifle fire would drown in the Great Western Sea. The Great Spirit was obviously angry with the red people, particularly those of her own Mohawk nation who were severely reduced in numbers. In her most melancholy moments, Coocoochee felt that she and her children were the only remnants of her race, and feared that when they went to sleep in the ground, nobody would be left to gather their bones for a proper celebration of the Feast of the Dead.[38]

In a more optimistic frame of mind, Coocoochee joyously contemplated the distant spirit land, the rewarding future of all the brave and good members of her nation. This beautiful realm, ten times larger than the entire American continent, lay far beyond the western ocean. There, the changing seasons brought no extremes of heat or cold, wet or drought, and nobody became sick, old, or incapacitated. Corn and beans, pumpkins and melons grew spontaneously from the earth, along with trees laden with delicious fruits. The meadowlands were perpetually green, and fragrant flowers bloomed continuously; springs were clear and cool; the deep, gently flowing rivers held endless varieties of fish; and the woodlands were stocked with innumerable herds of buffalo, deer, rabbits, and every species of game, with open patches for a variety of berry bushes. Projecting above this scene were trees larger than anyone had seen before, trees spreading their leafy branches high among the stars. This paradise, exclusively for Indian people, contained everything imaginable to gratify the senses and delight the mind.[39]

Although Coocoochee's spiritual and healing abilities gave her a special status in the community, her everyday life followed a pattern common to all women of her situation. The bark cabin in which she lived was constructed in a fashion typical of homes in all the surrounding villages. The framework over the fourteen by twenty-eight foot area was constructed of small saplings. Some were planted firmly in the ground to serve as posts and studs supporting the ridge poles. Others were tied to the skeletal frame with thongs of hickory bark, making girders, braces, and rafters. The exterior covering of the cabin consisted of large pieces of elm bark seven or eight feet long that had been pressed flat to prevent curling, fastened to the poles with more hickory thongs. The narrow doorway scarcely six feet high opened on the western wall of the cabin. When the entrance needed to be closed off, it was blocked with another large sheet of bark held in position by braces.

The interior of the original cabin was a single common room, bordered on two sides by frame couches covered with deerskins and blankets that served for sitting and sleeping space. On the ground in the center of the room directly under the smoke opening in the roof was the fireplace. Over it, a wooden trammel, suspended from a ridge-pole, supported a cooking kettle. Coocoochee's household possessions varied little if any from those used by pioneer white women all across frontier America. She had a large brass kettle for washing and for boiling sap during sugar-making season in the spring. A second kettle of copper was deep and close-covered for preparing hominy, the basic Indian dish of corn softened by soaking with wood ashes. She also had a few knives, pewter and horn spoons, wooden bowls, tin cups, woven sieves, a variety of baskets, and a block for pounding corn.[40]

Coocoochee's personal supply of worldly goods, and in fact the capital wealth of all the allied Indian towns, was increased with the supplies brought back in November, 1791, when General Arthur St. Clair's army expedition from Fort Washington was soundly defeated in a battle about seventy miles south of The Glaize.[41] Intensely prosecuted Indian warfare in 1791 and 1792 also brought many captives to the towns, adding an interesting variety to local society at The Glaize.

In the spring of 1792, a prisoner of incredible strength and agility, William Moore, was brought from the Ohio River shore to Blue Jacket's village, a mile from Coocoochee's cabin. Because of his formidable physical prowess, demonstrated before he was finally taken captive, Moore ran the gauntlet with his hands tied. In spite of this handicap, he bounded so swiftly between the lines of stick-wielding Indians, using his knees, heels, and elbows so adroitly, simultaneously swinging his head with great force, that his opponents were knocked about on both sides. Coocoochee had great admiration for Moore, who repaid her kind attitude by building an addition to her home. The second room often served as a pantry and spare bedroom but was also used as her private sanctuary for spiritual ceremonies.[42]

For seven months, beginning in July, 1792, Coocoochee's family included a young captive, an intelligent and resilient eleven-year-old lad named Oliver Spencer, whom White Loon had taken during a reconnaissance tour along the Ohio River near Cincinnati. Although she at first did not relish the added responsibility, the hungry boy with a badly scratched body and blistered feet was too pitiful to be ignored. Overcoming the problems of language communication, Coocoochee directed Oliver to bathe in the river, then lie on a blanket in the scorching sun for three or four hours. Meanwhile, she boiled a strong potion of red oak, wild cherry bark, and dewberry roots, which Oliver drank frequently and occasionally used to soak his feet. Within a few days, he felt perfectly cured.[43]

The chief event in Coocoochee's life during the spring season of 1792 was her observance of the Feast of the Dead, an occasion for reburial of her husband's remains. The new grave was placed a short distance from her dwelling, near the warpath from Detroit crossing the Maumee River and leading toward the Ohio River. In this location, Coocoochee could communicate with her husband, and his spirit could be invigorated by viewing the warriors as they went on their military expeditions, until his probation period was over and he traveled to his final abode in the delightful spirit land.

Cokundiawsaw was buried in a sitting posture, facing west, accompanied by all the material objects necessary for a warrior and hunter: his rifle, tomahawk, knife, blanket, and moccasins. Friends attending the ceremony tossed in other articles, presents for his journey. At the head of the grave they placed a red-painted post about four feet high, with the image of a face carved near the top, and underneath marks for the nineteen scalps he had taken in battle. On important occasions thereafter, scalps with hair of different length and color could be seen attached to a long, slender pole, swaying in the wind over his grave.[44]

A second important occasion for Coocoochee was the Green Corn Ceremony performed about the middle of August. This harvest festival, commonly observed from the Caddo country of East Texas to the Creek towns in Florida, was also an annual event for the Shawnee. The all-day celebration at Coocoochee's home began with serious oratory in the morning, then continued after a midday meal with games, dancing, and drinking. Participants included Coocoochee's daughter and George Ironside, her three

sons and their wives, a few other Shawnee families, and the captive William
Moore. Following the custom of Indian gatherings, the morning ceremony
began with the ritual of passing a pipe around the circle of seated participants. Highlight of the morning was a speech by a respected elder who first
thanked the "Great Spirit" for the generous gifts they all had received and
later shouted defiance against the "pale faces" who were encroaching on Indian land. To climax his rhetorical display, the elder exhorted the warriors
to drive back the "Big Knives" to the region south of the Ohio River. This
inspiring finale brought the audience to their feet with shouts of approval.
Shortly they turned to sports events.[45]

Footraces were first on the schedule, followed by a series of wrestling
matches and a special test of strength in retaining a grip on a slippery length
of greased leather thong. In preparation for this portion of the festivities,
William Moore had built a viewing stand behind Coocoochee's cabin. This
structure consisted of a raised platform with a rear wall and roof to shield
the older guests from the sun as they watched the athletic events. As a special privilege, Moore was allowed to join in the wrestling competition and
managed to throw one of the leading Shawnee contestants. This dangerous
victory he managed to dismiss as a lucky accident rather than evidence of
superior strength, since he knew that it was clearly unwise to demean his
captors' physical ability.[46]

Coocoochee had prepared a feast for all her guests. She served fish, venison, boiled "jerky" made from dried beef, stewed squirrels, squashes, roast
pumpkins, and several varieties of corn dishes. These included succotash
made of corn and beans, corn on the cob, corn bread, and a batter poured
into cornleaf molds and baked in the ashes of the fire. Eating utensils were
wooden bowls and spoons fashioned from wood, horn, or tin.[47]

Following a short interval of after-dinner smoking, a small keg of rum
was brought out and passed around. When the liquor appeared, the men immediately gave all their knives and weapons to Coocoochee for safekeeping
before continuing with the sports events. Among all Indians, this precaution was taken before commencing a "frolic" in order to prevent personal
injury as a consequence of clumsy or quarrelsome drinking behavior. Later
in the afternoon, the recreation turned to social dancing led by a traditional
singer who accompanied his own songs with the rhythmic beat of a small
drum, adjusting the tempo for each number. Forming two circles, men and
women circulated in opposite directions.

By evening, when the Green Corn Festival reached the last stage of an intoxicated revel, William Moore, George Ironside, and young Oliver Spencer had all departed. At the last moment, White Loon challenged a fellow warrior to one more wrestling match and was severely burned when he was thrown into the fire, a misfortune that brought the day's celebration to a sudden halt.[48]

Although sharing a jug of rum had become an established custom at all major social functions, Coocoochee and other Indian women were occasionally terrorized by the behavior of their male relatives as a consequence of a private drinking bout. The most frightening sound to drift through the night air was the disjointed song of a weary reveler, giving warning as he proceeded erratically on the homeward trail. Living in an isolated location, Coocoochee was seldom troubled, but one late-winter evening her son Black Loon came close to bringing tragic violence to her home. Her young prisoner Oliver Spencer, whom she had come to regard as a son, unfortunately had offended Black Loon. Returning from a "frolic" at Little Turtle's Miami village, located about four miles up the Maumee River, Black Loon veered off the river path toward Coocoochee's cabin, with vengeance in mind.

Alerted to potential danger by the approaching sound of the drunken "ki-ou-wan-ni" refrain, Oliver sprang from his bed, seized a blanket and dashed outside to crouch behind the house. In his hiding place, he heard Black Loon thrust open the door and inquire his whereabouts. When Coocoochee insisted that the boy was absent, Black Loon in a demented rage slashed his knife through the deerskins on Oliver's bunk, then seized the sleeping cat and threw it into the fire, holding the poor animal on the coals with his foot. Coocoochee pushed her son aside, grabbed the shrieking and dying cat, threw it outside into the snow, and then sent Black Loon on the path toward Blue Jacket's town. Fortunately, such a dreadful incident occurred very seldom.[49]

In the general exchange of hospitality, Coocoochee often visited friends in the neighboring villages of "The Glaize" region, accompanied by the three children who were part of her household. Late in July, 1792, they all attended a reception at Blue Jacket's home, a special occasion on his return from an extensive diplomatic journey among the tribes farther west. Blue Jacket's town consisted of perhaps thirty or forty bark cabins housing a population of about three hundred people. Vegetable gardens and pasture lands for horses and cattle lay behind the town, while the extensive acreage of unfenced cornfields were across the river separated from potentially marauding livestock.

Blue Jacket himself was a handsome man, dignified in bearing. His wife was half-French, the daughter of a Shawnee woman and Colonel Duperon Baby, prominent Detroit resident and former Indian agent.[50] Blue Jacket maintained a broad range of contacts among the regional Indian tribes, French inhabitants, and British officials in Detroit and Montreal.

Notable guests at Blue Jacket's reception were The Snake, chief of the Shawnee town nine miles further down the Maumee River, and Simon Girty of the British Indian department.[51] Captured by the Seneca as a child, Girty was one person in the gathering who might be able to communicate with Coocoochee in her native Mohawk, since both Indian nations spoke very similar Iroquoian languages. Thoughtfully considering his reputed earlier connection with her daughter, Coocoochee still preferred to avoid the hardy veteran of frontier warfare, identified by whites as an infamous renegade who led the Indians against his own compatriots.

Simon Girty's appearance at the age of fifty-three would make him conspicuous in any group. He had a dark, shaggy head, low forehead, sunken gray eyes, heavy eyebrows meeting at the bridge of a short flat nose, and thin and compressed lips—features combined to present a forbidding appearance. He was clad in Indian attire, but lacked the decorative ornaments and heavy silver earrings usually worn by Indian men. Knotted about his head was a silk scarf, pulled low over one eye to conceal an ugly scar. Girty inferred that it came from a sabre wound at St. Clair's defeat; but according to local reports, he had been struck with a tomahawk wielded by the Mohawk leader Joseph Brant, about whom he had made disparaging remarks following a joint expedition across Ohio in 1781. Even at Blue Jacket's social event, Simon Girty wore a pair of silver-mounted pistols stuck handily in his belt, and by his side hung a short dirk that served the ordinary purposes of a knife.[52]

Aside from her periodic visits to Blue Jacket's town, Coocoochee often crossed the Maumee River to see her daughter and George Ironside.[53] For Coocoochee, it was a joy to see her daughter happily married to a kind and humane man, who thoughtfully provided presents for his mother-in-law. Occasionally she traveled a few miles further up the Auglaize River past the trading town to see Wapanoo. She was troubled by the fact that her eldest son was sometimes given to surly moods which his wife bore with considerable grace and patience.[54]

Much of the satisfaction of Coocoochee's day-by-day existence came from the children in her household. In 1792, Sotonegoo at the age of thirteen was a cheerful girl with laughing eyes. Her half brother, whom Coocoochee called Simon although his mother had given him a Mohawk name, possessed the characteristic energy of a ten-year-old and had grown somewhat willful and headstrong due to his grandmother's indulgence. Oliver Spencer made a place for himself in the family group, sharing the responsibilities divided among the three children. These included keeping the horse out of the five-acre corn field, gathering firewood in the oak and hickory forest on the table land behind the cabin, washing the lye from the corn to make good hominy, gathering berries, and tending the vegetable garden.[55]

In early spring time their sugar-making equipment was loaded on the horse and taken a few miles away to a rude shelter set aside for this purpose. In a good season, they produced more than a hundred pounds of maple sugar, which was carefully stored in small packages. The children had their ball games, pastimes, and recreation, too. The boys could practice their skill with a reed blowgun or shoot fish with arrows in the clear water of the Maumee. Oliver Spencer became a practiced hunter, and once with the aid of the family dog brought back a huge wild cat. Coocoochee devoted considerable time to his proper education. He soon learned Shawnee, and appreciated the traditional tales she recounted during a winter's evening. She also taught him Indian dances, and laughingly ridiculed the English country dances and hornpipes he performed for her.[56] Although she clearly thought Oliver would remain with her, messages circulated throughout the British and American settlements resulted in arrangements for his return to his family by way of Detroit. He left shortly after the maple sugar season of 1793.[57]

In the early fall of 1792, prior to young Spencer's departure, the tempo of life in Coocoochee's neighborhood changed rapidly from languid summer leisure to bustling activity as preparations were under way for an intertribal council of great import. Over a thousand allied Indians were gathering around Captain Johnny's Shawnee town, located on the east bank of the Auglaize River about a mile south of the traders' town. Cheerful refrains of *voyageurs*' songs floated up from boats on the Maumee transferring provisions from the British base at the Maumee rapids to a storehouse in the trading community opposite Coocoochee's home. The French baker could scarcely keep up with the demand for bread. After a series of preliminary conferences and ten days of deliberations, the council decided to insist on the Ohio River boundary line for white settlement, although pioneers had already advanced along the northwest side into present-day Ohio.[58]

The intertribal council at The Glaize was followed by an interlude of buoyant optimism for Coocoochee and her people. In mid-October, spies reported that supplies were being transported under strong convoy to the three American outposts north of Cincinnati. The Indians immediately organized a joint force of two hundred Shawnee and Miami warriors under the leadership of Little Turtle, the Miami who had directed the defeat of General St. Clair the previous year. On their way to join the Miami camped near the traders' town, White Loon and Black Loon, along with a contingent of fifty Shawnee from The Snake's and Blue Jacket's towns, stopped at Coocoochee's cabin to get her opinion concerning the prospects for their military enterprise.

Acceding to their request, the old woman retired to her private room for nearly an hour of communion with her sources of spiritual power. Above the low humming of her voice, sticks could be heard striking the cabin walls and iron kettles. When she reappeared, wildly excited expressions animated her countenance. Her message was conveyed partially with a grand gesture. Standing before the Shawnee war party, she stretched out both arms at her sides and slowly drew her fingertips together to form a circle of maximum circumference. At the same time she exultantly exclaimed "Meechee! Meechee! Meechee!," repeating the Shawnee adjective signifying "great." The Shawnee confidently joined the rest of the warriors, interpreting this revelation as a forecast of "Many scalps, many prisoners, and much plunder."[59]

The expedition returned a month later after a victorious encounter with Kentuckians and American troops near Fort St. Clair, fifty miles north of Cincinnati. The booty included a good many horses as well as tents, kettles, blankets, and staple foods. White Loon and Black Loon were among the fortunate possessors of fine new horses. Grateful for the inspiring aid she had given them, the Shawnee brought to Coocoochee six blankets, several pounds of tobacco, and a small keg of whiskey.[60]

By the next year, the portents for the future of Coocoochee's people were not encouraging. The fateful decision to maintain the Ohio River boundary line for white settlements was affirmed in 1793. General Anthony Wayne's carefully planned campaign against the Indians at The Glaize, outlined in 1792, was drawing to a climax. In mid-summer of 1794, "The Big Wind," as Indians called General Wayne, sent his troops northward on the warrior path that crossed the Maumee River near Coocoochee's home. Warned by a deserter, the Indian people were able to flee down the Maumee River, where the warriors regrouped for a final encounter and were defeated in August at the Fallen Timbers, near Perrysburg, Ohio. On the site of the trading town, Wayne built Fort Defiance. All the Indian towns and the cornfields lining the shores of the Maumee were set afire, and the former inhabitants became dependent upon the British Indian department for food, dispensed at a refugee camp on Swan Creek on the outskirts of modern Toledo, Ohio.[61]

The subsequent life of Coocoochee, the Mohawk medicine woman living among the Shawnee, is a matter of conjecture, although fragments of information have come to light concerning her family and associates. George Ironside's next home was near Malden on the Ontario side of the Detroit River, where he later became British Indian Superintendent. This was very likely the residence as well of Coocoochee's daughter, for Ironside's son later stated that his mother came from a Shawnee community.[62] Black Loon and White Loon spent the early years of the nineteenth century in the Shawnee towns of northwestern Ohio, centered at Wapakoneta on the upper Auglaize River. Black Loon died during the War of 1812, in which he served in the American forces; White Loon lived at least to the 1830s, maintaining regular contact with Oliver Spencer, who became a prosperous resident of Cincinnati.[63]

Coocoochee may have stayed with any branch of her family, or perhaps lived at Blue Jacket's next town, located near a Wyandot community on the Detroit River at present-day Gibralter, Michigan. Blue Jacket himself died about 1811. Probably Coocoochee joined her husband in the spirit land before she found herself living in still another warpath; the Detroit River became a war zone in 1812.

During her most active years, Coocoochee's life displayed an outward pattern of periodic refugee existence, as she was recurrently buffeted by the advance of frontier warfare. Despite many vicissitudes, she drew on inner strength to preserve a way of life that had meaning and integrity in the tradition of her people. Although her warrior husband was killed at the prime of life, her four children and her grandchildren remained close to her, mutually reinforcing the family ties so highly valued in Indian society. In addition, Coocoochee achieved a position of respect and influence in the multitribal society into which her life was cast—an ultimate personal triumph.

Appendix

Oliver M. Spencer was about eleven years old in 1792 when he was captured near Cincinnati by Coocoochee's son, who brought the child to her. Spencer was returned to his family after seven months living with her, and later he became a Methodist Episcopal minister. This account was written about 1834 for publication in the periodical The Western Christian Advocate. *Readers will notice that although Spencer framed his narrative in his Christian point of view, as a child he acknowledged Coocoochee's spiritual power and recognized the importance of religion in her life, although his language disparaged her beliefs, as was typical of narratives written for this type of audience. However, readers will note that Coocoochee's personality, parenting style, and interpretation of history are evident in this text, as is her method of helping Spencer to assimilate into the culture through dance, and her amusement and even revulsion at elements of Euro-American culture.*

The Indian Captivity of O. M. Spencer, *ed. Milton Milo Quaife (Chicago: Lakeside Press, 1917), 77–81, 115–17, 119–22, 126–27, 171.*

Cooh-coo-cheeh, the old squaw in whose charge Wawpawmawquaw had left me, being in that advanced stage of life in which we seek for rest and quiet, apprehending no doubt from my squalid appearance and diseased state an increase of her cares and labors, at first received me with reluctance; but surveying my emaciated form and examining my scratched and festered limbs, my swelling feet, retaining when pressed the print of the finger, and my toes, from the friction of the sand collected in my moccasins in frequently fording creeks, raw and worn almost to the bone, her pity was excited, some of the dormant feelings of the mother were awakened, and she soon began to apply herself to my relief. Having first effected at the river a complete ablution of my person, she proceeded to wash my clothes, in the meantime compelling me to lie on a blanket for three or four hours under the scorching sun until my back was one entire blister; then boiling a strong decoction of red oak and wild cherry bark and dewberry root, of which I drank frequently, and in which I occasionally soaked my feet for several days, she effected in a short time a perfect cure.

She was a princess of the Wolf tribe of the Iroquois formerly living on the Sorel. Her person, about the ordinary stature, was stout and clumsy; her features were rather homely and her expression generally harsh and repulsive, though at times when her thoughts were withdrawn from the deep and weightier matters of futurity, or when, no longer conversing with the spirits of other worlds, she felt that she was an inhabitant of this and resumed her interest in its concerns, she was cheerful and occasionally quite sociable, relating many pleasant stories and amusing incidents of her early life. She was, besides, a sort of priestess to whom the Indian applied before going on any important war expedition, inquiring whether they should be successful; and from whom they generally received answers framed in such obscure and ambiguous terms so to confirm and increase her reputation, even when an expedition was most disastrous. Cooh-coo-cheeh was also esteemed a very great medicine woman, eminently skilful in the preparation of specifics believed to be of great efficacy, but whose extraordinary virtues were more particularly attributed to her powerful incantations and her influence with the good spirits, with whom she professed to hold daily intercourse.

Her husband had been a distinguished war chief of the Mohawks. . . .

After this signal defeat [likely in a Revolutionary War–era battle] and loss of the Mohawks, the husband of Cooh-coo-cheeh with his family, consisting of his wife, three sons, and a daughter, had removed from the St. Lawrence and settled at the Shawnee village a mile below the mouth of the Auglaize. In the victory of the Indians over a part of the army of Harmar under Hardin and Wyllys, in October, 1790, in a furious charge made against the regulars, while in the act of tomahawking a soldier he received a mortal wound from a bayonet, and dying on his way home was buried on the bank of the Maumee about twenty miles from the battle-ground.

Soon after his death his widow chose her residence and erected her bark cabin on the spot not occupied by her; and having only a few months before, at the feast of the dead, with pious affection removed the remains of her late husband from their first resting place, interred them only a few rods above her dwelling, near to the war path, so that not only she might enjoy the happiness of conversing with him, but that his own spirit might be refreshed from viewing the warriors as they crossed the Maumee on their war expeditions, until having ended his probation and being prepared for his journey, he should travel to the final abode of good spirits in the land far west, abounding with game, and enjoy all those several delights which in the mind of an Indian constitute heaven. . . .

About the middle of October the Indians, learning through their spies that either an expedition against some of their towns was contemplated by the Americans or that provisions were on their way to supply the outposts under a strong convoy, soon assembled a force of two hundred warriors (Shawnees and Miamies) under the celebrated Little Turtle and marched to attack them. On their way to join the Miamies, who had encamped near the point, the two Loons and about fifty Shawnee warriors from Snake's town and Blue Jacket's village halted near our cabin and sent to consult Cooh-coo-cheeh about the success of their expedition. The old woman immediately entered her sanctuary, where she remained nearly an hour, during part of which time, sitting under the shed, I could hear the noise as of a stick striking the sides of the cabin and the beds and particularly the kettles within it; and afterward a low humming sound of the voice, at which time I supposed she was uttering her incantations. Coming out soon after with a countenance unusually animated, though with a look of great wildness, she stretched out both arms and then gradually bringing the tips of her fingers together as if encircling something exclaimed, 'Mechee! mechee! mechee!' which the Indians, instantly interpreting to be 'Many scalps, many prisoners, and much plunder,' reported to the party, who, flushed with the confident expectation of success, immediately proceeded to join the main body.

I had never before seen so large a force of Indian warriors, and while I could not but admire their fine forms and warlike appearance as they marched in single file to the river or stood erect in their canoes, with their rifles in their hands, crossing the Maumee, I shuddered at the thought of the lives that would be taken and the hundreds that through their instrumentality would soon be made widows, orphans, and childless. Young as I then was I could not help at times looking on the old woman with superstitious fear, mingled with awe. I did not believe that she was divinely inspired, but thought it more than probable that she held intercourse with evil spirits; nor was that fear and awe lessened when about the middle of November the Indians under Little Turtle returned victorious, having defeated a body of troops, principally Kentuckians (or Semonthe, as they termed them) near Fort St. Clair, taking several scalps, a large number of horses, and a great deal of baggage. Wawpawmawquaw and his brother had each a good horse and a number of new blankets; and some of the Indians packed home tents, camp kettles, and many other articles. The Shawnees gave Cooh-coo-cheeh six blankets and several pounds of tobacco, besides a small keg of whiskey (part of their spoils) in gratitude for the aid which they doubted not she had afforded them in achieving their victory; while their late success, if possible, increased their confidence in her supposed supernatural power.

[*Spencer and the family dog killed a wildcat while out collecting firewood.*]
. . . Leaving my wood and shouldering my prize I marched home, and with no small exultation threw my load down before Cooh-coo-cheeh, who, raising her hands with surprise, exclaimed, "Waugh haugh-h! Pooshun!" It proved, indeed, to be a large male wild cat; an animal equally insidious and dangerous, according to its size and strength, as a panther; and which, but

for the presence of the dog and my ignorance of its nature and of my danger, might have destroyed me. This exploit, with which the old woman associated great courage and daring, raised me very much in her estimation. She heard all the particulars of the affair with great satisfaction, and frequently saying, "Enee, wessah" (that is right, that is good), said I would one day become a great hunter, and placing her forefingers together (by which sign the Indians represent marriage) and then pointing to Sotonegoo, told me that when I should become a man I should have her for a wife.

I had now acquired a sufficient knowledge of the Shawnee tongue to understand all ordinary conversation and, indeed, the greater part of all that I heard (accompanied, as their conversation and speeches were, with the most significant gestures); and often in the long winter evenings listened with much pleasure and sometimes with deep interest to Cooh-coo-cheeh, as she told of the bloody battles of her nation, particularly with the Americans; of the great prowess of her ancestors; their chivalrous exploits and "deeds of noble daring," or related some interesting events of her early life; her courtship and marriage; the great strength, bravery, and activity of her then young husband, Co-kun-di-aw-thah, and her own youthful charms. Her memory seemed a great storehouse out of which she brought "things new and old." In almost all her tales, however, whether tragic or mirthful, whether of great achievements in the battle and in the chase, or whether relating some diverting incident or humorous story, she mingled many superstitious ideas and spoke much of supernatural agency and of her own frequent intercourse and conversation with departed spirits. To the beaver she not only gave the faculty of reason, but the power of speech; and I shall ever recollect the song, said by her to have been sung by a beaver to an almost desponding hunter, stayed by a freshet and half starved; encouragingly telling him that the high waters would soon subside and that beyond the stream he would find plenty of game—

Sawwattee sawwatty,
Sawwattee sawwatty,
Sawawkee meechee noo kakoohonny;
Kooquay nippee ta tsa;
Waugh waw waugh whaw,
Waugh waw waugh whaw.

Cooh-coo-cheeh took much pains to teach me to dance; an accomplishment not so easily acquired as from the great simplicity of their steps might at first be supposed; grace with them consisting principally in the motions of the body; the action of their limbs being rather adapted to facilitate and perfect these (and not, as with us, at least in former days, the chief exhibitors of grace and skill) and it required much practice to combine both successfully. Having seen my elder instruct my younger sister in dancing, I had learned several steps, particularly the balancer and single and double chasser, and sometimes for the amusement of Cooh-coo-cheeh I gave her a specimen of the manner of our dancing. With the slower and more simple steps she seemed to be amused, occasionally laughing heartily at what to her appeared so ludicrous; but when I attempted a hornpipe, whirling around frequently, or capered along in a double chasser, so ridiculous did it appear to her, manifesting, as she thought, such a want of grace and dignity that usually with some marked expression of contempt she put a stop to my further exhibition.

... That evening she seemed more than usually disposed to converse with me, and repeating her inquiries about my parents, their rank in society, how long they had lived on the Ohio, and many such questions, asked me particularly of the place of their former residence; and when I told her that they once lived not far from the seashore, and near New York; and that their forefathers were English, who came from the Islands on the eastern side of the great salt lake, south and east of us, her brow for a moment seemed deeply clouded and the mournful tones of her voice betrayed her mingled feeling of melancholy and regret. She spoke of the first landing of the 'pale-faces' from their monstrous canoes with their great white wings, as seen by her ancestors; of their early settlements, their rapid growth, their widely spreading population, their increasing strength and power, their insatiable avarice, and their continued encroachments on the red men; who, reduced by diseases, thinned by civil wars, and diminished by their long and various struggles, first with the British (Met-a-coo-se-a-qua) then with Se-mon-the (the Americans or Long-knives), were no longer powerful; and that they would not be satisfied until they had crowded the Indian to the extreme north to perish on the great ice lake; or to the far west until, pushing those who should escape from their rifles into the great waters, all would at length be exterminated. She spoke of the anger of the Great Spirit against the red men, especially those of her own nation, nearly all of whom had perished; and that herself and her children, the remnant of her race, would soon sleep in the ground, and that there would be none to gather them at the feast of the dead or to celebrate their obsequies.

. . . Nearly forty years have since passed away; our rivers teem with commerce; their banks are covered with farms, with houses, villages, towns, and cities; the wilderness has been converted into fruitful fields; temples to God are erected where once stood the Indian wigwam, and the praises of the Most High resound where formerly the screams of the panther or the yell of the savage only were heard. O, 'what hath God wrought!' But where are the friends and companions of our youth? Our parents, where are they? Mine have long since 'slept with their fathers.' Wawpawmawquaw, who only a short time since had for several years previously paid me an annual visit, has gone to the land of his fathers, and almost all of those of whom in my narrative I had spoken are no longer 'dwellers upon earth.'"

Notes

1. Gary Nash and David Sweet, comp., "Cucuchi, Curandera," in *La Lucha por Supervivencia en la America Colonial* (Mexico, D.F.: Fondo de Cultura Económica, 1987).

2. Biographical sketch of Coocoochee is reconstructed from basic information in Oliver M. Spencer, *The Indian Captivity of O. M. Spencer*, ed. Milo M. Quaife (Chicago, 1917; reprint, New York, 1968). Young Spencer at age eleven lived in Coocoochee's home in northwestern Ohio from July 1792 to February 1793.

3. In 1758 a Delaware chief forcefully voiced the Indians' objections during a council with a British emissary: "D——n you, why do not you and the French fight on the sea? You come here only to cheat the poor Indians, and take their land from them." Christian Frederick Post, "Two Journals of Western Tours [1758]," in Reuben Gold Thwaites, ed., *Early Western Travels* (New York, 1966), 1:212.

4. Howard H. Peckham, *Pontiac and the Indian Uprising* (Chicago, 1961), 41-43. Braddock's defeat during his expedition against French-held Fort Duquesne (present Pittsburgh) on July 9, 1755, was a factor in strengthening French influence among Indians for the balance of the warfare, which continued to 1761.

5. Spencer identified her people as "the Wolf tribe of the Iroquois formerly living on the Sorel" (Spencer, *Captivity*, 77). The name "Sorel" was given to the present-day Richelieu River flowing northward in New York from Lake Champlain to enter the St. Lawrence River northeast of Montreal, Quebec. See Samuel Holland, "A Map of the River St. Lawrence (1773)," MS. Crown Collection, 119:23, photostat, The Newberry Library, Chicago.

6. For details of these campaigns, see Edward P. Hamilton, *The French and Indian Wars* (New York, 1962), 182, 195–99, 291–304. Although intercolonial warfare began in 1754, war in Europe was not officially declared until after the fall of Minorca in 1756, the date marking the beginning of the Seven Years' War, which ended with the Treaty of Paris in 1763.

7. All four children were born before 1770. Spencer, *Captivity*, 79. The only grandchildren reported by Spencer were those of her daughter who apparently was the eldest

of her children. Key dates in Coocoochee's personal life are estimates based on Spencer's observations and general information about Indian marriage and family patterns.

8. The boundary established by the Treaty of Fort Stanwix (present Rome, New York) was considered definitive by Indian people, although British military leaders doubted its enforceability. American authorities confirmed the boundary at the outset of the Revolutionary War in treaties signed at Pittsburgh. Repercussions in the Ohio country are interpreted by Randolph C. Downes, *Council Fires on the Upper Ohio* (Pittsburgh, 1940), 141–43.

9. Spencer erroneously assumed that Coocoochee's family came directly to Blue Jacket's town, located in 1792 on the Maumee River about a mile east of present-day Defiance, Ohio. Since only Ottawas were living on the lower course of the Maumee River at that time, it is reasonable to assume that the family went to the town where Blue Jacket lived in 1770, on Deer Creek in the Scioto River valley. Blue Jacket's residence is noted by David Jones, *A Journal of Two Visits Made to Some Nations of Indians on the West Side of the River Ohio in the Years 1772 and 1773* (Burlington, 1774; reprint, New York, 1865), 52.

10. Thomas Hutchins, "The Route from Fort Pitt to Sandusky, and Thence to Detroit," in Charles A. Hanna, *The Wilderness Trail*, 2 vols. (New York and London, 1911), 2:204. For map location see Helen Hornbeck Tanner and Adele Hast, "Indian Villages, Ohio, Pennsylvania and New York, 1760–1794," in Lester Cappon, ed. *Atlas of Early American History* (Princeton, 1976), 21. Information on the Shawnee towns is summarized by Erminie Wheeler-Voegelin, "An Ethnohistorical Report on the Indian Use and Occupancy of Royce Area 11, Ohio and Indiana," in Helen Hornbeck Tanner and Erminie Wheeler-Voegelin, *Indians of Ohio and Indiana Prior to 1795*, 2 vols. (New York, 1974), 2:145–48.

11. Jones, *Journal*, 55–56.

12. Downes, *Council Fires*, 11–12.

13. Helen Hornbeck Tanner, "The Greenville Treaty," in Tanner and Wheeler-Voegelin, *Indians of Ohio and Indiana*, 1:90–94. For complete documentary history, see Reuben Gold Thwaites and Louise Phelps Kellogg, eds., *Dunmore's War* (Madison, 1905).

14. American and British leaders urged Indians to remain neutral until 1777. Tanner and Wheeler-Voegelin, *Indians of Ohio and Indiana*, 1:96–97.

15. New locations of the towns of the Shawnees and their allies, principally in Logan County, Ohio, are mapped by Tanner and Hast in Cappon, *Atlas*, 21. For descriptions of towns, see Tanner and Wheeler-Voegelin, *Indians of Ohio and Indiana*, 2:651–53.

16. The girl was an "orphan," age thirteen in 1792. Spencer, *Captivity*, 82. Shawnee warriors suffered casualties during two major periods of hostilities in 1780: (1) British and Indian expedition that captured 350 Kentuckians at Ruddells and Martins Stations in May, and (2) retaliatory attack on Chillicothe near present-day Xenia, Ohio,

and Piqua on the lower Mad River in October. Charles Gano Talbert, *Benjamin Logan, Kentucky Frontiersman* (Lexington, 1962), 105–16.

17. As a child, Simon Girty was a captive of the Seneca; his brother James lived with the Shawnee. They later became Indian traders and deserted American-held Pittsburgh to serve the British Indian service in Detroit. Simon was considered the leading renegade. Consul W. Butterfield, *History of the Girtys* (Cincinnati, 1890), 8–15, 47–51, 74.

18. Rev. David Jones met James Girty in the Shawnee country in 1773. Jones, *Journal*, 60. In 1783, James Girty established Girty's Town at present-day St. Mary's, Ohio.

19. Louise Phelps Kellogg, *Frontier Retreat on the Upper Ohio, 1779–1781* (Madison, 1917), 378–79. The death of ninety pacifist Moravian Indians is known as the "Gnadenhütten Massacre." Consul W. Butterfield, *An Historical Account of the Expedition against Sandusky* (Cincinnati, 1873), 36–38.

20. Butterfield, *Expedition*, 63, 151–52, 216–17. Major DePeyster to General Haldimand, Detroit, January 7, 1783, *Michigan Pioneer and Historical Collections* 20 (1892): 87; Talbert, *Benjamin Logan*, 172–76.

21. Talbert, *Benjamin Logan*, 18, 239.

22. Simon Girty to Capt. A. McKee, October 11, 1786, *Michigan Pioneer and Historical Collections* 24 (1895): 34–35.

23. Major John Hamtramck to W. Sargeant, July 20, 1790, Winthrop Sargeant Papers, Massachusetts Historical Society, transcript in Ohio Valley–Great Lakes Ethnohistorical Archives, Indiana University.

24. A vivid account of the trading community at Fort Miami and nearby Indian towns was written by Henry Hay, "Journal of Henry Hay," ed. Milo M. Quaife, *Wisconsin Historical Society Proceedings* (1914): 208–61. The silversmith was John Kinzie, an important trader at Chicago in 1812. A. T. Andreas, *History of Chicago*, 3 vols. (Chicago, 1884–86), 1:100–102. Blue Jacket also had a residence. Antoine Gamelin, "Journal," in W. H. Smith, ed. *The St. Clair Papers*, 2 vols. (Cincinnati, 1882), 2:157.

25. Hay, "Journal," 332 n. 77.

26. Talbert, *Benjamin Logan*, 219–20.

27. *Kentucky Gazette*, August 25, 1787, photostat from Lexington Public Library by University of Michigan Library, 1918, copy in The Newberry Library, Chicago.

28. Following passage of the Northwest Ordinance in 1787, Marietta was established at the mouth of the Muskingum River in 1788, and settlements were founded near present-day Cincinnati in 1788 and 1789. Samuel P. Hildreth, *Pioneer History* (Cincinnati, 1848), 193, 207, 223. The federal government tardily made plans in 1788 to purchase from the Indians lands already being settled. Tanner and Wheeler-Voegelin, *Indians of Ohio and Indiana*, 1:118–21; Henry Knox, Secretary of War, to the President of the United States, June 15, 1789, *American State Papers*, Class 2: *Indian Affairs*, 2 vols. (Washington DC, 1832), 2:13.

29. Josiah Harmar to Henry Knox, November 23, 1790, Harmar Papers, vol. 11, pp. 16–28, Letter 8, Clements Library, Ann Arbor; *American State Papers, Indian Affairs*, 2:132–34.

30. Spencer, *Captivity*, 80–82.

31. The migration to Spanish Louisiana was noted by the trader Francois Vigo. Vigo to Sargeant, April 12, 1792, Winthrop Sargeant Papers, Massachusetts Historical Society, transcript in Ohio Valley–Great Lakes Ethnohistorical Archives, Indiana University. See also Zenon Trudeau to Louis Lorimer, May 1, 1793, in Louis Houck, ed., *The Spanish Regime in Missouri*, 2 vols. (Chicago, 1909), 2:51.

32. The area of present-day Fort Wayne, Indiana, was gradually abandoned by the Miami and their Shawnee and Delaware allies. They were dependent on the British for supplies in the winter of 1791–92. Alexander McKee to John Johnson, January 28, 1792, *Michigan Pioneer and Historical Collections* 24 (1895): 366.

33. Spencer, *Captivity*, 85, 89, 95, 111, 116. Delaware communities are described by Hendrick Aupaumut, "A Narrative of an Embassy to the Western Indians," ed. B. H. Coates, *Memoirs of the Historical Society of Pennsylvania* 2, pt. 1 (1827): 97–99.

34. Spencer, *Captivity*, 95–96.

35. Spencer stayed overnight at this dwelling before being turned over to Coocoochee. Spencer, *Captivity*, 74.

36. Spencer, *Captivity*, 89, 111.

37. Spencer, *Captivity*, 77–78, 87.

38. Spencer, *Captivity*, 120, 127.

39. Spencer, *Captivity*, 128.

40. Spencer, *Captivity*, 83–84, 86–87.

41. General St. Clair's account of his defeat at present-day Fort Recovery, Ohio, is in *American State Papers, Indian Affairs*, 2:137–38. The incident is regarded as the most humiliating defeat ever suffered by an American army. Loss is stated as 630 out of a total force of 1,400. Reginald Horsman, *Matthew Elliott, British Indian Agent* (Detroit, 1964), 68–69.

42. Spencer, *Captivity*, 97–98, 100–101.

43. Spencer, *Captivity*, 41–44, 77.

44. Spencer, *Captivity*, 80–82.

45. Spencer used the terms "Great Spirit" and "pale face" in his interpretation of the speech. Spencer, *Captivity*, 102–4.

46. Spencer, *Captivity*, 105–6, 111–12.

47. Spencer, *Captivity*, 106–7.

48. Spencer, *Captivity*, 112–13.

49. Spencer, *Captivity*, 111.

50. Lyman Draper, interview with Nanette Caldwell, Draper Mss. S17, 176 (1863), Wisconsin Historical Society, Madison.

51. Spencer, *Captivity*, 90–91.

52. Spencer, *Captivity*, 92–93.

53. Spencer, *Captivity*, 95–97.

54. Spencer, *Captivity*, 74–75.

55. Spencer, *Captivity*, 123.

56. Spencer, *Captivity*, 117–21, 125–26.

57. Spencer, *Captivity*, 126, 129.

58. Young Spencer was apparently unaware of the magnitude of the council that took place so close to Coocoochee's home. Capt. Hendrick, who brought an American peace message to the confederated tribes, reported his reactions. Hendrick Aupaumut, "Narrative," 117. The British Indian agent, Alexander McKee, sent minutes of the deliberations to his superiors after the meetings were ended on October 7, 1792. McKee, "Proceedings of a General Council of Indian Nations," *Michigan Pioneer and Historical Collections* 24 (1895): 483–98.

59. Spencer, *Captivity*, 115–16.

60. Spencer, *Captivity*, 117.

61. Richard C. Knopf, ed., *Anthony Wayne: A Name in Arms* (Pittsburgh, 1960), 351–55.

62. George Ironside to Mudge, April 11, 1831, Record Group 10, Indian Affairs V, p. 569, Public Archives of Canada, Ottawa. This information was provided by James A. Clifton, University of Wisconsin–Green Bay.

63. Spencer, *Captivity*, 111, 171.

8. Leadership within the Women's Community

Susie Bonga Wright of the Leech Lake Ojibwe

REBECCA KUGEL

New Introduction by Rebecca Kugel

I first encountered Susie Bonga Wright as a historic figure when I was conducting research for my dissertation on nineteenth-century Ojibwe political life. That was in the early 1980s, when the field of Native American history had just begun the florescence that continues to the present. Conventional historical wisdom at the time held that the documentary record contained few references to Native peoples, and that almost no writings by Native peoples themselves existed. I encountered quite the opposite situation. In the Minnesota Historical Society archives in St. Paul, I found literally hundreds of documents written by Ojibwes, with further abundant materials written about Ojibwes by observant non-Natives. Susie Bonga Wright's two letters, plus references to her in the correspondence of others, were among the trove of source materials—letters, diaries, journals, interviews, newspaper accounts, court testimony, fur traders' ledgers, baptismal records—that I located.

With such a wealth of sources, I did not at first realize that the documents revealed the past selectively. Political issues predominated in Ojibwe correspondence—quite logically, I felt, because political concerns mattered greatly to nineteenth-century Ojibwes as the balance of power with the United States shifted and Ojibwes lost both political autonomy and economic security. There was an unintended gender dimension to this emphasis, however, since political diplomacy and negotiations, especially with outsiders, were conducted by Ojibwe men. Political leaders, too, were almost always men. Such a view of politics as exclusively a male domain might accord with Euro-American notions of appropriate gender behavior, but it did not adequately explain Susie Bonga Wright and her contemporaries, for the record made it clear that she was not a one-of-a-kind figure. The limits of my sources became obvious: the records identified Ojibwe women leaders and showed that they exercised forms of leadership that both paralleled and intersected with male leadership. But because the usual locus of their political activity was outside the spaces identified as political by Euro-Americans, these women were not recognized as the leaders they were and their activities were rarely described.

Ethnohistorical theory provided me with a context for framing these too-brief descriptions of a female political arena. Eleanor Leacock (1978) theorized gender relations in hunter-gatherer societies similar to the Ojibwes. She argued that gender relations in what she termed "egalitarian societies" were based on gender complementarity rather than gender hierarchy. The egalitarianism and personal autonomy in such societies applied to women as well as to men, Leacock argued; women "held decision making power over their lives and activities to the same extent that men did over theirs" (247). At the same time, complementarity suggested a substantial degree of gender segregation in work roles. Such circumstances clarified Susie Bonga Wright's activities on behalf of the Ojibwe Women's Meetings. She acted within an Ojibwe tradition of gender complementarity in politics, where men and women, as complements that made up the social whole, met separately to discuss current events and make decisions, which they expressed in later joint meetings. References in my sources to joint sessions of the Men's and Women's Meetings confirmed this.

A second work of ethnohistorical theory, Clara Sue Kidwell's article on Native women as cultural mediators (1992), also contributed to my understanding of Susie Bonga Wright. There was ample cultural and historical evidence that Ojibwe women viewed themselves as cultural mediators of the kind Kidwell was describing. Growing up and assuming a leadership role at a time of social innovation and change, Bonga Wright could understand her work as a mediator between Ojibwe women and their Euro-American Episcopalian allies as part of the culturally appropriate work she, as an Ojibwe woman, had been raised to perform.

My exploration of Susie Bonga Wright's life was my first effort to reconstruct Ojibwe women's history, and one of my major concerns was to locate Bonga Wright within an Ojibwe cultural context. I think ethnohistory, with its combined anthropological and historical emphases, worked well in allowing me to reconstruct her leadership activities. As I reread the article for this volume, however, I wondered what insights feminist theory could bring to the lives of Ojibwe women. The documentary record, even when abundant, still tends to slight Native women; any methods that allow us to tease out Native women's experiences from these sources are worth investigating.

References

Kidwell, Clara Sue. 1992. "Indian Women as Cultural Mediators." *Ethnohistory* 39 (spring): 97–107.

Leacock, Eleanor Burke. 1978. "Women's Status in Egalitarian Society: Some Implications for Social Evolution." *Current Anthropology* 19 (2): 247–55, 273–75.

Leadership within the Women's Community
Susie Bonga Wright of the Leech Lake Ojibwe (1997)

Historically, the lives of Native American women have been misunderstood by the dominant society.[1] They have been characterized as oppressed and powerless drudges (the "squaw" stereotype) or as exotic and compliant helpers of the male European colonizers (the "princess" stereotype). In recent years, numerous scholars, both Native and non-Native, have issued calls to move beyond this inadequate polarization and reexamine the lives and work of Native women.[2]

Perhaps no realm of female activity is less accessible than leadership. There is great irony in this, for Europeans and, later, Euro-Americans, were struck by Native women's political presence and participation. Along the eastern coast of North America, the earliest English colonizers encountered women in positions of leadership. John Smith made note of the "Queene of Appamatuck" in his first communications; the Puritans likewise observed that the leader of the Massachusetts confederacy, on whose lands they had established their colony, was a woman, the "squa-sachim of Puckanokick." In the eighteenth century, John Adair, an English trader in the Southeast, disparagingly described the Cherokees as "under petticoat government," and long before Adair's complaint that Cherokee women exercised too much political power, both English and French colonists had come to recognize and respect the political influence of Iroquois women. In addition, and of particular interest to this study, there exists in the early nineteenth century a remarkable portrayal of Netnokwa, a female political leader in a multiethnic Ojibwe-Odawa community.[3]

Yet the Europeans and Euro-Americans who were so keenly aware of Native women's influence and participation in public councils rarely recorded—and presumably, were rarely aware of—other forms of female political activity that took place away from council meetings. In part this is due to the fact that the interests of Europeans and Euro-Americans, revolving largely around trade relations, diplomacy, and military affairs, were issues concluded in the council meeting forum. They had little reason to look elsewhere, to other social groups or social settings. From this situation numerous questions arise concerning Native women's political participation. For instance, were Native women's political expressions confined only to the public councils? Were certain women recognized as leaders among women, within kinship groups such as clans or extended families? How were such female leaders selected, and what were their responsibilities? And of course, how did Native women's political activity vary between tribal groups?

This chapter examines, within a specific tribal setting, a form of female political activity outside the realm of the public council. Given the scanty documentary record respecting women's activities, this work can provide only a partial glimpse, and raises questions it cannot answer. Yet in revealing, however imperfectly, the political activities of Native women from a particular tribal background, the Minnesota Ojibwes, at a particular point in time, the last quarter of the nineteenth century, it suggests much about the range of political activity in which Native women engaged, and, perhaps more important, the goals their political actions were meant to achieve.

Susie Bonga Wright, from the Minnesota Ojibwe community of Leech Lake, emerges from a small selection of documents in the 1870s and 1880s as a leader and spokeswoman for an important female constituency within her community. Bonga Wright's actions offer a view into the functioning of a distinct women's community, but they also allow an examination of the ways in which women's leadership was challenged and channeled by the growing dominance of Euro-American society. While only sketchily portrayed in the documents, her personal life reveals additional information that illuminates her leadership role, both in its traditional and innovative dimensions. Further, her life, as a person of mixed African and Ojibwe ancestry, the daughter of an influential fur trader, also lends itself to an examination of the changing intersections of race, class, and gender.[4]

Like other midwestern Indians, the Ojibwes understood gender relations as complementary. Men and women were social halves that made up a whole. To Ojibwe minds, this was clearly demonstrated economically on a daily basis—male hunters provided the meat portion of the family's diet, and female farmers contributed the products of the earth: grains, vegetables, and fruits. An obvious component of Ojibwe gender complementarity was the significant sex segregation of male and female work. This is not to say that men and women worked in isolation from each other, for this was not ordinarily the case. Indeed, men and women often worked in physical proximity to one another, but on gender-specific aspects of a task. What gendered work roles do indicate is that the Ojibwes perceived women and men as having differing areas of expertise and interest.[5]

Not surprisingly, given the gender-segregated organization of much of Ojibwe life, women and men formed separate political councils. One Ojibwe community made this division explicit in 1882, identifying "two persons as our leaders[,] one for the men & the other for the women." These two political bodies met together to create community policy, with the leader of the women's council presenting female opinion "to the men at their Meeting." While only the female leader, or *ogimakwe,* spoke, in keeping with Ojibwe political protocol, all other interested women could and did attend these joint meetings.[6] Ojibwe women also operated independently as a political entity. Assuming that Euro-Americans also divided political activity along gender lines, they worked to establish connections with organizations they understood to be Euro-American women's councils. In 1878, for instance, three prominent Ojibwe women wrote the wife and daughter of the Indian agent, emphasizing the "very pleasant feelings [that] have existed between us."[7]

Ojibwe women also addressed issues within their communities. In the 1820s, for example, a visitor observed that when the Leech Lake community had obtained alcohol and a general village revel was taking place, it was "the usual practice" for the women to confiscate all weapons and police the community while the men drank, preventing the intoxicated from injuring themselves or others. Such female drinking patrols existed in Ojibwe communities until at least the 1870s.[8]

Yet the most ubiquitous circumstance under which Ojibwe women organized themselves involved coordinating and directing their daily and seasonal work, much of which was performed in groups. The work of farming, gathering wild foods, and processing all foodstuffs; the construction of housing; and the manufacture of clothing, bedding, domestic containers, and utensils; not to mention child care, required women to organize and lead their activities. One female leader, Susanna Roy, discussed her work coordinating the labor of other women, organizing "the women [to] work making things."[9]

This most mundane level of activity may well have been the most important, however. The daily environment of a work group provided an obvious forum for political debate, and indeed, in the work group setting, Ojibwe women discussed issues and formulated their opinions. As late as the 1890s, missionary worker Pauline Colby observed that the work groups remained the arena for Ojibwe women "to discuss all affairs of interest to them." Echoing descriptions of more formal council meetings, Colby noted the egalitarian nature of these political discussions. Any woman might "rise and make an address" to the others, Colby noted, and all opinions were given "respectful attention." Susie Bonga Wright's career likewise demonstrates the significance of the work group for female leaders. While she participated in the multiple layers of female political activity, "speaking for" her supporters in a variety of contexts and regularly communicating with interested Euro-American women, the work group remained a central focus of much of her political activity.[10]

Born around 1850, Susie Bonga grew to young adulthood during some of the most difficult times the Ojibwes had known. Pressured by the growing physical and economic dominance of the United States during the 1850s and 1860s, the Minnesota Ojibwes had ceded most of their lands in the Treaty of 1855. The results had been calamitous. The reduced and fragmented land base could not sustain the older hunting/gathering and trapping economy, and the Ojibwes slid rapidly into poverty. Economic and social decline were accompanied by bitter political divisions, as Ojibwe communities split over strategies for dealing with the growing American presence. Unable to sustain themselves from the land, the Ojibwes found themselves increasingly dependent on cash payments from the U.S. government. This dependence, they learned to their dismay, made them increasingly vulnerable to additional American demands, both for more land cessions and for the dramatic cultural changes Euro-Americans called "civilization."[11]

American policy respecting Native Americans in the mid- to late nineteenth century involved the near-complete transformation of Native people. Federal government policymakers and well-meaning Euro-American reformers envisioned a two-pronged program simultaneously involving conversion to Christianity and the adoption of an idealized variant of American agrarianism, a cluster of cultural attributes that Euro-Americans called "civilization." The Ojibwes (indeed, all Native Americans) were to embrace private property, especially with respect to landholding, and accept a market economy with gender roles for men as wage-earning farmers and women as housekeepers who did not earn wages for their societally undervalued housework. Political matters were to be decided by a majority of the adult males. Ojibwe children were to attend schools where the civilized values would be sternly inculcated. On more visible and daily levels, the Ojibwes were to adopt the housing, clothing, foods, and language of Euro-Americans.[12]

In the face of this onslaught, the Ojibwes, including the people of Susie Bonga's village of Leech Lake, sought to preserve what they regarded as their cultural core. Daily manifestations of Euro-American culture such as housing and clothing styles did not concern them deeply. Indeed, as the Ojibwes had been involved in the fur trade since the 1600s, they had already adopted many items of Old World material culture. What the Leech Lakers struggled hard to preserve were a series of intangibles, valued and distinctive cultural attributes, ways of thinking and behaving that were sharply at odds with Euro-American cultural norms and expectations. They sought to continue their political decision-making process along aboriginal lines, basing decisions on unanimity rather than majority rule, and including both women and men as political participants. They further struggled to maintain an economic system based on egalitarian redistribution of resources contributed by both sexes rather than the private accumulation of wealth controlled by men. Beginning in the 1850s and gaining widespread support by the 1870s, sizable numbers of Ojibwes sought to turn the "civilization" program into a weapon they might wield in their own defense. Hard pressed to find means of self-support now that the resources of their former land base were denied them, the Ojibwes were particularly interested in the possibilities that increased reliance on agriculture seemed to promise.

At the same time, the Ojibwes also sought to cultivate ties with those groups of Euro-Americans heavily involved in administering the government's programs. Prominent in creating and administering the federal Indian policy were several Christian denominations and a host of religiously inspired individuals, a policy innovation begun during the presidency of Ulysses S. Grant. Deeply concerned about injustices toward Native peoples, determined to eliminate the near-legendary fraud and corruption of the Indian Office, such well-connected "friends of the Indian" could be mobilized in defense of Native interests.

Toward this end, important political leaders, their family members, and influential supporters on several Ojibwe reservations formally converted to Episcopalianism, the denomination that had maintained a presence in

Ojibwe country during the midcentury decades. At Leech Lake, in July 1880, the sister of the premier village leader, Flat Mouth, led an initial group of thirty-nine converts from notable families. Prominent among them were the Bongas, with ten family members, including Susie, converting.[13]

If the decades of Susie Bonga's youth had been difficult, the late 1870s and early 1880s were exciting times. Their adaptive revitalization strategy, the Ojibwes believed, was succeeding. They were learning a range of valued skills, from literacy in English to the mechanical knowledge to operate farming equipment. Conflicts with their Euro-American Episcopal friends, who decidedly did not envision an enduring Ojibwe cultural or political existence, had yet to arise. Instead, the two groups could focus on the obvious overlap in their goals. Euro-Americans and Ojibwes threw themselves into the work of constructing churches and organizing congregations. More compelling, from the Ojibwe perspective, were the simultaneous efforts to create the infrastructure they would need to become subsistence farmers. Land had to be cleared, plowed, and planted in Euro-American fashion with draft cattle and farm machinery; barns, outbuildings, and farmhouses had to be built; and the Ojibwes had to learn to equip and maintain these possessions, on which their new lifestyle was to be based.

The Episcopalians, like other denominations, advocated conventional Euro-American gender roles for Native peoples, and focused most of their time and energy on transforming the lives of Ojibwe men. They paid far less attention to Ojibwe women. Indeed, efforts to transform women's roles were often understood only within the larger context of altering male work. The Episcopalian head missionary, Joseph A. Gilfillan, a Euro-American, argued that as long as Ojibwe women continued their traditional subsistence pursuits (including agriculture), men would never accept their proper role of family provider. Once women were made into "housekeepers," however, Ojibwe men would be forced to adopt the corresponding male work of farming. Also suggestive of Episcopal priorities was the fact that they supported no female missionaries, who might reasonably be expected to focus their attention primarily upon Ojibwe women, for the first forty years of mission work.[14]

Nor were the wives of male missionaries to involve themselves in active proselytizing. Joseph Gilfillan made clear his feelings on the work proper for the sexes. Having determined that he and his wife could not both perform missionary work and maintain a household, he advocated a conventional and biblically sanctioned division of labor. Her husband, Harriet Cook Gilfillan recollected, "agreed with the Apostles that 'it is not meet for us to leave the word of God and serve tables.'" Rather than split the household work, "he took the 'Word' and she the 'tables.'" The Gilfillans regularly invited "for supper" "all the good Christian Indians . . . and their wives," with the goal of showing them "a Christian home." Prominently in evidence within that home were the proper male and female spheres. If Native men were to become yeomen farmers, Native women were being offered a familiar vision of female domesticity; they were to become Victorian True Women.[15]

Ojibwe women as well as men discovered that, in seeking to adapt the Euro-American civilization program to their own ends, they needed to learn a daunting range of new skills and work roles. Susie Bonga Wright and her contemporaries began living in log or frame houses equipped with heavy furnishings in place of their mothers' easily cleaned and easily transported bark *wigiwams*. They ceased to manufacture basic household items such as storage containers, dishes, and other cooking and eating utensils from forest resources, relying instead on more-fragile crockery that had to be carefully cleaned and maintained. They began cooking on woodstoves instead of open-pit fires, and they had to learn to process and prepare a range of new foodstuffs. As the Ojibwes began wearing Euro-American-style dress, women sought to learn to construct, clean, and maintain clothing and bedding made of wool and cotton instead of tanned animal skins. Ojibwe women evidently pursued knowledge of their half of the new agrarian lifestyle with an enthusiasm that initially gratified the Euro-American missionaries.[16]

It is in this environment of creative cultural adaptation that Susie Bonga Wright's leadership can be observed within the several arenas that constituted the female community. Deeply committed to the Ojibwe-directed program of social adaptation, Bonga Wright exemplified personally many of the qualities Ojibwe women sought to acquire. She had learned to maintain a household in such model fashion that she was judged "a very good housekeeper" by no less an authority than the patriarchal Joseph Gilfillan. She also had "considerable" Euro-American-style "learning," so that she spoke English "pretty well" and could converse knowledgeably on polite subjects. While the local Euro-American populace praised Bonga Wright as "a very rare girl" for conforming to their image of feminine domesticity, the Ojibwes esteemed her personal characteristics that accorded with their own long-standing leadership ideals. Her "good sense" and "wisdom" were qualities the Ojibwes expected of their leaders, and the fact that her words

and actions were "regulated by the greatest prudence" was far more important in Ojibwe eyes than her "zeal in the cause of religion," which impressed
Euro-Americans.[17]

At the same time that the Ojibwes valued the traditional leadership qualities Susie Bonga Wright displayed, there was no doubt that Euro-American
approbation enhanced her leadership standing in the classic Métis role as
bicultural mediator or broker. Because of her housekeeping skills and good
reputation, the Indian agent had hired her for one of the few secure, responsible jobs available to Native women, "the position of Matron of the Indian
[boarding] school" at Leech Lake, and locally, "the white people think there
is no person like Susie." Bonga Wright built on such expressions of esteem
to forge important ties, both to members of the local Euro-American elite
and in the wider network of religiously oriented Indian reformers.[18]

Such a brokering role was not without its own unique difficulties, however. Euro-Americans assumed Bonga Wright's wholehearted commitment
to their policy of eventual Ojibwe social and cultural absorption into the
larger Euro-American society. The Ojibwes, in stark contrast, trusted Bonga
Wright as a broker because she shared their goals of preserving their cultural core and revivifying their communities. Bonga Wright's reputation
and social skills gave her an avenue to exploit on the Ojibwes' behalf, and
many of her actions contained "coded" messages, revealing her continued
commitment to Ojibwe goals despite her apparent support for Euro-American policies. The unequal power relations between Ojibwes and Americans
dictated that such actions had to be subtle, and Susie Bonga Wright excelled
at performing actions open to dual interpretation. In one representative instance, she and other Leech Lake women sent beaded moccasins to Bishop
Henry Whipple's wife, Cornelia. From an Ojibwe perspective, the act reiter-
ated an alliance, the giving of gifts symbolizing the ties renewed between
two female communities. Euro-Americans viewed such acts in quite a different light, understanding "articles of Indian manufacture" as a "faint expression" of Christianized Indians' gratitude toward their Euro-American
benefactors.[19]

While Susie Bonga Wright's public acts and persona were important in
demonstrating her leadership capabilities, the critical arena in which she
exercised leadership was that core unit of the female community, the work
group. Ojibwe women who supported the revitalization effort continued to
perform much of their work in groups, as Ojibwe women had historically
done, and the work group remained the forum in which they discussed com-

munity issues and formulated their opinions. Within this aboriginal political context, Leech Lake women also emphasized their continued commitment to the traditional Ojibwe political goal of consensual, unanimous decision making. "We are all agreed in all we say and do," wrote Bonga Wright and four other influential women in 1882, signifying unanimity by their action of affixing all their names to the letter as well as by their words.[20]

If the Episcopal-inspired adaptations were to succeed, the female work groups would have been a critical component in their success. First and foremost, if Ojibwe women were going to support the proposed innovations, that support would be created, then mobilized, within the work groups. Bonga Wright clearly understood this. She spent much time discussing the proposed adaptive strategy, "getting the Indian women into her room," and "explaining . . . to them" what the adaptations entailed, carefully building the unanimous consent the Ojibwes recognized as constituting a legitimate political decision.[21]

In addition, much of the knowledge of the new domestic skills would have been imparted in the work-group setting. Bonga Wright herself noted this, observing that the women "bring sewing in which they need help" to the Episcopalian women's meetings. The enthusiasm with which Ojibwe women from Leech Lake and other communities attended these women's meetings "to learn knitting sewing cutting &c" also indicates their interest in acquiring the needed new domestic skills.[22]

Less obviously but just as critically, Susie Bonga Wright's activities also reflect the ways the Ojibwes sought to turn the Euro-American civilization program to their own advantage. One of the most public and visible portions of her work, organizing sewing bees and prayer meetings among the Leech Lake women, reveals a distinctive female variant of that process, one all the more fascinating because, superficially, the activities she organized seemed to conform so closely to the ideal of domesticity that Euro-Americans sought to impose on Native women.

In the early 1880s, Bonga Wright and other Leech Lake Episcopal women had "begun the good work" of organizing a sewing circle. Bonga Wright assured Bishop Whipple that meetings always opened with prayer and that the women "do not seek *earthly* reward." The Episcopal hierarchy approved heartily and encouraged all Ojibwe converts to commence such women's meetings. Not only did sewing circles allow Ojibwe women to perfect their new skills of housewifery, but they also engaged them in appropriately female charitable work.[23]

Beneath the surface of Susie Bonga Wright's pious remarks, however, lies another, more significant layer of meaning. At the same time they sought to learn the new skills, Bonga Wright and the other Episcopal women reaffirmed their commitment to the traditional Ojibwe redistributive economy. The new-style Anglo-American clothing and bedding made at the sewing bees was "*carefully* given to the needy." The women sought to reinforce community solidarity and avoid partisanship. "We have tried," they wrote, "To be *impartial*."[24]

In addition to their commitment to group solidarity and the traditional economy, the Episcopal Ojibwe women stressed other desired forms of behavior. They reserved their highest praise for one of their number because "she never for an instant had an angry mind to any one." This anonymous woman won community approbation for her efforts to ensure group harmony: "[I]f any of them were at enmity between themselves there was she standing in the midst trying to bring them together again." At the same time admirable behavior was praised, reprehensible acts were roundly condemned. Selfishness, viewed with especial antipathy in Ojibwe culture, was vigorously denounced. Bonga Wright's contemporary, Susanna Roy, was excoriated in 1879 when she behaved selfishly. Women complained that Roy had "taken one whole piece of the print [cloth]" for herself when "she ought to have given it to the most needy poor."[25]

Further evidence that the women of Susie Bonga Wright's sewing circle were continuing an older form of Ojibwe female political activity comes from their involvement in larger community issues. The women "boldly spoke" their opinions on community issues, working to ensure continued Ojibwe commitment to the values of group solidarity and egalitarian distribution of resources within the new framework of "civilization." They continued their more overt political activities, too, regularly attending and speaking at community councils where the men frequently noted that "the women are heer [*sic*] to hear what we say." This was not at all to the liking of head missionary Gilfillan, who blasted female political activity as "an injurry [*sic*] to the cause of [the] mission."[26]

Gilfillan's opposition to continuing female political activity reveals much about Euro-American expectations for Ojibwe converts. The Ojibwes had a different perspective, though, which is revealed in the writings of Canadian-born Ojibwe-Odawa missionary, John Johnson Enmegahbowh. It was his interpretation of gender roles, not Gilfillan's, that the converted Ojibwes supported. Where Gilfillan insisted on separate spheres and female subordination, Enmegahbowh emphasized women's integral importance to community rejuvenation. He urged that Ojibwe women "not keep silence" regarding community concerns. In his writings he described women as emotionally strong and physically courageous, as more unflinchingly committed to community well-being than men, and as stalwart partners whose example inspired their mates. The women's meetings, he felt, were "doing much good." Quite clearly, the "pro-civilization" Ojibwes expected female political activity to remain much as it had always been, centered in the work groups and female political councils, and staunchly supportive of community-defined goals.[27]

During these same decades, as the Ojibwes anticipated certain outcomes from their adaptive strategy, they were frequently and jarringly reminded that they now inhabited a world largely not of their own making. In an ironic twist, Susie Bonga Wright found herself and her leadership credibility profoundly challenged, *not* from the female world of her supporters, but from men, both Euro-American and Ojibwe. The very nature of the challenge mounted against Bonga Wright indicated how much had been altered. This male intervention in a domain that had always belonged to women also involved a series of issues that had no precedents in Ojibwe society. To her apparent consternation, the critique of Susie Bonga Wright's leadership capabilities was centrally involved in an unfolding Ojibwe dialogue concerning "race."

For the first time in the 1870s and 1880s, the Ojibwes were forced to confront Euro-American notions of "race." The Ojibwes had intermarried for two centuries with the peoples of the Old World, majoritively with Europeans but with the occasional African as well. By the nineteenth century, the Ojibwe population possessed a wide range of physical characteristics. Ojibwes understood people to belong to a variety of ethnic and national backgrounds, and identified individuals accordingly as French, British, American, Ojibwe, Menominee, Odawa, Dakota, and so forth. Skin color and phenotype were not, however, determining factors in assigning an ethnic identity. Cultural characteristics—the clothing one wore, one's religion, and perhaps most important, one's economic pursuits—were a wiser guide, to Ojibwe minds. Thus the Ojibwes had long considered the literate, multilingual, fur-trading, Christian, Afro-Ojibwe Bonga family to be French. Susie's grandfather, Pierre Bonga, of full African ancestry, was a fur trader whose mother tongue was French; his half-Ojibwe son, George, a long-time trader at Leech Lake, had been educated in Montreal and spoke French in addition to Ojibwe and

English. Their "race," as Euro-Americans conceptualized that term, was a point of interest to the Ojibwes, but it was not grounds for assigning them an identity. The African American population of Minnesota remained quite small in the nineteenth century, and the Bongas apparently did not consider themselves part of an African American community. Susie Bonga Wright's generation evidently understood themselves to be Ojibwe. According to her sister, Nancy Bonga Taylor, "we call one another as Indians." When Euro-Americans attempted to impose their conceptions of "race," the result for the Bongas was bewildering and painful.[28]

The dialogue involving "race" commenced when young Charles T. Wright, recently widowed son of Wabanakwad, the respected "head chief" at White Earth Reservation, and himself one of the influential Ojibwe Episcopal deacons, consulted Joseph Gilfillan concerning "the propriety of . . . marrying Miss Susie Bonga." The Episcopal church hierarchy approved of the match, with Gilfillan characterizing her as "wise, chaste and [a] good religious young woman." For Charles Wright, however, there was a major "sticking point": Susie Bonga's African ancestry. While Gilfillan assured his superiors that Susie Bonga "shows the negro blood but little," her family was well known in Ojibwe country and her ancestry was equally well known. Charles Wright had "heard that white people look down on . . . those of negro blood," and this information concerned him. The Episcopal Ojibwes expected him to succeed his father to a preeminent leadership position, and Wright worried about his effectiveness as a leader if an injudicious marriage left him open to "the ridicule of his companions."[29]

The few documents detailing the courtship of Charles Wright and Susie Bonga illuminate striking differences of perception between the men who contemplated the "fitness" of the marriage. Susie Bonga's "race," newly defined, was a central issue, of course, but its significance was very differently understood by Ojibwe and Euro-American men. Gender roles and gender role adaptation were also weighted differently. Taken together, the discussions of "race" and gender also highlight the nature of the challenge to Susie Bonga's leadership, revealing how external to her sources of power and legitimacy it was. Significantly, the people *not* heard from in the nearly two-year period that the marriage was under consideration were Ojibwe women. Without a doubt they had opinions on the subject, but their voices evidently did not find their way into the documentary record. On that final level, the power differential between men and women in Euro-American society was also revealed, reminding the Ojibwes that while men and women were both affected by the considerable intrusive power of Euro-American society, they were not affected in the same ways nor in equal measure.

For the Episcopalian hierarchy and head missionary Gilfillan, any issues raised by Charles Wright's proposed marriage had to be considered in the context of the overall success of the Episcopal mission endeavor. Central to Episcopal plans for continued success was a program of grooming young Ojibwe men for the clergy. Commencing their careers as deacons, these carefully selected young men were to form a cadre of dedicated proselytizers who would expand the mission work begun by the earlier generation. In their personal lives, the deacons and their wives were to serve as shining exemplars of all the attributes of the Euro-American "civilization" policy. For Gilfillan, upon whose shoulders fell the actual work of fulfilling these expectations, creating exemplary family lives for the deacons was tremendously problematic, commencing with the difficulty of finding "suitable" wives.[30]

Two concerns, both reflective of differing Euro-American and Ojibwe female gender roles, loomed particularly large. First, it was extremely difficult to find "among the Indian girls of marriageable age" young women "known to be pure." Although the Episcopalians struggled mightily to instill Euro-American sexual mores, the Ojibwes of the 1870s and 1880s still regarded premarital sexual activity as normal and natural for young people. In the second place was the problem of finding young women sufficiently knowledgeable about Euro-American housekeeping to be able to maintain what the Episcopalians deemed an appropriate household. The Episcopalians especially wished the deacons and their wives to exemplify the new "civilized" lifestyle with respect to such visible behaviors as dress, eating meals seated at a table at regularly appointed hours, and living in appropriately furnished and neatly kept-up Euro-American-style houses. The work of maintaining these domestic examples, of course, fell to the deacons' wives. Very few young Ojibwe women in the 1870s and 1880s could meet both these criteria. That Susie Bonga could made her a very likely spouse for an Ojibwe deacon, in the minds of the Euro-Americans. Since her African ancestry did not "show" in her physical appearance, Gilfillan felt her "blood" was not "an insuperable bar" to the marriage. Her piety, "spotless character," and qualifications as a good housekeeper far outweighed her mixed "racial" background.[31]

Reflecting Euro-American society's understanding that class was predicated on race, Gilfillan dismissed Charles Wright's concerns about Susie

Bonga's African ancestry. As an Indian, Wright could never achieve social equality with Euro-Americans, regardless of his professional and educational attainments, and so it little mattered if his wife had "[N]egro blood." That Wright had such concerns, Gilfillan believed, stemmed from unfortunate class pretentions; he considered himself "gentry." What Wright needed, in Gilfillan's estimation, was to focus more on his mission work and less on his presumed high social status. Although women's housework was undervalued in Euro-American society, it was centrally important for creating the lifestyle the missionaries wanted the Ojibwes to adopt, and thus became for them the defining characteristic of what constituted a good missionary's wife. For Charles Wright, a pious Ojibwe woman skilled in housekeeping "would advance his work far more than any [other] wife he could find[,] Indian or white."[32]

Charles Wright, of course, understood the situation very differently. "[B]eing the son of the Head Chief and expecting to succeed" his father, Wright viewed himself first and foremost as a *political* leader. Not only his father but his grandfather had been a prominent political leader, and the Ojibwes were willing to grant Wright a leadership role if he proved himself capable. Retaining political control of their own communities was a crucial component in the Ojibwes' revitalization effort. While the Euro-American Episcopalians viewed the Ojibwe deacons as the next generation of fervent proselytizers, the Ojibwes understood these young men as a sophisticated new generation of civil leaders, whose ability to speak, read, and write English would enable them to articulate Ojibwe concerns and defend Ojibwe interests effectively. The deacons revealed their priorities when they complained that their English-language training was insufficient. It was not enough that they "could read the Ojibway Book." What they sought, they reminded Bishop Whipple, was to "understand English." Charles Wright deliberately linked his roles as Ojibwe political leader and Christian preacher in his correspondence, signing himself "Charles T. Wright, Son of Chief White Cloud."[33]

Given Charles Wright's commitment to the revitalization effort and the central role he expected to play in it, political considerations weighed heavily in his choice of a mate (although, as an *ogima*'s son with political aspirations of his own, they would have been important in more aboriginal times as well). Ojibwe politics were kinship-based, and the Ojibwes expected that the female relatives of a male political leader would assume positions of leadership among women. Three of Susie Bonga's contemporaries demonstrated that this pattern still operated in the 1870s and 1880s. At her own community, Ruth Flat Mouth, the sister of the premier civil leader, was prominent within the women's community. At White Earth, Susanna Roy was the daughter of one civil leader and sister to another; Oge zhe yashik, also from White Earth, was the wife of "the chief." An *ogima*'s wife, if she demonstrated the requisite abilities, could become an important figure in the female political community. In Charles Wright's thinking, a "suitable" wife would be able to galvanize the women's community in support of the revitalization strategy. In her life and actions, she would uphold the cultural attributes the significant adaptations were meant to protect and enhance. By the 1880s it was no longer enough to consider Susie Bonga's qualifications in the traditional leadership arenas. All too aware of Euro-American racial attitudes, Charles Wright had to wonder if Susie Bonga's African ancestry would prevent other Ojibwes, newly sensitized to the significance of "[N]egro blood," from taking her seriously as an *ogimakwe*. And would his own standing as a leader be jeopardized if he married a woman with African ancestry?[34]

As he contemplated how the Ojibwes would view his marriage to Susie Bonga, Charles Wright must also have considered the reaction of Euro-Americans. In spite of his innocent remark about "whites looking down upon negroes but not at all on Indians," Wright could not have been blind to the anti-Indian racism of the local Euro-American population. Discrimination and prejudice against Ojibwes ran the range from small daily humiliations to occasional lynchings and murders.[35] As leaders of a new generation of Ojibwes, the Episcopal deacons self-consciously presented themselves to Euro-Americans as "civilized" and "Americanized." Their claims to political autonomy and just treatment were grounded in the assumption that by accepting "civilization" and Christianity they had removed any differences between themselves and Euro-Americans. If the Ojibwes cast their lot with African Americans, even persons such as Susie Bonga, whose African ancestry did not "show" and who had no ties to an African American community, did they risk becoming identified with that most despised of American "racial" minorities? Much about their daily lives already bore a disquieting resemblance to the treatment accorded African Americans. To avoid being permanently relegated to the lowest and most oppressed racial status, many Ojibwe people sought to distance themselves from African Americans. In such a setting, the African American ancestry of some Ojibwes became, suddenly, enormously problematic.[36]

Susie Bonga herself was tremendously upset by the controversy her proposed marriage caused, informing Charles Wright that "it would be a death-blow to her" if the marriage did not occur. The Episcopalians understood this remark in their own cultural terms as the normal female reaction to a broken engagement, and Gilfillan "heartily wish[ed]" that, "for the sake of the poor girl," the marriage would go forward. Yet neither Susie Bonga's words nor her actions support such an interpretation of Victorian distress. She publicly expressed herself as having "set her mind on marrying Charles Wright," and she remained "determined to have him" in spite of the controversy. It is also highly significant that Susie Bonga was financially independent. With a (relatively speaking) well-paying job as Matron at the Leech Lake boarding school, plus some money of her own, probably from the estate of her recently deceased father, Bonga did not need to marry for economic security, and indeed, had not. In her late twenties at the time of Charles' initial proposal, Susie was not considered a particularly young woman, either by Ojibwe or Euro-American standards of the day. Given her own solid commitment to the Ojibwe-directed adaptations of the 1870s and 1880s, it seems likely that Susie Bonga had not married previously because she had not found a young man who met *her* standards.[37]

As she considered the marriage proposal of a prospective tribal leader, Susie Bonga, the daughter of a politically prominent family, must have anticipated that her leadership talents and qualities would be closely scrutinized. She probably also assumed, with some confidence, that she would acquit herself well. Her abilities included her success as a broker mediating with Euro-Americans plus her leadership within the women's work groups at Leech Lake. She was deeply disconcerted when discussion focused instead on her "racial" background, newly and negatively defined. Suddenly, in 1880, a racial category that had scarcely existed in previous years mattered more than her firm commitment to Ojibwe community rejuvenation and her impressive personal adaptations in pursuit of that goal. Seen in this light, her remark to Charles Wright that "it would be a death-blow to her" if they did not marry takes on a far more tragic meaning than the conventional interpretation of a broken heart that the Euro-American Episcopalians assigned to it.[38]

Susie Bonga and Charles Wright did eventually marry two years later, but only "after great toil & trouble" over the vexing issue of her African ancestry. Ironically, once the marriage occurred, the "racial" issue seems to have died down; and Susie Bonga Wright's leadership abilities were seemingly unaffected. As Charles Wright's wife she commenced her sewing circle, and it was during these years, the early 1880s, that the Episcopal women were most active in community rebuilding work. By the 1890s, as Bonga Wright reached her forties and achieved the greater status the Ojibwes accorded a mature adult with children, she seems to have solidified a position of even greater respect in both the Ojibwe and Euro-American communities. Yet it is perhaps a reflection of the earlier controversy that, by the 1890s, Bonga Wright did not use her Euro-American name. Instead, she was known to Euro-Americans, including missionaries who saw her daily, either by her Ojibwe name, Chimokomanikwe, or as "Mrs Nashotah," the latter being an anglicization of Charles Wright's Ojibwe name, Nijode. Perhaps her Euro-American name, especially her surname, Bonga, was too much a reminder of the uncertain social status accorded her family in the Euro-American world of the late nineteenth century, and as such, better quietly dispensed with.[39]

Susie Bonga Wright's life is by no means completely revealed in the documentary record. Nevertheless, those aspects of her life that do emerge offer important insights into the lives and experiences of Native women. Ojibwe women participated in the political decision-making process of their communities, and continued to have a voice in internal tribal affairs at a time when Euro-Americans granted them no place in the political structures they sought to impose on Native people. Equally striking is the important role Ojibwe women played in their communities' efforts to retain their cultural integrity and some semblance of autonomy in the face of Euro-American domination.

On a second level, Susie Bonga Wright's experiences, in particular her political activities, also provide insights into the experiences of other midwestern Native women. The Ojibwes were not unique among midwestern Native Americans in their efforts to control their interactions with Euro-Americans and to direct the processes of cultural change. Across the Midwest, Native peoples engaged in creative dialogue with representatives of Euro-American (and, in earlier periods, European) cultures. Religious issues, in particular making sense of Christianity, were major concerns of long standing. The work of Carol Devens notwithstanding, the process was more complex than simple acceptance by men and rejection by women. In *The Middle Ground*, Richard White reveals the complexities of midwestern Native people's perceptions and utilizations of Christian religious teachings. In one instance, he notes, Illinois women in the 1690s embraced Catholic teachings, especially worship of the Virgin Mary, to assert a set of regenerated community norms in a time of "warfare, direct cultural challenge by Jesuits, population decline and . . . widespread violence against women." In many respects, then, the efforts of Susie Bonga Wright and her contemporaries to use Christianity creatively as a weapon in their own defense had a long history in the Midwest. The actions of the Illinois women, nearly two hundred years prior to Susie Bonga Wright's own efforts, underscore as well the enduring importance of female political action in midwestern Native communities.[40]

A second aspect of Susie Bonga Wright's life, her changing "racial" status, speaks poignantly to issues of cultural contact that scholars of the Midwest are only beginning to examine. Tamara G. Miller observes that, in the early nineteenth century, the Midwest was characterized by considerable ethnic and cultural diversity.[41] This observation can certainly be extended to the region's Native American population, which comprised dozens of independent political and cultural entities. The fur trade–based Métis society that spanned the region was composite by its very nature. As Americans, people whose political allegiance was to the United States (however varied their own regional or ethnic background), came to dominate the region, however, they sought to impose, among other things, their understandings of "race" on the disparate populations they encountered.

Euro-Americans explicitly rejected the *cultural* categorization of persons that had marked Native and Métis societies. Instead, they attempted to assign racial statuses on the basis of biological "facts." Such physical characteristics as skin color, hair color and texture, and eye color became particularly important indicators of "race." Most significantly, Euro-American "racial" categories were exclusive; they rejected intermediary statuses. One could be "Indian" or "white"; one could not be both. Thus the bicultural and bi-"racial" Métis found no place for themselves within the Euro-American system of racial classification. The Bongas, along with other "mixed-blooded" families, struggled to understand the new categorizations and the new "racial" identities open to (or denied) them. Because their non-Native ancestry was African rather than European, the Bonga family faced unique challenges to their sense of ethnic identity. Susie Bonga Wright's bewildered pain at the controversy over her marriage underscores the human cost involved in the Euro-American effort to redefine "race."[42]

The complexities of race and ethnic identity in the Midwest are by no means resolved by this examination of the life of Susie Bonga Wright. Just as Bonga Wright's political activities provide only a glimpse into Native women's political participation, so, too, her struggles to comprehend Euro-American conceptions of "race" underscore how much remains to be done on this topic. Continuing scholarly examination of differing cultural conceptions of "race" promises to expand further our understanding of cultural diversity among all the populations of that allegedly most homogeneous of regions, the Midwest.

Appendix: Selections from the Minnesota Historical Society Archives
Document 1

Susie B. Wright, Kate Reese, Elizabeth —— *, Maggie Selkirk, and Ruth* —— *to Henry B. Whipple, September 22, 1882, H. B. Whipple Papers, Box 16, Minnesota Historical Society.*

> Leech Lake Sept 22d 1882
> Rt Rev H. B. Whipple
>
> Our dear Friend
> We write to tell you that we have begun the good work in which you wished us to engage. We are enjoying it very much. We have our prayer meeting first and then engage in work—We are now well engaged in the work and enjoy it much. We meet at the house of those for whom we ~~are~~ have arranged to work—some bring sewing ~~as~~ in which they need help—There are of the very aged who need help 20. And the children of those who belong to the church number 34. One of our church members a grand son of George Bonga, is nearly blind. He is 25 years old. We are all agreed in all we say and do—and we all join in sending our love and gratitude.
> We are all strong in the Lord to do his work—and we hope the Lord will be with us always helping us in all our work for him.
> We do not seek *earthly* reward reward [*sic*] for this service—but only hope and pray that we may be able to serve the Lord that he will bring all to himself when he has done with us here.
> We all join our names
>
> > *Sus[i]e B. Wright*
> > *Mrs Kate Reese*
> > *Mrs Elizabeth* ——
> > *Mrs Maggie Selkirk*
> > *Miss Ruth* ——

We are very glad to add that the Indians are all very quiet now and are gathering cranberries

We wish we could tell you how much we love each other and how much we love you

Document 2

Susie B. Wright, Kate Reese, and Elizabeth —— to Henry B. Whipple, March 11, 1883, H. B. Whipple Papers, Box 16, Minnesota Historical Society.

Leech Lake March 11th 1883
Rt Rev H. B. Whipple

Our dear friend
We write to tell you that the goods you send came safely. We waited before writing till we had made up into garments the cloth sent. All were made happy—not only those who recd [received] garments but those of us who had the pleasure of making them and distributing them.

We have not yet given all as some are yet away.

We have *carefully* given to the needy what we had to given [*sic*]—trying to wisely distribute.

We *think* you would approve our work. We have tried to be *impartial*.

There were those who assisted in making garments who received nothing because they were not needy. We have followed your instructions as well as we could.

This is all now.

We all send our love and give you our daily prayer.

> *Susie B. Wright*
> *Mrs Kate Reese*
> *Mrs Elizabeth ——*

Document 3

The Episcopalians' head missionary opposes the efforts of the Indian agent to enroll a young Ojibwe woman in an exclusive boarding school in southern Minnesota where many wealthy Episcopalians sent their daughters, citing her lower-class background.

Excerpt from Joseph A. Gilfillan to Henry B. Whipple, February 25, 1874, H. B. Whipple Papers, Box 10, Minnesota Historical Society.

One of the girls in question was Lizzie Moore, who I understand, he [Agent Douglass] has so urgently wished you to take to Faribault to school. I cannot see the special need of removing her nor what his object was in that, as she now has employment in a good white family, and is in no more danger than any other girl on the Reservation. She is not one whom it would be desirable to have your young ladies associate with as an equal; I mean she has not been brought up in a station to be a fit companion for them.

Document 4

Joseph A. Gilfillan to Henry B. Whipple, December 3, 1875, H. B. Whipple Papers, Box 11, Minnesota Historical Society.

White Earth, Becker Co. Minn
Dec 3rd 1875

Dear Bishop,

At the weekly meeting of the Indian women on Thursdays, to learn knitting sewing cutting &c some of themselves proposed to work for several weeks to make articles of Indian manufacture to be sent as a present to you, in recognition, so far as they can, of your great kindness to them.

Those who were most active in getting it up, and in having their fellow Indian women join in it were the leaders of the Bands of women, whom you appointed many years ago, each to have several Indian women enrolled under them of whom they were to have a sort of spiritual Charge.

The names of these leaders are Cornelia E. Boardman, Mrs Alex Roy, Mrs Macudjiwence, Kakabishique, Emma Whitefisher.

As the result of their labors I send you today by freight—as the expense will be much less—a box filled with the work of the   present to you from them. I have attac[hed] name of the donor of each article to it. You will find the articles arranged by bands generally, that is the things contributed by Cornelia E. Boardman and her band are all in one place, the things by Mrs Roy and band in another, the things by Emma Whitefisher and band in another.

Please look in all the pockets; within all articles, as generally bags pockets &c have had smaller articles stuffed into them.

I also sent two mats made by the women, sending them separately as they were too large to be got into the box.

The Indian women have taken the greatest delight in preparing these things for you, and it is their own idea. Many of the things, particularly C. E. Boardmans, are the most beautiful I ever saw. They will be very much gratified if after having seen the articles you will write them a line if not too busy, letting them know whether you liked them or not.

Their present is but a very faint expression, dear Bishop, of the love they all have towards you.

The box was packed by Mrs Bodle. All well here.

No sickness and very few deaths among the Indians last summer and until now.

Respectfully Yours,
J. A. Gilfillan

Document 5

Letter of Mary Bird, enclosed with Susanna Roy to Henry B. Whipple, July 25, 1876, H. B. Whipple Papers, Box 11, Minnesota Historical Society.

We women whom you appointed leaders of Bands, has chosen one among ourselves whom we would wish to take general leadership of us, namely Mrs Roy Susanna. And we beseech you to write to us that you approve this arrangement. Our minds are all one on this subject; my mind Mary Bird or Kakabishique (who have written the last sentence enclosed in brackets) and the others all feel alike. We will try to do good to those who disturb us, to do as you wish us to do; to go forward in all that is good. I am sad today, for one of the women of my band has lost a son and though I try to comfort her I cannot.

That is all. We give hearty thanks to all those who have shown mercy to us, who live in your part of the world. The above written by Mary Bird.

Document 6

Excerpt from Mrs. J. J. Enmegahbowh, Mrs. E. W. Minogeshig, and Mrs. Anna Negaun to Mrs. Miss and Major Stowe, March 6, 1878, Lewis Stowe Papers, Box 1, Minnesota Historical Society.

White Earth March 6th 1878

Mrs Miss & Major Stowe & Little Georgy & all your children,—
Friends—We have examined ourselves thoroughly to see if there
has been anything in our hearts that we ever harbored the least
feeling against any of you at any time during your sojourned
with us.

   We are happy to say that we find nothing but rather always
more a very pleasant feelings have existed between us & therefore we parted with you as a true christian.

   Friends I know with sorrow of heart we bid you all farewell.
May the remainder of your lives be always happynes [happi-
ness].

   God bless you all is our prayers. Your true friends

> *Mrs J. J. Enmegahbowh*
> *" E. W. Minogeshig*
> *" Anna Negaun*

We are our way to our sugar camps & will not return home until
next Satturday

Document 7

*Native clergyman John Johnson Enmegahbowh writes to Bishop Whipple of
his concern that a prominent Ojibwe woman and her extended family have
stopped supporting the Episcopal mission because of conflicts with the Euro-
American head missionary over the work of the Women's Meeting.*

   *Excerpt from John Johnson Enmegahbowh to Henry B. Whipple, September
23, 1878, H. B. Whipple Papers, Box 13, Minnesota Historical Society.*

> She has entirely quit attending our church & the whole family
> caused by the sharp talk with my beloved brother Mr Gilfillan
> & with all her sisters too excepting Emma. In really [reality]
> Bishop I cannot & do not understand my brother Mr Gilfil-
> lan. He came to me thother [the other] day and ask me what
> I think about the women's meetings. I told him that I thought
> it was doing much good. He thought to the reverse an injurry
> to the cause of mission & that he never would visit the meet-
> ings &c &c.

Document 8

Joseph A. Gilfillan to Henry B. Whipple, May 20, 1880, Whipple Papers, Box 14, Minnesota Historial Society

> White Earth, Minnesota
> May 20th 1880
>
> Dear Bishop,
>   Rev Charles Wright of Leech Lake asks me to write you about the propriety of his marrying Miss Susie Bonga, daughter of the late George Bonga of Leech Lake whom you knew. She has the reputation of being an exceedingly wise, chaste and good religious young woman, one who is exceedingly highly thought of by all the white employes at Leech Lake, and respected by all Indians and whites. I know her perfectly; having seen her very often at Leech Lake, and she stayed with this ["this" crossed out] us at White Earth in our house on a visit for several weeks last summer. She has done a truly wonderful work at Leech Lake during the time of the other Mr Wright, and in fact I think it is owing in great measure to her that there are any Christians there atall, as she was the means of the conversion of most of them, getting the Indian women into her room one by one, praying with and for them, reading the scriptures and explaining them to them, leading them in their devotional meetings, and taking charge of them like a mother everywhere in Church and out. This is not a sudden bust [burst?] of zeal since Rev Charles Wright went there, as I saw her repeatedly in those meetings before the mission was started. In fact she has proved herself a very rare girl, such as as there are few any where Indian or white, and she has accomplished a great work at Leech Lake. She is a very good housekeeper, speaks English pretty well, has considerable learning, is of spotless character, and has been on all these accounts been advanced by the agent to the position of Matron of the Indian school, which she fulfills perfectly. Her distinguishing characteristics are her great wisdom and perfect good sense, and burning zeal in the cause of religion regulated by the greatest prudence. All her brothers ask her advice about their business and the white people think there is no person like Susie. I have never seen any Indian or Half-Breed like her since I

have been in the Indian country, and am quite sure there is none such anywhere to be found. She has set her mind on marrying Charles Wright, and as she has told him it will be a death-blow to her if she is disappointed. There is no doubt whatever that if she continues on as she has done in the past she would advance his work far more than any wife he could find Indian or white. He wishes to marry her, there is only one thing sticks in his mind, her negro blood. He has heard that white people look down on negroes or those of negro blood but not atall on Indians, and besides he is afraid of the ridicule of his companions, young Indians, who look down on negroes. She shows the negro blood but little; her hair is perfectly straight, and her lips not like the negro; but her brothers and sisters show it very much. When Charles Wright was here lately he asked my advice and I advised him to consult you before he did anything. There is one consideration to be taken into account that if he does not marry her it will be hard for him to find a suitable wife; for the young women at White Earth have all died off, and I think there are no good wives at Leech Lake or Red Lake. The only sticking point with him is the negro blood, and the apprehended ridicule of the young Indians. I have asked the clergymen at Red Lake. Rev George Smith highly approves of it; while Fred thinks they would ridicule Charles. For my part for the sake of the work and for the sake of the poor girl I heartily wish it could take place if the negro blood be not an insuperable bar, as judging by her past there is no such wife to be found anywhere.

In haste, Respectfully Yours, J. A. Gilfillan

P.S. You may write to Rev. Charles Wright or me. J. A. G.

Document 9

Wa ge ji ge zhik, Oge shi yashik, and G. B. Johnson to Henry B. Whipple, July 28, 1881, H. B. Whipple Papers, Box 15, Minnesota Historical Society.

Pembina Settlement July 23 1881
To our friend the Good Blackrobe

Dear friend,
    Since you passed through here & of all that you said to us &

our women we still keep in our memory. We have met together to consider about organizing meetings for this place & we have concluded to appoint two persons as our leaders one for the men & the other for the women We therefore ask you earnestly to assist us in any way that you may see it. There are two things that we would call your attention 1st—to send us by return of mail a paper that will protect us & our land from being taken from us by the palefaces 2nd We would like to have a flag for our Chief these are the two things we desire greatly. Also a paper to authorize us to have these meetings.

Your Friend Wa ge ji ge zhik Chief, leader of the meeting)
Our women will say a few words to you.

We are going to try an[d] do as you said to us women when you passed through here. We shall commence at once we hope you will do as you said to us. We have numbered our children there are sixteen altogether as you requested us to send you the number of our children Hoping you will help us all that you can we ask you a paper to authorize us to hold this meeting.

Your friend
Oge shi yashik the leader)

Appendix: Selections from Hilger's *Chippewa Child Life*

The next three selections are from Sister M. Inez Hilger's Chippewa Child Life *and Its Cultural Background. Older ethnographies such as Hilger's can be problematic because of their unacknowledged interpretive biases. Hilger was both a Catholic Sister of the Order of St. Benedict and a professional anthropologist. Thus she accepted not only the anthropological theories of her day, which viewed Native peoples as vanishing and their cultures as degenerating from pre-contact purity, but also Catholic teachings about human religiosity. At the same time, she showed remarkable sensitivity to her Ojibwe consultants. She protected their anonymity at a time when few anthropologists thought to do so; she did not press for information on sensitive subjects like indigenous religion. The following passages reveal Hilger's value as a source on Ojibwe women's lives. In the first excerpt, note that the women she describes cook at a communal fireplace and that three of the four families are related through the women (a mother and her two grown daughters). This is particularly interesting since the Ojibwe were patrilineal; it reminds us that just because a*

Native society traced descent through the father's family does not mean women were powerless or unimportant. Utilizing William Fenton's technique of "up-streaming" (looking for present-day cultural attributes in earlier sources), one can also read the letters of Susie Bonga Wright and her contemporaries, who lived fifty years before Hilger conducted her fieldwork, and discover remarkable cultural continuity in their lives. Bonga Wright's generation also lived and worked enmeshed in similar networks of female kinfolk and friends.

Sister M. Inez Hilger, Chippewa Child Life and Its Cultural Background, *Smithsonian Institution Bureau of American Ethnology Bulletin 146 (Washington DC: Government Printing Office, 1951), 127–28, 153, 33–34.*

A group of four families, probably not unlike those of early days, had settled on the Narrows of Red Lake for the fishing season of 1932. Women of two of the families were daughters of a third; the fourth family were friends—a young couple with a baby. The old couple occupied a canvas-covered tipi of 12 poles. Plus 2 used in controlling wind flaps that regulated the draft. One daughter and her family lived in a wigwam, a framework of saplings covered with canvas; the remaining two families lived together in a commercial canvas tent. Floors of all places were covered with bedding; corners were filled with wooden boxes and pasteboard cartons used in transporting belongings. Dishes and cooking utensils were seen on the outside of each home, indicating eating apart. Toward the center of the grouping, under a long rack, fire was smouldering in two places, charcoal being in evidence in a third. . . . The rack consisted of several stout 12-foot ironwood saplings, the ends of which either rested in crotches of two poles found at each end of the fireplace or were fastened to the poles with basswood fiber. The two end poles were firmly planted in the ground in the position of an X. All were held in position by being firmly tied together with basswood fiber. Pails and kettles used for cooking purposes were hanging from crotched sticks attached to horizontal poles. Astride the poles with bellies up hung skinned fish, slit down the back, backbone and entrails removed. These were being dried and cured in the smoke of the smouldering fires. "It will take about 2 days to smoke these fish; after that we can pack them to take home. These belong to me," remarked the old woman, "but there's room on the rack for everybody. We all cook here, too."

Although Hilger rarely analyzed the meaning of the ethnographic information she recorded, a researcher can draw many conclusions. As the second excerpt makes clear, Ojibwes traced descent through patrilineal clans (Hilger tran-

scribes the Ojibwe word as "do'dam"), a situation that might lead to the conclusion that women were substantially disempowered.

Warren, a native Chippewa, wrote that . . . his people . . . were as a body
divided into several large families, each of which was known and perpetuated by a symbol of some bird, animal, fish, or reptile, and called by them
totem or do'dam. He notes that the descent was invariably along the male
line; and that intermarriage never took place between persons of the same
symbol or family; "even, should they belong to different and distinct tribes,
as they consider one another related by the closest ties of blood and call one
another by the nearest terms of consanguinity" (Warren, 1885, vol. 5, p. 34).
Informants on all reservations were agreed that the do'dam was patrilin-
ear. Such remarks as the following were typical: "The do'dam is invariably
inherited from the father." "Children belong to the do'dam of their father;
never to that of their mother." "I have five boys and five girls and all belong
to the wolf do'dam, their father's do'dam." "You are always a member of
your father's do'dam; never of your mother's."

The third excerpt reveals that Ojibwe mothers retained important decision-
making authority over their children and that their husbands acquiesced in
that authority, though Hilger's consultants understood that acquiescence dif-
ferently. Such information sharpens our understanding of Native women's lives
in patrilineal societies, revealing that male descent systems did not automati-
cally deny women significant forms of authority.

Adoption of persons, however, was very prevalent in the old days, and is so
today: nearly all homes visited while making this study housed nonmem-
bers of families. Small children were, and are, adopted not only by relatives,
but also by friends. Older children and adult persons either chose a home
and asked to be adopted or they were invited to do so.

There were no adoption ceremonials. All that was necessary was a clear
understanding by the parties concerned. In the case of small children, the
parents' consent was required. One informant said she was present when
her dying mother arranged for the placing and adoption of her children;
she was old enough to remember the occasion well:

"Today, people have to arrange with the Agency [local U. S. Indian Ser-
vice] if they wish to adopt a child. It wasn't that way some years ago. Before
my mother died, she selected the relatives with whom she wanted all of
us children to stay; she might have selected friends or anyone else instead

of relatives. All of my mother's people talked with my mother and they decided among themselves who would take each child; we were five. If my father had been of the Chippewa Tribe, he would have had something to say and could have kept all of us if he had thought he could care for us; but since he is a Winnebago, he was not consulted. However, if mother had had no brothers nor sisters, my father could then have taken us. [She mentioned the names of three widowed Chippewa fathers on the reservation who were caring for their children.] But as things turned out, my oldest sister was given to my grandmother, my mother's mother; my brother was given to one of my mother's sisters; my two youngest sisters, to another sister; and another aunt raised me. I was treated just like the rest of my aunt's family; there was no discrimination shown as to food or work. At times, however, that is done; my brother was badly treated and the old lady with whom he was living struck him with a poker so that it penetrated his foot; she also hid bread from him. That is why he is now neglecting her."

An informant who had been willed a grandchild by her daughter said: "When mothers are certain of dying, they will their children to some-one—to relatives, or to the missionary, or to someone; the husband has nothing to say about it."

Notes

1. I would like to thank the Research Committee of the Academic Senate of the University of California, Riverside, for their support of this research; thanks also to Lucy Eldersveld Murphy, an editor of great patience, optimism, and unending good humor.

2. Recent treatments exploring new dimensions in Native women's lives include Clara Sue Kidwell, "Indian Women as Cultural Mediators," *Ethnohistory* 39 (spring 1992): 97–107; Sylvia Van Kirk, "Toward a Feminist Perspective in Native History," in William Cowan, ed., *Papers of the 18th Algonquian Conference* (Ottawa: Carleton University Press, 1987); see also Rayna Green, "The Pocahontas Perplex: The Image of Indian Women in American Culture," *Massachusetts Review* 16 (1975): 698–714.

3. Smith and Winslow quoted in Robert S. Grumet, "Sunksquaws, Shamans, and Tradeswomen: Middle Atlantic Coastal Algonkian Women during the 17th and 18th Centuries," in Mona Etienne and Eleanor Leacock, eds., *Women and Colonization: Anthropological Perspectives* (New York: Praeger, 1980), 43–62, 49, 50. Adair quoted in Theda Perdue, "The Traditional Status of Cherokee Women," *Furman Studies* 5 (1980): 19–25, 20. On Iroquois women see Diane Rothenberg, "The Mothers of the Nation: Seneca Resistance to Quaker Intervention," in Etienne and Leacock, *Women and Colonization*, 63–87; Judith K. Brown, "Economic Organization and the Position of Women among the Iroquois," *Ethnohistory* 17 (1970): 151–67; Cara B.

Richards, "Matriarchy or Mistake: The Role of Iroquois Women through Time," in Verne F. Ray, ed., *Cultural Stability and Cultural Change,* Proceedings of the 1957 Annual Meeting of the American Ethnological Society (Seattle: University of Washington Press, 1957), 36–45; and Anthony F. C. Wallace, *The Death and Rebirth of the Seneca* (1955; New York: Knopf, 1970). For Netnokwa see *The Falcon: A Narrative of the Captivity and Adventures of John Tanner* (1830; New York and London: Penguin Books, 1994). Anthropologists specializing in the study of Algonkian peoples, including the Ojibwes, observe that Netnokwa was not unique in her role as an important and respected female political leader; rather, the scarce documentary record has obscured the lives of other female political leaders. James McClurken, personal communication.

4. Kenneth Wiggins Porter, "Relations between Negroes and Indians within the Present Limits of the United States," *Journal of Negro History* 17 (July 1932): 287–367; and Porter, "Negroes and the Fur Trade," *Minnesota History* 15 (December 1934): 421–33.

5. Priscilla K. Buffalohead, "Farmers, Warriors, Traders: A Fresh Look at Ojibway Women," *Minnesota History* 48 (summer 1983): 236–44. Unfortunately, Ruth Landes's ethnographic classic, *The Ojibwa Woman* (1938; New York: Norton, 1971), contains no examination of women's political activities.

6. Wa ge ji ge zhik, Oge zhe ya shik, and George B. Johnson to Henry B. Whipple, July 28, 1882, Henry Benjamin Whipple Papers, Box 15, Minnesota Historical Society, St. Paul [hereafter MHS]; Susanna Roy to Whipple, April 13, 1882, Whipple Papers, Box 16, MHS. For the word *ogimakwe,* translated as "a female chief," see Bishop Frederic Baraga, *A Dictionary of the Ojibway Language* (Montreal: Beauchemin and Valois, 1878), pt. 2, 317.

7. Mrs. J. J. Enmegahbowh, Mrs. E. W. Minogeshig, and Mrs. Anna Negaun to Mrs. and Miss Stowe, March 6, 1878, Lewis Stowe Papers, Box 1, MHS.

8. Giacomo C. Beltrami, *A Pilgrimage in Europe and America, Leading to the Discovery of the Source of the Mississippi and Bloody River; with a Description of the Whole Course of the Former, and of the Ohio,* 2 vols. (London: Hunt and Clarke, 1828), 2:448. See untitled newspaper article from the *St. Anthony's Falls Democrat,* February 11, 1870, in Works Projects Administration, Minnesota Writers Project Annals, Subject Files, Box 170, "Nationality Groups—Indians, 1870-77" [hereafter WPA Papers], MHS (women confiscating weapons); William Whipple Warren, "History of the Ojibways, Based upon Traditions and Oral Statements," *Minnesota Historical Society Collections* 5 (1885): 3–394, 301; and Jedediah D. Stevens Diary, Jedediah Dwight Stevens Papers, MHS (Ojibwe efforts to monitor drinking behavior).

9. Susanna Roy to Whipple, April 13, 1882, Whipple Papers, Box 16, MHS. In addition to Landes, *Ojibwa Woman,* 124–77, anthropological descriptions of women's work include Frances Densmore, *Chippewa Customs* (1929; St. Paul: Minnesota Historical Society Press, 1979), 119–28 and passim; and Sister M. Inez Hilger, *Chippewa Child Life and Its Cultural Background,* Smithsonian Institution Bureau of

American Ethnology Bulletin 146 (Washington DC: Government Printing Office, 1951), 52, 55, 115–16, 129–30, 137–38, 141, 147, 156, 170–71. Mid-nineteenth-century ethnographic accounts discussing women's work are J. G. Kohl, *Kitchi-Gami: Life among the Lake Superior Ojibway* (1860; St. Paul: Minnesota Historical Society Press, 1985), 3–11, 29, 29–31, 46–47, 315–16, 412–14; and Warren, "History of the Ojibways," 186, 264–66, 337–38.

10. Pauline Colby, "Reminiscences," 1894–c. 1908, pp. 49, 65, MHS.

11. For Ojibwe socioeconomic decline and the political divisions thus engendered see Rebecca Kugel, "'To Go About on the Earth': An Ethnohistory of the Minnesota Ojibwe, 1830–1900" (Ph.D. diss., University of California, Los Angeles, 1986), esp. chaps. 4 and 5.

12. For American Indian policy during the second half of the nineteenth century see Francis P. Prucha, *American Indian Policy in Crisis: Christian Reformers and the Indian, 1865–1900* (Norman: University of Oklahoma Press, 1976).

13. "Leech Lake Confirmations," July 23, 1880, Whipple Papers, Box 38, MHS.

14. Joseph A. Gilfillan to Whipple, February 15, 1876, Whipple Papers, Box 11, MHS.

15. "Home Life," by Harriet Cook Gilfillan, n.d. [c. 1880s], Joseph A. Gilfillan Papers, Box 1, MHS; Gilfillan to Whipple, October 25, 1878, Whipple Papers, Box 13, MHS. For the True Womanhood ideal see Barbara Welter, "The Cult of True Womanhood, 1820–1860," *American Quarterly* 18 (1966): 151–74.

16. See Colby, "Reminiscences," 56, for the new knowledge and considerable physical labor involved in maintaining a Euro-American-style household.

17. Gilfillan to Whipple, May 20, 1880, Whipple Papers, Box 14, MHS.

18. Gilfillan to Whipple, May 20, 1880, Whipple Papers, Box 14, MHS. See Colby "Reminiscences," 82, 83, 93–94, and 103 for Bonga Wright's role as bicultural intermediary.

19. Gilfillan to Whipple, December 3, 1875, Whipple Papers, Box 11, MHS; Gilfillan to Whipple, June 10, 1887, Whipple Papers, Box 19, MHS.

20. Susie B[onga] Wright, Mrs. Kate Reese, Mrs. Elizabeth [blank in MS], Mrs. Maggie Selkirk, Miss Ruth [Flatmouth] to Whipple, September 22, 1882, Whipple Papers, Box 16, MHS.

21. Gilfillan to Whipple, May 20, 1880, Whipple Papers, Box 14, MHS.

22. Susie B[onga] Wright, Mrs. Kate Reese, et al. to Whipple, September 22, 1882, Whipple Papers, Box 16, MHS; Gilfillan to Whipple, December 3, 1875, Whipple Papers, Box 11, MHS.

23. Susie B[onga] Wright, Mrs. Kate Reese, et al. to Whipple, September 22, 1882, Whipple Papers, Box 16, MHS.

24. Susie B[onga] Wright, Mrs. Kate Reese, et al. to Whipple, March 11, 1883, Whipple Papers, Box 16, MHS.

25. Madjigishick to Whipple, January 5, 1887, Whipple Papers, Box 18, MHS; Mrs. C. Johnson to Whipple, August 15, 1879, Whipple Papers, Box 14, MHS. See A. Irving Hallowell, "Ojibwa Ontology, Behavior and World View," in Dennis Tedlock and

Barbara Tedlock, eds., *Teachings from the American Earth: Indian Religion and Philosophy* (New York: Liveright, 1975), 141–78, for the opprobrium attached to selfishness and greed.

26. John Johnson Enmegahbowh to Whipple, January 18, 1880, Whipple Papers, Box 14, MHS; "Committee of Ma ji gi zhik's Band" to Whipple, August 14, 1881, Whipple Papers, Box 15, MHS; Enmegahbowh to Whipple, September 23, 1878, Whipple Papers, Box 13, MHS.

27. Enmegahbowh to Whipple, January 18, 1880, Whipple Papers, Box 14; Enmegahbowh to Whipple, September 23, 1878, Whipple Papers, Box 13, MHS. For positive characterizations of women see Enmegahbowh, "The Death of Chief Tuttle," in *The Church and the Indians,* January 13, 1874, Whipple Papers, Box 10; Enmegahbowh to Whipple, March 7, 1876, May 1894, Whipple Papers, Boxes 11 and 22, MHS.

28. Testimony of Nancy [Bonga] Taylor, March 3, 1914, Ransom Judd Powell Papers, Box 6, MHS.

29. Gilfillan to Whipple, May 20, 1880, Whipple Papers, Box 14, MHS.

30. Pamphlet, "The Indian Deacons at White Earth," December 5, 1888, Gilfillan Papers, Box 1, MHS; Gilfillan to Whipple, November 13, 1876, October 10, 1878, Whipple Papers, Boxes 12 and 13, MHS (expectations for deacons).

31. Gilfillan to Whipple, May 20, 1880, Whipple Papers, Box 14, MHS; Gilfillan to Whipple, November 5, 1877, Whipple Papers, Box 12, MHS; Gilfillan to Whipple, May 20, 1880, Whipple Papers, Box 14, MHS; Gilfillan to Whipple, January 17, 1874, July 24, 1879, Whipple Papers, Boxes 10 and 13, MHS (traditional Ojibwe sexual mores); Gilfillan to Whipple, May 20, 1880, December 3, 1875, Whipple Papers, Boxes 14 and 11, MHS (expectations for deacons' wives).

32. Gilfillan to Whipple, May 20, 1880, Whipple Papers, Box 14, MHS; Gilfillan to Whipple, November 21, 1882, Whipple Papers, Box 16, MHS; Gilfillan to Whipple, May 20, 1880, Whipple Papers, Box 14, MHS.

33. Gilfillan to Gilbert, March 10, 1892, Fred Smith to Whipple, June 27, 1878, and Charles T. Wright to Whipple, June 25, 1892, Whipple Papers, Boxes 22, 13, and 22, MHS. Of the eight original deacons, seven were the sons of political leaders or their close supporters. See pamphlet "The Indian Deacons at White Earth," December 5, 1888, Gilfillan Papers, Box 1, MHS.

34. Gilfillan to Whipple, May 20, 1880, Whipple Papers, Box 14, MHS. See Susie B[onga] Wright, Mrs. Kate Reese, et al. to Whipple, September 22, 1882, Whipple Papers, Box 16, MHS (Ruth Flat Mouth); E. Steele Peake, "Reminiscences," c. 1856, Protestant Episcopal Church Diocese of Minnesota Papers, Box 46, volume 44, MHS (Susanna Roy); Gilfillan to Whipple, September 12, 1881, Whipple Papers, Box 15, MHS (Oge zhe ya shik).

35. Gilfillan to Whipple, May 20, 1880, Whipple Papers, Box 14, MHS. For the range of abuses the Ojibwe suffered, see Peake to Whipple, July 8, 1884, Whipple Papers, Box 17, MHS (Ojibwe men called "boys"); William H. Williams to Edward P. Smith, August 16, 1873, National Archives Microfilm Publications, Washington DC, Re-

cord Group 75, Microcopy 234 [hereafter NAMP, RG 75, M234], Roll 160: 635-36 (Ojibwes cheated by merchants); Enmegahbowh to Whipple, May 15, 1872, Whipple Papers, Box 9, MHS (Ojibwes fired on by Euro-American settlers); "Minnesota Justice—White and Red," newspaper article from the *St. Paul Pioneer,* December 10, 1872, NAMP, RG 75, M234, Roll 160: 585 (Ojibwes murdered in cold blood by Euro-Americans); "Lynch Law in Brainerd," newspaper clipping from the *Brainerd Tribune,* July 27, 1872, in WPA Papers, Box 170, MHS (lynchings).

36. See James H. Merrell, "The Racial Education of the Catawba Indians," *Journal of Southern History* 50 (August 1984): 363–84, for another Native people's efforts to comprehend Euro-American definitions of "race."

37. Gilfillan to Whipple, May 20, 1880, Whipple Papers, Box 14, MHS. See "Confirmations, Leech Lake," July 23, 1880, Whipple Papers, Box 38, MHS (Susie Bonga's age); Albion Barnard to Edward P. Smith, January 7, 1875, NAMP, RG 75, M234, Roll 162: 28 (George Bonga's death); James Bonga to Whipple, July 7, 1877, and Sela G. Wright to Whipple, July 7, 1877, Whipple Papers, Box 12, MHS (provisions of George Bonga's will).

38. Gilfillan to Whipple, May 20, 1880, Whipple Papers, Box 14, MHS.

39. Gilfillan to Whipple, January 16, 1882, Whipple Papers, Box 15, MHS; Colby, "Reminiscences," 82–83 (Bonga Wright is referred to as "Gemokomaniqua," Colby's rendering of Chimokomanikwe), 93–94, 98, 103 (she is referred to as "Mrs. Nashotah").

40. Richard White, *The Middle Ground: Indians, Empires, and Republics in the Great Lakes Region, 1650–1815* (Cambridge MA: Cambridge University Press, 1991), 67; Carol Devens, *Countering Colonization: Native American Women and Great Lakes Missions, 1630–1900* (Berkeley: University of California Press, 1992).

41. This essay on Susie Bonga Wright originally appeared in *Midwestern Women: Work, Community, and Leadership at the Crossroads,* ed. Lucy Eldersveld Murphy and Wendy Hamand Venet (Bloomington: Indiana University Press, 1997). The essay by Tamara G. Miller referenced here, "'Those with Whom I Feel Most Nearly Connected': Kinship and Gender in Early Ohio," also appeared in that volume.

42. Jacqueline Peterson, "Prelude to Red River: A Social Portrait of the Great Lakes Métis," *Ethnohistory* 25 (winter 1978): 41–67; Melissa L. Meyer, *The White Earth Tragedy: Ethnicity and Dispossession at a Minnesota Anishinaabe Reservation, 1889–1920* (Lincoln: University of Nebraska Press, 1994); also Tanis Chapman Thorne, "People of the River: Mixed-Blood Families on the Lower Missouri" (Ph.D. diss., University of California, Los Angeles, 1987).

Central Theme

The Kinship of Religous Affiliation

One of the most important European cultural elements that Native peoples encountered was the multiplicity of ideals, beliefs, and practices that composed Christianity. Whether Catholic or Protestant, Europeans agreed that Christianity was the only true religion and that their societies, founded on Christian precepts, represented the only truly civilized social order. Native societies, cultures, and religions, in contrast, were anything but divinely inspired, and Europeans expended enormous effort remaking, or "civilizing," Native peoples. This reformation encompassed every aspect of Native life, including economic production and inheritance practices, political organization and decision making, family structure, marriage, child rearing, and acceptable sexual activity. Native women would be particularly affected, since European societies were patriarchal. Indeed, European civilization and Christianization seemed calculated to disempower and dispossess Native women. And yet Native women converted to Christianity in much larger numbers than men, much to the puzzlement and chagrin of missionaries.

The articles in this section explore Native women's experiences with Christianity. Because of overlaps between them, they make interesting comparative reading. They involve the same Christian tradition, French Catholicism, allowing us to compare Native and missionary actions in related adjacent colonial environments. Each author utilizes the writings of French Jesuit missionaries, and the astute reader can consider to what degree these male missionaries in the field were writing what they thought their superiors in France wanted to hear, as well as to what degree they misinterpreted the motivations of their Native female converts. Each author also utilizes parish baptismal records, which reveal great usefulness in mapping family and kinship connections. The articles even discuss one person in common, the youthful Kaskaskia convert Marie Rouensa-8canic8e. Their very different conclusions speak to the many ways that historians can approach a problem and ask a question; they remind readers that historical documents can yield information on many subjects.

Carl Ekberg uses Marie Rouensa-8canic8e's remarkable life as a window into the development of French colonial society in present-day Illinois. Although he views the colony at Kaskaskia as unusual because it developed an agriculture-based economy rather than remaining tied to the fur trade, Ekberg interprets Rouensa-8canic8e's Catholic conversion as straightforward and complete. Indeed, his discussion of her strained relationship with her son Michel Accault suggests how thoroughly he believes Rouensa-8canic8e had accepted the cultural imperatives of French Catholicism. She threatened Accault with economic disinheritance, in itself more a European parental strategy to enforce obedience than a Native one, because he did not share her commitment to French life and religion and preferred living among unchristianized Native people.

Drawing inspiration from Clara Sue Kidwell's portrayal of Native women as cultural mediators, Susan Sleeper-Smith documents the lives of four women (including Rouensa-8canic8e) who married French men and utilized Catholic institutions, especially godparentage, to create expanded kinship networks that knitted together the far-flung villages of the fur trade. For these women, Catholicism involved neither patriarchal domination nor complete cultural assimilation; instead, it provided avenues to positions of prominence and autonomy, precisely because the women remained central to the kin networks of both Native and fur-trade societies.

9. Marie Rouensa-8canic8e and the Foundations of French Illinois

CARL J. EKBERG WITH ANTON J. PREGALDIN

New Introduction by Carl J. Ekberg

In Washington, D.C., the mantra is "Follow the money." In historial research a fruitful admonition is "Follow the footnotes." This was precisely the route I took when beginning my research on Marie Rouensa.[1] Natalia M. Belting's classic study, *Kaskaskia under the French Regime*, is a slim volume, but I was aware that it was based upon exhaustive research in the massive collection of Kaskaskia Manuscripts. That is, I knew that given the broad contours of Belting's study many of the topics appearing in this volume could not have been fully explored, that the Kaskaskia Manuscripts collection must contain riches that were not fully elaborated in her text. So, my approach was to read Belting's book (which is always a pleasure), to select a topic that interested me (Marie Rouensa-8canic8e, in this case), and to follow Belting's footnotes back to the Kaskaskia Manuscripts, those underutilized but indispensable sources for the colonial history of the Mississippi River valley. This turned out to be an effective approach, and yielded a treasure trove of documentation about Marie and her family. The Kaskaskia Manuscripts (and other manuscript collections) contain additional treasure troves awaiting future researchers willing to pursue this simple but rewarding approach.

The domestic life of Marie Rouensa was not a natural topic for a historian trained in the diplomatic history of seventeenth-century France. I took up the topic by virtue of my participation in a project being undertaken at the Illinois State Museum in Springfield. This museum had traditionally been devoted to prehistory, but a generous grant from the National Endowment for the Humanities funded the development of a historical component. Jan Wass was in charge of this project, and she decided that the new component would focus on domestic life in Illinois during the historical period and would be called "At Home in the Heartland."[2] She asked me to work up something pertaining to the French period (i.e., before 1763), and I set about finding suitable subject matter by proceeding in the manner outlined in the preceding paragraph. Because of the very large Indian presence in the "French" community of Kaskaskia and the constant intermingling of "Indianness" and "Frenchness" in that society, I immediately decided to find subject matter that would drive home this point.

Employing the strategy outlined in the first paragraph of this introduction, Belting's footnotes in *Kaskaskia under the French Regime* could have led me in several directions. Marie Rouensa was an obvious choice, but, for example, I could also have dwelt on the domestic life of Jacques Bourdon, whose life in Kaskaskia paralleled Marie's in so many ways. Bourdon, a French Canadian, was married in succession to two Indian women, and Marie, an Indian woman, was married in succession to two French Canadian men; Bourdon was captain of the Kaskaskia militia, and Marie's second husband, Michel Philippe, was as well; Bourdon was honored with burial beneath the nave of the parish church of the Immaculate Conception, and so was Marie.

The intertwined lives of Jacques and Marie provide evocative symmetry, a powerful reminder of the cross-racial nature of society in early-eighteenth-century Kaskaskia. Indeed, the wealth and eminence that both achieved suggest that racially mixed marriages were the surest avenue to worldly success in that society. In the American West from the mid-seventeenth century to mid-nineteenth, intimate relations—marriages, as well as more casual liaisons—oiled the gears of the fur trade and stimulated the generation of commerical wealth. Jacques and Marie were indubitably members of the early elite in Kaskaskia, and they remained friends and neighbors for two decades, until Jacques's death in 1723 at forty-three years of age. When Marie's son Jacques was baptized in July 1704, Bourdon served as godfather and conveyed his name to the newborn. Children, both boys and girls, were commonly christened with the name of one of their godparents in the Illinois country's Creole society.

My first foray into the history of the Illinois country came back in 1980 when the U.S. Corps of Engineers was preparing to build a dam on the Big River in Jefferson County, Missouri. Ed Jelks, a distinguished archaeologist at Illinois State University, was engaged to do part of the environmental impact analysis for the proposed dam, and he asked me to work with him on the French manuscripts pertaining to the region. This experience doing "public history" led me to write my first book on the Illinois country, *Colonial Ste. Genevieve: An Adventure on the Mississippi Frontier*. The dam was never built on the Big River, but the research done for the proposed project produced some useful results. After completing that book, I became involved with another "public history" initiative, the domestic-life project at the Illinois State Museum. This in turn led me to write *French Roots in the Illinois Country: The Mississippi Frontier in Colonial Times*. The point here hardly requires elaboration: crossing over from "academic history" to "public history" can often open one's mind and lead to new avenues of fruitful research.

Studying Indian women in the Mississippi River valley prior to 1800 requires certain paleographic skills—there is just no way around it. Having done a Ph.D. in the history of Bourbon France, I was lucky enough to come to Illinois country studies with a fair knowledge of French manuscripts. Nevertheless, making the transition from correspondence drafted by Louis XIV's diplomats at Versailles to marriage contracts drafted by royal notaries at early Kaskaskia demanded some devotion. Acquiring mastery of manuscripts written in French and often in difficult handwriting does not come easily. But the passionate student should face up to this challenge, for such mastery opens up enthralling vistas for pursuing topics in American history (such as Indian women) not otherwise accessible.

Marie Rouensa is becoming a popular figure in historical discourse, partly because she was an Indian woman, partly because adequate documentation exists to limn out her distinctive personality, and partly because she was a formidably tough and independent character—in short, she makes great copy, and we will doubtless continue to hear from her in the future.

Marie Rouensa-8canic8e and the Foundations of French Illinois (*1991*)

Marie Rouensa-8canic8e (8 represents the phoneme *ou*), a name like René Robert Cavelier de La Salle, is at once poetic and attached to a person of historical importance and of heroic stature. If Francis Parkman had continued his history of the Illinois country into the period following La Salle's death, he might have seized upon Marie Rouensa and used her life as the nucleus for the next stage of his story. Parkman's variety of romantic biographical history, splendid as it was, had gone out of fashion by the early twenti-

eth century. Clarence Walworth Alvord, in his magisterial *Illinois Country,*
1673–1818, did not elaborate upon the lives of individuals, choosing in the
manner of his time to dwell upon geography, politics, and institutions. Alvord briefly mentions Kaskaskia Chief Rouensa, Marie's father, but neither
Alvord nor Parkman had any interest in discussing the life of an Indian
woman, even one as important as Marie.[3]

In a 1944 article for this journal Floyd Mulkey devoted several paragraphs
to Marie, describing her as "Father [Jacques] Gravier's favorite convert,"
which she certainly seems to have been.[4] And Natalia Maree Belting, whose
1948 monograph on French Kaskaskia has yet to be superseded, devotes a
page to the historical importance of a single Indian woman, Marie Rouensa-
8canic8e, daughter of Chief Rouensa of the Kaskaskia tribe.[5]

The Jesuit Jacques Gravier described the seventeen-year-old Marie's conversion to Christianity at Peoria, probably in 1694:

> The girl made her first communion on the feast of the Assump-
> tion of Our Lady; she had prepared herself for it during more
> than 3 months—with such fervor, that she seemed fully pen-
> etrated by that great mystery. . . .
>
> Having heard me say that many Christians, penetrated with
> regret for their offenses and with sorrow for having crucified
> Jesus Christ by their sins, practice Holy severities upon them-
> selves, she . . . made for herself a girdles of thorns. This she wore
> for two whole days, and she would have crippled herself with
> it, had she not informed me of his mortification, when I com-
> pelled her to use it with more moderation.[6]

Young women of the Illini nation seemed more susceptible to the overtures of the Roman Catholic missionaries than were other members of the
tribes. Gravier noted that the "young women here greatly contribute to
bring prayer into favor, through the instructions and lectures that I hold for
them."[7] A few years later another Jesuit, Father Julien Binneteau, described
that issue at some length:

> The young men are no less opposed to the progress of Chris-
> tianity than are the jugglers [medicine men]. Among them are
> monsters of impurity, who abandon themselves without shame
> to the most infamous actions; this is the reason why we find
> hardly a single young man upon whom we can rely for the ex-

ercises of religion. The middle-aged men and the old men alone
have any constancy.

As a compensation, the women and girls have strong inclina-
tions to virtue—although, according to their customs, they are
the slaves of their brothers, who compel them to marry whomsoever they choose, even men already married to another wife.
Nevertheless, there are some among them who constantly resist,
and who prefer to expose themselves to ill treatment rather than
do anything contrary to the precepts of Christianity regarding
marriage.[8]

Gravier and Binneteau's observations were made during the mid-1690s.
A few years later, a nonmissionary observer remarked that although the Illinois were "much given to debauchery . . . the reverend Jesuit fathers, who
speak their language perfectly, manage (if one may say so) to impose some
check on this by instructing a number of girls in Christianity, who often
profit by their teaching, and mock the superstitions of their nation."[9] Thus,
different observers came to the same conclusion—young women were the
best avenues of access in the missionaries' effort to draw the Illinois into the
Roman Catholic faith.

Marie Rouensa was perhaps Gravier's favorite convert because she was
influential in persuading her father, Chief Rouensa, and his wife into abjur-
ing their pagan religion and becoming Christians. As Gravier noted:

The Chief of the Kaskaskia and his wife have, ever since the
marriage of the daughter with a Frenchman, been very assiduous at the instructions and have begged me to prepare them for
baptism. . . . These two worthy savages reflected so seriously on
all that their son-in-law and daughter told them respecting the
unfortunate condition of those who refuse my good advice that,
without speaking to me of it, they agreed that the chief should
publicly declare the resolution which he had taken to become a
christian.[10]

Thus, Marie's conversion set in motion a sequence of conversions, and that
sequence laid the basis for the founding of the Franco-Indian settlement of
Kaskaskia in 1703, a momentous event in early Illinois history.

Without Marie's cognizance, the conversion of those important members of the Kaskaskia tribe also set in motion an important French policy

in North America—making tribes dependent upon the French. Although strong-willed Marie made the leap between Indian culture and French colonial culture and led what seems to have been a successful and apparently fulfilling life as a wife to Frenchmen and a mother to their Métis children, most of her people were not so strong willed—or lucky. The close association of the Kaskaskia with the French colonists helped to promote the alcoholism and disease that ravaged the lives of individual Indians and doomed their culture. Historian Raymond E. Hauser observes that it was precisely the kind of assimilation that Marie Rouensa helped to foster that led to the rapid cultural disintegration and eventual destruction of her tribe.[11]

Marie married French *voyageur* Michel Accault (often spelled Acco or Aco). Born about 1646 in Poitiers, Accault was a resident of Canada by 1666. A trader, he had long frequented the Illinois country. He had been with La Salle and Henri de Tonti at the short-lived Fort Crèvecoeur in 1680, and later that year he accompanied the Recollect Louis Hennepin on his exploratory journey to the upper Mississippi Valley. By the early 1690s, Accault had become well known in the Illinois country.[12] Gravier described the circumstances surrounding Marie and Accault's marriage at Pimiteoui (Peoria) in 1694:

> Many struggles were needed before she could be induced to consent to the marriage, for she had resolved never to marry, in order that she might belong wholly to Jesus Christ. She answered her father and mother, when they brought her to me in company with the Frenchman whom they wished to have for a son-in-law, that she did not wish to marry; that she had already given all her heart to God, and did not wish to share it.[13]

According to Gravier's account, Marie eventually agreed to marry Accault in order to please her father and to facilitate Gravier's missionary work with the Kaskaskia tribe, for she wished "to please Jesus Christ alone."[14] Devotion to the Roman Catholic faith as it was conveyed to her by French Jesuit priests seems to have been a central element in Marie's life from the time of her conversion in 1694 to the moment of her death in 1725. Her first victory on behalf of her new religion was to reform the life of Accault himself, for as a voyageur he had been "famous in this *Ilinois* country for all his debaucheries."[15]

From Marie's marriage, we can project back in time to the approximate place and circumstances of her birth. La Salle's Fort St. Louis at "Le Rocher"

(Starved Rock) served as the principal base for the French presence in the Illinois country from the time of its construction in 1682–83 until La Salle's lieutenant and successor, Henri de Tonti, removed the post to Pimiteoui in 1691.[16] Across the Illinois River from Fort St. Louis lay the Kaskaskia village.[17] Marie Rouensa was born in that village in the late 1670s, sometime before the village was ravaged by the Iroquois in 1680. Her burial record states that at the time of her death at Kaskaskia in 1725 she was "about forty-five years old," which would place her birth in 1680, making Marie but fourteen years old at the time of her marriage in 1694.[18] Gravier, however, stated plainly that she was seventeen years old in 1694, and Gravier is probably the most accurate source on that issue.[19] Another French observer of the Illinois tribe remarked that "girls marry under eighteen," which would tend to corroborate Gravier's observations.[20]

Marie Rouensa's life began in violent, chaotic times. She was but an infant when her village was destroyed by the Iroquois attack of 1680. Using wonderful prose—although suffused with typical nineteenth-century ethnocentrism—historian Francis Parkman described the scene as "a plain once swarming with wild human life, and covered with Indian dwellings; now a waste of devastation and death. . . . The field was strewn with broken bones and torn and mangled corpses. A hyena warfare had been waged against the dead. La Salle knew the handiwork of the Iroquois. The threatened blow had fallen, and the wolfish hordes of the five cantons had fleshed their rabid fangs in a new victim."[21]

Pressure from the Fox and Iroquois tribes—in addition to lack of firewood, game, and adequate water—encouraged the French and their Indian allies to begin a southward migration in 1691, eventually resulting in the founding of Kaskaskia.[22] The first leg of the migration led to Pimiteoui at the lower end of Lake Peoria, where Marie and Accault were married. Gravier surely performed the ceremony, but because surviving church registers begin later, there is no official record of the marriage.[23] Gravier himself described the circumstances of the wedding and also the legitimate birth of their son, Pierre Accault, on March 20, 1695, at Pimiteoui.[24]

From Pimiteoui the Kaskaskia continued their southward migration, settling in 1700 on the west bank of the Mississippi at the mouth of the Des Peres River (the name suggests an association with *Les pères Jesuites*) near the present site of St. Louis.[25] After a seven-year hiatus, Marie Rouensa and Michel Accault again appear in the written records. On February 22, 1702, Father Pierre Gabriel Marest, a Jesuit colleague of Gravier's, baptized their second son, Michel Accault *fils*, who was destined to become the rebel in Marie's large family.[26]

Early in the winter of 1703, Marie with her two sons—one an infant and the other eight years old—accompanied what remained of the Kaskaskia tribe together with a handful of Jesuit missionaries and fur traders to the terminal point of their prolonged migration. The reasons for that final move, with its portentous consequences for early Illinois history, are not entirely clear. It seems likely, however, that pressure from hostile tribes west of the Mississippi, especially the Sioux, prompted the small band of Kaskaskia to return to the east side of the Mississippi and move farther south.[27]

Although the French presence in the Illinois country had revolved exclusively around missionary work and the fur trade during the last two decades of the seventeenth century, one wonders if the site of Kaskaskia was not selected with agriculture in mind. The alluvial land between the Kaskaskia and Mississippi rivers was among the richest anywhere in the world. The outpost of Kaskaskia established a new economic basis—the production of wheat and maize—for the French presence in the middle Mississippi Valley.[28]

It is not clear whether Michel Accault settled at Kaskaskia. At about the time of the new town's founding he disappears entirely from the written record. He must have died shortly after the birth of his second son, although Jesuit missionaries did not record his burial. The daughter of the chief of the Kaskaskia was not likely to remain a widow for long, however, especially when she possessed the character and talents of Marie. On January 22, 1704, less than two years after the birth of Michel Accault *fils*, Marie bore a daughter, Agnès, by her second French husband, Michel Philippe.[29]

For the next twenty years the only documents pertaining to the marriage and household of Marie and Philippe are the records of their children's baptisms by the various Jesuits who served as missionaries and from 1719 as parish priests in Kaskaskia. Fathers Gabriel Marest, Nicholas Ignace de Beaubois, and Jean Baptiste Le Boullenger recorded the baptisms of Marie and Philippe's six children, three boys and three girls, over a fifteen-year period. Sometimes the godparents were French, sometimes Indian, sometimes persons of mixed blood. Remarkably for that time and place, all of Marie's eight known children survived the hazards of infancy and lived to share in her estate.[30]

Except for the marriage, baptismal, and burial records kept by the Jesuits, documents pertaining to Kaskaskia's first twenty years are rare indeed.

Extrapolating from the few existing records of 1703 to 1723 and projecting back by using the more plentiful records from later time periods, we may make the following generalizations about early Kaskaskia: The Jesuit missionaries were the guiding force of the community in civil affairs as well as religious; the population was composed heavily of inhabitants of mixed blood, as French voyageurs settled down and married Indian women; agriculture on the rich bottomland developed rapidly and competed with the fur trade as the economic basis of the settlement; slavery, both Indian and black, became an important component of the work force.[31] A rare description of early Kaskaskia was left by Jean Pénicaut, a soldier who ascended the Mississippi from the French outposts on the Gulf of Mexico in 1711, seven years before the founding of New Orleans:

> This region . . . is one of the finest of all of Louisiana and possesses some of the richest soil. There is wheat that is as good as French wheat, and there are all sorts of vegetables, tubers, and herbs. . . .
>
> Close to the village [of Kaskaskia] there are three grist mills: a windmill belonging to the Jesuit fathers, which is much used by the *habitants*, and two other horsemills. . . .
>
> There is a large church in the village, where there are baptismal fonts. This church is very tidy inside, and there are three chapels—the large one of the choir and two on the sides. There is also a belltower with a bell.[32]

During 1717–1718 the French royal government restructured the administration of its possessions in North America. The Illinois country was removed from Canadian jurisdiction and incorporated into Louisiana, and all of Louisiana (including the Illinois country, or Upper Louisiana) was placed under the control of a royal chartered enterprise, the French Company of the Indies. In autumn of 1718 a convoy of bateaux carrying administrators and French marines departed New Orleans, the newly founded capital of Louisiana. The remote Illinois country was about to be brought into the official structure of French colonial North America; it would have a fort (Fort de Chartes), civil and military officers, royal notaries, and militia companies.[33]

The extensive changes wrought after 1718 had far-ranging effects upon the lives of Marie, Philippe, and the many children of their household. Most important, Philippe's life became more settled. A fur trader when he arrived in the Illinois country, he devoted himself increasingly to agriculture and the acquisition of property. No longer a reckless voyageur with a hankering to take to his canoe each spring, he became part of the local power elite. With the coming of French officials and a military commandant, a Kaskaskia militia company was organized. Philippe served as a lieutenant. His illiteracy did not impede his rise to prominence; he was married to the daughter of an Indian chief and was the owner of extensive property that included both black and Indian slaves.[34]

Originally, the Kaskaskia Indians, French Canadians, and persons of mixed blood all lived in the same community. In 1719, however, an Indian village was established as a separate entity several miles farther up the Kaskaskia River. Indian wives of French Canadians, of course, remained in French Kaskaskia. There is no direct evidence of how Marie felt about the distancing of her people, but her later actions suggest that she became increasingly attached to French ways and the Roman Catholic faith. Indeed, she seems to have been a proselyte who became, as it were, *plus royaliste que le roi.* She worked closely with the Jesuits in their efforts to bring the local Indians into the Catholic church, and she worried about her second son, Michel Accault *fils,* who preferred an Indian mode of existence to life in French colonial Kaskaskia.[35]

Diron d'Artaguiette, a French officer stationed in the Illinois country in 1723, described the Kaskaskia settlement as being located "in a vast prairie" and "composed entirely of farmers who live there very comfortably."

> Their houses are all built of frame timbers on the ground. The chimneys are of stone, of which they could very easily build their entire houses, as the stone there is of very good quality and ready at hand. . . . There is also a church there, which is certainly the finest in the colony. This church is ministered to by a Jesuit who performs the functions of curate. . . . A half league higher up on the bank of the same river, is the Indian village of the Illinois, who number about 200 warriors.[36]

A census taken at Kaskaskia in 1723 listed a total population of 193 souls—not including black or Indian slaves—sixty-one *habitants* (resident farmers), forty-one white laborers, thirty-seven women (including Indian wives), and fifty-four children.[37] Because of the relative shortage of women, many Frenchmen in early Kaskaskia married Indian women. Of the twenty-one baptisms recorded between 1701 and 1713 in the records of the parish of the Immaculate Conception of Kaskaskia, eighteen mothers were Indian and, with one exception, the fathers French.[38]

Such was the village of Kaskaskia when Marie Rouensa was preparing for her death in 1725. On June 13, Jesuit priest Jean Baptiste Le Boullenger, royal notary Du Vernay, interpreter Jacques Lalande, and an additional witness who signed his name Yue Pinet assembled at the residence of Marie and her husband to draft a last will and testament for Marie, "who was in bed ill in body, although clear of mind and understanding and free of will."[39] Apparently Marie and Michel Philippe had not concluded a marriage contract at the time of their marriage two decades earlier. If they had, under the Customary Law of Paris, which applied throughout French North America, a will would not have been necessary for allocating her possessions. Under the customary law, disposition of property was dealt with in the marriage contract.[40] It is clear from Marie's will, however, that she wished to conform to the inheritance practices as set forth in the law, for she requested that her estate be divided according to "La Coutume."[41] Thus, the total estate of Marie and Michel Philippe would be divided between him and all of Marie's children, including those by her first husband, with Philippe receiving one half and the children sharing equally the other half. An unusual feature of Marie's will is that she declared that her second son Michel Accault be "disinherited because of his disobedience, as well as the bad conduct he has exhibited towards me and the entire family." Father Le Boullenger dictated the will to notary Du Vernay in French, and then Jacques Lalande read it twice over to Marie in the Illinois language.[42] Marie was obliged to seek permission from the Superior Council in New Orleans for her disinheritance of her son, which was apparently granted.[43]

Marie's requiring, or at least desiring, a translation of her will into the Iliniwek language raises the interesting issue of just how Gallicized she had become after two French husbands and residence in "French" Kaskaskia. She had certainly become a *dévote* in the Roman Catholic church, but perhaps she spoke Iliniwek rather than French in her household. It is likely that both Accault and Philippe had acquired some skills in Indian languages, as had many French-Canadian voyageurs.

One week later, a group of men again assembled at Marie's sickbed in order to record a codicil to her will. As before, Le Boullenger and Yue Pinet were present. On this occasion, however, Louis Turpin served as interpreter, and in the absence of a royal notary, Jean-Baptiste Girardot, commandant at Kaskaskia, witnessed the document that was drafted by Father Le Boullenger. Marie was still "clear in mind" despite the fact that she had but a few days to live. The codicil she dictated pertained to Michel Accault, whom she had earlier disinherited:

> I have pity for my son Michel Aco, who has chagrined me with his folly and his flight, and I no longer wish to deprive him absolutely and forever of his claim to my possessions. Should he return and repent, my wish is that he should have the right to his possessions. If, however, he is unfortunate enough to persist in his folly, never to repent, and to remain among the savage nations, I wish to transfer his possessions to his brothers and sisters. They will become the owners of them and he will no longer have any claim to them.[44]

It is a bit odd that a full-blooded Indian woman would disinherit her son for choosing to "remain among the savage nations." Marie also justified her disinheritance of Michel Accault "as much for his disobedience as for the marriage that he has contracted despite his mother and his relatives."[45] Michel must have taken an Indian wife who had not been baptized into the Christian church, for there is no record of their marriage in the Kaskaskia parish register.

Marie—the only woman so honored—was buried under the floor of the Immaculate Conception parish church in Kaskaskia on June 25, 1725, having expressed that wish in her will.[46] Burial under the floor of the parish church clearly indicated Marie's high status in the community. It is not clear, however, how much of that status derived from her being the daughter of Chief Rouensa, how much from her wealth and marriage to a Frenchman, and how much from her having become a devout and zealous Roman Catholic. It is likely that the latter was most important to the Jesuits who arranged for her burial.

As Marie requested, her estate—held in common with her second husband, Michel Philippe—was divided in accordance with the Customary Law of Paris. Philippe received one half and also remained custodian of the shares, 2,861 livres each, for six of Marie's eight children. Pierre Accault, Marie's eldest son, took possession of his own share, as did Agnès Philippe Chassin, who was married to Nicolas Chassin, the *garde magasin* (storekeeper) at Fort de Chartres. As the children married or became of age, Philippe settled their inheritances on them.[47]

Shortly after Marie's death, appraisers compiled an inventory of her estate and that of her widower. Appraisal was necessary whenever anyone of substance died in French North America in order that the inheritance be divided in accordance with the customary law. The appraisers of Marie's estate included two witnesses, Jacques Lalande and Antoine Carrière, who represented Michel Philippe; two others, Antoine Boisseau and Léonard Billeron *dit* La Fatigue, represented the eight children. Those four men were joined by a neutral fifth witness, Jean Baptiste Potier. The large estate required two days for appraisal, and the entire inventory was recorded by royal notary André Perillaud.[48]

The inventory, which appears at the end of this article, tells us interesting things about an extraordinary woman. It reveals how a full-blooded Indian woman was able to make a remarkable transformation from a neolithic, pagan culture to a European culture and rise to a position of prominence, becoming one of the wealthiest persons in the community. Few families in Kaskaskia owned five slaves and had estates worth more than 45,000 livres.[49] Marie's apparent insouciance about owning slaves, including Indian slaves, suggests the extent to which slavery was accepted as the norm in French colonial Illinois society; the Jesuits themselves owned numerous slaves.[50] We will never know how Marie viewed slavery. Indian tribes often held slaves, and obviously her ideas were not based on racism and were quite different from those held on southern plantations.

Marie's estate also reveals an important transformation in the economic base of French colonial Illinois. When Kaskaskia was founded in 1703, hunting, trapping, and fur trading reigned supreme as the occupations of virtually all French and French Canadians in the region. That was surely the case with Marie's first husband, Michel Accault, who had lived and died a voyageur. But it is apparent from the inventory—which is dominated by agricultural land and farm buildings, animals, and implements—that Michel Philippe had largely forsaken his days in a canoe and in the woods for the sedentary life of the *habitant*, or resident farmer. By the 1720s the Illinois country was no longer merely a missionary center and fur-trading region; it was well on its way to becoming the largest cereal grain producing area in all of French North America.

The high status of Marie Rouensa, as revealed in the extent of her material wealth as well as by the fact that she was accorded the honor of being buried inside of the Kaskaskia parish church, is borne out by the marriages contracted by many of her immediate descendants. Those marriages to persons of patently high social status indicate that the Indian blood in Marie's descendants did not entail any social stigma for those persons in French Louisiana.[51]

In the years following Marie's death, her descendants spread widely through the small world of French Illinois on both sides of the Mississippi. That is not surprising, for the colonial settlements were remarkably inter- dependent, and many of the first settlers on the west bank at Ste. Genevieve and St. Louis came from the older communities on the east side of the river. A rare phenomenon in Marie's family, however, is that so many of her descendants settled on the Gulf Coast of Louisiana. Lower Louisiana was settled mostly by Europeans, with a minority coming from Canada (i.e., the true Acadians); on the other hand, most Illinois country settlers came from Canada, with a significant minority coming from Europe via New Orleans. The interchange of populations between New Orleans and Kaskaskia, how- ever, was surprisingly small.

As already noted, Marie's daughter Agnès married Nicolas Michel Chas- sin. After his death the widowed Agnès married René Roy, a surgeon major at Fort de Chartres. At the next generation, Agnès Chassin, daughter of Ag- nès and Nicolas Chassin, married Jean François Tisserand de Montchar- vaux, an aristocratic French officer who served at several posts in Upper Louisiana and became commandant at the Arkansas Post in 1739. Another daughter of Marie and Michel Philippe, Elizabeth, married an officer from Fort de Chartres, Alexandre de Celle Duclos, and their daughter Elizabeth Duclos married Pierre-Frédéric d'Arsensberg, an aristocrat of Swedish ex- traction who served as an officer in the French army. Elizabeth's brother, Joseph Duclos, married Marie Jeanne Fontaille Saucier, widow of Francois Saucier, the military engineer who designed the stone Fort de Chartres.

The foregoing summary, which extends only two generations beyond Marie Rouensa, suffices to demonstrate that her children and grandchil- dren married into the highest levels of Louisiana society. By the third gener- ation those upper-class marriage connections had carried her descendants throughout French Louisiana.

Extant documents from early Illinois history permit us to trace Marie Rouensa's life through her marriages to two French-Canadian voyageurs, through the birth of eight children, through the founding of Kaskaskia in 1703, and finally to her death and the division of her substantial estate in 1725. As interesting as Marie's life is, however, those documents provide us with much more than merely a fascinating biography. The written records also deal with virtually every aspect of early Illinois history: the migration of the Kaskaskia tribe from the upper Illinois River valley to the Kaskaskia River in southern Illinois; the central role played by Jesuit missionaries in colonial Illinois history; the founding of Kaskaskia, which became the metropole of French Illinois and the first capital of the state; Indian and French relations in the Illinois country; the use of the Customary Law of Paris as the legal foundation; the varieties of material culture that characterized the early French settlements; slavery, both Indian and black, as it developed in colonial Illinois. All of those important issues appear in the remarkable collection of civil and religious documents that provide a basis for examining some aspects of Marie Rouensa's life and for reconstructing portions of Illinois's earliest history.

The story of Marie Rouensa's family ended as she would have wanted. Not only did many of her descendants marry well, but her wayward son Michel Accault repented and returned to Kaskaskia. In 1728 he reconciled with his stepfather and received his share of Marie's estate, 2,861 livres.[52]

Appendix: Inventory of Marie Rouensa's Estate

Inventory of the estate of Marie Rouensa, Kaskaskia Manuscripts, Randolph County Courthouse, Chester, Illinois (microfilm in Illinois State Historical Library, Springfield), 25.8.16.1, translated from the French by Carl J. Ekberg.

Note*: The arpent was the usual way in which real estate was measured. There was both a linear arpent (approximately 192 English feet) and a superficial arpent (approximately .85 of an acre). It is not always easy to know which arpent is referred to in documents from the time. When unspecified, arpent usually refers to a linear unit, "arpent de face." The minot—approximately the same as one bushel—was a standard French unit for measuring the volume of such products as maize, wheat, and even salt. In the middle Mississippi Valley, French colonists usually built their houses with vertical logs, which were either planted in the earth palisade fashion* (poteaux-en-terre) *or placed upright on sills* (poteaux-sur-solle)*. Framed structures, and sometimes those of upright logs on sills, were often referred to as* de charpente. *Francs and livres were of the same value.*

16 August 1725 at Sieur Michel Philippe's house

Agricultural land of 5 facing arpents located in the prairie of Monsieur de Melique, bordering on one side of the land of the late Charles Dany and on the other side to Jacques Philippe
Estimated at 2000 livres

More land of 4 facing arpents bordering on one side Guillaume Pottier
and on the other side Cadron, which has been cleared to be sown
with 30 minots of wheat
Estimated at 3000 livres

More land located in the North Point of the village of Kaskaskia, bordering on the one side Sieur Lalande and several other *habitants*
Estimated at 2000 livres

Another piece of land located in the village of Kaskaskia close to the
petite riviere . . . in the common. . . .
Estimated at 300 livres

A lot of 3 arpents located in the village of Kaskaskia bordered on the one
side by the lot of the late Sieur Bourdon and on the other by Guillaume Pottier
Estimated at 500 livres

A barn located on a lot
Estimated at 550 livres

A barn located on a lot
Estimated at 1100 livres

Another lot located in the village of Kaskaskia containing one arpent
of land, . . . facing the church. On this lot there is a house of *poteaux-en-terre* 36 by 20 feet in which there is a stone fireplace, with
neither floor nor interior walls. And another framed [*de charpente*]
40 by 22 feet . . . a small cabin . . . stable of *poteaux-en-terre*. The lot
is half enclosed with pickets of mulberry.
Estimated at 5500 livres

A house 36 feet long and 20 feet wide located on a three-quarter arpent
lot bordering the Reverend Jesuit Fathers. . . . The said lot is enclosed with pickets.
Estimated at 2500 livres

The planks necessary in order to plank . . .
700 livres

The ironwork necessary for . . .
400 livres

Two cauldrons of red copper, one of 14 to 15 pots and the other of 10 to
    12 pots, together
300 livres

Three pair of tongs and one pot hook
75 livres

One bed of straw and rope
20 livres

Six minots of shallots @ 15 livres/minot
90 livres

Two kegs of oil containing 50 pots @ 3 livres/pot
150 livres

Six minots of small wheat @ 12 livres/minot
72 livres

One old cotton sheet
20 livres

Seventeen sickles, some good, some bad
68 livres

Three iron cooking spoons
30 livres

Five iron axes @ 25 livres each
125 livres

One pound of salt
60 livres

Twenty pounds of pepper . . . @ 4 livres/pound
80 livres

Three old . . . out of service
30 livres

Two iron salt spoons
20 livres

One pirogue of cottonwood, about 40 [?] feet long
40 livres
Sunset for the day

17 August 1725 in the a.m.

Twelve pigs @ 80 francs each
960 francs

Two medium size pigs @ 50 francs
100 francs

Seventeen little ones 25 francs ea.
425 francs

Eight picks totaling
80 francs

Four flails, two good, two out-of-service
60 francs

Six minots of wheat in flour
72 francs

Two augers and one . . .
30 francs

One crosscut and one rip saw
80 francs

Twelve stacks . . . of shingles made . . . for the cabin of 40 feet that is next
to the church of Kaskaskia.
180 francs
Stopped at midday

17 August 1725 in the p.m.

Six beefs
3600 livres

Four cows
2400 livres

Two heifers @ 500 livres ea.
1000 livres

Two male horses @ 500 livres ea.
1000 livres

One mare
600 livres

One old negro named Pierrot and one negress named Brinbelle, mar-
    ried
2400 livres

Two more negroes, one named Carod and one named Gollon, married
3500 livres

One Indian boy slave named Chinchchinan
600 livres

Two carts, one for oxen, one for a horse
300 livres

Two plows, equipped and ready to plow
500 livres

Eighteen pewter spoons
36 livres

Three and three-quarters ells of green serge @ 10 livres/ell
37 livres 10

Two ells of red fabric for leggings @ 15 livres/ell
30 livres

Five ells of white serge @ 10 livres ea.
50 livres

Fourteen and a half ells of cloth @ 8 livres/ell
116 livres

Four trade guns @ 40 livres ea.
160 livres

Two copper candelabra with their mouchette and its holder
25 livres

Eight small pewter plates @ 6 livres ea.
48 livres

Four plates and a small platter of pewter
36 livres

One pewter basin
36 livres

A salting tub containing about 300 pounds of bacon
300 livres

Two large brass cauldrons
100 livres

One brass milk bucket and two . . . a *boire*
50 livres

Three copper cauldrons without lids
250 livres

Two iron kettles with lids
150 livres

Two frying pans
50 livres

One copper coffee pot, one casserole kettle with legs and handle [*poêlon*]
    and one large stirring spoon of iron
30 livres

One grill in poor condition
15 livres

One pair of . . . and one cow
220 livres

About one minot of salt
75 livres

Eight trade picks
80 livres

One clipper [*buchet*] for working vines
10 livres

One walnut table with two drawers
100 livres

Five chairs and 2 armchairs of walnut
120 livres

Forty minots of peas @ 15 livres/minot
600 livres

Fifty pounds of bulk lead
50 livres

One hundred livres of . . .
100 livres

Sixty pots of oil estimated at 3 livres/pot
180 livres

Eight plat . . . @ 10 livres ea.
80 livres

Seven minots of flour
84 livres

Two boxes of old iron and nails
150 livres

Ten pots of oil [?] estimated 3 livres/pot
30 livres

One . . .
30 livres

One hayfork
10 livres

Fifty minots of maize estimated @ 5 livres/minot
250 livres

Twelve hundred laths @ 15 livres/1000
18 livres

Eight minots of oats @ 5 livres/minot
40 livres

Nine tons of wood, of which seven tons are debarked and 2 tons are cut
100 livres

A small horse-drawn cart
25 livres

The materials for two wheels
30 livres

Forty-eight fat poultry
192 livres

The harvest of French wheat [bled francais], which is sheaved and in the
barn, estimated at 3300 livres

Approximately 19 to 20 arpents of land sown in maize that has not been
harvested. When the harvest is done, Sieur Michel Philippe will be
obliged to make an inventory of the maize in order to hold in account for the heirs of the late Marie Rouensa, his wife; they will pay
Sieur Michel Philippe their share of the costs of the harvest.
. . . . . livres

Six cartloads of hay estimated @ 30 livres per *charrette*
180 livres

Six livres of scrap iron
3 livres 12

A lockplate for a gun
10 livres

A cassette with lock and key
10 livres

The inventory was closed between 10 and 11 a.m. in the presence of the same
witnesses and appraisers who signed. It amount to the sum of 45,214 livres
2 sous, not including the maize on the stalk, which although included in the
inventory has not been appraised. Done in Kaskaskia, 17 [18?] August 1725.

Appendix: Excerpts from *The Jesuit Relations*

The Jesuit Relations *are reports written by missionary priests for their superiors and supporters in Europe for the purpose of documenting their attempts
at converting Native people to their version of Christianity. The writers' objectives were not only to inform but also to convince readers that the missions were
worthy ventures and that continued funding was money well spent. Readers
of these excerpts from a letter by Father Jacques Gravier will notice his contempt for indigenous religion and other elements of culture and his attempts
to manipulate the community to his advantage. Also evident is the autonomy*

and authority that this situation afforded to Marie in this conflict. We also see
the role of Marie's mother in the community, and we hear echoes of Marie's
voice translated and paraphrased through Gravier, who had evidently learned
at least some of the local dialect. Gravier wrote this in French, but it has been
translated into English, thus Marie's words are twice removed.

Excerpts from the "Letter by Father Jacques Gravier in the form of a Journal
of the Mission of l'Immaculée Conception de Notre Dame in the Illinois country," February 15, 1694, from Reuben Gold Thwaites, ed., The Jesuit Relations
and Allied Documents: Travels and Explorations of the Jesuit Missionaries
in New France, 1610–1791, vol. 64 (Cleveland: Burrows Brothers Company,
1900), 179, 181, 193, 195, 197, 205, 207, 217, 219, 227, 229, 233.

> The chief of the *Kaskaskia* and his wife have, ever since the mar-
> riage of their daughter with a frenchman been very assiduous
> at the instructions, and have begged me to prepare them for
> baptism. Their son-in-law, forced by the reproaches of his con-
> science, has admitted to his father- and mother-in-law that all
> the falsehoods which he had told to discredit the missionaries
> were but fictions. . . . These two worthy savages reflected so seri-
> ously on all that their son-in-law and daughter told them re-
> specting the unfortunate condition of those who refuse my good
> advice that, without speaking to me of it, they agreed that the
> chief should publicly declare the resolution which he had taken
> to become a christian. To make this act more solemn, he gave
> a feast to the chiefs of all the villages. . . . The same evening, his
> wife gave a feast to all the women of her village, to inform them
> also that she intended to become a christian. The better to try
> them, I let neither of them know what I had learned. From that
> time, they urged me to baptize them; I granted them that favor
> after they had given me several proofs of their desire to perform
> the duties of christians. To make the ceremony of their baptism
> more profitable and more imposing, I proclaimed throughout
> the village that all were to be present at their baptism. I was very
> glad that many witnessed it. . . .
>
> . . . [T]he fervor of her who is married to Sieur Ako has noth-
> ing of the savage in it, so thoroughly is she imbued with the
> spirit of God. She tells me the thoughts and the elevated senti-
> ments that she has regarding God,—with such ingenuousness

that I cannot sufficiently thank God for revealing himself so intimately to a young savage in the midst of an infidel and corrupt nation. Many struggles were needed before she could be induced to consent to the marriage, for she had resolved never to marry, in order that she might belong wholly to Jesus Christ. She answered her father and mother, when they brought her to me in company with the frenchman whom they wished to have for a son-in-law, that she did not wish to marry; that she had already given all her heart to God, and did not wish to share it. Such were her very words, which had never yet been heard in this barbarism. Consequently her language was received with displeasure; and—as I frankly stated that such sentiments were not those of a savage, and that God alone could have inspired her with them—her father, her mother, and still more the frenchman who wished to marry her, were convinced that it was I who made her speak thus. I told them that God did not command her not to marry, but also that she could not be forced to do so; that she alone was mistress to do either the one or the other, in the fear of offending God. She made no answer either to all the entreaties or to all the threats of her father and mother, who went away quite chagrined, and thinking of nothing but venting their anger against me,—imagining that it was I who prevented their daughter from giving her consent.

As I went through the village calling the savages to prayers, the father stopped me when I passed before his cabin, and told me that, inasmuch as I was preventing his daughter from obeying him, he would also prevent her from going to the chapel; at the same time he came out of his cabin, rating me and inveighing against me, and barring the way to those who followed me. A portion of the *Kaskaskia* nevertheless came to the chapel, and so did the *Peouareoua*, who went round the village to escape his sight. He had just driven his daughter out of the house after depriving her of her upper garment, her stockings, her shoes, and her petty ornaments, without a single word of remonstrance or a single tear from her....

... During those 2 days the chief of the *Kaskaskia* made every effort to obtain his daughter's consent, by dint of caresses and of threats. He assured her that, if she obeyed him not, she would be treated most rigorously by him; that assuredly prayers would no longer be said to God; that he would go to war, and that she would see him no more. She came to me, and assured me that God strengthened her; that she was still resolved to consecrate her virginity to God; that she had wept for 2 days on account of this conspiracy against prayer, of which her father was the instigator; and that she feared that her father would become still more furious and proceed to extremities. "All the threats against me trouble me not," she said, "and my heart is content. But I fear for God's word, because I know my father and my mother." "Fear not," I said to her, "prayer is the homage paid to God." "My father has had pity on me," she said, "and I have an idea—I know not whether it is a good one. I think that, if I consent to the marriage, he will listen to you in earnest, and will induce all to do so. I wish to please God, and for that reason I intend to be always as I am in order to please Jesus Christ alone. But I thought of consenting against my inclination to the marriage, through love for him. Is that right?" These are all her own words and I merely translate her Ilinois into French. "My daughter," I said to her, "God does not forbid you to marry; neither do I say to you: 'Marry or do not marry.' If you consent solely through love for God, and if you believe that by marrying you will win your family to God, the thought is a good one. But you must declare to your parents that it is not their threats that make you consent to the marriage." She came to the latter decision. As the urgent solicitations continued, she said to her mother: "I pity my father. I feel no resentment against him for his treatment of me, and I fear not his threats. But I think that I shall grant his request, because I believe that you and he will grant me what I ask." Finally, she told her father that she consented to the marriage. . . .

. . . On another occasion I asked her whether she loved the Blessed Virgin, and what she said to her. "I know not whether I do wrong in calling her *my mother*," she replied; "I pray to her with every endearing term, to be pleased to adopt me as her daughter. What should I do were she not my mother, and did she not look upon me as her daughter? Am I capable of guiding myself? I am still but a child, and know not yet how to pray. I beg her to teach me what I should say to her, that she may protect me against the Demon—who assails me on all sides, and would cause me to fall had I not recourse to her, and did she not receive me in her arms, as a good mother receives her frightened child." She also told me, very ingenuously, that she begged her not to be angry at her for bearing her beautiful name of Mary; that she always remembered, while saying her rosary, to pray to Our Lady's beloved son Jesus, our Captain, that she might not sully the Holy name that she bore, and that he might not be angry at her for calling Our Lady her mother. "No," I said to her, "she is not angry because you call her mother. Continue to speak thus to her; she will cheerfully listen to you, and will look upon you as her daughter so long as you really love her son." This good girl displays admirable care in getting the children and young girls of her village baptized, and it gives her great pleasure to be chosen as Godmother. She herself brings the children of her relatives, as soon as they are born—in order, as she says, that they may at once cease to be slaves of the Devil, and become children of God. And when she learns that a child who has been baptized is dead, she rejoices at this, and begs it to intercede with God for her, and for the whole village. The grown girls and the young women who have been baptized she induces, whenever she can, to come to her home, that she may instruct them; and she tries to inspire them with horror for dances, for night assemblies, and for evil of all kinds, and to instruct them regarding confession. From time to time, she brings me one that I may confess her; and occasionally she comes to me, quite disconsolate, to say: "I have not been able to persuade such a one; she dreads confession. Try to speak to her yourself," she says to me; and informs me of all kinds of things that she adroitly discovers. Her discretion and virtue give her marvelous authority, especially over those to whom she speaks of prayer without even any aged women finding fault with her—reproving them sometimes more energetically than I myself would do. What efforts did she not make to induce her father and mother to become christians! She frequently added tears to her entreaties; and, since their baptism, she ceases not to remind them of the promises that they made to God. . . .

. . . When I asked her why she was so desirous of teaching the children, she replied that it was because God specially loved them; that their souls still retained the beauty that they had received in baptism; and that as yet they knew not evil. . . .

. . . Since the *Kaskaskia* have returned from hunting, so many people come after prayers all together to catechism—which is taught throughout the winter in my lodge, because it is too cold in the chapel—that there is not enough room for all. As she taught it as well as I, during the day, to the children, there were but few during the months of October and November at the conferences and instructions that I gave them. To the adults I explained the whole of the New Testament, of which I have copper-plate engravings representing perfectly what is related on each page. At the beginning she herself, her husband, who is a Frenchman, her father, her mother, and those of her cabin were the only persons present at the explanation that I gave of these pictures during an hour and a half; but curiosity to see the pictures, rather than to hear the explanations that I gave, attracted a great many.

This young woman, who is only 17 years old, has so well remembered what I have said about each picture of the Old and of the New Testament that she explains each one singly, without trouble and without confusion, as well as I could do—and even more intelligibly, in their manner. In fact, I allowed her to take away each picture after I had explained it in public, to refresh her memory in private. But she frequently repeated to me, on the spot, all that I had said about each picture; and not only did she explain them at home to her husband, to her father, to her mother, and to all the girls who went there,—as she continues to do, speaking of nothing but the pictures or the catechism,—but she also explained the pictures on the whole of the Old Testament to the old and the young men whom her father assembled in his dwelling. . . .

My sins and the malice of men have not prevented God from pouring down abundant blessings on this mission of the Ilinois. It has been augmented by two hundred and six souls whom I baptized between the 30th of March and 29th of November, 1693. Many children among that number are already in heaven and pray to God for their parents' conversion. Since the chief of the *Kaskaskia* has been baptized with his wife and family, consisting of 15 persons, he blushes not for the gospel, and ceases not to exhort and instruct the young men of his village night and day. I observe, thanks be to God, that he is listened to as well as his wife, who is ever in the chapel at the head of all those of her sex. I was greatly surprised, at the end of the night, to see her come, accompanied by all the women, to make a fine present of tallow to the chapel (this is the wax of the country). She told me, in the name of all, that they offered it to God, to light the chapel when I said the great prayer—that is, during mass. . . .

Notes

1. Marie was illiterate and left no signature. Early Kaskaskia parish records consistently give her name as "Marie 8canic8e." On the other hand, later civil records in the Kaskaskia Manuscripts associated with her succession refer to her as Marie Rouensa (or Roensa, Roinsa, or Rouenssa). I have found no original source document that uses the 8cate8a form. It is not clear how and when the 8cate8a inaccuracy was introduced, but it was perpetuated in Marthe Faribault-Beauregard, ed., *La population des forts français d'Amérique* (Montreal: Editions Bergeron, 1984), as well as by this author in the original version of the article reproduced here.
2. This extensive exhibit is still in place at the Illinois State Museum and may be accessed via the museum's website.
3. Clarence Walworth Alvord, *The Illinois Country, 1673–1818*, Centennial History of Illinois, vol. 1 (Springfield: Illinois Centennial Commission, 1920), 32n, 104. For a discussion of the 8 phoneme see Virgil J. Vogel, *Indian Place Names in Illinois* (Springfield: Illinois State Historical Library, 1963), 24n–25n. Since Marie Rouensa never learned to write, we have no personal letters, diaries, or journals. Documentation concerning her life, however, is relatively rich for a personage of the early Illinois country. She appears repeatedly in Jesuit correspondence, local notarial records, and Kaskaskia parish records. It is rare to link three discrete sets of documents to a particular individual.
4. Floyd Mulkey, "Fort St. Louis at Peoria," *Journal of the Illinois State Historical Society* 37 (1944): 306–7.
5. Natalia M. Belting, *Kaskaskia under the French Regime*, Illinois Studies in the Social Sciences, vol. 29 (Urbana: University of Illinois Press, 1948), 14. Mary Borgias Palm also mentions Marie in *The Jesuit Missions of the Illinois Country, 1673–1763* (Cleveland: n.p., 1931), 38.
6. Rueben Gold Thwaites, ed., *The Jesuit Relations and Allied Documents: Travels and Explorations of the Jesuit Missionaries in New France, 1610–1791* (Cleveland: Burrows Brothers, 1896–1901), 64:211–15.

7. Thwaites, *Jesuit Relations*, 64:177.

8. Thwaites, *Jesuit Relations*, 65:67.

9. "Memoir of De Gannes Concerning the Illinois Country," in *The French Founda-tions, 1680–1693*, ed. Theodore Calvin Pease and Raymond C. Werner, Collections of the Illinois State Historical Library, vol. 23 (Springfield: Illinois State Histori-cal Library, 1934), 361. Judith Franke, director of the Illinois State Museum at Dick-son Mounds, recently reexamined the authorship of this memoir. She is confident that the author was Pierre-Charles de Liette, that he was a cousin of Henri De Ponti, that he was active in the Illinois country from the late 1680s to ca. 1720, and that he was *not* the commandant at Fort de Chartres during the late 1720s: that comman-dant was Charles-Henri de Liette. No one has identified De Gannes: he seems to have been a scribe or secretary in Quebec, who never visited Illinois country.

10. Thwaites, *Jesuit Relations*, 64:179–81. Modern authorities are also interested in the relative ease with which Jesuit missionaries converted the younger women of the Illinois tribe. For example, see John A. Walthall and Elizabeth D. Benchlev, *The River L'Abbe Mission*, Studies in Illinois Archaeology no. 2 (Springfield: Illinois His-toric Preservation Agency, 1987), 79.

11. Raymond E. Hauser, "The Illinois Indian Tribe: From Autonomy and Self-Suffi-ciency to Dependency and Depopulation," *Journal of the Illinois State Historical So-ciety* 69 (1976): 135.

12. Pease and Werner, *French Foundations*, 265n; Alvord, *Illinois Country*, 82, 104n; Palm, *Jesuit Missions*, 38; Benjamin Sulte, *Histoire des Canadiens Francais, 1608–1880* (Montréal: Wilson & cie, 1882–84), 4:52–63, 64–78.

13. Thwaites, *Jesuit Relations*, 64:195.

14. Thwaites, *Jesuit Relations*, 64:205.

15. Thwaites, *Jesuit Relations*, 64:213.

16. Mulkey, "Fort St. Louis," 301–16. Mulkey calls Marie Rouensa "Marie Aramipinchi-coue," for which he cites the unreliable transcriptions in C. J. Eschmann, trans., "Kaskaskia Church Records," in *Transactions of the Illinois State Historical Society* (1904), 395. I have not located a *manuscript* that uses that name for Marie. Baptismal records of her children in Faribault-Beauregard, *Forts francais d'Amérique*, 2:108, 146 (those transcriptions are not impeccable but are more reliable), refer to Marie as "Marie Rouensa, fille du chef des Kaskaskias" and "Marie Rouensa-8cate8a."

17. See Margaret Kimball Brown, *Cultural Transformation among the Illinois: The Ap-plication of a Systems Model to Archaeological and Ethnohistorical Data* (1973; re-print, Ann Arbor: University Microfilms International, 1977), 15–16.

18. Faribault-Beauregard, *Forts francais d'Amérique*, 2:205.

19. Thwaites, *Jesuit Relations*, 64:229.

20. "De Gannes Memoir," 330.

21. Francis Parkman, *La Salle and the Discovery of the Great West* (London: Macmillan, 1893), 192–93.

22. Emily J. Blasingham, "The Depopulation of the Indians, Part I," *Ethnohistory* 3

(1956): 199–200; Palm, *Jesuit Missions*, 23–26, 35–48; Wayne C. Temple, *Indian Villages of the Illinois Country*, Illinois State Museum Scientific Papers, vol. 2, pt. 2 (1958; reprint, Springfield: Illinois State Museum, 1977), 30–35.

23. Thwaites, *Jesuit Relations*, 64:195–213. Gravier takes great pains to explain that Marie had become a devout Roman Catholic before her marriage.

24. Faribault-Beauregard, *Forts francais d'Amérique*, 2:108. This is the first record in the registers of the parish of the Immaculate Conception, which are now preserved in the archives of the Diocese of Belleville. The Immaculate Conception did not officially become a canonical parish until 1719, when it was located at Kaskaskia. Pierre Accault seems to have been sent to school in Quebec (Palm, *Jesuit Missions*, 38). He later returned to Kaskaskia. Pierre obviously received some schooling, for by 1725 he was able to sign his name, "Pierre Ako," with relative ease; see Kaskaskia Manuscripts, 25:8:17:1, Randolph County Courthouse, Chester, Illinois (microfilm in Illinois State Historical Library, Springfield). The documents are cataloged by year (two digits only), month, day, and sequence in the total number of transactions recorded that day. Both Alvord (*Illinois County*, 104n) and Mulkey ("Fort St. Louis," 307) give the wrong birth date for Pierre Accault based on an error in Eschmann, "Kaskaskia Church Records," 394–95.

25. Gilbert J. Garraghan, "The First Settlement on the Site of St. Louis," *Illinois Catholic Historical Review* 9 (1927): 342–47.

26. Faribault-Beauregard, *Forts francais d'Amérique*, 2:107–8.

27. Garraghan, "First Settlement," 346–47; Palm, *Jesuit Missions*, 42–45.

28. Thwaites, *Jesuit Relations*, 69:219; Antoine Simon Le Page du Pratz, *The History of Louisiana*, ed. Joseph G. Tregle Jr. (1774; reprint, Baton Rouge: Louisiana State University Press, 1975), 182.

29. Agnes Philippe was baptized at Kaskaskia by Father Pierre Gabriel Marest (Faribault-Beauregard, *Forts francais d'Amérique*, 2:146).

30. Faribault-Beauregard, *Forts francais d'Amérique*, 2:146. Since baptismal record keeping was sporadic from 1695 to the formation of Kaskaskia parish in 1719, the number of children Marie actually had is uncertain.

31. For black slavery in the Illinois country, see Carl J. Ekberg, "Black Slavery in Illinois, 1720–1765," *Western Illinois Regional Studies* 12 (1989): 5–19.

32. "Relation de Pénicaut," in *Découvertes et Etablissements des Francais*, ed. Pierre Margry (Paris: Maisonneuve Frères et Ch. Leclerc, 1879–88), 5:489–91.

33. Edward B. Jelks, Carl J. Ekberg, and Terrance J. Martin, *Excavations at the Laurens Sites: Probable Location of Fort de Chartes I*, Studies in Illinois Archaeology no. 5 (Springfield: Illinois Historic Preservation Agency, 1989), 6–9.

34. Kaskaskia Manuscripts, 27:2:11:2; Palm, *Jesuit Missions*, 49; Belting, *Kaskaskia*, 14–15.

35. Palm, *Jesuit Missions*, 49; Belting, *Kaskaskia*, 14–15. The exact circumstances of the creation of the French and Indian Kaskaskia villages remain unclear.

36. "Journal of Diron d'Artaguiette," in *Travels in the American Colonies*, ed. Newton D. Mereness (New York: Macmillan, 1916), 67–68.

37. Kaskaskia census of 1723, colonial series, C13A, VIII, 226, Archives Nationales, Paris.
38. Faribault-Beauregard, *Forts francais d'Amérique*, 2:107–81.
39. Kaskaskia Manuscripts, 26:6:13:1. Anton J. Pregaldin suggests that "Yue Pinet" may have been Hubert Finet, who married at Kaskaskia in 1731 and appears in the 1732 census of the Illinois (Charles R. Maduell Jr., comp. and trans., *The Census Tables for the French Colony of Louisiana from 1699 through 1732* [Baltimore: Genealogical Pub. Co., 1972], 151). A Hubert Finé embarked for Louisiana from France in 1719 (Belting, *Kaskaskia*, 98).
40. For marriage contracts in French Louisiana and the uses of the Customary Law of Paris in such contracts, see Hans Baade. "Marriage Contracts in French and Spanish Louisiana: A Study in Notarial Jurisprudence," *Tulane Law Review* 53 (1978): 1–92.
41. Kaskaskia Manuscripts, 25:6:13:1.
42. Kaskaskia Manuscripts, 25:6:13:1.
43. Kaskaskia Manuscripts, 25:6:14:1.
44. Kaskaskia Manuscripts, 25:6:20:1.
45. Kaskaskia Manuscripts, 25:6:14:1.
46. Kaskaskia Manuscripts, 25:6:13:1; Belting, *Kaskaskia*, 15.
47. Kaskaskia Manuscripts, 38:10:20:1 and 38:10:20:22.
48. Kaskaskia Manuscripts, 25:8:16:1.
49. During the mid-1720s, annual wages for an *engagé* in the Illinois country were 50 livres plus a pair of French shoes. See Margaret Kimball Brown and Laurie Cena Dean, *The Village of Chartres in Colonial Illinois, 1720–1765* (New Orleans: Polyanthos Press, 1977), 871.
50. According to the 1752 census of the Illinois country, the Jesuits owned thirty-two black slaves. See Loudoun Collection, Manuscript 426, Huntington Library, San Marino, California.
51. Anton J. Pregaldin compiled the genealogical data in this paragraph and the two following.
52. Kaskaskia Manuscripts, 28:11:13:1.

10. Women, Kin, and Catholicism

New Perspectives on the Fur Trade

SUSAN SLEEPER-SMITH

New Introduction by Susan Sleeper-Smith

The ways in which social history fostered the resurgence of Native history and the founding of women's history and gender studies has affected traditional scenarios of encounter. Robert Berkhofer's call for Indian studies to be written not as demise but as rebirth and resurgence has influenced my rethinking of this time period, especially the role that women played in that revitalization.[1] The new literature in Indian history that has emerged, particularly Richard White's *The Middle Ground*, has reenvisioned the Great Lakes as a coherent region where Indians dominated the social landscape and remained as politically powerful as the French, and where changes arose from cultural borrowing and diverse ethnic values. My interest was in how women were involved in negotiating many of those cultural changes.

Previous historians had written women out of encounter history, but I discovered that there were numerous references to women as wives, translators, and mediators. This article represents an attempt to correct those deficiencies and suggests one way that we may begin to reconsider the role that Native women played in the changes that occurred during the seventeenth and eighteenth centuries.

The documents that shape this article are often regarded as the evidence for early French communities, but if Indians readily borrowed French cultural forms to re-create familiar social landscapes, we can also use these documents to look at the types of social change which involved Indians. Baptismal and marital registers form the core of this research and are extremely valuable in identifying Indian women. The priests often included both Indian and Christian names, the identity of parents and godparents, and village affiliation. In creating genealogical charts from these registers, I found that many of these women appear repeatedly as baptismal sponsors. Comparing these registers across the breadth of this Great Lakes colonial region, it becomes apparent that these Indian women were important figures at multiple sites, from Detroit to Vincennes to Michilimackinac to Kaskaskia. By the end of the French colonial period there were so many Indian women married to French men that a network of Catholic kin seemed to link all of the families involved in the fur trade. In the language of assimilationist historians, these Indian women became Frenchwomen. But the evidence for such assimilationist paradigms is highly problematic. Sylvia Van Kirk's *Many Tender Ties* and Jennifer Brown's *Strangers in Blood* uncovered women's involvement in the fur trade, demonstrating that the exchange of goods for furs depended on marriage to Indian women who remained linked to their communities.[2] The women in my article were distinguished not only by their involvement in the fur trade but also by their Christianity. While we are still unsure what that faith meant, we can explore how the structures of Catholicism opened new avenues for women. Nancy Shoemaker's article on Kateri Tekakwitha in *Negotiators of Change* provided a glimpse into how Catholicism acted as a means of empowerment. I used that model for my own research, adding an exploration of how networks of these women, serving as godparents, gave them increasing power in the fur trade.[3]

I have also borrowed from Laurel Thatcher Ulrich's *Good Wives* and her *A Midwife's Tale* the sense that women's lives represented a variety of roles. There is much to suggest that the Indian women, like the "deputy husbands" of New England, were called on to act as surrogates for their husbands, to accept articles in trade, to judge the quality of furs, to distribute gifts, and to serve as traders themselves when their husbands were away.[4] These households were dominated not by the patriarchical cultures of Puritan New England but rather by kin networks and a greater flexibility in male and female roles. For example, Marie Rouensa, in making out her will, demanded that it be translated into her native language, revealing that, despite two French husbands and several children, the family was conversant in her language, not her husband's French tongue.

Finally, rather than seeing the past as a link to explain the present, I have envisioned an unfamiliar realm. In a seventeenth- and eighteenth-century world where the majority of the Great Lakes population was Indian, we need to look for the evidence of that Indian world, to imagine familiar sources differently, and to uncover the ways in which Indians adapted to meet the challenges presented by the encounter process.

Women, Kin, and Catholicism
New Perspectives on the Fur Trade (2000)

Scholars who have studied the fur trade of the western Great Lakes offer conflicting interpretations of its impact on Native American societies. Those who view the trade as synonymous with the intrusion of market forces, particularly the pursuit of profit, generally link both indigenous decline and the depletion of animal populations with the trade. Other scholars contend that the fur trade had overarching political and diplomatic ramifications, however, and that profit making was often subordinated to maintain the Algonquian-French alliance.[5] Most recently, Richard White has envisioned the fur trade as integral to an ever-evolving arena of cultural negotiation that he labeled the "middle ground." For White, "the creation of the middle ground involved a process of mutual invention" created by "people who shared neither their values nor their assumptions about the appropriate way of accomplishing tasks" and "which grew according to the need of people to find a means, other than force, to gain the cooperation or consent of foreigners."[6]

This article focuses on four Native women, married to French fur traders, whose lives offer insight into the process of sociological and cultural adaptation that occurred as Indian villages of the western Great Lakes became increasingly involved in the trade. This essay suggests that the conception of White's *Middle Ground* is a viable way in which to describe interaction between Indians and Euro-Americans and that it should be expanded to emphasize the prominent role that Native women played as cultural mediators. The Indian women who married fur traders were "negotiators of change."[7] They lived in a region where the exchange process occurred primarily at wintering grounds or in villages, and, because trade had social as well as economic ramifications, intermarriage played an integral role in the trade's evolution. Traders who married these women thus had an advantage over their rivals. Marriage, either in the "manner of the country" or performed by missionary priests, assured traders inclusion as members of indigenous communities and facilitated access to furs.[8]

A fur trader's presence enhanced the importance of the community where he lived and simultaneously enhanced his wife's authority and prestige among her people. Native women did not marry out; rather, they incorporated their French husbands into a society structured by Native custom and tradition.[9] Although access to trade goods enhanced the power and influence of the Native women, they did not simply reinvent themselves as French. Although early Jesuit records, particularly marital and baptismal registers, provide the opportunity to study such women's lives, unfortunately they also effectively mask indigenous identity. Many women were simply identified by their baptismal names or by the surname of their husbands.

The Native women who are the focus of this article can be identified in Jesuit records by both their Indian and Christian names. Because we are aware of their Native ancestry, we can consequently see how they were involved in the creation of Catholic kin networks. These women repeatedly served as godmothers to numerous children of mixed ancestry. Over time this Catholic kin network became increasingly more complex, as large numbers of such children and godchildren entered the fur trade. Baptism and marriage provided the means through which this diverse and real fictive kin network could be continually expanded. Marital and baptismal records suggest that these networks, created by Catholicism, facilitated access to peltry while simultaneously allowing these women to negotiate for themselves positions of prominence and power. Also, many of the traders who married into these networks became prominent fur-trade figures. Therefore, by the mid-eighteenth century an identifiable Catholic kin network had evolved that was compatible with and often parallel to that of indigenous society.

Female members—especially of the Barthe, Bourassa, Chaboyer, Chevalier, La Framboise, and Langlade families—appear frequently in baptismal registers of the western Great Lakes. These women were godmothers to each other's children and grandchildren, and their surnames span generations. The godparenting roles modeled by mothers were emulated by daughters and granddaughters.

The contention that Catholicism had important social ramifications that enhanced female autonomy contradicts the view that Catholicism instituted a male patriarchal order, which increasingly subordinated Native women to men. This later perspective, espoused in Carol Devens' *Countering Colonization* and Karen Anderson's *Chain Her by One Foot*, views Christianity as the means through which indigenous female autonomy was subverted.[10] These conclusions do not appear uniformly applicable to all Native communities in the western Great Lakes. Instead, this article suggests that Catholicism could also serve as pathway to social prominence.[11] The Jesuits generally recruited catechizers or instructors among Native women. These females were often the most visible proof of Jesuit success. It would have been foolhardy for these priests to foster female subjection to the authority of men, whom the Jesuits frequently despised. Indeed, most missionary priests viewed the fur-trade husbands of these converts as licentious drunkards who undermined Christian ideals; the Jesuits even vigorously supported a seventeenth-century royal policy that banished traders from the western Great Lakes. The Jesuits also frequently dismissed the elders of Native communities, many of whom scorned Christianity. Therefore, it would have been problematic for the Jesuits to support the establishment of a male patriarchal order that subjected their pious female converts to the authority of male fur traders and unconverted head men.

Just as the profit-making dimensions of the fur trade were mediated by the Algonquian-French political alliance, the repressive patriarchal order was mediated by the Jesuits' reliance on Native women. During the eighteenth century these women were also the beneficiaries of the dramatic decline in the number of Jesuit priests. Not only did missionary fervor wane, but in the last quarter of the century the Jesuits were temporarily disbanded. In the absence of priests, many female converts fashioned a type of "frontier Catholicism" in which they assumed the role of lay practitioners.

Amid the dynamics of this changing social landscape, Indian women who married fur traders relied on the interface between two worlds to position themselves as mediators between cultural groups, to assume leadership roles in religious training, to influence commodity production, and eventually, at least in a few cases, to establish themselves as independent traders. Through it all these women retained their Indian identity, as evidenced by their language, names, and tribal affiliations. More important, they relied on their Catholicism to maintain relative autonomy in relation to their husbands. The complicated dynamics of such behaviors are evidenced by four women, whose lives spanned the seventeenth and eighteenth centuries. Two of the women were Illini: Marie Rouensa-8cani8e[12] and Marie Madeleine Réaume L'archevêque Chevalier.[13] Each used Catholicism to resist and reshape indigenous societal constraints. Rouensa lived during the early years of the fur trade, when Catholicism was shaped by Jesuit missionaries. Réaume lived later in the eighteenth century, when priests were few in number, lay practitioners became increasingly important, and "frontier" or "folk" Catholicism emerged.[14] Over time, the syncretic nature of

Catholicism facilitated the creation of an ever-expanding kin network that extended the parameters of women's worlds from those of their immediate family and community to fur-trade posts throughout the Great Lakes and Mississippi River valley.

These women used the fictive ties created by godparenting to create ever-expanding kinship networks, and by the end of the eighteenth century these networks had evolved as strategic alliances that enabled some Native women to successfully establish themselves as independent fur traders. This was the case for Magdelaine Marcot La Framboise and Thérèse Marcot Lasaliere Schindler, who were raised in Odawa communities and were incorporated from birth into the Catholic kin networks of fur-trade society.[15] They negotiated the hazardous world of the late-eighteenth- and early-nineteenth-century fur trade when Frenchmen were displaced, first by the English and later by American traders. Both La Framboise and Schindler prospered because their centrality in indigenous kin networks gave them access to a stable supply of furs. These women retained their independence because they were at the locus of Catholic kin networks that were rooted in indigenous communities and that structured Great Lakes fur-trade society.[16]

These women, who have appeared tangentially in the fur-trade literature, have been depicted either as historical outliers or as women who did not challenge traditional spheres of male authority.[17] White used Rouensa to exemplify the cultural inventions of an evolving middle ground, when compromise, rather than force, convinced Rouensa to marry the fur trader Michel Accault. After her marriage, Rouensa disappeared from the "middle ground."[18] Marriage was not her gateway to invisibility, however. Marriage, coupled with her Catholicism, afforded access to power and prestige, which is apparent when examining the whole of Rouensa's life.[19]

Her centrality as a historical actor resulted from the economic and social adaptations that Indian communities experienced as they became increasingly involved in the western Great Lakes fur trade. Rouensa's village, located just south of Lake Michigan, became involved in the fur trade in the late 1670s, when Robert La Salle established a French presence in Illinois Country. Her father was an important headman among the Kaskaskia, one of the seven nations of the Iliniwek Confederacy.[20] In 1790 he arranged for Rouensa to marry a fur trader who had ventured west with La Salle in 1679.

Among the Kaskaskia, women were free to reject such arranged marriages. But in the 1690s, when the Fur Trade Wars engulfed the Great Lakes, access to trade goods and alliances with the French were considered important strategies that countered Iroquois hostilities. Rouensa would have experienced tremendous community pressure to accede to her father's request and to the wishes of her village. Had she acquiesced to such pressure, her behavior would have escaped historical attention. But Rouensa refused to marry, and she turned to the Jesuit Father Jacques Gravier for support.

Rouensa was one of Gravier's more prominent female converts among the Kaskaskia, of whom the Jesuits converted more women than men. Their efforts reinforced the Illini matrifocal households, which linked women in communal living arrangements and encouraged female conversions.[21] A 1712 Jesuit letter described how this process occurred among the Illinois: "We call those instructors, who in other missions are called catechists, because it is not in the Church, but in the wigwams that they instruct the catechumens and the proselytes."[22]

Gravier's enthusiastic search for converts encouraged these young women to speak out, and he (perhaps inadvertently) provided the tools for social empowerment to them.[23] In turn, female proselytes used Christianity to challenge the traditional wisdom of the tribal elders. Many young women became known for "mock[ing] the superstitions of their nation."[24] "Although this nation is much given to debauchery, especially the men, the Reverend Fathers of the Jesuits, who talk their language with perfect ease manage . . . to impose some check on this by instructing a number of girls in Christianity, who often profit by their teaching, and mock at the superstitions of their nation, which often greatly incenses the old men and daily exposes these Fathers to ill treatment, and even to being killed."[25] Given this scenario, it is not surprising that the Jesuits could "find hardly a single young man upon whom we can rely for the exercises of religion."[26]

Christian conversion enabled Rouensa to position herself as a teacher among her people. She expanded the culturally innovative dimensions of the middle ground when she translated Gravier's Christian message into her Kaskaskia language. Because she was an effective mediator of that message, Gravier loaned Rouensa books with pictures that supplemented her Christian storytelling and privileged her among the Kaskaskia: "Not only did she explain them at home . . . speaking of nothing but the pictures or the catechism—but she also explained the pictures on the whole of the Old Testament to the old and young men whom her father assembled in his dwelling."[27]

Gravier further reinforced such behaviors of young female proselytes when he shared with them stories of female saints. Virtue and mystical experiences produced European celibates, and strong similarities in indigenous behavior encouraged the Kaskaskia converts to dedicate their lives to the church. Illini women who traditionally elected to remain single usually entered warrior society. Christian conversion created an alternative option, and, facing the threat of an undesirable marriage, Rouensa "resolved to consecrate her virginity to God." Catholic conversion encouraged her to resist a proposed marriage, even though it was arranged by her parents. Her professed devotion to virginity, to the love of Christ, intensified when her parents chose for her husband Michel Accault, a fifty-year-old grizzled veteran of the fur trade. Rouensa called on Gravier to defend her decision to remain a celibate Catholic woman:[28] "She had resolved never to marry, in order that she might belong wholly to Jesus Christ. She answered her father and her mother, when they brought her to me in company with the frenchman whom they wished to have for a son-in-law, that she did not wish to marry; that she had already given all her heart to God."[29]

Gravier supported his young convert's decision. To have abandoned her would have resulted in the inevitable loss of his female congregation. Gravier was ridiculed by the fort commandant, and Rouensa's father banned his people from attending mass. Few attended, and although Gravier proposed prayer as the solution for the impasse, Rouensa proposed a more practical solution. She consented to marry the disreputable French trader if her parents agreed to become Christian converts. They readily assented to her demands.

In this manner Rouensa used Catholicism to reshape an otherwise potentially dismal outcome.[30] A marriage "in the manner of the country" would have given her minimal control over a husband who was "famous in this Illinois Country for all his debaucheries."[31] Now she could demand Christian reformation of Accault's character. As the priest's able assistant, Rouensa helped define what was expected of a Christian husband, and she relied on both her parents and her community to apply the necessary social pressures. Her parents' conversion was soon followed by the baptism of an additional two hundred people, and Gravier, obviously pleased with Rouensa's solution, counted more than three-fourths of the Kaskaskias present during catechism.[32]

Catholic marriages were sanctioned by Illini headmen, and consequently Christian strictures about the sanctity of marriage were incorporated into enforceable communal norms. Rouensa's father publicly proclaimed that "the black gowns were the witnesses of true marriage; and that to them alone God had given orders to pray for all who wished to be marry, and they would be truly married."[33] Although marriage "in the manner of the country" often acquired long-range stability, marriage partners like Accault, better known for their wayward ways than their faithful behavior, were problematic husbands. Not surprisingly, after his marriage Accault publicly proclaimed himself a reformed man. Surrounded by Christian Indians, he atoned for his sins. The sincerity of Accault's confession may be questioned, but Rouensa's matrifocal household, as well as her larger community, relied on Christian strictures about the sanctity of marriage to establish the invisible but effective links that ensured a reliable supply of well-priced trade goods.

French fur traders were eager to marry Native women with extensive kin networks, particularly socially prominent women like Rouensa. The exchange of trade goods for peltry occurred on a face-to-face basis, and along a kinship continuum. Kin networks controlled access to furs, and marriage ensured Euro-American men inclusion as kin. When French traders married Illini women, they joined their wives' households. This gave women, who controlled productive resources, increased access to trade goods. Trade goods reinforced ritual gift-giving and enhanced both the power and prestige of matrifocal households and individual women.

Households, like that of Rouensa, remained rooted within indigenous society and proved highly resistant to any efforts to impose patriarchal authority. Gravier was justifiably reluctant to accord Accault authority over his wife, for she was both an effective Catholic proselytizer and a more rigorous and faithful Christian than her husband. In this instance Catholicism proved to be a socially innovative mechanism that enhanced female authority. Simultaneously, access to trade goods reinforced the continued viability of Rouensa's matrifocal household, when it came under the stress of recurrent relocations. For Rouensa, her household, and her community, Accault was a desirable spouse, but only because this amorous adventurer was transformed into a reliable presence. Rouensa effected Accault's transformation, with the enthusiastic assistance of Gravier.

Such households not only frustrated attempts to impose hierarchical notions of European authority on Native women, they also fostered the expansion of the western fur trade. Native women became active participants in the trade because they controlled access to productive resources, particularly agricultural produce. European fur traders in the western Great Lakes were dependent on the indigenous food supply. Trade permits allowed each recipient only two canoes for the upper country, and men who married into these indigenous households were able to devote the limited cargo space of transport canoes almost entirely to trade goods. That was because the matrifocal households to which they were connected produced an agricultural surplus sufficient to feed not only their immediate family but also to feed the more transient fur trade population.

In Native American society agriculture was considered women's work, and in Illinois Country matrifocal households produced rich grain and vegetable harvests. Most historians have assumed that crops like wheat were not grown by Native people because they required extensive milling, but in Illinois Country wheat was harvested by both Indians and Jesuits. In Father Gabriel Marest's Iliniwek village on the Kaskaskia, two leagues from the Mississippi,[34] the Jesuits had their own mill, while the Illini operated two mills.[35]

During Rouensa's life the Kaskaskia migrated south to settle on the Mississippi's rich alluvial lands near St. Louis. Rouensa was left a widow after seven years of marriage to Accault, after which she married another Frenchman, Michel Philippe. He arrived in Illinois Country as an obscure *voyageur*, or canoeman, who probably earned less than a thousand livres a year.[36] For the next twenty years the Kaskaskia baptismal records detail the evolution of their increasingly large family. Rouensa gave birth to six more children, and by her death in 1725 she had amassed an estate that was sufficient to probate and inventory. The estate was divided between her second husband and her children from both marriages.

Before her death, Rouensa dictated her will to Father Baptiste Le Boullenger, and it was written down by a notary. The will was then read to her twice, in her Illini language. Her request that the document be written in her native tongue indicated that Rouensa's household and children were probably conversant in her language, rather than in her husband's French tongue. Each of her children, upon maturity or marriage, received 2,861 livres from an estate valued at 45,000 livres. Her property included several agricultural tracts of land. Two substantial houses, each thirty-six by twenty feet with stone fireplaces, were located within the Kaskaskia village. There were two barns filled with hay to feed the livestock: oxen, thirteen cows, three horses, thirty-one pigs, and forty-eight chickens. There were ox and horse carts and plows to cultivate the fields. Rouensa owned four African slaves (two couples, both married) as well as an Indian slave.[37] The female slaves probably planted and harvested the oats, wheat, and maize. The male slaves were more likely to work in the fur trade, but they were also woodcutters, for there were nine tons of wood, cut and debarked. The barns also contained wheat and oats. The wheat, valued at 3,300 livres, had been sheaved but not yet ground at the nearby mill. Nineteen to twenty arpents of maize or Indian corn remained to be harvested.[38]

The community of Kaskaskia itself underwent a complex evolution as a result of these relationships. It was a mature settlement, which historians have often erroneously identified as founded by the French. The fur traders intermarried among the indigenous people. Although numerous French names appear in marital and baptismal registers, Native women baptized by missionary priests assumed Christian names. During the first twenty years following European contact, there were few French women. As a consequence, of the twenty-one baptisms recorded by the Jesuits, only one was the child of a French woman.[39] There was a ready market in supplying fur traders as well as in shipping agricultural produce and furs north to Montreal and, in some instances, south to New Orleans. The establishment of Kaskaskia in close proximity to Cahokia created a new center of farming activity in the American Bottoms. Rouensa's household profited from the fur trade.[40]

Over time, communities like Kaskaskia evolved as a blending of indigenous and French cultures, but for the first generation they were more Illini than French.[41] Agriculture, for instance, remained the province of women. The continuity of these matrifocal households encouraged French husbands to become traders rather than farmers. But fields mounded in Indian fashion or cultivated by the small French *en bardeau* plows led travelers to condemn French men as lazy, simply because Native women's agricultural work was invisible to these Euro-American outsiders. These women also resisted the women's work associated with French households. Among the probated wills and inventories of the river community residents there were none of the traditional tools associated with French home industry—spinning wheels, looms, or even knitting needles.[42] In these communities it appears that indigenous gender roles gave women the management and allocation of resources. Even in the Illinois lead mines in the Fox-Wisconsin riverway region, women engaged in mining and seem to have influenced mining techniques and access to the mines.[43]

The fur trade and Catholicism enhanced not only the authority of women, but it also accorded them new avenues to social prominence. Women became Christian instructors. They also rang the chapel bells that summoned Catholic Indians to services in the morning and evening.[44] One of the most important figures at the River L'Abbe Mission, the French colonial church for the Cahokia Indians on Monks Mound, may have been the Illini woman who was buried with the chapel bell.[45] It was Rouensa who achieved one of the highest honors, however, for she was buried inside the Kaskaskia mission church.

Illini Catholicism was a shared female experience that was initially facilitated by Jesuit missionaries who consciously shaped Catholicism to be compatible with Indian beliefs and practices. Catholicism was then taught to Indian women by other female converts and was probably transformed even further by the verbal transmission process. By the mid-eighteenth century when Jesuit priests declined in number and when the order was suppressed in 1773, these Catholic women thus emerged as Catholicism's primary proselytizers. It was therefore not surprising that Catholicism then appealed to larger numbers of Native people.[46]

Catholicism acquired increased centrality in the fur trade because of its social ramifications. During the eighteenth century, female converts used their "frontier" Catholicism to construct kin networks, both real as well as fictive. Native women married to fur traders served as godmothers to each other's children, and during the eighteenth century these women constructed kinship ties with distant and dispersed communities throughout the western Great Lakes region. In the interface of two disparate worlds, these women relied on long-established kinship behaviors to recreate the familiar within a Christian context. Catholicism did not entail the dissolution of indigenous culture.

Distinctive Métis communities eventually evolved from these Catholic kin networks as mixed-ancestry women married Frenchmen or mixed-ancestry fur traders. Métis communities existed at important fur-trade posts, like Michilimackinac and Green Bay, but at smaller fur-trade communities the lives of these women continued to be shaped by the indigenous communities in which they lived. The power of habit structured their lives, just as it organized Indian society and enabled traditional economies to meet the demands of an emerging transatlantic market economy.[47]

Catholic kin networks were indispensable to the fur trade because they linked the larger fur-trade posts (the centers of exchange) with the smaller fur-trade posts (the sources of supply). How that kinship system operated is apparent in the life of another Illini woman, Marie Madeleine Réaume, the daughter of Simphorose Ouaouagoukoue and Jean Baptiste Réaume.[48] She was born early in the eighteenth century, shortly before Rouensa's death. Although both were Illini women and Catholic converts, their lives differed dramatically. Unlike Rouensa, Réaume had neither social prominence nor was her conversion of particular significance to any of the Jesuit fathers. She did not possess sufficient wealth to leave legacies for her children. In every respect she was a less conspicuous historical figure, and consequently she left no written records or will for the perusal of curious historians. But Réaume's life was illustrative of the prominent role women played in the evolution of fur-trade communities. Her life bridged two disparate worlds and illustrated how kin networks linked indigenous and French societies. Exchange remained embedded in social relationships, kinship mediated that process, and Catholic kin networks linked the distant fur-trade outposts of an expanding fur-trade society. For Native people, however, trade remained a process of collective exchange, while for Europeans exchange was an increasingly individualistic transaction within an emerging transatlantic market economy.[49]

Réaume, like the other women discussed in this article, was married "in the eyes of the church." Her husband was Augustin L'archevêque, a licensed trader in the Illinois Country.[50] During the course of their sixteen-year marriage, Réaume gave birth to six children and remained relatively anonymous until her husband's death.[51] Her name then started to appear in the fort's reimbursement records. Now identified as the Widow L'archevêque, she was reimbursed by the St. Joseph commandant for "one fat pig, a heifer, an ox, four pairs of snowshoes, a bark canoe, and another fat pig." Other invoices indicate that the widow also supplied sacks with wheat, oats, and corn.[52] It is clear that Réaume's household produced both a marketable agricultural surplus as well as specific goods for the trade.[53] Her agricultural holdings paralleled those of Rouensa, although they were far less significant. Réaume had "ten houses, good lands, orchards, gardens, cattle, furniture, [and] utensils."[54] Such women, and the agriculturally oriented communities in which they lived, were common throughout the Great Lakes. As far north as Michilimackinac, other Indian communities served as agricultural suppliers of the trade. At Waganagisi (L'Arbe Croche or Crooked Tree) the Odawa "raised large surpluses of corn and vegetables, produced fish, and later maple sugar, and manufactured canoes, snowshoes, and clothing essential to the Great Lakes fur trade."[55]

These communities experienced seasonal population shifts, but they acquired an increasingly larger core of permanent residents. Réaume, for instance, lived at Fort St. Joseph for almost seventy years; because of this longevity, she gradually established under the umbrella of Catholicism fictive and real kin networks that linked her household with similar fur-trade communities throughout the Great Lakes.[56]

Réaume's first attempt to expand her familial and fictive kin network to other prominent fur-trade families took place after her husband's death.[57] She had kin connections in the Illinois Country, but it was Michilimackinac that was emerging as the most important entrepôt of the eighteenth-century fur trade. In the summer of 1748, the thirty-eight-year-old widow traveled north to Michilimackinac. This was a journey of more than three hundred miles, which she made in a birch bark canoe with her three-year-old son and her two eldest daughters, seventeen-year-old Marie Catherine and fifteen-year-old Marie Joseph Esther. Réaume relied on baptism and marriage to incorporate her family into the more prominent Catholic kin network of Michilimackinac. Members of the Bourassa and the Langlade families served as godparents to Réaume's son and as witnesses at the weddings of her daughters.[58] The ceremonies and celebrations completed, Réaume returned to St. Joseph. Both daughters and their fur-trader husbands returned to St. Joseph and became part of Réaume's household.[59]

After the marriage of Réaume's daughters, increasingly complex behavioral strategies enveloped this entire household and included not just the children but also Réaume herself. Three years after the 1748 trip to Michilimackinac, Réaume, then forty-one years old, gave birth to a son. The child's father was a prominent Michilimackinac trader, Louis Thérése Chevalier, whom Réaume later married at the St. Joseph mission.[60] Chevalier was thirty-nine.[61] Although Chevalier had married among the Odawa, he nevertheless married this forty-two-year-old widow and relocated to the southeastern shore of Lake Michigan.

The apparent marital strategy of Réaume was to join her prosperous agricultural household to Michilimackinac, which was the most important trading outpost in the western Great Lakes. For Chevalier marriage extended his already extensive kin network and provided him with an entrée into the prosperous St. Joseph trade. Following Chevalier's marriage to Réaume, the Chevaliers garnered a substantial portion of the St. Joseph trade. Chevalier's father had traded there in 1718, but he subsequently did not receive a permit for the area. His eldest sister and her husband had lived in the community for more than twenty years, but reimbursement invoices signed by the post commandant were for Louis Deshêtres's work as a blacksmith. The Chevaliers were Michilimackinac traders who were long denied entrée into the St. Joseph trade. The other men in the Chevalier family had all married Native women on the western shore of Lake Michigan. In fact, Chevalier himself had married, in the manner of the country, an Odawa woman before his Christian marriage to Réaume, through whom he planned to enter the St. Joseph trade.[62]

The Chevalier kin network was gradually integrated into the St. Joseph community. One of Réaume's daughters married Chevalier's younger brother, Louis Pascal Chevalier.[63] Another daughter married her stepfather's Montreal trading partner, Charles Lhullic dit Chevalier. The groom was a recent widower age forty-five; the bride, Angelique L'archevêque, was twenty-one.[64] Réaume's youngest daughter, seventeen-year-old Anne, also married a fur trader, and they initially remained part of the St. Joseph community.[65]

Marriage integrated these two distant families, and in time the offspring migrated to other fur-trade communities. Mobility strengthened kinship ties not only with Michilimackinac but also to the south, creating a network that became increasingly important to the entire St. Joseph River valley when the British took control of the western Great Lakes. During the 1850s Réaume's two eldest daughters, their husbands, and their children moved to Fort Pimiteoui, now Peoria, and eventually to Cahokia.[66] Réaume's fourth daughter, Marie Amable, and her husband also eventually joined their L'archevêque kin at Cahokia.

Geographically distant kin links were also greatly reinforced by the godparenting roles that siblings played to each other's children. For example, Réaume's daughters were frequent godparents to their nieces and nephews.[67] After they no longer lived in the Fort St. Joseph community, they returned annually when missionary priests arrived from distant posts. Louis Chevalier's siblings also became godparents to the L'archevêque grandchildren, and Réaume's daughters were godmothers of the Chevalier grandchildren.

During the mid-eighteenth century an important demographic shift took place when Fort St. Joseph reverted to a predominantly indigenous settlement, and an increased number of Potawatomis became Catholic converts. By 1755 there was no longer a resident priest. In addition, many of the French families who had earlier lived at St. Joseph had now moved to Detroit.[68] Consequently, Réaume became the community's most important lay practitioner.[69] She employed Catholicism as a socially integrative tool that incorporated increased numbers of Native people. *Panis*, or Native slaves, and Indian women were baptized at the St. Joseph mission church. Réaume, for instance, was the godmother to Marie Jeanne, a thirteen-year-old slave, as well as to Thérèse, a forty-year-old Potawatomi woman.[70] One Miami couple, Pierre Mekbibkas8nga and his wife, had their "indian style marriage" sacramentally sanctioned by a visiting priest.[71] The incorporation of their four adult daughters through baptism revealed even more strongly the influence of the L'archevêque-Chevalier family. One daughter selected Louis Chevalier as her godfather; two other daughters chose Réaume as their godmother.[72]

The French departure did not signal the demise of St. Joseph as a fur-trade community. Instead, the number of furs harvested increased dramatically. More engagements or contracts for hiring canoemen were issued in this decade than in any previous period, and fur exports increased.[73]

By 1755, Réaume and Louis Chevalier were linked through trade and intermarriage to the Potawatomi villages of the St. Joseph River valley. Their son, Louison, probably married among the Potawatomi. In this smaller fur-trade community, on the banks of the St. Joseph River, Réaume and Chevalier remained part of an indigenous kin system.

Kinship facilitated fur-trade exchange and had political, as well as social and economic, dimensions. French authority over the North American interior rested on the hegemony of these kin networks. The French traders living among Native people were central to New France's highly effective communications network that linked distant western outposts. French traders relayed messages, solicited warriors, and mediated potentially disruptive disputes. Following the French and Indian War, when the British displaced the French, these kin networks frustrated the transfer of power. The garrisoning of former French forts proved an explosive event, when fur traders failed to assume their traditional role as mediators. Instead, in the uprising of 1763, they remained passive observers as the forts at Le Boeuf, Michilimackinac, Miami, Ouiatenon, Presqu'Isle, St. Joseph, Sandusky, and Verango fell to Native American forces.[74]

England lacked a sufficient presence to govern through force, and when the English ignored or attempted to displace French traders and their Native wives, this threatened to destabilize a highly complex, kin-related world of the upper Great Lakes region. Although Chevalier was described by the British as "so connected with the Potawatomis that he can do anything with

them," his influence was actually attributable to his wife.[75] Réaume had
lived at Fort St. Joseph for more than fifty years and had incorporated Chevalier into her kin network.[76] Communities like St. Joseph were the locus
of Catholic kin networks, and women like Réaume were the demographic
links in a world defined by kinship. Her behavior followed the pattern of
godparenting common in the western Great Lakes. She was the godmother
to the children of her children, her slaves and their offspring, fellow Native
American converts, and even the children of unconverted Native women.
Eventually, Reaume's kinship network extended south to St. Louis, Cahokia,
and Kaskaskia; north to Michilimackinac; and west to Green Bay. Both her
mother and first husband were people of the Illinois Country. Her uncle Simon Réaume was considered the most important trader at Fort Ouiatenon
until his death in the 1730s.[77] Her father eventually established himself as a
Green Bay trader, and her younger sister, Suzanne, was raised in that community. Réaume's oldest daughter was the godmother to Suzanne's son.[78]
Réaume's marriage to Chevalier was the impetus for incorporation of the
Chevalier kin at Michilimackinac into the Fort St. Joseph community. Chevalier's Montreal trading partner[79] and his younger brother (Louis Pascal
Chevalier) both married Réaume's daughters.[80]

Kinship facilitated the exchange process and had important social ramifications as well. The kinship ties that linked traders through female kin
networks at St. Joseph mediated fur-trade exchange in the western Great
Lakes. Jesuit baptismal registers reveal a great deal about the nature of
kinship and describe a complex social system wherein one was less an
individual and more a member of a larger kinship group.[81] The kin networks that evolved from intermarriage between fur traders and Native
American women were rooted in and paralleled, extended, and further
complicated those of Native American society. The more visible dimensions of these interrelationships were personified by the Catholic kin networks of women like Réaume.

English commandants who ignored women such as Réaume and their
French fur-trader husbands thwarted effective governance in the western
Great Lakes. Those Francophobic English commandants who advocated removal of French fur traders failed to appreciate that many mixed ancestry
offspring were now indistinguishable from the Indian people among whom
they lived. In 1780, when Patrick Sinclair, the Michilimackinac commandant responsible for the St. Joseph post, ordered the forcible removal of
the forty-eight French people resident at St. Joseph, including Réaume and

Chevalier, he learned a bitter lesson about the folly of ignoring these kinship ties.[82] Shortly after their arrival, the English fur traders sent to Fort St. Joseph were attacked by Réaume's Illinois kin network. This force was composed of her immediate family, her son-in-law, and thirty of his friends. Although this first raid was unsuccessful, it was followed by a larger, more effective force from Cahokia, Kaskaskia, and St. Louis, with Madeleine's son, thirty-year-old Louison Chevalier, as the guide and interpreter. The Potawatomi reckoned the number to be "one hundred white people and eighty Indians," while other estimates placed the number at sixty-five white men and a large Native American contingent.[83] Young Louison Chevalier ensured the attack's success because he divided the British goods among the St. Joseph Potawatomi. The attack proved devastatingly effective, and the invaders were gone when the British arrived the next day.[84]

The St. Joseph invasion is often described as a minor skirmish of the Revolutionary War, but such descriptions fail to appreciate the extent to which such events reflected fur trade rather than military rivalries. This 1781 incident prevented the establishment of British traders in the St. Joseph River valley and secured the economic interests of the L'archevêque-Chevalier kin network.

Kinship facilitated the exchange process, and by the beginning of the nineteenth century, access to the best peltry in the western Great Lakes was increasingly controlled by these complex kin networks. When the American Fur Company entered the Great Lakes trade, company managers relied on this established kinship network and chose to supply two Odawa women, rather than their male competitors. They were Thérèse and Magdelaine Marcot, who were born into the St. Joseph kin network. They were part of an intermediate link that joined that river valley to the Odawa community fifty miles farther north, in the Grand River Valley. Direct access to trade goods encouraged their emergence as independent traders.

Thérèse and Magdelaine were the children of an Odawa woman known as Thimotée and a French trader named Jean Baptiste Marcot. Marcot was a St. Joseph trader and, along with the Chevaliers, his family had been forcibly removed in 1781.[85] Thimotée returned with the children to her Odawa community in the Grand River valley, while her husband relocated to present-day Wisconsin.[86] He was killed in 1783, when Thérèse and Magdelaine were young children of three and four. They were raised as Odawa, since their mother was the daughter of Chief Kewinaquot (Returning Cloud).[87] Both children were baptized at Michilimackinac, and their godparents were members of generationally prominent fur-trade families, part of the Chevalier, Barthe, and La Framboise kin networks. Thérèse and Magdelaine, despite being Catholic and the daughters of a French father, were identified as Odawa by the missionary priest.[88]

At first, the lives of both Thérèse and Magdelaine were remarkably similar to that of Marie Rouensa and Marie Madeleine Réaume L'archevêque Chevalier. Like their predecessors, Thérèse and Magdelaine were raised in indigenous society and married French fur traders. They married young, at fourteen, and their husbands paid the bride-price required by the Odawa. Magdelaine remained in the Grand River valley with her husband, Joseph La Framboise, and he traded among her people; Thérèse moved with her fur-trader husband, Pierre Lasaliere, to the St. Joseph River valley.[89] After several years Lasaliere and Thérèse separated, and he moved to the west side of Lake Michigan to join the Wisconsin trade.[90] Like her mother, Thérèse returned to raise her daughter in her Odawa village in the Grand River valley. Then in 1799 she took her nine-year-old daughter to Michilimackinac to be baptized.[91] Once again, the Michilimackinac priest identified both Thérèse and her child as Odawa, not French. After her husband's departure, Thérèse remained an attractive marital prospect because of her dual-kinship heritage. Her second husband was an Anglo fur trader, George Schindler, who started trading among the Odawa in 1800.[92]

Early in the nineteenth century the lives of the two sisters changed dramatically. In 1804 their country marriages were consecrated by a missionary priest at Michilimackinac. Well-known Catholic fur-trade families witnessed the event, including their old friends the Chevaliers from St. Joseph. Joseph La Framboise had lived with Magdelaine for ten years and they had two children.[93] After Thérèse's marriage to Schindler, Thérèse moved to his house on the island. Now legal kin, the La Framboise and Schindler families also formed a business partnership. They planned to obtain trade goods from Claude La Framboise, Joseph's brother in Montreal, but unfortunately the business alliance never fully materialized.[94] In 1806, several years after the Michilimackinac celebration of his marriage, Joseph was killed by an irate Indian.[95] Magdelaine buried her husband and continued on her journey to the Odawa wintering ground with her infant son Joseph, two slaves (Angelique and Louison), and twelve voyageurs.[96]

After her husband's death, Magdelaine, then in her twenties, emerged as an independent trader. She chose not to remarry, unlike Marie Rouensa and Marie Madeleine Réaume. Magdelaine's centrality in the Catholic kin networks of fur-trade society, her social prominence as a young Odawa woman, and her experience in the fur trade coincided with trader John Jacob Astor's eager search for an entrée into the Great Lakes trade. Kinship worked to Magdelaine's advantage and encouraged her independence. For the next fifteen years, until she retired from the trade in 1822, she traveled annually between the Grand River valley and Michilimackinac to exchange peltry for trade goods. She lived among her Odawa kin in the Grand River valley, and each year wintered with them. Magdelaine established herself as Madame La Framboise, obtained trading licenses, first from the British and then, after the War of 1812, from the Americans. She hired voyageurs to accompany her, secured trade goods on credit, and returned each June to Michilimackinac to sell her furs and resupply her outfit.

Several years after Joseph La Framboise's death, a stroke left George Schindler an invalid.[97] Thérèse, like Magdelaine, became an independent fur trader, but traded at L'Arbe Croche, the Odawa community closest to Michilimackinac. Thérèse's operations rapidly expanded. She often served as Magdelaine's supply source for the Grand River valley trade, but she also supplied a large number of French fur traders, men drawn from her kin network.[98] She sold goods to traders from the Barthe, Chevalier, and La Framboise families, all members of her fictive kin network. Men from her Catholic kin network appeared regularly on the pages of her fur-trade journals. Thérèse increasingly acquired prominence as a supplier, while her sister Magdelaine remained an active, independent trader.[99]

In 1816, when the American Fur Trade Company acquired greater control of the Great Lakes trade, it incorporated both women. By 1818 their supplies came from the American Fur Trade Company.[100] Magdelaine may have earned as much as five thousand to ten thousand pounds a year, while the average fur trader probably earned no more than a thousand pounds a year. The Grand River territory shipped about one hundred packs of furs a year to Michilimackinac. In 1800 furs were valued at twenty pounds per pack, and Magdelaine secured the majority of furs exported from the Grand River valley. She eventually retired from the fur trade and moved next door to her sister on Michilimackinac.[101]

These women negotiated for themselves positions of prominence in an era when the fur trade proved to be a precarious male venture. Many independent male traders were eliminated when John Jacob Astor and the American Fur Company gained control of the Great Lakes trade. The furs Thérèse Schindler and Madame La Framboise had first sold to Ramsay

Crooks, Astor's representative in the Great Lakes, established their standing credit with Astor's newly formed American Fur Company.[102]

Marie Rouensa, Marie Magdelaine Réaume L'archevêque Chevalier, Magdelaine Marcot La Framboise, and Thérèse Marcot Lasaliere Schindler were part of a world where identity was defined not by nationality but by kinship. Kin networks, like those of the St. Joseph community, characterized every fur-trade community in the western Great Lakes. The fictive and familial relationships created by the umbrella of frontier Catholicism further strengthened and expanded an already complex indigenous kinship system.[103] The Catholic kin network, in which these women played so prominent a role, served a socially integrative function, which enhanced the role and importance of these women.

In 1680 and 1711, Rouensa and Réaume were born into a demographically chaotic and socially unstable world. The Fur Trade Wars pitted Iroquois against the Algonquian-speaking people. The Jesuits contributed to that social disruption when they condemned fur traders as licentious and dismissed shamans as "jugglers." Indian women emerged as the cultural mediators of this eighteenth-century landscape. The Jesuit presence offered Native women an opportunity to interface between two disparate worlds, and as Catholic converts these women constructed an ever-expanding world of real and fictive kin under the umbrella of Western religion. They raised children conversant with European and indigenous cultures, drew a livelihood for themselves and their households from the emerging market economy, and facilitated the evolution of the fur trade in the western Great Lakes. Fur-trade exchange was clearly much more than the simple economic transaction of a marketplace economy; instead, it was defined by kinship and friendship. The fur trade remained collective on one side and individualistic on the other, and this world of individual and collective exchange was bridged by Native women. These women's lives mirrored the complex interactions of indigenous societies and demonstrated how traditional economies met the demands of an emerging transatlantic economy.

Great Lakes people defined themselves by their relatives, while Anglo outsiders identified them as French or Native American. During the nineteenth century a distinctive Métis society developed from the intermarriages within kin networks, especially those involving the more prominent fur-trade families, such as the Barthes, Chevaliers, Bourassas, Langlades, and La Framboises, who resided in the larger fur-trade communities like

Detroit, Michilimackinac, Green Bay, and St. Louis.[104] At Fort St. Joseph, the forcible removal of the French traders and their families abruptly terminated a society evolving in that direction. Social boundaries remained ill-defined and children of Native American mothers and fur-trade fathers identified themselves as French or Canadian, but many preferred their indigenous identity. Réaume's son Louison, for example, was referred to by the British as Indian. Chevalier's son, Amable, by his first wife, became an important Odawa headman.[105] The Great Lakes kin network, with its diversity and multiplicity of names and identities, can never be fully untangled. It led to anonymity but simultaneously determined one's social position.

Change for these women was always defined by the extensive kin networks that controlled and mediated the exchange process of the fur trade. Three of these women were the daughters of fur traders, and many of their daughters married fur traders. Marriage served as a planned extension of familial kin networks, further extended through the fictive kinship of Catholic ritual. Therefore, as offspring moved to other fur-trade communities, mobility became the warp on which the fabric of the fur trade was woven.

Native women married to fur traders played a pivotal role in brokering social change. These multilingual translators fostered the spread of Christianity among Great Lakes people, just as they mediated the face-to-face exchange of goods for peltry. These women suggest alternative perspectives from which we might revise prevailing views about the fur trade and Catholicism. Native women were "negotiators of change," and Rouensa, Réaume, Schindler, and La Framboise were indicative of how that occurred and how women were active participants and emerged as central actors in the colonial era of the western Great Lakes.

Appendix

Susan Sleeper-Smith's documentary evidence included the Jesuit Relations, *reprinted following Carl Ekberg's article, and church records, in addition to other sources. Here follow some samples of the baptismal records from St Joseph and Mackinac Island, both in the present state of Michigan. They were translated from the French and reprinted, maintaining the original spelling of names and rather casual approach to capitalization and punctuation.*

Sleeper-Smith used these and other sources to understand the relationships between the people in her article, but readers will find a great deal of additional information here. These types of records include information about family ties and other social relationships, slavery, births (and therefore sexual relations) outside of marriage, literacy, tribal affiliation, and many other topics. The official attitudes of the church about marriage and the distinctions regarding "legitimate" marriages and children are evident. Readers will also notice the patriarchal habit of listing men before women, the practice of lay baptism in the case of weak newborns (which was carefully checked by priests), and the fact that married women often used their maiden rather than their married surnames. Priests thought it was important to tell for some godmothers the names of their husbands, but for godfathers, the reverse was not the case. Readers may notice that in some cases it was the godmother who bestowed the new name on the person being baptized. Also, note that some persons had titles, suggesting a higher social status than others. Some of the records are open to interpretation as to what they mean.

Tips for understanding:

"8" when used in a word indicates the phoneme "ou"

"dit" (pronounced "dee") between parts of a surname indicates that the family sometimes used the first part and at other times the second part of the name. For example Charles Personne dit LaFond might be called Charles Personne or Charles LaFond. The second, or "dit name" was preferred, in general.

"pani" or "panise" refers to an Indian slave. The most common slaves were captives from the Pawnees of the Great Plains, so that the term referring to the tribe came to be equivalent to "slave" in the Midwest. Some slaves designated as "panis" were actually from other Native nations.

"Saki" here refers to the Sauk people; "Outaois" to the Odawas, also known as Ottawa people.

"J. Bte." refers to the common name Jean Baptiste.

The name "L'archeveque" was sometimes "Larche." Many given names appear with different spellings. Spelling was not standardized.

Keep in mind that the original documents were old and often hard to read, so the transcribers may have incorrectly copied some information. Again, the originals were in the French language. For the readers' convenience, we have numbered the entries.

Appendix: The St. Joseph Baptismal Register

The following quote and ten extracts originally appeared in "The St. Joseph Baptismal Register," ed. Rev. George Paré and M. M. Quaife, Mississippi Valley Historical Review *13, no. 2 (1926): 203, 212, 213, 214, 216, 218, 219, 222, 225, 237.*

In the register I have tried to give a faithful rendering of the original even in cases where a little transposing would render the entries less ambiguous. However, I have taken some liberties in the matter of punctuation, generally by inserting it where there was none, to make the entries more readable. Empty brackets enclose words or parts of words which are absolutely illegible. Wherever possible to determine, the number of brackets corresponds to the number of illegible words. Words or parts of words in brackets denote missing or illegible words which can be plainly inferred from other entries.

> *George Paré*

(1) *March 7, 1729*

In the year 1729 the 7th of March I J. bap. Chardon priest and missionary of the society of Jesus at the river St. Joseph baptized Joseph son of Jean baptiste Baron voyageur from the parish of boucherville at present settled in this post and of Marie Catherine 8ekioukoue Married in the eye of the church, baptized the 8th of March the day following his birth. the godfather was Mr. Louis-coulon de Villiers junior and the Godmother Marie Rheaume daughter of Sieur Jean baptiste Rheaume interpreter and of Simphorose ouaouagoukoue married in the eyes of the church.

> *J. B. Chardon M. of the soc. of Jesus*
> *Louis de villier*
> *marie reaume*

(2) *January 13, 1731*

In the year 1731 the 13th of January I, C M Mesaiger priest and missionary of the society of jesus at the river St joseph, baptized marie catherine daughter of augustin larchevesque of quebec settled here and of marie rheaume married in the eyes of the church, born [the night before] the 12th. The godfather was [Nico]las coulon de villiers commanding [for the king in this post] and the godmother catherine ouekioukoue wife of jean baptiste baron

> *C M Mesaiger miss of the soc. of jesus*

(3) *January 26, 1731*

In the year 1731 I, C M Mesaiger priest and Missionary of the river St joseph, baptized this 26th of January Louis son of antoine Deshestres born in new england and at present resident and blacksmith in this post and of charlotte chevalier married in the eyes of the church, born the night before The Godfather was Mr Louis Coulon De villiers esquire and cadet in the troops of his majesty. The godmother marie Rheaume wife of Augustin L'archevesque

        villiers

        C M Mesaiger missionary of the society of jesus

(4) *June 21, 1738*

The same day I supplied the ceremonies of Holy baptism to Marie Charles legitimate daughter of augustin l'archevesque and of marie Reaume his wife, born the 22nd of november of the year 1736 and baptized the 23rd of the month by Mr de lusignan commander of the post in the absence of the missionary. the godfather was Mr. alexis de Langis esquire and the godmother charlotte chevalier wife of deshetres. done at the river St Joseph this 21st of june 1738

        Chev de langis Pr. du jaunay miss. of the soc. of jesus

        charlotte chevalie

(5) *April 28, 1740*

In the year one thousand seven hundred and forty the twenty eighth of april I the undersigned jan Baptiste Lamorinie priest of the society of jesus and missionary at the present time at the mission of the river St joseph baptized the slave girl of Monsieur Larche of the panise nation [] 13 years old and named marie jeanne. she had for godfather Jean Le faivre voyageur and for godmother marie magdelaine Reaume married to Sieur Larche and they signed with me

        jean baptiste Lamorinie priest of the society of jesus

        Benoist, witness

        jean le faivre

        marie madelaine

(6) June 29, 1741

In the year one thousand seven hundred and forty the 27th of june was born Charles joseph mainard, son of Monsieur francois mainard interpreter at the post of the River St joseph and of Charlote janne robert, who was baptized by Monsieur Charles benoist because he seemed to be in danger of death as the said monsieur certified to me and the 29th of june of the year one thousand seven hundred and forty one I supplied the usual ceremonies in such a case. his godfather was Monsieur Charles benoist and the godmother Marie magdelaine reaume wife of Sieur augustin Larche residing in the said post and for this I signed

> *jean Baptiste Lamorinie e soc jesu*
> *Charles Benoist*
> *marie madelene la larche*

(7) April 28, 1752

Today the twenty eighth of the month of april of the year one thousand seven hundred and fifty two I solemnly baptized in the church of this mission a young girl about two years old, little daughter of pierre mekabekanga daughter of sip8assan and pi8alam8 whom they called 8ikapsinin. the godfather was jan dit curisv [] and the godmother Angelique l'archeveque who gave her at baptism the name angelique. done at St joseph the year and day as above

> *p. du jaunay miss of the soc of Jesus*
> jandc c arj

(8) May 1, 1752

Today the first day of the month of may of the year one thousand seven hundred and fifty two I solemnly administered Holy Baptism to three sisters, daughters of pierre mekabe[kanga]. the first a widow about 26 or 27 years old who was called temagas8kia took the name of marguerite, the second about 25 years old who is married to pi8assin still unconverted and who is called [] took the name of marie madelene, the third about 15 or 16 years old who was called [] took in Holy baptism the name of susanne.

all three desired Holy baptism and were sufficiently instructed.
[] [] the godmother of marguerite is marguerite of the saki nation. the other godparents signed with me at St joseph the year
and day as above

> *p. du Jaunay miss of the soc of Jesus*
> *Jean baptise lefebvre*
> *marie madelene chevallier*
> *Louis Hamelin*
> *the godmother susanne wife of Bolon*

(9) April 23, 1753

In the year one thousand seven hundred and fifty three the
twenty third of april I the undersigned priest of the society of
jesus and exercising the functions of missionary supplied the
ceremonies of Holy baptism according to the usages of our Holy
mother the church to marie Catherine daughter of charlotte *father unknown* born the fourteenth of april of the same year one
thousand seven hundred and fifty three and baptized the same
day by Louis chevailler according to the right form as he has testified, because of the danger of death. the godfather was Louis
paschal chevailler and the godmother angelique Larchevesque
who signed with me. the godfather the godmother declared she
could not sign at St joseph this twenty third of april one thousand seven hundred and fifty three

> *jean Baptiste Lamorinie of the society of jesus*
> *Louis paschal chevalier*

the mother of this girl was married to antoine St francois*

*This sentence in the manuscript is written in Latin. The mother was
Charlotte L'archevêque, as shown *post* by the baptismal entry for Nov. 13,
1755.—*George Paré.*

(10) March 21, 1773

The twenty first of march one thousand seven hundred and seventy three by us missionary priest were baptized pierre born
The Twenty eighth Of october one thousand seven hundred
and sixty nine [October 28, 1769] and francois born The third
of august one thousand seven hundred and seventy two [Au-

gust 3, 1772] [sons of] Jean Roc morin and of therese of the potawatami nation who by marrying legitimized the aforesaid children. The godfather of pierre was paschal Chevallier and the godmother magdeleine Larcheveque. The godfather of francois [was] Louis Chevallier and the godmother Catherine St francois wife of Nicolas LeCompte. of these some signed with me and others declared they could not sign

> *Louis Chevallir junior*
> *P. Gibault Priest*

Appendix: The Mackinac Baptismal Register

The four excerpts that follow are from "The Mackinac Register, 1695–1821: Register of Baptisms of the Mission of St. Ignace de Michilimakinak," ed. Reuben Gold Thwaites, Wisconsin Historical Collections *19 (1910): 24, 25, 86. Translation is from a transcript of the original, which is kept in the parish church of Ste. Anne at Mackinac.*

(11) *July 7, 1748*

I Supplied the ceremonies of holy baptism to and baptized conditionally Augustin, son of the late Augustin l'archevêque and of Marie Reaumé, his wife, residing at St Joseph. The said child was born at St joseph on January 9, 1746, and was privately baptized the same day. The godfather was m$^{r.}$ Augustin moras de l'anglade, esquire; and the godmother m$^{lle.}$ Bourassa, the elder.
* * *

> *P. DU JAUNAY, miss. of the society of Jesus*

Asterisks (* * *) indicate that portions of the entry have been omitted. These omissions are mere repetitions of formal phrases, conveying no specific information concerning the event or the persons interested, and are the same for each entry. Liberty has also been taken with the form of the date—the spelled-out style of the original being reduced to briefer numerical form.

(12) *July 21, 1748*

I supplied the ceremonies of holy Baptism to and baptized conditionally Catherine, daughter of Charles personne dit la fond, blacksmith, and of Susanne Réume, his wife, residing at la Baye. The said child was born at la Baye on the 14th of April last and was privately baptized, being considered in danger of death. The godfather was Mr de Coulonge; and the godmother Catherine l'archevêque, wife of Sieur joutras.

* * *

> P. DU JAUNAY, miss. of the society of Jesus
> COULONGE
> CATHERINE LATHRE [LARCHE]
> SUSANE REAUME

(13) August 1, 1786

I, the undersigned Priest, baptized Therese, about ten years old, daughter of Sieur Jean Baptiste Marcot and of Thimotée, of the Outaois nation, his lawful wife. The Godfather was Mr. Jean Baptiste Chevalier; and the Godmother $M^{d.}$ Carignan, who signed with us.

> PAYET, Missn. priest.
> PILLET CARIGNAN; J. Bapte CHEVALIER

(14) August 1, 1786

I, the undersigned Priest, baptized Magdelaine, about six years old, legitimate daughter of Sieur Jean Baptiste Marcot and of Thimotée of the Outaois nation. The Godfather was Sieur Antoine Barthe; and the Godmother Madame Charles Gauthier, who declared that she could not sign her name.

> PAYET, Missn. priest.
> ANTOIN BARTHE

Notes

I would like to thank David Trask, Nancy Shoemaker, and Jeani O'Brien-Kehoe for their insightful comments, assistance, and encouragement. I am also grateful to people who commented on earlier versions of this paper: Helen Hornbeck Tanner, Alfred Young, and participants at the Newberry Library Seminar in Early American History; to my History Department colleagues David Bailey, Lisa Fine, and Maureen Flanagan, and to those who participated in our Department Seminar; to members of the National Endowment for the Humanities American Indian Ethnohistory Seminar organized by Gary Anderson at the University of Oklahoma, especially Jacki Rand, Lee Anne Howe, Bob Craig, and Eldon Lawrence; to R. David Edmunds, who encouraged my initial research in ethnohistory in 1995 and have remained faithful mentors; to Daniel Richter, who has repeatedly and insightfully commented on my work at conferences. In addition, the participation of Lucy Eldersveld

Murphy and Alice Nash as copresenters on Organization of American History and ethnohistory panels have proved invaluable. This article has also benefited from the suggestions and comments of the anonymous reviewers for Ethnohistory.

To readers familiar with French spelling and phonetics, the spelling of some names in this article may appear nonstandard (e.g., "Angelique" rather than Angélique). Occasionally, they vary among different holders of the same name. These are not typographical errors; on the contrary, I have sought to reproduce faithfully the spellings as given in the St. Joseph Baptismal Register and other primary sources in the interest of facilitating further research into these families. Where possible, the Dictionary of Canadian Biography *has been used to standardize spelling.*

1. Robert F. Berkhofer, "The Political Context of a New Indian History," *Pacific Historical Review* 40 (August 1971): 357–82.

2. Sylvia Van Kirk, *Many Tender Ties: Women in Fur-Trade Society, 1670–1870* (Norman OK, 1980); Jennifer S. H. Brown, *Strangers in Blood: Fur Trade Company Families in Indian Country* (Vancouver, 1980).

3. Nancy Shoemaker, "Kateri Tekakwitha's Tortuous Path to Sainthood," in Shoemaker, ed., *Negotiators of Change: Historical Perspectives on Native American Women* (New York, 1995).

4. Laurel Thatcher Ulrich, *Good Wives: Image and Reality in the Lives of Women in Northern New England, 1650–1750* (New York, 1980) and *A Midwife's Tale: The Life of Martha Ballard, Based on Her Diary, 1785–1812* (New York, 1990).

5. Harold Innis, in *The Fur Trade in Canada* (Toronto, 1970), views the North American fur trade as an extension of a European economic system. Lewis O. Saum describes the effect of trade as not simply economic but also destructive of indigenous cultures in *The Fur Trader and the Indian* (Seattle, 1965), and Donald F. Bibeau discusses at length the literature that supports similar perspectives in "Fur Trade Literature from a Tribal Point of View: A Critique," in *Rendezvous: Selected Papers of the Fourth North American Fur Trade Conference,* ed. Thomas C. Buckley (Saint Paul MN, 1981), 83–91. Carolyn Gilman discusses the idea that the fur trade was exemplative of how a common ground of understanding was established between two cultures "without sacrificing their unique characteristics and without annihilating one another" in *Where Two Worlds Meet: The Great Lakes Fur Trade* (Saint Paul MN, 1982), 1–4. More recently, Richard White, in *The Middle Ground: Indians, Empires, and Republics in the Great Lakes Region, 1650–1815* (New York, 1991), asserts that the trade was a cultural compromise in which Europeans accommodated to the customs of Native people. Bruce J. Bourque and Ruth Holmes Whitehead explore the idea that Native people were assertive and early participants in the trade in "Tarrentines and the Introduction of European Trade Goods in the Gulf of Maine," *Ethnohistory* 32 (1985): 327–41.

6. The western Great Lakes was referred to by the French as the *pays d'en haut* and initially included all of the "lands bordering the rivers flowing into the northern Great Lakes and the lands south of the lakes to the Ohio." See White, *Middle Ground,*

x–xi, 50, 52. For an explanation of the "middle ground," see chapter 2, pp. 50–93.

7. Clara Sue Kidwell, "Indian Women as Cultural Mediators," *Ethnohistory* 39, no. 2 (1992): 97–107. The phrase "negotiators of change" is borrowed from Nancy Shoemaker's *Negotiators of Change.*

8. "Marriage 'after the custom of the country' was an indigenous marriage rite which evolved to meet the needs of fur trade society. . . . Although denounced by the Jesuit priests as immoral, the traders had taken their Indian wives according to traditional Native marriage rites and distinct family units had developed." Van Kirk, *Many Tender Ties*, 28. These marriages combined Indian and European marriage customs; the unions, although not always permanent, were neither casual nor promiscuous. For a further explanation of how marriage *á la facon du pays* became institutionalized as integral to the Great Lakes fur trade, see especially Jacqueline Peterson's "Prelude to Red River: A Social Portrait of the Great Lakes Métis," *Ethnohistory* 25 (1978): 48, 41–67, which shows how "the force of tribal custom . . . French peasant practices and the *coutume de Paris*" encouraged intermarriage. See also Brown, *Strangers in Blood*, 62–63; also Jacqueline Peterson and Jennifer S. H. Brown, eds., *The New Peoples: Being and Becoming Métis in North America* (Fort Garry, Manitoba, 1985), especially Peterson's "Many Roads to Red River: Métis Genesis in the Great Lakes Region, 1680–1815," 37–73. See also Sylvia Van Kirk's "The Custom of the Country: An Examination of Fur Trade Marriage Practices" and John E. Foster's "The Origin of the Mixed Bloods in the Canadian West" in *Essays on Western History*, ed. Lewis H. Thomas (Edmonton, Alberta, 1976), 49–68, 71–80.

9. Sylvia Van Kirk, "Toward a Feminist Perspective in Native History," in *Papers of the Eighteenth Algonquian Conference*, ed. José Mailhot (Ottawa, 1987), 386.

10. For a discussion of missionization among Native American women that relies on an assimilationist model, see Karen Anderson, *Chain Her by One Foot: The Subjugation of Women in Seventeenth-Century New France* (New York, 1991); Carol Devens, *Countering Colonization: Native American Women and Great Lakes Missions, 1630–1900* (Berkeley, 1992); Eleanor Burke Leacock, "Montaignais Women and the Jesuit Program for Colonization," in *Myths of Male Dominance: Collected Articles on Women Cross-Culturally*, ed. Leacock (New York, 1981), 43–62.

11. For the parallel circumstance of Catholic women among the Iroquois, see Shoemaker, "Kateri Tekakwitha's Tortuous Path," 49–71; and Natalie Zemon Davis, "Iroquois Women, European Women," in *Women, "Race," and Writing in the Early Modern Period*, ed. Margo Hendricks and Patricia Parker (New York, 1994), 243–61.

12. The number 8 appears throughout the St. Joseph Baptismal Register and indicates the phonetic equivalent for parts of Native American languages that were not spelled in French. *8* was a digraph or shorthand for *ou*. [Editors' note: Sleeper-Smith's original article used the spelling "8cate8a" for the second part of Marie Rouensa's surname; we have changed it here to conform to the corrected name, "8cani8e," per Carl Ekberg's more recent research.]

13. Before their conversion to Catholicism the Illini were polygamous, and this has been attributed to the high ratio of women to men. Early observers reported that women outnumbered men four to one, and for this reason men married the younger sisters of their first wives. Village dwellings consisted of substantial oblong cabins that housed from six to twelve families. Consequently, village houses brought substantial numbers of women together. These women also exercised control over productive resources, and men turned over the food of the hunt to them. Women owned all household possessions, while a man's property consisted only of his weapons and clothes. Clarence Walworth Alvord, *The Illinois Country, 1673–1818* (Chicago, 1920), 41–46.

14. The term "frontier Catholicism" suggests that lay Catholics were instrumental in the spread of Catholicism in the western Great Lakes. This was a result of the scarcity of priests, a situation worsened in 1762 by the secularization of the Jesuits. The role laypeople played in the transmission of dogma is unclear. The term "baptized conditionally" appears frequently in baptismal registers and indicates that a child had previously received lay baptism when a priest was unavailable.

15. The Odawa were semi-sedentary and moved their villages only when the soil was no longer fertile or when enemies threatened attack. Women remained resident in the village, while hunting parties were an all-male activity. Although divorce was uncommon, when it did occur the children remained with the women. Children belonged to the women, and for this reason it appears that descent was traced through women. James E. Fitting and Charles E. Cleland, "Late Prehistoric Settlement Patterns in the Upper Great Lakes," *Ethnohistory* 16 (1969): 295–96; W. Vernon Kinietz, *The Indians of the Western Great Lakes* (Ann Arbor, 1990), 270–74.

16. All four women—Marie Rouensa-8cani8e, Marie Madeleine Réaume L'archevêque Chevalier, Magdelaine Marcot La Framboise, and Thérèse Marcot Lasaliere Schindler—were Catholic, hence the presence of Christian names.

17. Carl J. Ekberg with Anton J. Pregaldin, "Marie Rouensa-8canic8e and the Foundations of French Illinois," *Illinois Historical Journal* 84 (fall 1991): 146–60; John E. McDowell, "Therese Schindler of Mackinac: Upward Mobility in the Great Lakes Fur Trade," *Wisconsin Magazine of History* 61 (winter 1977–78): 126–27; David A. Armour, "Magdelaine Marcot La Framboise," *Dictionary of Canadian Biography* (Toronto, 1991), 7:582–83; John E. McDowell, "Madame La Framboise," *Michigan History* 56 (winter 1972): 271–86; Keith R. Widder, "Magdelaine La Framboise, Fur Trader and Educator," in *Historical Women of Michigan: A Sesquicentennial Celebration*, ed. Rosalie Riegle Troester (Lansing, 1987), 1–13.

18. White, *Middle Ground*, 70–75.

19. See Louise Tilly, "Gender, Women's History, and Social History," *Social Science History* 13 (1989): 339–480 (esp. 447), which suggests that women's history become more analytical and address issues central to the historical agenda.

20. The Algonquian-speaking Illinois included several groups: the Cahokia, Chipussea, Coircoentanon, Kaskaskia, Michigamea, Moingwena, Peoria, and Taponero.

The French referred to the area as the "Illinois Country," which included the present state of Illinois plus eastern Missouri and eastern Iowa. Emily J. Blasingham, "The Depopulation of the Illinois Indians," *Ethnohistory* 3 (1956): 193. The term *Iliniwek* comes from *Ilini*, or man; *iwek* is the plural termination, and was changed by the French to *ois*. Alvord, *Illinois Country*, 31.

21. In a matrifocal household the woman is the focus of the relationship but not the head of the household. Women evolved as the center of economic and decision-making coalitions with their children, despite the presence of a husband-father. Raymond Smith, "The Matrifocal Family," in *The Character of Kinship*, ed. Jack Goody (New York, 1973), 124–25.

22. From Father Gabriel Marest, Missionary of the Society of Jesus, to Father Germon of the same Society, November 9, 1712, *Lettres édifiantes* (Toulouse, 1810), 6:207.

23. Raymond E. Hauser, in "The *Berdache* and the Illinois Indian Tribe during the Last Half of the Seventeenth Century," *Ethnohistory* 37 (1990): 54, suggests that the status of Illinois women was limited by sororal polygyny and that brothers played an important role in the selection of a husband. The conversion to Catholicism would have clearly ended the practice of polygyny as well as the marital influence exercised by men.

24. "Memoir of DeGannes Concerning the Illinois Country," in *The French Foundations, 1680–1692*, ed. Theodore Calvin Pease and Raymond C. Werner, *Collections of the Illinois State Historical Library* (Springfield, 1934), 23:361.

25. Mary Borgias Palm, *The Jesuit Missions of the Illinois Country, 1673–1763* (Cleveland, 1933), 25; "Memoir of DeGannes," 38–40.

26. Reuben Gold Thwaites, ed., *The Jesuit Relations and Allied Documents, Travels and Explorations of the Jesuit Missions in New France, 1610–1791* (Cleveland, 1896–1901), 65:67.

27. Thwaites, *Jesuit Relations*, 64:229.

28. Thwaites, *Jesuit Relations*, 64:205, 195–205.

29. Thwaites, *Jesuit Relations*, 64:195.

30. Rouensa married Accault within the church. Gravier described the circumstances of the wedding and baptized their first son, Peter Accault, on March 20, 1695, at Pimiteoui. For the baptism see "Kaskaskia Church Records," *Transactions of the Illinois Historical Society*, vol. 2 (Springfield, 1904), 394; Marthe F. Beauregard, *La population des forts francais d' Amérique* (Montreal, 1982), 2:108.

31. Thwaites, *Jesuit Relations*, 64:213.

32. Thwaites, *Jesuit Relations*, 64:233; Palm, *Jesuit Missions*, 26.

33. Thwaites, *Jesuit Relations*, 64:209.

34. Palm, *Jesuit Missions*, 42.

35. Pierre Margry, ed., *Découvertes et établissements des Français dans l'ouest et dans le sud de l'Amérique septentrionale, 1614–1698* (Paris, 1879–88), 5:375–586; Father Gabriel Marest to Father Germon, in Thwaites, *Jesuit Relations*, 66:218–95; also in Father Watrin's summary of his work among the Kaskaskia, in Thwaites, *Jesuit Relations*, 70:218–95.

36. Margaret Kimball Brown and Laurie Cena Dean, *The Village of Chartres in Colonial Illinois, 1720–1765* (New Orleans, 1977), 871; Ekberg, "Marie Rouensa," 156.

37. For a description of African American slavery in Illinois country see Carl J. Ekberg, "Black Slavery in Illinois, 1720–1765," *Western Illinois Regional Studies* 12 (1989): 5–9. For Native American slavery in the Great Lakes see Russell M. Magnaghi, "Red Slavery in the Great Lakes Country during the French and British Regimes," *Old Northwest* 12 (summer 1996): 201–17.

38. An arpent is a French unit equal to about .84 acres or, when used as a linear measurement, 192 English feet. Winstanley Briggs, "Le Pays des Illinois," *William and Mary Quarterly* 47 (1990): 38.

39. Palm, *Jesuit Missions*, 42; Beauregard, *Forts francais d' Amérique*, 2:107–81.

40. Daniel H. Usner, in *Indians, Settlers, and Slaves in a Frontier Exchange Economy* (Chapel Hill NC, 1992), 7, indicates that the Illinois country was under the political administration of New Orleans but was economically more integrated with the Great Lakes.

41. Palm, *Jesuit Missions*, 42–43, 80.

42. Susan C. Boyle, "Did She Generally Decide? Women in Ste. Genevieve, 1750–1805," *William and Mary Quarterly* 44 (1987): 783–84.

43. Lucy Eldersveld Murphy, "Autonomy and the Economic Roles of Indian Women of the Fox-Wisconsin River Region, 1763–1832," in Shoemaker, *Negotiators of Change*, 72–89, esp. 81–82.

44. Gilbert J. Garraghan, "New Light on Old Cahokia," *Illinois Catholic Historical Review* 2 (1919): 99–146.

45. John A. Walthall and Elizabeth D. Benchley, *The River L'Abbe Mission: A French Colonial Church for the Cahokia Illini on Monks Mound*, Studies in Illinois Archaeology no. 2 (Springfield, 1987), 71–73.

46. Thomas Hughes, *History of the Society of Jesus in North America* (London, 1917), 2:418–19.

47. See chapter 3, "Structures, Habitus, Practices," in Pierre Bourdieu, *The Logic of Practice* (Stanford, 1980), 52–65.

48. Marie Madeleine Réaume's father was the trader Jean Baptiste Réaume. The first official reference to him was in 1720, when the governor of New France, Vaudreuil, sent him to the reestablished Fort St. Joseph post with two canoes loaded with gifts for the Miamis. In 1717 her father served as the post interpreter and later he moved to Green Bay. Marie Madeleine Réaume first appears in the St. Joseph Baptismal Register when she was listed as a godmother, in March 1729, and was identified as the daughter of Simphorose Ouaouagoukoue and the post's interpreter, Sieur Jean Baptiste Réaume. "St. Joseph Baptismal Register," ed. Rev. George Paré and M. M. Quaife, *Mississippi Valley Historical Review* 13 (June 1926–March 1927): 212.

49. For an explanation of exchange in indigenous societies see Marcel Mauss, *The Gift: The Form and Reason of Exchange in Archaic Societies* (New York, 1990).

50. Variant spellings for *L'archevêque* include *Larchesveque* and *Larche*. Certificate,

Montreal, signed de Villiers, July 18, 1745, Archives Nationales, Colonies, Versailles (Paris), C^{11}A, 117, 325. In 1741 Augustin L'archevêque contracted to hire canoemen to accompany him to Illinois Country. For engagements or contracts hiring voyageurs at St. Joseph from 1722 to 1745 see *Rapport de l'Archiviste de la Province de Québec* (1929–30): 233–465.

51. The daughters lived to maturity, but the son probably did not reach adulthood. The first daughter, Marie Catherine, was born the day after her mother and father were married. She was baptized on January 13, 1731. Her godfather was the post commandant, Nicholas Coulon de Villiers, and her godmother was Marie Catherine, of the Illinois nation. "St. Joseph Baptismal Register," 213. The second daughter, Marie Esther (referred to as Marie Joseph Esther), was born sometime in 1733 and baptized one year later at Michilimackinac on January 1, 1734. "The Mackinac Register, 1696–1821: Register of Baptisms of the Mission of St. Ignace de Michilimackinak," *Collections of the State Historical Society of Wisconsin*, 19:4 [hereafter "Mackinac Register: Baptisms"]. The third daughter, Marie Anne, was twenty-one months and eight days old at the time of her baptism at St. Joseph in April 1740. Her godfather was Nicholas Coulon de Villiers, the post commandant, and her godmother was her older sister, Marie Joseph Esther. "St. Joseph Baptismal Register," 218. The fourth daughter, Marie Amable, was baptized at St. Joseph on July 27, 1740, by the post commandant, Nicholas Coulon de Villiers, and subsequently by Father Lamorine on June 29, 1741. The godparents were Claude Caron and Charlotte Robert, the wife of the post interpreter. "St. Joseph Baptismal Register," 219. The fifth daughter, Angelique (Agathe), was baptized in March 1744. Her godfather was Monsieur de Lespiné de Villiers, a cadet in the troops of the colony's marine detachment, and her godmother was her oldest sister, Marie Catherine. "St. Joseph Baptismal Register," 221.

52. Joseph Peyser, *Fort St. Joseph Manuscripts: Chronological Inventory and Translations* (Niles MI, 1978), 121, 104.

53. The seventeenth-century Jesuits attested to the lushness of the Saint Joseph River valley and to the profusion of wild grapes that grew along riverbanks. The dune area around southern Lake Michigan also produced large quantities of huckleberries, wild currants, gooseberries, and blackberries. Plum, crab apple, and cherry trees grew along the river bottoms. James A. Brown, *Aboriginal Cultural Adaptations in the Midwestern Prairies* (New York, 1991), 60; Thwaites, *Jesuit Relations*, 55:195.

54. "Petition of Louis Chevallier," reprinted from the Haldimand Papers, Canadian Archives, Ottawa, *Michigan Pioneer and Historical Society: Collections and Researches* [hereafter MPHC] 13 (1889): 61.

55. James M. McClurken, "Augustin Hamlin, Jr.: Ottawa Identity and the Politics of Persistence," in *Being and Becoming Indian*, ed. James A. Clifton (Chicago, 1989), 85.

56. These communities had a settled agricultural appearance. There were agricultural fields, log cabins, framed houses, and fruit orchards. The usual markers of Eu-

ropean society, houses and cabins, were also indicative of Native American society. At Réaume's St. Joseph village, a French carpenter had even built a house for a Potawatomi headman. A jail was even constructed by the blacksmith Antoine Deshêtres. It was made of stone and measured eight feet by ten feet. Certificate, St. Joseph, signed Piquoteé de Belestre, May 13, 1750, Archives Nationales, Colonies, Versailles (Paris), C¹¹A, 96: 313. The post interpreter Pierre Deneau dit Detailly submitted a certificate to receive a thousand livres for building a house for a medal chief. Certificate, St. Joseph, April 30, 1760, Archives Nationales, V7, 345: 99. Ottawa: National Archives of Canada.

57. In Ste. Genevieve, Illinois Country, French widows were more active in the local economy and were more likely to file legal grievances than either single or married women. Boyle, "Did She Generally Decide?" 788–89.

58. Augustin L'archevêque was baptized on July 7, 1748. He probably never reached adulthood. His godfather was Augustin Langlade, and his godmother was Marie Catherine Lerige Bourassa. "Mackinac Register: Baptisms," 24–25; Marie Catherine married Jean Baptiste Jutras (Joutras) at St. Ignace on July 7, 1748. He was a trader from Trois Rivieres. Witnesses included Legardeur de St. Pierre Verchere, Bourassa, Langlade, and Charles Langlade. "Mackinac Register, 1725–1821: Register of Marriages in the Parish of Michilimackinac," *Collections of the State Historical Society of Wisconsin*, 18:475 [hereafter "Mackinac Register: Marriages"]. The wedding of Marie Joseph Esther and Jacques Bariso de La Marche took place at Saint Ignace on August 2, 1748. Some witness signatures were illegible, but those of Langlade and Bourassa are legible. "Mackinac Register: Marriages," 476. The bridegroom was probably related to the Montreal merchant with whom Réaume's father had traded. In 1729 Jean Baptiste Réaume owed Charles Nolan LaMarque 4,000 livres in furs. *Rapport de l'Archiviste de la Province de Québec* (1929–30): 244–408. Joseph Esther was twice widowed, and at the age of forty-six, on June 8, 1779, she married Thomas M. Brady. He became the Indian agent at Cahokia. She had children and grandchildren living in Cahokia until well into the 1800s. Mildred Webster and Frederick Krause, *Fort Saint Joseph: De la Poste de la Rivière St. Joseph, 1690–1780* (Privately printed, 1990), 115.

59. Catherine married Jean Baptiste Jutras (Joutras). Her youngest daughter, Esther, married Jacques Bariso de La Marche. He was the son of a Montreal merchant, which would have guaranteed the St. Joseph community an adequate and annual supply of trade goods.

60. The Chevaliers were a large French family. There were seventeen children. Jean Baptiste Chevalier and his wife, Marie Francoise Alavoine, probably moved from Montreal to Michilimackinac in 1718. Baptismal registers at Michilimackinac and St. Joseph provide information about fifteen of the seventeen children born to Chevalier and Alavoine: five, possibly six, children were born in Montreal; eleven were baptized at St. Ignace. The four children born in Montreal included Charlotte (1712), Marie Anne (Chabouillez) Catherine (1714), Michel Jean Baptiste

(1715, died young?), and Marie Josephe (1718). The eleven children baptized at the St. Ignace Mission included Constance (1719), Louis Therèse (1720), Marguerite Josephe (1723), Marie Magdaleine (1724), Anne Charlotte Veronique (1726), Charles (1727), Joseph Maurice (1728), Louis Pascal (1730), Anne Therèse Esther (1732), Angelique (1733), and Luc (1735). John M. Gram, "The Chevalier Family and the Demography of the Upper Great Lakes" (unpublished paper, Mackinac Island State Park Commission, Lansing MI, 1995).

61. Their marriage coincided with the baptism of their son, Louis, who was born in October 1751 and was baptized by his uncle, Louis Pascal Chevalier. In April 1752 he was baptized by the priest, Father DuJaunay. His godfather was his oldest step-sister's husband, Joutras, and his godmother was another stepsister, Madeleine Chevalier. "St. Joseph Baptismal Register," 223.

62. Gram, "The Chevalier Family," 20.

63. Marie Magdelaine L'archevêque appears to have been one of Madeleine's daughters, but this cannot be confirmed by the baptismal registers. Louis Pascal was baptized at Michilimackinac on July 22, 1730. He died before January 1, 1779. He and his wife had four children baptized at St. Joseph between 1758 and 1773. "St. Joseph Baptismal Register," 223 n. 38; "Mackinac Register: Marriages," 490; "Mackinac Register: Baptisms," 3; Webster and Krause, *Fort Saint Joseph*, 120–21.

64. The Chevaliers were partners, but they were not related. Charles Lhullic Chevalier's trading partner now became his stepfather-in-law. Charles and Angelique were married at St. Joseph, where three of their children were later baptized. Chevalier died in 1773; he was about sixty-four. His death was the last entry in the St. Joseph Baptismal Register. Webster and Krause, *Fort Saint Joseph*, 115–17; Dunning Idle, "Post of the St. Joseph River during the French Regime, 1679–1761" (PhD diss., University of Illinois, 1946), 253–54 n. 104; "St. Joseph Baptismal Register," 230.

65. The register does not mention the marriage of Anne L'archevêque and Augustin Gibault. When she served as godmother to the daughter of her sister Marie Joseph in 1756, she was identified as Anne L'archevêque. By 1758 she was identified as Gibault's wife. "St. Joseph Baptismal Register," 228, 230.

66. Marie Amable married Jean Baptiste Francois Lonval. Lonval's ties were to the fur-trade community at Trois Rivières. The Lonvals settled in Cahokia, where they appear on the 1787 Cahokia census. Webster and Krause, *Fort Saint Joseph*, 117–18; "St. Joseph Baptismal Register," 231, 233–34.

67. Both Joseph Esther's and Marie Amable's children were baptized at the Fort Saint Joseph Mission. Four of Esther's children were baptized there. In 1753 her sister Catherine was the godmother to her sixteen-month-old son, Louis, and to her three-year-old son, Etienne Joseph. Esther's sister Anne was the godmother to her three-year-old daughter, Marie Joseph. In 1756, Esther's sister Magdeleine was the godmother to her five-month-old daughter, Angelique. "St. Joseph Baptismal Register," 225, 225–26, 228. In 1761, Amable's two-month-old daughter was baptized at St. Joseph. "St. Joseph Baptismal Register," 233–34.

68. The prolonged absence of priests at frontier missions led lay Catholics and even non-Catholics to perform baptisms. Priests were only intermittently assigned to the St. Joseph Mission, but they did serve continuously from 1750 to 1761. During other times the post was reliant on the missionary priests assigned to the Illinois Country; generally these priests resided at either Cahokia or Kaskaskia. Growth of the frontier Catholic church was hampered in 1762, when the French government decreed secularization of the Jesuits. The Supreme Council of New Orleans put the decree into effect on July 3, 1763. Father Meurin was allowed to remain in the Illinois Country at Ste. Genevieve on the Spanish side of the river. Priests from other orders were at the Saint Joseph mission in 1761, 1768, and 1773. A new missionary priest, Father Gibault, was assigned to the Illinois Country in 1773. "St. Joseph Baptismal Register," 204–5; George Paré, *The Catholic Church in Detroit, 1701–1888* (Detroit, 1951), 78–103. For an account of the banishment see Thwaites, *Jesuit Relations.*

69. The term "baptized conditionally" appears frequently in baptismal registers and indicates that a child had previously received lay baptism when a priest was unavailable. For an explanation of this phrase see "Mackinac Register: Baptisms," 7 n. 25.

70. "St. Joseph Baptismal Register," 218, 238.

71. Pierre Mekbibkas8nga's godfather was Mr. Marin de La Perrière, and his godmother was Madeleine de Villiers, de La Perrière's wife. Marie's godfather was Louis Metivier, a master carpenter, and her godmother was Marie Fafard, Metivier's wife. Five years later, Marie died. "St. Joseph Baptismal Register," 221–23.

72. On April 22, 1752, one of Pierre's daughters, 8abak8ik8e, was baptized. She was about thirty-five years old and took Marie as her Christian name. Louis Chevalier signed as the godfather. On May 1, 1752, three more of Pierre's children, all women, were baptized; one was twenty-six or twenty-seven, the second was twenty-five, and the third was fifteen or sixteen. The eldest, a widow and identified as Temagas8kia, took the name Marguerite. Her godmother was Marguerite of the Saki nation. Both of the other daughters elected Marie Madeleine Réaume Chevalier as their godmother. The middle daughter was identified as being married to Pi8assin, who was listed as still unconverted. The third daughter took the name Suzanne. "St. Joseph Baptismal Register," 222–23.

73. Idle, "Post of the Saint Joseph River," 182; *Rapport de l'archiviste de la Province de Québec* (1929–30): 233–465.

74. Howard Peckham, *Pontiac and the Indian Uprising* (Detroit, 1994); Ian K. Steele, *Warpath: Invasions of North America* (New York, 1994), 237–42; Charles E. Cleland, *Rites of Conquest: The History and Culture of Michigan's Native Americans* (Ann Arbor, 1994), 134–43; White, *Middle Ground*, 269–314; Gregory Evans Dowd, "The French King Wakes up in Detroit: Pontiac's War in Rumor and History," *Ethnohistory* 37 (1990): 254–78; Gregory Evans Dowd, *A Spirited Resistance: The North American Indian Struggle for Unity, 1745–1815* (Baltimore, 1992).

75. "To General Gage from Lt. Campbell, April 10, 1766," Gage Papers no. 308, Ayers

Manuscript Collections, Newberry Library, Chicago; "To General Haldiman from A. S. DePeyster, August 15, 1778," MPHC, 9:368.

76. British traders who attempted to break the exclusionary St. Joseph trade barrier met a dire fate. In 1773 four English traders were murdered near St. Joseph by the Potawatomi. Chevalier was suspected, but the British were reluctant to remove him. Gérard Malchelosse, "Genealogy and Colonial History: The St. Joseph River Post, Michigan," *French Canadian and Acadian Genealogical Review* 7, nos. 3–4 (1970): 189.

77. Joseph L. Peyser, "The Fate of the Fox Survivors: A Dark Chapter in the History of the French in the Upper Country, 1726–1737," *Wisconsin Magazine of History* 73 (winter 1989–90): 110; R. David Edmunds and Joseph L. Peyser, *The Fox Wars: The Mesquakie Challenge to New France* (Norman OK, 1993), 144.

78. "Mackinac Register: Baptisms," 25.

79. The Chevaliers were partners, but they were not related.

80. Louis Pascal was baptized at Michilimackinac on July 22, 1730. He died before July 22, 1740. Pascal and his wife had four children baptized at the mission church between 1758 and 1773. "St. Joseph Baptismal Register," 223; "Mackinac Register: Marriages," 490; "Mackinac Register: Baptisms," 3.

81. Three baptismal registers and one wedding register are part of this research: "St. Joseph Baptismal Register," 202–39; "Mackinac Register: Baptisms," 1–161; "Mackinac Register: Marriages," 469–513; "Kaskaskia Church Records," *Transactions of the Illinois State Historical Society*, vol. 2 (1904), 395–413.

82. Memorial of Louis Joseph Ainsse, August 5, 1780, MPHC, 13:58–59, 10:415. The pretense for removal was Governor General Haldimand's order that the traders whose loyalty was questionable be prevented from living among the Indians. Haldimand to DePeyster, May 6, 1799, MPHC, 9:357–58; Keith R. Widder, "Effects of the American Revolution on Fur Trade Society at Michilimackinac," in *The Fur Trade Revisited: Selected Papers of the Sixth North American Fur Trade Conference, Mackinac Island, Michigan, 1991*, ed. Jennifer S. H. Brown, W. J. Eccles, and Donald Heldman (East Lansing, 1994), 307.

83. "Indian Council held at Detroit 11th March, with the Pottewatimies from St. Josephs, Terre Coupe, and Coeur de Cerf," MPHC, 10:453–54.

84. The attack from Cahokia was led by Thomas Brady and Jean Baptiste Hamelin. Brady had married Réaume's widowed daughter, Marie Joseph, and Hamelin kin were frequent godparents for St. Joseph children. Descriptions of the attack on and destruction of Fort St. Joseph include Joseph Peyser, ed., *Letters from New France: The Upper Country, 1686–1783* (Chicago, 1992), 219–21; A. P. Nasatir, "The Anglo-Spanish Frontier in the Illinois Country during the American Revolution, 1779–1783," *Illinois State Historical Society Journal* 21 (1928): 291–358; Ralph Ballard, *Old Fort St. Joseph* (Berrien Springs MI, 1973), 46–48; Malchelosse, "St. Joseph River Post," 204–6; Rufus Blanchard, *The Discovery and Conquest of the Northwest* (Chicago, 1880), 165–66; B. A. Hinsdale, *The Old Northwest* (New York, 1888), 173–

74; Charles Moore, *Northwest under Three Flags* (New York, 1900), 257–60; John Francis McDermott, *Old Cahokia: A Narrative and Documents Illustrating the First Century of Its History* (St. Louis, 1949), 31–32, 200; Clarence W. Alvord, "The Conquest of St. Joseph Michigan, by the Spaniards in 1781," *Michigan History* 14 (1930): 398–414.

85. Thimotée is also called Marie Neskesh by the Jesuits. Thérèse was ten and Magdelaine six when they were baptized on August 1, 1786. "Mackinac Register: Baptisms," 86.

86. "Census of the Post of St. Joseph," MPHC, 10:406–7.

87. In 1783, Marcot was killed by Indians at the portage between the Fox and Wisconsin rivers. His widow returned to her native Odawa village to raise her children among her people. Magdelaine was the youngest of seven children. McDowell, "Therese Schindler."

88. Baptisms of Native American women occurred most frequently during the summer months, and multiple baptisms took place in a day.

89. "Marguerite-Magdelaine Marcot (La Framboise)," *Dictionary of Canadian Biography*, 7:582; Milo M. Quaife, *Lake Michigan* (Indianapolis, 1944), 201–6.

90. "Mackinac Register: Baptisms," 86, 117, 118; 11:164–65.

91. "Mackinac Register: Baptisms," 117–18.

92. Quaife, *Lake Michigan*, 115.

93. "Mackinac Register: Marriages," 507–8.

94. George Schindler to Solomon Sibley, July 9, August 22, 1807, and Claude La Framboise to John Kinzie, June 11, 1807, Solomon Sibley Papers, Burton Historical Collection, Detroit Public Library; McDowell, "Therese Schindler," 131.

95. Claude La Framboise to John Kinzie, June 11, 1807, Sibley Papers.

96. Elizabeth Thérèse Baird, "Reminiscences of Early Days on Mackinac Island," *Collections of the State Historical Society of Wisconsin*, 14:38–39.

97. Baird, "Reminiscences of Mackinac Island," 22; Elizabeth Thérèse Baird, "Reminiscences of Life in Territorial Wisconsin," *Collections of the State Historical Society of Wisconsin*, 15:213.

98. "Account Book of Mackinac Merchant," Michigan Manuscripts, C, in Archives Division, State Historical Society of Wisconsin, Madison; MPHC, 37:143, McDowell, "Therese Schindler," 135–36.

99. Baird, "Reminiscences of Mackinac," 22; Baird, "Reminiscences of Territorial Wisconsin," 213; "Account Book of a Mackinac Merchant"; MPHC, 27:143; McDowell, "Therese Schindler," 128, 135–36.

100. Ida Amanda Johnson, *The Michigan Fur Trade* (Grand Rapids MI, 1971), 130–31; *Dictionary of Canadian Biography*, 7:582.

101. Gordon Charles Davidson, *The North West Company* (Berkeley, 1918), 72; McDowell, "Madame La Framboise," 278.

102. John Denis Haeger, *John Jacob Astor: Business and Finance in the Early Republic* (Detroit, 1991), 149–52.

103. When increased numbers of mixed-ancestry offspring migrated to larger fur-trade communities such as Michilimackinac, Green Bay, and St. Louis, they increasingly married among themselves. These intermarriages resulted in the emergence of a distinctive Métis community. As the number of mixed heredity offspring continued to increase, these young women of mixed marriages appeared with increasing frequency as the spouses of French fur traders, but these favored marital choices had kin networks rooted in indigenous society. Kinship networks ensured access to peltry and ensured viability as a fur trader. Women with extensive kinship networks remained the most desirable marriage partners. It was for this reason that Marie Madeleine, at age forty, was a desirable fur-trade widow.

104. For a description of the St. Louis community, see especially Tanis C. Thorne, *The Many Hands of My Relations* (Columbia MO, 1996).

105. DePeyser to Gen. Haldimand, August 15, 1778, MPHC, 9:368; DePeyser to Gen. Haldimand, March 8, 1780, MPHC 10:378–79; DePeyser to Sinclair, March 12, 1780, MPHC, 9:580–81; "Return," MPHC 16:116; Mr. Claus to Secretary Foster, May 22, 1815, MPHC, 16:115; the birth and baptism of Amable's two daughters, Marie and Marie Louise, are detailed in *Collections of the State Historical Society of Wisconsin*, 19:93, 95.

Central Question

Did Native Women Lose Power after Colonization?

The following two articles were crafted to answer a central question, in this case an inquiry into whether Native women lost power and/or status as their nations were increasingly dominated by the U.S. government and Euro-American institutions such as Christian missions and schools. Theda Perdue's 1989 essay examined Cherokee experiences during the century before the forced removal of 1838–39, while Nancy Shoemaker's 1991 essay looked at Seneca women in a later era, 1848–1900. These studies can be seen as following in the wake of American women's history research during the 1960s and 1970s, which had focused on ways that political changes and a rising ideology of domesticity had negatively affected white women during the nineteenth century. Both Perdue and Shoemaker argued that a straight declension model was not nuanced enough to address the question. Both also noted that, for the periods in question, they evaluated Native women's status relative to men *in their own communities* precisely at a time when *all* Native people were losing power relative to the United States. In this context, Perdue noted a decline in some indicators of Cherokee women's power, while Shoemaker found less significant losses for Seneca women.

These scholars used a number of variables to assess changes in their respective tribal groups. With regard to women's authority, they inquired into the extent to which women's political participation continued or declined, particularly in response to changing and formalizing political structures. They also examined the implications of matrilineality for politics, inheritance, and property issues, and the extent to which Euro-American efforts to substitute patriarchal patterns affected women's power.

Another set of variables related to questions of women's autonomy, including women's family roles. Again questions arose relative to matrilineality, such as whether women or their husbands were considered heads of households and whether wives could control their own property. Other issues were the freedom to choose one's husband, the availability of divorce, the absence of stigmas attached to sexual relations outside of marriage, and the evidence that women might choose to limit their childbearing. Domestic violence and access to education were mentioned briefly, and economic options were considered as well.

Both Perdue and Shoemaker considered whether family roles increasingly conformed to patriarchal norms of nineteenth-century Euro-American society, and came to different conclusions, although for Perdue it was the elites who were more likely to adopt the non-Native ideals. Neither scholar found a public-private dichotomy to be useful to analyzing women's social and political roles, and in fact, women's roles as mothers had traditionally been the basis of their political participation in both societies. While Perdue found that shifts in the political structure disempowered Cherokee women in significant ways, Shoemaker concluded that Seneca women were able to maintain a certain amount of authority in spite of changes.

These authors used a wide range of sources; we reproduce here samples of petitions, laws, census data, and reports of contemporary non-Native observers.

11. Cherokee Women and the Trail of Tears

THEDA PERDUE

New Introduction by Theda Perdue

This essay marks the beginning of a shift in my thinking about women in Cherokee society. In an earlier essay, "Southern Indians and the Cult of True Womanhood," published in *The Web of Southern Social Relations: Essays on Family Life, Education and Women* (Athens: University of Georgia Press, 1985), I had adopted the declension model, and I charted a decline in the status of Cherokee women as a result of U.S. Indian policy and the activities of Christian missionaries. This essay, which focuses on removal, incorporates some of that analysis, but I pay far more attention to the changing power dynamic within Cherokee society and between the Cherokee Nation and the United States. By the time I wrote *Cherokee Women: Gender and Culture Change, 1700–1830* (Lincoln: University of Nebraska Press, 1998), I had come to the conclusion that women's power and status were remarkably consistent and stable.

One reason for that reinterpretation is that I began to look more closely at non-elite women, even in this essay, rather than focus on the women who attended mission schools and married planters, as I had done in the first essay. As in every field of history, non-elites tend to leave fewer records and participate less publicly in the events that are recorded. This is true, of course, for men as well as women. But I discovered that these non-elites were present in the documentary record if I did not let the elites obscure them. Non-elite women lost their homes, spent the summer of 1838 in stockades, suffered harassment from soldiers, and buried their children along the trail of tears. What can their story tell us? The opposition of women's councils to land cessions reflects an ancient association between the land and women.

Even less abstractly, the refusal of a woman to surrender her food to intruders and her efforts to extinguish the fire threatening her cornfield suggests a persistence of traditional culture. The stockade experiences epitomize the vulnerability of indigenous women in colonial situations, and the loss of children by rich and poor women demonstrates the equalizing effect that U.S. policy, shaped in part by racism, had on Indian people.

Did the status of women decline? Of course, but I now think that we must examine that decline in the context of colonization. All Indian people suffered as a result of the European invasion of the Americas, and whether men or women suffered more is beside the point. At the very end of this essay, I am pointing in that direction. In terms of the relationship between Cherokee men and women, I no longer think that declension is a particularly satisfactory theoretical model. What happened was far more complicated than a single model—or my earlier conclusions—can support. How do I feel about contradicting myself? I am relieved that I have had more than one idea in my career. I enjoy revisiting evidence, assumptions, and conclusions, and I am thrilled when I see something new in my own research or in the work of other scholars. History, after all, is about seeking the past, since, minus a time machine, we will never really find it.

Cherokee Women and the Trail of Tears (1989)

One hundred and fifty years ago, in 1839, the United States forced the Cherokee Nation west of the Mississippi River to what later would become the state of Oklahoma. The Cherokees primarily occupied territory in the Southeast that included north Georgia, northeastern Alabama, southeastern Tennessee, and southwestern North Carolina. In the three decades preceding removal, they experienced a cultural transformation. Relinquishing ancient beliefs and customs, the leaders of the Nation sought to make their people culturally indistinguishable from their white neighbors in the hope that through assimilation they could retain their ancestral homeland. White land hunger and racism proved too powerful, however, and the states in which the Cherokees lived, particularly Georgia, demanded that the federal government extinguish the Indians' title and eject them from the chartered boundaries of the states. The election of Andrew Jackson in 1828 strengthened the states' cause.

While President Jackson promoted the policy of removing eastern Indians to the west, he did not originate the idea. Thomas Jefferson first suggested that removal beyond the evils of "civilization" would benefit the Indians and provide a justification for his purchase of Louisiana. In 1808–10 and again in 1817–19, members of the Cherokee Nation migrated to the west as the Cherokee land base shrank. But the major impetus for total removal came in 1830 when Congress, at the urging of President Jackson, passed the Indian Removal Act, which authorized the President to negotiate cessions of Indian land in the east and transportation of native peoples west of the Mississippi. Although other Indian Nations such as the Choctaws signed removal treaties right away, the Cherokees refused. The Nation's leaders retained legal counsel and took its case against repressive state legislation to the United States Supreme Court (*Cherokee Nation v. Georgia,* 5 Peters 1). The Cherokee Nation won, however, on the grounds that the Cherokees constituted a "domestic dependent" nation-not a foreign state under the U.S. Constitution. The state's failure to respond to the decision and the federal government's refusal to enforce it prompted an unauthorized Cherokee faction to negotiate removal. In December 1835, these disaffected men signed the Treaty of New Echota, by which they exchanged the Cherokee Nation's territory in the southeast for land in the west. The United States Senate ratified the treaty, and in the summer of 1838 soldiers began to round up Cherokees for deportation. Ultimately, the Cherokees were permitted to delay until fall and to manage their own removal, but this leniency did little to ameliorate the experience the Cherokees called the "trail of tears." The weather was unusually harsh that winter; cold, disease, hunger, and exhaustion claimed the lives of at least 4,000 of the 15,000 people who travelled the thousand miles to the west.[1]

The details of Cherokee removal have been recounted many times by scholars and popular writers. The focus of these accounts has tended to be political: they have dealt primarily with the United States' removal policy, the negotiation of removal treaties, and the political factionalism which the removal issue created within Cherokee society. In other words, the role of men in this event has dominated historical analysis. Yet women also were involved. In the sesquicentennial year of the Cherokees' arrival in the West and on the occasion of the inaugural issue of the *Journal of Women's History*, it seems appropriate to reexamine the "trail of tears" using gender as a category of analysis. In particular, what role did women play in removal? How did they regard the policy? Did their views differ from those of men? How did the removal affect women? What were their experiences along the "trail of tears"? How did they go about reestablishing their lives in their new homes in the West? How does this kind of analysis amplify or alter our understanding of the event?

The Treaty of New Echota, by which the Cherokee Nation relinquished its territory in the Southeast, was signed by men.[2] Women were present at the rump council that negotiated the treaty, but they did not participate in the proceedings. They may have met in their own council—precedents for women's councils exist—but if they did, no record remains. Instead, they probably cooked meals and cared for children while their husbands discussed treaty terms with the United States commissioner. The failure of women to join in the negotiation and signing of the Treaty of New Echota does not necessarily mean that women were not interested in the disposition of tribal land, but it does indicate that the role of women had changed dramatically in the preceding century.

Traditionally, women had a voice in Cherokee government.[3] They spoke freely in council, and the War Woman (or Beloved Woman) decided the fate of captives. As late as 1787, a Cherokee woman wrote Benjamin Franklin that she had delivered an address to her people urging them to maintain peace with the new American nation. She had filled the peace pipe for the warriors, and she enclosed some of the same tobacco for the United States Congress in order to unite symbolically her people and his in peace. She continued: "I am in hopes that if you Rightly consider that woman is the mother of All-and the Woman does not pull Children out of Trees or Stumps nor out of old Logs, but out of their Bodies, so that they ought to mind what a woman says.[4] The political influence of women, therefore, rested at least in part on their maternal biological role in procreation and their maternal role in Cherokee society, which assumed particular importance in the Cherokee's matrilineal kinship system. In this way of reckoning kin, children belonged to the clan of their mother, and their only relatives were those who could be traced through her.[5]

The Cherokees were not only matrilineal; they also were matrilocal. That is, a man lived with his wife in a house which belonged to her, or perhaps more accurately, to her family. According to the naturalist William Bartram, "Marriage gives no right to the husband over the property of his wife; and when they part she keeps the children and property belonging to them."[6] The "property" that women kept included agricultural produce—corn, squash, beans, sunflowers, and pumpkins—stored in the household's crib. Produce belonged to women because they were the principal farmers. This economic role was ritualized at the Green Corn Ceremony every summer when an old woman presented the new corn crop. Furthermore, eighteenth-century travelers and traders normally purchased corn from women instead of men, and in the 1750s the garrison at Fort Loudoun, in present-day eastern Tennessee, actually employed a female purchasing agent to procure corn.[7] Similarly, the fields belonged to the women who tended them, or rather to the women's lineages. Bartram observed that "their fields are divided by proper marks and their harvest is gathered separately."[8] While the Cherokees technically held land in common and anyone could use unoccupied land, improved fields belonged to specific matrilineal households.

Perhaps this explains why women signed early deeds conveying land titles to the Proprietors of Carolina. Agents who made these transactions offered little explanation for the signatures of women on these documents. In the early twentieth century a historian speculated that they represented a "renunciation of dower," but it may have been that the women were simply parting with what was recognized as theirs, or they may have been representing their lineages in the negotiations.[9]

As late as 1795, women still played some role in the negotiation of land transactions. Nancy Ward, the Beloved Woman of Chota, spoke to the treaty conference held at Hopewell, South Carolina, to clarify and extend land cessions stemming from Cherokee support of the British in the American Revolution. She addressed the assembly as the "mother of warriors" and promoted a peaceful resolution to land disputes between the Cherokees and the United States. Under the terms of the Treaty of Hopewell, the Cherokees ceded large tracts of land south of the Cumberland River in Tennessee and Kentucky and west of the Blue Ridge Mountains in North Carolina. Nancy Ward and the other Cherokee delegates to the conference agreed to the cession not because they believed it to be just but because the United States dictated the terms of the treaty.[10]

The conference at Hopewell was the last treaty negotiation in which women played an official role, and Nancy Ward's participation in that conference was somewhat anachronistic. In the eighteenth century, the English as well as other Europeans had dealt politically and commercially with men, since men were the hunters and warriors in Cherokee society and Europeans were interested primarily in military alliances and deerskins. As relations with the English grew increasingly important to tribal welfare, women became less significant in the Cherokee economy and government. Conditions in the Cherokee Nation following the American Revolution accelerated the trend. In their defeat, the Cherokees had to cope with the destruction of villages, fields, corn cribs, and orchards which had occurred during the war and the cession of hunting grounds which accompanied the peace. In desperation, they turned to the United States government, which proposed to convert the Cherokees into replicas of white pioneer farmers in the anticipation that they would then cede additional territory (presumably hunting grounds they no longer needed).[11] While the government's so-called "civilization" program brought some economic relief, it also helped produce a transformation of gender roles and social organization. The society envisioned for the Cherokees, one which government agents and Protestant missionaries zealously tried to implement, was one in which a man farmed and headed a household composed only of his wife and children. The men who gained power in eighteenth-century Cherokee society—hunters, warriors, and descendants of traders—took immediate advantage of this program in order to maintain their status in the face of a declining deerskin trade and pacification, and then diverted their energy, ambition, and aggression into economic channels. As agriculture became more commercially viable, these men began to farm or to acquire African slaves to cultivate their fields for them. They also began to dominate Cherokee society, and by example and legislation, they altered fundamental relationships.[12]

In 1808, a Council of headmen (there is no evidence of women participating) from Cherokee towns established a national police force to safeguard a person's holdings during life and "to give protection to children as heirs to their father's property, and to the widow's share," thereby changing inheritance patterns and officially recognizing the patriarchal family as the norm. Two years later, a council representing all seven matrilineal clans, but once again apparently including no women, abolished the practice of blood vengeance. This action ended one of the major functions of clans and shifted the responsibility for punishing wrongdoers to the national police force and tribal courts. Matrilineal kinship clearly did not have a place in the new Cherokee order.[13]

We have no record of women objecting to such legislation. In fact, we know very little about most Cherokee women, because written documents reflect the attitudes and concerns of a male Indian elite or of government agents and missionaries. The only women about whom we know very much are those who conformed to expectations. Nancy Ward, the Beloved Woman who favored peace with the United States, appears in the historical records while other, less cooperative Beloved Women are merely unnamed, shadowy figures. Women such as Catherine Brown, a model of Christian virtue, gained the admiration of missionaries, and we have a memoir of Brown's life; other women who removed their children from mission schools incurred the missionaries' wrath, and they merit only brief mention in mission diaries. The comments of government agents usually focused on those native women who demonstrated considerable industry by raising cotton and producing cloth (in this case, Indian men suffered by comparison), not those who grew corn in the matrilineage's fields.[14] In addition to being biased and reflecting only one segment of the female population, the information from these sources is secondhand; rarely did Indian women, particularly traditionalists, speak for themselves.

The one subject on which women did speak on two occasions was land. In 1817 the United States sought a large cession of Cherokee territory and removal of those who lived on the land in question. A group of Indian women met in their own council, and thirteen of them signed a message which was delivered to the National Council. They advised the Council:

> The Cherokee ladys now being present at the meeting of the Chiefs and warriors in council have thought it their duties as mothers to address their beloved Chiefs and warriors now assembled.
>
> Our beloved children and head men of the Cherokee nation we address you warriors in council[. W]e have raised all of you on the land which we now have, which God gave us to inhabit and raise provisions[. W]e know that our country has once been extensive but by repeated sales has become circumscribed to a small tract and never have thought it our duty to interfere in the disposition of it till now, if a father or mother was to sell all their lands which they had to depend on[,] which their children had to raise their living on[,] which would be bad indeed and to be removed to another country[. W]e do not wish to go to an unknown country which we have understood some of our children wish to go over the Mississippi but this act of our children would be like destroying your mothers. Your mother and sisters ask and beg of you not to part with any more of our lands.[15]

The next year, the National Council met again to discuss the possibility of allotting Cherokee land to individuals, an action the United States government encouraged as a preliminary step to removal. Once again, Cherokee women reacted:

> We have heard with painful feelings that the bounds of the land
> we now possess are to be drawn into very narrow limits. The
> land was given to us by the Great Spirit above as our common
> right, to raise our children upon, & to make support for our
> rising generations. We therefore humbly petition our beloved
> children, the head men and warriors, to hold out to the last in
> support of our common rights, as the Cherokee nation have
> been the first settlers of this land; we therefore claim the right
> of the soil. . . . We therefore unanimously join in our meeting to
> hold our country in common as hitherto.[16]

Common ownership of land meant in theory that the United States government had to obtain cessions from recognized, elected Cherokee officials
who represented the wishes of the people. Many whites favored allotment,
because private citizens then could obtain individually owned tracts of land
through purchase, fraud, or seizure. Most Cherokees recognized this danger
and objected to allotment for that reason. The women, however, had an
additional incentive for opposing allotment. Under the laws of the states in
which the Cherokees lived and of which they would become citizens if land
were allotted, married women had few property rights. A married woman's
property, even property she held prior to her marriage, belonged legally to
her husband.[17] Cherokee women and matrilineal households would have
ceased to be property owners.

The implications for women became apparent in the 1830s, when Georgia claimed its law was in effect in the Cherokee country. Conflicts over
property arose because of uncertainty over which legal system prevailed.
For example, a white man, James Vaught, married the Cherokee Catherine
Gunter. She inherited several slaves from her father, and Vaught sold two of
them to General Isaac Wellborn. His wife had not consented to the sale, so
she reclaimed her property and took them with her when the family moved
west. General Wellborn tried to seize the slaves just as they were about to
embark, but a soldier, apparently recognizing her claim under Cherokee
law, prevented him from doing so. After removal, the General appealed to
Principal Chief John Ross for aid in recovering the slaves, but Ross refused.
He informed Wellborn: "By the laws of the Cherokee Nation, the property
of husband and wife remain separate and apart and neither of these can sell
or dispose of the property of the other." Had the Cherokees accepted allotment and come under Georgia law, Wellborn would have won.[18]

The effects of the women's protests in 1817 and 1818 are difficult to determine. In 1817 the Cherokees ceded tracts of land in Georgia, Alabama, and Tennessee, and in 1819 they made an even larger cession. Nevertheless, they rejected individual allotments and strengthened restrictions on alienation of improvements. Furthermore, the Cherokee Nation gave notice that they would negotiate no additional cessions—a resolution so strongly supported that the United States ultimately had to turn to a small, unauthorized faction in order to obtain the minority treaty of 1835.[19]

The political organization which existed in the Cherokee Nation in 1817–18 had made it possible for women to voice their opinion. Traditionally, Cherokee towns were politically independent of one another, and each town governed itself through a council in which all adults could speak. In the eighteenth century, however, the Cherokees began centralizing their government in order to restrain bellicose warriors whose raids jeopardized the entire nation and to negotiate as a single unit with whites. Nevertheless, town councils remained important, and representatives of traditional towns formed the early National Council. This National Council resembled the town councils in that anyone could address the body. Although legislation passed in 1817 created an Executive Committee, power still rested with the Council, which reviewed all Committee acts.[20]

The protests of the women to the National Council in 1817 and 1818 were, however, the last time women presented a collective position to the Cherokee governing body. Structural changes in Cherokee government more narrowly defined participation in the National Council. In 1820 the Council provided that representatives be chosen from eight districts rather than from traditional towns, and in 1823 the Committee acquired a right of review over acts of the Council. The more formalized political organization made it less likely that a group could make its views known to the national government.[21]

As the Cherokee government became more centralized, political and economic power rested increasingly in the hands of a few elite men who adopted the planter lifestyle of the white antebellum South. A significant part of the ideological basis for this lifestyle was the cult of domesticity, in which the ideal woman confined herself to home and hearth while men contended with the corrupt world of government and business.[22] The elite adopted the tenets of the cult of domesticity, particularly after 1817, when the number of Protestant missionaries, major proponents of this feminine ideal, increased significantly and their influence on Cherokee society broadened.

The extent to which a man's wife and daughters conformed to the idea quickly came to be one measure of his status. In 1818 Charles Hicks, who later served as Principal Chief, described the most prominent men in the Nation as "those who have for the last 10 or 20 years been pursuing agriculture & kept their women & children at home & in comfortable circumstances." Eight years later, John Ridge, one of the first generation of Cherokees to have been educated from childhood in mission schools, discussed a Cherokee law which protected the property rights of a married woman and observed that "in many respects she has exclusive & distinct control over her own, particularly among the less civilized." The more "civilized" presumably left such matters to men. Then Ridge described suitable activities for women: "They sew, they weave, they spin, they cook our meals and act well the duties assigned them by Nature as mothers." Proper women did not enter business or politics.[23]

Despite the attitudes of men such as Hicks and Ridge, women did in fact continue as heads of households and as businesswomen. In 1828 the *Cherokee Phoenix* published the obituary of Oo-dah-less, who had accumulated a sizable estate through agriculture and commerce. She was "the support of a large family," and she bequeathed her property "to an only daughter and three grandchildren." Oo-dah-less was not unique. At least one-third of the heads of household listed on the removal roll of 1835 were women. Most of these were not as prosperous as Oo-dah-less, but some were even more successful economically. Nineteen owned slaves (190 men were slaveholders), and two held over twenty slaves and operated substantial farms.[24]

Nevertheless, these women had ceased to have a direct voice in Cherokee government. In 1826 the Council called a constitutional convention to draw up a governing document for the Nation. According to legislation which provided for election of delegates to the convention, "No person but a free male citizen who is full grown shall be entitled to vote." The convention met and drafted a constitution patterned after that of the United States. Not surprisingly, the constitution which male Cherokees ratified in 1827 restricted the franchise to "free male citizens" and stipulated that "no person shall be eligible to a seat in the General Council, but a free Cherokee male, who shall have attained the age of twenty-five." Unlike the United States Constitution, the Cherokee document clearly excluded women, perhaps as a precaution against women who might assert their traditional right to participate in politics instead of remaining in the domestic sphere.[25]

The exclusion of women from politics certainly did not produce the removal crisis, but it did mean that a group traditionally opposed to land cession could no longer be heard on the issue. How women would have voted is also unclear. Certainly by 1835, many Cherokee women, particularly those educated in mission schools, believed that men were better suited to deal with political issues than women, and a number of women voluntarily enrolled their households to go west before the forcible removal of 1838–39. Even if women had united in active opposition to removal, it is unlikely that the United States and aggressive state governments would have paid any more attention to them than they did to the elected officials of the Nation who opposed removal or the 15,000 Cherokees, including women (and perhaps children), who petitioned the United States Senate to reject the Treaty of New Echota. While Cherokee legislation may have made women powerless, federal authority rendered the whole Nation impotent.

In 1828 Georgia had extended state law over the Cherokee Nation and over white intruders who invaded its territory. Georgia law prohibited Indians, both men and women, from testifying in court against white assailants, and so they simply had to endure attacks on person and property. Delegates from the Nation complained to Secretary of War John H. Eaton about the lawless behavior of white intruders: "Too many there are who think it an act of trifling consequence to oust an Indian family from the quiet enjoyment of all the comforts of their own firesides, and to drive off before their faces the stock that gave nourishment to the children and support to the aged, and appropriate it to the satisfaction to avarice."[26] Elias Boudinot, editor of the bilingual *Cherokee Phoenix*, even accused the government of encouraging the intruders in order to force the Indians off their lands, and he published the following account:

> A few days since two of these white men came to a Cherokee house, for the purpose, they pretended, of buying provisions. There was no person about the house but one old woman of whom they inquired for some corn, beans &c. The woman told them she had nothing to sell. They then went off in the direction of the field belonging to this Cherokee family. They had not gone but a few minutes when the woman of the house saw a heavy smoke rising from that direction. She immediately hastened to the field and found the villains had set the woods on fire but a few rods from the fences, which she found already in a full blaze. There being a very heavy wind that day, the fire spread

so fast, that her efforts to extinguish it proved utterly useless. The entire fence was therefore consumed in a short time. It is said that during her efforts to save the fence the men who had done the mischief were within sight, and were laughing heartily at her!

The Georgia Guard, established by the state to enforce its law in the Cherokee country, offered no protection and, in fact, contributed to the lawlessness. The *Phoenix* printed the following notice under the title "Cherokee Women, Beware": "It is said that the Georgia Guard have received orders, from the Governor we suppose, to inflict corporeal punishment on such females as shall hereafter be guilty of insulting them. We presume they are to be the judges of what constitutes *insult*."[27]

Despite harassment from intruders and the Guard, most Cherokees had no intention of going west, and in the spring of 1838 they began to plant their crops as usual. Then United States soldiers arrived, began to round up the Cherokees, and imprisoned them in stockades in preparation for deportation. In 1932 Rebecca Neugin, who was nearly one hundred years old, shared her childhood memory and family tradition about removal with historian Grant Foreman:

> When the soldier came to our house my father wanted to fight, but my mother told him that the soldiers would kill him if he did and we surrendered without a fight. They drove us out of our house to join other prisoners in a stockade. After they took us away, my mother begged them to let her go back and get some bedding. So they let her go back and she brought what bedding and a few cooking utensils she could carry and had to leave behind all of our other household possessions.[28]

Rebecca Neugin's family was relatively fortunate. In the process of capture, families were sometimes separated and sufficient food and clothing were often left behind. Over fifty years after removal, John G. Burnett, a soldier who served as an interpreter, reminisced: "Men working in the fields were arrested and driven to stockades. Women were dragged from their homes by soldiers whose language they could not understand. Children were often separated from their parents and driven into the stockades with the sky for a blanket and the earth for a pillow." Burnett recalled how one family was forced to leave the body of a child who had just died and how a distraught mother collapsed of heart failure as soldiers evicted her and her three children from their homes.[29] After their capture, many Cherokees had to march miles over rugged mountain terrain to the stockades. Captain L. B. Webster wrote his wife about moving eight hundred Cherokees from North Carolina to the central depot in Tennessee: "We were eight days in making the journey (80 miles), and it was pitiful to behold the women & children, who suffered exceedingly—as they were all obliged to walk, with the exception of the sick."[30]

Originally the government planned to deport all the Cherokees in the summer of 1838, but the mortality rate of the three parties that departed that summer led the commanding officer, General Winfield Scott, to agree to delay the major removal until fall. In the interval the Cherokees remained in the stockades, where conditions were abysmal. Women in particular often became individual victims of their captors. The missionary Daniel Butrick recorded the following episode in his journal:

> The poor Cherokees are not only exposed to temporal evils, but also to every species of moral desolation. The other day a gentleman informed me that he saw six soldiers about two Cherokee women. The women stood by a tree, and the soldiers with a bottle of liquor were endeavoring to entice them to drink, though the women, as yet were resisting them. He made this known to the commanding officer but we presume no notice was taken of it, as it was reported that those soldiers had those women with them the whole night afterwards. A young married woman, a member of the Methodist society was at the camp with her friends, though her husband was not there at the time. The soldiers, it is said, caught her, dragged her about, and at length, either through fear, or otherwise, induced her to drink; and then seduced her away, so that she is now an outcast even among her own relatives. How many of the poor captive women are thus debauched, through terror and seduction, that eye which never sleeps, alone can determine.[31]

When removal finally got under way in October, the Cherokees were in a debilitated and demoralized state. A white minister who saw them as they prepared to embark noted: "The women did not appear to as good advantage as did the men. All, young and old, wore blankets which almost hid them from view."[32] The Cherokees had received permission to manage their own removal, and they divided the people into thirteen detachments of approximately one thousand each. While some had wagons, most walked. Neugin rode in a wagon with other children and some elderly women, but her older brother, mother, and father "walked all the way."[33] One observer reported that "even aged females, apparently nearly ready to drop in the grave, were traveling with heavy burdens attached to the back." Proper conveyance did not spare well-to-do Cherokees the agony of removal, the same observer noted:

> One lady passed on in her hack in company with her husband, apparently with as much refinement and equipage as any of the mothers of New England; and she was a mother too and her youngest child, about three years old, was sick in her arms, and all she could do was to make it comfortable as circumstances would permit. . . . She could only carry her dying child in her arms a few miles farther, and then she must stop in a stranger-land and consign her much loved babe to the cold ground, and that without pomp and ceremony, and pass on with the multitude.[34]

This woman was not alone. Journals of the removal are largely a litany of the burial of children, some born "untimely."[35]

Many women gave birth alongside the trail: at least sixty-nine newborns arrived in the West.[36] The Cherokees' military escort was often less than sympathetic. Daniel Butrick wrote in his journal that troops frequently forced women in labor to continue until they collapsed and delivered "in the midst of the company of soldiers." One man even stabbed an expectant mother with a bayonet.[37] Obviously, many pregnant women did not survive such treatment. The oral tradition of a family from southern Illinois, through which the Cherokees passed, for example, includes an account of an adopted Cherokee infant whose mother died in childbirth near the family's pioneer cabin. While this story may be apocryphal, the circumstances of Cherokee removal make such traditions believable.[38]

The stress and tension produced by the removal crisis probably accounts for a post-removal increase in domestic violence, of which women usually were the victims. Missionaries reported that men, helpless to prevent seizure of their property and assaults on themselves and their families, vented their frustrations by beating wives and children. Some women were treated so badly by their husbands that they left them, and this dislocation contributed to the chaos in the Cherokee Nation in the late 1830s.[39]

Removal divided the Cherokee Nation in a fundamental way, and the Civil War magnified that division. Because most signers of the removal treaty were highly acculturated, many traditionalists resisted more strongly the white man's way of life and distrusted more openly those Cherokees who imitated whites. This split between "conservatives," those who sought to preserve the old ways, and "progressives," those committed to change, extended to women. We know far more, of course, about "progressive" Cherokee women who left letters and diaries which in some ways are quite similar to those of upper-class women in the antebellum South. In letters they recounted local news such as "they had Elick Cockrel up for steeling horses" and "they have Charles Reese in chains about burning Harnages house" and discussed economic concerns: "I find I cannot get any corn in this neighborhood, so of course I shall be greatly pressed in providing provision for my family." Nevertheless, family life was the focus of most letters: "Major is well and tryes hard to stand alone he will walk soon. I would write more but the baby is crying."[40]

Occasionally we even catch a glimpse of conservative women who seem to have retained at least some of their original authority over domestic matters. Red Bird Smith, who led a revitalization movement at the end of the nineteenth century, had considerable difficulty with his first mother-in-law. She "influenced" her adopted daughter to marry Smith through witchcraft and, as head of the household, meddled rather seriously in the couple's lives. Interestingly, however, the Kee-Too-Wah society which Red Bird Smith headed had little room for women. Although the society had political objectives, women enjoyed no greater participation in this "conservative" organization than they did in the "progressive" republican government of the Cherokee Nation.[41]

Following removal, the emphasis of legislation involving women was on protection rather than participation. In some ways, this legislation did offer women greater opportunities than the law codes of the states. In 1845 the editor of the *Cherokee Advocate* expressed pride that "in this respect the Cherokees have been considerably in advance of many of their white brethren, the rights of their women having been amply secured almost ever since they had written laws." The Nation also established the Cherokee Female Seminary to provide higher education for women, but like the education women received before removal, students studied only those subjects considered to be appropriate for their sex.[42]

Removal, therefore, changed little in terms of the status of Cherokee women. They had lost political power before the crisis of the 1830s, and events which followed relocation merely confirmed new roles and divisions. Cherokee women originally had been subsistence-level farmers and mothers, and the importance of these roles in traditional society had made it possible for them to exercise political power. Women, however, lacked the economic resources and military might on which political power in the Anglo-American system rested. When the Cherokees adopted the Anglo-American concept of power in the eighteenth and nineteenth centuries, men became dominant. But in the 1830s the chickens came home to roost. Men, who had welcomed the Anglo-American basis for power, now found themselves without power. Nevertheless, they did not question the changes they had fostered. Therefore, the tragedy of the trail of tears lies not only in the suffering and death which the Cherokees experienced but also in the failure of many Cherokees to look critically at the political system which they had adopted—a political system dominated by wealthy, highly acculturated men and supported by an ideology that made women (as well as others defined as "weak" or "inferior") subordinate. In the removal crisis of the 1830s, men learned an important lesson about power; it was a lesson women had learned well before the "trail of tears."

Appendix

In this selection, Ward's speech is introduced by the council speaker, the Tassel of Chota. This excerpt is instructive because it shows that Cherokee male leaders recognized women like Nancy Ward as legitimate leaders and spokespersons in their own right. The phrase "one of our beloved women" also reveals that Ward was not an anomaly, that Cherokees regularly recognized beloved women as political figures. Ward's speech originally appeared in "Treaty of Hopewell, 1785," American State Papers, *Class 2, Indian Affairs, 2 vols. (Washington DC, 1832), 1:41.*

I have no more to say, but one of our beloved women has, who has born and raised up warriors.—[A string of beads.]

The War-woman of Chota then addressed the commissioners:

I am fond of hearing that there is a peace, and I hope you have now taken us by the hand in real friendship. I have a pipe and a little tobacco to give the commissioners to smoke in friendship. I look on you and the red people as my children. Your having determined on peace is most pleasing to me, for I have seen much trouble during the late war. I am old, but I hope yet to bear children, who will grow up and people our nation, as we are now to be under the protection of Congress, and shall have no more disturbance.—[A string, little old pipe, and some tobacco.]

The talk I have given is from the young warriors I have raised in my town, as well as myself. They rejoice that we have peace, and we hope the chain of friendship will never more be broke.—[A string of beads.]

Robert Sandford was an explorer on behalf of Barbadian planters interested in establishing settlements in the Carolinas. Not understanding that women's roles in Cherokee society differed from those of English women in colonial America, in 1929 the editor of his narrative, Alexander S. Salley, was perplexed by the women's participation and suggested in the footnote reproduced here that the women were signing away their "dower" rights to property as potential future widows. "Robert Sandford's Relation of 1666" and editor's footnote in Narratives of Early Carolina, 1650–1708, *ed. Alexander S. Salley Jr. (New York: Barnes & Noble, 1929), 90.*

When Wee were here a Capt. Of the Nation named Shadoo (one of them which Hilton had carried to Barbados) was very earnest with some of our company to goe with him and lye a night att their Towne, which he told us was but a smale distance thence. I being equally desirous to knowe the forme, manner and populousnesse of the place, alsoe what state the Casique held . . . and foure of my Company vizt: Lt. Harvy, Lt. Woory, Mr. Thomas Giles and Mr. Henry Woodward, forwardly offring themselves to the service, having alsoe some Indians aboard mee who constantly resided there night and day, I permitted them to go with this Shadoo. They returned to me the next morning with great Comendations of their entertainment, but especially of the goodnesse of the land they marcht through and the delightfull situation of the Towne Telling mee withal that the Cassique himselfe appeared not (pretending some indisposition) but that his state was supplied by a Female, who received them with gladness and Courtesy, placeing my Lt. Harvey on the seat by her.

Footnote 2: By a deed, dated March 10, 1675, "the Casseques naturall borne Heires and sole owners and Proprietors of great and the lesser Cassoe lying on the River of Kyeawah the River of Stonoe and the freshes of the River of Edistoh," for themselves, their "subjects and Vassalls" conveyed the "said parcel and parcels of land called by the name and names of great and little Cassoe with all the Timber on said land and all manner of the appurte-

nances any way belonging to any part or parts of the said land of lands"
to the Lords Proprietors of Carolina. The deed is signed (with marks and
seals) by the great cassique, three lesser cassiques, eleven Indian captains
and fourteen women captains, the consideration being "a valuable parcel
of cloth, hatchets, Beads and other goods and manufactures." It is probable
that the signatures of the women were secured to serve the purpose of a
renunciation of dower, the deed being otherwise legally executed. Seven
white men witnessed it. (Records of the Register of the Province of South
Carolina, 1675–1696, p. 10—a manuscript volume in the office of the Historical Commission of South Carolina.) Numbers of other similar deeds
executed later by Indians and signed by their women captains are on record
in South Carolina. (p. 90)

*Captain Rayd. DeMere to Governor Lyttelton, Fort Loudoun, January 2d, 1757,
from William L. McDowell, Jr.,* Documents Relating to Indian Affairs, 1754–
1765 *(Columbia SC: University of South Carolina Press, 1970), 303.*

I am under no Apprehensions that when the French comes a great many
of these Indians will go there to receive Presents from them, and to drink
some *de leur Eau de Vie* [an alcoholic beverage] which may corrupt them.
That Villain the Emperor has bragged that we should soon be in want of
Provisions by which Means it will be an easy Matter to starve or take us.
As to this he may guess right if we do not get some Supply; there is but five
cannoe Loads of Corn bought. I have sent an Indian Wench (who has been
very serviceable in purchasing of Corn for us) with some Truck to buy all
the Corn she can, for want of necessary trifling Things that the Indians like,
we are obliged to pay very dear for Corn, for they will give no more for a
Thing of Value than for a Trifle suppose they like it. . . . The Traders have
no Goods proper for the purchasing of Corn; had it not been for the few
Things I sent for to supply my Men with, I do not know what we should
have done. Your Excellency may depend I shall do whatever I can to get as
much Corn as possible without any Delay.

*James Adair, a Scots-Irish trader who lived in the South for four decades, pub-
lished a book about his experiences in 1775. The following selections are from
Adair's* History of the American Indian, *ed. Samuel Cole Williams (Johnson
City TN, 1930), 112, 152–53.*

[A] crier informs them of the good tidings, and orders an old beloved
woman to pull a basket-full of the new-ripened fruits, and bring them to

the beloved square. As she before had been appointed, and religiously prepared for that solemn occasion, she readily obeys, and soon lays it down with a cheerful heart, at the out-corner of the beloved square.

The Cheerake are an exception to all civilized or savage nations in having no laws against adultery; they have been a considerable while under a petticoat-government, and allow their women full liberty to plant their brows with horns as oft as they please, without fear of punishment.

Benjamin Hawkins, a Euro-American from North Carolina, served in that state's legislature and the U.S. Senate before being appointed an Indian agent by President George Washington in 1796. The following is an excerpt from a diary of one of his voyages. Benjamin Hawkins, Letters of Benjamin Hawkins, *1796–1806, vol. 9 of* Georgia Historical Society Collections *(Savannah GA, 1916), 110–11.*

March, 28, 1797

    We sat [*sic*] out early from our encampment N.W.; in 16 minutes to thro' [*sic*] a narrow pass . . . pass a creek . . . arrive at a large creek . . . go down . . . to Little Tellico; here I saw 28 gun men who collected on being informed that I should be here accompanied with General Pickins. I addressed a short speach to them relative to our visit. They expressed pleasure at seeing us, and confidence in our exertions to restore order between the red and white people. One of them informed me that five of their hunters who went towards Cumberland were missing and he was apprehensive they had been killed. We procured some corn of the women and proceeded on.

Appendix: Three Selections from *Laws of the Cherokee Nation*

Laws of the Cherokee Nation: Adopted by the Council at Various Periods *(Wilmington DE: Scholarly Resources Inc., 1973 [facsimile edition], originally published 1852, by Cherokee Advocate Office, Tahlequah, Cherokee Nation), 3–4, 14–15, 18.*

Resolved by the Chiefs and Warriors in a National Council assembled, That it shall be, and is hereby authorized, for the regulating parties to be organized to consist of six men in each company; one Captain, one Lieutenant and four privates, to continue in service for the term of one year; whose duties it shall be to suppress horse stealing and robbery of other property within their respective bounds, who shall be paid out of the National annuity, at the rates of fifty dollars to each Captain, forty to the Lieutenant, and thirty dollars to each of the privates; and to give their protection to children as heirs to their fathers' property, and to the widow's share whom he may have had children by or cohabited with, as his wife, at the time of his decease, and in case a father shall leave or will any property to a child at the time of his decease, which he may have had by another woman, then, his present wife shall be entitled to receive any such property as may be left by him or them, when substantiated by two or one disinterested witnesses.

> Accepted—
> BLACK FOX, *Principal Chief,*
> PATH KILLER, *Sec'd.*
> TOOCHALAR.
> CHAS. HICKS, *Sec'y to Council.*
> Brooms Town 11th Sept., 1808

Be it known, That this day, the various clans or tribes which compose the Cherokee Nation, have unanimously passed an act of oblivion for all lives for which they may have been indebted, one to the others, and have mutually agreed that after this evening the aforesaid act shall become binding upon every clan or tribe; and the aforesaid clans or tribes, have also agreed that if, in future, any life should be lost without malice intended, the innocent aggressor shall not be accounted guilty.

Be it also known, That should it happen that a brother, forgetting his natural affection, should raise his hand in anger and kill his brother, he shall be accounted guilty of murder and suffer accordingly, and if a man has a horse stolen, and overtakes the theif [sic], and should his anger be so great as to cause him to kill him, let his blood remain on his own conscience, but no satisfaction shall be demanded for his life from his relatives or the clan he may belong to.

By order of the seven clans.

> TURTLE AT HOME, Speaker of Council.
> Approved—
> BLACK FOX, *Principal Chief,*
> PATHKILLER, *Sec'd,*
> TOOCHALER.
> CHAS. HICKS, *Sec'y to the Council*
> Oostanallah, April 10, 1810

New Town, Cherokee Nation, November 2d, 1820. Resolved by the National Committee and Council, That each District shall be entitled to four members to represent them in the National Council, and that each member shall be allowed one dollar per day for their services during the sitting of the Councils, and that a Speaker to the Council be appointed and allowed one dollar and fifty cents per day for his services, and the clerk of the Council be allowed two dollars and fifty cents per day, and that the two principal Chiefs, viz: The Path Killer, shall be allowed one hundred and fifty dollars per annum, and Charles R. Hicks, two hundred dollars per annum, considering the burden of writing and interpreting which devolves on him entitles him to this difference; and

Be it resolved, also, That each Committeeman be allowed two dollars per day, and the President of the Committee be allowed three dollars and fifty cents per day, and their clerk two dollars and fifty cents per day, during the sitting of the National Council; and a member of the Committee shall be chosen as an Interpreter, and be allowed fifty cents per day in addition to his pay.

> By order of the National Committee.
> *JNO. ROSS, Pres't Com.*
> *EHNAUTAUNAUEH, Speaker of Council. his mark.*
> Approved—
> *PATH X KILLER.*
> *CHAS. R. HICKS*
> *A. McCOY, Clerk.*
> New Town, Cherokee Nation, November 2d, 1820

Resolved by the National Committee and Council, That the Cherokee Nation be organized and laid off in Districts, and to be bounded as follows . . . and that each District shall hold their respective Councils or Courts, on the following days;

> The first Mondays in May and September for Coosewatee District; and the
> Second Mondays in May and September, for Amoah District; and on the
> First Mondays in May and September, for Hickory Log District; and on the
> Second Mondays in May and September, for Etowah District; and on the

First Mondays in May and September for Aquohee District; and on the
Second Mondays in May and September, for Tauquohee District; and
each of the Councils or Courts shall sit five days for the transac-
tion of business at each term.
By order of the Committee and Council.
CHAS. R. HICKS

Notes

1. The standard account of Cherokee removal is Grant Foreman, *Indian Removal: The
Emigration of the Five Civilized Tribes of Indians* (Norman OK, 1932), 229–312. Also
see Ronald N. Satz, *American Indian Policy in the Jacksonian Era* (Lincoln NE, 1975);
Dale Van Avery, *Disinherited: The Lost Birthright of the American Indian* (New York,
1966); William G. McLoughlin, "Thomas Jefferson and the Beginning of Cherokee Nationalism, 1806 to 1809," *William and Mary Quarterly*, 3d ser., 32 (1975): 547–
80; Thurman Wilkins, *Cherokee Tragedy: The Story of the Ridge Family and The Dec-
imation of a People* (New York, 1970); Gary E. Moulton, *John Ross: Cherokee Chief*
(Athens GA, 1978); Russell Thornton, "Cherokee Population Losses during the Trail
of Tears: A New Perspective and a New Estimate," *Ethnohistory* 31 (1984): 289–300.
Other works on the topic include Gloria Jahoda, *The Trail of Tears* (New York, 1975);
Samuel Carter, *Cherokee Sunset: A Nation Betrayed* (Garden City NY, 1976); John
Ehle, *The Trail of Tears: The Rise and Fall of the Cherokee Nation* (New York, 1988). A
good collection of primary documents can be found in the *Journal of Cherokee
Studies* 3 (1978). For the context in which the removal policy developed, see Francis
Paul Prucha, *American Indian Policy in the Formative Years: The Indian Trade and
Intercourse Acts, 1790–1834* (Cambridge MA, 1962). Not all Cherokees went west; see
John R. Finger, *The Eastern Band of Cherokees, 1819–1900* (Knoxville, 1984).
2. Charles J. Kappler, ed., *Indian Affairs: Laws and Treaties*, 5 vols. (Washington DC,
1904–41), 2:439–49.
3. While some similarities to the role of women among the Iroquois exist, the differences are significant. Both had matrilineal kinship systems and practiced the
same fundamentally sexual division of labor, but the Cherokees had no clan mothers who selected headmen, an important position among the Iroquois of the Five
Nations. The Cherokees were an Iroquoian people, but linguists believe they separated from the northern Iroquois thousands of years ago. Certainly, the Cherokees
had been in the Southeast long enough to be a part of the southeastern cultural
complex described by Charles Hudson in *The Southeastern Indians* (Knoxville,
1976). Yet where women were concerned, the Cherokees differed from other southeastern peoples. James Adair, an eighteenth-century trader, gave the following analysis: "The Cherokees are an exception to all civilized or savage nations in having
no laws against adultery; they have been a considerable while under a petticoat-
government, and allow their women full liberty to plant their brows with horns as

oft as they please, without fear of punishment" (James Adair, *Adair's History of the American Indian*, ed. Samuel Cole Williams [Johnson City TN, 1930], 152–53). Indeed, Adair was correct that Cherokee women enjoyed considerable sexual autonomy. Furthermore, they seem to have exercised more political power than other eighteenth-century native women in the Southeast. Earlier sources, however, describe "queens" who ruled southeastern peoples other than the Cherokee. See Edward Gaylord Bourne, ed., *Narratives of the Career of Hernando de Soto*, 2 vols. (New York, 1922), 1:65–72. Consequently, the unusual role of women in Cherokee society cannot be attributed definitively to either Iroquoian or southeastern antecedents.

4. Samuel Hazard, ed., *Pennsylvania Archives, 1787*, 12 vols. (Philadelphia, 1852–56), 11:181–82. See also Theda Perdue, "The Traditional Status of Cherokee Women," *Furman Studies* 5 (1980): 19–25.

5. The best study of the aboriginal Cherokee kinship system is John Phillip Reid, *A Law of Blood: The Primitive Law of the Cherokee Nation* (New York, 1970). Also see William H. Gilbert, *The Eastern Cherokees* (Washington DC, 1943); and Alexander Spoehr, *Changing Kinship Systems: A Study in the Acculturation of the Creeks, Cherokee and Choctaw* (Chicago, 1947).

6. William Bartram, "Observations on the Creek and Cherokee Indians, 1789," *Transactions of the American Ethnological Society* 3, pt. 1 (1954): 66.

7. William L. McDowell, ed., *Documents Relating to Indian Affairs, 1754–1765* (Columbia SC, 1970), 303; Henry Timberlake, *Lieut. Henry Timberlake's Memoirs, 1756–1765*, ed. Samuel Cole Williams (Johnson City TN, 1927), 89–90; Benjamin Hawkins, *Letters of Benjamin Hawkins, 1796–1806*, vol. 9 of *Georgia Historical Society Collections* (Savannah GA, 1916), 110; Adair, *Adair's History*, 105–17.

8. William Bartram, ed., *The Travels of William Bartram*, ed. Mark Van Doren (New York, 1940), 90.

9. Alexander S. Salley, ed., *Narratives of Early Carolina, 1650–1708* (New York, 1911), 90.

10. *American State Papers*, Class 2: *Indian Affairs*, 2 vols. (Washington DC, 1832), 1:41. For Nancy Ward, see Ben Harris McClary, "Nancy Ward: Last Beloved Woman of the Cherokees," *Tennessee Historical Quarterly* 21 (1962): 336–52; Theda Perdue, "Nancy Ward," in *Portraits of American Women*, ed. Catherine Clinton and Ben Barker-Benfield (New York, 1991), 83–100.

11. Prucha, *American Indian Policy*, 213–49; Bernard W. Sheehan, *Seeds of Extinction: Jeffersonian Philanthropy and the American Indian* (Chapel Hill NC, 1973); Robert F. Berkhofer Jr., *Salvation and the Savage: An Analysis of Protestant Missions and American Indian Response* (Lexington KY, 1965).

12. William G. McLoughlin, *Cherokee Renascence in the New Republic* (Princeton, 1986); William G. McLoughlin, *Cherokees and Missionaries, 1789–1839* (New Haven, 1984); Henry T. Malone, *Cherokees of the Old South: A People in Transition* (Athens GA, 1956); Theda Perdue, *Slavery and the Evolution of Cherokee Society, 1540–1866* (Knoxville, 1979).

13. *Laws of the Cherokee Nation: Adopted by the Council at Various Times, Printed for the Benefit of the Nation* (Tahlequah, Cherokee Nation, 1852), 3–4.

14. Rufus Anderson, *Memoir of Catherine Brown, A Christian Indian of the Cherokee Nation* (Philadelphia, 1832); Hawkins, *Letters*, 20.

15. Presidential Papers Microfilm: Andrew Jackson (Washington, 1961), Series 1, Reel 22; also mentioned in *Journal of Cyrus Kingsbury*, February 13, 1817, Papers of the American Board of Commissioners for Foreign Missions, Houghton Library, Harvard University, Cambridge MA (hereafter cited as American Board Papers).

16. Brainerd Journal, June 30, 1818, American Board Papers.

17. For women's property rights in the United States, see Mary Beard, *Woman as a Force in History: A Study in Traditions and Realities* (New York, 1946); Marylynn Salmon, "Women and Property in South Carolina: The Evidence from Marriage Settlements, 1730–1830," *William and Mary Quarterly*, 3d ser., 39 (1982): 655–85; Marylynn Salmon, "Equality or Submersion? *Feme Covert* Status in Early Pennsylvania," in *Women of America*, ed. Carol Berkin and Mary Beth Norton (Boston, 1979); Marylynn Salmon, "'Life Liberty and Dower': The Legal Status of Women after the Revolution," in *Women, War, and Revolution*, ed. Carol Berkin and Clara Lovett (New York, 1980); Norma Basch, "Invisible Women: The Legal Fiction of Marital Unity in Nineteenth-Century America," *Feminist Studies* 5 (1979): 346–66; Norma Basch, *In the Eyes of the Law: Women, Marriage, and Property in Nineteenth-Century New York* (Ithaca NY, 1982); Albie Sachs and Joan Hoff-Wilson, *Sexism and the Law: A Study of Male Beliefs and Legal Bias in Britain and the United States* (New York, 1979); Suzanne Lebsock, *The Free Women of Petersburg: Status and Culture in a Southern Town, 1784–1860* (New York, 1984).

18. Louis Wyeth to R. Chapman and C. C. Clay, May 16, 1838, Memorial of Isaac Wellborn to Martin Van Buren, n.d., Writ of the Morgan County (Alabama) Court, June 9, 1838, Letters Received by the Office of Indian Affairs, 1824–1881, Record Group 75, National Archives, Washington DC; Joel R. Poinsett to Mathew Arbuckle, December 17, 1838, John Ross to Joel R. Poinsett, July 18, 1839, John Ross Papers, Thomas Gilcrease Institute, Tulsa, Oklahoma.

19. Charles C. Royce, *Indian Land Cessions in the United States* (Washington DC, 1900), 684–85, 696–97.

20. V. Richard Persico Jr., "Early Nineteenth-Century Cherokee Political Organization," in *The Cherokee Indian Nation: A Troubled History*, ed. Duane H. King (Knoxville, 1979), 92–109.

21. *Laws of the Cherokee Nation*, 14–18, 31–32.

22. The classic article is Barbara Welter, "The Cult of True Womanhood, 1820–1860," *American Quarterly* 18 (1966): 151–74. Also see Glenda Matthews, *"Just a Housewife": The Rise and Fall of Domesticity in America* (New York, 1987). In *The Plantation Mistress: Woman's World in the Old South* (New York, 1982), Catherine Clinton points out that southern women, particularly from the planter class, did not exactly fit the model for northern women. Yet Cherokee women may have conformed

more closely to that model than many other southern women because of the influence of northern missionaries. See Theda Perdue, "Southern Indians and the Cult of True Womanhood," in *The Web of Southern Social Relations: Essays on Family Life, Education and Women*, ed. Walter J. Fraser Jr., R. Frank Saunders Jr., and Jon L. Wakelyn Jr. (Athens GA, 1985), 35–51. Also see Anne Firor Scott, *The Southern Lady: From Pedestal to Politics, 1830–1930* (Chicago, 1970), 3–21; Mary E. Young, "Women, Civilization, and the Indian Question," in *Clio Was a Woman: Studies in the History of American Women*, ed. Mabel E. Deutrich and Virginia C. Purdy (Washington DC, 1980).

23. Ard Hoyt, Moody Hall, William Chamberlain, and D. S. Butrick to Samuel Worcester, July 25, 1818, American Board Papers; John Ridge to Albert Gallatin, February 27, 1826, John Howard Payne Papers, Newberry Library, Chicago.

24. *Cherokee Phoenix*, July 2, 1828; Census of 1835 (Henderson Roll), Record Group 75, Office of Indian Affairs, National Archives, Washington DC; R. Halliburton Jr., *Red over Black: Black Slavery among the Cherokee Indians* (Westport CT, 1977), 181–92. Robert Bushyhead, a native Cherokee speaker from Cherokee, North Carolina, identified the gender of names on the Henderson Roll.

25. *Laws of the Cherokee Nation*, 79, 120–21.

26. George Lowrey, Lewis Ross, William Hicks, R. Taylor, Joseph Vann, and W. S. Shorey to John H. Eaton, February 11, 1830, Letters Received, Office of Indian Affairs, 1824–1881, National Archives, Washington DC.

27. *Cherokee Phoenix*, March 26, July 16, 1831.

28. Foreman, *Indian Removal*, 302–3.

29. John G. Burnett, "The Cherokee Removal through the Eyes of a Private Soldier," *Journal of Cherokee Studies* 3 (1978): 183.

30. Capt L. B. Webster, "Letters from a lonely Soldier," *Journal of Cherokee Studies* 3 (1978): 154.

31. Journal of Daniel S. Butrick, n.d., Payne Papers. There is another Butrick journal in the American Board Papers. The one in the Payne Papers is as much a commentary as a personal narrative.

32. J. D. Anthony, *Life and Times of Rev. J. D. Anthony* (Atlanta, 1896).

33. Foreman, *Indian Removal*, 302–3.

34. "A Native of Maine, Traveling in the Western Country," *New York Observer*, January 26, 1839.

35. A good example is B. B. Cannon, "An Overland Journey to the West (October–December 1837)," *Journal of Cherokee Studies* 3 (1978): 166–173.

36. "Emigration Detachments," *Journal of Cherokee Studies* 3 (1978): 186–87.

37. Butrick Journal, Payne Papers.

38. Story related by unidentified member of an audience at Warren Wilson College, Black Mountain NC, January 1983.

39. Butrick Journal, April 30, May 2, 1839, American Board Papers.

40. Edward Everett Dale and Gaston Litton, eds., *Cherokee Cavaliers: Forty Years of*

Cherokee History as Told in the Correspondence of the Ridge-Watie-Boudinot Family (Norman ok, 1939), 20–21, 37–38, 45–46. For comparison, see Scott, *Southern Lady*; and Clinton, *Plantation Mistress*.

41. *Indian Pioneer History,* 113 vols. (Oklahoma Historical Society, Oklahoma City), 9:490–91; Robert K. Thomas, "The Redbird Smith Movement," in *Symposium on Cherokee and Iroquois Culture,* ed. William N. Fenton and John Gulick (Washington DC, 1961).

42. *Cherokee Advocate,* February 27, 1845; Rudi Halliburton Jr., "Northeastern Seminary Hall," *Chronicles of Oklahoma* 51 (1973–74): 391–98; *Indian Pioneer History,* 1:394.

12. The Rise or Fall of Iroquois Women

NANCY SHOEMAKER

New Introduction by Nancy Shoemaker

I wrote the first version of this article on Iroquois women's history for a graduate seminar in American women's history, a course I took at the end of my graduate course work after I had spent years specializing in American Indian history. In this seminar on women's history, I became frustrated by the gap between the rich and complex histories of white and African American women that we read and the shallowness and uncritical acceptance of assumptions whenever the historical literature mentioned American Indian women. For the seminar's assigned research project, I chose to investigate Iroquois women's history for two reasons. First, I knew at that point that my dissertation would be a comparison of five tribes' demographic histories in the twentieth century, so it made sense to conjoin these projects somehow. Second, as one of the referees of my article said of Iroquois women's history, when I later submitted this article to a journal for review, this topic is the "old chestnut," meaning that Iroquois women's history had been worked on and worked on and worked on, and here it was, still a problem. For all the inquiry, debates, and theorizing over the role of women in Iroquois history, I still considered the questions being asked limiting and misguided. Since the Seneca Nation of Indians was one of the five tribes to be included in my dissertation, and since the Senecas are an Iroquois nation, I determined to focus on Seneca women's history in the nineteenth century.

I then devoted myself to collecting any information I could, looking through the usual sources for American Indian history: federal government records, especially those kept by the Bureau of Indian Affairs; censuses, both in the form of published, aggregated statistics and the raw manuscript forms; and a particularly valuable source at the Buffalo and Erie County

Historical Society, the papers of Maris Bryant Pierce, a Seneca man especially active in internal Seneca politics and legal administration.

Reading through my article again for the purposes of this collection, I
think the appeal I make to historians to ask more complex questions and to
expect ambivalence—not to write simple narratives in which some vague
concept of "women's power" rises or falls over time—still holds up fifteen
years later. However, I am a much better historian now, through experience, and realize that there are many more sources of information out there
that I could have found and used. Most palpably, almost immediately after
publishing this article, Joan Jensen's article on nineteenth-century Seneca
women was reprinted in the first edition of *Unequal Sisters*.[1] I felt terrible.
How could I not have seen her article before? I justified its absent citation
in my article by its having been published originally in *Sex Roles*, a sociol-
ogy journal that ordinarily I would not be familiar with, nor would it have
come up in my searching through indexes of humanities journals. Still, I
had missed in my research the one secondary source closest to the topic of
my own research.

More important, for future scholarship on this topic, I believe there are
other types of primary sources that I did not try to use but which, if I were
researching this topic now, I would. Nineteenth-century Iroquois women's
lives must to some extent be documented in the records of the surrounding county and state. I never looked for New York State court records or for
newspaper articles, nor did I consider borrowing from genealogical forms
of research and hunt down marriage, estate, church, and school records and
then attempt to trace the life histories of individuals.

The impressive research behind a book such as Renée Sansom Flood's
Lost Bird of Wounded Knee, which is able to illuminate the life of one Indian
woman in incredible detail, suggests to me that such research on individuals presents the most promising new direction for Indian women's history
and for American Indian history in general.[2] By putting aside for a while
the "tribe" as the standard unit of historical analysis—Senecas, Iroquois,
Navajos, Cherokees, and so on—and by working instead to reconstruct the
lives of individuals, we would naturally produce histories that are rich and
complex, attuned to ambivalence and a variety of experiences.

Two of the three documents that follow the essay are petitions Seneca
women of the Cattaraugus Reservation wrote to assert their rights as the
women of the tribe. The third document excerpts entries for four families
(selected randomly) from the manuscript schedules of the Allegany (Seneca

Nation) Reservation portion of the 1915 New York State census. I did not do an extensive analysis of the 1915 census in my article "The Rise or Fall of Iroquois Women," because it fell outside the dates I had set for the scope of my project. I have, however, been long intrigued by the latent value in these censuses, heretofore, so far as I know, never analyzed by scholars. The New York State censuses, of 1915 and also 1925, are interesting because they include unusual questions designed with the Iroquois population in mind. For example, "clan" is not usually asked in censuses conducted in the United States, but whoever compiled this questionnaire recognized the significance of clans among the matrilineal Iroquois.

The Rise or Fall of Iroquois Women (1991)

Now that women's history has established itself as a legitimate field of academic inquiry, there has been an outpouring of revisionist interpretations. Women in colonial America, who in older histories appeared to be economically powerful and emotionally fulfilled, are being recast as more complex historical characters constrained by a variety of social rules and limitations. Similarly, the view of nineteenth-century American women as victims of domesticity is no longer a convincing interpretation as scholars point to more and more evidence of Victorian women nurturing domesticity as a kind of empowerment.

These flourishing debates have focused on the history of white, middle-class women and make our knowledge of other American women seem egregiously undeveloped. American Indian women are one group whose history remains shadowy. When packaged by academics for an academic market, their history tends to follow a prepackaged formula, much like the history of white women before revisionism set in. For the period before European contact, American Indian women are generally depicted as powerful and respected members of their communities. Then colonization, cousin to industrialization, initiated a loss of women's power and status.

This type of narrative history—sometimes called a declension narrative because change is cast in terms of a decline—is especially prominent in the history of Iroquois women. In the nineteenth century, numerous publications on the Iroquois, most of which were based on historical and ethnographic accounts of the Senecas (the westernmost of the six Iroquois tribes), helped spawn a popular image of Iroquois women as something akin to North American Amazons.[3] Interest in the role of women in Iro-

quois society continues today. Most of this interest, however, has focused
on the period after European contact and before colonization, roughly the
seventeenth and eighteenth centuries. Very little historical research has
looked at Iroquois women after colonization, when some of the most radical changes in Iroquois society occurred. And yet, it is widely thought that
Iroquois women lost status and power. As one scholar has put it, "the position of Seneca women came more and more to resemble the position of the
women of the white man."[4]

This paper proposes an alternative strategy for looking at the experience
of one group of Iroquois, the Senecas, after colonization. Instead of trying to prove that women lost power or gained power—as though power
were absolute and measurable—I will focus on how women's political
rights, economic roles, and individual freedoms changed in the context of
colonization. All Senecas lost power as they were confined to ever-smaller
reservations, threatening both subsistence and cultural traditions. There is
little evidence, however, showing that Seneca women became increasingly
subordinate to Seneca men.

The Golden Age for Iroquois Women?

The idea of a decline in Seneca women's social position relies on their being
powerful members of society at an earlier point in history. The most recent
scholarly research on Iroquois women in the period before the American
Revolution has investigated the sources of Iroquois women's political influence. Judith Brown argued that Iroquois women were influential because
they controlled the means of production. However, Elisabeth Tooker has
argued that the relationship between men and women in the household
was one of economic exchange rather than economic dominance and that
the political participation of Iroquois women was limited. Their power
came from the group's matrilineal, not matriarchal, social organization.[5]
In the language of women's history, Iroquois women probably had more
influence in the private sphere than in the public.

Iroquois women acquired their reputation for great political influence
partly because clan mothers, the eldest women of certain lineages, had the
right to choose successors to office among the eligible men in their clans.
Their other political activities were not as visible. Some women attended
councils, but few women spoke. More often, women designated someone
to speak for them. For much of his life, the famous Seneca leader Red-Jacket
was a designated speaker for the women. Although women were not at the

center of political discussions, they were diligent lobbyists. Before or after councils, women occasionally took aside participants to make their positions clear.[6]

In seventeenth- and eighteenth-century Iroquois society, women probably experienced the same limitations as women in western society. Iroquois women were confined to a domestic sphere and participated in political decision making when their roles as wives and mothers allowed it. However, in Iroquois society the roles of wife and mother may have had a political significance not accorded women's roles in other cultures.

A superficial survey of Seneca history in the nineteenth century would imply that women's position had lost some of its former importance. Changing economic roles for women and frequent revisions in Seneca government may have affected the nature of women's political participation. Moreover, in the nineteenth century the Senecas did accept many aspects of American culture. By 1900, all Senecas dressed much like their white neighbors and had Anglicized names, 94 percent of the adult population could speak English, and almost all children attended school.[7]

A closer look at Seneca history from roughly 1848 to 1900—a period for which there is some, albeit scant, primary research material—suggests that women retained their independence within the domestic sphere despite the many changes occurring in their communities. Persistently, the Senecas, like the other Iroquois tribes, fought to maintain their political sovereignty. Among the many battles to control their own political and economic affairs were efforts to preserve institutions safeguarding the social rights of women: property and inheritance customs, marriage and divorce, and matrilineal descent. Despite pressures from the federal government, New York State, and missionaries, Seneca political leaders, who were men, defended women's rights as part of the larger effort for community survival.

The Seneca Nation

At the beginning of the nineteenth century, the Senecas were recovering from the disruptions of the Revolutionary War. Having fought on the side of the British, they were forced to locate on several small reservations in the western part of New York State when the war ended. At this time, the Senecas had little contact with whites. Only a few Senecas, mostly men, spoke English. The women cultivated the land. The men hunted and traded furs, and some were learning to be blacksmiths and sawmill operators.

Quaker missionaries came to live and teach at the Seneca reservations in the early 1800s, and they initiated a revolution in housing styles and the fencing of land. Since Quakers believed that Christian faith followed on the heels of civilization, they limited their proselytizing to technological and economic innovation. Thus, Quaker missionaries encouraged men to farm, women to spin and knit, and children to read and write. In the 1820s and 1830s other Protestant missionaries—who, unlike the Quakers, had explicit goals to create Christian converts—settled on the reservations and established schools and churches despite widespread Seneca resistance.[8]

An important Seneca religion, the Longhouse Religion, originated among the Senecas around 1800. The Seneca prophet Handsome Lake preached a new morality, consisting primarily of traditional Seneca beliefs and incorporating some Christian beliefs and social values brought to the Senecas by the Quakers. Among other preachings, Handsome Lake urged husbands and wives not to separate and reprimanded mothers for giving their daughters medicines that would cause abortions. Thirty years after Handsome Lake's death, some Senecas revived his prophecies and established the Longhouse Religion in an attempt to preserve traditional beliefs.[9]

For much of the nineteenth century, competing factions tried to dominate Seneca political decision-making. Even though Christians and the so-called pagans lived in separate communities on each of the four Seneca reservations—Buffalo Creek, Tonawanda, Cattaraugus, and Allegany—factions did not always follow along the lines of religious disagreement. Factions arose over land and annuity issues, and very often college-educated Christians spoke for both factions because they were intellectually well equipped to mediate between Indians and whites. Political divisions intensified in the 1830s and 1840s as the Senecas deliberated over a land sales and removal treaty with the U.S. government. Corruption among Seneca chiefs, fraudulent treaty negotiations, and the resulting loss of the Buffalo Creek Reservation and part of Tonawanda led the Cattaraugus and Allegany Senecas to depose their chiefs in 1848 and establish the Seneca Nation. The Tonawanda Senecas, numbering only a few hundred, maintained a separate government so that Seneca chiefs at other reservations would not be able to sign away the rest of their reservation. The remainder of this paper will deal primarily with members of the Seneca Nation.[10]

The Seneca Nation government survives today, with most of their reservation lands intact. Although a few Senecas moved to Indian Territory in the 1840s, the Senecas escaped all the other major government policy programs designed for Indians. Their land was not allotted to individuals under the 1887 Allotment Act, and they did not restructure their government with the 1934 Indian Reorganization Act. They did, however, lose much of Allegany Reservation to a flood-area when the Kinzua Dam was built in the 1960s.[11]

Women's Political Participation

The 1848 change in government marks a crucial change in Seneca politics. The Senecas abandoned the traditional civic leadership of chiefs and adopted a written constitution with elected officials. Diane Rothenberg has interpreted the 1848 change in government as a disenfranchisement of women because the constitution decreed that only men over the age of 21 could vote.[12] Even though the constitution preserved some of the former powers of the clan mothers—by giving them voting rights on land sales issues—other women were denied the right to vote or seek political office until the 1960s.[13]

However, instead of taking away women's political privileges, the revolution in Seneca government probably prevented further loss of women's political power. Anthropologist William Fenton termed the 1848 revolution in government a "transition from a kinship state to a territorial government" because the adoption of a written constitution with elected officials effectively separated family from politics.[14] But the transformation had been gradually occurring in the decades before 1848 as chiefs began to act as independent agents.

The constitution emerged during factional disputes about land sales, and by several accounts the "warriors and squaws" were partly behind the effort to establish unbreakable laws for the Senecas.[15] Thirty or more years before, at the 1797 Treaty of Big Tree, U.S. treaty negotiators began by ignoring the chiefs; they arranged preliminary meetings with the chief women and warriors instead. According to a later New York State study of the state's Indians, treaty negotiators recognized that "the lands belong to the warriors, because they form the strength of the Nation, and to women, as the mothers of the warriors."[16] But in the 1830s and 1840s, many chiefs were signing land sales treaties in saloons and hotel rooms, away from the public council as traditional Seneca politics demanded.[17] A written constitution ensuring elected officials was therefore an attempt to restrain the increasing power of the chiefs. Women advocated the constitution perhaps because the family's loss of political power threatened their own position in Seneca society.

Throughout the nineteenth century, women seem to have been most

politically visible when major issues divided the nation, and by the mid-
1800s they adopted new forms of political participation as lobbying tools.
Although women did not sign treaties or agreements with the government,
they occasionally collected other women's signatures on petitions, and
women's organizations like the W.C.T.U. on the Cattaraugus Reservation
raised issues that would ultimately be brought to the Seneca Nation Council for a vote. After the revision of Seneca government in 1848, women sent
out several petitions to President Zachary Taylor and others. Speaking "in
behalf of a large majority of the mothers, wives, and daughters," they asked
that the new government be allowed to stand. These women petitioners also
advocated distribution of annuities to heads of families, instead of to chiefs,
because, as they said, "we women have an equal right to our annuities with
the men, and with the Chiefs."[18] Women petitioners implied that as mothers or potential mothers, they spoke for future generations of Senecas: "It
is by our pain and sorrow that children are brought into the world, and we
therefore are interested in whatever concerns the welfare of our children."[19]
Thus, even though the form of lobbying was new, using their roles as wives
and mothers to legitimize their right to political participation shows some
continuity with the past. Public politics, newly defined as voting and office
holding, remained an activity for men.

Seneca political life did come to resemble that of whites in that the constitution identified men as the community's leaders, and petitioning allowed women some access to politics. Women supported the revision in
government with the hope that leaders would be held accountable for their
actions but also because the new government probably gave women some
security in a rapidly changing society. Most of the Seneca Nation's laws,
set down in print in 1854, institutionalized economic and social independence for women. The constitution established civil courts, called Peacemaker Courts, to adjudicate the Nation's laws on each of the two Seneca
Nation reservations. New York State had previously assumed jurisdiction
in most criminal cases, but disputes over property and divorce were to be
resolved by the three elected judges serving as peacemakers. Council and
Peacemaker Court records suggest that there was confusion about how to
apply the new laws. But whether these elected officials decided cases on the
basis of tradition or the new laws, women's rights in property and divorce
settlements—and consequently their economic and social freedoms—were
preserved.[20]

Women's Economic Role

As with political participation, women's economic role changed but did not necessarily suffer as the Senecas began to have more contact with whites. One visitor to a Seneca reservation in 1838 remarked that a Seneca wife lived with her husband out of love because "the wife is more useful and important to the husband than he is to her" and because "she can obtain her own means of support better than he can." This observer also noted that Seneca women advised their husbands "in the mightiest matters and have immense influence, for they may leave when they choose and when not treated kindly invariably do so."[21] In 1838 the women still tended their cornfields, while men's contributions to the household through hunting and fur trading were constrained by animal depletion. Eventually, however, changes in the Seneca economy would create more opportunities for men.

From first contact, missionaries and later government agents tried to change the Senecas' traditional gender roles. They aimed to confine women's domestic sphere entirely to the home, whereas previously women had worked in the cornfields as well as in the home. At first glance, the efforts of missionaries and the U.S. government to make farming an occupation for men seems to have met with some success. The U.S. census suggests that by 1900 men had replaced women in the farming industry, for 65 percent of the adult men compared to 3 percent of the adult women were listed as farmers or farm laborers.[22] These occupation listings, however, may reflect the enumerators' cultural biases more than anything else. Enumerators recorded "farmer" for almost all heads of households living on a farm, and "farm laborer" for all other men living in farm households.[23] In 1900, women, whether Seneca or white, may have had more occupations than enumerators credited them with because women were not expected to work outside the home.[24]

Men replaced women as farmers to some degree, but the importance of farming in the Seneca economy was declining in the nineteenth century. Without capital, Seneca farmers had a difficult time competing with neighboring whites. And, even though many women supposedly were encouraging their sons to take up farming, few men chose to invest heavily in it. Some men preferred wage labor, and for a few years in the first half of the nineteenth century, Seneca men preferred the quick profits of selling timber over other income. Farming was a riskier investment for Senecas than for whites because the Senecas were continually being threatened with re-

moval west and later with allotment of their lands in severalty. Such a state
of uncertainty did not encourage land improvement. Government agents'
annual reports on Seneca conditions generally admitted that only a few
Seneca men succeeded as farmers.[25] As with political power, wealth tended
to concentrate in the hands of a few men.

In the late nineteenth century, the Seneca economy depended largely on
the leasing of land and wage labor. Men had more opportunities to earn
wages than women and worked for the railroad, logging companies, a glue
factory near the Allegany Reservation, and as laborers on farms owned
by both Indians and whites. Although most Senecas lived on farms, they
rented much of their farmland out to neighboring whites who had the capital necessary for growing and marketing farm produce. Leasing income,
more than farming income or wage earning, supported many of the Cattaraugus and Allegany residents, including women property holders. Among
the Senecas there were no restrictions on women owning and inheriting
property, and most Senecas adhered to traditional concepts of property
throughout the nineteenth century. Husbands' and wives' estates were never
combined; each kept their own property. When one of them died, however,
they often bequeathed some of their property to their spouse and some to
their children.[26]

The change in Seneca government and the 1854 written Laws of the Seneca
Nation may even have favored women more than men in property decisions.
The laws codified traditional procedures for family inheritance and dictated
that husbands and wives would each keep control of their own property. But
the laws also borrowed new property concepts from Euro-American practices, like the "widow's third." The Seneca laws set a minimum inheritance
right for widows to one-third of their husband's estate.[27] By the end of the
nineteenth century, some of the Christian Senecas, frustrated by the traditional inheritance practices, began to litigate inheritance decisions. But since
Christians were almost always the minority in the Seneca Nation, the court
usually decided in favor of tradition. When uncertain about how to decide
cases based on tradition—for instance, if no witnesses knew for sure whether
the husband or wife owned property in dispute—the peacemakers fell back
on the written laws as the basis for making a just decision.[28]

Missionaries and government agents attempted to assimilate the Senecas
to Western concepts of property holding but met with little success. Government agents particularly disapproved of the ten-day feasts held among
the conservative Senecas. For ten days after someone's death, relatives and

friends gathered to mourn and redistribute the deceased's property. If the dead person had left a will or an oral bequest, his or her wishes were followed. Land was bequeathed as well, since any improved land belonged to the person who had improved it. The only restriction on land inheritance was that land could only be passed on to other Senecas.[29] Government agents objected to the ten-day feasts because property did not always fall to the people they considered the rightful heirs. As one agent said in 1889, "In some cases I find that upon the death of the wife the dead feast is made and the relations not only divide up the property of the wife, who is dead, but also that of the husband, who is living."[30] In this particular case, witnesses testified that the wife had bought the property, and thus the court ruled against the husband's claim and upheld the deceased wife's original bequest.[31] When one agent interfered in a property dispute relating to a marital separation, council members of the Seneca Nation complained to the Commissioner of Indian Affairs, emphasizing that "Women with us have the right to hold property separate and apart from her husband and her rights are always respected when husband and wife separate."[32]

Besides earning income from their property through leasing land and subsistence farming, women could also work for wages. The 1865 New York State census enumerator claimed that Indian women's farming skills earned them the same wages as male farm laborers, but he does not say how many women took advantage of this.[33] Wage earning more often was subject to American norms for what constituted women's work, and so women's choices were generally limited to domestic labor, teaching, and nursing. Although one woman worked as a farm laborer and another as a laborer for the railroad, most employed Seneca women in 1900 worked as housekeepers, laundresses, and cooks.[34]

Other sources of income for women included treaty annuities and selling beadwork, baskets, and berries. Some women on the Cattaraugus Reservation made substantial income from selling crafts and fruit, partly because Cattaraugus was only about twenty miles from the growing city of Buffalo, which was in turn close to the thriving tourist trade at Niagara Falls.[35] The annuities, which after 1848 were distributed among all Senecas equally, may have had more symbolic power than spending power. Both the U.S. government and the state of New York paid annuities consisting of bales of gingham cloth and several thousand dollars for each Iroquois tribe. In 1900, annuities amounted to less than $5.00 per individual, and women could often earn that much in a single day by picking berries.[36]

Seneca men had increasingly more economic opportunities than Seneca women did, but they were not the sole breadwinners of the nuclear family model. Women were able to earn independent incomes. The most reliable and perhaps most profitable source for economic security was not gender but membership in the Seneca Nation. Although annuities did not provide much income, the Seneca Nation periodically received monetary settlements from court cases, land leases, and the sale of mineral and gas rights. Much of the Nation's money reputedly went for bribing voters, in which case men would have benefited more than women, but there were several substantial payments made to all individual members of the tribe in the late nineteenth century.[37] And of course, women could own and lease their own land.

Women, Family, and Society

Seneca women's changing relationship to family and society is difficult to uncover since any documents they may have produced themselves are not available in the historical record. The only resources are census data, collected by whites, and debates between Indians and whites about family institutions—matrilineage, marriage, and divorce.[38] What information is available shows that Seneca family relations did not come to resemble those of whites. Missionaries and government agents pressured the Senecas to accept whites' social norms, but the Senecas in turn tried to retain their traditional customs.

Most of the pressure on the Senecas to conform to whites' concept of the nuclear family was subtle and bureaucratically enforced. Missionaries and government agents always treated men as heads of families and disregarded other patterns of family authority. When families came to the courthouse to collect their annuities, the agents expected males to put their mark for their wife and children. However, accounts of annuity day suggest that most men and women went to pick up their annuities together.[39] Also, as the Senecas adopted Anglicized surnames, they adopted a patrilineal naming system. Apparently, Seneca women at first resisted using whites' naming patterns. The 1865 census enumerator told about how Seneca women reluctantly named their children after their husband, preferring instead to "name them after the grandfather and others."[40]

Although the Senecas adopted a patrilineal naming system, they retained aspects of their matrilineal social organization. Surnames may have followed the father, but tribal membership followed the mother and today still follows the mother among the New York Iroquois. Thus, the benefits of tribal membership—being able to live on the Seneca Nation reservations and sharing in annuities and other treaty settlements—only belonged to people whose mothers were members of the Seneca Nation.

Government officials thought matrilineage unfair and illogical, but few people living on the Seneca Nation felt matrilineal tribal inheritance should be abolished. Indian Affairs administrators considered tribal membership a racial issue and would have preferred that the degree of "Indian blood" be used as the standard. Also, the United States, unlike Canada, never enforced a patrilineal tribal inheritance system on its Iroquois reservations.[41] U.S. policy did not interfere with Seneca tribal inheritance partly because reservations were always viewed as temporary, but also because few Indians complained. In the 1880s, one disgruntled Cattaraugus Seneca man repeatedly requested that the government remove from the reservation the five white men who had married Seneca women and whose children were thus considered Senecas. But agents and members of the Council refused to listen to him, pointing out that the complainant was himself a descendant of a white woman who had been adopted into the tribe in the eighteenth century.[42]

More frequent complaints came from members of other Iroquois Nations—the Onondagas, Cayugas, and Oneidas—who lived on the Seneca reservations. Occasionally, situations arose where entire families were asked to leave when the Seneca relative they lived with died. These non-Seneca residents of the Seneca Nation lobbied council members and U.S. government officials, but they did not intend that matrilineage should be abandoned. Instead, they suggested other Iroquois should be made permanent citizens of the Seneca Nation, especially the Cayugas, who had no reservation of their own. Since only Senecas could vote or be elected to leadership positions in the Seneca Nation, the minority of non-Senecas who had married into Seneca families usually found the council resistant to change.[43]

Since matrilineal descent determined tribal membership, women may have felt they had more freedom of choice in marriage partners than men. A Seneca man marrying a white woman would have Indian children who had no tribe and who therefore had no rights to Seneca Nation lands or benefits. A Seneca woman, no matter whom she married, could rest assured that her children were guaranteed residence on the reservations and other rights as members of the Seneca Nation.

However, the matrilineal social system limited some of women's choices within the household. Women were not always free to marry whomever they chose. As is common in matrilineal societies, a woman's male relative could influence a woman's marital decisions. For instance, when William Crouse moved in with Susan John and her parents, sometime around 1830, it was entirely her and Crouse's decision. As she described their decision at a later inheritance hearing, "We made a bargain to live together as man and wife and we did live together." But Susan John's uncle, presumably her mother's brother, eventually broke up the relationship and forced Crouse to leave because Crouse and John were members of the same clan.[44] Seneca social organization prohibited clan endogamy. And in the 1830s, one couple about to be married by one of the Protestant missionaries was forced to postpone the marriage indefinitely because the woman's brother strongly opposed Christianity.[45] Women generally made their own marital decisions, although their relatives could influence them.

By 1900, Seneca social organization had undergone significant changes that greatly altered certain social rules regarding marriage. The prohibitions against clan endogamy weakened and marriage rules generally relaxed. Still, Seneca marital relations in 1900 did not bear much similarity to marriage among whites. For much of the nineteenth century, a Seneca woman married in one of two ways. She could marry in a Christian ceremony, or, as most often happened, she could simply live with somebody. Few marriages involved a ceremony or other action which suited missionaries' and government agents' standards of legality. Although one man told a missionary that his wife was trying to arrange a Christian marriage so that he would never be able to leave her, it is not clear from the evidence which kind of marriage most women preferred.[46] Even Christian ceremonies could end in divorce, easily granted by the peacemakers' courts after 1854. Divorce rules did not favor either sex, but women appear to have sought divorce more often than men. There were no special criteria for divorce, and most divorcing couples simply separated without having to legalize the divorce through the courts. According to one source, Seneca women sought legal divorce at the peacemakers' courts only when they wanted to protect their property.[47]

One as yet unexploited resource for Seneca women's history is census data. Unfortunately, the earliest census of the Senecas that provides information on individuals within a household and that is still extant in manuscript form is the 1900 U.S. census. Analysis of 1900 U.S. census data suggests

Table 1. Marriage Patterns for Seneca Women and Neighboring U.S. Population (Rural* New York, Pennsylvania, and Ohio), 1900

	Seneca	Rural New York, Pennsylvania, Ohio
Singulate mean age at marriage	20.5	22.5
Percent never married, women 45–54	2.2	11.0
Marital status, women, 15–44**		
% Married	62.3	54.6
% Married, spouse absent	5.4	4.6
% Widowed	7.0	2.4
% Divorced	0.9	.1
% Never married	24.4	38.3
Number of women, 45–54	89	429
Number of women, 15–44	419	1,940

Sources: Seneca Census Data; 1900 U.S. Census Public Use Sample (ICPSR).
*Rural = places with fewer than 2,500 people.
**Standardized to age distribution of U.S. women in 1900.

that in 1900 marriage among the Senecas was a different sort of institution than marriage among other U.S. residents. To compare marriage and childbearing patterns for the Senecas and their white neighbors I used a sample of women living in rural New York, Pennsylvania, and Ohio drawn from the 1900 U.S. Census Public Use Sample.[48]

As can be seen in Table 1, almost all Seneca women married sometime in their life and married at a very young age. Considering the easy access to divorce, surprisingly few Seneca women were divorced. Since the 1900 census did not ask how many times people had married, it is not possible to know how many divorced or widowed women remarried. Even though most Seneca women married at some time in their lives, they had a much higher incidence of separation and widowhood than women in the general population.

Seneca women also had different childbearing patterns. The most striking difference between the Senecas and the U.S. population in their region was in patterns of illegitimacy (see Table 2). Of course, the concept of "illegitimacy" did not exist in Seneca society. The 1854 written laws explicitly stated that children born out of wedlock to Seneca mothers were legitimate and fully entitled members of the Seneca Nation. And there is no suggestion in the records that within Seneca society there was any social stigma attached to unmarried women having children. The laws also listed procedures for ensuring fathers of such children would contribute economically

Table 2. Childbearing Patterns for the Senecas and Neighboring U.S. Population, 1900

	Seneca	United States
Percent of never-married women 15–44 with 1 or more children	14.3	0.6
Estimated mean age at birth of last child, married women, spouse present, 40–49	33.0	34.9
Number of never-married women, 15–44	84	738
Number of currently married women, 40–49	58	313

Sources: Seneca Census Data; 1900 U.S. Census Public Use Sample (ICPSR).

to their upbringing.[49] In Seneca society women may not have needed marriage to make childbearing socially respectable, but since nearly all women married eventually, being married was clearly a cultural norm.

Another childbearing choice, probably made mostly by women in Seneca society, was to limit their families. Seneca women started their childbearing early and ended it early also, suggesting that once they had reached their preferred family size, they tried to prevent further childbearing. Data from the 1900 census shows that among Seneca women who lived to at least age 40, the mean age at the birth of their last child was 33 years, nearly two years below that of American women. Such a low age at stopping childbearing suggests that in 1900 Seneca women, like women in the general population, were practicing deliberate family limitation.[50]

Seneca family limitation may have had the same origins as family limitation in the general population; both may have been related to the late-nineteenth-century U.S. fertility decline. However, there is evidence that Seneca women had practiced some form of family limitation for several hundred years before. In the early 1800s, Handsome Lake preached against abortion, and several decades later a plant well known among the Senecas to cause abortions still grew on the reservations.[51]

Seneca women's reasons for limiting their fertility are not clear. An early nineteenth-century biographer of Red-Jacket claimed that the Seneca population had been decreasing because of "the reluctance of their women to bear children, prompting them to employ means to prevent an increase of maternal responsibilities." In their own words, supposedly, "they have become tired of bearing children to be slain in war."[52] Yet, Seneca folklore says that the number of children a woman has is outside her control, that the children are like knots on a string and each woman has within her a deter-mined number of children waiting to be born.[53] In the nineteenth century, this traditional belief in one's predestined childbearing fate was still held among the so-called pagans. One old woman, in conversing about death with a missionary campaigning for new converts, told him that she had once died but had to come back because she had not yet borne all her chil-dren.[54] Regardless of when Seneca women started practicing fertility con-trol, attitudes toward family limitation were probably not borrowed from Euro-Americans.

Thus, during the nineteenth century, Seneca social relations did not come to resemble those of whites. Whether women in Seneca society were better off than other American women remains an open question, how-ever. Matrilineage, fertility limitation, and easy access to divorce imply that women had some social rights, but such social features as high marriage and illegitimacy rates could support contrary arguments of women's social dependence or independence.

Conclusion

Throughout the nineteenth century, the Senecas accommodated Euro-American culture but never accepted it entirely. Politically, the Seneca Na-tion adopted a Euro-American-style constitution, but this was largely a preventive measure. They were not forsaking traditional Seneca politics but were trying to preserve their democratic political process. Economi-cally, they reorganized traditional gender roles to a degree—men became farmers and probably had more opportunities for earning income than women did—but farming as a source for Seneca livelihood declined in importance. For the most part, Seneca incomes depended on the leasing of land and other economic benefits available to members of the Seneca Nation.

As one aspect of Seneca social organization and belief, women's posi-tion in society may have survived the onslaughts of colonization. Since the Senecas protected some of their traditional social organization, including matrilineal descent, and continued to prefer flexible marriage customs, there is no reason to believe that Seneca society and family life incorpo-rated any other Euro-American features. The question of women's status and influence begs an ambiguous response. It could be argued that if there were more evidence available for a thorough history of Seneca women, a decisive answer might finally be reached. However, the use of a declension

narrative to explain Iroquois women's history is in itself problematic because the pre-decline starting point, the extent of women's power in "traditional" Iroquois society, remains unresolved after 100 years of contention.
Since numerous revisions in the history of other American women have led
to increasing uncertainty about women's power in colonial and Victorian
America, perhaps ambiguity is a progressive step forward to a more sophisticated understanding of Iroquois women's history.

Appendix

*Committee in Behalf of the Women of the Cattaraugus Reservation to Philip
E. Thomas [of the Society of Friends], October 13, 1868, in National Archives,*
Correspondence of the Office of Indian Affairs, Letters Received, 1824–1881,
microfilm collection M234, reel 587.

> To our Respected Friend Philip E. Thomas
> The women of the Cattaraugus Reservation wish to address you
> a few words in this time of our trouble; & we do so the more
> cheerfully because we know that the Friends are always labour-
> ing to promote the welfare of the females among the Indians, &
> to improve their condition. We would also request you to secure
> in our behalf all the influence of the Society of Friends so that
> our words may be strengthened & become sufficiently powerful
> to be heard and regarded by the Secretary of War & obtain from
> him the help which we desire. We wish you to inform the Sec-
> retary of war that we women have an equal right to our annui-
> ties with the men, and with the Chiefs. We are all on the same
> footing as to the amount we are entitled to receive, Chiefs &
> warriors, men, women & children. We were glad when we heard
> the Secretary had instructed our new agent to pay the annuities
> for this year to the heads of families. We see no other way by
> which our rights can be secured to us, and justice done alike to
> all. We hope you will urge the Secretary to confirm his former
> instructions; for we were greatly perplexed & troubled when the
> agent was induced to delay the payment on the grounds that the
> chiefs insisted on the observance of the old custom in regard to
> it. We ask for our just rights and nothing more, but we repeat
> it we do not feel that our rights will be safe if these instruc-
> tions to the agent shall be reversed. We regret that the Agent

should have thought it necessary to delay a strict compliance with his instructions but we do not yet feel disheartened, for we have confidence that the secretary will manifest a due regard to our rights. Only we beg leave to repeat our request that you will bring all the weight of your influence & that of your Society to bear upon this question that he may be willing to confirm his former decision and give every Indian, women & children no less than others the opportunity of receiving that which of right belongs to each.

With great respect ??? ????? ??? and we would desire to add that we have already suffered greatly for the proceedings of the Chiefs through whose instrumentality our poverty has been increasing upon us and we wish to entreat that we may never again hereafter be exposed to be deprived by them of our rights, but that we and our children from time to time may be permitted to receive the full and proper share which rightfully belongs to us.

We are fully sensible that it is a hard case to have a difficulty with the chiefs but we feel that we have been wronged by them, and our children have suffered already and for a long time past, through their avarice & pride, and we believe the things which they have said in justification of themselves are not true. It is by our pain & sorrow that children are brought into the world, and we therefore are interested in whatever concerns the welfare of our children; we have therefore examined this subject and are satisfied that the party who are laboring to bring about an equal division of the whole of our annuities are the party really striving for the best interests of our children. We have taken the same view of the matter which was taken by the old men long since dead who first entered into these arrangements. They decided that every individual man, woman & child had an equal right to our monies and to our land,—in short to all our national property, that it was so from the beginning and that it always should be so. We have taken the liberty to express our views because we believe this to be the real truth, and we would earnestly desire the President & the Secretary of War to secure to us now & to our posterity in all time to come the fulfillment of the original stipulation, that as long as wood should grow or water run or a Seneca live to behold the light of the sun these annuities should be faithfully paid & righteously distributed.

With great respect your obliged friends

their marks

Betsey X Snow

Done in presence of

Julia Ann X Dennis

Joseph S. Walton

Jane X Scott

Asher Wright

Gaa' nah hoh X

Polly X Johnson

Martha X Phillips

Committee in behalf of the women of the Cattaraugus Reservation

Committee in Behalf of the Women of the Cattaraugus Reservation to President Zachary Taylor, April 2, 1849, in National Archives, Correspondence of the Office of Indian Affairs, Letters Received, 1824–1881, *microfilm collection* M234, *reel 587.*

To his Excellency, Gen. Zachary Taylor, President of the United States of America.

The undersigned, Mothers, heads of families, wives, and grown up daughters of the Seneca Nation of Indians, residing in Western New York, would respectfully represent to our Father the President, that we have heard with extreme regret, that an educated young man from among our sons and brothers, is at Washington, importuning the President to undo the good which had been done for our people by his predecessor, and to destroy the effect, so far as the Senecas are concerned, of the wise regulation, that a portion of all the Indian annuities should be distributed just at seed time, every spring, in order to facilitate and encourage agriculture.

We wish our sons to be industrious, to be in the field stirring the soil betimes, procuring a bountiful harvest as the fruits of God's blessing upon their own honest exertions; not leaving it for the women to raise the corn, as did their hunting, fishing and fighting forefathers.

The days of hunting & fishing, and we trust also of Indian fighting, are gone by forever; and it pains us exceedingly, that an educated son of ours; and one, too, who, if he would consult the well being of his people, might be so smart a man and useful; should now be trying, either of his own will, or under the direction of those, whom, if they had sought the public good, we should still have rejoiced to call our Chiefs, to thwart the wishes of his people, check the pursuits of agriculture, and bring embarrassing and perplexing want upon the destitute who have been relying upon the stability of the counsels of the U.S. Government for the relief of their necessities. We have many and (to us) weighty reasons why our father the President should not heed the petition of our son whom we did not send to speak for us to the President; but lest it should be thought that Indian women have tongues that never tire, we only add, that it is the earnest prayer of the undersigned, in their own behalf, and in behalf of a large majority of the Mothers, wives, and daughters of the Seneca nation, that the recognition of the new Government may be permitted to stand; and that we may be paid our annuities according to the rule adopted in 1847 for the payment of all the tribes receiving annuities from the Government; i.e., during the current month, and your Memorialists as in duty bound will ever pray

Betsey X Bennett   Old Miss Logan X

Mrs X Jones

Lucy X Jemison

Mrs X Button (?)   4th mo 2nd 1849 In convention

Mrs X Hoinloy (?)   I witnessed the forgoing

Polly X Johnson   Signatures

Mrs X Joes   J.S. Walton

Go wa da oo X

Hannah X Luke

Mary X Snow

Widow Destroyer Town X

Mrs X Bennitt

Jane X Scott

Mrs Fox X

Mrs Cooker X

Sally Fox X

Polly X Half Town

Eliza X Toconsen (?)

Emily Isaac X

Table 3. New York State Census, Allegany (Seneca Nation) Reservation, 1915, Manuscript, excerpts (on microfilm at the New York State Library, Albany, New York)

Name	Relationship to Head of Family	Birth	Sex	Clan	Occupation	Acres Cultivated	Where Educated	Speaks English	Christian or pagan
Watt, Libbie	Head	1870	F	Heron	Housework	39	Res.	Y	P
Watt, Hiram	Husband	1860	M	Deer	Farmer		Res.	Y	P
Watt, Clarence	Son	1895	M	Heron	Farmer		Quaker inst.	Y	P
Watt, Cecelia	Daughter	1899	F	Heron	School		Quaker inst.	Y	P
Watt, Harry	Son	1901	M	Heron	Farmer		Quaker inst.	Y	P
Watt, Loretta	Daughter	1903	F	Heron	School		Quaker inst.	Y	P
Watt, Effie	Daughter	1906	F	Heron	School		Quaker inst.	Y	P
Doctor, Lillie	None	1870	F	Heron	Housework		Res.	Y	C
Pierce, Jennie	Head	1886	F	Unk.	Housework	0	State school	Y	
Pierce, Harry	Husband	1880	M		Farm laborer		Res.	Y	
Pierce, Andrew	Son	1910	M					Y	
John, Carrie	Head	1874	F	Wolf	Housework	20	Res./Quaker	Y	P
John, Franklin	Husband	1874	M	Heron	Farmer		Res./Quaker	Y	P
John, Ulysses	Son	1896	M	Wolf	Farmer		Res.Quaker	Y	P
John, Leland	Son	1898	M	Wolf	Section Hand RR		Res./Quaker	Y	P
John, Franklin, Jr.	Son	1901	M	Wolf	School		Quaker inst.	Y	P
John, Adelbert	Son	1905	M	Wolf	School		Res.	Y	P
John, Asa	Son	1907	M	Wolf				Y	P
Redeye, Casler	Father	1829	M	Bear			Res.	Y	P
Kittle, Ellanor	Head	1820	F	Wolf	Housework	4		N	P
Jimeson, Howard	Son	1863	M	Wolf	Farm laborer			Y	

Notes

1. Joan M. Jensen, "Native American Women and Agriculture: A Seneca Case Study," in *Unequal Sisters: A Multi-Cultural Reader in U.S. Women's History*, ed. Ellen Carol DuBois and Vicki L. Ruiz (New York: Routledge, 1990), 51–65. Orig. published in *Sex Roles* 3 (1977).

2. Renée Sansom Flood, *Lost Bird of Wounded Knee: Spirit of the Lakota* (New York: Scribner, 1995).

3. Lewis Henry Morgan, *League of the Iroquois* (Secaucus NJ: Citadel Press, 1962); Lewis Henry Morgan, *Ancient Society, or Researches in the Lines of Human Progress from Savagery Through Barbarism to Civilization* (Tucson: University of Arizona Press, 1985); Frederick Engels, *The Origin of the Family, Private Property and the State, in the Light of the Researches of Lewis H. Morgan* (New York: International Publishers, 1942); William M. Beauchamp, "Iroquois Women," *Journal of American Folk-Lore* 13 (April–June 1900): 81–91; Alexander A. Goldenweiser, "Functions of Women in Iroquois Society," *American Anthropologist* 17 (April–June 1915): 376–77; Martha C. Randle, "Iroquois Women, Then and Now," in *Symposium on Local Diversity in Iroquois Culture*, ed. William N. Fenton, Bureau of American Ethnology Bulletin 149 (Washington DC: Smithsonian Institution, 1951): 167–80; Cara E. Richards, "Matriarchy or Mistake: The Role of Iroquois Women through Time," in *Cultural Stability and Cultural Change: Proceedings of the 1957 Annual Spring Meeting of the American Ethnological Society*, ed. Verne F. Ray (Seattle: American Ethnological Society, University of Washington, 1957), 30–45.

4. Diane Rothenberg, "The Mothers of the Nation: Seneca Resistance to Quaker Intervention," in *Women and Colonization*, ed. Mona Etienne and Eleanor Leacock (New York: J. F. Bergin, 1980), 82; see also Anthony F. C. Wallace, *The Death and Rebirth of the Seneca* (New York: Knopf, 1969); Elizabeth H. Pleck, "Women's History: Gender as a Category of Historical Analysis," in *Ordinary People and Everyday Life: Perspectives on the New Social History,* ed. James B. Gardner and George Rollie Adams (Nashville: American Association for State and Local History, 1983), 58.

5. Judith K. Brown, "Economic Organization and the Position of Women among the Iroquois," *Ethnohistory* 17 (summer–fall 1970): 151–67; Elisabeth Tooker, "Women in Iroquois Society," in *Extending the Rafters: Interdisciplinary Approaches to Iroquoian Studies*, ed. Michael K. Foster, Jack Campisi, and Marianne Mithun (Albany: State University of New York Press, 1984), 109–23.

6. William L. Stone, *The Life and Times of Red-Jacket, or Sa-go ye wat ha; Being the Sequel to the History of the Six Nations* (New York: Wiley and Putnam, 1841); Tooker, "Women in Iroquois Society"; Donald H. Kent and Merle H. Deardorff, "John Adlum on the Allegheny: Memoirs for the Year 1794," *Pennsylvania Magazine of History and Biography* 84 (July, October 1960): 265–324, 435–80; Walter Pilkington, ed., *Journals of Samuel Kirkland: 18th-Century Missionary to the Iroquois, Government Agent, Father of Hamilton College* (Clinton NY: Hamilton College, 1980).

7. Commissioner of Indian Affairs, *Annual Report*, 1900 (Washington DC: Govern-

ment Printing Office, 1900), 646–47; Manuscript Schedules of the 1900 U.S. Census, National Archives, T623, reels 1011, 1034 (New York State, Cattaraugus and Erie Counties, Allegany and Cattaraugus Reservations) [hereafter cited as Seneca Census Data]. I collected census data from the manuscript schedules of the 1900 U.S. census for 2,017 individuals (all residents of Allegany and Cattaraugus reservations except for children living at the Thomas Indian Orphan Asylum).

8. Thomas S. Abler and Elisabeth Tooker, "Seneca," in *Northeast*, ed. Bruce G. Trigger, vol. 15 of *Handbook of North American Indians* (Washington DC: Smithsonian Institution, 1978), 505–17; Elisabeth Tooker, "Iroquois since 1820," in *Handbook of North American Indians*, 15:449–65; Mrs. Harriet S. Caswell, *Our Life Among the Iroquois Indians* (Boston: Congregational Sunday-School and Publishing Society, 1892); Halliday Jackson, *Civilization of the Indian Natives* (Philadelphia: Marcus T. C. Gould, 1830); Rayner Wickersham Kelsey, *Friends and the Indians, 1655–1917* (Philadelphia: Associated Executive Committee of Friends on Indian Affairs, 1917).

9. Arthur C. Parker, "The Code of Handsome Lake," in *Parker on the Iroquois*, ed. William N. Fenton (Syracuse: Syracuse Press, 1968); Anthony F. C. Wallace, "Cultural Composition of the Handsome Lake Religion," in *Symposium on Cherokee and Iroquois Culture*, ed. William N. Fenton and John Gulick, Bureau of American Ethnology Bulletin 180 (Washington DC: Smithsonian Institution, 1961), 143–51; Wallace, *Death and Rebirth of the Seneca*; Anthony F. C. Wallace, "Origins of the Longhouse Religion," in *Handbook of North American Indians*, 15:442–48; Merle H. Deardorff, "The Religion of Handsome Lake: Its Origin and Development," in Fenton, *Symposium on Local Diversity in Iroquois Culture*, 79–107.

10. Maris Bryant Pierce Papers, Buffalo and Erie County Historical Society, Buffalo; Thomas Abler, "Factional Dispute and Party Conflict in the Political System of the Seneca Nation, 1845–1895: An Ethnohistorical Analysis" (Ph.D. diss., University of Toronto, 1969); Thomas S. Abler, "The Kansas Connection: The Seneca Nation and the Iroquois Confederacy Council," in Foster, Campisi, and Mithun, *Extending the Rafters*, 81–93; Robert F. Berkhofer Jr., "Faith and Factionalism among the Senecas: Theory and Ethnohistory," *Ethnohistory* 12 (spring 1965): 99–112.

11. See Laurence M. Hauptman, *The Iroquois and the New Deal* (Syracuse: Syracuse University Press, 1981) and *The Iroquois Struggle for Survival: World War II to Red Power* (Syracuse: Syracuse University Press, 1985).

12. Seneca Nation Constitution, Section 5, in National Archives, *Correspondence of the Office of Indian Affairs (Central Office) & Related Records. Letters Received, 1824–1881* (M234), reel 573; Rothenberg, "Mothers of the Nation," 81.

13. Abler, "Factional Dispute and Party Conflict," 17.

14. William N. Fenton, "From Longhouse to Ranch-type House: The Second Housing Revolution of the Seneca Nation," in *Iroquois Culture, History and Prehistory*, ed. Elisabeth Tooker (1967; reprint, Albany: University of the State of New York, 1970), 21.

15. Maris Bryant Pierce Papers.

16. New York State Assembly, *Report of the State of New York, Appointed by the Assembly of 1888: Assembly Document 51* (Albany: Troy Press Company, 1889), 19.

17. Maris Bryant Pierce Papers; Abler, "Factional Dispute and Party Conflict."

18. Committee in Behalf of the Women of the Cattaraugus Reservation to President Zachary Taylor, April 2, 1849, in *Correspondents of the Office of Indian Affairs, Letters Received*, reel 587.

19. Committee in Behalf of the Women of the Cattaraugus Reservation to Philip E. Thomas, October 13, 1848, in *Correspondence of the Office of Indian Affairs, Letters Received*, reel 587.

20. Seneca Nation Constitution; "Laws of the Seneca Nation," passed January 28, 1854, in *Correspondence of the Office of Indian Affairs, Letters Received*, reel 596; miscellaneous court records in Maris Bryant Pierce Papers.

21. Frank H. Severance, ed., "Journals of Henry A. S. Dearborn," in *Publications of the Buffalo Historical Society 7* (Buffalo: Buffalo Historical Society, 1904), 111–12.

22. Seneca Census Data.

23. New York State censuses—available in manuscript form for 1845, 1915, and 1925 (New York State Library, Albany)—show how enumerators with different interpretations of census questions could influence final results. The 1915 and 1925 censuses included questions sensitive to Iroquois cultural differences (such as clan and the name of each child's mother). Perhaps enumerators reacted to the more typical questions in the same spirit, for some enumerators chose to list women as heads of households whenever possible while others chose to list men. For the question "number of acres of land cultivated," the responses are ambiguous as to whether men or women owned or farmed more land. Most enumerators listed responses for this question for the household head only, and so if taken at face value, the 1915 census would suggest that on the Allegany Reservation women owned (or farmed, depending on how "acres cultivated" was understood) almost all the land, while on the Cattaraugus Reservation men owned all the land.

24. For more on how the U.S. Census Office dealt with women's occupations in the past, see Margo A. Conk, "Accuracy, Efficiency and Bias: The Interpretation of Women's Work in the U.S. Census of Occupations, 1890–1940," *Historical Methods* 14 (spring 1981): 65–72.

25. Thomas Donaldson, *Extra Census Bulletin. Indians. The Six Nations of New York* (Washington DC: U.S. Census Printing Office, 1892), 49.

26. Donaldson, *Six Nations of New York*, 80.

27. "Laws of the Seneca Nation," 21.

28. See miscellaneous wills and court records in Maris Bryant Pierce Papers and in Indian Collection Papers, Buffalo and Erie County Historical Society.

29. Donaldson, *Six Nations of New York*, 80.

30. Commissioner of Indian Affairs, *Annual Report*, 1889 (Washington DC: Government Printing Office, 1890), 266.

31. Marvin Crouse Testimony, New York State Assembly, *Assembly Document 51*, 816–19.

32. George Jimeson et al. to Commissioner of Indian Affairs, December 23, 1844, in *Correspondence of the Office of Indian Affairs, Letters Received*, reel 585.

33. Franklin B. Hough, ed., *Census of the State of New York for 1865* (Albany: Charles Van Benthuysen & Sons, 1867), 602.

34. Seneca Census Data.

35. Severance, "Journals of Henry A. S. Dearborn," 35–225; Donaldson, *Six Nations of New York*, 50.

36. Commissioner of Indian Affairs, *Annual Report*, 1900, 306.

37. Commissioner of Indian Affairs, *Annual Report*, 1897 (Washington DC: Government Printing Office, 1898), 207; Abler, "Kansas Connection," 91.

38. While the census data is useful for analyzing demographic behavior, it has limited value for discerning power relationships within the household. Women's occupations, as previously discussed, have a reputation of high undercount. Even more problematic is the census's treatment of household headship: enumerators clearly expected men to be heads of households. There is evidence suggesting that members of some households felt differently. On the manuscript schedules of the 1900 census for the Seneca, there are some women listed as heads who were later crossed out, to have their husband's name written over instead and the entire household listing rearranged. Presumably, as soon as the enumerators realized who lived in the household they could structure it to fit cultural norms.

39. Donaldson, *Six Nations of New York*, 77.

40. Hough, *Census of the State of New York for 1865*, 603.

41. William N. Fenton, "Locality as a Basic Factor in the Development of Iroquois Social Structure," in Fenton, *Symposium on Local Diversity in Iroquois Culture*, 43.

42. D. Sherman to Commissioner of Indian Affairs, March 16, 1878, in *Correspondence of the Office of Indian Affairs, Letters Received*, reel 595.

43. *Correspondence of the Office of Indian Affairs, Letters Received*; Commissioner of Indian Affairs, Annual Reports, 1850–1907.

44. Susan John's testimony, from William Crouse inheritance proceedings, in *Correspondence of the Office of Indian Affairs, Letters Received*, reel 594.

45. Frank H. Severance, ed., "Journals of Rev. Thompson S. Harris," *Publications of the Buffalo Historical Society* 6 (Buffalo: Buffalo Historical Society, 1903), 330.

46. Severance, "Journals of Rev. Thompson S. Harris," 327.

47. Donaldson, *Six Nations of New York*, 54.

48. The U.S. Census Public Use Samples are available from the Inter-University Consortium for Political and Social Research, Ann Arbor, Michigan. The 1900 Public Use Sample is described in Stephen N. Graham, "1900 Public Use Sample. User's Handbook (Draft Version)" (Seattle: Center for Studies in Demography and Ecology, University of Washington, 1980).

49. "Laws of the Seneca Nation," 22.

50. For a discussion of the measure for estimating the mean age of stopping childbearing and its implications for fertility control, see Michael Haines, *Fertility and Occupation: Population Patterns in Industrialization* (New York: Academic Press, 1979).

51. Parker, "Code of Handsome Lake," 30. For more on Iroquois birth control practices in the early contact period, see William Engelbrecht, "Factors Maintaining Low Population Density among the Prehistoric New York Iroquois," *American Antiquity* 52 (January 1987): 13–27.

52. Stone, *Life and Times of Red-Jacket*, 401.

53. Parker, "Code of Handsome Lake," 30.

54. Asher Bliss Journal, January 1833, Bliss Family Papers, New York State Library.

Using Gender as a Tool of Analysis

Economics

Until very recent times, in almost every human society, economic production has been gendered. Certain tasks have been regarded as the domain of women, while other work has been seen as appropriately performed by men. Human beings have no universal agreement concerning what work is properly male and what work is properly female, as the long, squalid history of the "squaw drudge/lazy male" stereotype of Native North American peoples makes sadly clear. But the fact that some work is viewed as male and some as female has shaped human perceptions of themselves (and allowed them to vilify Others) for centuries. The multiple theories suggesting why economic work is gendered, whether they are based on biological explanations or religious authorization, are beside the point in this discussion. What is significant here is that, because economic work is gendered, it is a particularly fruitful avenue for the historian to explore. The economic activities of men and women in a given society, the actual labor they perform, and the social recognition accorded them on the basis of that labor nearly always reveal important but differing components of their lives.

Investigations of the intersections of gender and economic production in Native societies have revealed important information about Native women, often when other sources have been absent or unavailing. As the two articles in this section show, gender relations and economics were structured and transformed in very different ways in eighteenth-century southern New England, as studied by Jean O'Brien, and in the nineteenth-century Wisconsin-Illinois region, as studied by Lucy Eldersveld Murphy. The two authors also creatively utilized what might be called unintentional historical sources—wills and other legal documents, census returns and business records—that were created to serve immediate social needs and unintentionally provide later historians with information.

O'Brien's reconstruction of Native life in eighteenth-century New England focuses on Native women's economic strategies during the century that saw Native peoples quietly and inexorably dispossessed of their land base. O'Brien's research reminds us that Native peoples' attachment to their land was not just sentimental; land was also a source of sustenance and economic security. Its loss was devastating and plunged Native peoples, especially women, into poverty. O'Brien also finds that Native women's experiences of economic dispossession and marginalization were different from men's in large part because of the patriarchal assumptions about women brought by the colonizing English.

The second study reveals a very different reality. Murphy examines the fairly peaceful relations among Sauks, Meskwakis, and Ho-chunks (or Winnebagos) and the small towns of southern Wisconsin that had their origin in and owed their continued existence to the fur trade. Women, both of Native and mixed Native and European descent, were central to maintaining these peaceful and reciprocal relations, Murphy argues, and had worked out ways of incorporating outsiders into their communities over the course of centuries. She also describes how Native peoples attempted to incorporate Anglo-American lead miners into their societies using these same tried-and-true strategies, and considers why these efforts failed.

13. "Divorced" from the Land

*Resistance and Survival of Indian Women
in Eighteenth-Century New England*

JEAN M. O'BRIEN

New Introduction by Jean M. O'Brien

Locating sources that capture pre-twentieth-century American Indian history is difficult enough, but finding documents that illuminate Indian women's lives during this time is an even more formidable challenge. In the case of New England, several accounts offer commentary on Indian women and gender roles in the seventeenth century, filtered through cultural lenses that require careful consideration in order to account for biases. (See excerpt from William Wood, *New England's Prospect*, originally published in 1634.) These ethnographic observations provide snapshots of Indian women's lives at the time of sustained and intensive interaction with the English. As such, they also purportedly capture Indian social and cultural worlds prior to a time when European invasion introduced fundamental transformations in Indian America.

These documents thus provide the means for capturing bygone worlds that shaped Indian women's experiences in New England. Yet too often scholarship focuses exclusively on recapturing the "pre-contact" history of Indian peoples. When I conceived "'Divorced' from the Land" (in response to an invitation to present a paper on matrilineality and patrilineality in comparative perspective), I decided to shift instead to the eighteenth century for two basic reasons. First, I could find very little historical or ethnohistorical literature that did so. And second, I wanted to foreground the fact of social and cultural change in Indian New England. Although Indian women (and men) dramatically transformed their ways of being in the world in dialogue with English colonialism, such changes represented creative adaptations that have ensured New England Indian survival into the present. A tendency for observers to assume that Indian culture change constituted a diminishment of Indianness has, in my view, contributed to the notion that Indian peoples—and especially New England Indians—had disappeared, or somehow became less Indian. Such assumptions rob Indian people of the capacity for change and create artificial criteria for Indian people as they continually remake themselves for the future.

After I decided to focus on the eighteenth century, the next challenging step was to locate the sources for illuminating that historical moment. As the English extended their reach over Indian New England, their attention to recording Indian lives diminished, thus considerably thinning the documentary record. Indian women (and men) did continue to appear (albeit less frequently) in county and commonwealth documents in Massachusetts, where my previous work had focused. I had already collected many of these documents, and when I decided to write the article I went back and collected more. (Several of these documents are reproduced or excerpted here.)

In framing my article, I juxtaposed material from the seventeenth and nineteenth centuries to illuminate some of the major changes one might consider when comparing portrayals of Indian women. This comparison provides a way to pose questions about what distinguished their experiences, and sets a context for then focusing on their eighteenth-century experiences. Most of the eighteenth-century documents I used for this article are petitions by or on behalf of Indian women and families to the Massachusetts General Court and probate documents generated when Indians died with estates that were then subsumed within the English legal system. Both sets of documents contain valuable information about social and cultural changes of Indian women and families. They illuminate how gender roles had been transformed, how Indian peoples made a living in the wake of their dispossession, and how they retained aspects of earlier material culture in combination with the adoption of new ways of being in the world that ensured their survival. Yet these documents also require care: virtually all of them were produced because the petitioner or petitioners faced substantial problems that required alleviation, and thus might suggest that all Indians faced dire circumstances at the time. The fact that Indians struggled as the English surrounded and dispossessed them cannot override the equally important fact that Indian people in New England survived.

One final note: this article originally appeared in the volume that followed the conference for which I wrote it.[1] When Colin Calloway asked to reprint it for a volume on Indian survival in New England, I asked him if I could rewrite it. Several things about the first version bothered me, and the rewrite allowed me address those nagging concerns. Today it could use yet another rewrite to reflect the continued development of literature in the field. Such is history.

"Divorced" from the Land
Resistance and Survival of Indian Women
in Eighteenth-Century New England (1997)

In 1624, Edward Winslow, Governor of Plymouth colony, observed about Native Americans that "[t]he women live a most slavish life; they carry all their burdens, set and dress their corn, gather it in, and seek out for much of their food, beat and make ready the corn to eat and have all household care lying upon them."[2] Winslow's use of the term "slavish" in this passage is instructive. The portrayal of the Native American woman as "squaw drudge" who toiled endlessly for her "lazie husband" was both a common English analysis of Native American division of labor in the northeastern woodlands and a commentary upon English expectations about gender roles.[3] Observers viewed Indian women as "slaves" because, unlike English women, they performed virtually all of the agricultural labor in their societies.[4] In fact, most labor the English would have regarded as male work was performed by Indian women.

The "squaw drudge" permeated early observations of Native Americans in the Northeast. Two centuries later, different kinds of images of Indian women could be found in local accounts. Consider the following: "The last Indian here was 'Hannah Shiner,' a full-blood who lived with 'Old Toney,' a noble-souled mulatto man . . . Hannah was kind-hearted, a faithful friend, a sharp enemy, a judge of herbs, a weaver of baskets, and a lover of rum."[5] This description, taken from a nineteenth-century history of Medford, Massachusetts, reflects not just the passage of time but also the extent to which relations, roles, and expectations had changed on both sides of a sustained cultural encounter.

The juxtaposition of these two fundamentally different portrayals reveals crucial changes in the circumstances of Indian women in New England. Four key structural changes differentiate the historical eras from which the

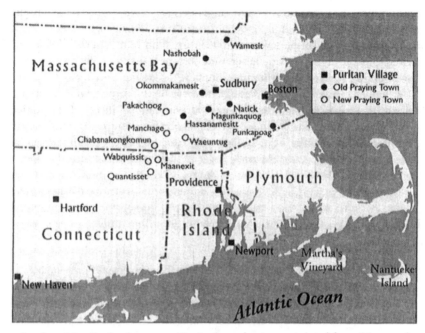

4. Southern New England communities in the early 1670s, reprinted from *Dispossession by Degrees: Indian Land and Identity in Natick, Massachusetts, 1650–1790* by Jean M. O'Brien by permission of the Univeristy of Nebraska Press. © 1997 by the University of Nebraska Press.

images come. First, Indian societies that were "tribal" and politically independent prior to intensive colonization became effectively "detribalized" and politically encompassed by the late seventeenth century. By this time, most Indian individuals and families were incorporated into English communities, mostly in small clusters that rendered Indians virtually invisible within the context of the now-dominant New English society. Second, the prosperity of Indian societies, based on diversified agricultural economies and intensive use of seasonally available plant and game resources, was undermined as the English gained possession of nearly all Indian land by the end of the seventeenth century. The central element of the Indian economy was thus eliminated, requiring fundamental changes that resulted in the recasting of Native gender roles. Third, Indian societies that stressed communal values, sharing, and reciprocity were thrust into a market economy with the advent of colonization. Immersion in the market left Indians at the mercy of English legal institutions and affected the shape of Native social welfare practices. And fourth, Indians were quickly rendered a minority population within their own homelands by the astounding success of the English demographic regime, which was coupled with Indian struggles caused by imported diseases and military encounters. These structural changes compelled Indians to see the landscape in a different way, requiring them to make massive adjustments, and eliciting myriad and contradictory responses.[6]

As they successfully dispossessed and displaced Indians, the heirs of English colonialism seized the power to define the rules governing the social order, and they constructed surviving New England Indians as peculiar and marginal. Local historians underscored the "disappearance" of the Indian population by singling out individuals such as Hannah Shiner as representing the "last survivor" of their "tribe." Even so, historians used their representations of Indians as peculiar and marginal, as hopelessly "other," to continue to constitute and affirm an English identity. They presented Indians such as Hannah Shiner as the complement to "Englishness," thereby reminding themselves of the persistent difference between Indian survivors and themselves. But more than just reinforcing the difference between Indians and themselves, the ways in which they used this binary operated to emphasize English dominance.[7]

The English colonial regime imposed a different landscape, one requiring Indians to transform their relationship to the land. Gender figured prominently in this transformation. The English aimed to "divorce" Indians from their possession of the land in order to establish themselves and English culture in their place. New England Indians' agricultural, hunting, fishing, and gathering economy was interpreted as wasteful, and the sedentary agriculture pursued by English men was seen as the only proper pursuit for Native men. Yet even as they pursued the larger project of English colonialism (replacing Indians and Indian ways of using the land with English people using the land in English ways), colonists also aimed to convert surviving Indians to English culture. As they separated Indians from possession of virtually all their land, colonists also sought to "divorce" Indian women from their role as agriculturalists, replacing them with male Indians working drastically reduced plots of land to the exclusion of hunting and other older economic pursuits. From the perspective of the English, "divorce" from the land would fulfill the biblical directive to "subdue the earth and multiply" by bringing land into agricultural production to sustain a growing English Christian population. And it would also place Indian women and men in a "proper" relationship to the land. In the most crucial sense, however, the English failed to "divorce" either Indian women or Indian men from the land. Although in narrow legal terms the English succeeded in imposing their own rules for possessing the land, New England Indians did not monolithically embrace English gender ways. They remained crucially connected to the land that sustained their kinship and visiting networks and their own sense of proper place.[8]

In addressing the transformations accompanying the cultural conflicts between Indians and English colonists, I will focus on the issue of "gendered division of labor" rather than on the important problem of lineality in the northeastern woodlands, which also involved different conceptions of how gender ought to operate. Use of the dichotomous construction of matrilineal/patrilineal obscures much diversity in the ordering of families, reckoning of descent, ordering of power relations, and much more. Because of the paucity of early sources that provide detailed information on social organization, combined with the early occurrence of devastating epidemics throughout the region, there is much we will never know about the "precontact" shape of social organization in the northeastern woodlands. Indian peoples in early New England were concerned overwhelmingly with resisting and surviving English incursions, and the disruptions of epidemics that accompanied early contact certainly must have obscured their previous shape at least to some extent. About all that is evident is that, by the eighteenth century, patrilineal naming practices predominated among Indians; whether this was the case because it had always been so, or because the English imposed these forms on Indians in bureaucratic transactions, is not so clear.[9]

About a gendered division of labor, much more seems to be apparent. Most scholars agree that women performed most agricultural labor (except growing tobacco), built and transported bark or mat wigwams from place to place, manufactured baskets and pottery, gathered shellfish and wild foodstuff, processed hides, made clothing, and raised children. Men also made some household tools and were the principal woodworkers, making canoes and fortifications, for example.[10]

By 1700, Native American groups in New England had a long history of encounters with Europeans. Indians reeled from the impact of imported epidemic diseases, with many groups suffering demographic declines on the order of 90 percent. Military conquest followed quickly on the heels of the epidemiological disasters. The last major war in southeastern New England ended in 1676, terminating the political independence of those Native groups who had hitherto avoided encompassment by the English. These events effectively ended the autonomy of Indian groups in that region and rendered many aspects of the aboriginal economy obsolete through massive displacement and dispossession. Under the cumulative impact of the colonial experience, a great many New England Indians found themselves landless, a diasporic population vulnerable to the institutions of English colonialism.[11]

Missionary sponsorship had secured land bases for several Indian groups in the seventeenth century as part of English efforts to transform Indian cultures. Here, the English expected Indians to alter their gender roles in conformity with English cultural prerogatives.[12] Indian groups were allowed to retain small plots of land provided they would express responsiveness to missionary messages about cultural change. The English expected Indians to erect compact, English-style towns in order to fix them in particular places, directed men to forego hunting in favor of agricultural duties, and trained women in "household skills," especially spinning and weaving. Indians were encouraged to adopt English work habits, individual ownership of land, English tastes in material culture, and values structured by a market economy. Some Indians experimented with cultural transformations along these lines, but success in the market economy did not follow so easily. Many Indians were landless at the beginning of the eighteenth century, and, as their land was transformed into a commodity, Indian landowners continued to lose land.[13] Many were encompassed within the flourishing English settlements, finding niches in colonial economies, performing agricultural and nonagricultural labor.

Although some Indians steadfastly resisted English influences on their life-ways, and others struggled within the market economy, still others borrowed extensively from English culture as a means of accommodating to English colonialism. In some senses, Jacob and Leah Chalcom symbolized Indian transformation as conceptualized by the English. Chalcom purchased land, established an English-style farm, and built a frame house in Natick, Massachusetts, an important mission town established seventeen miles southwest of Boston. He was involved actively in the local land market, buying and selling small parcels from time to time as he strove to upgrade his farm. The cultural priorities of this family are visible in their childrearing practices. The Chalcom children were literate, and the daughters were given dowries upon their marriages to local Indian men.[14] After his death, Chalcom's estate included a thirty-acre homelot and "Buildings thereon," plus other lands, an assortment of household goods and husbandry tools, a horse, a cow, and books. After debts against his estate were discharged, fifty-two acres of land remained to be divided among his heirs.[15]

The women in Chalcom's family had made corresponding changes in their lifeways, including their separation from agricultural tasks. Leah Chalcom and her widowed daughters, Esther Sooduck and Hepzibeth Peegun, inherited land from their husband and father, respectively. Finding themselves without husbands, they pondered what to do with their inheritance. In 1759 they petitioned the Massachusetts General Court to sell their forty-six acres, arguing that "as your Petitioners [have been] brought up to Household business, [we are] incapable of improving said lands."[16] They requested that their lands be sold and the money be put out to earn interest for their income and support, a strategy adopted by a number of women. The implication here is quite clear: these women were no longer farmers and were thus unable to "improve" the land except insofar as it represented a monetary resource. The mother and daughters recognized that English financial strategies could sustain them and prolong the nurturing functions of land from which they were effectively torn loose. Putting money "at interest" constituted one strategy for women who had maintained clear "legal" connections to the land. Their decision not to use the land for gardening, as English women often did, in part reflected their perception that if they chose to keep the land it would "speedily be exhausted by frequent Law-Suits."[17]

The "Household business" to which Leah Chalcom and her daughters referred reflects the efforts of English missionaries to realign Native American gender roles. Biblical imperatives motivated missionaries who aimed to train Indian women in English skills for structuring a household, and to integrate Indian families into the market economy. In 1648, missionary John Eliot wrote that: "[t]he women are desirous to learn to spin, and I have procured Wheels for sundry of them, and they can spin pretty well. They begin to grow industrious, and find something to sell at Market all the yeer long[.]"[18] Some Indian women continued to pursue these tasks that missionaries had pushed so vigorously in the early years of intensive English-Indian contact. Fifteen percent of inventories of Indian estates from Natick filed between 1741 and 1763 listed spinning wheels.[19] Ruth Thomas, who died in 1758, was described in her probate docket as a weaver; Esther Freeborn and Hannah Lawrence, sisters who both left wills, were described as spinsters.[20]

Esther Sooduck, also a weaver, died in 1778. Her probate documents vividly evoke the kinds of changes Indian women confronted even though very few accumulated and held onto material goods as successfully as Esther had.[21] Her house, described as "much out of repair," nonetheless contained an impressive array of furnishings and sat upon thirty acres of land. Included among her belongings were a bed and bedstead, a chest, a trunk, a rug, a table and two chairs, plus knives, forks, and pewter. She read her two old Bibles with "speticals." She owned two spinning wheels as well as baskets and "Baskets Stuf."[22] Apparently merged in her economic pursuits were English skills (spinning and weaving) and Native American artisanal production (basket-making).

Native American women displayed transformations in their work habits, material life, aesthetic emphases, and even physical their appearance. Hannah Lawrence owned several articles of clothing when she died in the 1770s, including several gowns and aprons (one of them linen) as well as quilted petticoats and a pair of shoes with buckles.[23] Cloth replaced animal skins; petticoats and gowns were substituted for skirts and leggings. These accommodations were rooted in more than a century of profound cultural change. And in many ways, they represent an *up*rooting, a broken connection: English-style clothing signified the distance women had moved from their former way of life. Eighteenth-century economic adaptations no longer produced the materials for older ways of clothing production, and adopting English style probably reflected not just this reality but also newer Indian tastes.

There were many ways in which Native American women in eighteenth-century New England *were* divorced from the land: the colonial experience reoriented their relationship to the land in tangible and not so tangible ways. English ideals for cultural change aimed to realign the Indians' gendered economy and make room for English people to subdue the land in English ways. For Indian women this meant a stark separation: once the principal producers of the crucial agricultural element of subsistence economies, women were expected to sever the vital connection they had to the soil as its principal cultivators and nurturers. Though the English who wanted to accomplish these changes may not have noticed, their models for transformation went well beyond a simple shift in the gendered organization of labor. On the practical level, knowledge and skills were altered drastically, and the content of material life was dramatically recast. On the ideological level, less visible reverberations can only be imagined in individual and corporate identity, belief systems, and other deeply rooted cultural values. The tensions accompanying these transformations can be glimpsed in one possible explanation for the ultimate failure of Indian men as farmers in a market economy, which suggests that their reluctance to tend crops stemmed from their view that these "effeminate" pursuits properly remained women's work.[24] In refusing English gender ideals, many Indian men resisted this foundational concept of English colonialism.

Leah Chalcom, Esther Sooduck, Hannah Lawrence—all of these women came from one kind of Indian community. They all lived in Indian-dominated towns, their land ownership sanctioned by the English, who conferred "possession" of these reduced plots of land according to English legal principles. At least in this nominal sense, they were beneficiaries of missionary endeavors.[25] Although they were relatively successful in emulating English ways, as the eighteenth century unfolded, the slow but steady dispossession of Indian landowners allowed fewer Indians to replicate earlier successes. Other Indians were uprooted utterly almost from the beginning of their contact with the English. They adjusted to English invasion differently, mapping out alternative kinds of lifeways. After the 1660s, for example, "The remnant of the Pocumtuck Confederacy, adopting in part the English costume, had gathered about the English in the valley towns. . . . Here they lived a vagabond life, eking out, as they could, a miserable existence on the outskirts of civilization. . . . So hampered, their stock of venison or beaver, with which to traffic for English comforts, was small, and the baskets and birch brooms made by the squaws ill supplied their place."[26]

This is a stark outline of the principal difficulties Indians faced in making the transition to landlessness within a society emphasizing the market. With the possibilities for hunting gone, and no land—what remained? Production of Indian crafts constituted one possibility for women, who remained important in the economy and maintained this earlier economic role, which was possible even when landless. In their artisanal production, women continued to cultivate the specialized knowledge required to gather materials for fashioning baskets and other crafts. Their craftwork represented a revealing accommodation to dispossession: reaping basket stuff did not require "possession" of the land. At the same time, in marketing Indian goods, they earned an income and reinforced their "Indianness" in the popular perception.

Craft production by Indian women constituted one of the crucial threads that ran through the seventeenth, eighteenth, and nineteenth centuries in New England. Indian women in the eighteenth century were engaged especially in basket making as an economic activity, but other artisanal skills were added as well.[27] In 1764, Abigail Moheag attested that she was "64 years of Age and . . . a widow [for] more than fifteen years and hath . . . by her Industery in the business of making Brooms Baskets and horse Collars; Supported her Self till about two years ago She was taken sick."[28] The inventory from Hannah Speen's estate listed "baskets and barkes, brombs and bromb-sticks."[29] Craftwork, including the production of "new" items like horse collars, moved from the periphery of women's economic activities to the center as Indian women became enmeshed in the market and were no longer engaged in farming. For some women, craft production was fundamentally redefined. No longer one activity in an integrated economy, performed seasonally and for purposes largely internal to the household, artisanal activities became specialized and divorced from seasonal rhythms, and a principal means to get a living.

Wage labor constituted another possibility for Indian women. It remains unclear just what kind of work Indian women were doing, or what it was they received in return. In 1755, the circumstances of some Indian women at Mattakeset were such that "at present they live among White People, and work with them for a living."[30] The formula in these kinds of situations may have involved the contribution of unskilled and unspecialized labor, perhaps domestic work, in exchange for small wages or even some degree of basic sustenance. The existence of small clusters of Indians in virtually every Massachusetts town suggests that the lives of English colonists and Indians were intertwined in ways we are only beginning to understand.[31]

Disruption of Native societies extended to every sphere, requiring their constant adjustment. Marginal individuals, that is, those with few relatives or friends, Indian or non-Indian, and little in the way of economic resources, suffered the most. Prior to Indian enmeshment in the market, caretaking and nursing constituted central kinship obligations. During the eighteenth century, as kinship networks thinned, families became fractured, and involvement in the market made prosperity precarious at best. Individuals could no longer count on thick networks of relatives to care for them when they were in need of shelter, sustenance, or support. Nursing and caretaking became commodified and unreliable. Even when an intact family was in place, taking on caretaking obligations in this changed context could spell the economic ruin of a precariously established family. These developments represented the cumulative effect of generations of demographic decline, military conquest, economic disruption, and cultural transformation. Abigail Speen reported to the General Court in 1747 that she had: "by Reason of her great age & infirmities ... been long and still is Unable to do anything to Support herself, & so having cast herself on Mr. Joseph Graves of Sd Natick [an Englishman]; She has been kind entertained & Supported at his House now for near two years, & has nothing to recompense Sd Graves with nor to procure for her the Necessaries of Life for the time present & to come."[32] This woman had land, and she liquidated the remainder of her estate in order to pay Graves. No doubt he realized that his "investment" was secured by that plot of land she owned in Natick. This replacement of Indian kinship obligations with market-driven social welfare occurred throughout New England and accounted for much dispossession of Indian peoples who might otherwise face legal proceedings for debts they accumulated.[33]

Just as Abigail Speen cast herself on Joseph Graves, Indian women cast themselves upon other Indian women, too. What differed in the eighteenth century was that these women were not necessarily relatives, and that nursing or caretaking was often given in exchange for monetary compensation. The administrators of the estate of Elizabeth Paugenit, for example, allowed nearly two pounds to Hannah Awassamug "for nursing."[34] Sarah Wamsquan was cared for by Eunice Spywood, among others. Englishman John Jones petitioned the General Court in 1770, setting forth Sarah's dire circumstances and begging: "let something be done that Shall Speedily relieve the poor person that has her—or they will perish together."[35] Town authorities did not always countenance such arrangements. In 1765, when "Sarah Short a molatto woman Last from Wrentham [was] Taken in by Esther Sodeck," Natick selectmen feared she would become a town charge and warned her that she should leave the town.[36]

Banding together just to survive, these women struggled within a radically changing world. Often their situation was complicated by the dramatic transformations accompanying their dispossession, which stretched Indian communities thinly across the landscape to form a network of small clusters of families throughout southeastern New England. One response was to move constantly in search of a niche. As landlessness accelerated throughout the eighteenth century, a pattern of Indian vagrancy emerged: this pattern, accepted by the dominant society as natural, was also an accommodation strategy. Indian women, especially, were described as wandering from place to place, a characteristic that was associated in the public mind particularly with Indians. An Englishman of Dorchester petitioned the General Court in 1753 as follows: "An Indian Woman called Mercy Amerquit, I think Born Somewhere about Cape-Cod, but had no settled Dwellingplace any where, . . . Strolled about from one Town & Place to another, & sometimes she wrought for Persons that wanted her work[. She] came to my House . . . and desired liberty to tarry a little while, and your Petr condescended, expecting that she would go some other place in a little time (as their manner is) and what work she did for your Petr she was paid for as she earned it."[37] It is clear from this passage that English observers expected Indians to "wander." Their semi-sedentary lifeways had always been regarded most simplistically as nomadism. In the eighteenth century this translated into constant movement, "from one Town & Place to another . . . as their manner is." In this case, an arrangement seems to have been negotiated that involved Mercy Amerquit performing labor for wages as well as for her temporary residence with the narrator. He expected her to "go [to] some other place in a little time," and the arrangement was regarded as rather unexceptional. The only reason this relationship was documented at all was because Amerquit died while in the petitioner's residence and he sought to recover money he expended for her burial.

The story of Mercy Amerquit was by no means unique. An Englishman from Roxbury reported to the General Court about sixty-year-old Hannah Comsett, who became ill at his house: "She informs that her Mother was born at Barnstable, she at Scituate, and that for 30 years past she has been [strolling] about from Town to Town geting her living where she could but never lived During that time the space of one year at any Town at any time."[38] Though Hannah Comsett's mobility seems rather astounding, there are so many similar stories available that it is certain it was not an aberration.

The mechanisms behind Indian vagrancy were complex. Prior to the arrival of the English, Indian societies in New England reaped abundance from economies that depended upon knowledge about and extensive use of resources and a semi-sedentary lifeway. Scheduled mobility lay at the center of this system. In the eighteenth century, Indian migrations may have been scheduled, but if so, they were motivated by very different priorities, since they could no longer rely on movements governed by independently composed Indian communities to and from places that "belonged" to them in the strict legal sense. Probably kinship ties and some knowledge of labor markets entered into movements, but for women like Mercy and Hannah, there seemed to be nothing particularly patterned about their shifting about. Perhaps it was setting about to track the occasional charitable English colonist that spurred on the solitary and needy Indian women, from whom a different kind of resource might be procured. One important element that differentiated earlier migratory practices from new patterns was their largely individual nature; this new "vagrancy" drew upon older

patterns and places, but was not necessarily kin-group sponsored movement with planned, deliberate ends in mind. At the heart of the problem
lay landlessness, whether it had resulted from military conquest in the seventeenth century or from failure in the market economy in the eighteenth.
"Divorced" from the land initially when their economic role was redefined
along English lines, a much more literal separation had been accomplished
for most by the middle of the eighteenth century.

The situation of these women hints at two recurrent themes regarding
Indian women in eighteenth-century New England. First, transiency is
graphically described in a manner consistent with the emerging problem of
landless poverty in New England more generally. The "wandering Indian"
had much in common with the "strolling poor,"[39] although the fact that the
English categorically distinguished between the two offers testimony for
their separatist views about race. The problem of Indian women seems to
have been compounded, however. The extent to which these are stories of
women alone, or mostly alone, is the second theme and it is most striking.

Where were the men? The evidence suggests that, despite the missionary model of settled agriculture performed by men within nuclear families
on family farms, transiency also remained characteristic even of landown-
ing Indian men. Most Indian landowners lost what they had over time, and
the tendency for Indian men to enter service in two areas (military service
and the emerging whaling industry) contributed to a grossly distorted sort of
transiency.[40] As a result of their participation in these activities, Indian men
were absent for extended periods of time, engaged in dangerous pursuits that
seriously jeopardized their lives and well-being and compromised their ability to function effectively within the English-dominated society. Whaling, in
fact, fostered the same sort of debt peonage that proved so devastating in
fur trade relationships.[41] These orientations contributed to uncertainty and
instability for Indian families and also reduced the number of Indian men
available as desirable spouses. Interpretations of the involvement of Indian
men in the military and labor at sea have stressed the continuity in skills and
culturally determined priorities they offered them.[42] But some men also abandoned their families to escape their predicaments; evidence may be found in
scattered narratives of Indian men "absconding" as difficult circumstances
evolved into insurmountable economic and legal problems. Such was the
case for Eunice Spywood's husband, who "Some Years Ago Absconded and
left her in very distressing Circumstances, and he . . . never returned."[43]

An important cumulative effect of English colonialism was to reconfigure the relationships among Indian mobility, a gendered division of labor, and household structures. The semi-sedentary Indian economy entailed a gendered mobility that assumed that women and men would be apart for periods of time: men departed central villages for hunting and fishing, leaving women to tend crops and gather wild plant resources near their villages, for example.[44] But these periods of separation were scheduled, part of the seasonal rhythm of life, and as such they rendered neither women nor men helpless. Newer patterns of male mobility (such as participation in the whaling industry and the military) that drew upon older Indian lifeways frequently left women alone to experience harsher circumstances than before, when kin-based social welfare and flexible marriages had provided them with the means to alleviate their wants.[45] At least for women like Mercy Amerquit and Hannah Comsett, mobility was circumscribed by virtue of their being separated from men. And whereas whaling and military service may have reformulated earlier patterns of Indian male mobility, allowing men to resist the redefinition of gender in economic and social roles, the wives of these men—women like Eunice Spywood—were defined as "responsibilities" in new ways and experienced far greater hardship as a result of their men's flight. The English nuclear family model thus reconfigured kin responsibilities and marriage, leaving Indian women newly vulnerable to "divorce" in dramatically different ways.

Whatever the underlying motivations, Indians of both sexes experienced hardship as a direct result of participation of Indian men in military service, especially. The social and demographic impact of the Seven Years' War on Indian enclaves in New England was enormous. In 1756, a cluster of Indians at Mattakesett in Pembroke, Massachusetts, pleaded to the General Court "that Several of us [have] in the late Warrs, lost our husbands & Sons, & Some of our Sons [are] yet in Sd Service, & that some of us are old, blind, & bed rid & helpless poor Creatures, Many of us [are] old Women & want help."[46] Indians of Eastham and Harwich in Barnstable County, Massachusetts, complained that many of their men "Have Died in ye Service & left their Squa & Children in Distressing Circumstances."[47] In 1761 Ezra Stiles reported that in Portsmouth, Rhode Island, "4 Ind. Boys [had] enlisted in the service . . . only one Boy more in Town, & he [is] about 10 y. old. I can't find . . . any Ind. Men in Town, . . . but several Squaws, perhaps 8 or 10." At Milford, Connecticut, there were twenty male Indians in 1755, at the beginning of the Seven Years' War, but in 1761 "not one: but 3 or 4 Squaws."[48]

Even when they did return, many Indian men were rendered incapable of working to support themselves or their families as a result of war-related disabilities. Thomas Awassamug complained to the Massachusetts General Court in 1761 that "he having been engaged . . . as a Soldier . . . for more than thirty years past, has indured inexpressible hardships, and fatigues and thereby brought on him the Gout, and many other ailments . . . And [he has] no means of support." Awassamug sought to stir compassion by describing in detail his "deplorable Circumstances," and to clarify his own relationship with the colony by reminding the magistrates that he had "jeopardized his life in so many . . . very dangerous Enterprizes against those of his nation who remain Savage, and in behalf of his friends, the English."[49] The General Court allowed a small sum to be paid out of the public treasury for his temporary relief.

No comprehensive evidence is available to investigate the precise dynamics of demographic change for Indians in eighteenth-century New England. Several censuses gathered by Stiles in his journeys through the region are suggestive, however. In addition to his more random observations, Stiles compiled detailed lists of residents by household from three Indian communities he visited in 1761 and 1762. In these communities, widows constituted heads of households in proportions ranging from 29 percent (Mashantucket Pequot in Groton, Connecticut) to 52 percent (the "Potenummekuk" Indians in Eastham and Nauset, Massachusetts). These figures suggest that the tribulations outlined above were not idle and unconnected complaints.[50]

One solution to the apparently growing problem of unbalanced sex ratios and insufficient numbers of Indian men was for Indian women to find spouses among free or enslaved African Americans, who occupied similarly marginal positions in New England. The dynamics of intermarriage between Indians and African Americans are difficult to map precisely from the surviving documentary record. Impressionistic evidence does exist. Stiles observed in 1761 that "At Grafton [Massachusetts] . . . I saw the Burying place & Graves of 60 or more Indians. Now not a Male Ind. in the Town, & perh. 5 Squaws who marry Negroes." A nineteenth-century history of Needham, Massachusetts, noted that there was "a colony of negroes, with more or less Indian blood, dwelling along the south shore of Bullard's Pond (Lake Waban)."[51] Clearly, intermarriage did occur, as yet another kind of accommodation on the part of Indian women, representing an important demographic shift for Native populations of the northeast.

Equating "Indianness" with "blood quantum" (the perceived importance of "pure" blood lines) in rigid ways, English observers failed to understand the demographic and cultural changes that were reconfiguring "race" in New

England. Intermarriage, which blurred the picture for those who looked for racial "purity," helped the Native population of New England to survive the devastating consequences of English colonization. Most colonists who noticed Indians just lamented what they saw as an inevitable process of extinction. Some vaguely grasped the complex process of vagrancy and intermarriage that was so central to eighteenth-century accommodations, even if their cultural blinders rendered them incapable of analyzing the changes. In 1797, the minister at Natick observed: "It is difficult to ascertain the complete number of those that are now here, or that belong to this place, as they are so frequently shifting their place of residence, and are intermarried with blacks, and some with whites; and the various shades between these, and those that are descended from them, make it almost impossible to come to any determination about them."[52] Indians became, like other groups displaced by the colonizing impulse of the English, a diasporic population defined by the complex transformations and dislocations brought about by English colonialism. In the end, the migratory pattern and complexities of intermarriage created an erroneous impression in the minds of English observers that the Native population was simply and inevitably melting away.[53]

In truth, monumental Indian adjustments spanned the entire colonial period and stretched into the nineteenth century. Both precontact Native American societies in the northeast and early modern European societies were organized according to particular expectations about gender roles. In New England, Indian women were responsible for most agricultural tasks, for gathering wild foods, building houses, most craft production, and child-rearing. Men were warriors, diplomats, hunters, and fishermen, and they aided women in agricultural production by clearing fields. This way of organizing society came into direct conflict with English expectations, and the ability to maintain an economy that perfectly reflected older Native gender roles ran into the hard realities of changing circumstances. The loss of political independence and the massive displacement of Indians within their homelands brought tremendous changes that affected Indian women and men in different ways. Hunting and fishing became marginal, diplomacy became obsolete, and military involvement was transformed into economic activity. Agriculture was enormously altered in technique and organization: it became predominantly if not exclusively a male activity for Indian landowners, and it became a diminishing element of the Indian economy as Indians continued to lose land throughout the eighteenth century.

Although English expectations for change within Indian culture (encapsulated most fully in missionary platforms) called for altering the gendered Indian division of labor, the English did not fully succeed in "divorcing" Indian women (or men) from the land. Even though they quite successfully dispossessed Indians, Indians remained in the homelands that continued to sustain their kin, community, and sense of place. Indian women and men found creative solutions for resisting displacement and surviving as Indian people in a milieu theoretically designed to erase their difference completely.

How does all of this connect to Hannah Shiner? The manner in which she is portrayed in the nineteenth-century account that I began with, compared to how she might have been characterized in the seventeenth century, speaks volumes. This Indian woman is not described generically, as most Indian women were when regarded as members of a tribal unit, but as an individual with an Anglicized name. Her categorization as an Indian is based on the observer's judgment of her (pure) genealogy. And her husband is seen as a "mulatto," a mate who probably could trace some African American heritage. Hannah Shiner was assigned several traits, including two ("judge of herbs" and "weaver of baskets") that were associated in the public imagination with "Indianness," and especially with Indian women. They also suggest trades, or means of support, that had always been female activities. Hannah Shiner symbolizes the tumultuous changes experienced by Native peoples in seventeenth- and eighteenth-century New England. Indian peoples survived the catastrophe of English colonization, and they resisted the erasure of their Indianness. Men and women experienced the fundamental transformations in their lifeways differently. "Divorced" from the land in some respects but, crucially, not in others, many women displayed the characteristics that are visible in this brief description of Hannah Shiner. Apparently accepted and incorporated as an individual member of the community of Medford, Massachusetts, Hannah Shiner represents a particular kind of transformation, though not of the sort English missionaries had in mind. "Marginal" and a bit "exotic," she was portrayed as a bit of "local color," a tangible tie to what seemed to be (but was not) an increasingly distant Indian past. Her configuration by a local historian as such was precisely what Anglo-Americans needed for her to continue to represent the "otherness" necessary for the ongoing construction of their own difference.

Appendix: William Wood's *New England's Prospect*

Published in London in 1634, William Wood's New England's Prospect *is regarded as an unusually important early natural history and ethnography by a writer mired in some obscurity. Likely based on approximately four years of personal observation and crafted in part as promotional literature and justification for colonialism,* New England's Prospect *found a ready audience in England that resulted in the publication of a second edition the following year.*[54] *The following is an excerpt from chapter 19 of Wood's book.*[55]

"Of Their Women, Their Dispositions, Employments, Usage by Their Husbands, Their Apparel, and Modesty"

To satisfie the curious eye of women-readers, who otherwise might thinke their sex forgotten, or not worthy a record, let them peruse these few lines, wherein they may see their owne happinesse, if weighed in the womans ballance of these ruder *Indians*, who scorne the tuterings of their wives, or to admit them as their equals, though their qualities and industrious deservings may justly claime the preheminence, and command better usage and more conjugall esteeme, their persons and features being every way correspondent, their qualifications more excellent, being more loving, pittiful, and modest, milde, provident, and laborious than their lazie husbands. Their employments be many: First their building of houses, whose frames are formed like our garden-arbours, something more round, very strong and handsome, covered with close-wrought mats of their owne weaving, which deny entrance to any drop of raine, though it come both fierce and long, neither can the piercing North winde find a crannie, through which he can conveigh his cooling breath, they be warmer than our *English* houses; at the top is a square hole for the smoakes evacuation, which in rainy weather is covered with a pluver;[56] these bee such smoakie dwellings, that when there is good fires, they are not able to stand upright, but lie all along under the smoake, never using any stooles or chaires, it being as rare to see an *Indian* sit on a stoole at home, as it is strange to see an *Englishman* sit on his heeles abroad. Their houses are smaller in the Summer, when their families be dispersed, by reason of heate and occasions. In Winter they make some fiftie or threescore foote long, fortie or fiftie men being inmates under one roofe; and as it their husbands' occasion these poore tectonists[57] are often troubled like snailes, to carrie their houses on their backs sometime to fishing-places, other times to hunting-places, after that to a planting place, where it abides the longest: an other work is their planting of corne, wherein they exceede our *English* husband-men, keeping it so cleare with their Clamme shellhoes, as if it were a garden rather than a corne-field, not suffering a choaking weede to advance his audacious head above their infant corne, or an undermining worme to spoile his spurnes.[58] Their corne being ripe, they gather it, and drying it hard in the Sunne, conveigh it to their barnes, which be great holes digged in the ground in forme of a brasse pot, seeled with rinds of trees . . . An other of their employments is their Summer processions to get Lobsters for their husbands, wherewith they baite their hookes when they goe a fishing for Basse or Codfish. This is an everyday's walke, be the weather cold or hot, the waters rough or calme, they must dive sometimes over head and eares for a Lobster, which often shakes them by their hands with a churlish nippe and bids them adiew. The tide being spent, they trudge home two or three miles, with a hundred weight of Lobsters at their backs, and if none, a hundred scoules meete them at home, and a hungry belly for two dayes after. Their husbands having caught any fish, they bring it in their boates as farre as they can be water, and there leave it; as it was their care to catch it, so it must be their wives paines to fetch it home, or fast: which done, they must dresse it and cooke it, dish it, and present it, see it eaten over their shoulders; and their loggerships[59] having filled their paunches, their sweete lullabies scramble for their scrappes. In the Summer these *Indian* women when Lobsters be in their plenty and prime, they drie them to keepe for Winter, erecting scaffolds in the hot sun-shine, making fires likewise underneath them, by whose smoake the flies are expelled, till the substance remain hard and drie. In this manner they dry Basse and other fishes without salt, cutting them very thinne to dry suddainley[60] before the flies spoile them, or the raine moist them, having a speciall care to hang them in their smoakie houses, in the night and dankish weather.

In summer they gather flagges,[61] of which they make Matts for houses, and Hempe and Rushes, with dyeing stuffe of which they make curious baskets with intermixed colours and protractures of antique Imagerie: These baskets be of all sizes from a quart to a quarter, in which they carry their luggage. In winter time they are their husbands Caterers, trudging to the Clamm bankes for their belly timber, and their Porters to lugge home their Venison which their lazienesse exposes to the Woolves till they impose it upon their wives shoulders. They likewise sew their husbands shooes, and weave coates of Turkie feathers, besides all their ordinary household drudgerie which daily lies upon them, so that a bigge bellie hinders no businesse, nor a childebirth takes much time, but the young Infant being greased and sooted, wrapt in a Beaver skin, bound to his good behaviour with his feete up to his bumme, upon a board two foote long and one foote broade, his face exposed to all nipping weather; this little *Pappouse* travells about with his bare footed mother to paddle in the Icie Clammbankes after three or foure days of age have sealed his passeboard and his mother's recovery.

Appendix: Selections from the Massachusetts Archives

The next six documents can be found in the Massachusetts State Archives at Columbia Point, Boston, the depository of the official records produced and collected by the commonwealth since 1629. All of these documents are found in the collection of documents relating to Indian affairs. The first is from volume 32, document 65.

Petition of Mattekeset Indian Guardians[62] responding to Memorial of Patience & others

. . . One of them namely Peter Job is but a New Comer there, and with Respect to the Said Patience and her Grandson Caleb and Others that have dwelling Houses there, the Said Guardians Set out to them Such Portions as they Thot Proper after inquiring into their Circumstances and Manner of living by their Neighbours the white people; and which were at the time of it to Their Sattisfaction exprsed to the Guardians from the Indians [own?] Mouths. With Respect to Others of the Subscribers it did not appear to the Said Guardians that they were proper Owners of Land ther. Tho: their Relations who were originally Foreigners,[63] were Suffer'd by the Sachems[64] to make Some Improvement there formerly, and Since Decd and their Habitations Demolished, and the Petitioners being women, are not in a Capacity to build Houses, and as at present they live among White People, and worke with them for a living.

> *Samll Bradford*
> *Jonah Edson*
> *Nathaniel Smith, Guardians*

Massachusetts Archives, volume 32, document 375.

The Petition of John Robinson of Dorchester in ye County of Suffolk, and Province aforesaid, Gentleman, Humbly, Sheweth,

That an Indian Woman called Mercy Amerquit, I think Born somewhere about Cape-Cod, but had no settled Dwellingplace any where, but strolled about from one Town & Place to another, & sometimes wrought for Persons that wanted her work, came to my House in Dorchester aforesaid, sometime in ye Month of October 1751, & brought with her a young Child of about Two Months old in her arms, and desired liberty to tarry a little while, and your Petr condescended, expecting that she would go to some other place in a little time (as their manner is) and what work she did for your Petr she was paid for as she earned it; But about ye middle of January following, she was taken Sick of a tedious Sickness & very Delirious, That after about 20 Days Sickness she Died, leaving her young Child upon your Petrs Hands; That your Petr was obliged out of meer Humanity as she was in his House; & so extreme bad, to send for a Physician for her, & to provide things for her that were necessary for her in her Sickness, & to nurse her, and also after she Died to Bury her; That your Petr Expended upon her ye Sum of Three Pounds Fifteen Shillings & Ten Pence, as appears by ye following Accompt . . .

[Petition was dismissed by the Council, September 11, 1753]

The following is an excerpt from a petition that complains of the encroachment of Englishmen, especially upon their ancient whaling beaches. Massachusetts Archives, volume 33, document 10.

The Humble Petition of us the Subscribers In Behalf of our Selves and Brethren Indian natives of ye Towns of Eastham and Harwich in ye County of Barnstable and Province Aforesd Humbly Sheweth.

. . . that we were Never more in a Distressing Case [than?] at present: As many of our Nation Have Entred into ye Warr with the English Against ye French and Indians in Alliance with them And many of them Have Died in ye Service & Left their Squa & Children in Distressing Circumstances. And as there is Many Old Crippled Indians among us that stand in Great Need of Relief all Which is under a Greater Necessity of making ye Best Improvements of What Little Lands that are Still Left in our Hands . . .

> *Isaac James*
> *Joshua Ralph*
> *Joshua Jethro*
> *James Oliver*
> *John Ralph Jen*
> *[?]*
> *Thomas [?]*
> *Samuel [?]*
> *Amos Laraninc*

Massachusetts Archives, volume 33, document 106–107

The Petition of Leah Chalcom, Esther Sooduck, and Hepzibeth Peagun, Indian women of Natick in the County of Middlesex

That Your Petitioners being [posses?] of about Forty six acres of land in Said Natick, the fee where of is in themselves: As also of a small right in the Common and undivided lands in said Natick which is of small value; And your Petitioners being brought up to Household business, are incapable of improving Said lands: And their Predecessor/under whome they hold their present possession/ having many Years Ago, Sold Twenty Acres of very valuable land in Said Natick, the title where of having Since failed, Your Petitioners (being Subjected by Law) having paid for the Said lands and Secured the title thereof & the present occupants, and thereby involved themselves in debts to the value of about thirty five pounds Lawful money: And unless they Are impowered to Sell Some of their Lands, to discharge the Same, the whole of their Estate will speedily be exhausted by frequent Law-Suits; And as the [Remaining?] part of their Said Estate would be of More Advantage if Sold and the money at intrest in the hands of their Trustees or the money at intrest in the hands of their Trustees or Guardians, the Intrest thereof /and only that/ to be applyed to their yearly support, as they Shall need the Same—Therefore your Petitioners Pray that Your Excellency and this Honll Court will grant them power to Sell their Said lands already laid out, and their Common Rights, their Said debts being paid, the remainder of ther proceeds to be kept at Intrest for their support as above & Your Petitioners in duty bound Shall Ever Pray [&c]

> Natick June 1 1759
> *Leah Chalcom*
> *Esther Sooduck*
> *Hepzibeth Pegun [their marks]*
> *endorsed by John Jones & Jos. Buckminster, Guardians*
> granted Oct 17 1759

Massachusetts Archives, volume 33, document 300–301

The Petition of Abigail Moheag of Natick . . . Indian woman

Humbly Sheweth that your Petitioner is 64 years of Age and hath been a widow more than fifteen years and hath no child nor any Relation nearer

than a remote cousen and your Petitioner hath by her Industery in the business of making Brooms Baskets and horse Collars; Supported her Self till
about two years ago She was taken Sick of a long fever and hath had weak and
Ill turns at times ever Since and is in no wise able to Support her Self and it
is Improbable that She ever will: and your Petitioner is now Indebted to the
docter and others for the Necessaries of Life four or five Pounds L = M = and
your Petitioner hath no house Nor any Sort of Shelter of her own to repair to:
but has been and Now is in a Suffering Condition and Stands in Great Need
of Relief for She is Entirely Deprived of any Shelter; for her Cousens house
where She used to live is taken Down and Carried off and Your Petitioner
knows not of any Place where She can Get in if She Should be Sick—

And your petitioner having a free hold in lands in Natick the fee hereof
is in her and she is willing to Sell Some Part of it now to Pay her Debts
and for her Support and to Build your Petitioner a Small log house about
ten or twelve feet Square that She may hav a house of her own where She
may work if She be able and lie warm when She is Sick and Not be obliged
to travel from one Place to another and Expose her health as heretofore
and as your Petitioner is Not able to Say how Much it will take to Pay her
Debts already Contracted and to build her Such a house as aforementioned
and much More to Say what She Shall Stand in need of for the future: So
She does not Pray for liberty to Sell a Certain Number of acres: hopeing
therefore that this honoured Court Can rely on the fidelity of our Guardians Your Petitioner humbly Prays that this Honoured Court will Grant her
Power to Sell So much of her Real Estate as the Guardians Shall think of
real necessity for the Purposes above Mentioned: And Your Petitioner as in
Duty Bound Shall Ever Pray

> Abigail Moheag [her mark]
> Natick June ye 4 1764
> endorsed John Jones, Jos. Buckminster
> granted with Advise & Consent of Guardians

Massachusetts Archive, volume 33, document 513–514

Sir

I am desired by Eunice Spywood to write to you, but I don't
know what was done on her Petition, and what she further
needs. I cannot indulge her any farther than to Set forth Certain
facts that have been heretofore Collected from Sarah Wampsquan, the pauper mentiond in the Said Eunices Petition. Vizt

That the parents and grandparents of the said Sarah dwelt at Bil-
lerica in the County of Middlesex; That her Grand-parents were
Sachems and owned that Town and lands adjacent—That her
parents came occasionally to Natick when her mother was pregnant with the Said Sarah, and tarrying a few days she was born
there, (at that time Natick was not incorporated, nor an English
family in it,)—That she Said Sarah was carryed to Woodstock
or Pomfret, and kept there till she was seven years old—Then
bound to Deacon Braddish of Cambridge, whom she served till
she was eighteen—Then went to service with Doctor Dalhone
of Boston 2 or 3 years—and then marryed to an Indian belonging to Cape-Cod whose name was Lawrence—he dying, she
marryed to Solomon Wampsquan of Natick, who has been dead
near 20 years. That her last husband was not a Proprietor in
Natick, nor his predecessors:—That this poor woman is in advanced age—one side Dead with the Dead Palsey[65]—uncapable
of helping or even feeding herself—She has begged from door
to door till about three years ago—when she could not Travel
one mile in a day, and could not labour with her hands, which
she was willing to do when able, and was honest as far as I know;
And as she is also a human being, my heart has been greatly
moved for her many a time, in particular in July last, when the
Revd mr Badger the minister of Natick, (who had from year
to year been exceedingly burthened with her and other poor
Indians, who have been cast upon him one way or other) was
at the General Assembly praying for the relief of the said Sarah,
and at the Same time remonstrating against her being made
the Charge of Natick—while mr Badger was thus employed
from week to week at his own expense—this poor woman was
brought in the night, and put into his necessary-house—in his
absence . . . and from thence she was Carryed to this Eunice
Spywood's—and has been there ever Since. Upon the whole, the
Indians are not able to support her—nor themselves,—and the
English of Natick are already Over-Stocked with their own poor,
Some of whom I know suffer for want: This poor woman has
been supported by this Province—Pray Let Something be done
that Shall Speedily relieve the poor person that has her—or they
will perish together—I have no expectation that the District of

Natick will pay Eunice Spywoods acct for the time past nor take Care of the Said Sarah Wampsquan for the future: Or if they Should be ordered by this Court, I may not say it will not be legal, but it will be attended by such delays, as will not answer the good intentions of the Legislature, and will prove and in-let to as many other Indians to come, as shall hear of it—And Towns that shall have an Indian in them will be likely to send him when he shall want relief—Sir, I can say no more than this—That I hope the Assembly will revive the Petition of Eu-nice Spywood—and order her acct to be paid out of ye Province Treasury—I doubt not of the wisdom of the Assembly of which you are a member—and hope you will be directed in this and all your proceedings—as shall most promote the Interest of the publick, and of individuals.

> *I am sir, yr friend and Humble servt—John Jones*
> *Dedham April 4 1770*

To Capt Eleazer Kingsbury a member of the Honble House of Representatives in Cambridge

Appendix: Probate Documents of the Middlesex County Court

The following probate documents can be found in the public records of the Middlesex County Court. They relate to the settlement of the estates of two Indian women of Natick, Massachusetts. The first set of documents is a will and attached estate inventory, divided into personal and real property sections, for Hannah Speen. Middlesex County Court, Probate Records, Cambridge MA, #21027, Hannah Speen, Will, 1742.

In the name of God amen. I Hannah Speen of Natick in the County of Middlesex in the Province of Massachusetts Bay in New England widow & Relick of John Speen Late of Sd Natick Deceased, Indian Being weak in Body but of sound & perfect mind & memory; but apprehending myself near to Death; Do Make Constitute & ordain this to be my Last will & Testa-ment; that is to say; first of all I Give & bequeath my immortal soul into the hands of God who gave it, to be justifyed, sanctyfied & Saved by the Spirit of God & in the name of Christ; & my Body to Christian & Decent Burial at the discretion of my Executr & as touching such outward Estate as God has given me I will give bequeath & dispose of it in manner of following—that is to say first

Imprimus[:] I Give & Bequeath Unto my well beloved son Joseph Speen & my Beloved Daughter Hannah, all the Yearly Rents & Interest of the Meguncog Money[66] which belongs to me, to be Received by them in Equal parts, if sd Joseph be alive & Live to return; but if not I give it all to sd Hannah; & upon Condition she shall dye without Heirs of her Body I give sd Money in Equal parts to my two sons hereafter mentioned. & inasmuch as the sd Joseph and Hannah will (if Living,) be Heirs to all their sd Fathers Estate—therefore

Item[:] I Give & bequeath unto my two sons Samuel Speen & Zachary Speen alias Maynard, all my Lands & Estate which belongs to me in [Natic?] as the only Heir to my Father & Brothers Decd to be Equally Divided between them; to them & their Heirs and assigns forever, they to be put out & brought up, in ye fear of God, at the Discretion of my Executor

Finally I Constitute ordain & appoint my trusty & well beloved friend Isaac Coolidge of Sherborn in sd County of Middlesex to be my Sole Executor of this my Last Will & Testament, desireing & fully inpowering him to see all & every part of it duely Executed according to the true Intent thereof; hereby revoking disannuling & making void all former or other Wills by me made, & Constituting appointing ordaining & Ratifying this to be my Last will & Testament, In Witness whereof I the said Hannah Speen have hereunto sett my hand & seal this twenty six Day of April Anno Domini one thousand seven hundred & forty two & in the fifteenth year of the Reign of his Majesty King George the Second—

> *Signed sealed, published pronounced*
> *& declared, In the Presense of—*
> *Thomas Russell*
> *Jonathan Lealand*
> *Benjamin Kendall*
> *Hannah Speen [hir mark]*

An Inventory of the Estate of Hannah Speen Late of Natick Decd widow taken by us the subscribers being sworn october ye 18th 1742 as was shewn to us by Capt. Isaac Coolidge Executor of her Last will and testament Which is as follows viz:

Imprimus	to books 7s	
	to wearing apparel 18.7.6	1:14
Item	to beding 10-4-0	

to pewter and brass 1:3:8
to earthenware and glass bottles 0:4-9   14:10
to Iron ware 1-10:0
to wooden ware 1:1:6
to one old [berthmettle?] skillet 0:4:0

Item   to baskets and barkes, brombes and brombsticks   1:11:0
to one knife 1:6   4:7:6
to two old Chests 1:10:0
to six chairs 1:4:0

Item   wampon[67] and suckenhock[68] 6:10:0

                                              Total   27:2:3

Real Estate
to her Rights in Natick Lands £170   170:0:0
The administr mentions a Sum of money which he has recd for Land Sold
belonging to the Deceasd—which he will add to the inventory when the
General Court shall have determined what proportion of it he ought to
stand chargd with

Thomas Russell
Jonathan Lealand
Benjn Kendall
appraisers
sworn before ye Judge
Middlesex [?] Octobr 18 1742 mr. Isaac Coolledge the ad-
minstr—presented the forgoing & made Oath that the same
contains a full & proper Inventory of the Estate of the be-
forenamed Decd so far as came to his Hands & Knowledge,
& promised if more Shall appear he would cause the same
to be added.
Jos. [?] Remington [J prob?]

An Inventory of the Real Estate of Hannah Speen Late of Natick in the
County of Middlesex Deceased as the Same was Shewn to us by Isaac Coollidge Esqr and was Taken by us the Subscribers Being Thereunto appointed
and Sworn march ye 4th 1744 and is valued as followeth; That is to Say:

Impri To one Lot Lying the ye plantation of Natick aforesd
Containing 84 acres att 5£ pr acer old tenor   420-0-0
To one Lot Containing 43 ½ acers att £3 pr acer   130-10-0

To one Lot Containing 16 ½ acers att 5£ pr acer 82-10-0
To one acer of meadow Land att £18   18-0-0
Item To one half of a Dweling house att £50   50-0-0
                                                      £701-0-0

Natick March ye 16th 1744
Thomas Russell
Jonathan Lealand
Benjamin Kendall
apprisers
March 18 1744 Major Isaac Coollidge the adminr sworn as
usual before S. Danforth J. [pro. & Regr?]

A second, and much smaller, set of probate documents pertains to the estate of
Esther Sooduck. Middlesex County Court, Probate Records, Cambridge, MA,
#20860, Esther Sooduck, Will, 1778

Inventory of Esther Sooduck "Late of Natick Indian Woman Deceasd Taken
the 20th: Day may 1778 and as follows Viz

To one Bed L9-0-0 to a rug 15s to one Bedsteld L12   10:7-0
To one Cedar Tub 15s to Small log [?] one Table 16s   11=1-0
To Two Chairs 2s to one Chest 12s *one Trunk* 10s   1=4-0
To knives and forks 2s to old Puter 1s to one Pot 18s   1=1-0
To one kettle 18s *to two old Bibles 3s* to Baskets 2s   1=3-0
To Baskets Stuf 1s To one Tramel 3s to fire Shovel Tongs [?] 2=11-0
To one Hamer 3s To Old Iron 2s to one mat 1s to [?]   0=7-0
To one Box and lime 1s to one Glas Bottle 1s   0 2-0
To one Bed board 3s *to one Cotton Gownd* 72s   3=15-0
To one Spinning Whel 6s to one small [ditto] 16s   1=2-0
To one ax 12s to one Pair Speticals 4s To Brick 10s   1=6-0
To one mug 1s to Six yards Black Calaminco L5-8-0   5=9-0
     Total of the Personal Estate   L 30=3-0
To About Thirty Acres of Land and a Small Dwelling House thereon
                                                             75=0-0
Total of the Real and Personal Estate   105:3-0

          Daniel Travis

362 JEAN M. O'BRIEN

Notes

For their valuable suggestions in revising the originally published version of this paper, I wish to thank Lisa Bower, Lisa Disch, and Jennifer Pierce.

1. *Gender, Kinship and Power*, ed. Mary Jo Maynes, Ann Waltner, Brigette Soland, and Ulrike Strasser (New York: Routledge Press, 1996).
2. Quoted in Howard S. Russell, *Indian New England before the Mayflower* (Hanover NH: University Press of New England, 1980), 96.
3. William Wood, *New England's Prospect* (1634), as quoted in *The Indian Peoples of Eastern America: A Documentary History of the Sexes*, ed. James Axtell (New York: Oxford University Press, 1981), 119. See Rayna Green, "The Pocahontas Perplex: The Image of Indian Women in American Culture," *Massachusetts Review* 16 (1975): 698–714, for an analysis of Pocahontas as literary convention and national symbol, and how Native American women have been conceptualized according to the dichotomy between "princess" and "squaw."
4. Women's labor accounted for well over half of Indian subsistence in most northeastern woodland cultures. Agricultural production alone contributed approximately 65 percent to the diet. See M. K. Bennet, "The Food Economy of the New England Indians, 1605–1675," *Journal of Political Economy* 63 (1955): 369–97.
5. Charles Brooks, *History of the Town of Medford, Middlesex County, Massachusetts* (Boston: James M. Usher, 1855), 80–81.
6. William Cronon, *Changes in the Land: Indians, Colonists, and the Ecology of New England* (New York: Hill and Wang, 1983). James H. Merrell has analyzed these massive structural changes in Indian-English relations by looking at the important shift in whose "customs" governed encounters between peoples. James H. Merrell, "'The Customes of Our Countrey': Indians and Colonists in Early America," in *Strangers within the Realm: Cultural Margins of the First British Empire*, ed. Bernard Bailyn and Philip D. Morgan (Chapel Hill: University of North Carolina Press, 1991), 117–56.
7. On Indian dispossession and the negotiation of the social order in colonial New England, see Jean M. O'Brien, *Dispossession by Degrees: Indian Land and Identity in Natick, Massachusetts, 1650–1790* (New York: Cambridge University Press, 1997). On the last survivor trope in New England, see William S. Simmons, *Spirit of the New England Tribes: Indian History and Folklore, 1620–1984* (Hanover NH: University Press of New England, 1986), 3–4. On the forging of distinctive European/colonial identities with reference to Native peoples and imported African slaves, see the studies collected in *Colonial Identity in the Atlantic World, 1500–1800*, ed. Nicholas Canny and Anthony Pagden (Princeton: Princeton University Press, 1987); Roy Harvey Pearce, *Savagism and Civilization: The Study of the Indian in the American Mind* (Baltimore: Johns Hopkins University Press, 1953); and Richard Slotkin, *Regeneration through Violence: The Mythology of the American Frontier* (Middletown CT: Wesleyan University Press, 1973).
8. On the process of missionization see, for example, James Axtell, *The Invasion*

Within: The Contest of Cultures in Colonial North America (New York: Oxford University Press, 1985); and O'Brien, *Dispossession by Degrees* (especially ch. 2).

9. Scholars of this region have argued positions with regard to social organization across a wide spectrum: as matrilineal or patrilineal societies, as bilateral, or as some blend of these general rules. Lewis Henry Morgan, "Systems of Consanguinity and Affinity of the Human Family," *Smithsonian Contributions to Knowledge*, 218 (Washington DC: Smithsonian Institution, 1870), and Lorraine Williams, "A Study of 17th Century Central Community in the Long Island Sound Area" (Ph.D. diss., New York University, 1972), are most often cited by those who argue for the matrilineality of southeastern New England groups. William S. Simmons and George F. Aubin, "Narragansett Kinship," *Man in the Northeast* 9 (1975): 210–31, argue for the patrilineal reckoning of political leadership and tribal identity and suggest that exogamous matrilineal clans may have existed to regulate marriage. In general, Kathleen Bragdon has agreed: "'Another Tongue Brought In': An Ethnohistorical Study of Native Writings in Massachusett" (Ph.D. diss., Brown University, 1981). Elise Brenner suggests that a bilateral kinship system was in place: "Strategies for Autonomy: An Analysis of Ethnic Mobilization in Seventeenth Century Southern New England" (Ph.D. diss., University of Massachusetts, 1984). Those who argue for patrilineal or a bilateral system focus on the lack of evidence for matrilineality from the seventeenth century. Dean R. Snow, *The Archaeology of New England* (New York: Academic Press, 1980), and William A. Starna, "The Pequots in the Early Seventeenth Century," in *The Pequots in Southern New England: The Fall and Rise of an American Indian Nation*, ed. Laurence M. Hauptman and James D. Wherry (Norman: University of Oklahoma Press, 1990), 33–47, have argued that the inconclusive nature of the evidence might signal differences in degree and/or be the result of the chaotic conditions surrounding conquest, which required flexible social responses and at least the periodic appearance of matrilineal or bilateral kinship systems. I am indebted to my research assistant, Margaret Rodgers, for helping me sort out this literature.

10. Robert Steven Grumet, "Sunksquaws, Shamans, and Tradeswomen: Middle Atlantic Coastal Algonkian Women during the 17th and 18th Centuries," in *Women and Colonization: Anthropological Perspectives*, ed. Mona Etienne and Eleanor Leacock (New York: Praeger, 1980), 43–60; Snow, *Archaeology of New England*; Neal Salisbury, *Manitou and Providence: Indians, Europeans, and the Making of New England, 1500–1643* (New York: Oxford University Press, 1982); and William Cronon, *Changes in the Land*. Debate over gender roles in this region centers on the permeability of the boundaries between women's and men's work, and implications of the meaning of gendered division of labor for the relative power and status of women and men in these societies.

11. See especially Francis Jennings, *The Invasion of America: Indians, Colonialism, and the Cant of Conquest* (New York: Norton, 1976); Salisbury, *Manitou and Providence*; Cronon, *Changes in the Land*; and O'Brien, *Dispossession by Degrees*.

12. Axtell, *Invasion Within*; and Theda Perdue, "Southern Indians and the Cult of True Womanhood," in *The Web of Southern Social Relations*, ed. Walter J. Fraser Jr., R. Frank Saunders Jr., and Jon L. Wakelyn (Athens: University of Georgia Press, 1985), 35–51.

13. The process of gradual loss of individually owned land in one missionized Indian town is documented in my book *Dispossession by Degrees*.

14. Massachusetts Archives, 31 (1730), doc. 175 [hereafter cited as Mass. Arch., vol. (year), doc.]; and Mass. Arch., 32 (1753), 417–18.

15. Middlesex County Probate Docket no. 4124, Jacob Chalcom, Admin. (1756) [hereafter cited as Middlesex Probates]. For a discussion of the diverse cultural patterns of Indian adjustment to the English, see O'Brien, *Dispossession by Degrees*, especially ch. 5.

16. Mass. Arch., 33 (1759), 106–76.

17. Mass. Arch., 33 (1759), 106–76. On English women and gardening, see Laurel Thatcher Ulrich, *Good Wives: Image and Reality in the Lives of Women in Northern New England, 1650–1750* (New York: Vintage Books, 1980). On the loss of individual Indian-owned land through legal prosecutions, see O'Brien, *Dispossession by Degrees*.

18. Thomas Shepard, *The Clear Sun-shine of the Gospel Breaking Forth Upon the Indians in New-England* (London: Printed by R. Cotes for John Bellamy, 1648), reprinted in Massachusetts Historical Society, *Collections*, 3d ser., 4 (1834), 59.

19. O'Brien, *Dispossession by Degrees*, ch. 6.

20. Middlesex Probates, 22411, Ruth Thomas, Admin. (1758); Esther Freeborn, Worcester County Probate Docket no. 22322 (1807) [hereafter cited as Worcester Probates]; and Hannah Lawrence, Worcester Probates, 36457 (1774).

21. Probate documents for several hundred Indian estates in Massachusetts were filed throughout the eighteenth century and have been preserved in county court records. Probate procedures seem to have been followed most vigorously when English creditors to Indian estates sought payment. The majority of Indians died intestate; divisions of Indian estates then almost always followed English estate law quite closely, with provisions made for "widow's thirds," a double share given to the eldest son, and equal shares to other children.

22. Esther Sooduck, Middlesex Probates, 20860, Will (1778).

23. Hannah Lawrence, Worcester Probates, 36457 (1774).

24. This is a common theme. See especially Anthony F. C. Wallace's classic work *The Death and Rebirth of the Seneca* (New York: Knopf, 1970), as well as a critique offered by Diane Rothenberg, "The Mothers of the Nation: Seneca Resistance to Quaker Intervention," in Etienne and Leacock, *Women and Colonization*, 63–87.

25. Indian women could obtain title to land as individuals within the landholding system of Massachusetts, but most Indian women gained access to land as wives and children, as heirs to estates. In the process of dividing land in early eighteenth-century Natick, Massachusetts, nineteen individuals were designated proprietors,

with principal rights to all of the land within the town. One of these was a woman; the rest were men. O'Brien, *Dispossession by Degrees*, ch. 4.

26. George Sheldon, *A History of Deerfield, Massachusetts* (Greenfield MA: E. A. Hall and Co., 1895), 1:71.

27. Ann McMullen and Russell G. Handsman, eds., *A Key into the Language of Wood-splint Baskets* (Washington CT: American Indian Archaeological Institute, 1987).

28. Mass. Arch., 33 (1764), 300.

29. Hannah Speen, Middlesex Probates, 21027, Will (1742).

30. Mass. Arch., 32 (1755), 675–76.

31. See, for example, John A. Sainsbury, "Indian Labor in Early Rhode Island," *New England Quarterly* 48 (1975): 378–93. Sainsbury found that "35.5 percent of all Indians in [Rhode Island] were living with white families in 1774; and if the Indians still living on the Charlestown reservation are excluded, the figure rises to 54 percent." He suspected they were "rent-paying lodgers." (Quotations are from p. 379.) In examining vital records from all over Massachusetts to identify Indians who were connected to the town of Natick, I located at least one Indian in each of 113 towns. Taking nine very distinctive surnames of Natick Indians, I located individuals with the same surnames in twenty towns. O'Brien, *Dispossession by Degrees*, ch. 6.

32. Mass. Arch., 31 (1747), 529. Speen was petitioning the General Court for permission to sell all of her remaining land so that she could reimburse Graves for caretaking. Massachusetts erected a system of oversight for Indian land that required General Court permission in order for Indian individuals to sell land to non-Indians. O'Brien, *Dispossession by Degrees*, ch. 3.

33. O'Brien, *Dispossession by Degrees*, ch. 6.

34. Middlesex Probates, 17057, Elizabeth Paugenit, Will (1755).

35. Mass. Arch., 33 (1770), 513.

36. Natick Town Records, First Book of Records for the Parish of Natick, 1745-1803, Morse Institute, Natick, Massachusetts.

37. Mass. Arch., 32 (1753), 375–76.

38. Mass. Arch., 32 (1751/2), 230.

39. Douglas Lamar Jones, "The Strolling Poor: Transiency in Eighteenth-Century Massachusetts," *Journal of Social History* 8 (1975): 28-54; and Jones, "Poverty and Vagabondage: The Process of Survival in Eighteenth-Century Massachusetts," *New England Historical and Genealogical Society Register* 133 (1979): 243–54.

40. Richard R. Johnson, "The Search for a Usable Indian: An Aspect of the Defense of Colonial New England," *Journal of American History* 64 (1977): 623–51; Daniel Vickers, "The First Whalemen of Nantucket," in *After King Philip's War: Presence and Persistence in Indian New England*, ed. Colin G. Calloway (Hanover NH: University Press of New England, 1997); Laurie Weinstein, "'We're Still Living on Our Traditional Homeland': The Wampanoag Legacy in New England," in *Strategies for Survival: American Indians in the Eastern United States*, ed. Frank W. Porter III (Westport CT: Greenwood Press, 1986), 91.

41. Vickers, "The First Whalemen of Nantucket."

42. See especially Johnson, "Search for a Usable Indian"; and Vickers, "First Whalemen of Nantucket."

43. Mass. Arch., 33 (1762), 204.

44. Cronon, *Changes in the Land*.

45. O'Brien, *Dispossession by Degrees*, ch. 6. On English colonialism and the institution of Indian marriage, see Ann Marie Plane, "'The Examination of Sarah Ahaton': The Politics of 'Adultery' in an Indian Town of Seventeenth Century Massachusetts," in *Algonkians of New England: Past and Present*, ed. Peter Benes, The Dublin Seminar for New England Folklife Annual Proceedings, 1991 (Boston: Boston University, 1993), 14–25; and Plane, "Colonizing the Family: Marriage, Household, and Racial Boundaries in Southeastern New England to 1730" (Ph.D. diss., Brandeis University, 1994).

46. Mass. Arch., 32 (1756), 710.

47. Mass. Arch., 33 (1757), 10.

48. Franklin B. Dexter, ed., *Extracts from the Itineraries and Other Miscellanies of Ezra Stiles D.D. LL.D. 1755–1794* (New Haven: Yale University Press, 1916), 117, 149.

49. Mass. Arch., 33 (1761), 170.

50. Stiles, *Itineraries* ("Potenummekuk"), 170, ("Nyhantic" in Lyme, Connecticut—47 percent widow-headed households), 130; and Stiles, "Memoir of the Pequots," in Massachusetts Historical Society, *Collections*, 3d ser., 10 (1834), 102–3.

51. Stiles, *Itineraries*, 203; and George Kuhn Clarke, *History of Needham, Massachusetts, 1711–1911* (Cambridge MA: University Press, privately printed, 1912), 558. Determining the degree of intermarriage between Indians, African Americans, and whites is problematic lacking vital records that systematically note the race of the individuals. Even when race is designated in vital records, labels such as "colored" and "mulatto" only indicate that intermarriage had occurred at some time in the past. Clerks did not necessarily use these labels consistently, either. Certainly intermarriage had been occurring between Indians and African Americans over the course of the eighteenth century. Intermarriage with the English was proscribed by legal statute. See Jack D. Forbes, "Mulattoes and People of Color in Anglo-North America: Implications for Black-Indian Relations," *Journal of Ethnic Studies* 12 (1984): 317–62.

52. Stephen Badger, "Historical and Characteristic Traits of the American Indians in General, and Those of Natick in Particular, in a Letter from the Rev. Stephen Badger of Natick, to the Corresponding Secretary," Massachusetts Historical Society, *Collections*, 1st ser., 5 (1790), 43.

53. O'Brien, *Dispossession by Degrees*, ch. 6.

54. "Introduction," by Alden T. Vaughan in William Wood, *New England's Prospect*, edited with an introduction by Alden T. Vaughan (Amherst: University of Massachusetts Press, 1977), [1]-14.

55. William Wood, *New England's Prospect: A True, Lively, and Experimentall Descrip-*

tion of that Part of America, Commonly Called New England: Discovering the State of that Countrie, both as it Stands to our New-Come English Planters; and to the Old Native Inhabitants.* I am grateful to the James Ford Bell Library at the University of Minnesota for providing access to this volume.

56. Not in the *Oxford English Dictionary*, but it clearly refers to the covering over the smoke-hole of a wigwam.
57. Builders.
58. Roots.
59. A derisive word to describe a slow, lazy, or idle person.
60. Suddenly.
61. A reed or such-like plant.
62. English individuals appointed by the commonwealth to protect Indian interests.
63. Referring to Indians from other locales in New England.
64. Indian leaders.
65. Paralysis, probably caused by a stroke.
66. Interest money earned due to the sale of a parcel of land called Magunkog in the Algonquian language.
67. Wampum—Indian medium of exchange and diplomatic symbolism, produced out of shells, and adopted by the English as an early medium of exchange.
68. Probably a bible or a book in the Massachusett language. My thanks to John Nichols in sorting out this translation.

14. To Live among Us

Accommodation, Gender, and Conflict in the Western Great Lakes Region, 1760–1832

LUCY ELDERSVELD MURPHY

New Introduction by Lucy Eldersveld Murphy

This essay began as a conference paper and was based on research I did for my dissertation (later published as *A Gathering of Rivers: Indians, Métis, and Mining in the Western Great Lakes, 1737–1832*).[1] It asks a central question: Why were frontier relations between Native people and others sometimes harmonious and in other situations conflicted? To answer this question I used three tactics: first, a comparative analysis of social relations in fur-trade towns and lead-mining communities that existed near one another; second, examination of economic activities in a particular area; and, finally, a focus on gender roles and gender relations. I determined that differences in levels of hierarchy or equality between and within groups (both gender and social strata or classes) were important in explaining why some people got along and others did not.

The influence of Clara Sue Kidwell's and Jennifer Brown's scholarship is evident in this article, as I looked for examples of Native women's mediation and matrifocal families, while understanding that I would not always find these patterns. I also recognized that Native gender roles and gender relations differed from those of Euro-Americans, as scholars such as Eleanor Leacock, David Smits, and others noted.

Researching the economic history of a region with an eye to gender requires a creative approach to sources and an ability to read carefully. General questions were: Who produced and/or exchanged what? How did economic production link people or divide them? This research builds on methods of women's history that consider domestic production—the work that sustains a family in and around the household—as part of a larger conception of local, regional, and international production and trade. It also asks the usual questions about gender: What did women do? Was it different from what men did? How strongly did people feel about the sex-typing of work? What were gender relations like, both within and between groups? It helps if we think of communities as being formed by families rather than by individuals, and documents such as Indian agent Thomas Forsyth's "List of the Sac and Fox half breeds" can help us to understand who the families were.

One can use a wide range of sources to understand the economy, including memoirs, letters, estate inventories, and merchants' lists of purchases and sales as well as exported and imported goods. If we approach them looking for answers to our basic questions, many of these same sources can help us to understand related social relations. For example, does dairying equipment, such as butter churns, appear in a mixed family's estate inventory? Was butter imported into a community? Do letters or travelers' reports mention whether European grains were grown (suggesting male plow-farming), or was maize still grown in hills with beans and squash (suggesting Native women working the field)?

Elizabeth Baird's memoir presents a unique window into the fur-trade families and communities of the nineteenth-century Midwest because it offers a woman's perspective. Baird, the granddaughter of one of the women mentioned in Susan Sleeper-Smith's article, was an elite Métis woman in a mixed marriage, and her reminiscences tell us much about both elite and lower-status women. Her writings reveal the tensions of different expectations based on cultural differences as well as the negotiation of gardening and dairying within her own family. (Another interesting revelation is that Elizabeth's Scots-Irish mother-in-law was much stricter with the Baird children than was Elizabeth, who evidently used typical Native parenting styles—more gentle and permissive—a difference that made it hard for them to share child care. Typically, Anglo families were quicker to use physical punishment and more restrictive rules with children.)

The memoirs of Elizabeth Baird and of other observers, of course, must be used with an understanding of the writers' points of view. Moses Meeker, for example, provides a classic example of the "squaw drudge" stereotype in his description of Native women lead miners, in his comment that "the men would not work." If we examine a wide range of other sources about Native men's and women's activities, it becomes clear that Native men were plenty busy, but with other types of production and service work, much of it unrelated to mining. Yet even though Meeker used the stereotype in his memoir, we can still extract information about what women did by using the source carefully.

To Live among Us
Accommodation, Gender, and Conflict in
the Western Great Lakes Region, 1760–1832 (1998)

Elizabeth Thérèse Fisher of Mackinac Island received a note from her fiancé one Saturday evening in late March 1824. Henry Baird, a young Irish lawyer, wrote to his fourteen-year-old Métis sweetheart to inquire "at what time [she] would be ready to go to the Sugar-Camp tomorrow" and told her, "if you will ride with me and inasmuch as you have said 'If you please' to me I will be happy to have the pleasure of your Company."[2]

In the days and years ahead, Elizabeth and Henry would learn a great deal from each other. In their new home in Green Bay, Wisconsin, the young wife, who spoke French, Ottawa, and Ojibwe but little English, taught her spouse the nuances of the French Creole and Native American cultures of the region; the husband helped his wife learn English as she taught herself to read, and he trained her as a legal assistant in his law office, where she served as the interpreter for most of his clients. But first, Henry would experience the joys of maple sugar making. Both the intimacy and the sugar production were typical of the mixed-race Creole communities of the Midwest in the late eighteenth and early nineteenth centuries.[3]

By contrast, in November 1827, just three years later and two hundred miles to the southwest of Green Bay, an Indian woman lay dying. "Her face was much lacerated, and one eye apparently put out," wrote newly appointed Indian agent Joseph Street, who was passing through the lead-mining region known as Fever River when he saw two Indians carrying her away in a blanket. He was shocked to learn that she "had the evening before been drinking much whiskey, and that a white man knocked her down and stamped on her head with his foot." Although the Menominee woman was "well known at this place, and reputed a good Indian," local officials took no action to investigate the murder. Violence in the lead-mining area had become all too common, and local government agents either could not or would not follow Street's recommendation to keep "a more vigilent eye . . . upon the hetrogenus mass" of white miners.[4] Over the course of a decade,

5. Fox-Wisconsin region, ca. 1830, reprinted from *A Gathering of Rivers: Indians, Métis, and Mining in the Western Great Lakes, 1737–1832*, by Lucy Eldersveld Murphy, by permission of the University of Nebraska Press. © 2000 by the University of Nebraska Press.

between 1822 and 1832, such men seized the lead region from Indian miners, forcing them out of the area entirely.

Why did some patterns of Indian-white relations lead to peaceful coexistence and integrated communities, while others resulted in conflict and Indian removal? This essay examines two communities that existed within the same region during the early nineteenth century: one based on the fur trade and the other on lead mining. There were several similarities between these two. Both were established in the area of southern Wisconsin, northern Illinois, and eastern Iowa among mostly Mesquakie, Sauk, and Winnebago people (although some Menominees, Potawatomis, and other Indians also lived in the region). Both communities were based on exporting partially processed natural resources—animal pelts and pig lead—to be processed further elsewhere. Although the fur-trade towns were founded well before the mining communities, they persisted into the 1820s and existed contemporaneously with the mining camps and towns. Indian miners had aunts and cousins living in the fur-trade towns and often went there to visit or trade.

In one type of community, fur-trade towns, Indians, whites, and Métis people coexisted peacefully as neighbors, relatives, employers, and workers; but in another, in the lead-mining region, Indian-white relations degenerated into hopeless conflicts. Examining the dynamics of social and economic interaction in the two communities may help to explain why accommodation succeeded in one place and failed in another. Although the term "accommodation" is sometimes used to suggest that indigenous or minority groups acquiesced in their own exploitation and oppression, I do not mean to use the word in that way here. I do mean "accommodation" as successful integration of Indian people into communities, economies, and societies in which people of European descent also lived and participated.

I will argue that women's actions, gender relations, and the negotiation of gender roles were crucial to the creation of the culturally syncretic fur-trade communities and that an examination of these same factors can illuminate reasons for Indian removal and the ultimate triumph of monoculturalism in the mining district. Ultimately, the ways that each community expressed domination and mutuality in gender, race, and intracommunity relations determined whether accommodation would be possible.

During the century between the end of the Fox Wars in 1737 and the Black Hawk War of 1832, the land between Lake Michigan and the Mississippi became ethnically diverse, experiencing several waves of immigration.

Winnebago, Sauk, Mesquakie, Menominee, and other Native peoples living in the region were joined by French Canadian fur traders, who married Native women, lived in Indian villages, and then founded Creole fur-trade towns after 1760. Although the region was technically under British control after the Seven Years' War, in reality the residents were practically independent. A few men from England and Scotland moved into the region, but the Creole towns continued to be places where French and Native languages prevailed. Finally, Anglophone immigrants from the United States arrived in large numbers after the War of 1812. A particularly intense period of Anglo migration into the lead-mining area took place after 1822, a phenomenon referred to here as the "lead rush."[5]

The fur-trade centers at either end of the Fox-Wisconsin waterway grew after the Seven Years' War and developed a culture that was neither purely European nor Native American but had elements of both. This culture will be referred to here as "Creole"—a distinctive regional multiethnic blend having roots in many Indian and European traditions. Virtually all of the husbands were French Canadian, and nearly all of the wives were Native American during the 1760s and 1770s, after which grown Métis children joined the ranks of householders.[6] These towns were not only multiracial but also multiethnic; a typical family might include a French Canadian husband, a wife of mixed Sauk and Mesquakie ancestry, their Métis children, and kin, servants, and other employees with Pawnee, Dakota, Menominee, Scottish, or even African ethnic heritages. Their neighbors might represent several different ethnicities. I use the general term "Creoles" to refer to all of the residents who participated in this culture, regardless of race or ethnicity. Although they were participants in a Creole culture, most of them were bicultural; that is, they understood, identified with, and participated in other cultures some of the time. Probably ethnicity and culture were more important concepts than race to Creoles, but outsiders did think in racial terms.

Creole communities were rooted in relationships established when immigrants entered Indians' neighborhoods. Midwestern Indians assimilated newcomers through a process that incorporated individuals into family units, a tradition probably dating from the precontact era. Outsiders became kin through marriage or, less frequently, adoption. Kinship bound strangers to their neighbors through ties of obligation, which regulated conduct. Outsiders who rejected this assimilation could expect no cooperation from Indians, because their rejection would be seen as evidence of bad intentions. Native customs allowed polygyny as well as divorce, making Indian matchmakers suspicious of the European who protested that he was already married or preferred a long courtship to make sure of compatibility. The possibility of divorce might have comforted young women whose marriages were arranged. As a result of the pressure and the opportunities, traders compromised on their own culture's marriage taboos to marry local daughters (sometimes qualifying these unions as "country marriages" in their correspondence with outsiders). As the Indians wished, economic relationships then became personal.[7] Initially, fur traders spent at least some of the year with their Indian kin in the Native villages, but after 1760 some of these families established separate towns, maintaining ties with friends and kin in the Indian villages.

Creole culture was created by husbands and wives, parents and children, employers and employees, and neighbors in their everyday lives and personal relationships. They communicated, learned, taught, adapted, and negotiated the details of daily life. Language was the most fundamental skill people needed for accommodation, and many wives were expected to learn, teach, and interpret across cultures, as Elizabeth Baird's experience makes clear.

If outsiders married local Indian and Métis women in order to gain entry into the region's economy and to get interpreting assistance, wives had their own set of expectations. They were frequently willing to play the role of "cultural mediator," as Clara Sue Kidwell has explained. This role was a respected one in Indian society; they and their kin expected appropriate treatment. Furthermore, Native women were used to a certain amount of autonomy with regard to economic production, and related resources such as sugar groves and cornfields were considered to belong to them. Finally, women in this region were not particularly subordinate to Indian husbands, although younger people were expected to defer to their elders' wishes.[8] We should not be surprised, then, that Native-descended women took active roles in shaping the emerging Creole culture and economy, creating accommodation.

The Creole towns were hierarchical systems with a handful of elite fur traders at the top, generally Euro-American and Métis men and their Métis and Indian wives and children. These elites employed "retainers"—contract workers and tenant farm families—and owned a few Indian slaves. In the middle were a few moderately successful traders and small farmers and the occasional artisan or professional. Wives, daughters, sons, and other kin helped with family business activities. Occasionally, women traded in their own names if widowed or if their husbands retired, but most frequently men were the official heads of household and business. Similar towns and cultures appeared throughout the Great Lakes and upper Mississippi Valley at places as far apart as Mackinac and Saint Louis. More than fifty such communities were founded during the late eighteenth century; by the late 1820s, as many as ten to fifteen thousand people called them home, according to Jacqueline Peterson's estimate. The population of Prairie du Chien was probably between six hundred and eight hundred in 1816, and perhaps nine hundred to eleven hundred people lived in Green Bay at that time.[9] Creole towns coexisted with Indian villages nearby.

Accommodation in the Creole communities entailed considerable teaching, learning, adaptation of traditional practices, and negotiation of gender roles. Compromises were made at the personal level. Although the Creoles were, as fur traders, taking part in an international economy, they also created domestic economies, and it is at this level that we can see the dynamics of syncretism.

A look at Native and Creole maple sugar production illustrates not only learning and adaptation in domestic production but also women's active roles in the processes. Sugar making had long been part of the seasonal economy of the Great Lakes Indians, whose many homes included the family sugar camps. After the autumn corn harvest, they moved from the summer villages to winter hunting grounds and then, in March, to these sugar camps, situated in a grove of maple trees.[10]

For Indians, the month or so of sugar making was a festive event at which women managed the boiling of maple tree sap, continuing day and night, while children helped or played nearby and men chopped wood for the fires and hunted to provide meat for the whole party. The tree sap was collected in birch-bark buckets. Before metal pots were acquired in trade, women used pottery, wood, or bark vessels and concentrated the sap by dropping hot stones into it, boiling it in birch-bark trays, or freezing it. European-made kettles increased the ease of boiling the sap a great deal, so they were eagerly adopted. The women stored sugar in birch-bark containers of various sizes called mococks, which they sometimes decorated with fancy quillwork and used as special gifts.[11]

Indians had produced commodities for trade to other communities for many centuries before European contact, a practice they continued when the European presence provided additional markets. By the early nineteenth century, Indian women made maple sugar a commodity of major importance. The Indians of northern Illinois and southern Wisconsin sold more than seventy thousand pounds of maple sugar in 1816, for example, not counting what they made for their own consumption. The Indian women around Green Bay alone produced twenty-five thousand pounds of maple sugar in one season. Fur traders, in their correspondence with one another, speculated on the prospects of a season's sugar, as they did with pelt production. As late as the 1890s, Indians in east-central Wisconsin were still selling maple sugar to their white neighbors.[12]

In the Creole communities of the Great Lakes, families accepted and adapted sugar traditions. They continued the spring tradition of moving to sugar camps called *sucreries*. Sugar making was well adapted to a lifestyle of seasonal migration, as practiced not only by Native Americans but also by Creoles, many of whom traveled extensively in the fur trade. Green Bay was deserted during the spring sugar production. An observer, Albert Ellis, commented that Creoles moved "from their home cabins on the River bank, into the deep wood, often many miles distant; taking generally most of their household treasures, even to their chickens." Elizabeth Fisher took Henry Baird to her grandmother's sugar camp, where the family owned more than a thousand trees.[13] Because sugar making was considered women's work, skills—and ownership of sugar bushes—were passed from Indian mothers to Métis daughters.

Creole sugar-making methods were quite similar to Indian techniques and continued to be under women's management. Many of the "better class of the French" preferred to refine their sugar more than did Indians, however, which had the effect of whitening it. They strained the syrup and then added a special clarifying agent, Ellis noted: "Here came in the product of the chickens, to-wit, the eggs, the whites of which were broken in the boiling syrup, when all impurities immediately came to the surface and were removed." Like Indian women, Métis women also might sell their excess sugar, the refined sugar being more desirable than the regular. Ellis recorded: "Some of the more enterprising and forehanded, bought syrup and . . . coarse sugar of their Indian retainers, and their less able neighbors, and went into the purifying process on a large scale, and thus largely increased their product for the season. A few families of this class had a preference in the sugar market at the frontier trading posts, their mococks, branded with their names, always being first sought, at advanced prices."[14]

The sugar season neatly coincided with the French Creole Easter celebration, and this festival combined elements from several cultures: day and night sugar boiling and celebrating, feasting on Easter eggs and crepes with maple syrup, and the ringing of the sugar bush with "the merry violin and the dance."[15]

Creoles continued the tradition of special gifts. Métis girls gave their boyfriends maple sugar candy wrapped in a strip of birch bark, which they called a "billet doux" (love letter—literally, a "sweet note"). Mothers such as Marguerite Griesie Porlier, who was part Menominee, expressed their love to distant children by promising to send a mocock of sugar.[16]

Processes involved in cultural fusion are evident in this description of Creole sugar production. First, teaching took place when Indian women taught their Métis daughters and granddaughters the basics of production. Second, the concept of sugar production as an area of women's management was passed from the Indian to the Creole culture. Maple sugar making was not practiced in Europe, so European-descended men had no traditions sex-typing the work differently.[17] That meant men and women did not have to negotiate control over this type of production. Third, even so, European traditions such as Easter celebrations, poultry keeping, and crepe making could be introduced—presumably by men—to make the endeavor bicultural. Fourth, the Indian and Métis women of Creole communities chose to continue producing Native commodities, not only for their own families but sometimes also for market. That is one of the ways they actively influenced Creole economies. Last, although both Creole and Indian communities produced sugar, Creoles also purchased Indian-made sugar either to refine further or to resell. Creoles do not seem to have appropriated Native sugar camps, except those that daughters inherited from Native foremothers. Thus, there was more cooperation than competition for resources or economic roles.

Other forms of production raised issues that required the negotiation of gender roles. Just as maple sugar production was new to Europeans, dairying and bread making were new to Indians. But although sugar making was passed from Indian women to Métis women, transmission of these Euro-American skills in Creole society was more problematic, owing to the gendered nature of work. In all of this region's cultures, some jobs and skills were sex-typed whereas others were nongendered. For example, interpreting could be done by men or women, whereas hunting was considered by all to be men's work.[18] Creoles encountered differences in cultural perceptions about the types of work women ought to do, and they had to find compromises. Disputes regarding women's production were often solved by hiring others to do certain kinds of work or by purchasing commodities women did not wish to make.

Creoles kept cattle for meat, but other uses for these animals raise interesting issues concerning gender roles in these multicultural, multiracial communities. In European and Euro-American communities, people also used cows for dairying. In Euro-American communities in eastern North America, milking and butter making were usually considered women's work, although men cared for the animals. Native Americans, however, had no such traditions, since they had not kept livestock. In fact, historian Rebecca Kugel has found that, to the northwest, in present-day Minnesota, some Ojibwes were wary of cattle because they believed them to have spiritual power, which could become malevolent.[19]

Some Indian and Métis women resisted taking up dairying, as did some white and Métis men. The wife of trader Julien Dubuque, appearing only in the written records as "Madame," was said to be Mesquakie. She seems to have avoided learning these skills: when her husband died in 1810, although there were seven cows on their farm, no butter churn or other dairying equipment was listed on his estate inventory.[20]

Several documents demonstrate that some dairying was done during the early nineteenth century in Green Bay and Prairie du Chien. Besides an 1811 letter that mentions a "milkhouse" on land that had belonged to a U.S. agent at Prairie du Chien, legal papers dated 1805 refer to Jacob Franks's "seven milch cows" on his farms at Green Bay.[21] Did Franks's wife, Thérèse LaRose, a Métisse, milk these cows? If so, where did she learn how? If not, who did milk them?

Learning sometimes took place outside the region. Some Métis daughters of traders went to Mackinac, Montreal, Saint Louis, or other towns to be educated at boarding schools. Elizabeth Baird's mother, Marianne Lasaliere Fisher, ran such a school for teenagers at Mackinac, where "the girls were taught to read, write, and to sew. . . . In addition, they were taught general housekeeping." That could have included some dairying, as there was a "maid who milked" at that home. Some other Métis daughters spent time with Euro-American aunts and other family members who lived elsewhere. Girls who brought Euro-American domestic skills into Green Bay or Prairie du Chien were soon wives and mothers, who taught daughters, nieces, and cousins the skills they had learned. Even so, their application of the lessons was bound to be selective: some were ignored, others altered or embellished. For this reason, perhaps, butter continued to be imported into the 1820s.[22]

Elizabeth Baird's memoir reveals some of the difficulties her family encountered as they tried to negotiate dairying. Whether it was because of her Indian ancestry or personal taste, Elizabeth hated dairying. She wrote, "All who know of my great dislike of milk, especially cream, may imagine what I suffered in taking care of milk and making butter." Henry and other family members, however, liked and wanted dairy products, but Elizabeth apparently resisted milking. At first, rather than importing butter and dispensing with milk as other families apparently did, they tried to hire others to do the dairying. She and Henry hired a "man servant" from Montreal to chop wood, bring in water, take care of the horse and cow, and milk the cow. "The latter," she recalled, "he considered almost a disgrace."[23] She also remembered: "My husband was an Irishman and of course never milked a cow. His mother in after years used to say 'a gentleman from Dublin never did.'" If the manservant disliked milking because he considered it women's work, Henry resisted because he considered it inappropriate to both his class and gender. When their servants quit several years later, Elizabeth had to milk, which shocked Henry's mother, who apparently thought this inappropriate labor for a "lady." A combination of inherited ideas about the gender- and class-appropriateness of dairying seems to have made everyone in the Baird household try to avoid milking the cows, including Elizabeth, who felt that such work was not rightly part of her wifely duties.[24]

Ultimately, Elizabeth got her wish. A few days after the servants quit and left her to milk, she was kicked and injured by an apparently malevolent cow, so her husband "declared that I never should milk again, and *I never did.*" Did she consciously or unconsciously provoke the cow? We cannot know. Fortunately, occasional work could sometimes be arranged with Creole women from the local community; one might hire a neighbor to help out for a few days. Thus, the Bairds again turned to hired labor to resolve their gender-role conflicts and engaged a Madame LaRose, who came across the river in her canoe twice a day, her baby strapped in a cradleboard, to milk the five cows until more permanent servants could be found.[25] The negotiations got Henry his dairy products and Elizabeth her freedom from responsibility for them.

The butter at issue in the dairying disputes would be spread on the basic Euro-American staple, bread, which many Indians loved as well. The unique feature of wheat bread was the leavening, usually yeast. Although Indians made a type of unleavened corn bread, wheat bread was introduced into the region by Europeans, for whom bread baking was often housewives' work. But if husbands wanted wheat bread, that could be a problem for Native and Métis wives, whose mothers generally had not passed along these skills. At Prairie du Chien the problem of bread baking was effectively solved when Michel Brisbois, a prominent trader and farmer, set up a bakery. He traded bread tickets worth fifty loaves of bread for each one hundred pounds of flour, and the tickets became a kind of circulating medium "to buy trifles of the Indians with."[26] Again, gender-role conflicts were solved by buying the product rather than expecting women to produce it.

At Green Bay there were fewer ways to negotiate, and, somehow, people learned to bake bread. Residents ground locally grown wheat with two-person hand mills to make flour until the first horse mills were set up in 1809. An Ojibwe wife of an interpreter made bread in a bake kettle at a fireplace.[27] Elizabeth Baird's experiences as a fourteen-year-old bride learning to make bread—a food she liked much more than milk or butter—suggest one way the skill was transmitted.

As a third-generation Métisse, Elizabeth had eaten plenty of bread in her short life growing up in Mackinac, but she had never learned how to make it. There, as at Prairie du Chien, people bought bread from bakeries, so she had never seen it made. Her first biscuits were "heavy," and her crumpets—"laid in a dry pan and baked by an open fire"—were "a little more palatable." Fortunately, "we were young and healthy, nothing hurt us, and we did not become the victims of dyspepsia, as one might imagine." At last, a neighbor befriended her: "Good old Mrs. Irwin . . . gave me my first instruction in bread-making, telling me the secret of light bread and giving me a cup of yeast to experiment with." Elizabeth was not completely satisfied with the results, but she kept trying and one day invited Mrs. Irwin's husband for dinner. She recalled: "I cannot now tell what we had for dinner, but I do know we had *bread*, which lies heavy upon me yet in memory. However, our new friend assured me that he liked just such bread, an assertion which put an end to my apologies, that were made in such broken English, that they were not soon forgotten, being a great source of amusement in after years."[28]

Although there were virtually no white women in these Creole communities before the War of 1812, Creole men wanted Euro-American women's products. Some Native and Métis women learned to milk cows, make butter, and bake bread, whereas others resisted. Compromises between European-descended men and Native-descended women sometimes included either buying bread and butter rather than producing them at home, or hiring others to produce them. The scattered resistance suggests that it was more difficult to negotiate domestic production across culture and gender lines than it was to adapt Native women's production, such as sugar making, to Creole society.

Farming also required compromise, and in this case the solutions that Creoles worked out were influenced by gender, race, and class. Negotiation across cultures was difficult enough when one taught skills to—or organized an activity with—people for whom the type of production was new. But Creoles also confronted conflicting gender roles in their fields and gardens, and their actions were complicated by the ambivalence that many of them seem to have felt toward farming.

Indigenous people of the Midwest considered farming to be women's work, and the Winnebago, Sauk, and Mesquakie women were apparently quite successful at it. For example, during the 1760s, Jonathan Carver recorded, the women at Lake Winnebago raised "a great quantity of Indian corn, beans, pumpkins, squash, and water melons." They planted beans among the corn, letting the cornstalks support the winding vines, and, because they used no tools more complicated than a hoe, they had no need for draft animals. The Sauk women's production was substantial enough to make the "Great Town of the Saukies" famous as "the best market for traders to furnish themselves with provisions of any within eight hundred miles of it." From 1805 into the 1820s, Sauk and Mesquakie women at the Turkey River and around Rock Island raised thousands of bushels of corn annually, cultivated more than three hundred acres, and raised "sufficient corn to supply all the permanent and transient inhabitants of the Prairie des Chiens," according to another observer.[29]

With this degree of agricultural success, it is little wonder, then, that Sauk and Mesquakie men were not the least bit interested in learning what U.S. government agents termed "the advantages of employing the plough, harrow, etc." In fact, Indian men showed their contempt for the efforts of agricultural agent William Ewing in 1806 by shooting his draft animals full of arrows.[30] They rejected not just the adoption of new tools but a complete change of gender roles that would have meant adopting Euro-American systems of property relations and concentration of wealth while completely reorienting a worldview that linked women, land, and reproduction.

In spite of European and Euro-American traditions in which farm wives kept a "kitchen garden," missionaries and government policy makers could not imagine Indian agriculture as successful so long as women and not men were in charge of it. They clung to their own gendered ideas about farming even when these ideas were not particularly effective.

With the exception of Indian women, most Creoles seem to have had mixed feelings about the actual farming work. Indian women living in the Creole towns did farm there, and, as mentioned earlier, Indian women from neighboring villages provided produce to Creoles wishing to buy it. Métis women were often wives in middling or elite families who hired help whenever possible and, like other Creoles, bought food from Indians living nearby. Métis men had as uncles and grandfathers Indian men who scorned the idea of men's farming, and they had as fathers white and Métis traders who had selected their occupations based on personal preference.

For example, John W. Johnson, who ran a U.S. government trading post at Bellevue on the Mississippi River, wrote to his superior in 1809 that, although he wanted "to improve the mind of the Indians particular in so valueable a point as agriculture" and had apparently been asked to take charge of a demonstration farm at the garrison, he felt that the twelfth of April was too late in the season "to Commence for the present year," since he had neither "hands" nor a "team." If Tapassia, Johnson's Sauk and Mesquakie wife, read the letter, she must have laughed.[31] While her kinswomen were preparing their fields nearby, Euro-American men's reliance on the supposedly superior white agricultural methods meant that grain could not be grown without draft animals or hired men.

Did Tapassia teach John Native agricultural methods or, perhaps, did she set up her own garden? Did he eventually teach her to use a plow? What were the work arrangements in bicultural, multiracial marriages in which traditional gender roles denominated each partner the proper farmer?

Unfortunately, the evidence for this couple and for others like them is scanty. John doubtless knew of Ewing's humiliation three years earlier and preferred simply to trade peacefully at Bellevue without enduring the additional hard work of farming and possible ridicule of his Indian customers and in-laws. But after moving to Prairie du Chien seven years later, John apparently did have some input with regard to planting, since he wrote to a friend in 1816 asking for some garden seed and commented, "I have an ellegant situation for a garden."[32]

Most farming was for home consumption before 1816. By one account, Green Bay families of that era had on average only two or three acres under cultivation. Before the War of 1812, most husbands were, at best, part-time farmers; some might have agreed with Missouri Métis men, who, Tanis Thorne argues, "firmly held the idea that agriculture was the work of slaves and women."[33] How did they organize the farm work?

The elite families owned a number of farms, which were farmed by tenant families, the men of which worked for the elites as voyageurs and laborers. Since these men were often called away in their capacities as boatmen or other fur-trade workers during the growing season, their wives did a substantial amount of the farm work. Morgan L. Martin, who moved to Green Bay in 1827, wrote, "All these enclosures of men more or less employed as laborers by the traders, were cultivated by their women, whom they called *wives*, but really Indian women with whom they lived after the Indian custom."[34]

A few records of mixed couples in which the wives were Métis do exist. Like middling and elite couples elsewhere, these couples hired others to do the farm work whenever possible, but sometimes family members had to work together. Henry and Elizabeth Baird hired men to do their farm work; when all the hired help quit, owing to the meddling of Henry's parents, Elizabeth and her father-in-law had to take care of the vegetable gardening (Henry was too busy with his law practice). But Elizabeth's mother-in-law, a city woman, "could not see how a lady could put her hands into the dirty ground." In addition, Elizabeth wrote: "My husband always planned a flower garden which I was expected to attend. I tried to do so but my cares were too great." She resisted enough to get some help, she remembered: "Yet we did have a flower garden for I planted the seeds and father Baird would help me in weeding."[35]

Another couple, the Gagniers, lived near Prairie du Chien in 1827 and had a slightly different approach. The wife, Teresa, was French and Sioux, and the husband, Regis, was French and African. They had as a boarder an elderly "discharged American soldier by the name of Solomon Lipcap," according to an early resident who knew them. Apparently, their white Anglo boarder helped with the cultivating, as he was reportedly "at work hoeing in the garden near the house" when they were all attacked by Indians during the Winnebago Revolt of 1827.[36]

Creoles created accommodation within families, neighborhoods, and towns. They adapted Native assimilation customs by intermarrying but forming their own communities. Native-descended women mediated between Euro-American immigrants and indigenous people, as eventually did their husbands and children. By teaching, learning, and adapting languages and lifeways, they created syncretism on a personal level. Gender relations were clearly at the center of this process.

Gender roles were an area of potential conflict for Creoles, who responded in a variety of ways. Some Indian wives took charge of the farming; some couples in mixed marriages counted on tenant families, boarders, or hired workers to cultivate their land or milk their cows. Some, like the Dubuques, dispensed with dairying altogether. Some bought bread and butter with furs and other products—even maple sugar. The spirit of creative accommodation took a variety of forms. If Indian wives' farm work differed from Métis women's, the Native women were probably less interested in dairying or raising poultry, and their husbands were probably less active cultivators. Conversely, Métis wives seemingly incorporated more Euro-American domestic activities into their routines, such as laundry and butter and bread making, which gave them less time to cultivate their land.

Native-descended women shaped these towns in economic as well as social ways. The economies of Creole communities did not exactly mirror Euro-American patterns, and fur-trade families did not confine their activities solely to securing pelts in exchange for dry goods. Women as well as men determined what would be produced, and how.

Long-term accommodation like that in the Creole towns could have prevailed at the lead mines, but it did not. After the 1820s—a decade of Indian-Anglo coexistence at the mines during which conflict became endemic—the Indians were forced out. A number of factors contributed to this outcome, but unsuccessful gender relations were central to the discord.

Clear similarities existed between the fur-trade economy and lead production. As in the fur trade, mining meant extracting the region's natural resources for export. At first, also like the fur trade, indigenous workers gathered the product to be exported by white traders. Lead mining was a part of the Indians' seasonal economy in this region, as was hunting for fur-bearing animals. The sex ratio among immigrants who participated in the mining economy was unbalanced, only slightly less so than among fur-trade immigrants. And yet, in spite of these similarities and in spite of a few exceptional instances of intermarriage, cooperation, and integration, Indians and Euro-Americans could not find common ground in the mining district.

Native Americans had dug lead (also known as "galena") in the upper Mississippi Valley for at least four thousand years, had traded it as far away as the present states of Ohio, Mississippi, Georgia, and the province of Ontario, and had used it to make ornaments and sparkling paint. Generally this was a midsummer activity that took place while young men were away on the summer hunt. During the seventeenth century, the French learned about the upper Mississippi Valley lead mines and apparently taught Indians to smelt ore and to make molds for crafting objects out of melted lead.[37]

The French colonial presence increased both Native and French demand for lead in several ways. First, to the south in the Illinois country, French traders accepted lead along with furs in exchange for trade goods beginning in the seventeenth century. Second, one of the most important items traded to the Indians was the gun, valued because the technology both enhanced men's ability to hunt and increased their military prowess. Although Indians depended on Europeans for gunpowder, they could make their own musket balls with lead, so Native demand for galena increased with Indian men's participation in the fur trade during the eighteenth century. Furthermore, both international wars and local intertribal conflicts stepped up demand. Sauks, Mesquakies, and Winnebagos traded the lead within their own communities, to members of other tribes, and to Euro-American traders.[38]

During the late eighteenth century, Indians increased their lead mining, thereby diversifying their economies and reducing their dependence on furs as commodities to be sold for trade goods. Anticipating the interest of the U.S. government and individual Anglophone miners, they tried to forestall Euro-American encroachment on the mining lands by keeping all whites out of the mining area except a few traders who became kin through marriage to Indian women. These men also traded for furs, and their wives were traditional mediators.[39]

One such wife was the Sauk-Mesquakie woman Mawwaiquoi, who married Samuel C. Muir, a Scottish lead trader and physician. After their marriage, Muir resigned his position as a surgeon with the U.S. Army. By 1820 they had a post on an island opposite the Mesquakie village at present-day Dubuque, Iowa, where Indian women could sell the lead they dug. Later, Muir and Mawwaiquoi moved to Puck-e-she-tuk at present-day Keokuk, Iowa, and then to the mining center at Galena. They had five children. Galena's early history records that Muir treated Mawwaiquoi "with marked respect." "She always presided at his table, and was respected by all who knew her, but never abandoned her native dress."[40]

From 1788 to 1832 a few wives like Mawwaiquoi and husbands like Samuel

Muir linked the Sauk, Mesquakie, and Winnebago lead miners to markets in Saint Louis, Prairie du Chien, and elsewhere. As long as Euro-American men like Muir were more interested in trading than mining lead, the Indians continued to specialize as producers, maintaining an active role and the ability to control the region and its trade. Indian women were central to mining and consequently to the diversity of production it represented.

Early-nineteenth-century observers uniformly described the principal Indian lead miners as female, although children or elderly men might help out. For example, in 1818 a traveler passed by the Mesquakie lead mines near the Mississippi River and remarked, "The women dig the ore, carry it to the river where they have furnaces, and smelt it." The strongly sex-typed nature of this work is clear from another traveler's observation that "the warriors and young men, hold themselves above it." A white miner recalled: "When the Indians mined, . . . there were often fifty or a hundred boys and squaws at work, on one vein. They would dig down a square hole, covering the entire width of the mine leaving one side not perpendicular, but at an angle of about forty-five degrees, then the deer skin sacks attached to a bark rope, they would haul out along the inclining side of the shaft, the rock and ore."[41] The Indians' tools also included pickaxes, hoes, shovels, crowbars (some of them made out of old gun barrels), and baskets. Eventually they also bought tin pails to replace the homemade containers. They broke up mineral deposits by heating the rocks with fire and then dashing cold water on them.[42]

In 1822 the U.S. government sent troops to force the Indians to allow Anglophone miners to dig there. The first group included James Johnson and eight of his male workers, four black and four white. At least some of these blacks were probably slaves. About four dozen other Anglos came in that year.[43]

From 1822 through the Black Hawk War of 1832, the mineral region east of the Mississippi experienced a full-fledged lead rush. About four thousand whites and one hundred blacks arrived in the region seeking wealth and adventure, founding towns such as Galena, Mineral Point, Hardscrabble, and New Diggings and spreading out in twos and threes across the rolling countryside.[44]

For a few years the Indians, blacks, and whites lived and mined as neighbors, but by 1827 accommodation began to fall apart. The U.S. federal government supported and protected the Anglophone miners in exchange for 10 percent of the lead they produced, but it implemented policies that tolerated and encouraged lawlessness and trespass on Indians' rights and resources. During the course of this decade the self-styled Americans seized the lead mines and the exploitation process from the Sauk, Mesquakie, and Winnebago people. The Winnebago Revolt of 1827 and the Black Hawk War were, in part, protests against this seizure.

But at the beginning of Euro-American involvement in the mining district, conflict was not foreordained. For a few years in the early 1820s, Indians, blacks, and whites lived and worked in the area of Fever River (later called Galena River) in relative peace. In August 1823 between five hundred and two thousand Indians tolerated their neighbors, seventy-four whites and blacks. Anglo mining techniques differed from Indian: the men sank shafts, placed windlasses across the openings to control buckets for the lead and workers, and used explosives to break up large concentrations of the mineral. One observer found the contrast entertaining: "The Indian women proved themselves to be the best as well as the shrewdest miners. While Col. Johnson's men were sinking their holes or shafts, in some instances the squaws would drift under them and take out all the mineral or ore they could find. When the men got down into the drift made by the women, the latter would have a hearty laugh at the white men's expense."[45] Some of these early miners described the community for a writer in the 1870s, a half-century later. They remembered that around 1823 there were perhaps eight log cabins in the immediate vicinity of "the Point"—later called the town of Galena—"but the river bottoms, ravines and hillsides were thickly dotted with the wigwams of the Sacs and Foxes, who . . . were engaged in hunting and fishing, and supplied the whites with a large portion of their meats, consisting of venison, game, fish, etc. The squaws and old men, too old to hunt, raised the most of the mineral which supplied the furnaces." Indian and white boys fished and prospected together.[46] Native economic practices continued apace, while the newcomers proved to be customers for Indian hunters. For a few years, Indians and whites were able to mine side-by-side, yielding accommodation. The small number of Anglos during this early period probably contributed to tolerance on both sides.

A settlement at Gratiot's Grove seemed to promise that accommodation was possible at the mines. The small Creole community, founded by the Gratiot brothers and their families, was central to the rapid acceleration of the lead rush in 1826. The impetus for this sudden expansion of mining began when Winnebago miners discovered a particularly rich prospect about fifteen miles northeast of Galena in 1825 or 1826. At the same time, Henry and John Gratiot of Saint Louis decided to seek opportunities in a free state because they opposed slavery; they arrived in the mining region in 1825 and were joined by their families in 1826.

The Gratiots were in some ways typically Creole. The brothers were American-born men of French ancestry, and they spoke French in addition to English. Women in the Gratiot family connected them to established midwestern Creole communities: their mother was a member of the powerful Chouteau fur-trade family of Saint Louis, a connection the Indians acknowledged when they respectfully dubbed Henry "Chouteau"; Henry's wife, Susan Hempstead Gratiot, had kin at Prairie du Chien. No doubt through the Chouteau fur-trade empire they had many other connections there. Clearly, they knew well the French Creole culture with which the region's Indians had become familiar.[47]

Another woman, an interpreter named Catherine Myott, brought the Gratiots and the Winnebagos together. Myott was a Winnebago Métisse and an important woman in several communities. Her father, Nicholas Boilvin, was the U.S. Indian agent at Prairie du Chien until his death in 1827. She was between thirty and forty years old, according to the 1830 census, with a daughter between five and ten years old. A skilled linguist, she spoke Winnebago and French and possibly English as well; Winnebago leaders had great respect for her.[48]

Interpreters who could speak Winnebago and English were rare in the region, and this created problems for Anglophone immigrants. Winnebago, a Siouan language, is unrelated to Algonquian languages of the region such as Sauk, Mesquakie, Ojibwe, and Ottawa, so it was difficult for people who spoke Algonquian tongues to pick up. Boilvin's successor as agent at Prairie du Chien, Joseph Street, who spoke only English, was extremely frustrated by this problem.[49]

With the help of Catherine Myott, the Gratiots negotiated for rights to mine and live in the region, paying three hundred dollars in trade goods and provisions. No one recorded what promises the Gratiot brothers made to the Winnebagos, but the agreement probably stated that the Gratiots would accept Winnebago lead, furs, and other products in trade for the high-quality merchandise Indians knew their Chouteau family connections commanded. In addition, the Winnebagos likely realized that, with Anglo miners flocking to the area throughout the summer of 1826, it would be impossible to keep whites completely out and so decided to accept the elite French Creole Gratiots in the hope that the Gratiots would be able to maintain peaceful relations there. Susan Hempstead Gratiot's kin ties at Prairie du Chien, where Catherine Myott also had relatives, were probably an important consideration from the Winnebago point of view, since Prairie du Chien residents had proven themselves to be tolerable neighbors. In 1831, Henry Gratiot's appointment as U.S. Indian subagent to the Winnebagos formalized existing relations between them and the Creoles.[50]

After 1826 a multilingual community grew up around Gratiot's Grove, including perhaps twenty Francophone families (both Creole and Swiss) and Anglos such as Esau and Sally Johnson. (The Swiss were refugees from the Selkirk colony of Canada's Red River.) Residents included a few sons of Prairie du Chien families, including the Heberts, who had Mesquakie kin; the Gagniers, who had Dakota kin; and the St. Cyrs, who had Winnebago relatives and were stepcousins of Catherine Myott.[51] Gratiot's Grove was not ethnically typical—in terms of the demographics of the whole lead-mining region, Francophones and foreign-born immigrants represented only a very small minority of lead rushers—but the settlement gave whites a foothold in the Winnebago mineral area.

News of the wealth of the lead deposits around Gratiot's Grove did stimulate migration markedly by 1827. According to one estimate, the mining region's white and black population increased from two hundred in 1825, to one thousand in 1826, to four thousand by 1827. No more than 3 percent of these were African Americans. Some blacks in the region were slaves, although the legality of slavery was repeatedly challenged in the new courts, and Indian slavery was being phased out gradually.[52]

In what was a typical prologue to Native assimilation, many Indians made special efforts to observe and befriend blacks and whites, monitoring their activities as they established relationships. For example, James Beckwourth, one of the African American men working for James Johnson as a hunter and miner, later recalled being befriended by the Indians, who showed him "their choicest hunting-grounds" and often accompanied him. Beckwourth remarked that this increased his "knowledge of the Indian character," and, no doubt, the relationships were equally educational for his Native companions.[53]

Another relationship arose when Old Buck—a Mesquakie leader whose band had for years worked the famous mines called the "Buck Lead"—made friends with a Yankee smelter named Horatio Newhall, who wrote to his brother in 1828 that the Mesquakie leader had camped the previous winter near his Sinsinawa River furnace. "Himself and sons often visit me in town.

. . . I have been at his lodge twice." Old Buck took the next logical step by trying to arrange a marriage between his daughter and Newhall, but Newhall refused.[54]

Such associations helped the Indians to understand the immigrants and to observe and police men like Newhall and Beckwourth. By the late 1820s, Native American men spent more and more of their time and energy policing the region, trying to control the lead rushers.[55]

In spite of intruding Anglophone miners, Indians continued to mine for lead through the 1820s. Mesquakies mined at and around the old Mines of Spain west of the Mississippi (from which whites were excluded until 1832) and around the Fever River until the mid-1820s. Winnebagos, and to a lesser extent the Sauks, mined between the Rock and Wisconsin rivers, east of the Mississippi. They sold lead to merchants and smelters like Muir, Newhall, and the Gratiots and also to other Indians.[56]

Women continued through this period to be the principal Indian miners. Young and middle-aged Indian men might prospect, smelt, and guard the mines, but exposure to Anglophone views that digging ore was men's work did not alter Indian men's convictions that mining was for women and their assistants, the elderly and children. Native mining techniques continued to differ from whites', indicating that Indians and Anglos did not mine together. Sometimes Indians prospected for whites, but beyond that Indians and whites did not cooperate in mining. Indian men, for their part, showed little interest in playing more than auxiliary roles even in Native mining.[57]

That Indian and white miners did not incorporate each other's mining techniques underscores the extent to which each worked independently from people of the other race. Not only did Indians and Anglos fail to cooperate in lead mining, but after 1826 they also failed to achieve peaceful relations, integration, or toleration. Instead, relations between Indians and Anglos became increasingly hostile. Anglo miners invaded even areas the U.S. government acknowledged belonged to the Indians, destroyed their cornfields, and killed and scared away the game. Blood was spilled during the Winnebago Revolt of 1827 and the Black Hawk War of 1832. Both of these conflicts expressed Indian resistance to Anglo immigration and incursions on Indian land, and both resulted in more Indian land cessions.[58]

This outcome was not, however, inevitable. Even once the U.S. government had made clear that it would back whites' mining efforts in the region, accommodation was possible. Gratiot's Grove serves as an example of what might have been much more pervasive. There mining operations resembled Creole sugar production: both Indians and whites dug lead, just as Indians and Creoles both made maple sugar. Whites bought minerals from Indians and whites, just as Creole traders bought sugar from both. Indians kept some of both their sugar and their lead for their own use and to trade with other Indians. In both Gratiot's Grove and the fur-trade towns, kinship linked residents to the local Indians and their friends; communication was possible by way of bilingual residents. Although there is no evidence the Gratiots married Native women, they employed Catherine Myott to mediate with their Winnebago neighbors and took pains to be on friendly terms with them. Other Métis people also were residents. Not surprisingly, relations at Gratiot's Grove were apparently much more peaceful than elsewhere at the mines.

By contrast, Anglos at the mines did not make the connections that could have permitted negotiation leading to peaceful coexistence or even cultural syncretism. When Indians tried to assimilate them, they resisted. Their economic organization, abusive behavior, and traditional gender relations isolated them.

One reason that Anglos and Indians were more often in conflict than accord at the mines after the mid-1820s was that they generally had no relationships other than those of neighbor. If they had been co-workers they might have developed lasting patterns of cooperation, but they did not work together. Indian women were not among the wage workers or slaves mining for white bosses such as James Johnson—owing, no doubt, to disinterest on the women's part and to sex-typed notions of mining on the part of the small number of mining entrepreneurs—so they were not co-workers. Indian men clearly had no interest in digging for ore under any circumstances, because they considered it women's work.

In addition, most Anglo miners were self-employed and in no position to recruit employees. U.S. government policy makers aimed for a system of exploiting the mines that would be egalitarian—that is, open to men of all social ranks. In fact, Lieutenant Martin Thomas, superintendent of the U.S. lead mines, with his resident agents and the approval of the secretary of war, constructed a system that they hoped would discourage speculators and favor individual miners. Rather than selling the mineral lands outright, the government established the leasing system, so that men with little or no capital could profit alongside the elites.[59] The leasing system made land titles unavailable, discouraging the permanent settlement that might have encouraged marriage.

Although Creoles negotiated gender roles, Anglo and Indian lead miners did not. One might suppose that a husband-wife mining team composed of an Indian wife and a white or black husband could have been extremely productive, but if this ever occurred there is no record of it. For that matter, white and black women apparently never mined. Sally Johnson, Esau's wife, for example, provided domestic support but did not dig. Anglophone men did not think that wives should dig lead. Gender roles with regard to mining were at least as rigid for whites as for Indians.

In addition to the fact that Anglo lead rushers and Indians were not co-workers, accommodation was hampered by their having no language in common. The Indians spoke their own languages, of course: Winnebago (a Siouan language) or Sauk/Mesquakie (Algonquian dialects). Some of them also spoke French and Ojibwe, the latter being the lingua franca of the region up to this point. But most of the immigrants who came to dig lead spoke little besides English.

One exception was Horatio Newhall, the Yankee smelter and physician who was befriended by his neighbor Old Buck. In 1827, Newhall wrote to his brother: "I have made me a Dictionary of the most common words in their language so that by the help of this I can understand them tolerably well."[60] Old Buck recognized the potential for mediation, but when Newhall declined to marry Old Buck's daughter, he missed an opportunity to form a lasting alliance. Yet Newhall was only adhering to his culture's marriage customs of monogamy, endogamy, and strong distaste for divorce.

For others, marriage could have bridged the language barrier, as Elizabeth and Henry Baird learned. Mawwaiquoi and Samuel Muir were among only a handful of biracial couples at the mines; it seems that only the earliest Anglo men in the lead region married Native women, and they were traders rather than miners. Like Newhall, few lead rushers planned to stay in the region for very long; most expected to make some money and return home in a season or a few years. In addition, many of them harbored prejudices against the "heathen" and "savage" indigenous people.[61] Both of these factors—impermanence and intolerance—tended to deter marriages with local women, who preferred to stay and no doubt resented the racism.

Native women in the lead-mining region did not leave records of their impressions of the Anglo men. Initially, they might have viewed men who mined lead as effeminate and therefore not likely husbands. Records left by others, however, indicate that male miners' relations with Indian women during the 1820s were increasingly exploitative and violent, treatment that Indian men protested vehemently.

The immigrants used and abused Indian women sexually. For example, about 1823 mining boss Moses Meeker recalled, "Indians . . . offer[ed] lewd women to the whites for whisky, which too many of the young men accepted to their sorrow." A few years later, Winnebago leaders complained to their Indian agent that "some of the white people are insulting to the Indians and take liberties with their women." In 1827, after a drinking party Anglo boatmen had sponsored, several Winnebago women were abducted and taken aboard a boat ascending the Mississippi to supply Fort Snelling, provoking an attack by Winnebago men on the boat as it descended the river.[62]

Many Anglo miners also exhibited patterns of misogynistic violence. It was also in 1827 that a white miner in Galena knocked down a Menominee woman and stamped on her head, killing her. White and black men in the mining area also abducted, enslaved, and beat black women and girls on occasion, and a few white wives found themselves abused and abandoned by husbands who became alcoholics and gambling addicts.[63] It is little wonder, then, that many Indian women avoided contact with the Anglophone miners.

Who were these immigrants, and why did they think and act in these ways? Of the adult lead rushers, 97 percent were white and 77 percent male in 1830 (although they perceived 95 percent of their population to be male). They were generally restless young people of all social ranks participating in a cultural rite, the customary wandering that young Anglo men performed during their late teens and twenties before settling down and forming families. Some of them sought wealth, some were just adventurous, others were seeking both excitement and fortune. Going to the lead mines was only one of several journeys many of the young men had undertaken; others included visiting friends and relatives on different parts of the frontiers, working as a farmhand, seeing the sights of such cities as Cincinnati or Saint Louis, riding a flatboat to New Orleans, serving in the army, even engaging as a clerk to a Missouri River fur trader. The women were generally adventurous sisters and wives, and a few were servants.[64]

For many of these young men, going to Fever River, as the lead district was generally called, also meant escaping from parental and social control and from the conventions and comforts of life with women. Slightly more than half of the households in the lead-mining region in 1830 consisted of young men only. They called this way of living "keeping Bachelor's Hall," and it meant a man could leave his dirty clothes wherever he wanted, drink and gamble to his heart's content, and do whatever he wanted on the Sabbath. When they wearied of keeping Bachelor's Hall, these men waxed sentimental about womanhood.[65] But in the meantime, they sometimes beat, raped, killed, kidnapped, and abandoned the women in the region. They also fought and killed each other. Although they might sometimes have fantasies about beautiful young Indian women, keeping Bachelor's Hall by definition excluded females. That might explain why they perceived the region's sex ratio to be even more skewed than the census takers reported. Under other circumstances and later in life, many if not most of these men would be restrained, law-abiding citizens, but during the 1820s too many of them were rude, brash, violent, and racist as they sought to dominate others. Their experience at the mines was strongly gendered.

For every Horatio Newhall or Henry and Susan Gratiot who made friends with an Indian or Métis neighbor and tried to find links of communication and negotiation, dozens of other lead rushers made no connections. Part of their difficulty was the incompatibility of their gender-role expectations with Native patterns. Their vision of the possible did not include women—particularly women of color—in roles of mediation, certain commodity production, teaching across cultures, or interpreting; neither did they consider intermarriage an option. Their patterns of dominating and exploiting women were too strong to be replaced by the mutuality of negotiation and compromise.

In both the Creole towns and the mining district, social relations were characterized by domination and subordination on the one hand and mutuality on the other. The patterns of these relations differed markedly, however. Creole communities were socially, politically, and economically stratified societies in which a few elite families exercised considerable control over the middling and poorer sort and the small number of slaves. Paradoxically, gender, intercultural, and race relations were characterized by negotiation and compromise indicative of mutuality if not equality.

By contrast, during the lead rush of the 1820s, Anglo men too often tended to dominate and exploit women rather than seek compromise. In addition, they resisted mutuality in race relations, ultimately seeking to conquer and displace the indigenous people. However, egalitarian ideals for intragroup relations created a society that had a few weak elites, a few slaves, and a mass of uncontrolled equals seeking to assert themselves over others, especially women and Indian men. Of course, Indians and non-Native women often objected, resisted, and withdrew from negotiation. Ironically, those who tended toward mediation rather than confrontation, such as Horatio Newhall and the Gratiots, were the lead rush district's weak elites.

Accommodation required personal relationships: communication, teaching, learning, cultural understanding, compromise, and commitment. Creole communities could incorporate Indians, whites, and Métis people and could coexist peacefully with nearby Indians not only because they depended on one another economically but also because the former included kin and friends of the latter. In centers where cultures combined, people worked out compromises in negotiations that were frequently gendered. Usually, women were central to accommodation, and when it broke down, both gender roles and gender relations explain important elements of its failure.

The Creole mining community at Gratiot's Grove demonstrates that accommodation might have succeeded at the mines. There, sincere effort, kin ties, and mediation brought people together. Catherine Myott linked the Gratiots and their local lead rushers to the Winnebago residents, as her mother had linked the Indians to her father, Indian agent Nicolas Boilvin, in a country marriage. Characteristic of Anglo unwillingness to recognize Native-descended women's powerful roles as mediators, Boilvin's successor Joseph Street blasted the custom of country marriages between agents or traders and local women. The monolingual Street, who apparently did not try to enlist Catherine Myott's aid, was unable to find an English-Winnebago interpreter. He declared that it was "almost impossible to hold a council with the" Winnebagos and had to try communicating by speaking English to his interpreter, who rendered the speech into Mesquakie or Ojibwe. These words were then translated into Winnebago by a bilingual Winnebago. "Much, tho, is entirely lost on both sides," he found. Street never saw the connection between his rejection of women as mediators and his frustration with trying to understand the Indians. Not surprisingly, the Winnebagos seemed to prefer Henry Gratiot, to Street's chagrin.[66]

The Anglo miners were forerunners and representatives of the expanding United States. They were also people who failed to reach accommodation with Indians; a look at Native and Anglo mining demonstrates how gendered the experience of their failure was. They could neither specialize nor cooperate to reach accommodation with the indigenous people, for reasons that had a good deal to do with Indian women's experiences, with gender relations between groups, and with conflicting gender roles. Gender certainly cannot explain all aspects of human relations on this frontier, but it can illuminate a great deal.

Mawwaiquoi and Samuel Muir and their children moved back to Puck-e-she-tuk from Galena around the time of the Black Hawk War. We may wonder whether their move was motivated by growing racism at the mines. According to an early history of the region, Muir died in the cholera epidemic of 1832 soon after the family moved, leaving "his property in such condition that it was wasted in vexatious litigation." Mawwaiquoi was "left penniless and friendless, became discouraged, and, with her children . . . returned to her people on the Upper Missouri."[67] Clearly, the region had become inhospitable to some women and children of color.

Although the Anglos of the lead-mining region failed to develop a society in which Indians had a role, the multicultural Creole communities persisted. Although Anglos, to a greater extent in Green Bay and a lesser extent in Prairie du Chien, swelled the population, came to dominate in business and politics, and imposed the use of English as the court language, the Creole people and culture continued to play an important, if poorly recognized, role in Wisconsin. Elizabeth Baird, like thousands of other holdovers from the Creole frontier, lived out her life in the American Republic that had taken over her homeland.

Some Indians found ways to triumph over the government policies of removal. Officially relocated after 1827 to a series of reservations in Iowa, Minnesota, North Dakota, and Nebraska, hundreds of Winnebagos quietly resisted and returned to Wisconsin. Following the Black Hawk War, the Sauk and Mesquakie people were forced west of the Mississippi, confined to Iowa, and later moved to Kansas. During the early 1850s, however, a group of about one hundred Mesquakies, fed up with Kansas, returned to Iowa, bought land, and established a community at Tama, which is still in existence. By 1869 another two hundred had joined them.[68] In a sense, a degree of accommodation was restored with the return of these Indians.

After Henry and Susan Gratiot died, their daughter kept in touch with many Winnebagos, according to her husband. "For many years after [her] marriage . . . and up to 1860, many of the surviving members of the tribe would come almost annually to visit her at her home in Galena. . . . Bringing their blankets with them, they would sometimes remain for several days, sleeping on the floor of her parlors."[69] Even in the midst of the mining district, where accommodation lost out during the 1820s, remnants of the personal relationships that persisted in nearby Creole communities could occasionally, briefly, be found.

Appendix

In approximately 1824, Thomas Forsyth, U.S. Indian agent to the Sauk and Mesquakie ("Fox") Indians, wrote two copies of the following "List of the Sac and Fox half breeds." The version here follows the one he kept for himself in his own notebook. The version he submitted to the government did not include the names of the Indian wives in the last column, but included only the names of the children's fathers and the tribal affiliation of the mothers. Thus, the Indian women were erased in the official record, and the patriarchal family concept of Euro-American society would have appeared to U.S. officials to have been replicated in these mixed families. We must take care not to assume that these families were patriarchal. Forsyth submitted a similar report in 1830. Names were sometimes spelled differently in different documents.

Thomas Forsyth Papers, Lyman Draper Manuscripts, microfilm, 2T, pp. 21–23, State Historical Society of Wisconsin, Madison.

Table 4. A List of the Sac and Fox half breeds, who claim land according to the Treaty made at Washington City with the Chiefs Sac and Fox Tribes on 4th August 1824, which children are supposed to be now living and aged as follows.

No	Names	Age	Residence	Remarks
1	Elizabeth	43	Prairie du Chien	Children of
2	Marguerite	41	do[1]	Pierre Antailla
3	Maria	37	do	and
4	Theoditte	32	do	Pokoussee
5	Euphrosine	30	do	a Fox
6	Isaac	28	do	woman
7	Isidore	26	do	
8	Chroystome	22	do	
9	Marie Louise	16	Prairie du Chien	Children, Augustus
10	Frances	12	do	Hebert & Fox Woman
11	Margaret	10	do	Cheenaeipaukie
12	Pierre Jaundron	15	Prairie du Chien	Son to Pierre Jaundron & Kayawiscoquoi Fox woman
13	Lisette	36	Prairie du Chien	Bazil Giard & Macoutchequoi Fox Woman
14	Mary	28	do	

No	Names	Age	Residence	Remarks
15	Victoire	49	Portage des	Nicholas Blondeau
16	Maurice	45	Sioux	& Keepaikeoa
17	Angelique	42	"	Fox Woman
18	Frances	39	Cahokia	
19	Amelie	9	Portage des	Maurice Blondeau
20	Catherine	9	Sioux	& Peeavie, Sac & Fox
21	Elizabeth		Maremeck	Louis Honoré & Qusewatatche[2]
22	Francois	49	Prairie des Moins	Francis Monbreau & Mautcha, Sack
23	Elizabeth	12	St. Charles Convent	George Hunt & Pasoquey, Sac & Fox
24	Eliza	13	St. Louis	John W. Johnson by
25	Mary	11	Female Academy	Tapassia, Sac &
26	Rosella	8	Florissant	Fox Woman
27	Louisa		Galena	Doctor S. C. Muir
28	James		"	by
29	Jane		"	Mawwayquoi, a Sack & Fox woman
30	Thomas		Rock River with Indians	John Connolly by Checom is quoa, Sack
31	1 child		Florrissant	James Campbell by Peweni, Sac & Fox
32	1 child		Rock River	Nadeau by Paupaugee, Sac & Fox
33 & 34	2 children		State of Missouri	Louis Gonniville, sister to Braspiqui, Sack
35	Amilia	18	Cahokia	Joseph Gonniville,
36	Laurent	12		a Sack half Breed and
37	Jean	9		Francis Blondeau
38	Maurice	6		Fox half Breed
39	Betsy		Fever River	Amos Farrar & Black Thunder, a Fox woman
40 41 42 43	4 children		Portage & Prairie du Chien	St. Johns, by Masackque, Sack woman
44	Baptiste[3]	25	Rock River	His father unknown, mothers name is To she sa quoi, Sack

No	Names	Age	Residence	Remarks
45	Antoine	19	St. Louis	Pierre Courville by a half breed woman, making him quarter breed, and many others are on this list

¹This is an abbreviation for "ditto"

²This woman's name was left off the 1824 list but included in Forsyth's 1830 list

³In 1830, Forsyth listed this man as Baptiste Bousie

Elizabeth Thérèse Fisher Baird's memoirs were serialized in the Green Bay State Gazette *between December 4, 1886, and November 19, 1887. A member of an important fur-trade family, Baird was born at Prairie du Chien, Wisconsin, in 1810, and raised at Mackinac Island by her mother and maternal relatives. Her ancestors were Ottawa, Chippewa (or Ojibwe), Scottish, and French. At age fourteen she married Henry Baird, a young Scots-Irish lawyer, and the couple moved to Green Bay. Although English was her fourth language, after Odawa, Ojibwe, and French, she crafted her memoir in English. It offers a rare glimpse of frontier life from the point of view of an elite, Native-descended woman.*

Elizabeth T. Baird, "O-De-Jit-Wa-Win-Wing, Contes du Temps Passe," Wisconsin Historical Society Library, Henry and Elizabeth Baird Papers, box 4, folder 9, State Historical Society of Wisconsin.

No. V

A visit to the sugar camp was a great treat to the young folks as well as to the old. In the days I write of sugar was a very scarce article. Loaf sugar and muscovada were all *some* markets afforded, not ours. But maple sugar was largely manufactured in the northwest and all in this region became accustomed to the flavor and many preferred it to the other sugar. All who were able possessed a sugar camp. My grand-mother had a sugar camp on Bois Blanc Island, about five miles east of Mackinac.

About the first of March nearly half of the inhabitants of our town, as well as many from the garrison, would move to Bois Blanc to prepare for the work. Would that I could describe the lovely spot! Our camp was delightfully situated in the midst of a forest of maple, or a maple grove.

One thousand or more trees claimed our care, and three men and two women were employed to do the work. . . .

NOW FOR THE WORK:

All the utensils used in making sugar were made of that daintiest of material, birch-bark. The *casseaux* to set at the tree to catch the sap was a birch-bark dish, holding from one to two gallons. The pails for carrying the sap were of the same material and held from three to four gallons of sap. The men placed a *gauje* or yoke on their shoulders, then a bucket would be suspended on each side. The women seldom used this yoke, but assisted the men in carrying the buckets, doing so in the usual manner. . . .

MAPLE SYRUP AND SUGAR

By this time the sap must be boiling. It takes over twenty-four hours to make the sap into syrup and the boiling of the sap is usually begun in the morning. The fire is kept bright all day and all night. Two women were detailed to watch the kettles closely, for when the sap boils down nearly to syrup, it is liable to boil over at any moment. The women therefore stand by with a branch of hemlock in hand and as soon [as] the liquid threatens to boil over they dip the branch in quickly and it being cool, the syrup is settled for awhile, when at this stage it requires closest watching. When the sap has boiled down about one-half, the women have to transfer contents of one kettle to another as the kettles must be kept full for fear of scorching the top of the kettle, which would spoil all. . . .

MAKING THE SUGAR

. . . For the sugar cakes, a board of bass-wood about five or six inches wide, with moulds set in, in form of bears, diamonds, crosses, rabbits, turtles, spheres, etc. When the sugar was cooked to a certain degree it was poured into these moulds. For the granulated sugar, the stirring is continued for a longer time; this being done with a long paddle which looks like a mush stick. This sugar had to be put into the mocock while warm as it would not pack well if cold. This work was especially difficult; only a little could be made at a time, and it was always done under my grandmother's immediate supervision. . . .

No. XXVI

Our farm life began under a series of difficulties. We had to move into our new home before the house was finished as we had sold our Shantytown home to the Sisters or nuns. . . .

I have already spoken of the cholera and Indian scare. When all fear had subsided, my good Margaret Bourassa [a hired domestic worker] was married, which left me with a young, good-natured girl, but one who knew nothing of housework.

FARM LIFE

We had two men who attended to the plowing and planting, taking care of the horses and pigs and milking five cows. The girl took care of the chickens.

Here I found myself entire mistress of the farm, with these hired persons besides my three children, my husband and myself to care for. I was, however, young and not easily discouraged. I worked hard, and who did not in those days? . . .

Had my husband been a farmer and not a lawyer, comforts would have been added sooner to our home. But his law business had to be attended to, which only gave him part of a day at home, sometimes not that. Mechanics were scarce so he could not employ one for any length of time, which made it tedious to get things fixed to our liking. We did try to get a little settled as we were expecting Mr. Baird's father and mother, who were coming to make their home with us.

They came in August. It was hard, indeed, to offer such a home to any city lady. Mr. Baird's mother felt the change greatly but his father was satisfied anywhere there was a garden.

We, of course, had a large garden laid out and my husband always planned a flower garden which I was expected to attend. I tried to do so but my cares were too great. Yet we did have a flower garden for I planted the seeds and father Baird would help me in weeding. He was a very industrious man, but Mother Baird "could not see how a lady could put her hands into the dirty ground."

My husband having to be away nearly all day, his father quite assumed the mastership of the whole premises, although not so requested as we had two faithful men who understood their business well and my husband trusted his whole work to them. One was an old man by the name of Crowle, who did not wish to be meddled with; the other was a young man who did not like the interference any better. The men entered their complaints to my husband about his father and the maid entered hers to me about the mother. Both my husband and myself tried our best to point out things as they were to the old folks, but it was of no use. One day when the men came to dinner they announced their intention of leaving directly after dinner, saying they would not work for us as long as there was a second master on the place. They announced their intention of going down to see Mr. Baird. Then my girl said she was going, also. She said I could not get a girl who would work for me as long as I was not mistress of my house. So they all left. . . . What was I to do? There were five cows to milk, besides all of the rest of the work to do! I had but two children at home and their grandmother offered to take care of them. But as she ruled children with a rod of iron they were not willing to stay with her. This annoyed her very much. She said to her son that she always got along with children until she met with these French children, who would have nothing to do with her. Our children spoke both French and English, always speaking French to each other and, of course, to me.

There was nothing for me to do when I was thus left by our servants but to go and milk the cows, which again shocked the old lady. We lived in this manner about one week, when to our great joy our good Mr. Charles Mette arrived from Mackinac, whom Mr. Baird had engaged to take care of the farm.

Mr. Mette brought a young servant girl for me from Mackinac, named Betsey. She was an Indian girl. . . .

But before I conclude the history of the hard work of the farm before Mr. Mette came, I must tell of

A GREAT COMMOTION

that occurred one day. In the morning I went early to milk, and as it was a sultry day the horse flies were tormenting the cows so greatly that I could scarcely do anything with them. I came to one who would not stand still, but at last I finally quieted her and began to milk when she kicked me so as to throw me against a large box which was in the barnyard. My head struck this box and I fainted. It so happened a boy was passing at the time and he gave the alarm. My husband was terribly frightened not knowing how great an injury I had received. He declared that I never should milk again, and *I never did.*

Mother Baird had to get the breakfast that morning.

My husband galloped off after a doctor and our old friend, Dr. Ward, soon returned with him. I knew before my husband left that I was not much hurt but they could not believe me as I did not present a very healthy appearance.

We were fortunate enough at this time to get Madame LaRose to assist us. She lived on the west side of the river, opposite our home. She came in a dug-out or wooden canoe, at both morning and evening to milk the cows and at appointed times she would stay and do any hard work, such as scrubbing the kitchen and scouring the tin pans. She would bring her baby, tied in its cradle or board.

All who know of my great dislike of milk, especially cream, may imagine what I suffered in taking care of milk and making butter. That great antipathy to milk and cream has never left me, although I have learned to eat butter.

The following excerpt describes maple sugar production in the early nineteenth century. Readers will note the casual reference to "Indian retainers" working for fur-trade families, and the identification of Métis young women as "French."

Albert G. Ellis, "Fifty-four Years' Recollections of Men and Events in Wisconsin," State Historical Society of Wisconsin Collections 7 (1876): 220–22.

The Easter festival was the most joyous of the calendar; with most of them it was celebrated in the deep forests, where they had before repaired, for one of their chief industries, the making of maple sugar; which requires a little more special notice. It was a source of the greatest amusement, as well as profit, occupying two or three months of every year, and engaged nearly the whole population, male and female, children and all. They probably got the art from the Indians, and greatly improved on the savage mode. About the first to the fifteenth of February, preparations were made throughout the settlement for repairing to the *sucrerie*, or sugar-bush—for moving from their home cabins on the river bank, into the deep wood, often many miles distant; taking generally most of their household treasures, even to their chickens; and they made the business worthy of their preparations. Some of them had as many as five hundred, eight hundred, and some one thousand sugar trees tapped. A few of their sugar-houses were quite large, and as good as those at the river, well furnished with buckets, store troughs, kettles, etc. The ground was neatly cleared of underbush [*sic*], and roads made to every part of it. The first business of the season, after arriving at the *sucrerie*, was to provide a good store of fuel for purposes of boiling; next to overhaul and repair the buckets, which had been carefully stored in the sugar-house the spring before. These buckets were made from the birch bark—nothing else would suffice. This bark, it may be added, is taken from the tree by the Indians in June, and made an object of merchandise, like peltries, by the traders. These various preparations would consume perhaps a month before the commencement of the sap-running season.

The product of those *sucreries* of the better class of the French, was a fair article of sugar, of ready sale, and in some respects preferable to the best muscovado. They had learned to use the utmost neatness and caution to keep out all impurities, and had attained to great perfection in the purifying process. All the sap was strained through a fine sieve into the kettles—the syrup was strained twice before granulating; and here came in the product of the chickens, to-wit, the eggs, the whites of which were broken in the boiling syrup, when all impurities immediately came to the surface and were removed. The sugar, when strained off and cooled, was quite fair and pure. Some of the more interprising and fore-handed, bought syrup and coarse sugar of their Indian retainers, and their less able neighbors, and went into the purifying process on a large scale, and thus largely increased their product for the season. A few families of this class had a preference in the sugar market at the frontier trading posts, their mococks, branded with their names, always being first sought, at advanced prices.

As before stated, the Easter festival was generally observed at those *sucre-ries*; for this reason those who had the chickens, and could do it, took them into the woods, made houses for them, and saved a store of eggs for this festival. Then it was that their friends at the settlement, the Americans and army officers, were invited to visit them, and the invitations were rarely declined. The American citizens, the gentlemen and ladies of the army, found no greater enjoyment than one of these spring festivals, celebrated among their French and half-breed entertainers in the depth of the great maple woods, in their commodious sugar-houses. There was never-failing good cheer, somewhat enlarged, perhaps, by their visitors in a picnic style; which was followed with strains of the merry violin and the dance, and at length the guests retired with pleasing, vivid recollections of the Easter festival among the French, at the *sucreries*. These frolics were often enlivened by an old fashioned "candy-pull," when the French girls presented their sweet-hearts, on parting, with a cake of candy, folded in a strip of birch bark, which they called their "billet doux."

The following memoir discusses the lead-mining region. The stereotypical "squaw drudge" is evident, as is the use of the word "squaw," yet there is useful information here.

Moses Meeker, "Early History of Lead Region of Wisconsin," State Historical Society of Wisconsin Collections *6 (1872): 271–72, 280–82.*

After much delay, I commence to write, at the request of the Historical Society, the early history of the Lead Mining Region of Wisconsin, which will necessarily embrace much of my own history, having been connected with almost all the early transactions in this section of the country.

In the spring of 1822, when residing in Cincinnati, and engaged in the manufacture of white lead, it became necessary for me to visit St. Louis, to purchase a stock of pig lead. On arriving there, I learned that Col. James Johnson, of Kentucky, was fitting out an expedition to work the lead mines on Fever River, on the east side of the Mississippi. . . .

About this time there appeared an advertisement in the papers, that the President proposed to lease to individuals one-half of a section of land on the Upper Mississippi lead mines. . . . [So he went to the mining region, where Sauk and Mesquakie Indians had lead mines.]

. . . In the month of August [1823], I had the census taken; there were seventy-four persons, men, women and children, white and black; my company numbering forty-three of them. Col. Johnson had four black men with him, one of whom was James P. Beckwourth, afterwards a mountaineer of notoriety.

There were about five hundred Indians; their women quite industrious miners, but the men would not work. They would form an inclined plane where they went deep. I saw one place where they dug forty-five feet deep. Their manner of doing it was by drawing the mineral dirt and rock in what they called a *mocock*, a kind of basket made of birch bark, or dry hide of buckskin, to which they attached a rope made of rawhide. Their tools were a hoe made for the Indian trade, an axe, and a crowbar, made of an old gun barrel flattened at the breach, which they used for removing the rock. Their mode of blasting was rather tedious, to be sure; they got dry wood, kindled a fire along the rock as far as they wished to break it. After getting the rock hot, they poured cold water upon it which so cracked it that they could pry it up. At the old Buck Lead, they had removed many hundred tons of rock in that manner, and had raised many thousand pounds of mineral or lead ore.

The Buck Lead was discovered by an Indian who was called by that name, about one and a half miles from Galena, and had been worked by Old Buck and his wife, and such of his friends as he chose to invite to join him, for some fifteen years, as I was informed by the Indian traders. . . .

Col. J. Johnson purchased the right of working the Buck and Cave leads of the Indians in 1822; and the following year, the Indians were at work at different places on the same range. The Indian women proved themselves to be the best as well as the shrewdest miners. While Col. Johnson's men were sinking their holes or shafts, in some instances the squaws would drift under them and take out all the mineral or ore they could find. When the men got down into the drift made by the women, the latter would have a hearty laugh at the white men's expense.

In the following excerpt, Esau Johnson recalled an event on July 4, 1828, when he and a friend were searching for lost cattle.

Esau Johnson Papers, Group C, pp. 1, 2, State Historical Society of Wisconsin, Branch, Wisconsin Room, Karrmann Library, University of Wisconsin, Platteville.

We followed the Indian trail about a Southwest course across the Ridge down into the head of a valley that went to Old Spotted Arms Village a Winnebago Chief There the Indians had Corn growing and a trail going Southeast from there. We followed that trail till we came to what is called the Shoogar River diggings There was a parsel of Indians digging I went to one hole that certainly was forty feet deep Two Indians Were there on

top and two Squaws down in the hole diggings digging The Indians had
small tin pails with ropes to them The Idinds [Indians] let the pails down
the Squaws filled them the Indians then halled them up by hand by raising
them up catching hand under hand till they raised it up then went & emp-
tyed it returned and let it down again to be filled so they kept at work while
I stayed They certainly had over one hundred thousand lbs I then went to
their camps ... They had fiftytwo Furnices in blast making lead They were
along a spring Brook where the Bank was four or five foot high There they
had dug holes that were round into the Bank ...

*Horatio Newhall to Isaac Newhall, March 1, 1828. Horatio Newhall Papers,
microfilm, Illinois State Historical Library, Springfield*

> Galena. Fever River. Ill.
> March 1st 1828
> Dear Brother
> I rec'd your letter of 18th Dec. a few weeks since. We have had
> but two mails this winter ...
>   The "Old Buck" The Fox chief, who discovered, the famous
> "Buck Lead" the largest body of mineral ever found on Fever
> River, & which Col. Johnson worked out while he was at these
> mines in 1820-1 has been encamped all winter within a mile
> of my furnace. —Himself & sons often visit me in town. And
> I have made me a dictionary of the most common words in
> their language, so that by the help of this I can understand them
> tolerably well.—I have been at his lodge twice.—He wants me
> to marry his daughter, Because, he says, I am a great man. He is
> the chief of his Band. Has at his lodge the American flag. & the
> Musick of his Band. That is to say a keg with head of Deer Skin.
> Rattles &c. &c. Together with the Tomahawk, war clubs &c &c
> which are the public property of the Band.& which they use in
> their war dances, scalp dances &c &c.
>   Remember me to all enquiring friends & believe me to be
>   *Yours truly,*
>   *Horatio Newhall*
>   Isaac Newhall Esq.
>   Merchant
>   Salem
>   Massachusetts

Notes

I would like to thank Allan Kulikoff, Rebecca Kugel, Neal Salisbury, and Christine Heyrman for their helpful comments on an earlier draft of this essay.

1. Lucy Eldersveld Murphy, *A Gathering of Rivers: Indians, Métis, and Mining in the Western Great Lakes, 1737–1832* (Lincoln: University of Nebraska Press, 2000).

2. Henry S. Baird to Elizabeth T. Fisher, March 20, 1824, Henry and Elizabeth Baird Papers, box 1, folder 1, State Historical Society of Wisconsin, Madison [hereafter SHSW]. Probably Elizabeth had the note read and translated for her by a family member.

3. Elizabeth T. Baird, "O-De-Jit-Wa-Win-Wing; Comptes du Temps Passe," Baird Papers, box 4, folder 9, SHSW.

4. Joseph M. Street to Secretary of War, November 15, 1827, Indian Office Miscellaneous Files, 1826–1827, Pension Building, SHSW.

5. I use the term "Creoles" to refer to people who lived in communities such as Prairie du Chien and Green Bay that had a culture neither purely European nor Native American but had elements of both. These people included Frenchmen, Indian women, their mixed-race children, and sundry others. "Métis" refers to people of mixed European and Native American ancestry. "Anglophones" and "Anglos" refer to English-speakers. In the context of the lead-mining region, it should be understood that these people had immigrated from the United States. I use these labels, with some reservations, in preference to the term "Americans," which can be misleading.

6. Sixty wives and mothers were identified from 1817 Prairie du Chien church records with other sources. Eleven were Dakota, five Mesquakie, two Ojibwe, and one each Pawnee, Sauk, Menominee, and Winnebago. Twenty-two were Métis, two were French-African, and one was known to be French. The ethnicity of the other thirteen was not ascertained. See James L. Hansen, "Prairie du Chien's Earliest Church Records, 1817," *Minnesota Genealogical Journal* 4 (1985): 329–42. Additional information about ethnicity was provided by James H. Lockwood, "Early Times and Events in Wisconsin," SHSW *Collections* 2 (1856): 125–26; and M. M. Hoffmann, *Antique Dubuque, 1673–1833* (Dubuque IA, 1930), 51–59. Nearly all male householders, however, had at least some French ancestry. Only three English names were among twenty-nine householders at Prairie du Chien before 1785. Even among seventy-two adult male residents who lived there about 1820 whose names could be identified, only eleven had English names; all the others, except a Mandan freedman, had French names. See Hansen, "Prairie du Chien's Earliest Church Records"; U.S. Congress, *American State Papers: Documents, Legislative and Executive, of the Congress of the United States . . .* , 38 vols. (Washington DC, 1832–61), Class 8, *Public Lands*, 8 vols., ed. Walter Lowrie et al., 5:47–98, 270–72, 283–328 [hereafter cited as *American State Papers, Public Lands*].

7. Sylvia Van Kirk, *Many Tender Ties: Women in Fur-Trade Society, 1670–1870* (Norman OK, 1980); Jennifer S. H. Brown, *Strangers in Blood: Fur Trade Company Fami-*

lies in Indian Country (Vancouver, 1980); Jacqueline Louise Peterson, "The People in Between: Indian-White Marriage and the Genesis of a Métis Society and Culture in the Great Lakes Region, 1680–1830" (Ph.D. diss., University of Illinois at Chicago Circle, 1981); Tanis Chapman Thorne, "People of the River: Mixed-Blood Families on the Lower Missouri" (Ph.D. diss., University of California, Los Angeles, 1987); Bruce M. White, "Gender and Trade in the Lake Superior Region in the Eighteenth Century," paper presented at the conference "Crucibles of Cultures: North American Frontiers, 1750–1820," sponsored by the Institute of Early American History and Culture, The Historic New Orleans Collection, and the Newberry Library, November 18, 1994, New Orleans; Nancy Oestreich Lurie, ed., *Mountain Wolf Woman, Sister of Crashing Thunder: The Autobiography of a Winnebago Indian* (Ann Arbor, 1961).

 8. Clara Sue Kidwell, "Indian Women as Cultural Mediators," *Ethnohistory* 39 (1992): 97–107; Lucy Eldersveld Murphy, "Autonomy and the Economic Roles of Indian Women of the Fox-Wisconsin River Region, 1763–1832," in *Negotiators of Change: Historical Perspectives on Native American Women*, ed. Nancy Shoemaker (New York, 1995), 72–89.

 9. For a more thorough discussion of the social order of Creole towns, see Lucy Eldersveld Murphy, "Economy, Race, and Gender along the Fox-Wisconsin and Rock Riverways, 1737–1832" (Ph.D. diss., Northern Illinois University, 1995), chap. 3. Population figures are difficult to estimate because the towns swelled so much during summer months with fur-trade workers, who wintered in Indian hunting regions but summered in town, and hundreds of Indians, who came to town to trade in fall and spring on their journeys from and to their summer villages. However, Jacqueline Peterson estimated the Prairie du Chien population at 370 in 1807 and about 600 in 1816, and the Green Bay population at 533 in 1796 and 900 in 1816. Probably several hundred more could be added during the busy seasons. See Peterson, "People in Between," 133, 136.

10. Donald Jackson, ed., *Black Hawk: An Autobiography* (1955; reprint, Urbana IL, 1990), 89–95; H. A. Schuette et al., "Maple Sugar: A Bibliography of Early Records," Wisconsin Academy of Sciences, Arts, and Letters, *Transactions* 29 (Madison, 1935): 209–36; Schuette et al., "Maple Sugar: A Bibliography of Early Records, II," *Transactions* 38 (1946): 89–184. For those wishing to study maple sugaring in early America, this extensive bibliography, which quotes relevant sections from primary sources, is a good starting place.

11. Margaret Holman and Kathryn C. Egan, "Maple Sugaring," *Michigan History* 74 (March–April 1990): 30–35; Milo Milton Quaife, ed., *Alexander Henry's Travels and Adventures in the Years 1760–1776* (Chicago, 1921), 69–70, 143–44; Thomas Ridout, "An Account of My Capture by the Shawanese Indians," *Western Pennsylvania Historical Magazine* 12 (1929): 18; Frances Densmore, "Uses of Plants by the Chippewa Indians," *Forty-fourth Annual Report of the Bureau of American Ethnology* (Washington DC, 1928), 308–13.

12. Gary A. Wright, "Some Aspects of Early and Mid-Seventeenth Century Exchange Networks in the Western Great Lakes," *Michigan Archaeologist* 13 (1967): 181–97; Thomas Forsyth Papers, Lyman Draper Manuscripts, microfilm, 3T:63, SHSW; Mary Maples Dunn to the author, June 29, 1993. At this time, the Native American population of the region was around twelve thousand. See Helen Hornbeck Tanner, ed., *Atlas of Great Lakes Indian History* (Norman OK, 1987), 139–411. For an example of fur traders' correspondence, see John Lawe to [——], April 25, 1824, Green Bay and Prairie du Chien Papers, microfilm, reel 1, 10152, SHSW.

13. Ebenezer Childs, "Recollections of Wisconsin since 1820," SHSW *Collections* 4 (1857–58): 161; Albert G. Ellis, "Fifty-Four Years' Recollections of Men and Events in Wisconsin," SHSW *Collections* 7 (1876): 220; Baird, "O-De-Jit-Wa-Win-Wing," chap. 5; Schuette et al., "Maple Sugar" (1946), 134.

14. Baird, "O-De-Jit-Wa-Win-Wing," chap. 5; Jacques Porlier to J. Jacques Porlier, March 11, 1815, Green Bay and Prairie du Chien Papers, reel 1; Ellis, "Recollections," 221.

15. Ellis, "Recollections," 221; Baird, "O-De-Jit-Wa-Win-Wing," chap. 5.

16. Ellis, "Recollections," 222; Jacques Porlier to J. Jacques Porlier, March 11, 1815, Green Bay and Prairie du Chien Papers, reel 1; "Life at La Baye" exhibit, Heritage Hill State Park, Green Bay, Wisconsin.

17. The term "sex-typing" is used to refer to gendered concepts of work in Julie A. Matthaei, *An Economic History of Women in America: Women's Work, the Sexual Division of Labor, and the Development of Capitalism* (New York, 1982), 187–97.

18. There was at least one woman hunter in this area, however: an Ojibwe woman named O-cha-own, who lived alone not far from Green Bay during the late eighteenth century. See Augustin Grignon, "Seventy-two Years' Recollections of Wisconsin," SHSW *Collections* 3 (1857): 259.

19. Joan M. Jensen, *Loosening the Bonds: Mid-Atlantic Farm Women, 1750–1850* (New Haven CN, 1986), 93; Rebecca Kugel, "Of Missionaries and Their Cattle: Ojibwa Perceptions of a Missionary as Evil Shaman," *Ethnohistory* 41 (1994): 227–44.

20. Julien Dubuque Estate Inventory, June 11, 1810, Chouteau Maffitt Collection, Missouri Historical Society, Saint Louis.

21. Nicholas Boilvin to William Eustis, March 5, 1811, Prairie du Chien Papers, Nicholas Boilvin Letters, SHSW; Agreement, Jacob Franks and John Lawe, Lawe Collection, item 2151, July 3, 1805, box 1, folder 1, Chicago Historical Society.

22. Baird, "O-De-Jit-Wa-Win-Wing," chaps. 3, 11; American Fur Company Account Book, 120, 186, 187, 191, Chicago Historical Society.

23. Neither would he do housework "that was considered degrading." See Baird, "O-De-Jit-Wa-Win-Wing," chap. 13.

24. Baird, "O-De-Jit-Wa-Win-Wing," chaps. 11, 26.

25. Baird, "O-De-Jit-Wa-Win-Wing," chaps. 25, 26. (Madame LaRose might have been the estranged wife of Jacob Franks, owner of the "milch cows.")

26. One Yankee woman who moved into the area in 1830 claimed that a common greeting of Indians to whites at that time was "I have no bread." See [Juliette M. Kinzie],

Wau-Bun; The "Early Day" in the North-West (1856), ed. Nina Baym (Urbana IL, 1992), 92; Lockwood, "Early Times," 125.

27. Grignon, "Recollections," 254; William Arundell, "Indian History," *Miners' Journal* (Galena), October 30, 1830, typescript, Archives, file 1809, SHSW; Lockwood, "Early Times," 120; John Shaw, "Personal Narrative of Col. John Shaw, of Marquette County, Wisconsin," SHSW *Collections* 2 (1855): 229–30; Thomas Anderson, "Personal Narrative of Capt. Thomas G. Anderson, 1800-28," SHSW *Collections* 9 (1892): 149.

28. Baird, "O-De-Jit-Wa-Win-Wing," chap. 12.

29. Norman Gelb, ed., *Jonathan Carver's Travels through America, 1766–1768* (New York, 1993), 71–72. Both Carver and Peter Pond commented on the "great quantities" and "Grate Crops" raised by the Sauk women during the 1760s and 1770s. See Charles M. Gates, ed., *Five Fur Traders of the Northwest* (Saint Paul MN, 1965), 41; P[ierre] de Charlevoix, *Journal of Voyage to North-America*, 2 vols. (London, 1761), 2:121; Gelb, *Carver's Travels*, 74 (quotation); Elliott Coues, ed., *The Expeditions of Zebulon Montgomery Pike*, 3 vols. (New York, 1895), 1:294; Major Morrell Marston to Rev. Jedidiah Morse, November 1820, in Emma Helen Blair, ed., *The Indian Tribes of the Upper Mississippi Valley and Region of the Great Lakes*, vol. 2 (Cleveland, 1912), 151; Lockwood, "Early Times," 112.

30. Marston to Morse, in Blair, *Indian Tribes of the Upper Mississippi Valley*, 2:179–80; Donald Jackson, "William Ewing, Agricultural Agent to the Indians," *Agricultural History* 31 (April 1957): 4–7.

31. John W. Johnson to William Clark, April 12, 1809, Clark Papers, Missouri Historical Society. The land had previously been tilled. If Tapassia was like most other full-blood Indians of this time, of course, she would have been illiterate. See Forsyth Papers, Draper MSS, 2T:22a. It is unclear when they married, but they had the first of three children in 1811.

32. Johnson to Theodore Hunt, July 6, 1816, Lucas Collection, Missouri Historical Society. Johnson wrote that he had inherited a garden when he moved, leading us to assume that he could have saved seed for the following year, but perhaps he wanted a greater variety. One wonders if Tapassia asked her friends and relatives for seed too.

33. Ellis, "Recollections," 218; Grignon, "Recollections," 254; Thorne, "People of the River," 199.

34. *American State Papers, Public Lands*, 5:47–98, 270–72, 283–328; "Lawe and Grignon Papers, 1794–1821," SHSW *Collections* 10 (1888): 139–40.

35. Other such couples include the Rolettes and the Lawes. See Baird, "O-De-Jit-Wa-Win-Wing," chaps. 14, 18, 26; Jeanne Kay, "John Lawe, Green Bay Trader," *Wisconsin Magazine of History* 64 (1980): 2–27.

36. Lockwood, "Early Times," 161.

37. Ronald M. Farquhar and Ian R. Fletcher, "The Provenience of Galena from Archaic/Woodland Sites in Northeastern North America: Lead Isotope Evidence," *American Antiquity* 49 (1984): 774–85; John A. Walthall et al., "Galena Analysis and

Poverty Point Trade," *Midcontinental Journal of Archaeology* 7 (1982): 133–48; John A. Walthall, Stephen H. Stow, and Marvin J. Karson, "Ohio Hopewell Trade: Galena Procurement and Exchange," in *Hopewell Archaeology: The Chillicothe Conference*, ed. David S. Brose and N'omi Greber (Kent OH, 1979), 247–50; John A. Walthall, *Galena and Aboriginal Trade in Eastern North America* (Springfield IL, 1981), 20. Other useful sources on Native mining include Janet Doris Spector, "Winnebago Indians, 1634–1829: An Archeological and Ethnohistorical Investigation" (Ph.D. diss., University of Wisconsin, Madison, 1974); Karl J. Reinhard and A. Mohamad Ghazi, "Evaluation of Lead Concentrations in Eighteenth-Century Omaha Indian Skeletons Using ICP-Ms," *American Journal of Physical Anthropology* 89 (1992): 183–95; Reuben Gold Thwaites, ed., "Narrative of Spoon Decorah," SHSW *Collections* 13 (1895): 458–59; Kristin Hedman, "Skeletal Remains from a Historic Sauk Village (11RI81), Rock Island County, Illinois," in Thomas E. Emerson, Andrew C. Fortier, and Dale L. McElrath, eds., *Highways to the Past: Essays on Illinois Archaeology in Honor of Charles J. Bareis, Illinois Archaeology* 5 (1993): 537–48.

38. Phillip Millhouse, "A Chronological History of Indian Lead Mining in the Upper Mississippi Valley from 1643 to 1840," 1–5, Collections of the Galena Public Library, Galena, Ill.; Jeanne Kay, "The Land of La Baye: The Ecological Impact of the Green Bay Fur Trade, 1634–1836" (Ph.D. diss., University of Wisconsin, Madison, 1977), 175–76; Thwaites, "Narrative of Spoon Decorah," 458; Jackson, ed., *Black Hawk*, 92.

39. Murphy, "Economy, Race, and Gender," chap. 4; Thomas Auge, "The Life and Times of Julien Dubuque," *Palimpsest* 57 (1976): 2–13; William E. Wilkie, *Dubuque on the Mississippi, 1788–1988* (Dubuque IA, 1987).

40. Thomas Forsyth, "A List of the Names of the Half-Breeds, Belonging to the Sauk and Fox Indians, Who Claim Land according to the Treaty Made at Washington City, on the 4th August 1824 . . . ," Forsyth Papers, Draper MSS, 2T:23; Isaac R. Campbell, "Recollections of the Early Settlement of Lee County," *Annals of Iowa*, 1st ser., 5 (1867): 889–90; Henry Rowe Schoolcraft, *Travels through the Northwestern Regions of the United States* (1821; reprint, Ann Arbor, 1966), 344-45; Sac-Fox Half-breeds, Thomas Forsyth, 1830, vol. 32, *Records of the Superintendent of Indian Affairs, St. Louis*, 11, 15, Kansas State Historical Society, Topeka; quote from *History of Jo Daviess County, Illinois* (Chicago, 1878), 234–35.

41. Edward Tanner, "Wisconsin in 1818," SHSW *Collections* 8 (1879): 288; Schoolcraft, *Travels*, 344–45; Lucius H. Langworthy, "Dubuque: Its History, Mines, Indian Legends, Etc.," *Iowa Journal of History and Politics* 8 (1910): 376.

42. Schoolcraft, *Travels*, 343–44; Moses Meeker, "Early History of the Lead Region of Wisconsin," SHSW *Collections* 6 (1872): 281; Reminiscences of Esau Johnson, Group C, 1–3, Esau Johnson Papers, State Historical Society of Wisconsin, Branch, Wisconsin Room, Karrmann Library, University of Wisconsin, Platteville.

43. Joseph Schafer, *The Wisconsin Lead Region* (Madison, 1932), chaps. 3, 4; Reuben Gold Thwaites, "Notes on Early Lead Mining," SHSW *Collections* 13 (1895): 271–92; Meeker, "Early History," 271–96; *History of Jo Daviess County*, 226–57.

44. U.S. Census Office, *Fifth Census; or, Enumeration of the Inhabitants of the United States, 1830* . . . (Washington DC, 1832), Michigan Territory, Iowa County, and State of Illinois, Jo Daviess County; Consolidated Returns of Mineral and Lead Manufactured, 1827–1829, Historical Collections of the Galena Public Library.

45. *History of Jo Daviess County*, 243; Meeker, "Early History," 280–81, 282; Thwaites, "Notes on Early Lead Mining," 271–92; Henry R[owe] Schoolcraft, *A View of the Lead Mines of Missouri* . . . (New York, 1819), 90-106.

46. *History of Jo Daviess County*, 243.

47. [Marie G. Dieter], *The Story of Mineral Point, 1827-1941* (1941; reprint, Mineral Point WI, 1979), 17–18; Elihu B. Washburne, "Col. Henry Gratiot—A Pioneer of Wisconsin," SHSW *Collections* 10 (1888): 244–45; George Davenport to O. N. Bostwick, January 29, 1826, Chouteau-Papin Collection, Missouri Historical Society.

48. Washburne, "Col. Henry Gratiot," 235–45; Hansen, "Prairie du Chien's Earliest Church Records," 330; Elizabeth Taft Harlan, Minnie Dubbs Millbrook, and Elizabeth Case Erwin, eds., *1830 Federal Census: Territory of Michigan* (Detroit, 1961), 244; Henry Dearborn to Nicolas Boilvin, April 10, 1806, SHSW *Collections* 19 (1910): 314–15; Ellen M. Whitney, ed., *The Black Hawk War, 1831–1832*, 2 vols. (Springfield IL, 1973), 2:324 n. 5, White Crow speeches, April 28, June 3, 1832, 2:321, 507, 509. However, she didn't speak Sauk (2:319 n. 1); Adèle Gratiot, "Mrs. Adèle P. Gratiot's Narrative," SHSW *Collections* 10 (1888): 267.

49. Joseph Street to James Barbour, January 8, 1828, Joseph Street, "An Estimate of Expenses," September 1, 1828, Letters Received by the Office of Indian Affairs, microcopy 234, reel 696, National Archives, Washington DC.

50. Thomas Forsyth to William Clark, August 15, 1826, Forsyth Papers, Draper MSS, 4T:259; Gratiot, "Gratiot's Narrative," 267; Washburne, "Col. Henry Gratiot," 253; Whitney, *Black Hawk War*, 2:36 n. 4, 77 n. 1.

51. Caleb Atwater, *Remarks Made on a Tour to Prairie du Chien; Thence to Washington City in 1829* (Columbus OH, 1831), 190; Alvin M. Josephy, *The Artist Was a Young Man: The Life Story of Peter Rindisbacher* (Fort Worth, 1970), 47–55; Harlan, Millbrook, and Erwin, *1830 Federal Census*, 109; Hansen, "Prairie du Chien's Earliest Church Records," 330.

52. [Dieter], *Story of Mineral Point*, 17–18; R. W. Chandler, "Map of the United States Lead Mines on the Upper Mississippi River," 1829, copy in author's possession; U.S. Census Office, *Fifth Census* . . . *1830*, Jo Daviess County, Illinois, and Iowa County, Michigan Territory; Murphy, "Economy, Race and Gender," chap. 5; Russell M. Magnaghi, "Red Slavery in the Great Lakes Country during the French and British Regimes," *Old Northwest* 12 (1986): 201–17.

53. James P. Beckwourth, *The Life and Adventures of James P. Beckwourth as Told to Thomas D. Banner* (1852; reprint, Lincoln NE, 1972), 22.

54. Horatio Newhall to Isaac Newhall, March 1, 1828, 4, Horatio Newhall Papers, microfilm, Illinois State Historical Library, Springfield.

55. On Native American police work, see Murphy, "Economy, Race, and Gender," chap. 5.

56. George Davenport to O. N. Bostwick, January 29, 1826, Chouteau-Papin Collection; Nicholas Boilvin to William Eustis, February 11, 1811, typescript, State Historical Society of Wisconsin, Branch, Wisconsin Room, Karrmann Library; Thwaites, "Narrative of Spoon Decorah," 458.

57. Reminiscences of Esau Johnson, C-2, Esau Johnson Papers.

58. Gov. Lewis Cass to the Secretary of War, July 10, 1827, in Clarence Edwin Carter, ed., *The Territorial Papers of the United States*, vol. 11, *The Territory of Michigan* (Washington DC, 1943), 1101–3. General works on the Black Hawk War include Cecil Eby, *"That Disgraceful Affair": The Black Hawk War* (New York, 1973); Anthony F. C. Wallace, *Prelude to Disaster*, ed. Ellen M. Whitney (Springfield IL, 1970); Roger L. Nichols, *Black Hawk and the Warrior's Path* (Arlington Heights IL, 1992); and Black Hawk's autobiography, Jackson, ed., *Black Hawk*.

59. James E. Wright, *The Galena Lead District: Federal Policy and Practice, 1824–1847* (Madison WI, 1966), 19–20. "The working men are those that suit us best and not the speculators," one of Thomas's agents wrote, a sentiment all policy makers seem to have shared (19). Although Indians continued to mine in the region up to the Black Hawk War of 1832, they did not figure in this system. (Apparently, Indians did not have to pay the 10 percent of their lead that whites and blacks did.) Unfortunately, egalitarian ideals in the mining region brought chaos in social relations, and the government failed to put in place any controls. No fort was built in the region; the court system was remote and weak. The system turned several thousand white men loose in Indian country, and the system's agent consciously encouraged conflict and violence.

60. Horatio Newhall to Isaac Newhall, March 1, 1828, Horatio Newhall Papers.

61. For example, Horatio Newhall to Isaac Newhall, March 1, 1828, Horatio Newhall Papers; Edward Langworthy, "Autobiographical Sketch of Edward Langworthy," *Iowa Journal of History and Politics* 8 (1910): 346.

62. Meeker, "Early History," 290; Forsyth to Clark, June 10, 1828, Forsyth Papers, Draper MSS, 6T: 84; Reminiscences of Esau Johnson, B-43, Esau Johnson Papers; Whitney, *Black Hawk War*, 2:793 n. 3; [Dieter], *Story of Mineral Point*, 18.

63. *Miners' Journal*, September 13, 1828; *Louisa I. Holmes v. Roland R. Holmes*, April term, 1832, *Sally George v. Alexander George*, April term, 1832, *Dunkey v. William Morrison, Leonard Bryant and Mary Bryant v. Alexander Neavill and Elias Griggs*, all in Jo Daviess County Court Records, Galena Public Library, on loan to the Karrmann Library.

64. *Fifth Census . . . 1830*, Michigan Territory, Iowa County and State of Illinois, Jo Daviess County; Chandler, "Map of the United States Lead Mines on the Upper Mississippi River"; E. Langworthy, "Autobiographical Sketch," 347. Some sources on the lead-mining region are Schafer, *Wisconsin Lead Region*; J. E. Wright, *Galena Lead District*; Gratiot, "Gratiot's Narrative," 261–75; reminiscences by the Langworthy brothers in the *Iowa Journal of History and Politics* 8 (1910); Meeker, "Early History," 281; Horatio Newhall Papers and early Galena newspapers, Illinois State His-

torical Society, Springfield; Friedrick G. Hollman, *Auto-Biography of Fredrick G. Hollman* (Platteville WI, [1870?]); reminiscences of Esau Johnson, Esau Johnson Papers; Jo Daviess County Court Records, Galena Public Library; letters in various collections of the Missouri Historical Society.

65. For example, L. H. Langworthy, "Dubuque," 383; Reminiscences of Esau Johnson, B-28, Esau Johnson Papers. See, for examples of sentimentality, Coelebs, "Home," *Advertiser* (Galena), August 16, 1829, Coelebs, "Marriage," "Sonnet to Miss M**** C*****," August 30, 1828, W., "The Indian Girl," July 25, 1828.

66. Street to Barbour, Secretary of War, January 8, 1828, September 1, 1828 (quotations), Letters Received by the Office of Indian Affairs, Prairie du Chien, microfilm, Newberry Library, Chicago; Street to Cass, August 26, 1831, in Whitney, *Black Hawk War*, 2:147–54.

67. Campbell, "Recollections," 890; Sac-Fox Halfbreeds, Thomas Forsyth, 1830, vol. 32, 11, 15; *History of Jo Daviess County*, 235 (quotation).

68. Nancy Oestreich Lurie, *Wisconsin Indians* (Madison WI, 1987), 10, 18–20; Lurie, "Winnebago," in William C. Sturtevant, gen. ed., *Handbook of North American Indians*, vol. 15, *Northeast*, ed. Bruce G. Trigger (Washington DC, 1978), 700; Kay, "The Land of La Baye," 416–18; William T. Hagan, *The Sac and Fox Indians* (Norman OK, 1958), 205–32, 261.

69. Washburne, "Col. Henry Gratiot," 258.

Oral History

Listening to Native Voices

An important goal in writing Native history is to hear and take seriously as historical sources the voices and words of Native people. While a shortage of records written by Native people can sometimes make this difficult, scholars may find oral interviews to be useful in achieving this objective. Anthropologists have long relied on fieldwork, including conversations with Native people about their history and culture, while historians have typically been trained to base their work on documents, particularly for the period before 1900. Interdisciplinary methodologies such as ethnohistory and its younger, larger cousin, American Indian Studies, have encouraged scholars to incorporate both types of research.

Scholars looking for the voices of Native women may find them in a number of places. The records of interviews collected by anthropologists, including Native anthropologists, during the twentieth century are obvious and valuable sources, but other, lesser-known records exist as well. New Deal contract workers of the Federal Writers Project recorded interviews with many Native peoples from various tribes. In addition, miscellaneous historians, officials, government committees, and tribal community members recorded oral narratives during the last several centuries.

We reprint here excerpts from Nancy Lurie's classic anthropological collaboration with Mountain Wolf Woman. Readers will note not only the substantial amount of historical and cultural information included in Mountain Wolf Woman's narrative of her life during the late nineteenth century, but also the way one becomes acquainted with her personality and values through her choice of topics to discuss, and with the rhythms of her speaking style. At the same time, this project presents the combined efforts of Lurie, Mountain Wolf Woman, and the latter's grandniece Frances Thundercloud Wentz, who provided careful assistance with the translation.

Michelene E. Pesantubbee's article, "Beyond Domesticity: Choctaw Women Negotiating the Tension between Choctaw Culture and Protestantism," not only connects the past to the present but also uses interviews with contemporary Native people to make a point about the persistence of certain women's roles in Choctaw communities. Pesantubbee's article is also informed indirectly by an older interview taken in 1901. Researching the Treaty of Dancing Rabbit Creek in 1830, H. S. Halbert interviewed Joe Jones, also known as Conteatubbee, a ninety-two-year-old Choctaw man who had been present at the treaty deliberations. Although transcripts of this interview are not available, it informed Halbert's 1902 article, which in turn informs Pesantubbee's essay, revealing women's important roles in the political process.[1]

Note

1. H. S. Halbert, "Story of the Treaty of Dancing Rabbit," *Publications of the Mississippi Historical Society* 6 (1902): 401–2.

15. Mountain Wolf Woman, Sister of Crashing Thunder

The Autobiography of a Winnebago Indian

EDITED BY NANCY OESTREICH LURIE
Excerpts

New Introduction by Nancy Oestreich Lurie

Mountain Wolf Woman dictated her story in 1958, nearly fifty years before the present publication. While she traced her life from the horse-and-buggy era to air travel, by the time of her birth in 1884 the Winnebago—or Ho-Chunk, as the Wisconsin branch of the tribe is now officially designated—had long adapted to dealing with the larger society on its and their own terms. Material culture was by then overwhelmingly drawn from the industrialized American economy. She was part of the first generation of Ho-Chunk women (and many men) to attend school, speak English, drive a car; at the same time, her values, beliefs, attitudes were enduringly Ho-Chunk. Her children and most of her grandchildren have died, and few people now remember her personally. The community in which she lived, the Indian Mission near Black River Falls, Wisconsin, is greatly changed, as can be said of the Winnebago tribe as a whole. When I first visited in 1945, and for many years thereafter, the community had no electricity and water was obtained by the bucketful from a number of pumps. Aunt Stella, as I called Mountain Wolf Woman, died in 1961, the year her story was published. The lag between recording and publication was taken up by translation and editing; the translation by Frances Thundercloud Wentz is not only accurate but preserves the literary flavor of Ho-Chunk discourse of Aunt Stella's generation. I shall be forever grateful to Frances.

The year following Aunt Stella's death, enormous changes were set in motion as the tribe was finally able to organize under the Indian Reorganization Act of 1934 with their own constitutional government. Federal Indian policy in the 1950s had been directed toward dismantling Indian societies. Improved housing was a priority for the new tribal Business Committee, along with encouraging advanced education and dealing with problems of health, welfare, and employment. By the 1980s Indian gaming began to make a big economic difference for some tribes, and the Wisconsin Winnebagos were in the forefront of this development. They have amended their Constitution and expanded their governing structure, now called the Ho-Chunk Nation Legislature. A large complex of new buildings houses the offices of the Ho-Chunk government and various programs at the headquarters near Black River Falls and at the other communities across central Wisconsin. The Ho-Chunk have three casinos.

I am at the Indian Mission as I write this, staying in my "modern" wigwam, a style developed by World War I, that retains the old arched framework but is covered with roofing paper and equipped with floor, windows, door, stove, and chimney. I have electricity but not running water. In fact, I have the sole remaining privy at the Mission. When the modern housing projects began, I felt the distinctive Ho-Chunk wigwam that was ubiquitous when I began my research should be documented, so I had one built in 1978. It still serves as a place to stay during my good-weather visits. Old friends bring their grandchildren to see how the Indians used to live around here, and we laugh about the reversal of roles.

Although there is a struggle to maintain the Ho-Chunk language, the old ceremonies Mountain Wolf Woman described flourish, benefiting from increasing individual affluence, as do services of the Native American Church, her religion of choice. The seasonal powwows now draw enormous crowds and pay out huge contest dance prizes. She would still feel at home here, enjoying new conveniences and opportunities.

Are there other life stories to be told? Probably, but they don't need the mediation of an anthropologist. Some Ho-Chunk people now have degrees in anthropology . . . and law, and medicine, and other professions. Like Mountain Wolf Woman, who could have assimilated into the so-called mainstream culture and society, they are still around being Ho-Chunk and working in the Ho-Chunk interest. They can tell their own stories. I hope they will.

Mountain Wolf Woman, Sister of Crashing Thunder
The Autobiography of a Winnebago Indian (1961)

Autobiographies are published for a variety of reasons. Authors often disclaim any personal importance but justify making their memoirs public because of close association with the great people and stirring events of their time. Individuals whose roles are of obvious historical significance frequently explain that a sense of social responsibility requires that they make known the underlying influences and motivations of their actions. Mountain Wolf Woman has told her story for a reason that is at once simpler and more complex than those usually adduced. Her niece asked for the story. Among the Winnebago Indians, a strong sense of obligation to relatives prevails, as well as the reciprocal sense of right to call upon them as the need or desire for favors may arise. The fact that the kinship in this case is one of adoption and not of blood makes it no less binding from a Winnebago point of view.

Our relationship stems from my adoption by Mountain Wolf Woman's parallel cousin, Mitchell Redcloud, Sr. According to Winnebago reckoning, they are classified as brother and sister because their fathers were brothers. Thus, Mountain Wolf Woman is my aunt. I had met Redcloud during the summer of 1944. . . . When I began my senior year at the University of Wisconsin the following fall, I learned that Redcloud was a cancer patient at the Wisconsin General Hospital on the university campus. I visited him frequently and my questions about Winnebago culture helped relieve the tedium of existence in a hospital ward. . . . He was eventually scheduled for surgery, and fearing that he might not survive the operation, presented me with a cherished and valuable legacy—adoption as his daughter. . . .

Thus, when I met Mountain Wolf Woman in the summer of 1945 while working at the Winnebago community of Black River Falls, Wisconsin, she greeted me as her niece. My aunt soon proved to be not only a valuable informant, but a good friend as well. Her personality and her own experiences as an individual became as interesting to me as the ethnographic data about the Winnebago which she could provide. I felt that her autobiography would be of great interest both as a literary document and as a source of insights for anthropological purposes. I was inspired, naturally, by the fact that the first full-length autobiography of an American Indian edited and published by an anthropologist, Paul Radin, had been that of a Winnebago, Crashing Thunder.[1] The example set by Radin in 1920 has been followed by the publication of a number of autobiographies of American Indians and other native peoples. However, few such life histories have been collected from women. Therefore, Mountain Wolf Woman's story takes on particular significance in scholarly terms, since it is the account of a woman from the same tribe as Crashing Thunder. However, I knew Mountain Wolf Woman almost a year before I learned that she is the sister of Crashing Thunder. Thus, a unique opportunity was presented to obtain an autobiography which would be valuable not only for its own sake but also for its comparative importance in regard to Radin's work.

Mountain Wolf Woman readily agreed to my request for her story, but a great deal of time elapsed before we could actually begin work on the project. In the first place, I realized that a request of such magnitude would require a commensurate gift as a matter of reciprocal kin obligations. I was obliged for many years to use any field funds I received for more general research on the Winnebago. Then there were technical problems. Mountain Wolf Woman's household was crowded with small grandchildren she was rearing and she did not have the leisure or quiet to write her story in the Winnebago syllabary script, let alone in English which she would find even more difficult. Furthermore, I was fully occupied for several years with teaching and other research.

It was not until 1957 that I could begin to give serious thought to the long-delayed work with Mountain Wolf Woman. By that time she was able to put her household in the temporary charge of an adult granddaughter in order to stay with me. . . . We worked together at my home for almost five weeks during January and February of 1958.

We began our task by discussing the best manner of procedure. She soon became accustomed to using a tape recorder and decided she preferred it to writing her story in the Winnebago syllabary script that her brother had employed. She also chose to speak Winnebago rather than English as it allowed for easier recall and discussion of events. However, to aid me in the task of translation, she repeated the entire story on tape in English using the Winnebago recordings as a guide. . . .

The transcription of Mountain Wolf Woman's story was doubtless one of the most pleasant ways imaginable of doing "field work." Mountain Wolf Woman is a delightful companion, witty, empathic, intelligent and forthright. During the course of our work she thought of herself as a visiting relative. When my teaching schedule interrupted our work, she found ways to occupy her time, and even between daily recording sessions she was never idle. Indeed, she is incapable of idleness and equates personal contentment with useful activity. She sewed clothing for herself, and even split wood for the fireplace when she felt in need of exercise. Because my birthday occurred during the course of her visit she decided to make me a gift in the form of elaborate floral beading of the buckskin dress I wear for lectures of a popular nature, explaining, "The girls wearing fancier dresses to powwows nowdays."

Appendix B

In this excerpt from Appendix B, Nancy Oestreich Lurie discussed both men's and women's roles during the transitional era of the nineteenth- and early twentieth centuries. She compared the narratives of Mountain Wolf Woman and of her brother, Crashing Thunder.

... [There was] a fundamental difference between males and females generally among the Winnebago. In large part, Mountain Wolf Woman's autobiography is a predictable reflection of the greater self-confidence enjoyed by women in comparison to men in a culture undergoing rapid and destructive changes. As was true of many American Indian groups, the roles of wife, mother and homemaker for which the Winnebago girl was prepared could be fulfilled in adulthood despite the vagaries of acculturation. There is another dimension that might be considered as well. Even in aboriginal times and on through the late historic period, warfare meant men would be absent for varying times and necessitated a degree of self-reliance among Winnebago women. Later, despite the terrible disruption of domestic life because of government removals and resettlement on a series of reservations, women still had to care for children, prepare meals, mend clothing and carry out other familiar tasks as a matter of survival.

Winnebago boys were prepared for traditional roles as warriors, hunters and shamans long after these roles stood little chance of effective fulfillment. For example, Crashing Thunder sought to be a respected warrior by taking part in the killing of a Potawatomi Indian. His father understood and appreciated his motives, but in the opinion of white officialdom he was an accomplice in a pointless murder (pp. 148–67).

The sense of personal adequacy displayed by Mountain Wolf Woman can be attributed to more than the greater continuity and stability of female roles. Cultural change has indeed affected the lives of Winnebago women, but in contrast to men, they have benefited by the change to some extent.

Their socially humbler roles have acquired greater economic power at the expense of the more prestigious male roles. Traditionally, the Winnebago male provided game, the primary subsistence item of the group as well as the main source of clothing. This continued to be the case during the long period of the fur trade when even the peltry animals trapped by men brought new wealth in material goods to the Winnebago. Women raised garden produce and gathered wild foods, and though they contributed significantly to the family larder their offerings were not held in the high esteem accorded venison or bear meat.

Within the lifetime of Mountain Wolf Woman's oldest sibling it became extremely difficult to subsist by hunting and gardening. White settlers began to occupy the lands of the Winnebago and the tribe was driven from its homeland. Trapping became ever less profitable while the Winnebago became increasingly more dependent on the trader's stock as necessary to their existence. When they became involved in a cash economy, the Winnebago cast about for new sources of subsistence. They found a solution to their economic problems in harvesting fruit and vegetable crops for white employers or selling wild vegetable produce to white people. Although both men and women engaged in these tasks, gathering and agricultural activities were matters with which women were identified and in which they traditionally excelled.

Finally, the tourist trade of the last sixty years has become exceptionally important to the Winnebago and has given women an added source of income in the production of bead-work and basketry. Although basketry is a relatively new craft learned from more easterly tribes, it has on occasion been the mainstay of many Winnebago families. Mountain Wolf Woman takes her productive activities so much for granted that she does not even mention that during most of her adult life and throughout her wide travels and changes of residence she has made baskets to obtain cash. She implies that men are the providers and speaks approvingly of her second husband as industrious. In plain fact, she has always contributed a large amount to the family income and furthermore exercised primary control over family finances.

Mountain Wolf Woman is a practical person. Her story lacks the emotional intensity of personal crises, indecision and violence found in her brother's autobiography. Though interlarded with general descriptions of Winnebago customs, the theme of Crashing Thunder's personal story is the seeking of a satisfactory way of life on the part of an ambitious but frustrated individual. He finds it ultimately in the value system of the peyote religion. Mountain Wolf Woman's narrative is primarily the story of the Winnebago over the last seventy-five years. She devotes attention to matters that concerned her family and the entire Winnebago tribe before her birth, and she ends her story with an account of her children, grandchildren and great-grandchildren. They will continue the story of the Winnebago long after she is gone.

Chapter 1: Earliest Recollections

. . . It was about the time that my older sister Bald Eagle was born that they went to Nebraska.[2] Mother used to say they were taken to Nebraska that winter; they were moved from one land to another. Many Winnebago were moved to Nebraska and there mother took her three children. Grandmother had relatives in Nebraska. Grandmother was the oldest daughter in her family. In Nebraska she saw her sisters, the second and third daughters. They were very eager to see their relatives. But, mother said, some of the Wisconsin Winnebago did not like the removal. Some even cried because they were taken there. However, mother used to say, "The fact that we would see my relatives made me happy that we were going. And when we reached the Missouri River, our uncles came to meet us. When they heard we were coming, Squeaking Wing and Captures The Lodge and a third uncle Hágaga came to meet us."

As their uncle Squeaking Wing came through the train he called out, "Bends The Boughs, where is she? Bends The Boughs, where is she?"[3] At last he found them and there was much rejoicing when they saw one another. Brother Crashing Thunder was dressed in a fringed buckskin outfit, and when my uncles saw him they lifted him up in the air and they said, "Oh, how cute our nephew is!" Eventually they arrived at the reservation.

It was winter. Everyone had his own camping outfit, and they all made their homes here and there. They built wigwams. Then spring came and mother said that the Winnebago died in great numbers. Deaths occurred almost every day. When someone died, the Winnebago carried away their dead, crying as they walked. All those who had a death in the family cried as they walked along. They were going to the graveyard, and there was much weeping.

Mother was frightened. "Why do we stay here?" she said. "I am afraid because the people are all dying. Why do we not go back home?" They were with some uncles at the time. The first was called Good Village, the next was called Big Náqiga and the third was called Little Náqiga. In the spring they moved to the Missouri River where they cut down some big willow trees and made dugout canoes big enough for two, mother said. She must have been talking about fairly big boats that they made. There in the spring when the weather is very pleasant, mother used to say, a large group went down the Missouri River. Thus she returned home with some of her relatives. They went down the Missouri to River's Mouth Place as they used to call St. Louis. From there they travelled back on the Mississippi River, they travelled upstream on the Mississippi.

Eventually they stopped at a certain place where they saw some white people. Nobody knew how to speak English, so they said, "Where is Hénaga? Where is Hénaga? He is the only one who knows the name of that place." They meant Captures The Lodge, who was just a little boy. When they brought him they said to him, "Say it! Say it!" He was the only one who knew that one word, and he said, "Prarsheen? Prarsheen?" I guess he was saying "Prairie du Chien." Then the white people understood him,—and said it was Prairie du Chien. They stopped there for a while and eventually they left and arrived at La Crosse. They lived there for a time and then they moved out towards Black River Falls.

It seems that many Winnebago came back to Wisconsin. My family were evidently not the only ones who returned. Also, some of the Winnebago in Wisconsin lived way out in the country a great distance from any town. These people said that they had not been found so they did not go to Nebraska, mother said. Thus, not all of the Winnebago left in the removal.

It must have been at this time that my parents took up land, that is, a homestead. Some of them acquired homesteads there at Black River Falls.[4] However, father was not interested in such things. Even when they were in Nebraska his brother said, "Register, older brother, claim some land for yourself and claim some for your children." But father did not do it, so they did not have any land in Nebraska. Mother and her uncles did not take any land, but some of the Winnebago took land in Nebraska so they had property, but eventually they sold it.[5] However, my parents did not realize what they were doing and that is why they acted as they did. Some of the Indians took homesteads but father did not understand so he did not take a homestead. That was when my mother took a homestead. There was an old man who was a grandfather to us who took land. His name was Many Trails. I used to see him; he was a little old man. He said to my mother, "Granddaughter, why do you not claim some land? I claimed some and if you take a homestead right next to me, then we can live beside each other." So mother took forty acres.

Indians did not look ahead to affairs of this sort. They never looked to the future. They only looked to the present insofar as they had enough to sustain themselves. This is the way the Indians used to live. The fact that my father did not care to obtain any land was because he was a member of the Thunder Clan. "I do not belong to the Earth," he said, "I do not belong to the Earth and I have no concern with land." This is why he was not interested in having any land. But mother was also one,—one of the bird clan people; she belonged to the Eagle Clan. She said, "By this means we will have some place to live," and so she took forty acres. Here my father built the log house where we usually lived. . . .

Chapter 2: Livelihood

In March we usually travelled to the Mississippi River close to La Crosse, sometimes even across the river, and then we returned again in the last part of May. We used to live at a place on the edge of the Mississippi called Caved In Breast's Grave. My father, brother-in-law and brothers used to trap there for muskrats. When they killed the muskrats my mother used to save the bodies and hang them up there in great numbers. When there were a lot of muskrats then they used to roast them on a rack. They prepared a lot of wood and built a big fire. They stuck four crotched posts into the ground around the fire and placed poles across the crotches. Then they removed the burning wood and left the embers. They put a lot of fine wood crisscross and very dense on the frame. On this the muskrats were roasted, placed all above the fireplace. As the muskrats began roasting, the grease dripped off nice and brown and then the women used long pointed sticks to turn them over and over. The muskrat meat made a lot of noise as it cooked. When these were cooked, the women put them aside and placed some more on the rack. They cooked a great amount of muskrats.—When they were cooled, the women packed them together and stored them for summer use.

In the spring when my father went trapping on the Mississippi and the weather became very pleasant my sister once said, "It is here that they dig yellow water lily roots." So, we all went out, my mother and sisters and everybody. When we got to a slough where the water lilies were very dense, they took off their shoes, put on old dresses and went wading into the water. They used their feet to hunt for the roots. They dug them out with their feet and then the roots floated up to the surface. Eventually, my second oldest sister happened upon one. My sister took one of the floating roots, wrapped it about with the edge of her blouse and tucked it into her belt. I thought she did this because it was the usual thing to do. I saw her doing this and when I happened upon a root I took it and did the same thing. I put it in my belt too. And then everybody laughed at me! "Oh, Little Siga is doing something! She has a water lily root in her belt!" Everybody laughed at me and yelled at me. My sister had done that because she was pregnant. I suppose she did that to ward off something because she was pregnant. Thus she would not affect the baby and would have good luck finding the roots.[6] Because I saw her do that, I did the same thing, and so they teased me.

When they dug up a lot of roots in this fashion they put them in a gunny sack, filling it half full and even more. Then we carried them back to camp and my mother and all my sisters scraped them. The roots have an outside covering and they scraped that off and sliced them. — They look something like a banana. The women then strung the slices and hung them up to dry in order to store them. They dried a great amount, flour sacks full. During the summer they sometimes cooked them with meat and they were really delicious.

Upon returning home, mother and father planted a garden in front of the log house where we usually lived. Nearby stood the well that my father had made. . . . The water was icy cold. The Indians used to come there for water. It was very good water that we had.

At the time we were there when mother and father planted a garden, the blueberries ripened and we picked blueberries. There were pine trees all around where we lived, the kind of pine trees that are very tall and look as if they had been trimmed all up the trunk almost to the top. That is the way it used to be around our home. The pine trees were very dense and there was no underbrush. Under the trees the blueberries grew in profusion. All the Indians picked blueberries. They came carrying boxes on their backs and when they filled the boxes they left. At that time they used to come to our house for water, and when they brought the water up, the turning wheel would say, "gink, gink, gink, gink."

All the berry pickers carried boxes on their backs. The boxes were square and were divided into four square compartments. There were two holes on opposite sides of the box and cords were strung across these holes. They called these boxes waŋkšíkwak'ʔín, that is, carry on a person's back. They used to carry them by horseback too, a pair slung in front and in back of the person riding the horse. This is the way they went to town to sell the berries.

There they bought food for themselves, bringing the berry boxes back full of groceries. This is the way that they earned money.

They were paid a good price; fifty cents a quart is the price they used to get toward the beginning of the season, and as the season wore on, toward the end, they got a quarter. They saved their money and they even bought horses. Some of the Indians had no wagons and that is why they let the horses carry the berries, but some of them had wagons. Thus the Indians came through history.[7] That is the way they procured food for themselves. They saved food and they saved money.

When various foods were ripe the people dried them. They also steamed things underground. They harvested a lot of corn and carried it home on their backs. When I was a little girl our family was large. I was the youngest and I had three older brothers and two older sisters. Another older sister and I were the younger ones. When they harvested the gardens, they harvested a great amount. They steamed the corn. In the evening they dug a pit and heated stones there in a big fire. They put the stones in the pit and when the stones became red hot they took out all the wood and embers and put in the corn husks. Then they put in the fully ripe corn and covered it with more husks. Finally they covered it with the earth that had been dug out. They covered the pit but they left four holes in which they poured water. We used to hear the red hot stones make a rumbling sound.

Then, very early in the morning they opened the pit with great care. They removed the earth very carefully and finally when they reached the husks they took them out. Eventually they reached the corn and it was thoroughly cooked. It was really hot! They took the corn out and put it on the husks. Sometimes other people heard about it and worked with my family. The helpers came and spread out a big piece of canvas on which they put the corn. Then they used metal teaspoons or clam shells to scrape the corn off the cobs. They used to dry it and after it was dried you could see sackfuls of corn standing here and there. They dried the corn in the sun and put it in white flour sacks. Some corn was allowed to remain on the stalks after it was ripe. This they saved for seed. In addition to saving seed they made hominy of this dried corn. They mixed it with ashes and popped it to make hominy.

Squash was also dried. The women pared the squash, cut it in two and sliced it to form rings. They cut down forked trees, peeled them, and strung the squash on poles they laid across the forks. A lot of squash hung on this framework. The Indians generally dried squash in this way and saved it for winter.

They used to dry blueberries too, berries they did not sell. They dried the blueberries and cooked them in the winter time. The blueberries were boiled with dried corn and I used to think this was delicious. That is what we used to eat.

They used to dig a hole to save whatever they were not going to use during the winter. They kept out whatever they thought they would need for that winter and they saved in the hole what they would eat in the spring. Seed was also buried in the ground. They made a hole and buried things in it and took them out as they were required. "Dig up that which is buried," they used to say.

They also dried Indian potatoes. My grandmother and my mother's younger sister and I used to gather them.—Indian potatoes grow wild, where it is wooded with dense hazel bushes, near creeks. The vines of the Indian potatoes are like strings stretched out, a lot of strings extending in all directions. That is the way the vines grow, tangled up around the bushes. The women would try poking here and there with a hoe and then they would hit upon them. The potatoes would be linked to each other as if they were strung together. Then they would dig a lot of them. After they dug them up, they cut up the links and dried them. When they cooked these things they added sugar and boiled them until the water was gone, and then we peeled off the skins. Oh, they were really delicious things!—

Stealing from mice is something I never did but aunt and grandmother told me about it. They would go off in the brush, in the woods, and steal wild beans from the mice. These mice know how to store things. Running back and forth, the mice carried things to a particular place. Their little trails showed the way they went into their little holes in the ground. There they gathered very many of those wild beans. Grandmother said that when a family had a lot of little boys it used to be said of the last born, the youngest one, that he is married to one of these mice. It was that boy who used to find the storehouses. That is why they used to say the little boys married little mice. Mother's brothers were all big and they did not have any little boy. Even my youngest uncle was grown up, but they used to say, "Squeaking Wing's wives have stored some things, let us go look for some of them." They always found some. Grandmother used to say that some women knew very well how to look for wild beans. They would stand some place and look around. "There is one over there!" they used to say, and "There is one right here too!" When they scraped away the leaves and the earth there the holes used to be, just all full of wild beans. They would take them and save them. —Sometimes they said they found a bucketful, I do not know how big a bucket they meant. Those beans were very good; I ate some of them. When I went to Nebraska they gave me some there. I cooked them in the same way I cook any beans. The beans that we eat today are good, but wild beans are much more delicious.

When I was small the Winnebago generally went to pick cranberries after they were through taking care of their gardens.[8] We used to do that too. When we arrived at the marsh there were many Indians who camped together there and picked cranberries. The men used rakes and the women picked by hand. As the women were picking and they reached the edge of the ditch, they all sat on the edge of the ditch in a long row, side by side.[9] They picked ahead of themselves in a straight line, a bushel-sized box at each woman's side. They would put aside as many boxes as they thought they would fill so they would not run out of boxes. They left their boxes as they filled them, and if you looked down a line you could see the row of filled boxes. As they filled each box they took along another empty box. At noon they went back to the camp to eat. Some people even brought their lunches along and ate there at the marsh. I used to think it was great fun when we took food and ate outside.

That is what people did in the fall. They were making money to save. When they finished there they went deer hunting. They were trying to earn money for themselves and they probably earned quite a bit but I did not know what they were earning. The women used to pick into a big dishpan and when it was full it was emptied into the box. We children used to pick too. We used small pails. Wherever mother sat, I used to sit next to her and I would pick cranberries. When I filled the pail I emptied it into mother's bushel box. My sister did the same thing on the other side of mother. That is what I used to do.

When we were there a peddler of general merchandise often came around. When he said the word for a white man's shirt, he would say, "šorot." He was a white man with black hair and black mustache and he did not know how to speak English. When this peddler came they would all call out, "Oh, šorot is here!" They used to call him šorot.

The Indians were making money and that is why they used to come around and sell things. Somebody came around selling pies. I used to think that was very nice. Mother often bought things from these peddlers and then we used to eat pie. After all, the Indians were using campfires outside and could not bake pies and cakes, and so they had a bakery shop there at the marsh.

That cranberry picking place is gone now. Iron Mountain Marsh they used to call it and I do not even know the English name for it. That cranberry marsh no longer exists because at one time a big forest fire came through there. When the people fled they said that they had to put the old people in the ditches. They could not flee with them in time so they put the old people in the water in the ditches. I believe the marsh ceased to exist at that time. The entire stand of cranberry bushes was burned up.

After cranberry time they went on the fall migration to hunt deer. That is what we always did, we went travelling to hunt deer. At that time my father did not have to buy any deer license. They never used to pay for such things. When they went deer hunting the white people did not spy on them. That is how it used to be at that time. They killed as many deer as they deemed necessary. We used to travel a certain distance east of Neillsville where there used to be a woods. There were not many white people around at that time. That is where we used to go in the fall. That is where we used to live and almost immediately the hunters used to bring in deer. They wrapped the deer in autumn leaves and carried the deer on their backs. As they were approaching you could see the red leaves moving along here and there, as they came home with the freshly killed deer. Just as soon as we arrived, the first day, they always brought home game. It was always this way. Sometimes they even used to bring in a bear.

Four or five households of Indians migrated to this area where they built long wigwams; my father and my brothers, also my brother-in-law Cloud, and another brother-in-law Little Náqiga as well as their relatives, and sometimes our uncles came there too. Our family was large enough to require a two-fireplace wigwam. We lived in a rush wigwam. My grandmother and my mother made our house of cattail matting. The wigwam was covered with mats of cattail stalks. The inside of the house was never smoky. I suppose that was because it was properly made. It was very pleasant to live in a rush wigwam. My older sister White Thunder and my brother-in-law Cloud lived next door, but they lived in a large round wigwam. Another person who lived in a big round wigwam was Cloud's brother who was called Big Thunder. Big Thunder's wife's name was Axjiŋwiŋga—and I do not know what that would mean in English. Her mother's name was Four Women and her husband's name was Daylight.

One time when we had been living there only a short time, as I recall, this old man, Daylight, died. When he was about to die he was very sick. He was really very sick but he said that he wanted to see the daylight, he wanted to go outside. He said this as he lay there. Upon hearing this my mother came home. She had evidently gone to visit him. She said, "My sons, he is to be pitied that he is saying this. Go and carry him. Take him outside. Let him see the daylight." So, my older brothers did as they were told to do. Then the old man said as he lay there, "Daylight, at one time I knew this daylight well. That accounts for my name; they called me Daylight. But nothing can be done to help me, so I am going away. At one time there was a certain food of which I was fond, skunk meat. If you should kill a skunk, cook it and think of me as you do so. Think of me and scatter some tobacco for me. Whatever you want when you do this, it will be granted to you." That is what the old man said. That is the way the old people were; the old people were supposed to be respected. "Respect those old people," mother and father used to say to us. That is what we used to do. We respected the old people, but today they do not respect the old people.

Notes

1. Paul Radin, *Crashing Thunder* (New York, 1926).
2. The Winnebago ceded their homeland, which comprised most of southern Wisconsin and the northwestern corner of Illinois, in the course of three treaties with the government in 1829, 1832, and 1837. The tribe maintained that the last treaty was signed under duress, was misrepresented to them, and was signed by unauthorized tribesmen. Part of the tribe felt that they were outnumbered and outarmed and the best course was to submit to the terms of the treaty. They accordingly moved to a reservation in Iowa, but in 1846 were moved to another reservation in northern Minnesota. In 1855 they were again forced to cede their land and were moved to a reservation in southern Minnesota where they exhibited a remarkable willingness to become acculturated and accept a farming economy. They anticipated receiving patents in fee to plots unofficially distributed among the families by their agent. However, the Sioux uprising in Minnesota in 1862 was used as an excuse to force their removal from their improved lands although as a group they had taken no part in the uprising. They were taken to Crow Creek in South Dakota in cold weather and suffered great hardships and reduction in population. Fearing for their lives they fled down the Crow Creek to the Missouri River in dugout canoes. Eventually, most of them settled among the Omaha in Nebraska. In 1865 they were allowed to exchange their Crow Creek land for a reservation in Nebraska along the Missouri River. . . .

   Meanwhile, a part of the tribe consistently resisted efforts to remove them from the contested Wisconsin land involved in the treaty of 1837. Despite four removals by armed troops they always returned, their ranks swelled by dissatisfied members of the treaty-abiding faction. The last attempt to remove the Winnebago was made in 1874, the removal discussed by Mountain Wolf Woman.

3. This is the name of Mountain Wolf Woman's mother.

4. After the removal of 1874 the government stopped trying to keep the Winnebago out of Wisconsin and allowed them to take up forty-acre homesteads which were to be tax-free and inalienable for twenty years. Most of these homesteads have passed from Indian ownership through sales or tax default and the remaining ones are of little use agriculturally since they have been divided into ever smaller parcels through inheritance over several generations. The land itself was for the most part rather poor and the Wisconsin Winnebago used the homesteads as headquarters where they planted gardens but which they abandoned for long periods to hunt, trap, or gather wild foods. Often they found the timber stripped from the land by whites during their protracted absences. Gradually, the Wisconsin Winnebago formed settlements of a few dozen to several hundred people near white communities throughout central Wisconsin from Wittenberg on the east to La Crosse on the west. The settlements are located on mission lands, government lands, or lands bought or rented by the Winnebago.

5. Allotment in severalty was carried out on the Nebraska reservation some time after the removal of 1874, but enrollments were made as early as 1865 with the understanding that this land would be secured to the Indians without further removals. Hence the advice of Mountain Wolf Woman's uncle to her father to register and assert his claim to Nebraska land.

6. The Winnebago observe a number of prenatal taboos relating to the health and personality of the child after birth, but the custom noted in this context refers to the belief that pregnant women must take special precautions to protect the fetus when engaging in unusual activities such as wading in search of *cerap*. There is also a general feeling that pregnant women are apt to be unsuccessful in such quests unless they take such measures. Mountain Wolf Woman found this incident very amusing and laughed when she heard it played back on the tape.

7. This rather curious phrase is intended to imply that the Winnebago are always adaptable and self-sufficient, not that they traditionally sold blueberries to white people.

8. That is, after the harvest and storage of garden produce.

9. The description of gathering cranberries is inserted here from a later recording. Mountain Wolf Woman decided to describe the seasonal cycle in detail after realizing that she had discussed a few of the seasonal food activities and omitted others, hence the frequent insertions of data in this chapter. Although the Winnebago had picked cranberries for many years to sell to white people, by the time Mountain Wolf Woman was a child, cranberry marshes were already being operated on a commercial basis by white owners who hired Indian laborers. The description of the work requires clarification. Formerly sections of marshland were drained off into ditches and became sufficiently dry for men to go through and rake the berries into containers and for women to sit on the ground gleaning berries after the raking process.

16. Beyond Domesticity

Choctaw Women Negotiating the Tension
between Choctaw Culture and Protestantism

MICHELENE E. PESANTUBBEE

New Introduction by Michelene E. Pesantubbee

In the spring of 1993 I embarked on my journey to visit different Oklahoma Choctaw churches and to interview Choctaw people about their experiences as Choctaw Christians. I originally interviewed Choctaw Protestants as part of my dissertation project on Choctaw culture retention in Choctaw churches. My experiences that year raised a number of questions about Choctaw women's leadership in the church and in earlier traditional communities. Thus, upon completion of my dissertation I turned my attention toward a study of the construction of Choctaw gender roles.

As I drove toward Choctaw country I felt a sense of unease mixed with the anticipation of getting firsthand accounts of Choctaw Christians negotiating church and culture. The unease remained my constant companion as I struggled to find some sense of balance between the academic study of religion and the reality of delving into the lives of people whose culture had been probed and dissected for centuries. In graduate school we had discussed the dangers of imposing change on the people we interview by the very nature of the questions we asked. An objective scholar supposedly did not pose leading questions or offer opinions. Yet, I as a Choctaw person who had grown up during the heady times of American Indian culture revitalization in the 1960s and 1970s felt a sense of responsibility to educate other Choctaws about their cultural heritage and history as colonized people. Perhaps due to my inexperience in interviewing people, or my own

desire to better understand what I observed in a couple of the churches I
visited, a few leading questions found their way into the interviews.

Fortunately for me, Christianity is a proselytizing religion with a tradition of witnessing. Most Choctaw Christians I met were willing to talk
about their churches, although a few were careful not to reveal too much
about their own Choctaw traditional beliefs lest such information get back
to their churches. In fact, on a couple of occasions I was asked to turn the
tape recorder off, which I did. The Choctaws I spoke with felt strongly that
Choctaw churches differed from white churches in culturally distinct ways.
Each noted the use of Choctaw language in the church, Sunday meals with
Choctaw dishes, and Choctaw gospel singing, especially all-night singing.
Some spoke about Sunday school and Bible school activities that incorporated Choctaw cultural themes. However, the similarities ended there due
primarily to generational differences.

I met some elder Choctaw Christians who spoke from experience and
not from ancestral memory (meaning stories handed down from generation to generation over a long period of time). Their responses indicated to
me that their knowledge of Choctaw culture was limited to the experiences
of their parents and grandparents, who were also Christians. For example,
one elder Methodist Choctaw man stated that the Choctaws never danced
[traditional religious dances]. When I told him that my research indicates
they did, and that some contemporary Choctaws dance, he clarified his
statement by saying that he had personally never seen or heard of dancing
among the Choctaws. Another Choctaw male, in response to my question
about Choctaw dances, said, "I know I've seen that over at Mississippi. But
I used to say, you know, that Choctaws don't dance. It's just the other tribes,
I use to say. But I found out Choctaws do dance. When we went to Mississippi, that's where I saw the Choctaws all dancing. So I had to come back
and say we do dance" (interview, May 2, 1994).

Although my research was directed toward the experiences of the elders,
I spoke to a few younger Choctaws. They had grown up during a time of
American Indian cultural revitalization inside and outside of Choctaw
country and were more familiar with some traditional activities, including
dances. They had a different attitude toward revitalizing Choctaw culture
than some of the elders, as one man explained: "In the early seventies a
group of Choctaws from Oklahoma went to Mississippi and learned the
Choctaw dances which is different from the powwow style. And there were
attitudes toward that. I would say at that time the group of people that

were between the ages of sixty and eighty or eighty-five were very much against the Choctaw dancing and considered it to be sinful" (interview, July 31, 1993).

Among the elders I spoke to, the women tended to be more open to re-vitalization of Choctaw culture within and outside the church. One young Choctaw man whom I interviewed noted the importance of women in maintaining Choctaw cultural identity within the church. A few elder men, however, expressed disapproval of the inclusion of certain Choctaw cul-tural practices in the church, most particularly, dancing. I also spoke with one Choctaw woman who felt strongly that Choctaw dancing should not be part of church activities. From observations and interviews I learned that women more than men encouraged language use in the church, taught Sunday school and Bible school, and included Choctaw cultural activities as part of their lessons, and in the case of the Presbyterian church, to be lay ministers. I recall attending a Choctaw gospel singing where one of the song leaders gave the page numbers out in Choctaw only. She told the con-gregation that if they could not speak Choctaw, then they were not really Choctaw.

I wondered about women's leadership in the churches. I knew that among white Americans women often attended church in greater numbers than men. As I became more aware through observations that the same was true of Choctaw churches, I began inquiring more about women's leadership. One young man told me, "Yes, as an intern, summer intern for Choctaw Parish last summer I noticed that at several of our camp meetings during the summer, that most of the leadership was women. And, I don't object to that. I think that's great. But at the same time, you know, my question is what happened to all the men and why aren't they involved in the commu-nity, or in the church, in the life of the church" (interview, July 31, 1993).

Although women had a greater presence in the church, I also perceived a mostly unspoken attitude that women were not the decision-makers at higher levels. I realized that both men and women had reservations about women as administrators of their churches. They could be lay pastors or Sunday school teachers but not ordained ministers who could administer rites of baptism, marriage, and funerals. In fact, I met only one Choctaw female ordained minister (who I already knew) in all the churches I visited among the Methodists, Presbyterians, and Baptists. At one Baptist church the pastor, a full-blood Choctaw, emphasized his declaration that women were subservient to men by drawing a triangle on a large easel pad and writing the word *God* at the apex, *men* in the middle, and *women* at the bottom. He then proceeded to tell the teenage girls in the audience not to marry Choctaw men because they make the worst Christians. He said that Choctaw men don't make their wives stay at home where they belong.

As I sat in the back of the church quietly listening to the minister, I wondered how this hierarchical, bounded model of society meshed with the historically interdependent, communal structures of pre-Protestant Choctaw society. If Choctaw women were confined to homes and fields and men to the hunt and war, then how did Choctaw society survive so long in a world where uncertainty and change always demanded adaptation? Questions such as these compelled me to research traditional Choctaw gender roles.

I had read Theda Perdue's study of Cherokee women and the changes they experienced as a result of missionization. In her article "Southern Indians and the Cult of True Womanhood," Perdue argues that Cherokee women learned to be true women according to the ideals of nineteenth-century white society "primarily through the work of Protestant missionaries" (1985, 41). She suggests that in the early nineteenth century Cherokee women borrowed selectively from the dominant white culture, but as Cherokee male leaders began to exclude women from many of their former activities, such as farming and participation in the political process, more distinct divisions arose between the roles and influence of males and females. More significant for the purposes of my work, she stated that "the influence of the cult of true womanhood probably far exceeded the modest number of women trained in mission schools" (46). I used the experiences of Cherokee women to inform my own approach to the study of Choctaw gender roles. Accordingly, I began my study with the theory that if the distinct divisions between men and women were a product of colonization, then at one time those roles must have been less distinct or less permanent. My research convinced me that at one time Choctaw women's roles were much more influential and flexible than previously believed.

Beyond Domesticity
Choctaw Women Negotiating the Tension
between Choctaw Culture and Protestantism (1999)

"In the daytime I see us as Christians so that we're Presbyterians, Methodists, Baptists, Pentecostals, whatever; but in the nighttime, then we become tribal [Choctaw] people again" (interview, May 2, 1994). This quote by an Oklahoma Choctaw Presbyterian minister suggests that a strong sense of Choctaw identity exists among Choctaw Protestants. Yet the idea of a strong Choctaw identity in the face of more than one hundred sixty years of intense missionization efforts seems oxymoronic. However, despite white American intentions of cultural genocide, Choctaw religio-cultural values and traditions still inform Choctaw identity, but because they are expressed within the context of Protestantism they exist relatively unnoticed. They exist, in part, because Choctaw women perpetuated Choctaw culture within Protestant churches. And they were able to do so because of white American assumptions about Choctaw gender roles. Women were assumed to have such minimal involvement in the religious, political, and economic life of the Choctaw that their activities elicited little concern on the part of missionaries.

Contrary to appearances, however, Choctaw women perpetuated Choctaw culture up to the present time and, ironically, did so within the alien structure of Protestant churches. To understand the process of culture retention within the Protestant church I draw on Angel Rama's study on narrative transculturation in Latin America. Rama argues that despite the homogenizing pressures of acculturation, local cultures resist total loss of their own culture for the acquired one. However, they resist "not by entrenching themselves rigidly within their traditions, but rather by engaging in processes of transculturation without giving up their souls." In other words, the cultures will go through a process of acculturation while preserving their particularity because, as Rama states, "modernity [acculturation] is unavoidable and to deny it is suicide as is also denying one's self in order to accept it" (1985, 33–34, 71; D'Allemand 1996, 363–64). Thus, to survive, a culture must find some way to negotiate the tension between acculturation and expression of culture.

One way in which the Choctaws resisted total acculturation, I argue, is through the actions of women under the imposed guise of domesticity. In this article I will look at how white American assumptions about gender roles provided a context in which Choctaw women could negotiate the tension between acculturation (in this case christianization) and culture retention. By tracing the changes in perceived and actual roles of women in eighteenth- and nineteenth-century Choctaw society we can gain insight into how Choctaw women kept their religio-cultural values and traditions alive through the structures of the Protestant churches. On the basis of the arguments of this study, I will offer a model for understanding Choctaw women's roles that goes beyond earlier assumptions about gender in Choctaw society that, in turn, will shed more light on the transculturation process among Protestant Choctaws.

Cult of True Womanhood

In 1755 an anonymous French writer described Choctaw women as "slaves to their husbands" who did "everything in the house, work the ground, sow, and harvest the crop" (Swanton 1931, 139). This image of oppressed Choctaw women persisted well into the nineteenth century. More than one hundred years later, Horatio Bardwell Cushman, a missionary who spent much of his life close to the Choctaw, expressed the same opinion when he characterized the wife of a warrior or hunter as "the slave of her husband" who does "all the drudgery work about the house and the hunting camp" (1899, 174). Not only were women perceived as slaves to their husbands, but they were also, as J. F. H. Claiborne, one-time Commissioner to the Choctaw, reported, "very submissive" (Swanton 1931, 139).

Choctaw women were not oppressed or submissive. These misconceptions about them arose from white American ideas of gender roles and what midnineteenth-century authors commonly referred to as "true womanhood" (Welter 1966, 151). This "cult of true womanhood" called for women to confine themselves to the domestic affairs of the home and leave economic and political pursuits to the men. In addition to confining themselves to concerns of the home, women were also expected to be submissive to men according to God's decree (159). In eighteenth- and nineteenth-century white America, ideally men farmed the land while women took care of the home. However, in traditional Choctaw society women owned and worked the fields. Thus, it appeared to missionaries and other white observers, who were appalled at the idea of women doing what they considered to be men's work, that Choctaw men forced women to work in the fields like slaves.

White American conceptions of true womanhood not only led to misconceptions about Choctaw women's roles but also contributed to changes in women's lives. According to Theda Perdue, in the nineteenth century white society began to impose its ideas of true womanhood on Choctaw women. She argues that southern indigenous women "could no longer behave in what was perceived to be a 'savage' or 'degraded' way" (1985, 35). As Choctaw women began to take on the characteristics of "true womanhood," they were increasingly seen by whites as powerless women confined primarily to domestic concerns of cooking, cleaning, sewing, and child-bearing.

The idea that women were limited to domestic concerns colored scholarly interpretations of women's experience. For instance, although colonization and missionization had a tremendous impact on women's roles, scholars have assumed that Choctaw women endured less change than men. In her article "Choctaw Women and Cultural Persistence in Mississippi," Clara Sue Kidwell, Choctaw historian, states that "women's roles as child bearers and contributors to subsistence were not threatening to white society and were less affected than those of men" (1995, 116). The underlying assumption of Kidwell's interpretation is that women were so disconnected from the powerful male world of politics, economics, and religion that their activities suffered less from colonization efforts. However, Choctaw women did not exist in a vacuum untouched by societal concerns. They experienced the traumatic effects of colonization as much as men did, but perhaps in different ways.

Choctaw women were also affected by intense missionization efforts, particularly by Presbyterians and Methodists. Although Choctaw leaders indicated their people were not interested in religious training, the missionaries labored vigorously to convert them to Christianity (Debo 1989, 14–16; ABCFM 1834, 243). In 1829 the Methodists reported that some thirteen hundred persons, mostly Choctaws, had experienced an emotional state associated with conversion, while the American Board of Commissioners for Foreign Missions records indicate that approximately 250 Choctaws had converted by the end of 1830 (Kidwell 1987, 68–69).

Although these conversions represented less than 8 percent of the population, missionization was having an impact on women's lives (Debo 1989, 45; Senate Exec. Doc. 512, 1833, 3:149). The few girls who attended mission schools were trained to become the archetypes of southern true womanhood. They learned to read scriptures and recite Christian prayers regularly, and they were taught white ways of sewing, cooking, and cleaning. Both girls and boys were taught that many of their customs were immoral. Influenced by the missionaries and highly motivated to adopt white ways, Choctaw leaders passed a number of laws that directly affected women. In 1822 Aboha Kullo Humma, chief of *Okla Hannali*, or the Southern District, passed laws making polygamy, infanticide, and divorce punishable by lashing (Cushman 1899, 87–88). Four years later leaders of all three districts of the nation passed a law that essentially took away matrilineal control of land by providing that a deceased man's property was to be divided between his widow and children (Kidwell 1995, 123).

When the Choctaws were removed to Indian Territory in the early 1830s, the missionaries followed them and continued their efforts. The missionaries were so successful that by the 1860s, 20 percent of the population was Christian (DeRosier 1972, 167; Debo 1989, 65, 78). For many Choctaws traditional ceremonies had been replaced by church camp meetings and Sunday schools, and they lived much like their white neighbors did. Choctaw women dressed the same as white women, and they patterned their daily lives after those of white women. Thus, it appeared that Choctaw women, for all intents and purposes, had become "white" women.

Pre-Nineteenth-Century Choctaw Women's Roles

Eighteenth- and nineteenth-century descriptions notwithstanding, Choctaw women were not submissive slaves to their husbands. In a society that valued and depended upon reciprocal relationships, women and men contributed to the well-being of their families and communities. Although the nature and extent of their contributions varied according to need and conditions, both engaged in all areas of Choctaw life. For example, women typically attended to local concerns such as gardens and fields, groves of fruit and nut trees, and homes. Men tended more to concerns away from home such as hunting, trading, and warring. However, women commonly accompanied men on their hunts, often traveling two or three hundred miles with them as they searched for deer, while others remained behind to care for the elderly and the young (Hudson 1994, 271–72).

As owners of the homes and fields women controlled the distribution of corn and other vegetables. Their contributions were important in a society that depended heavily upon an agriculturally based economy. According to John R. Swanton, an ethnologist, the Choctaw depended upon domesticated plants for their food more than any other southeastern society, and they raised enough corn to trade with their neighbors (1946, 817). While men often assisted during the height of the planting and harvesting seasons, women for the most part tended the fields and harvested them. In fact, corn, their most important domesticated plant, was given to them by Ohoyo Osh Chisba, a female supernatural (Hudson 1994, 272; Swanton 1931, 208–9). Women, who "had an exact knowledge of the country around them" and had particular groves that they visited each fall, also gathered wild vegetables, berries, fruits, and seeds (Hudson 1994, 270, 285–86).

The women, as mothers, also had many opportunities to teach their children about Choctaw traditions and values. A mother taught her daughters how to care for the homes and fields as well as by example about other aspects of Choctaw society. Although she did not directly train her sons, she influenced their training through their maternal uncles, who were responsible for the education of the young boys (Swanton 1931, 124–25). She also influenced her younger sons who were not yet old enough to leave her side. Younger sons and daughters, as well as elders, accompanied the mother in the fields, in the woods while she gathered wild foods, and as she worked around the home or at hunting camps.

Women also contributed to the Choctaw ritual cycle, which revolved around the planting and harvesting of corn. Corn itself was an essential ritual element of the annual green corn ceremony, which celebrated the harvest. More than a first fruits ceremony, the green corn ceremony was a time of social renewal and political decision-making and a time when social activities such as courting or marriage took place. This ritual marked a time when families and communities came together at a central ceremonial plaza to renew social relations through feasting and dancing. Feasting, an indispensable state function, demonstrated generosity and commitment to community and allies. Women not only prepared the feasts and attended to their homes in preparation for the ceremonies but also participated in the public functions of their towns whether in council or during dances (Swanton 1931, 97, 148–49, 221–26).

Although little information exists regarding women's roles during council gatherings, we do know that women participated in the decision-making process. According to Simpson Tubby, a Choctaw who spoke to Swanton, "if the women wanted a certain chief he was almost certain of election." He also stated that "if the head chief or a captain died suddenly and the vice-chief could not be present at an assembly which had already been summoned, the wife of the deceased took his place. . . . When she rose to speak . . . all kept quiet and listened attentively" (Swanton 1931, 100–101).

As the above account indicates, women had recognition, but it is difficult to ascertain the level of responsibility or status that they attained among their people because of the sexism inherent in white documentations of Choctaw society. For example, in the Choctaw language dictionary compiled by Cyrus Byington, *hatak asahnonchi* or *hatak asonunchi* is translated as "an elderly man; a presbyter" and the plural form as "elderly men; elders." But the female counterpart, *ohoyo kasheho*, is translated as "an aged woman; an aged female; an old wife" (1915, 137, 291). "Elder" or "presbyter" connotes respect and dignity, someone who has attained wisdom, while "aged" brings forth images of someone old and perhaps dependent.

The sexism of white society is perhaps more evident in the way whites documented honor titles. For example, throughout the Southeast honored or highly esteemed people were referred to as "beloveds." Turning again to Byington's dictionary, we find an entry for beloved man, *hatak holitopa*, but not for beloved woman. Yet, we know that there were honored women among the Choctaw. For instance, according to Simpson Tubby, women who were official messengers might be called *Mantema*, "to go and carry or deliver something sacred or particular"; *Onatima*, "when you get there give it (to him)"; or *Wakayatima*, "get up and hand it or deliver it." Tubby also told Swanton that wives of *mingoes* or band captains were given the titles *Nompashtika* or *Nompatisholi*, both meaning "speaker" (Swanton 1931, 121).

Although government records do not indicate the presence of women messengers or speakers during treaty negotiations or council meetings, these titles may still have been in use at least up to the time of removal in the early 1830s. An examination of the 1831 registers of Choctaws claiming reserves of land include personal names such as Onnatima,[1] also the title of a female messenger, and Mingohoyopa, which could be translated "this woman leader" or "this woman chief" or as the "wife of a *mingo*" (Senate Exec. Doc. 512, 1833, 3:39, 51; Byington 1915, 260).

The respect and influence of Choctaw women were clearly demonstrated during the council meeting that ended in the signing of the Treaty of Dancing Rabbit Creek in September 1830. In the center of a circle comprised of approximately sixty Choctaw councilmen, two United States commissioners, and several other whites who were connected in various ways to the commission sat seven Choctaw female elders. When one of the interpreters, Middleton Mackey,[2] first spoke, he addressed the women elders promising them that he would faithfully interpret to them everything said by the commissioners. He concluded by telling them, "and if I tell a lie, you may cut my neck off" (Halbert 1902, 382). As a white man who had been associated with the Choctaw for forty-five years, Mackey would have been familiar with Choctaw protocol. He demonstrated the respect and honor extended to female elders when he addressed them and empowered them to take his life if he failed at his job (DeRosier 1972, 127).

During the council meeting the women freely expressed their opinions. In one instance one of the female elders loudly voiced her indignation and disapproval when Killihota, a councilman, expressed his willingness to sell everything the Choctaw owned including their land and move west. The woman, incensed at Killihota's treasonous speech, threatened to cut him open with a butcher knife that she waved towards him. She accused him of having divided loyalties, a situation that would lead to the downfall of the Choctaw Nation. Two other councilmen successively arose and told Killihota that what the woman said about him was true. Killihota, distressed by the accusation of split loyalties, "stood for a few minutes with down-cast looks, then lifting his head he addressed the old women. 'You may hang me up,' said he, 'and cut my bosom open and you will see that I have only one heart and that for my people'" (Halbert 1902, 384–85).

Clearly, the women held a commanding presence among their people in the council meeting. Yet, despite the importance of this exchange between the women elders and Killihota, the commissioners for the United States did not record the women's presence, nor did they make mention of the heated discussion. Without the writings of Judge Antony Dillard of Alabama, who recorded the recollections of Colonel George S. Gaines, also of Alabama and the supplier of provisions at the meeting, we would not know that beloved women were present during council proceedings (Halbert 1902, 375, 384). If such a memorable scene had not been recorded by observers and participants at the council meeting, then it is reasonable to assume that other instances of women's presence at other council meetings also went unrecorded. More than likely, female elders, perhaps seven in number, participated in council meetings, including those held during green corn ceremonies.

Choctaw women were also known to take up arms in support of their communities. Bernard Romans, writing of his travels among the Choctaw in 1770 and 1771, said he was informed by a woman "that she kept a gun to defend herself as well as her husband did." He also wrote that several times he had "seen armed women in motion with the parties going in pursuit of the invading enemy" (Swanton 1931, 165). In another account, one by Jean-Bernard Bossu, a French naval officer, published in 1768, some Choctaw women accompanied their husbands to war. He described women carrying and passing arrows to the men while encouraging them to be brave in battle (Swanton 1931, 163). From these examples we can see that Choctaw women participated in the political life of the Choctaw during both peacetime and war. Unfortunately, their actions as well as the titles they might have earned remain largely unknown to us.

In addition to their economic and political activities, Choctaw women also achieved recognition as healers, diviners, and midwives. According to

Swanton, females were just as likely as men to be *alikchis* (doctors) of all specialties, and they were as successful in their practices as their counterparts. Women *alikchis* had herbal knowledge as well as ritual knowledge, and they were recognized as having the ability to foresee coming events (Swanton 1931, 118, 226; Cushman 1899, 307). Their treatments included emetics, cathartics, sweats, cold baths, scarification, cupping, and sucking. Prior to becoming *alikchis* both men and women might be appointed to serve as "medicine givers." A male medicine giver had to be present when a man took certain medicines, and a woman medicine giver had to be present when a female did (Swanton 1931, 235–36). But, as in the political life of Choctaw women, very little has been documented about their roles in the healing practices of the Choctaw.

Changing Women's Roles

As the examples above indicate, Choctaw women once held positions of importance in the economic, political, and religious life of their communities. By the 1800s, however, as the sexism and ethnocentrism of white society began to infiltrate the infrastructure of Choctaw society, their roles began to undergo change. This trend reflected changes that were taking place in white society. In nineteenth-century white America, males dominated the economic, religious, and political arenas. White women occupied the separate and secondary domestic domain, and, according to feminist scholar Denise Riley, they became willing inhabitants of the domestic sphere (1988, 66). White males and females expected the ideal woman to attend to the domestic affairs of the home only.

As white males interacted more and more with Choctaws—whether through marriage, trade, government negotiations, or missionization—they treated Choctaw women in accordance with their expectations of the ideal southern woman. Threatened by the influence and presence of Choctaw women, white men reacted in ways that increasingly pushed Choctaw women into the second-class status that their white counterparts were experiencing.[3] White males refused to negotiate with Choctaw women in both the political and economic arenas, silencing their voices in the public sphere. They helped confine women to the home by urging Choctaw men to take over farming responsibilities, thus stripping women of their primary means of contributing to the economic life of the town, which in turn affected their participation in the political and religious life of the Choctaws.

On a more personal level, intermarriage with white men significantly impacted Choctaw women's positions in the family and community. White patrilineal and patriarchal emphases contributed to the breakdown of the clan system that had supported a matrilineal society; it took away women's ownership of the home and other property; and child rearing became the responsibility of the father rather than of the mother and her maternal relatives (Eggan 1937, 42, 50; Gibson 1973, 79–80). These changes rendered women invisible, particularly to the non-Choctaw world. White male attitudes toward Choctaw women inevitably infiltrated the structure of Choctaw society. Political, economic, and religious concerns, once the shared responsibilities of men and women, slowly became male dominated, or so it seemed. Evidence indicates women continued to participate in all aspects of Choctaw life in the early nineteenth century. However, their presence in the public aspects of councils and trade negotiations began to decline in response to increasing pressures to conform to white expectations of gender roles.

Thus, Choctaw women were experiencing changes in their participation in the social structures of their society when news of their impending removal to Indian Territory reached them in September 1830. Less than a month after the Treaty of Dancing Rabbit Creek had been signed, somewhere between five and six hundred families were on their way to Greenwood Leflore's home where the 500-mile walk to Indian Territory would begin. They left Mississippi, vastly underprovisioned and under less than ideal conditions. They made the walk in the worst of winter conditions with inadequate supplies of food, clothing, shelter, wagons, and horses. Many died along the way as "old women and young children, without any covering for their feet, legs, or body, except a cotton under-dress generally," travelled on foot through swamps and often in heavy sleet (Senate Exec. Doc. 512, 1833, 1:720).

As a result of conditions, separations from the men who were hunting, and delays, on March 7, 1831, Lieutenant Jas. R. Stephenson reported that "of a thousand Choctaw emigrants reported to have been sent west by Leflore several months earlier, only eighty-eight had arrived; they were principally women and children and in all but a starving condition."[4] These survivors, weak from hunger and sickness, were forced to stay in some old log buildings that remained after Fort Towson had been abandoned two years earlier. The women set up their households in the dilapidated buildings as best they could. They arrived in Indian Territory to start a new life separated from the only homes they had known for generations and from their towns, the centers of their ceremonial and social life (Foreman 1989, 41–42; Senate Exec. Doc. 512, 1833, 1:852).

The process of acculturation that began in Mississippi continued in Indian Territory. Women increasingly conformed to the American image of the "ideal southern woman," an image strongly reinforced by the missionaries who relocated with the Choctaws. After removal, Choctaw leaders moved quickly to build churches and mission schools in their new homelands. As more and more Choctaws became involved with Christian missions, their society increasingly became like white society. Their clothing, homes, and education mirrored that of their white neighbors (Debo 1989, 78). On the surface, Choctaw women, like their white counterparts, appeared to be confined to a life of domesticity seemingly excluded from religious, political, or economic concerns.

Transculturation Process

An examination of life in Indian Territory indicates that Choctaw women continued to contribute to all areas of Choctaw society; however, they now did so through the medium of domestic activity. Since white society equated domesticity with the feminine and presumed that the concerns of the domestic sphere were separate from the real political concerns of men (Sampson 1993, 147), Choctaw women could indirectly influence the religious, economic, and political life of the Choctaw with little notice being taken by white society. Apparently the domestic sphere seemed innocuous not only to the general white population but, more importantly, to missionaries among the Choctaw. It was this notion of the domestic as being feminine and nonthreatening to the colonizing process that provided Choctaw women the means to perpetuate Choctaw culture in Protestant churches.

The missionaries struggled to rid the Choctaw of their remaining customs and rituals; however, they soon acquiesced to those activities where women and domestic activities were most visible. For example, although the missionaries tried to replace *yaiyas* (funeral cries) with Christian services, they were not able to do so. Instead, *yaiyas* became part of the Christian funeral service. During the *yaiyas* women periodically went to the grave of the deceased to weep and express grief to the memory of the dead. After the cry ended, the women prepared a feast for the mourners (Swanton 1931, 173; Cushman 1899, 145–46). Although men sometimes participated in the cry, the greater visibility of women at the *yaiyas* as well as the feasting led missionaries to dismiss *yaiyas* as a threat to missionization goals. Besides, *yaiyas* provided them with an opportunity to preach to the large gatherings of Choctaws who attended them. The lack of missionary concern with the supposed nonreligious, nonpolitical domestic activities of women has allowed *yaiyas* to continue up to the present day.

By the 1950s the length of *yaiyas* had been shortened and the ritual activities somewhat altered, but the basic form remained the same. In the early 1990s I asked several Choctaws about contemporary funeral practices. According to one seminary student, in Choctaw Parish, Presbyterian Church (U.S.A.), it is not uncommon for participants at three-day meetings or camp meetings to hold a memorial. Much like the one-year anniversary of the *yaiya*, the people take time to mourn the people who have died since the last time the meeting was held. A song is sung for the dead, usually in the Choctaw language (interview, July 31, 1993). In another instance, Bertram Bobb, Chaplain of the Oklahoma Choctaw Tribal Council, noted that many features of the cry still exist in rural areas, particularly in northern McCurtain County and eastern Pushmataha County. He said that wakes are often held in the home of the deceased, and feasting usually takes place at the house of the family of the deceased (interview, November 5, 1990).

Another example of missionary acquiescence to perceived domestic activities can be seen in their use of camp meetings as a forum to preach to Choctaws. Camp gatherings, once part of the earlier green corn ceremonies, became part of church life. In many ways, however, Choctaws experienced church camp meetings more as a Choctaw event than a Christian one. Large crowds gathered during the meetings, not always to attend services but rather to socialize with other Choctaws. Instead of camping around a central ceremonial plaza, families now set up camps all around the arbor where preaching took place. Just as in earlier times, each camp shared whatever it had, including food, labor, and stories.

When Choctaws began to build permanent church structures, they also erected permanent family camphouses that are still used today. The hospitality, reciprocity, and socializing that took place around ceremonial fires of earlier times continued at these camp gatherings. The missionaries did not discourage camp meetings because to them they were simply social gatherings where eating and visiting took place. These were domestic concerns of women that had little to do with religion. What the missionaries did not see, or perhaps what they ignored, was that the camp gatherings provided a way for women to express and perpetuate Choctaw values of reciprocity and redistribution, as well as language and identity through feasting, story-telling, and socializing.

That the missionaries responded differently toward women-centered activities than they did toward male-centered ones is clearly demonstrated by their reactions to *tolih* (stickball games). Like funerals and camp meetings, stickball games drew large crowds of Choctaws who set up camps, feasted together, and visited for several days. Yet the missionaries vehemently denounced ballgames and urged the federal government to ban them. The significant difference appears to be the focus on men. The warlike games, once played by men and women, had become a male sport steeped in religious ritual such as purification of players and performative prayer through dance. Players wore Choctaw religious symbols and used medicine and *isht ahollo* (witchery) to help them defeat their opponents. The missionaries considered such activities the domain of men and a threat to missionary goals.

Unlike *yaiyas* and camp meetings, which provided opportunities for preaching, *tolih* had always proved to be an impediment to the work of the missionaries. In May 1830 in response to the removal threat, Choctaw leaders in the southeastern district passed a resolution that stickball and dances should be encouraged instead of attendance at church services (*Missionary Herald* 1830, 254). Later, in Indian Territory the missionaries found themselves once again competing with *tolih* matches. Choctaws, Christian and non-Christian, would forego church camp meetings for a *tolih* match whenever one was in progress. The missionaries soon learned not to schedule a camp meeting at the same time as a *tolih* match (Benson 1860, 39).

The missionaries seemed to ignore the social aspects of the game; they only saw betting, conjuring, chanting, and ball playing—all considered male activities by whites. Under constant fire by the missionaries, *tolih* lost its draw as the national sport of the Choctaw by 1907. It was still played, but it became more a form of entertainment at community picnics or county fairs rather than a display of physical strength and supernatural power (Morrison 1987, 115). *Tolih* nearly died out, but in the 1970s it made a comeback as an exhibition sport. Women became active in the stickball game again, but they no longer played with ball sticks, nor did they play separately in the rough and skillful manner of past generations. Instead men and women played together in exhibition games.

By the time of the Civil War the distinctions between male-centered and female-centered activities already had been internalized by many Choctaw

Christians. Reverend Israel Folsom, a Choctaw missionary, wrote that the ball-play dance, war dance, eagle dance, and scalp dance were important national dances. The rest of them were insignificant and did not deserve notice (Cushman 1899, 308). The so-called important dances were men's dances. The ones he considered insignificant were the social dances, which, according to Cushman, were the only ones in which women were permitted to participate (Swanton 1931, 223; Cushman 1899, 156). However, according to George Catlin women also danced ballgame dances (Densmore 1943, 132).

Although there is little ethnographic documentation regarding the meaning of Choctaw social dances, it is reasonable to assume that they were once based in beliefs about human relationships with animals and other aspects of the world. According to Frank G. Speck and Leonard Broom, who observed a similar situation with the Cherokee, social dances are now perceived mainly as social forms, but some older people believed that the dances exerted an influence over animals and their associations with human beings (1951, 7). The distinction between the religious and the social or secular is a western one that has become part of Christian Choctaw ideology. Such a distinction undoubtedly led Swanton to comment that what the Choctaw lacked in ceremonialism, "they seem to have made up for in social dances and feasts" (1931, 221).

It is no surprise then that when Choctaw Christians began revitalizing social dances in the 1970s, they received support from most members of Choctaw Parish and the Executive Presbyter of Eastern Oklahoma Presbytery, Presbyterian Church (U.S.A.) (interview, May 2, 1994). The same was true for the United Methodists. Choctaw Methodists began powwow dancing in the 1970s particularly in the Talihina area. Many Choctaw Methodists and Presbyterians told me that dancing inside churches was frowned upon, but dancing outside on church grounds or exhibition dancing was deemed okay. The revival of social dances demonstrates a consistent attitude towards perceived women's activities by Christians, Choctaw and white. As women's dances, social dances were considered nonreligious and thus nonthreatening to the church.

Contemporary Choctaw Women and Culture Retention

Today Choctaw women who are members of Protestant churches continue to perpetuate Choctaw culture through a number of venues, many of which are conceived of as domestic activities. Outside the church structure, for example, one Choctaw woman, Juanita Jefferson, a member of St. Paul

United Methodist Church, organized a group of American Indian senior citizens to teach them Indian sign language, Choctaw and other indigenous gospel songs, and powwow dance steps. While signing and gospel songs are not Choctaw and, in fact, reinforce Christian ideals, these activities also reinforce Choctaw language, identity, and community. Choctaws gather to watch the signing or singing, and, as Alfonso Ortiz states, "there are, ideally speaking, no observers, only participants . . . dramas mobilize a community's moods and motivations and reflect their collective identity" (1972, 139). By watching and listening, observers reinforce and are part of the community. Powwow dancing, which is neither Choctaw nor Christian but rather of Plains Indian derivation, is accepted because it is perceived as a social activity of the church and not a ceremonial ritual.

Choctaw women also perpetuate Choctaw culture within the church structure itself. For example, when Presbyterian members of Choctaw Parish wanted someone to begin telling Choctaw stories at youth camps, they approached a female elder in 1983 and asked her to be a storyteller. She researched and developed Choctaw stories (primarily animal stories) over a two-year period, during which she told them to the children in English with Choctaw words mixed in or in Choctaw only (interview, May 2, 1994). Again, through storytelling language was reinforced as well as Choctaw values. And, like dances, storytelling was perceived as part of the nurturing of children by Christian Choctaws. Stories were tales to entertain and to reinforce cultural identity. The old traditional stories that connected the Choctaws to their heritage had validity as expressions of Choctaw culture, but the youth were not expected to accept them as valid religious teachings like those found in the Bible.

The greatest impact by women, however, occurred through the domestic functions of providing food and taking care of children and elders. In the past and even in the present day, whites have conspired to instill values of individualism and capitalism among Choctaws. Choctaw women, however, have countered those efforts through feasting and caretaking roles. Today a major component of Sunday services is the fellowship dinner after the sermon.[5] Members gather around a communal table and eat and visit before leaving the church. A young pastor aptly described the importance of providing for visitors and sharing one's food when he told me that Choctaws "will give their last meal from the table and put it in a potluck to share with everybody else" (Pesantubbee 1994, 223). Just as with the green corn ceremony of old, the women through preparation of food honor visitors and reinforce community. Through Sunday dinners Choctaws reinforce traditional ideals of reciprocity, communal sharing, and respect towards visitors and family members. One Choctaw pastor, in discussing the importance of sharing with me, described how the Choctaw women brought food to the church: "they would bring trunkloads of food, and that was the way of sharing. I think that's really what kind of sets the Choctaws apart from other churches" (interview, March 11, 1993).

Women also reinforce Choctaw traditions through their roles as caretakers of children, the elderly, and the sick. As I traveled around the Choctaw Nation in 1992 and 1993, I observed that if someone in the community needed aid, whether food or transportation to the doctor, women tended to help out in greater numbers than the men. The domestic concerns of family, health care, and education also are the responsibility of women within the church structure. In every Methodist, United Presbyterian (U.S.A.), and Southern Baptist Choctaw church I visited, women attended church in greater numbers by far than men did, and the majority of those men and women were elders. The second-largest group in the church was the young children. Thus, women more often than men were observed teaching Sunday School and Bible School to the children and elders. They not only taught the children about the Bible but also Choctaw songs and crafts, again reinforcing Choctaw culture and values. One summer intern for Choctaw Parish commented to me that the previous summer he noticed "that at several of our camp meetings during the summer, most of the leadership was women" (interview, July 31, 1993).

Church is also where women reinforce Choctaw traditional childcare practices. In school and on the playground Choctaw children behave according to western standards, but in the Choctaw church they behave as Choctaw children always have. In traditional Choctaw society adults did not discipline children with harsh words or spankings or separate them from adults during religious events because they were noisy. Children simply were not expected to behave as adults. This philosophy is evident in contemporary churches. In many of the churches I visited I watched children entertain themselves during services with toys or books and freely move about the sanctuary. They often walked up to the front of the church to stand near a parent or grandparent who was leading songs or praying (Pesantubbee 1994, 163–64). I have often observed a pastor raise his or her voice over the noise of the children rather than tell them to be quiet. As the primary caretakers of the children the women carry on the earlier practices of their ancestors.[6]

While teaching Sunday School, caring for children, or preparing feasts have provided women the means to perpetuate culture, their participation in the church has gone beyond the domestic. Today, women participate in pastoring and administration of churches, areas that typically have been dominated by men. While women have always been active on committees, pastoring by women was unheard of before midcentury. In the nineteenth and early twentieth centuries they were expected to be the models of piousness (Welter 1966, 152–53), to teach by example, but not to be the authorities in the public sphere of religion. Today women pastors are not unusual, and women lay preachers in Choctaw Parish are almost commonplace. Among Choctaw Presbyterians lay women responded to the shortage of male pastors in the 1970s by assuming pastoral duties. These women lay pastors, like their male counterparts, reinforce Choctaw identity by interspersing Choctaw with English during their sermons and by leading Choctaw hymns. At one United Methodist church I visited, the pastor related a Bible story using Choctaw symbols. She ended the story by saying Jesus would have made a good Choctaw.

Choctaw Christian women have taken Protestant Christianity, which was complicit in the suppression of Choctaw traditions and religious practices, and made it a forum for reinforcing Choctaw culture. They have been able to use the church to reinforce traditional ways because the church fulfilled many of the functions that their ceremonial structure once did. The songs and dances that once were part of their ceremonies have been replaced by all-night gospel singing, fifth Sunday singing, or revivals. Many of the features once found at green corn ceremonies are now part of gospel singings. Both are places for feasting, socializing, and honoring one another. Like at green corn ceremonies, women are involved in preparing food, singing songs, honoring people, planning events, and caring for others.

Gospel singings also reinforce a sense of community. It is a place where Christian and non-Christian Choctaws can come together as one people. One young Choctaw man who was training for the ministry told me that "when it's an all-night singing, people from all denominations are welcome, and a lot of times the people don't go necessarily to sing, but they go to socialize, to see other people . . . it is a valid form of worship, you know, singing praise, but at the same time, . . . I think it has some social meaning underneath there" (interview, July 31, 1993). That social meaning is the sense of Choctaw community generated by the singings. Gospel singings invigorate and renew community ties just as the green corn ceremonies once did.

The popularity of gospel singings may be due in part to the fact that they serve a social function but also because they are Christian oriented and thus are approved of by Christians both Choctaw and white. The all-night gospel singings may also be popular because they are decidedly Choctaw in form. They originated from an earlier pattern found in Choctaw social and ceremonial life—all-night dancing. Traditional dances took place at night, involved extensive singing, and served as occasions for reinforcing ties with friends and relatives. Those features carried over to gospel singings, which are also held at night and which draw large groups of Choctaws together who want to listen or sing or socialize. As the pastor of Choctaw Parish put it, people go to singings not because they are Christians but because they are Choctaws.

Today the Choctaw Nation is recognized by Choctaws and non-Choctaws as a Christian nation, and it is, but it is also still very much Choctaw in its values and its traditions, except that the context has changed. Instead of gathering at the ceremonial plaza, they gather at the church or campground. Wherever they gather, Choctaw women will be perpetuating Choctaw culture through their work in the domestic domain. White America may have assumed that Choctaw women were confined to the domestic sphere and thus exercised little influence on the religious and political life of the Choctaw. However, it was just this assumption about Choctaw women and domesticity that provided the means for Choctaw women to perpetuate Choctaw culture in Protestant churches. As long as Choctaw women were seen as nonthreatening to acculturation because they had been deliberately relegated to a life of domesticity, separated from the more powerful and public political, economic, and religious spheres of men, they could continue to express Choctaw values and traditions relatively unhindered (Riley 1988, 46; Sampson 1993, 146–47).

Conclusion

The underlying assumption in this interpretation of Choctaw women's roles in the transcultural process of maintaining Choctaw identity is that white America compartmentalized society into public and private spheres dominated by men and women, respectively. What whites did not realize was that while Choctaw society had gender distinctions, and at times the genders were separated from each other, they did not function independently of each other. Nor did the various concerns of society—economic, political, religious, and domestic—exist separately. All were connected and interdependent on each other. Thus, it would be shortsighted indeed to determine Choctaw women's roles in the transculturation process based on nineteenth-century concepts of gender and domesticity.

Just as the boundaries between functions of society were fluid, so too were the boundaries between male and female roles. For instance, an individual's responsibility might be determined by external forces such as famine or war. At such times the immediate concern of the town's survival might call for changes in roles that were not common in times of peace or plenty. While it is true that women were more likely to participate in peacetime activities than in wartime ones, it is also true that women might assume typically male roles at times of disaster. Thus, it would be misleading to assume that an individual's contribution to society depended solely upon gender and function. Rather, we must look for other determining factors of gender roles beyond the oppositional dichotomies of public and private concerns and male and female categories.

I would like to offer another model that is characterized by multiple complementary constituents rather than oppositional dichotomies such as submission/power and private/public roles. By discerning the multiple principles by which Choctaw gender roles are constructed we can better determine the various ways in which women participate in Choctaw society. For example, if we limit our analysis to the categories of submission/power and private/public, then we could erroneously conclude that men held more important and influential roles than women. However, in pre-nineteenth-century Choctaw society all functions were necessary and valued. It did not matter if it were a small child gathering a handful of nuts or an adult male defending his family from enemy attacks—both contributions were equally valid and integral ways of maintaining community life and solidarity. Thus, Choctaw women would not be considered less important than men if they limited their activities to domestic concerns, and men would not be more important than women if they dominated the religious, economic, and political life of Choctaw society. This is not to say that an individual could not gain status but rather that status depended upon one's accomplishments or abilities and not simply on the type of contribution one made.

Separating the functions of society into parts—domestic, economic, religious, and political—is also problematic because separation belies the notion of reciprocity and interdependence that lies at the heart of Choctaw community. In Choctaw society it did not make sense to disassociate one function from another. Religion was not separate from the domestic,

nor the domestic from the political, and so on. All functions were interdependent and necessary. If all functions are interdependent, then gender
roles must have been determined by factors other than separate functions
of society. In addition, to say one function is more powerful than another
is to say it is more important, again not recognizing the necessity and value
of all functions. Thus, it is arbitrary to study Choctaw gender roles only in
terms of western concepts of dichotomous oppositions. We must look for
culturally specific ways of studying Choctaw society.

A closer examination of Choctaw economic roles, for example, suggests
criteria other than oppositional dichotomous categories may have contributed to the determination of gender roles. Prior to the nineteenth century
women were primarily the horticulturalists and men the hunters. Yet, at
times men worked the fields and women accompanied men on their hunting trips. Obviously the boundaries between genders or between functions
(horticulture and hunting) blurred or shifted at times. We need to identify
those occasions when the boundaries were less distinct. By doing so we may
uncover additional, perhaps more relevant, criteria that contribute to the
determination of gender roles in Choctaw society. We can then use those
criteria to trace and understand changing gender roles and their impact on
the process of transculturation.

I suggest that a number of factors contribute to the determination of gender responsibilities including the complementary principles of local/distant,
safety/danger, and noncontact/contact with blood. We know women primarily were responsible for the fields, orchards, and wild food gathering—in
other words, local concerns. Men had responsibility for more distant matters: hunting, trading, and warring. However, there are times when considerations of safety/danger or noncontact/contact with blood counter concerns
with local/distant activities. For instance, to protect childbearers or potential
childbearers, women held jobs that were relatively safe, while men took on
more dangerous jobs. Thus, for the most part women gathered nuts, fruits,
and wild vegetables—local, safe activities. However, men collected honey, a
local task but one that involved the danger of bee attacks. During times of
famine men also would be the ones to raid the stores of acorns and other
nuts of bears and squirrels (Campbell 1959, 11, 15), again local but dangerous
activities. With respect to horticulture, a local, safe task, if the community
did not plant and harvest its crops in a timely manner, an important food
source could be lost. During these times of potential danger for crops and in
turn the community's well-being, men helped with a local task.

In each of the above examples we could argue from the dichotomous standpoint of horticulture/hunting that men were doing women's work. But since these activities included the element of danger, they became men's work. Continuing this same line of reasoning, men usually hunted, an activity involving distance and danger. Yet women often accompanied the hunters on their long trips. In this case concerns for safety determined women's responsibilities while away on hunting trips. Typically, women stayed at the hunting camps (which can be considered local) where they took care of the camp and processed the meats and hides, safe from the danger of frightened or injured animals.

Another factor involved in hunting is contact with blood, an important concern in Choctaw society. Whether it was a menstruating woman or a man returning from hunting or warring, each had been exposed to blood that had crossed the boundaries of the body and thus she/he was separated from the rest of the community. These concerns are apparent in the economic functions of Choctaw society. Thus, women typically did not hunt large game that would require them to cause blood to cross the boundaries of the animal's body. However, young girls often assisted boys in trapping small game, fishing, and collecting mussels (Campbell 1959, 11), food-gathering responsibilities that entailed little or no contact with blood. They were also relatively safe activities that took place close to home.

Although these three categories of local/distant, safety/danger, and noncontact/contact with blood do not exhaust all the possible ways of determining gender roles, they do demonstrate that the construction of historical Choctaw gender roles derives from a complex, interdependent system of variables that shift and change depending on circumstances. While dichotomous concepts like submission/power and domestic/public spheres provide particular ways of interpreting gender roles, in the case of Choctaw gender roles they limit and in some cases distort our views of them. As the preceding discussion indicates, every individual has a valid way of contributing to the needs of Choctaw society. That contribution is not limited to a particular function of society. Since the various functions of Choctaw society are inseparable, the actions of each individual have an impact on all areas of life whether direct or indirect. Rather than perceiving religious concerns as contained within or exercised by a particular segment of society such as males in the public sphere, we could, for example, examine how the manifestation of the religious is communal in nature within a flexible, interconnected structure. This is not to say that expressions of religiosity never inhere in the person but rather that personal expression is also simultaneously communal. In other words, in historical Choctaw society religiosity was not defined by individualistic, inflexible, or autonomous structures.

In the case of gender roles in Choctaw society it would seem appropriate to develop a theoretical model utilizing a concept of communal activity in a flexible structure in order to construct a viable, more encompassing picture of women's participation in Choctaw society. For example, we know that at least in one instance women elders sat in the "safe" center of councils, surrounded by male council members. If we look at councils as an expression of communal activity whose membership changes according to the criteria of local/distant, safety/danger, and noncontact/contact with blood instead of as the disassociated political and powerful domain of men, we can surmise instances when women would be present in them. We also can use these criteria to discern Choctaw women's involvement in other functions of society across time and place consistent with Choctaw communal structures. Once we set aside oppositional dichotomies as templates for determining gender roles, we also can begin to understand and identify the multiple and diverse ways in which Choctaw women (and men) negotiated the tension between retention of Choctaw cultural identity and acculturation to Protestant Christianity.

Notes

1. Various spellings of names and titles appear in the literature. In each instance I follow the spelling used by the source.
2. Halbert erroneously identified the interpreter as Middleton McKee.
3. See Hatley (1993, 148–54) for a discussion of white male attitudes toward Cherokee women, whom they considered "dangerously domineering in tribal marriages" and a threat to colonial proper authority.
4. One estimate indicates that 400 of the 1,000 Choctaws actually left Mississippi in December (DeRosier 1972, 132).
5. In Choctaw Parish churches are on a circuit and typically have dinner on those Sundays when a pastor is present. Among the Methodists in the Southeast District Sunday dinner is usually held once a month, for instance, the first Sunday of the month.
6. This approach to childcare is not universal in Choctaw churches. One young man recalled growing up in a Presbyterian church where children were expected to behave according to strict standards. At one Southern Baptist church I observed the pastor admonishing the children to be quiet and chastising parents for not controlling them.

References

American Board of Commissioners for Foreign Missions [ABCFM]. 1834. Minutes of the Tenth Annual Meeting of the American Board of Commissioners for Foreign Missions. In *First Ten Annual Reports of the American Board of Commissioners for Foreign Missions, with other Documents of the Board.* Boston: Crocker and Brewster.

Benson, Henry C. 1860. *Life among the Choctaw Indians, and Sketches of the South-West.* Cincinnati: L. Swormstedt & A. Poe.

Byington, Cyrus. 1915. *A Dictionary of the Choctaw Language.* Bureau of American Ethnology Bulletin, 46. Ed. John R. Swanton and Henry S. Halbert. Washington DC: Government Printing Office.

Campbell, T. N. 1959. "Choctaw Subsistence: Ethnographic Notes from the Lincecum Manuscript." *Florida Anthropologist* 12 (1): 9–24.

Cushman, H. B. 1899. *History of the Choctaw, Chickasaw and Natchez Indians.* 2nd ed. 1972. New York: Russell & Russell.

D'Allemand, Patricia. 1996. "Urban Literary Production and Latin American Criticism." *Bulletin of Latin American Research* 15 (3): 359–69.

Debo, Angie. 1989. *The Rise and Fall of the Choctaw Republic.* 1934. 2nd ed. Norman: University of Oklahoma Press.

Densmore, Frances. 1943. *Choctaw Music.* Bureau of American Ethnology Bulletin, 136. Washington DC: Government Printing Office.

DeRosier, Arthur H., Jr. 1972. *The Removal of the Choctaw Indians.* Knoxville: University of Tennessee Press, 1970. Reprint. New York: Harper & Row.

Eggan, Fred. 1937. "Historical Changes in the Choctaw Kinship System." *American Anthropologist* 3 (9): 34–52.

Foreman, Grant. 1989. *Indian Removal.* American Indian Civilization Series, 2. 1932. New ed. Norman: University of Oklahoma Press.

Gibson, A. M. 1973. "The Indians of Mississippi." In *A History of Mississippi*, 1:69–89. Hattiesburg: University College Press of Mississippi.

Halbert, H. S. 1902. "Story of the Treaty of Dancing Rabbit." *Publications of the Mississippi Historical Society* 6:373–402.

Hatley, Tom. 1993. *The Dividing Paths.* New York: Oxford University Press.

Hudson, Charles. 1994. *The Southeastern Indians.* 1976. Knoxville: University of Tennessee Press.

Kidwell, Clara Sue. 1987. "Choctaws and Missionaries in Mississippi before 1830." *American Indian Culture and Research Journal* 11 (2): 51–72.

———. 1995. "Choctaw Women and Cultural Persistence in Mississippi." In *Negotiators of Change*, ed. Nancy Shoemaker, 115-34. New York and London: Routledge.

Missionary Herald. 1830. "The Present Condition of the Mission, as Affected by the Proposed Removal of the Indians." 26/8.

Morrison, James D. 1987. *The Social History of the Choctaw Nation: 1865–1907.* Durant OK: Creative Infomatics.

Ortiz, Alfonso, ed. 1972. *New Perspectives on the Pueblos.* Albuquerque: University of New Mexico Press.

Perdue, Theda. 1985. "Southern Indians and the Cult of True Womanhood." In *The Web of Southern Social Relations,* ed. Walter J. Fraser Jr., R. Frank Saunders Jr., and Jon L. Wakelyn, 35–51. Athens: University of Georgia Press.

Pesantubbee, Michelene. 1994. "Culture Revitalization and Indigenization of Choctaw Churches." Ph.D. diss., University of California, Santa Barbara.

Rama, Angel. 1985. *Transculturacion Narrativa En America Latina.* 1982. Mexico City, D.F.: Siglo Vientiuno Editores.

Riley, Denise. 1988. *"Am I That Name?" Feminism and the Category of "Women" in History.* Minneapolis: University of Minnesota Press.

Sampson, Edward E. 1993. *Celebrating the Other: A Dialogic Account of Human Nature.* Boulder: Westview Press.

Senate Exec. Doc. 512. 1833. Correspondence on the Subject of Emigration of Indians. 23rd Cong., 1st sess., vols. 1 and 3.

Senate Exec. Doc. & Rep. 1830. "Extract of a Letter from John Donly to the Secretary of War." In Senate Executive Documents and Reports. 21st Cong., 2nd sess.

Speck, Frank G., and Leonard Broom. 1951. *Cherokee Dance and Drama.* Reprint. Norman: University of Oklahoma Press. 1983.

Swanton, John R. 1931. *Source Material for the Social and Ceremonial Life of the Choctaw Indians.* Washington DC: Government Printing Office.

———. 1946. *The Indians of the Southern United States.* Bureau of American Ethnology Bulletin, 137. Washington DC: Government Printing Office.

Welter, Barbara. 1966. "The Cult of True Womanhood: 1820–1860." *American Quarterly* 18 (2): 151–74.

Interviews

November 5, 1990. Bertram Bobb, Chaplain, Choctaw Tribal Council. Antlers OK: by telephone.

March 11, 1993. Anonymous. Los Angeles CA: Native American Ministry Project.

July 31, 1993. Anonymous. Sallisaw OK: Dwight Mission.

May 2, 1994. Eugene Wilson. Idabel OK: by telephone.

Source Acknowledgments

Chapter 1, "The Pocahontas Perplex: The Image of Indian Women in American Culture," by Rayna Green, originally appeared in *Massachusetts Review* 16 (autumn 1975): 698–714.

Chapter 2, "The 'Squaw Drudge': A Prime Index of Savagism," by David D. Smits with excerpts selected by the editors, originally appeared in *Ethnohistory* 29, no. 4 (1982): 281–306. Excerpts selected by the editors of this anthology.

Chapter 3, "Indian Women as Cultural Mediators," by Clara Sue Kidwell, originally appeared in *Ethnohistory* 39, no. 2 (1992): 97–107.

Chapter 4, "Woman as Centre and Symbol in the Emergence of Métis Communities," by Jennifer S. H. Brown, originally appeared in *Canadian Journal of Native Studies* 3, no. 1 (1983): 39–46.

Chapter 5, "Women's Status in Egalitarian Society: Implications for Social Evolution," by Eleanor Leacock with excerpts selected by the editors, originally appeared in *Current Anthropology* 19, no. 2 (1978): 247–75. Excerpts selected by the editors of this anthology.

Chapter 6, "Blood Ties and Blasphemy: American Indian Women and the Problem of History," by Kathryn Shanley with excerpts selected by the editors, originally appeared in *Is Academic Feminism Dead? Theory in Practice*, ed. The Social Justice Group at The Center for Advanced Feminist Studies, University of Minnesota (New York: New York University Press, 2000), 204–32. Excerpts selected by the editors of this anthology.

Chapter 7, "Coocoochee: Mohawk Medicine Woman," by Helen Hornbeck Tanner, originally appeared in *American Indian Culture and Research Journal* 3, no. 3 (1979): 23–41.

Chapter 8, "Leadership within the Women's Community: Susie Bonga Wright of the Leech Lake Ojibwe," by Rebecca Kugel, originally appeared in *Midwestern Women: Work, Community, and Leadership at the Cross-*

roads, ed. Lucy Eldersveld Murphy and Wendy Hamand Venet (Bloomington: Indiana University Press, 1997), 17–37.

Chapter 9, "Marie Rouensa-8cate8a and the Foundations of French Illinois," by Carl Ekberg with Anton J. Pregaldin, originally appeared in *Illinois Historical Journal* 84, no. 3 (1991): 146–59.

Chapter 10, "Women, Kin, and Catholicism: New Perspectives on the Fur Trade," by Susan Sleeper-Smith, originally appeared in *Ethnohistory* 47, no. 2 (2000): 423–52.

Chapter 11, "Cherokee Women and the Trail of Tears," by Theda Perdue, originally appeared in *Journal of Women's History* 1.1 (1989): 14–30.

Chapter 12, "The Rise or Fall of Iroquois Women," by Nancy Shoemaker, originally appeared in *Journal of Women's History* 2, no. 3 (1991): 39–57.

Chapter 13, "'Divorced' from the Land: Resistance and Survival of Indian Women in Eighteenth-Century New England," by Jean M. O'Brien, originally appeared in *After King Philip's War: Presence and Persistence in Indian New England*, ed. Colin G. Calloway (Hanover NH: University Press of New England, 1997), 144–61.

Chapter 14, "To Live among Us: Accommodation, Gender, and Conflict in the Western Great Lakes Region, 1760–1832," by Lucy Eldersveld Murphy, originally appeared in *Contact Points: American Frontiers from the Mohawk Valley to the Mississippi, 1750–1830*, ed. Andrew R. L. Cayton and Fredrika J. Teute (Chapel Hill: University of North Carolina Press, 1998), 270–303.

Chapter 15, *Mountain Wolf Woman: Sister of Crashing Thunder: The Autobiography of a Winnebago Indian*, edited by Nancy Lurie (Ann Arbor: University of Michigan Press, 1961), xi–xiv, 2–5, 8–17, 100–102, 112, 113, 114, 116, 117. Excerpts selected by the editors of this anthology.

Chapter 16, "Beyond Domesticity: Choctaw Women Negotiating the Tension between Choctaw Culture and Protestantism," by Michelene E. Pesantubbee, originally appeared in *Journal of the American Academy of Religion* 67, no. 2 (1999): 387–409.

Contributors

Jennifer S. H. Brown is Professor of History at the University of Winnipeg, Manitoba, and holds a Canada Research Chair in Aboriginal history; she is also Director of the Centre for Rupert's Land Studies. She has published widely on fur trade, Algonquian, and Métis history. Her books include *Strangers in Blood: Fur Trade Company Families in Indian Country* (1980); several coedited volumes, notably, *Reading beyond Words: Contexts for Native History* (1996), with Elizabeth Vibert; and *Telling Our Stories: Omushkego Legends and Histories from Hudson Bay* (2005), a collection of Cree stories told by Louis Bird.

Carl J. Ekberg is Professor Emeritus at Illinois State University, where he taught for twenty-eight years. His publications include *Colonial Ste. Genevieve: An Adventure on the Mississippi Frontier* (1985), *French Roots in the Illinois Country: The Mississippi Frontier in Colonial Times* (1998), *François Vallé and His World: Upper Louisiana before Lewis and Clark* (2002), and *Louis Bolduc: The Man and His House* (2002). His latest study, "Stealing Indian Women: The Price of Freedom in the Illinois Country," is forthcoming from the University of Illinois Press.

Christine Ward Gailey is Professor of Anthropology and former Chair of the Women's Studies Department at the University of California, Riverside. She has written extensively on contemporary kinship formation and on gender, race, and class dynamics in U.S. domestic and international adoption. Her long-term research on cultural resistance to state formation underlies her writings on the history of feminist anthropology and Marxist anthropology, and includes intellectual biographies of Eleanor Leacock, Stanley Diamond, and Richard Lee, who in concert forged a culturally attentive wing of Marxist anthropology that remains deeply committed to indigenous rights.

Rayna Green is currently Curator of American Indian History and American Food History at the National Museum of American History. With a PhD from Indiana University, she served on university faculties (e.g., Dartmouth College) before her twenty years of service to the Smithsonian Institution. Green's publications include *The British Museum Encyclopedia of Native North America* (1999), *Women in American Indian Society* (1992), *That's What She Said: Contemporary Fiction and Poetry by Native American Women* (1984), *Native American Women: A Contextual Bibliography* (1983), and many well-known essays on American Indians, American material culture, and American identity. She is also known for her work in museum exhibition and film and audio production.

Clara Sue Kidwell (Choctaw and Chippewa) is currently Director of the Native American Studies Program and Professor of History at the University of Oklahoma in Norman. Before joining the faculty there in 1995 she served for two years as Assistant Director of Cultural Resources at the National Museum of the American Indian, Smithsonian Institution. She has taught previously at the University of California, Berkeley; Dartmouth College; the University of Minnesota; and Haskell Indian Junior College, now Haskell Indigenous Nations University. Her publications include *Choctaws and Missionaries in Mississippi, 1818–1918* (1995); *A Native American Theology* (2001), coauthored with Homer Noley and George Tinker; and *Native American Studies* (2005), coauthored with Alan R. Velie.

Rebecca Kugel teaches Native American History at the University of California, Riverside. She is the author of *To Be the Main Leaders of Our People: A History of Minnesota Ojibwe Politics, 1825–1898* (1998). Her long-term research focuses on a number of aspects of Ojibwe history, including the operation of the historic political system in the eighteenth and nineteenth centuries and the construction of political speech and its use of distinctive metaphors. She has additional research interests in the cultural constructions of race among Great Lakes Native peoples and in Native women's history.

The late **Eleanor Burke Leacock** pioneered anthropological research on the impact of colonialism on indigenous peoples, particularly women. She taught at the Brooklyn Polytechnic Institute and at the City College of the City University of New York. Her best-known works include *The Montag-*

nais-Naskapi "Hunting Territory" and the Fur Trade, American Anthropological Association Memoir 78 (1954); *Women and Colonization,* edited with Mona Etienne (1980); and *Politics and History in Band Societies,* edited with Richard B. Lee (1982).

Nancy Oestreich Lurie is an anthropologist whose special interests are the history and culture of the North American Indians, cultural change and persistence, action anthropology, and museology. Her major field research has been with the Ho-Chunk (formerly known as Winnebago) Indians of Wisconsin and Nebraska and the Dogrib Indians of the Canadian Northwest Territories. Her career has included university teaching, serving as an expert witness on behalf of American Indian groups before the U.S. Indian Claims Commission and various courts, and employment as head curator of anthropology at the Milwaukee Public Museum. She is the author of *A Special Style: The Milwaukee Public Museum, 1882–1982* (1983).

Lucy Eldersveld Murphy is Associate Professor of History at the Ohio State University, Newark. Her research focuses on intercultural, interracial, and gender relations on midwestern American frontiers. Her current projects include *After the Fur Trade,* a study of Métis families in mid-nineteenth-century Wisconsin; and a team oral history project, "Discovering the Stories of Native Ohio." Her book *A Gathering of Rivers: Indians, Métis, and Mining in the Western Great Lakes, 1737–1832* (2000) examined a century of social and economic transformations in northern Illinois and southern Wisconsin. She is editor with Wendy Hamand Venet of the essay collection *Midwestern Women: Work, Community, and Leadership at the Crossroads* (1997).

Jean M. O'Brien (White Earth Ojibwe) is Associate Professor of History at the University of Minnesota, where she is also affiliated with the Departments of American Indian Studies and American Studies. She is the author of *Dispossession by Degrees: Indian Land and Identity in Natick, Massachusetts, 1650–1790* (1997). She has served on the national council for the American Studies Association and the American Society for Ethnohistory, and as a member of the Executive Committee of the Committee on Institutional Cooperation American Indian Studies Consortium.

Theda Perdue is Professor of History and American Studies at the University of North Carolina. Her publications include *Slavery and the Evolution* *of Cherokee Society, 1540–1865* (1979); *Nations Remembered: An Oral History of the Five Civilized Tribes* (1980); *Cherokee Editor* (1983); *Native Carolinians* (1985); *The Cherokee* (1988); *Cherokee Women: Gender and Culture Change, 1700–1835* (1998); *Sifters: Native American Women's Lives* (2001); *The Columbia Guide to American Indians of the Southeast* (2001); and *"Mixed Blood" Indians: Racial Construction in the Early South* (2003). She currently is working on a book about Indians in the segregated South.

Michelene E. Pesantubbee (Choctaw) is Associate Professor of Religious Studies and American Indian and Native Studies at the University of Iowa. She is the author of *Choctaw Women in a Chaotic World: The Clash of Cultures in the Colonial Southeast* (2005). She specializes in southeastern Native American religious traditions, Native American women and religion, and Native American religious movements. She currently is Secretary of the American Academy of Religion Board of Directors and serves on the steering committee for Women and Religion Section of American Academy of Religion.

Kathryn W. Shanley is Chair of the Native American Studies Department at the University of Montana and an enrolled Assiniboine (Nakoda) from the Fort Peck Reservation in Montana. She has published widely in the field of Native American literary criticism on issues of representation of Indians in popular culture, on gender, and about authors such as James Welch, Maria Campbell, Leslie Marmon Silko, Linda Hogan, Thomas King, and N. Scott Momaday. She recently edited *Native American Literature: Boundaries and Sovereignties* (2001) and is working on a book on Native American autobiography.

Nancy Shoemaker, Professor of History at the University of Connecticut, is the author of *A Strange Likeness: Becoming Red and White in Eighteenth-Century North America* (2004) and *American Indian Population Recovery in the Twentieth Century* (1999). She also edited the collection *Negotiators of Change: Historical Perspectives on Native American Women* (1995). Shoemaker's current research is on American Indians and the New England whaling industry.

Susan Sleeper-Smith is an Associate Professor in the History Department at Michigan State University. Her monograph *Indian Women and French*

Men: Rethinking Cultural Encounter in the Western Great Lakes was published in 2002. She also coedited *New Faces of the Fur Trade* (1998) and has articles in *Sixty Years War for the Great Lakes, 1754–1814* (2001, ed. David Curtis Skaggs and Larry L. Nelson) and *Transatlantic Rebels; Agrarian Radicalism in Comparative Context* (2004, ed. Thomas Summerhill and James C. Scott). She has also published in *Ethnohistory, Journal of American History, Reviews in American History, Journal of the Early Republic,* and *American Indian Culture and Research Journal*. Her research interests focus on the intersection of diverse cultures from the sixteenth through nineteenth centuries in North America, particularly in the Great Lakes.

David D. Smits is Professor of History at the College of New Jersey, where he has taught since 1971. He has been married for forty-three years and has three children and six grandchildren. He is a former Peace Corps volunteer who served among Guatemala's Mayan Indians. He is a lifelong student of Native American history and cultures and is the author of numerous articles on Native peoples, including "'Fighting Fire with Fire': The Frontier Army's Use of Indian Scouts and Allies in the Trans-Mississippi Campaigns, 1860–1890," *American Indian Culture and Research Journal* (1998); and "The Frontier Army and the Destruction of the Buffalo, 1865–1883," *Western Historical Quarterly* (1995).

Helen Hornbeck Tanner is a Senior Research Fellow at The Newberry Library, Chicago. She became affiliated with the library in 1976 as head of the project and editor of the *Atlas of Great Lakes Indian History* (1987). Although she occasionally taught courses in Latin American history at the University of Michigan, and introduced the first courses there in Indian-white relations in 1974, her chief career has been as a consultant and expert witness for Indian tribes presenting cases before the U.S. Indian Claims Commission in Washington DC and in state and federal courts in Michigan and Minnesota.